X Window System
User's Guide

OSF/Motif Edition

Volume Three

X Window System
User's Guide

OSF/Motif Edition

by Valerie Quercia and Tim O'Reilly

O'Reilly & Associates, Inc.

Printing and Revision History

Sept. 1988:	First Edition
July 1989:	Second Edition. Revised to reflect Release 3.
Oct. 1989:	Minor corrections.
May 1990:	Third Edition. Revised to reflect Release 4.
Jan. 1991:	Motif Edition.

Small Print

ISBN 0-937175-61-7

Table of Contents

10 Setting Resources 233

11 Customizing mwm 259

12 Setup Clients 283

PART THREE: Client Reference Pages

Figures

Examples

Tables

Preface

By convention, a preface describes the book itself, while the introduction describes the subject matter. You should read through the preface to get an idea of how the book is organized, the conventions it follows, and so on.

In The Preface:

Preface

The X Window System™ is a network-based graphics windowing system. It was developed by MIT and has been adopted as an industry standard. X provides the bare bones of a window system upon which almost any style of graphical user interface (GUI) can be built. One of the most popular user interfaces available in the market today is OSF/Motif™ developed by the Open Software Foundation.™

The *X Window System User's Guide, Motif Edition* describes window system concepts, the application programs (clients) commonly distributed with Version 11, Release 4 of X, and how you can expect programs to operate with OSF/Motif. (The *Motif Edition* is intended for those using X with the OSF/Motif interface. Another edition of the *X Window System User's Guide* is available for those using X without Motif.)

Assumptions

This book assumes that X is already installed on your system and that all standard MIT clients are available. In addition, although X runs on many different systems, this book assumes that you are running it on a UNIX® system and that you have basic familiarity with UNIX. If you are not using UNIX, you will still find this book useful—UNIX dependencies are not that widespread—but you may occasionally need to translate a command example into its equivalent on your system. This book also assumes that you are using a three-button pointer (e.g., a mouse) and that the operation of the *mwm* window manager is controlled by the *system.mwmrc* file provided with OSF/Motif 1.1. (If this is not the case, the book provides information that will allow you to understand how *mwm* is configured on your system.)

This book is written for both first-time and experienced users of the X Window System. First-time users should read the book in order, starting with Chapter 1, *An Introduction to the X Window System*.

Experienced users can use this book as a reference for the client programs detailed here. Since there is great flexibility with X, even frequent users need to check on the syntax and availability of options. Reference pages for each client detail command line options, customization database (resource database) variables, and other detailed information.

Organization

The book contains these parts:

Part One: Using X

Preface
Describes the book's assumptions, audience, organization, and conventions.

Chapter 1: An Introduction to the X Window System
Describes the basic terminology associated with the X Window System: server, client, window, etc. The most important X clients are described.

Chapter 2: Getting Started
Shows how to start the programs necessary to begin using X: the server, the first terminal window, and window manager. This chapter is tutorial in nature: you can follow along at a workstation as you read.

Chapter 3: Working in the X Environment
Teaches the skills necessary to begin working productively. Shows you how to add additional windows; exit from a window; use the tools of the display; perform some basic window manager operations using the *mwm* window manager; set up the display.

Introduces two methods of customizing X client programs: command line options and resource variables.

Compares a standard X application (created using the X Toolkit) with a Motif application (created using the Motif Toolkit).

Chapter 4: More about the mwm Window Manager
Describes additional window manager operations, such as resizing windows and changing the order of windows in the stack.

Chapter 5: The xterm Terminal Emulator
Describes how to use the *xterm* terminal emulator, the most frequently used client. Certain aspects of *xterm* operation described in this chapter, such as scrolling and "copy and paste," are common to other applications as well.

Chapter 6: Font Specification
Describes the somewhat complicated font naming conventions and ways to simplify font specification, including wildcarding and aliasing. Describes how to use the *xlsfonts*, *xfd*, and *xfontsel* clients to list, display, and select available display fonts.

Chapter 7: Graphics Utilities
Explains how to use the major graphics clients included with X, notably the *bitmap* editor.

Chapter 8: Other Clients
Gives an overview of other clients available with X, including window and display information clients, the *xkill* program, and several "desk accessories."

In describing various standard clients, this chapter highlights those features provided by the Athena widget set. This chapter also describes some of the features of applications written using the Motif widget set.

Part Two: Customizing X

Chapter 9: Command Line Options
Discusses some of the standard command line options accepted by most clients.

Chapter 10: Setting Resources
Tells how to create an *.Xresources* file to set default characteristics for client applications. This chapter also describes how to use *xrdb*, which saves you from having to maintain multiple *.Xresources* files if you run clients on multiple machines.

Chapter 11: Customizing mwm
Describes the *.mwmrc* file by showing the default file shipped by OSF and examines the purpose and syntax of entries. Explains various techniques for revising the *.mwmrc* file to modify existing menus and create new ones. Reviews the different types of resources that can be used to control *mwm*.

Chapter 12: Setup Clients
Describes how to set display and keyboard preferences using *xset* and how to set root window preferences using *xsetroot*. Also demonstrates how to use *xmodmap* to redefine the logical keynames and pointer commands recognized by X.

Part Three: Client Reference Pages

Extended reference pages for all clients.

Part Four: Appendices

Appendix A: System Management

Appendix B: Release 4 Standard Fonts

Appendix C: Standard Bitmaps

Appendix D: Standard Cursors

Appendix E: xterm Control Sequences

Appendix F: Translation Table Syntax

Appendix G: Athena Widget Resources

Glossary

Index

Bulk Sales Information

This guide is being resold by many workstation manufacturers as their official X Window System documentation. For information on volume discounts for bulk purchases, call O'Reilly & Associates, Inc., at 800-338-6887, or send email to linda@ora.com (uunet!ora!linda). For companies requiring extensive customization of the guide, source-licensing terms are also available.

xshowfonts.c and Other Free Programs

The source to *xshowfonts.c*, which is printed in Appendix B, *Release 4 Standard Fonts*, is also available free from UUNET (that is, free except for UUNET's usual connect-time charges). If you have access to UUNET, you can retrieve the source code using UUCP or FTP. For UUCP, find a machine with direct access to UUNET, and type the following command:

```
uucp uunet\!~uucp/nutshell/Xuser/xshowfonts.c.Z yourhost\!~/yourname/
```

The backslashes can be omitted if you use the Bourne shell (*sh*) instead of *csh*. The file should appear some time later (up to a day or more) in the directory */usr/spool/uucppublic/yourname*.

You don't need to have opened an account to UUNET to be able to access their archives via UUCP from within the United States of America. By calling 1-900-468-7727 and using the login "uucp" with no password, anyone may *uucp* any of UUNET's online source collection. (Start by copying *uunet!~/ls-lR.Z*, which is a compressed index of every file in the archives. Peruse this file to get an idea of what sorts of programs are available. The file *uunet!~nutshell/ls-lR.Z* contains a listing of the files contained in the nutshell subdirectory (example programs for our books.)) As of this writing, the cost is 40 cents per minute. The charges will appear on your next telephone bill.

To use FTP, you will need to find a machine with direct access to the Internet. The following example is a sample session, with commands in boldface.

```
% ftp uunet.uu.net
Connected to uunet.uu.net.
220 uunet FTP server (Version 5.99 Wed May 23 14:40:19 EDT 1990) ready.
Name (uunet.uu.net:ambar): anonymous
331 Guest login ok, send ident as password.
Password: ambar@ora.com (use your user name and host here)
230 Guest login ok, access restrictions apply.
ftp> cd nutshell/Xuser
250 CWD command successful.
ftp> binary (you must specify binary transfer for compressed files)
200 Type set to I.
ftp> get xshowfonts.c.Z
200 PORT command successful.
150 Opening ASCII mode data connection for xshowfonts.c.Z (5587 bytes).
226 Transfer complete.
ftp> quit
221 Goodbye.
%
```

The file is a compressed C program. To uncompress the program, type:

```
% uncompress xshowfonts.c
```

Acknowledgements

The first edition of this guide was based in part on three previous X Window System user's guides: one from Masscomp, which was written by Jeff Graber; one from Sequent Computer Systems, Inc., and one from Graphic Software Systems, Inc.; both of which were written by Candis Condo (supported by the UNIX development group). Some of Jeff's and Candis's material in turn was based on material developed under the auspices of Project Athena at MIT.

Most of the reference pages in Part Three of this guide have been adapted from reference pages copyright © 1990 the Massachusetts Institute of Technology, or from reference pages produced by Graphic Software Systems. Refer to the "Authors" section at the end of each reference page for details. Other copyrights are listed on the relevant reference pages.

Permission to use this material is gratefully acknowledged.

This guide was primarily developed using the MIT sample server on a Sun-3™ Workstation, with additional testing done on a Sony NEWS™ workstation running Sony's X implementation, a Visual 640 X Display Station™, and an NCD16™ Network Display Station.

We are grateful to Sony Microsystems for the loan of a Sony NEWS workstation and to Visual Technology Incorporated for the loan of a Visual 640 X Display Station. We appreciate the support of these manufacturers in helping us develop complete and accurate X Window System documentation.

We'd also like to thank the Open Software Foundation for permission to reprint the *system.mwmrc* file in Chapter 11, *Customizing mwm*. Special thanks to Elizabeth Connelly of OSF for arranging this.

Special thanks also to Dave Curry for his expert technical and editorial support.

Of course, the authors would like to thank the entire staff of O'Reilly and Associates for producing the book, and the staff of Cambridge Computer Associates, Inc., for lending their support.

Despite the efforts of these people, the standard authors' disclaimer applies: any errors that remain are our own.

Font and Character Conventions

These typographic conventions are used in this book:

Italics   are used for:

- new terms where they are defined.

- file and directory names, and command and client names when they appear in the body of a paragraph.

`Courier`   is used within the body of the text to show:

- command lines or options that should be typed verbatim on the screen.

  is used within examples to show:

- computer-generated output.

- the contents of files.

`Courier bold`   is used within examples to show command lines and options that should be typed verbatim on the screen.

`Courier italics`   are used within examples or explanations of command syntax to show a parameter to a command that requres context-dependent substitution (such as a variable). For example, *`filename`* means to use some appropriate filename; *`option(s)`* means to use some appropriate option(s) to the command.

Helvetica   is used to show menu titles and options.

These symbols are used within the *X Window System User's Guide*:

[ ]   surround an optional field in a command line or file entry.

$ is the standard prompt from the Bourne shell, *sh*(1).

%   is the standard prompt from the C shell, *csh*(1).

name(1)   is a reference to a command called *name* in Section 1 of the *UNIX Reference Manual* (which may have a different name depending on the version of UNIX you use).

Part One:

Using X

Part One provides an overview of the X Window System and concepts, and describes how to use the most important programs available in the X environment.

An Introduction to the X Window System
Getting Started
Working in the X Environment
More about the mwm Window Manager
The xterm Terminal Emulator
Font Specification
Graphics Utilities
Other Clients

1

An Introduction
to the X Window System

This chapter describes the features of a typical X display, while introducing some basic window system concepts. It also provides an overview of the X Window System's client-server architecture and briefly describes the most commonly used clients.

In This Chapter:

1
An Introduction
to the X Window System

The X Window System, called X for short, is a network-based graphics window system that was developed at MIT in 1984. Several versions of X have been developed, the most recent of which is X Version 11 (X11), first released in 1987.

X11 has been adopted as an industry standard windowing system. X is supported by a consortium of industry leaders such as DEC, Hewlett-Packard, Sun, IBM, and AT&T that have united to direct, contribute to, and fund its continuing development. In addition to the system software development directed by the X Consortium, many independent developers are producing application software specifically for use with X, including spreadsheets, database programs, and publishing applications.

First, we'll take a look at a typical X display and consider some general system features. We'll also briefly compare a standard X application (written with the X Toolkit) to a Motif application (written with the Motif Toolkit). Then we'll discuss what distinguishes the X Window System from other window systems. We'll also introduce some of the more important programs included in the standard distribution of X, and the *mwm* window manager shipped with OSF/Motif.

Anatomy of an X Display

X is typically run on a workstation with a large screen (although it also runs on PCs and special X terminals, as well as on many larger systems). X allows you to work with multiple programs simultaneously, each in a separate *window*. The display in Figure 1-1 includes five windows.

The operations performed within a window can vary greatly, depending on the type of program running it. Certain windows accept input from the user: they may function as terminals, allow you to create graphics, etc. Other windows simply display information, such as the time of day or a picture of the characters in a particular font, etc.

The windows you will probably use most frequently are *terminal emulators*, windows that function as standard terminals. The terminal emulator included with the standard release of X is called *xterm*. Figure 1-1 depicts three *xterm* windows. In an *xterm* window, you can do anything you might do in a regular terminal: enter commands, run editing sessions, compile programs, etc.

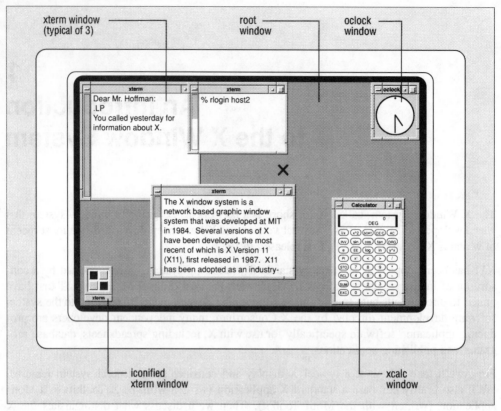

xterm window
(typical of 3)

root
window

oclock
window

xterm

Dear Mr. Hoffman:
.LP
You called yesterday for
information about X.

xterm

% rlogin host2

oclock

xterm

The X window system is a
network based graphic window
system that was developed at MIT
in 1984. Several versions of X
have been developed, the most
recent of which is X Version 11
(X11), first released in 1987. X11
has been adopted as an industry-

Calculator

DEG   0

1/x x^2 SQRT CE·C AC
INV sin cos tan DRG
e   EE   log ln y^x
PI   x!   <   >   /
STO 7   8   9   *
RCL 4   5   6   -
SUM 1   2   3   +
EXC 0   .   +/-   =

iconified
xterm window

xcalc
window

Figure 1-1. X display with five windows and an icon

The display in Figure 1-1 also includes two other application windows: a clock (called *xclock*) and a calculator (*xcalc*). X provides many such small utility programs—analogous to the so-called "desk accessories" of the Macintosh environment—intended to make your work easier.

The shaded area that fills the entire screen is called the *root* (or *background*) window. Application windows are displayed on top of this root window. X considers windows to be related to one another in a hierarchy, similar to a family tree. The root window is the root or origin within this hierarchy and is considered to be the *parent* of application windows displayed on it. Conversely, these application windows are called *children* of the root window. In Figure 1-1, the *xterm*, *xclock*, and *xcalc* windows are children of the root window.

As we'll see later, the window hierarchy is actually much more complicated than this "two generation" model suggests. Various *parts* of application windows are windows in their own right. For example, many applications provide menus to assist the user. Technically speaking, these menus are separate windows. Knowledge of the complexity of the window hierarchy (and the composite parts of an application) will become important when we discuss how to tailor an application to better suit your needs.

One of the strengths of a window system such as X is that you can have several processes going on simultaneously in several different windows. For example, in Figure 1-1, the user is logging in to a remote system in one *xterm* window and editing a text file in each of the two other *xterm* windows. (As we'll see in Chapter 5, *The xterm Terminal Emulator*, you can also cut and paste text between two windows.) Be aware, however, that you can only input to one window at a time.

Another strength of X is that it allows you to run programs on machines connected by a network. You can run a process on a remote machine while displaying the results on your own screen. You might want to access a remote machine for any number of reasons: to use a program or access information not available on your local system; to distribute the work load, etc. We'll discuss X's networking capabilities in more detail in the "X Architecture Overview" later in this chapter.

Now let's take another look at our sample display in Figure 1-1. Notice that the *xterm* windows overlap each other. Windows often overlap much like sheets of paper on your desk or a stack of cards. Be aware that overlapping does not interfere with the process run in each window. However, in order to really take advantage of windowing, you need to be able to move and modify the windows on your display. For example, if you want to work in a window that is partially covered by another window, you need to be able to raise the obscured window to the top of the window stack.

Window management functions are provided by a type of program called a *window manager*. The window manager controls the general operation of the window system, allowing you to change the size and position of windows on the display. You can reshuffle windows in a window stack, make windows larger or smaller, move them to other locations on the screen, etc. The window manager provides part of the user interface—to a large extent it controls the "look and feel" of the X Window System.

The window manager provided with OSF/Motif is called *mwm*, the *M*otif *w*indow *m*anager. The most distinguishing feature of *mwm* is the "frame" it places around all windows on the display. Notice that each top-level application window in the illustration is surrounded by this frame. As we'll see, by clicking a mouse or other pointing device on various parts of the window frame, you can perform management functions on the window.

The *mwm* window frame is a composite of several parts, the most prominent of which are shown in Figure 1-2.

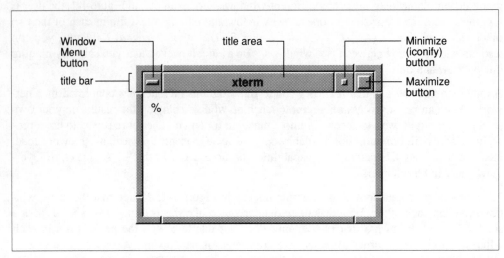

Figure 1-2. mwm frames each window on the display

The top edge of the frame is wider than the other three edges and features most of the window management tools. This wide horizontal bar spanning the top of the window is known as a *titlebar*. The large central portion of this top edge is called the *title area* mainly because it contains a text description of the window. (Generally, this is the application name, but as we'll see later, you can often specify an alternate title.) The titlebar also features three command buttons whose functionality we'll discuss in Chapter 3 and Chapter 4. We'll also see how to use the sides and bottom of the frame to resize a window and to raise it to the top of the window stack.

mwm attempts to create a three-dimensional appearance, which is somewhat more aesthetic than the look provided by many other window managers. You'll probably notice that window frames, various command buttons, icons, etc., appear to be raised to varying heights above screen level. This illusion is created by subtle shading and gives many display features a "beveled" look, similar to the beveled style of some mirrors.

mwm is intended to be used with the OSF/Motif graphical user interface. For those not using Motif, there are several other window managers available in the market today. In the standard distribution of X from MIT (as of Release 4), the official window manager is called *twm*. (*twm* originally stood for "Tom's window manager," in honor of its developer, Tom La-Strange. However, it has since been renamed the "tab window manager.") The *twm* window manager provides a different "look and feel" than *mwm*. Rather than framing application windows, *twm* simply provides each window with a titlebar, different from the *mwm* titlebar in style, but offering similar window management functions. Earlier releases of X supported a third window manager, *uwm*, the "universal window manager," which is still available as part of the user contributed part of the MIT X distribution. The contributed distribution includes several other window managers and still others are available commercially.

Aesthetics notwithstanding, one of the primary advantages *mwm* has over other window managers is inherent in the nature of a frame: it provides window management tools on four sides of the window. *twm*'s titlebar is a useful window management tool, but a titlebar is often covered by other windows in the stack. In most cases at least a part of a window's frame should be visible—and thus accessible to the user.

Also pictured in Figure 1-1 is an *icon*. An icon is a small symbol that represents a window in an inactive state. The window manager allows you to convert windows to icons and icons back to windows. You may want to convert a window to an icon to save space on the display or to prevent input to that window. Each icon has a label, generally the name of the program that created the window. The icon in Figure 1-1 represents a fourth *xterm* window on the display. Icons can be moved around on the display, just like windows.

The contents of a window are not visible when the window has been converted to an icon but they are not lost. In fact, a client continues to run when its window has been iconified; if you iconify a terminal emulator client such as *xterm*, any programs running in the shell will also continue.

If you've used other window managers, you may notice that icon symbols generated by *mwm* are somewhat larger and more decorated. The detail on icons is another aesthetic advantage of *mwm*.

All X displays require you to have some sort of pointer, often a three-button mouse, with which you communicate information to the system. As you slide the pointer around on your desktop, a cursor symbol on the display follows the pointer's movement. For our purposes, we will refer to both the pointing device (e.g., a mouse) and the symbol that represents its location on the screen as pointers. Depending on where the pointer is on the screen (in an *xterm* window, in another application window, on the root window, etc.), it is represented by a variety of cursor symbols. If the pointer is positioned on the root window, it is generally represented by an X-shaped cursor, as in Figure 1-1. If the pointer is in an *xterm* window, it looks like an uppercase I and is commonly called an *I-beam cursor*.*

A complete list of standard X cursors is shown in Appendix D, *Standard Cursors*. OSF/Motif provides some additional cursors. Some of the most common standard cursor shapes, as well as two Motif-specific cursors, are shown in Figure 1-3. As we'll see later, some applications allow you to select the cursor to use.

---

*Even though the actual image on the screen is called a cursor, throughout this guide we refer to "moving the pointer" to avoid confusion with the standard text cursor that can appear in an *xterm* window.

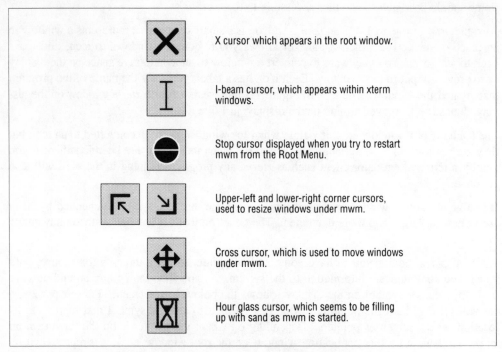

X cursor which appears in the root window.

I-beam cursor, which appears within xterm windows.

Stop cursor displayed when you try to restart mwm from the Root Menu.

Upper-left and lower-right corner cursors, used to resize windows under mwm.

Cross cursor, which is used to move windows under mwm.

Hour glass cursor, which seems to be filling up with sand as mwm is started.

Figure 1-3. Some standard cursors and two Motif-specific cursors

You use the pointer to manage windows and icons, to make selections in menus, and to select the window in which you want to input. You can't type in an *xterm* window until you select that window using the pointer. Directing input to a particular window is called *focusing*. When a window has the input focus, the window frame and the text cursor (if any) are highlighted, as in Figure 1-4. The window to which input is directed is often called the *active* window.

Be aware that the frame may be highlighted in different ways, depending on the version of *mwm* you are running and the color resources specified for your system. The frame may change from black to white, from grey to white, etc. In any case, the active window's frame will be a different color than the frames of all other windows on the display.

Most window managers require you to select the active window in one of two ways: either by moving the pointer so that it rests within the desired window or by clicking the pointer on the window. By default, the Motif window manager requires you to click the pointer on the window to which you want to direct input. This focusing style is commonly referred to as "click-to-type" or ("explicit focus"). However, as we'll see in Chapter 11, *Customizing mwm*, *mwm* can be customized to allow you to direct input focus simply by moving the pointer. This focusing style is commonly referred to as "real-estate-driven" (or "pointer focus").

The *twm* window manager uses the real-estate-driven style: you direct input focus by moving the pointer into the desired window and leaving it there. As long as the pointer remains within the window's borders, the keystrokes you type will appear in that window (when the

Figure 1-4. Focus on an xterm window

application accepts text input) or will somehow affect its operation (perhaps serve as commands). If you accidentally knock the pointer outside the window's borders, the keystrokes you type will not appear in that window or affect its operation. If you inadvertently move the pointer into another window, that window becomes the focus window. If you move the pointer onto the root window, the keystrokes are in effect lost—no application will interpret them.*

As previously mentioned, by default the Motif window manager uses the click-to-type focusing style: you must click the pointer on a window to focus input on that window. When you begin using X with *mwm*, you'll need to select the window to receive input by placing the pointer anywhere within the window and clicking the first (generally the leftmost) button. Once you select the focus window in this way, all input is directed to that window until you move the pointer and deliberately click on another window.

---

*In a few cases, the window manager may interpret these keystrokes. For example, you can customize *mwm* to display a menu when you type certain keystrokes while the pointer rests on the root window. See Chapter 11, *Customizing mwm*, for more information about mapping window manager functions to certain keys and pointer actions.

One of Motif's greatest strengths is that it allows you to choose the focus policy. This flexibility makes *mwm* a desirable choice for users with a variety of needs and work habits. As you might imagine, both focusing policies have their advantages. Click-to-type focus requires a little more work than pointer focus. (It's simpler to move the pointer than to move and click.) On the other hand, click-to-type focus is more precise—you can't inadvertently change the focus by moving the pointer.

We find click-to-type focus somewhat laborious. However, a touch typist, who is not inclined to look at the screen, might consider pointer focus too risky. It's possible to knock the pointer out of a window and lose a large amount of text before noticing. Another disadvantage of pointer focus is that it sometimes takes a moment for the input focus to catch up with the pointer, especially on slower machines. If you type right away, some keystrokes may end up in the window you left rather than in the new window. This is actually a bug that happens because of the additional overhead involved in complex window managers such as *mwm* or *twm*. Since you can change the focus policy rather simply, you might want to experiment with both methods. For now, we'll assume you're using the default click-to-type focus.

The most important thing to recognize is that focusing on the proper window is integral to working with an application running with a window system. If something doesn't work the way you expect, make sure that the focus is directed to the correct window. After you use X for a while, awareness of input focus will come naturally.

The pointer is also often used to display menus. Some X programs, notably *mwm* and *xterm*, have menus that are displayed by keystrokes and/or pointer button motions. More versatile than many other window managers, *mwm* provides two default menus, each representing a different menu "style."

The Window Menu is a "pull-down" menu that can be displayed on any window by placing the pointer on the small rectangular button in the upper-left corner of the frame and either clicking or pressing and holding down the first pointer button. Roughly defined, a pull-down menu is accessed from a graphical element that is always displayed, such as a command button or a menu bar. Figure 1-5 shows an *xterm* window with the Window Menu displayed by clicking the first pointer button in the menu button on the frame.

As you might infer from some of the menu items, you can use the Window Menu to move, resize, and otherwise manage the window on which it is displayed. When you display the Window Menu by clicking the first pointer button (as opposed to pressing and holding it down), the first the first item available for selection is surrounded by a box. In this case, the first available selection is Move. The first item on the menu, Restore, is used to change an icon back into a window; therefore, it is not useful at this time. The fact that Restore is not selectable is indicated by the fact that it appears in a lighter typeface. The Window Menu is discussed in detail in Chapter 4, *More about the mwm Window Manager*.

mwm also supports "pop-up" menus, which are displayed at the current pointer position. (Many X clients also use pop-up menus.) In addition to keyboard keys and pointer button motions, the location of the pointer plays a role in displaying menus. For example, *xterm* menus can only be displayed when the pointer is within an *xterm* window. Figure 1-6 shows the *mwm* Root Menu, which is generally displayed by placing the pointer on the root window and pressing and holding down the first pointer button.

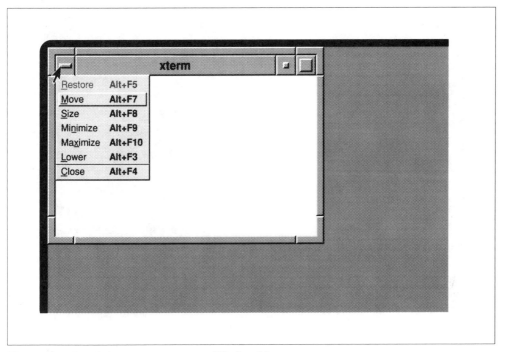

Figure 1-5. A pull-down menu: mwm's Window Menu

In Figure 1-6, the arrow next to the menu title represents the pointer. As you drag the pointer down the menu, each of the menu selections is highlighted. Regardless of the program, you generally select a menu item by dragging the pointer down the menu, highlighting the item you want, and releasing (or sometimes clicking) the pointer button. (*mwm* generally highlights an item by placing a rectangular box around it.) The Root Menu provides commands that can be thought of as affecting the entire display (as opposed to a single window). For example, the first menu item, New Window, creates a new *xterm* window on the local machine and display.

Though mwm's menus can be useful, you'll probably find that you perform most window management functions simply by using the pointer on the window frame. In Chapter 3, *Working in the X Environment*, we'll describe several of these functions. Keep in mind, however, that both of the menus can be useful in certain circumstances. For instance, the Window Menu may be useful when parts of the window frame are obscured by another window. The Root Menu can be customized to execute system commands, such as the *xterm* command initialized by the New Window menu item. It's fairly simple to add items to the Root Menu; you might want to add menu items to start some of the applications you use regularly. Chapter 11, *Customizing mwm*, describes how to add menu items and to perform a variety of modifications.

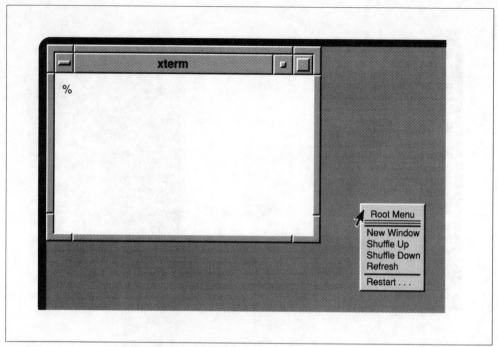

Figure 1-6. A pop-up menu: mwm's Root Menu

As we'll see in Chapter 8, *Other Clients*, some programs provide menus that you can display simply by placing the pointer on a particular part of the window, e.g., a horizontal menu bar across the top.

A final note about the X display: in X, the terms *display* and *screen* are not equivalent. A display may consist of more than one screen. This feature might be implemented in several ways. There might be two physical monitors, linked to form a single display, as shown in Figure 1-7. Alternatively, two screens might be defined as different ways of using the same physical monitor. For example, on the Sun-3/60 color workstation, screen 0 is color, and screen 1 is black and white. Each screen is the size of the monitor; you can only view one screen at a time. In practice, the two screen seem to be side by side: you can "scroll" between them by moving the pointer off either horizontal edge of the screen. By default, windows are always placed on screen 0 but you can place a client window on screen 1 by specifying the screen number in the -display option when starting the client. (See Chapter 3 for instructions on using the -display option.)

Figure 1-7. A display made up of two physical screens

Standard X Clients versus Motif Clients

The window manager running on a display helps determine the "look and feel" of an application. The *mwm* window manager frames each window on the display and allows you to manage a variety of application windows using the same mechanisms.

However, the look and feel of an application is not wholly determined by the window manager. In addition, the programming routines used to create the application also distinguish it. With the exception of *mwm*, all the applications we've looked at so far have been written (or rewritten) using what is known as the X Toolkit, developed at MIT.

The X Toolkit is a collective name for two subroutine libraries designed to simplify the development of X Window System applications: the X Toolkit (Xt) Intrinsics and the Athena widget set (Xaw). The Xt library consists of low-level C programming routines for building and using widgets, which are pre-defined user interface components or objects. Typical widgets create graphical features such as menus, command buttons, dialog boxes, and scrollbars. Widgets make it easier to create complex applications. A common widget set also ensures a consistent user interface between applications.

Remember that X does not provide a distinct graphical user interface (GUI). X is a basic window system upon which almost any style of GUI can be built. The X Toolkit provides a simplified approach to creating graphical user interface components—guidelines for writing and implementing widgets—rather than offering a set of components with a predefined look and feel. (However, the Athena widget set does provide X Toolkit applications with certain common features, many of which are mentioned in Chapter 8.)

In response to the need for a graphical user interface for X, the Open Software Foundation developed the Motif Toolkit. The Motif Toolkit is based upon the Xt Intrinsics and upon widget sets originally developed by two OSF sponsor companies, Digital Equipment Corporation and Hewlett-Packard. The Motif widget set was designed to emulate the look and feel of the IBM/Microsoft Presentation Manager, popular in the microcomputer world. An application coded using the Motif Toolkit has a distinct look and feel.

AT&T and Sun Microsystems have also developed a GUI—or more precisely, a specification for a GUI—called OPEN LOOK. At present the two major implementations of the OPEN LOOK specification are Sun's XView toolkit (which is not Xt based) and AT&T's OPEN LOOK widget set (which is Xt based). OPEN LOOK and Motif are the prime contenders to establish a graphical user interface standard in the market.

With the exception of *mwm* and a program called *mre* (the Motif resource editor), all of the clients discussed in this guide are standard X clients shipped by MIT. Most of these clients have been built with the X Toolkit and illustrate the use of many of the Athena widgets. When you run these standard clients with the *mwm* window manager, your environment is something of a hybrid—neither a vanilla X nor a Motif environment (with Motif applications in addition to the window manager).

A standard X client running with *mwm* is different from a true Motif application, one coded using the Motif Toolkit. At first look, they may seem very similar—when *mwm* is running all clients on the display are framed in the same way. In addition, certain graphical features provided by the Motif widgets are also provided, albeit with slight variations, by the Athena widgets. However, other features are unique to Motif.

Without dissecting every component or closely examining how it functions, let's briefly compare a standard X application to a Motif application, highlighting some of the major differences (primarily in appearance). Many features of Motif and standard X applications also *operate* differently. We'll examine the functionality of various Motif and Athena widgets in more detail in Chapter 8, *Other Clients*.

For the comparison, we'll use a Motif demo program called *mre*, the Motif resource editor. Developed at OSF by Mitch at OSF by Mitch Trachtenberg, *mre* assists you in editing your own resource specification file. The editing help *mre* provides is minimal, but the program clearly demonstrates many of the Motif widgets—as it was intended to do.

The standard X client we're using is *xclipboard*, which you use in concert with *xterm*'s "cut and paste" facility, described in Chapter 5. The *xclipboard* client provides a window in which you can paste multiple text selections and from which you can copy text selections to other windows. Similar to the clipboard feature of the Macintosh operating system. *xclipboard* is basically a storehouse for text you may want to paste into other windows, perhaps multiple times.

The *mre* window in Figure 1-8 contains a resource file to be edited. (Resources are a mechanism that allow you to customize the operation of X clients.) The *xclipboard* window in Figure 1-9 contains a long text selection "cut" from an *xterm* window. Some prominent features of each application are labelled. Both clients are illustrated without the *mwm* frame. (When the window manager is running, the frame creates a superficial resemblance among all clients on the display.)

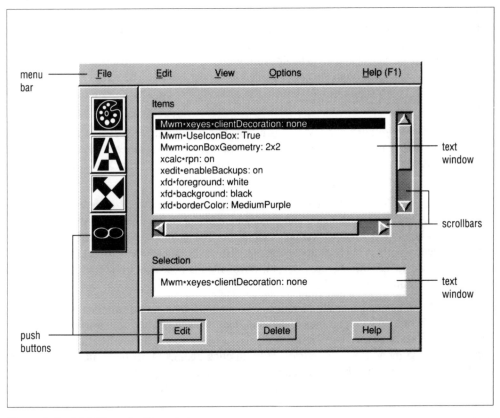

Figure 1-8. A Motif application: mre

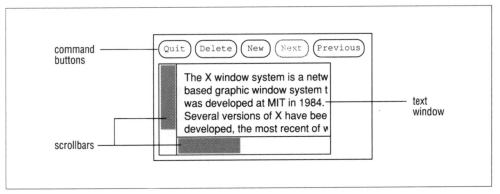

Figure 1-9. A standard X application: xclipboard

The most striking difference between the two clients is simply the amount of detail. Like the Motif window manager, the individual Motif widgets create a three-dimensional appearance. The subwindows labelled Items and Selection seem to be set in to the application window. The push buttons (and drawn buttons) are shaded to suggest that they are raised above the level of the application window. (The drawn buttons also feature bitmapped images, three of them rather elaborate.) The menu bar is shaded to appear raised. The scrollbars have clearly distinguishable components, all of which are shaded and contoured to maintain the 3-D impression.

By contrast, the *xclipboard* window seems almost like a preliminary sketch of an application. It is basically flat. The text window, command buttons, and scrollbars are rendered in simple lines, without contouring, and with virtually no shading (though a portion of each scrollbar is shaded).

Another difference is that the *mre* window has a menu bar. Each word on the menu bar is the title of a pull-down menu that you can access by placing the pointer on it and clicking (or pressing and holding down) the first pointer button. The *xclipboard* application doesn't provide any menus—it's a fairly simple program. However, some standard X clients (notably *xman* discussed in Chapter 8) provide pull-down menus accessed by pressing and holding down a pointer button.

Motif pull-down menus generally have a few advantages over pull-down menus provided by standard X clients. While you must press and hold down a pointer button to dislay a menu provided by a standard X client, you can display a Motif menu simply by clicking a pointer button—and the menu stays displayed until you click again. Motif menu items can also be invoked in multiple ways (including pointer actions and keystrokes); the only way to invoke an item from a standard X menu is by dragging the pointer down the menu and releasing the button. The various ways you can work with a Motif pull-down menu are described for *mwm*'s Window Menu in Chapter 4.

Despite differences in general appearance and complexity, *mre* and *xclipboard* have many analogous components. Both applications feature a subwindow containing text that can be edited. (*mre* actually has two such windows, labeled Items and Selection.)

Both applications feature buttons: push buttons in the *mre* window; command buttons in the *xclipboard* window. From a user's viewpoint, push buttons and command buttons are functionally equivalent (though you can invoke a push button's function in more ways). The Motif and Athena widget sets simply identify them by different names. The four push buttons on the left side of the *mre* window are actually called drawn buttons. Drawn buttons are just push buttons decorated with a bitmap rather than a text label.

Both the *mre* and *xclipboard* windows have a horizontal and a vertical scrollbar, which are used to look at text that is currently outside the viewing window. (These scrollbars are only displayed when the text read into the window extends beyond the bounds of the viewing area. If the text only exceeds the viewing area in one direction—either horizontally or vertically—only one scrollbar will be displayed.) The Athena scrollbar is basically rectangular (actually one rectangle within another). The Motif scrollbar is somewhat more elaborate. Notice the arrows on either end, for instance. These arrows are the hallmark of a Motif scrollbar and can help you readily identify a Motif application. The arrows also provide functionality not duplicated by the Athena scrollbar.

In general, once you've mastered the basics of working with the MIT client programs running under the *mwm* window manager, you should have no problem making use of any additional features provided by commercial applications built with the Motif widget set.

X Architecture Overview

Most window systems are *kernel-based*: that is, they are closely tied to the operating system itself and can only run on a discrete system, such as a single workstation. The X Window System is not part of any operating system but instead is composed entirely of user-level programs.

The architecture of the X Window System is based on what is known as a *client-server* model. The system is divided into two distinct parts: *display servers* that provide display capabilities and keep track of user input and *clients*, application programs that perform specific tasks.

In a sense, the server acts as intermediary between client application programs, and the local display hardware (one or perhaps multiple screens) and input devices (generally a keyboard and pointer). When you enter input using the keyboard or a pointing device, the server conveys the input to the relevant client application. Likewise, the client programs make requests (for information, processes, etc.) that are communicated to the hardware display by the server. For example, a client may request that a window be moved or that text be displayed in the window.

This division within the X architecture allows the clients and the display server either to work together on the same machine or to reside on different machines (possibly of different types, with different operating systems, etc.) that are connected by a network. For example, you might use a relatively low-powered PC or workstation as a display server to interact with clients that are running on a more powerful remote system. Even though the client program is actually running on the more powerful system, all user input and displayed output occur on the PC or workstation server and are communicated across the network using the X protocol. Figure 1-10 shows a diagram of such a network.

You might choose to run a client on a remote machine for any number of reasons. Generally, however, the remote machine offers some feature unavailable on your local machine: a more efficient or powerful processor; a completely different architecture better suited to a particular task; different application software; file server capabilities (and perhaps large data files you'd rather not transfer over the network). X allows you to take advantage of these remote features and to see the results on your local terminal.

The distinction between clients and the server also allows somewhat complicated display situations. For instance, you can access several machines simultaneously. (This can greatly simplify the work of a system administrator.) X also allows you to output to several displays simultaneously. This capability can be very helpful in educational situations. Hypothetically, a teacher could display instructional material to a group of students each using a graphics workstation or terminal hooked up to a network.

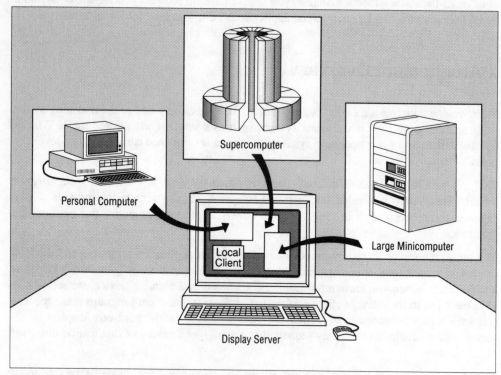

Personal Computer

Supercomputer

Local
Client

Large Minicomputer

Display Server

Figure 1-10. A sample X Window System configuration

There is another less obvious advantage to the client-server model: since the server is entirely responsible for interacting with the hardware, only the server program must be machine-specific. X client applications can easily be ported from system to system.

The X Display Server

The X display server is a program that keeps track of all input from input devices, such as the keyboard and pointer, and conveys that input to the relevant client applications; the server also keeps track of output from any clients that are running and updates the display to reflect that output. Each physical display (which may be multiple screens) has only one server program.

User input and several other types of information pass from the server to a client in the form of *events*. An event is a packet of information that tells the client something it needs to act on, such as keyboard input. Moving the pointer or pressing a key, etc., causes *input* events to occur.

When a client program receives a meaningful event, it responds with a *request* to the server for some sort of action affecting the display. For instance, the client may request that a window be resized to particular dimensions. The server responds to requests by a client program by updating the appropriate window(s) on your display.

Servers are available for PCs, workstations, and even for special terminals (generally called X terminals), which may have the server downloaded from another machine or stored in ROM.

Clients

As previously mentioned, a client is an application program. The standard release of X from MIT includes more than 50 client programs that perform a wide variety of tasks. X allows you to run many clients simultaneously: each client displays in a separate window. For example, you could be editing a text file in one window, compiling a program source file in a second window, reading your mail in a third, all the while displaying the system load average in a fourth window.

While X clients generally display their results and take input from a single display server, they may each be running on a different computer on the network. It is important to note that the same programs may not look and act the same on different servers since X has no standard user interface, since users can customize X clients differently on each server, and since the display hardware on each server may be different.

Remember that the server conveys input from the various input devices to the appropriate client application; likewise, the client issues output in the form of requests to the server for certain actions affecting the display.

In addition to communicating with the server, a client sometimes need to communicate with other clients. For example, a client may need to tell the window manager where to place its icon. Interclient communication is facilitated by the use of *properties*. A property is a piece of information associated with a window or a font and stored in the server. Properties are used by clients to store information that other clients might need to know, such as the name of the application associated with a particular window. Storing properties in the server makes the information they contain accessible to all clients.

A typical use of properties in interclient communication involves how a client tells the window manager the name of the application associated with its window. By default, the application name corresponds to the client's name, but many clients allow you to specify an alternative name when you run the program. A window manager that provides a titlebar needs to know the application name to display in that area. The client's application name is stored in the server in the property called WM_NAME and is accessed by the window manager.

See the *xprop* reference page in Part Three of this guide, and Volume One, *Xlib Programming Manual*, for more information about properties and the *xprop* client.

Several of the more frequently used client programs are discussed in the following sections.

The Window Manager

The way a kernel-based window system operates is inherent in the window system itself. By contrast, the X Window System concentrates control in a special kind of client application, called a window manager. The window manager you use largely determines the look and feel of X on a particular system.

The window manager shipped with OSF/Motif is called *mwm*. As we've discussed, *mwm* allows you to move and resize windows, rearrange the order of windows in the window stack, create additional windows, and convert windows into icons, etc. These functions are discussed more fully in Chapter 3 and Chapter 4.

mwm is compliant with the X Consortium's *Inter-Client Communication Conventions Manual* (ICCCM), introduced at Release 3. The ICCCM contains standards for interaction with window managers and other clients. It defines basic policy intentionally omitted from X itself, such as the rules for transferring data between applications, for transferring keyboard focus, for installing colormaps, and so on. As long as applications and window managers follow the conventions outlined in the ICCCM, applications created with different toolkits will be able to coexist and work together on the same server.

In this guide, we assume you are using *mwm*. Other popular window managers, such as *twm* (the tab window manager), *awm* (Ardent™ window manager), *rtl* (tiled window manager, developed at Siemens Research and Technology Laboratories, RTL), and *olwm* (the OPEN LOOK™ window manager), are also widely used.

If the *mwm* window manager has been customized at your site or you are using a different window manager, many of the concepts should remain the same. However, the actual procedures shown may differ. See Chapter 11, *Customizing mwm*, for a discussion of how to tailor *mwm* to your particular needs.

The xterm Terminal Emulator

X11 itself is designed to support only bitmapped graphics displays. For this reason, one of the most important clients is a terminal emulator. The terminal emulator brings up a window that allows you to log in to a multiuser system and to run applications designed for use on a standard alphanumeric terminal. Anything you can do on a terminal, you can do in this window.

xterm is the most widely available terminal emulator. *xterm* emulates a DEC® VT102 terminal or a Tektronix® 4014 terminal. For each *xterm* process, you can display both types of windows at the same time but only one is active (i.e., responding to input) at a time.

Running multiple *xterm* processes is like working with multiple terminals. Since you can bring up more than one *xterm* window at a time, you can run several programs simultaneously. For example, you can have the system transfer files or process information in one window while you focus your attention on a text-editing session in another window. As you might imagine, having what are in effect multiple terminals can increase your productivity remarkably. See Chapter 3, *Working in the X Environment*, and Chapter 5, *The xterm Terminal Emulator*, for more information about *xterm*.

The Display Manager

The display manager, *xdm*, is a client that is designed to start the X server automatically (from the UNIX */etc/rc* system startup file) and to keep it running. (X can also be started manually, as described in Chapter 2, *Getting Started*.) In its most basic implementation, the display manager emulates the *getty* and *login* programs, which put up the login prompt on a standard terminal, keeping the server running, prompting for a user's name and password, and managing a standard login session.

However, *xdm* has far more powerful and versatile capabilities. Users can design their own sessions, automatically running several clients and setting personal resources (such as keyboard, pointer, and display characteristics). The system administrator can also customize special *xdm* files to manage several connected displays (both local and remote) and to set system-wide X resources (for example, client default features). Resources are introduced in Chapter 3, *Working in the X Environment*, and discussed fully in Chapter 10, *Setting Resources*.

Many commercial vendors provide alternative display/session managers. If you are using a display manager other than *xdm*, many of the concepts should remain the same. However, the actual setup procedures may differ. See Appendix A, *System Management*, for a discussion of how to set up and customize the *xdm* display manager.

Introduction to X

Other X Clients

The standard distribution of X from MIT includes more than 50 client applications. The client you will probably used most frequently is *xterm*. We've grouped some of the other more useful applications as follows:

Desk accessories

xbiff	Mail notification program.
xclock, *oclock*	Clock applications.
xcalc	Desktop calculator.
xload	System load monitor.
xman	Manual page browser.

Display and keyboard preferences

xset	Allows you to set various display and keyboard preferences, such as bell volume, cursor acceleration, and screen saver operation.
xmodmap	Allows you to map keyboard keys and pointer buttons to particular functions.

Font utilities

xlsfonts	Lists available fonts.
xfd	Displays the characters in a single font.
xfontsel	Allows you to display multiple fonts sequentially and select a font to be used by another application.

Graphics utilities

bitmap	Bitmap editor.
atobm, *bmtoa*	Programs to convert ASCII characters to bitmaps and bitmaps to ASCII characters.

Printing applications

xwd	Dumps the image of a window to a file.
xpr	Translates an image file produced by *xwd* to PostScript® or another format, suitable for printing on a variety of printers.
xwud	Redisplays a window dump file created using *xwd*.

Removing a window

xkill	Terminates a client application.

Window and display information utilities

xlsclients	Lists the clients running on the display.
xdpyinfo	Lists general characteristics of the display.
xwininfo	Lists general characteristics of a selected window.
xprop	Lists the properties associated with a window.

These and other client applications are described in Chapters 5 through 8, and in Chapter 11. In addition, a reference page describing each client and listing its options appears in Part Three of this guide. As more commercial and user-contributed software is developed, many more specialized programs will become available.

Customizing Clients

Most X clients are designed to be customized by the user. A multitude of command-line options can be used to affect the appearance and operation of a single client process. A few of the more useful command-line options are introduced in Chapter 3. Chapter 9 discusses several options in detail. Part Three of this guide includes a reference page for each client that details all valid options.

X also provides a somewhat more convenient way to customize the appearance and operation of client programs. Rather than specifying all characteristics using command line options, default values for most options can be stored in a file (generally called *.Xresources* or *.Xdefaults*) in your home directory. Each default value is set using a variable called a *resource*;

you can change the behavior or appearance of a program by changing the *value* associated with a resource variable.

Generally, these resource values are loaded into the server using a program called *xrdb* (*X resource database* manager). Then the values are accessed automatically when you run a client. Storing your preferences in the server with *xrdb* also allows you to run clients on multiple machines without maintaining an *.Xresources* file on each machine.

There is a separate customization file for the *mwm* window manager called *.mwmrc*, which is also kept in your home directory. By editing the *.mwmrc* file, you can modify several aspects of the window manager's operation, such as the contents of menus, and the key and pointer button sequences used to invoke actions. See Chapter 11, *Customizing mwm*, for more information.

Client customization is introduced in Chapter 3, *Working in the X Environment*, and described fully in Part Two of this guide.

2

Getting Started

This chapter helps you start the X server, the first xterm *(terminal emulator)* *window, and the* mwm *window manager. These processes may be started* *automatically when you log in, or you may have to start them manually.*

In This Chapter:

Getting Started

2
Getting Started

Before you can begin using the X Window System, you must do three things:

- Start the X server.

- Start at least one *xterm* terminal emulator.

- Start a window manager. (Although you *can* run X without a window manager, this is fairly limiting.)

Depending on how X is configured on your system, some or all of these steps may be performed for you automatically. This chapter explains how you can tell if the X server, an *xterm* window, and the *mwm* window manager are being started automatically. This chapter also describes how to start these processes manually.

After you've started these preliminary processes, skip to the section "Typing in a Window Once mwm is Running," later in this chapter.

Starting X

Depending on how X is being run on your system, the initial screens you see and the way you log in will be slightly different.

On some systems the display manager, *xdm*, starts X and keeps it running. If your system is set up to use *xdm*, you log on in a special window provided for that purpose. If *xdm* is running, you should never have to start X manually.

On some systems, you may be required to log in at a prompt displayed on the full screen. In these situations, X may or may not be started automatically when you log in. If X is not started automatically, you must start it yourself from the command line, as we'll describe later in this chapter.

Be aware that X is very easy to customize. There are countless command options as well as startup files that control the way the screen looks or even what menus a program displays. If X has been customized on your system, or you are trying out X using someone else's system or login account, things may not work exactly as described here. Customizing the X environment is introduced in Chapter 3, *Working in the X Environment*, and described in detail in Chapters 9 through 12.

Logging On in the Special xdm Window

If the display manager, *xdm*, is running X on your system, you'll probably see a window similar to Figure 2-1 when you turn on your terminal.

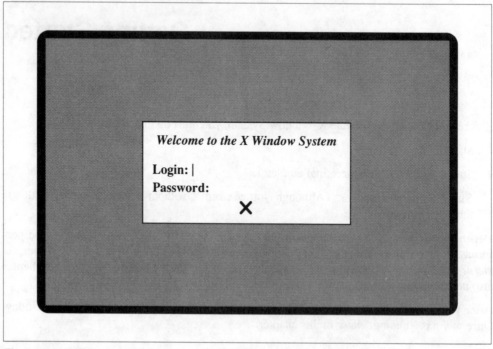

Welcome to the X Window System

Login: |
Password:

X

Figure 2-1. xdm login window

Log in just as if you were using a standard alphanumeric terminal. Without any user customization, the display manager executes a standard login "session," providing the first *xterm* window and starting the window manager. The *xterm* window will be displayed in the upper-left corner of the screen. If the Motif window manager is running, you will see the characteristic frame around the *xterm* window, as in Figure 2-2. The name of the application ("xterm") appears in the frame's title area.

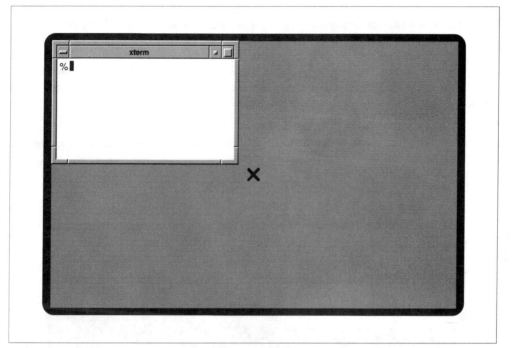

Figure 2-2. Window frame indicates that mwm is running

The frame provides a quick and easy way to move, iconify, resize, and otherwise manage windows on the screen. Some of the basic window manager functions are introduced in the section "Raising, Moving, and Iconifying Windows" in Chapter 3.

If the *mwm* window manager is running, skip to the section "Typing in a Window Once mwm is Running," later in this chapter. If the window manager is not running, skip to the section "Bringing Up the Window Manager," for instructions on how to start it.

Be aware that, in addition to *xdm*, other display/session managers are commercially available. For example, Digital Equipment Corporation provides a display manager called *dxsession*, which functions similarly to *xdm*. If your system is using a display manager other than *xdm*, the login procedure may be slightly different. Also keep in mind that system administration tasks will vary depending on which display manager you use. Appendix A, *System Management*, describes the tasks involved in setting up the *xdm* display manager to run X.

Logging In at a Full Screen Prompt

If you log in at a prompt displayed on the full screen, your system is probably set set up to work in one of three ways. First, some workstations may be set up to start the server, open up the first *xterm* window, and possibly even start the window manager automatically. If all of these processes are running when you log in, the initial *xterm* window will be framed, as in Figure 2-2. Once the server, initial *xterm*, and the *mwm* window manager are running, you can skip to the section "Typing in a Window Once mwm is Running."

Some systems are set up to start the server and initial *xterm* window when you log in, but not the window manager. If this is the case, your screen should then look something like the one in Figure 2-3.

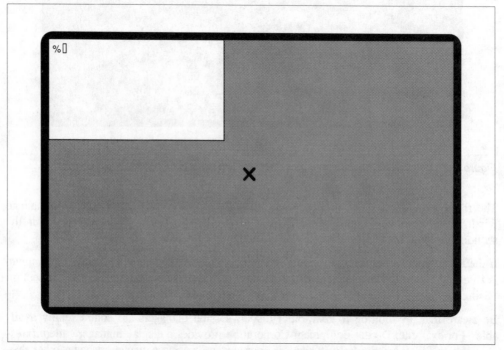

Figure 2-3. Workstation with login xterm window on the root window

If you have an *xterm* window without a frame, you must start *mwm* yourself. Skip to the section "Starting the Window Manager" later in this chapter.

Be aware, however, that on some systems, X is not started automatically. When you log in at the prompt displayed on the full screen, no windows are opened; instead the entire screen functions as a single terminal, as shown in Figure 2-4.

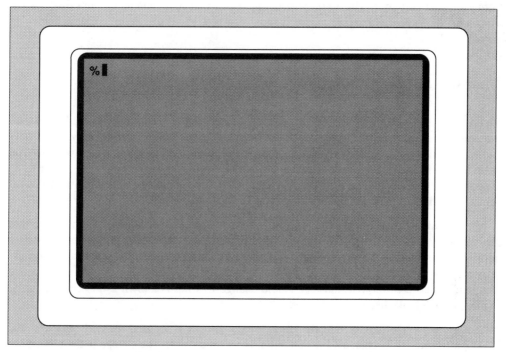

Figure 2-4. Workstation functioning as a single terminal: X isn't running

If no windows are displayed when you log on at a full screen prompt, you must start the X Window System manually.

Starting X Manually

To start X manually, first make sure that the X11 directory containing executable programs is in your search path.* If not, add the pathname */usr/bin/X11* to the path set in your *.profile* or *.login* file.

If another windowing system (such as SunView™) is running, you must first kill it.

Then at the system prompt, enter:

```
% xinit
```

---

*For more information on how to set your search path, see Appendix A, *System Management*. Note that the appropriate pathname to add may be different in vendor distributions.

The *xinit* program starts the X server and creates the first *xterm* window in the upper-left corner of your display.* The *xterm* window indicates that X is running on your display. (In Appendix A, *System Management*, we'll show you how to set things up so that X comes up automatically.)

Starting the mwm Window Manager

To bring up the *mwm* window manager, you must enter the *mwm* command in the login *xterm* window. As described in Chapter 1, *An Introduction to the X Window System*, you can only provide input to one window at a time. X does not automatically know which window you want to type in, even if only one window appears on the display, as in Figure 2-3. In order to type in the *xterm* window on the display, you must first focus input to that window. The window to which input is focused is often referred to as the active window.

When no window manager is running, you focus input simply by moving the pointer so that the cursor symbol on the screen rests within the window. Depending on where the pointer rests, the cursor symbol representing it on the screen differs. When the pointer rests on the root window, it appears as a large X (another indication that X is running). When you move the pointer into the *xterm* window, it should change to what is known as the I-beam cursor symbol, which looks like a very thin letter "I".

When you move the pointer into the *xterm* window, input is focused there. Notice that the rectangular text cursor changes from an outline to a solid color. The change in the text cursor is another indication that input is focused on the window. Once you've selected the *xterm* window as the active window, the characters you type will appear on the window's command line.

Start the *mwm* window manager by typing:

```
% mwm &
```

The screen will momentarily go blank. Then while *mwm* is starting up, the root window pointer changes to an hour glass that appears to be filling up with sand. When the hour glass is full, the *xterm* window will be redisplayed, this time with the characteristic frame, indicating that *mwm* is running.

---

*If *xinit* produces a blank background with no terminal window, software installation was not completed correctly. Reboot your workstation and try again. Before invoking *xinit*, look in the directory */usr/bin/X11* for a file whose name begins with a capital X but otherwise has a similar name to your workstation (e.g., Xsun). When you find one that seems a likely possibility, try this command:

```
% xinit -- Xname
```

If that works, link X*name* to X, and *xinit* will work correctly thereafter. For example:

```
% cd /usr/bin/X11
% ln Xsun X
```

X Window System User's Guide, Motif Edition

Note that it is important to run *mwm* in the background by typing an ampersand (&) at the end of the command line so you can continue to enter additional commands in the *xterm* window. If you neglected to do this on a system that supports job control, type Control-Z to suspend *mwm*, then use the *bg* command (see *csh*(1)) to place it in the background.

If the system you're on does not support job control, interrupt the process using the appropriate key sequence (Control-C on many systems) and start over.

Typing In a Window Once mwm is Running

Now that you've started the X server, the first *xterm* window, and the *mwm* window manager, you'll want to proceed by entering commands in the *xterm* window. However, if you type some characters, you'll find that the keystrokes do not appear in the *xterm*—or anywhere else on the display!

In order to type in a window when *mwm* is running, you must first move the pointer into the window and click the first button. As described in Chapter 1, this focus policy is commonly referred to as click-to-type or explicit focus. (When *mwm* is not running, you select the window to receive input—the active or focus window—simply by moving the pointer into that window.) Until you select the *xterm* window as the window to receive input, any keystrokes are lost.

This feature of *mwm* can be even more confusing if *mwm* is not started automatically when you log in. Before you start the window manager, you can focus input on a window simply by moving the pointer. As described in the preceding section, you must move the pointer into the first *xterm* window in order to enter the *mwm* command. However, once you run *mwm*, the focus policy changes to click-to-type. If you try to type additional characters without clicking on the window, the keystrokes will be lost.

To select the focus window when *mwm* is running:

1. Move the pointer into the *xterm* or other client window.

2. Click the first pointer button. (To click a pointer button, you press it down and release it without pausing. Pointer actions are explained in the section "Using the Pointer" in Chapter 3.)

The color of the window frame will change in some way, indicating that the window has the input focus. (Once you are running several windows simultaneously, it's important to be able to identify the focus window easily.) The color of the active window's frame depends on the version of *mwm* you are running and the color resources for your system.

When you are using explicit (click-to-type) focus and the other default *mwm* resources, selecting a window to receive input also raises that window to the top of the window stack. As we'll see in Chapter 11, *Customizing mwm*, this behavior is controlled by an *mwm* resource variable called `focusAutoRaise`, which is true by default when explicit focus is in effect.

If you are working with a stack of windows that overlap, selecting a focus window automatically raises that window to the top of the stack (in effect the front of the display).

Keep in mind that *mwm* is highly customizable. You can specify dozens of features, including the color of the active window's frame, the options available on menus, and how certain window management functions are invoked. As we've discussed, one of the most significant modifications you can make to *mwm* is to change the focus policy from click-to-type (or explicit focus) to real-estate-driven (or pointer focus).

3

Working in the X Environment

This chapter shows you how to begin working productively in the X environment. It describes how to:

• Open a second xterm *window,*

• Move windows; raise windows to the front of the display; convert windows to icons,

• Close an xterm *window,*

• Start other clients in convenient places on the display,

• Run clients on remote machines,

• Customize a single client process using command line options,

• Specify alternate default characteristics for a client using resource variables.

In This Chapter:

3
Working in the X Environment

At the end of the last chapter, you should've had the X server, the first *xterm* window, and the *mwm* window manager running. The current chapter illustrates some of the system's basic capabilities so you can begin working more productively. This chapter shows you how to:

- Open a second *xterm* window.

- Use the pointer to affect windows on the display.

- Raise, move, and iconify windows.

- Close an *xterm* window.

- Start additional client programs, on both local and remote machines.

- Organize the display.

This chapter also introduces some basic ways to customize X clients to better suit your needs.

Creating Other Windows

Once you focus input on the first *xterm* window, as described in Chapter 2, you can enter commands to open other client windows. For example, you can open a second *xterm* window by typing this command at the prompt in the first *xterm* window:

```
% xterm &
```

After a few moments, a second *xterm* window will be displayed on the screen. As we'll see later in this chapter, you can specify the location for a new window using a command line option (or in many cases using a resource variable stored in a file in your home directory). If you don't specify position on the command line (or in a resource file), by default *mwm* automatically places new windows offset from the upper-left corner of the screen, as shown in Figure 3-1.* The new *xterm* window displays a prompt from whatever shell you are using. In this case, the new window is running the UNIX C shell.

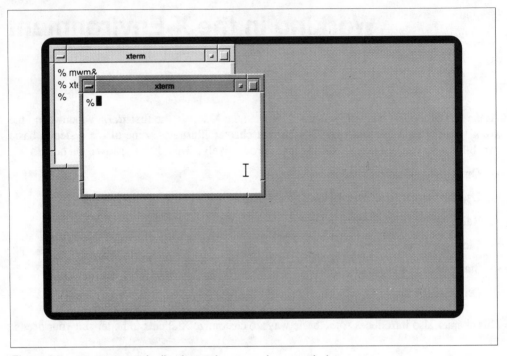

Figure 3-1. mwm automatically places the second xterm window

Notice that the second window's frame is a dark grey, indicating that input is focused on it. The first window's frame has changed from dark to light grey; it no longer has the input focus. It's important to be aware that when you start a new window (and click-to-type focus is being used), the new window automatically takes over the input focus.

In the default *mwm* configuration, to switch back and forth between windows you must move the pointer from one window to the other and click the first button. Notice that if you are working with a stack of windows that overlap, selecting a window as the active window automatically raises that window to the top of the stack (in effect, the front of the display).

---

*If you start multiple processes in a row, the windows will be placed progressively further from the upper-left corner (towards the opposite corner), so that no window completely overlaps another.

You can customize *mwm* to allow you to place new windows interactively using the pointer. This modification is performed by setting a resource variable called `interactivePlacement` to a value of true. See Chapter 11 for instructions on modifying *mwm*. See the *mwm* reference page in Part Three of this guide for more information about `interactivePlacement`.

Whatever you type will appear in the window with the highlighted frame. Try starting a command in both windows. For example, start up *vi* or another text editor in the second *xterm* window. Notice how you can switch back to the first window to type a new command, by moving the pointer and clicking—even if you leave *vi* in insert mode or some other command in the process of sending output to the screen. Whatever process was running in the window you left will continue to run. If it needs input from you to continue, it will wait.

You must always switch focus to work with multiple windows. However, *mwm* has complicated matters by placing the second *xterm* window in Figure 3-1 in a very inconvenient place. The second window overlies the first window and almost completely obscures it.

Windows commonly overlap on the display. The window manager allows you to change the position and size of windows so that you can work effectively in such situations.

The primary window management tool *mwm* provides is the window frame. The section "Raising, Moving, and Iconifying Windows," later in this chapter, shows you how to perform these functions simply by using the pointer on various parts of the frame. But before we can learn to perform these window management functions, we need to learn more about pointer actions.

Using the Pointer

You use the pointer to indicate a graphical element on the screen, such as a window, icon, or command button. Most pointers have three buttons. For our purposes, we'll refer to these buttons as first, second, and third, where the first button is the leftmost on the pointer, the second is in the middle, and third is the rightmost.* By placing the pointer on a particular element and then performing some button action (and possibly a pointer motion), you can invoke a variety of commands. The types of button actions and pointer motions you can perform are:

Click   To click a button, you press the pointer button down and release it. A click is a rapid action; there is no pause between the press and release. A double click is two full clicks in succession, with no pause between clicks. A triple click is three clicks in succession.

Press   To press a button, you push the button down and hold it down.

Release   After pressing a button down, you release it by letting up on the button.

Drag   To drag a graphical object (such as a window or icon) from one location on the screen to another: place the pointer on the object; press one or more pointer buttons; move the pointer to another location (dragging the object); and release the button(s).

---

*Keep in mind that "first" is a logical distinction made by X, not a physical one. The first logical pointer button generally corresponds to the leftmost button on the pointer. (Thus, in some contexts you may find the buttons referred to as left, middle, and right.) However, X allows you to change the correspondence of logical and physical buttons. For example, you can reassign the first logical button to be the rightmost button on the pointer. A lefthanded person might opt to reverse the order of the buttons. You remap pointer buttons using a client called *xmodmap*, which is described in detail in Chapter 12, *Setup Clients*.

Keep in mind that some commands or actions are invoked by a simple click on a particular graphic element, as illustrated by *mwm*'s click-to-type focus. Alternatively, some actions require a button press and pointer motion (i.e., dragging).

When dragging is used to move an object, the actual object does not appear in the new location until you complete the movement and release the pointer button. Instead, you appear to drag an outline representing the object. When you release the pointer button, the actual object appears in the new location. This effect is illustrated in the section "Moving a Window," later in this chapter.

Dragging is also commonly used to change the size of a window. Again, an outline indicates that the window's size is changing. When the outline approximates the size you want, you release the pointer button and the actual window is redrawn using the selected dimensions. Resizing a window is described in Chapter 4. The following sections describe how to perform the most basic window management functions, which require you to use the pointer in the ways we've discussed.

Raising, Moving, and Iconifying Windows

Figure 3-2 shows an *xterm* window "framed" by *mwm*. The window frame itself and several features of it are tools that allow you to manipulate the window using the pointer.

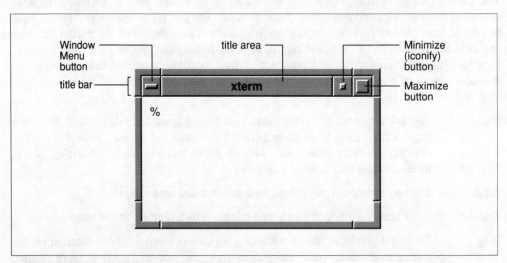

Figure 3-2. An xterm window framed by mwm

The wider top edge of the frame is the titlebar. The titlebar is composed of several parts including a title area (displaying the name of the application) and three command buttons (Minimize, Maximize, and Window Menu). Notice that whenever you move the pointer into the titlebar, the pointer changes to the arrow cursor.

Though it's not apparent from Figure 3-2, you can perform most window management functions by using the pointer on various part of the frame. The following sections explain how to perform some of the simplest and most necessary functions. The remaining functions you can perform using the frame will be discussed in Chapter 4, which also describes menu items and keyboard shortcuts that can be used as alternatives to the frame.

Raising a Window or Icon

We've already seen the necessity for raising windows on the display: frequently windows overlap. In order to work with a window that is all or partially covered by another window, you'll want to raise it to the top of the window stack. Using the default *mwm*, you raise a window with the following steps:

1. Place the pointer on any part of the window frame, except the three command buttons (Minimize, Maximize, and Window Menu).

2. Click the first pointer button. The window is raised to the top of the stack.

When you are using explicit (click-to-type) focus, this click also selects the window to receive input, i.e., makes the window the active window. Once you have raised a window to the top of the stack, you should be able to enter input and read output easily.

Windows may obscure icons on the display. (*mwm* does not allow one icon to obscure another.) If an icon is partially visible under a window, you can raise it using the following steps:

1. Place the pointer on the obscured icon.

2. Click the first pointer button.

The icon is raised to the top of the stack.

Figure 3-3 illustrates an icon being raised in front of a window.

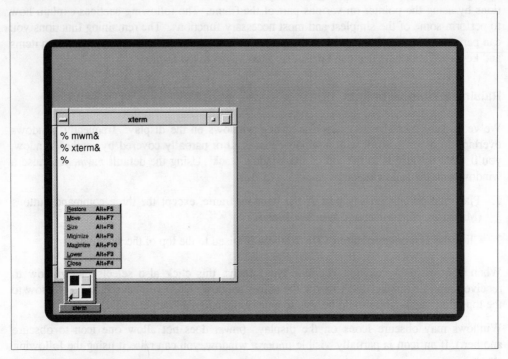

Figure 3-3. Raising an icon

Notice that in addition to being raised to the top of the window stack, a menu (called the Window Menu) is displayed over the icon. (This menu can be displayed from a window or from an icon and can be used to invoke several management functions on the window or icon. We'll discuss the Window Menu in more detail in Chapter 4.) To remove the menu, move the pointer off of the icon and menu and click the first button.

Notice also that the icon image appears to change when you raise the icon to the top of the stack. The icon label becomes wider and the label and the frame surrounding the icon are highlighted. These changes indicate that the icon has the input focus; thus the icon will interpret subsequent keystrokes as window manager commands. Even when you remove the Window Menu, the icon will retain the focus (and remain highlighted). When you direct focus to another window (or icon), the icon label will become normal again.

Moving a Window

In many cases you'll want to move a window from one location on the display to another. The largest part of the titlebar is known as the *title area*, primarily because it displays the name of the application. The title area allows you to move the window, using the following steps:

1. Place the pointer within the title area. The pointer changes to the arrow cursor.

2. Press and hold down the first pointer button.

3. Move the window by dragging the pointer. Figure 3-4 shows a window being moved in this way. When you begin to move the window, the pointer changes to a cross arrow pointer and a window outline appears. This outline tracks the pointer's movement. In the center of the screen, a small, rectangular box also appears, displaying the x and y coordinates of the window as you move it.

4. Drag the cross arrow pointer with the window outline to the desired location on your screen.

5. Release the first pointer button. The window will move to the selected location.

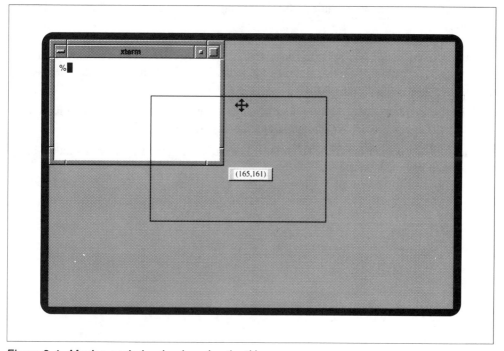

Figure 3-4. Moving a window by dragging the title area

With the default configuration of *mwm*, moving a window also selects that window as the active or focus window.

You can also move icons on the display. As we discussed in Chapter 1, an icon is a small symbol that (generally) represents a window in an inactive state. The next two sections describe how to convert a window to an icon and an icon back to a window. Once we've seen how to iconify a window, we'll also learn how to move an icon.

Converting a Window to an Icon

There are many circumstances in which it might be desirable to iconify a window:

- To prevent yourself from inadvertently terminating a window, as in the case of the login *xterm*.

- While running a program whose progress you don't need to monitor; if a window is tied up running a process and you don't have to see it, the window is just taking up space.

- If you are only using an application occasionally. For example, you might be running the *xcalc* calculator program, but only using it every hour or so.

- If you want to use several application windows, but only display a few at a time; this arrangement can be somewhat less confusing than a display crowded with windows. Having some windows iconified also frees you from constantly shuffling the stacking order.

The Minimize command button on the *mwm* frame allows you to convert a window to an icon (iconify it). The Minimize button appears immediately to the right of the title area, and is identified by a tiny square in its center. To iconify a window, use the following steps:

1. Place the pointer within the Minimize command button. The pointer simply has to rest within the button's outer border, not within the tiny square identifying it.

2. Click the first pointer button. The window is iconified. Figure 3-5 shows a window being converted to an icon in this way.

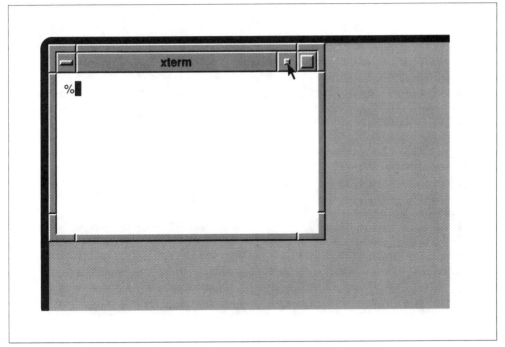

Figure 3-5. Converting a window to an icon with the Minimize button

By default, icons are displayed in the bottom left corner of the root window. *mwm* can also be set up to place icons in another location, to allow you to place them interactively using the pointer, or to organize icons within a window known as an *icon box*. In Chapter 11, *Customizing mwm*, we'll discuss the specifications necessary to set up an icon box.

Converting an Icon to a Window

To convert an icon back to a window (deiconify it), place the pointer on the icon and double click, using the first pointer button. The window is redisplayed in the position it appeared before it was iconfied.

Between the first and second clicks, you'll probably notice that another small window is displayed for an instant above the icon. This window is actually the Window Menu (which is also displayed when you raise an icon to the top of the stack). We'll discuss the Window Menu in more detail in Chapter 4, *More about the mwm Window Manager*.

Be aware, however, that if you pause too long between the two clicks in deiconifying a window, the second click will not be interpreted and the icon will not be converted back to a window. Instead the Window Menu will remain on the screen, as in Figure 3-6.

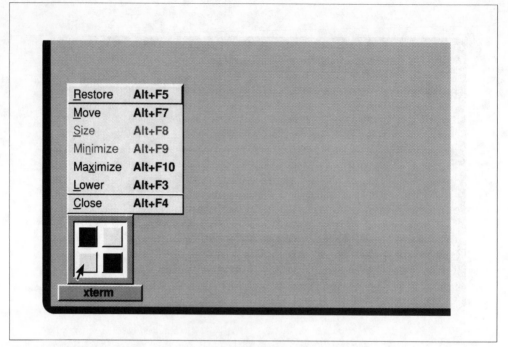

Figure 3-6. Window Menu being displayed over an icon

Notice that in addition to displaying the menu, the icon image has changed in the same way it did when we raised an icon. The wider label and the highlighted label and frame indicate that the icon has the input focus. (Remember, when an icon has the input focus, it will interpret subsequent keystrokes as window manager commands.)

Notice also that the first item on the menu, Restore, is surrounded by a box, indicating that it is available for selection. Restore means to restore an icon to a window. When the Window Menu is displayed above an icon, you can convert the icon to a window by placing the pointer on the Restore menu item and clicking the first pointer button. (Whenever a Window Menu item is boxed, you can also select it by pressing either the Return key or the space bar.)

If you want to remove the menu without invoking a command, simply move the pointer off the icon and menu and click the first pointer button. The menu will be removed; however, the icon will retain the input focus—the label and border will remain highlighted—until you focus input on another window or icon.

Moving an Icon

Moving an icon is similar to moving a window. To move an icon:

1. Place the pointer on the icon.

2. Press the first pointer button.

3. Move the icon by dragging the pointer. Figure 3-7 shows an icon being moved in this way. When you begin to move the icon, the pointer changes to a cross arrow pointer and an icon outline appears. This outline tracks the pointer's movement.

4. Drag the cross arrow pointer with the icon outline to the desired location on your screen.

5. Release the first pointer button. The icon will move to the selected location.

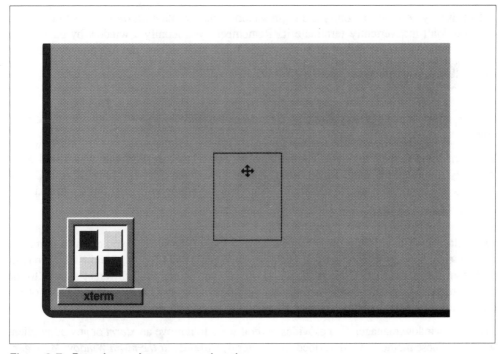

Figure 3-7. Dragging an icon to a new location

With the default configuration of *mwm*, moving an icon also selects that icon to receive the input focus.

Exiting from an xterm Window

When you are finished using an *xterm* window, you can remove it by typing whatever command you usually use to log off your system. Typically, this might be `exit` or Control-D. We'll close the second *xterm* window in Figure 3-8 by typing `exit`.

Notice that when we terminate the second *xterm* window, the first *xterm* window takes over the input focus. When explicit focus is being used and a window is terminated, the input focus reverts to the window that previously had the focus.

Be aware that terminating the login *xterm* window (the first *xterm* to appear) kills the X server and all associated clients. (If *xdm* is running X, the server will be reset but only after all client processes have been killed.) Be sure to terminate all other *xterm* windows before terminating the *xterm* login window. Also, if you are in an editor such as *vi*, be sure to save your data before you terminate the window.

In fact, it may be wise to iconify the login window and use other *xterm* windows instead, so that you don't inadvertently terminate it. Remember: you iconify a window by placing the pointer on the Minimize command button on the frame and clicking the first pointer button.

Alternatively, you can enter:

```
% set ignoreeof
```

in the login window. Then typing `exit` becomes the only way you can terminate the window.

Note that some C shell implementations have an `autologout` variable, which will automatically terminate the shell if there is no activity for a given period of time. If your C shell supports this feature, be sure to disable it in the login *xterm* window using this command:

```
% unset autologout
```

As an alternative to entering the command used to log off the system, you can also terminate an *xterm* window by selecting Send HUP Signal, Send TERM Signal, Send KILL Signal, or Quit from the *xterm* Main Options menu. (These menu options send different signals to the *xterm* process. Depending on what signals your operating system recognizes, some of the options may not work as intended. See Chapter 5 for more information.)

The *mwm* window manager also provides several ways to remove an *xterm* or any other client window. These methods are described in Chapter 4, *More about the mwm Window Manager*.

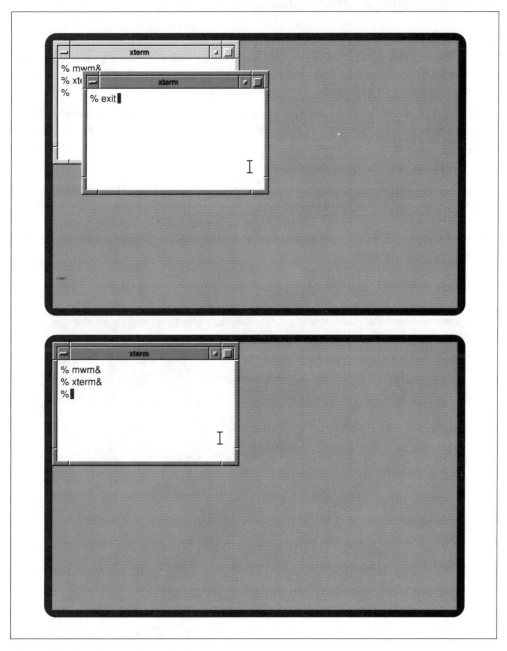

Figure 3-8. Closing an xterm window

Starting Additional Clients

Now that you know the basics of managing windows, you can start other X clients just like you can start another instance of *xterm*. The following sections describe how to open more client windows, place them on the display in convenient positions, and take advantage of X's networking capabilities by running clients on other machines.

To start a client, at the command line prompt in any *xterm* window, type the name of the client followed by an ampersand (&) to make the client run in the background. For example, by typing:

```
% oclock &
```

you can cause a window displaying a clock to be placed on the screen. The clock will appear in the upper-left quarter of the screen. You can then drag the *oclock* window to a more convenient location—say the upper-right corner, as in Figure 3-9. (Remember, to move a window, place the pointer on the title area, press the first button, drag the window outline to the desired location, and release the button.)

Figure 3-9. The oclock window

Though moving windows on the display is fairly simple, manually positioning every window is not particularly convenient. For most clients, X provides a way to specify a window's location (and also its size) automatically—using an option when you run the command. A window's size and position is referred to as its *geometry* and you set these attributes using the -geometry option. The use of this option is discussed in the section "Window Geometry: Specifying Size and Location," later in this chapter.

Unfortunately the developers of *oclock* neglected to provide an easy way to remove it. For instructions on removing an *oclock* window, see Chapter 8, *Other Clients*.

Command Line Options

Most X clients accept two powerful and extremely useful options: the -geometry option, which allows you to specify the size and location of a window on the screen; and the -display option, which allows you to specify on which screen a window should be created. (Most commonly, you'd use the -display option to run a client on a remote machine and display the window locally.)

The next few sections illustrate some typical uses of these important options. In explaining how to use them, we introduce some new, perhaps somewhat involved concepts (such as the way distances can be measured on your screen). Bear with us. We feel that you need to master the -geometry and -display options in order to begin to take advantage of the powers of X.

After explaining these options in detail, we'll briefly consider some of the characteristics you can specify using other common options.

Window Geometry: Specifying Size and Location

The command line option to specify a window's size and location has the form:

```
-geometry geometry
```

The -geometry option can be (and often is) abbreviated as -g, unless the client accepts another option that begins with "g."

The parameter to the geometry option (*geometry*), referred to as the "standard geometry string," has four numerical components, two specifying the window's dimensions and two specifying its location. The standard geometry string has the syntax:

```
widthxheight±xoff±yoff
```

Obviously, the first half of the string provides the *width* and *height* of the window. Many application windows are measured in pixels. However, application developers are encouraged to use units that are meaningful in terms of the application. For example, *xterm*'s dimensions are measured in columns and rows of font characters. More precisely, an *xterm* window is some number of characters wide by some number of lines high (80 characters wide by 24 lines high by default).

The second half of the geometry string gives the location of the window relative to the horizontal and vertical edges of the screen. Imagining the screen to be a grid (where the upper-left corner is 0,0), *xoff* (x offset) and *yoff* (y offset) represent the x and y coordinates at which the window should be displayed. The x and y offsets are also measured in pixels.

Many users may not be accustomed to thinking in terms of pixels. What exactly is a pixel? A pixel is the smallest element of a display surface that can be addressed by a program. You can think of a pixel as one of the tiny dots that make up a graphic image, such as that displayed by a terminal or a television.

Since a pixel is a tiny unit of measurement, gauging sizes and distances in pixels will take some practice. For instance, what are the dimensions of your screen in pixels? Your workstation or X terminal documentation may provide this information, or you may have to experiment by placing windows in order to figure out the approximate dimensions.

Keep in mind that monitors can vary substantially. The Sun 19-inch monitor has dimensions of 1152 x 900 pixels (these figures also comprise what is known as the screen's *resolution*). Since the horizontal and vertical dimensions of the viewing area are approximately 13.75 x 10.75 inches, each inch is equivalent to approximately 84 pixels (sometimes called dots) in both dimensions. By contrast, the 16-inch monitor on the Sony NEWS workstation has dimensions of 1280 x 1024 pixels. The actual viewing area is approximately 13 inches wide by 10 inches high. This can be translated to 98.5 dots per inch (dpi) horizontally and 102.4 dpi vertically.

What are the implications of such hardware differences in specifying client geometry? The size and location of client windows is related to the size and resolution of your screen. For example, if you specify a window with dimensions of 125 x 125 pixels, it will appear somewhat larger on the Sun monitor than on the Sony.

So how do we use the geometry option to specify a window's size and location? First, be aware that you can specify any or all elements of the geometry string. Incomplete geometry specifications are compared to the application's default settings and missing elements are supplied by these values. All client windows have a default size. For example, if you run an *xterm* window with the geometry option and specify a location but no dimensions, the application default of 80 characters by 24 lines is used.

If you don't specify the x and y coordinates at which to place a client window, the client may provide a default location; if the application doesn't provide a default and *mwm* is running, the window manager will automatically position the window in the upper-left quarter of the screen.

For now, let's just specify a window's location and let the size be the application default. The x and y offsets can be either positive or negative. If you specify positive offsets, you're positioning the left side and top side of the window. Negative offsets are interpreted differently. The possible values for the x and y offsets and their effects are shown in Table 3-1.

Table 3-1. Geometry Specification x and y Offsets

Offset Variables	Description
+xoff	A positive x offset specifies the distance by which the left edge of the window is offset from the left side of the display.
+yoff	A positive y offset specifies the distance by which the top edge of the window is offset from the top of the display.
-xoff	A negative x offset specifies the distance by which the right edge of the window is offset from the right side of the display.
-yoff	A negative y offset specifies the distance by which the bottom edge of the window is offset from the bottom of the display.

For example, the command line:

```
% xclock -geometry -10+10 &
```

places a clock of the default size in the upper-right corner of the display, 10 pixels from the top and right edges of the screen.

To place a window in any of the four corners of the screen, flush against its boundaries, use the following x and y offsets.

Offset Specification	Window Location
+0+0	Upper-left corner of the display.
+0-0	Lower-left corner of the display.
-0+0	Upper-right corner of the display.
-0-0	Lower-right corner of the display.

If you want a window placed away from one or both edges of the screen, the guesswork starts. How many pixels away from the left side of the screen? How many pixels down from the top? You'll have to experiment with placing some clients on your screen to get a better idea of x and y offsets.

It's actually a good idea to start some windows and move them around on your screen using the pointer. While you're dragging a window, check the x and y offsets displayed in the small box *mwm* places in the center of the screen. These coordinates are the positive x and y offsets of the window (i.e., the offsets relative to the upper-left corner of the screen). This method for gauging location is fairly reliable.*

---

*There seems to be a very slight delay between pointer motion and update to the *mwm* coordinate box. When you finish dragging the window, the last coordinates visible in the box may differ from the true coordinates by a pixel in either or both directions. But this variance is so trivial that you can supply the coordinates as part of the geometry string and come very close.

You can also place some windows in different places by dragging and then figure out their x and y offsets using the *xwininfo* client, described in Chapter 8, *Other Clients*. *xwininfo* gives you several statistics about a window, including the coordinates of its upper-left corner. However, since the client's results are affected by the presence of the frame, when *mwm* is running it's a little easier to move a window and check the coordinates box.

Now what about the size of a window? For *xterm*, the size of the window is measured in characters and lines (by default 80 characters by 24 lines). If you want to use a large VT100 window, say 100 characters wide by 30 lines long, you could use this geometry specification:

```
% xterm -geometry 100x30-0-0 &
```

This command creates a large *xterm* window in the lower-right corner of the screen, as illustrated by Figure 3-10.

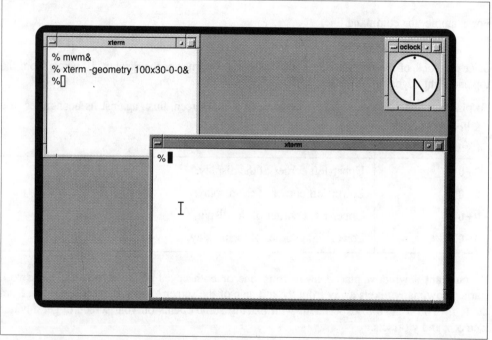

Figure 3-10. *xterm window sized and positioned with the -geometry option*

As stated previously, most of the standard clients (other than *xterm*) are measured in pixels. For example, *xclock* is 164 pixels square by default (exclusive of the *mwm* frame). A client's default dimensions may appear on its reference page in Part Three of this guide. However, you'll probably need to experiment with specifying sizes (as well as locations) on your display. (See Chapter 8, *Other Clients*, and the client reference page, for more about *xclock*.)

Be aware that the geometry option is not necessarily the only means available to specify window size and location. Several clients, including *xterm*, allow you to set the size and location of a window (and often its icon or an alternate window) using resource variables (in an *Xresources* or other defaults file). We'll introduce some of the basics of specifying resources later in this chapter. See Chapter 10, *Setting Resources*, for more detailed instructions on setting resources. See the appropriate client reference pages in Part Three of this guide for a complete list of available resources.

You should be aware that, as with all user preferences, you may not always get exactly what you ask for. Clients are designed to work with a window manager, which may have its own rules for window or icon size and placement. However, priority is always given to specific user requests, so you won't often be surprised.

Running a Client on Another Machine: Specifying the Display

We still have yet to take advantage of X's networking capabilities. Remember that X allows you to run a client on a remote machine across a network. Generally, the results of a client program are displayed on a screen connected to the system where the client is running. However, if you are running a client on a remote system, you probably want to see the results on your own display (connected to a local server).

Running a client on a remote machine may give you access to different software, it may increase the efficiency of certain processes, or benefit you in a number of other ways. We discussed some of the advantages of running a client on a remote machine in Chapter 1, *An Introduction to the X Window System*. See the section "X Architecture Overview" for details.

But how does running a client on a remote system affect how you work with the X display? Once a client is running, it doesn't. You can display the application window on your own screen, enter input using your own keyboard and pointer, and read the client's output in the window on your screen—all while the actual client process occurs on another machine.

However, by default a client creates its window on a display connected to the machine on which it is running. In order to run a client remotely and display its results locally, you must tell the client process where to display its window. For this purpose, X provides a command line option: `-display`. Like `-geometry`, the `-display` option is recognized by most X clients. The display option tells the client on which server to display results (i.e., create its window). The option has the syntax:

    -display [host]:server[.screen]

The `-display` option can be abbreviated as `-d`, unless the client accepts another option that begins with "d."

The argument to the display option is a 3-component *display name*. The `host` specifies the machine on which to create the window, the `server` specifies the server number, and the `screen` specifies the screen number.

In this context, "server" refers to a single physical display controlled by one X server program. (A display may be composed of multiple screens, but the screens share one keyboard and pointer.) Most workstations have only one keyboard and pointer and thus are classified as having only one display. Multiuser systems may have multiple independent displays, each running a server program. If one display exists, as in the case of most workstations, it is numbered 0; if a machine has several displays, each is assigned a number (beginning with 0) when the X server for that display is started.

Similarly, if a single display is composed of multiple screens (sharing one keyboard and pointer), each screen is assigned a number (beginning with 0) when the server for that display is started. Multiple screen displays may be composed of two or more physical monitors. Alternatively, two screens might be defined as different ways of using the same physical monitor. For example, on the Sun-3/60 color workstation, screen 0 is color, and screen 1 is black and white. Each screen is the size of the monitor; you can only view one screen at a time. In practice, the two screens seem to be side by side: you can "scroll" between them by moving the pointer off either horizontal edge of the screen.

Note that the `server` parameter of the display option always begins with a colon (a double colon after a DECnet node*), and that the `screen` parameter always begins with a period. If the host is omitted or is specified as `unix`, the local machine is assumed. If the screen is omitted, screen 0 is assumed.

Although much of the current X Window System documentation suggests that any of the parameters to the `-display` option can be omitted and will default to the local node, server and screen 0, respectively, we have not found this to be true. In our experience, only the `host` and `screen` parameters (and the period preceding `screen`) can be omitted. The colon and `server` are necessary in all circumstances.

On UNIX systems, the display name is stored in the DISPLAY environment variable. Clients running on the local system access this variable to determine which display to connect to. The DISPLAY variable is set automatically by the *xterm* terminal emulator. Thus it is set when you start X and the first *xterm* window. In most circumstances, *xterm* sets the server and screen numbers to 0, and either omits a hostname (the local host is assumed) or sets the hostname to "unix," a generic name, which also defaults to the local host.

If you run all processes on the local machine, you don't have to deal with issues concerning the display setting. Clients running locally access the DISPLAY variable and open windows on a display connected to the local host. However, if you want to run a process on a remote machine and display the results locally, things become more complicated. A client running on a remote machine does not have access to the DISPLAY variable on the local machine. By default, a client running on a remote machine checks the DISPLAY setting on *that* machine.

You can override the DISPLAY environment variable a client accesses by using the `-display` option when you run the command. Think of `-display` as a pointer to the physical display on which you want the window to appear. For example, say you're using a single display workstation and the display also has only one screen. The hostname of the workstation is *kansas*. In order to tell a client to connect to a display, you must identify it by its unique name on the network. (You cannot identify your display by the shorthand setting given to it by *xterm*—`unix:0.0`, `:0.0`, or some variation.) Let's assume that the complete display name for the workstation *kansas* is:

```
kansas:0.0
```

---

*By convention, DECnet node names end with a colon.

Now let's say you want to run an *xterm* window on a faster system—let's call it *oz*—on your network. In order to run an *xterm* on *oz* but display the window on your screen connected to *kansas* (the local server), you would run the *xterm* command using a remote shell* (*rsh*):

```
% rsh oz xterm -display kansas:0.0 &
```

The *xterm* process runs on *oz*, but you've directed the client to use the display and screen numbered 0 on *kansas*, your local system. Notice that `kansas:0.0` is the complete display name. Hypothetically, if the workstation (*kansas*) has only one screen or it has multiple screens but you want to specify screen 0, you can omit the screen number and the preceding period (`.0`).

Keep in mind that for this process to succeed, the remote system (*oz*) must have permission to "open" the local display (on *kansas*). (See "Server Access Control" in Appendix A, *System Management*, and the *xhost* reference page in Part Three of this guide, for more information.) If *oz* has not been granted access to the server running on *kansas*, the window will not be opened, and you may also get an error message similar to:

```
Error: Can't Open display
```

If your command fails happens, try entering the command:

```
% xhost +
```

in an *xterm* window running on your display. Then run the remote shell (*rsh*) again. If problems persist, consult Appendix A, *System Management*, the *xhost* reference page, or your system administrator.

The following command illustrates a common mistake:

```
% rsh oz xterm &
```

If you try to run a client using a remote shell and forget to direct the client to create its window on your own display, the window will not be displayed and you'll get an error message stating that the display cannot be opened.

In addition to specifying a local display, if permissions allow you can also use the display option to open a window on someone else's display. You might want to display a window on another user's screen for instructional purposes. Multiuser systems can even be set up to allow teachers to display educational material simultaneously to several students, each using an X display of some sort.

If you're working on *kansas* and you want to open an *xterm* window on the first display connected to *oz*, you could use the command:

```
% xterm -display oz:0.0 &
```

Note that you can only open a window on another display if the server running that display permits your server access. (Access must be granted from the remote server, perhaps using *xhost*.) If *oz* does not allow *kansas* access, this command will fail and an error message will indicate that the display cannot be opened.

---

*The command to run the remote process might be different depending on the available networking software. Ask your system administrator for the proper command.

Once You Run a Remote xterm using -display

A less than obvious repercussion of using -display to run a remote *xterm* is that the option sets the DISPLAY variable for the new *xterm* window—and that DISPLAY setting is passed on to all child processes of the client. Therefore, once you run an *xterm* on a remote system and correctly specify your own display, you can run any number of clients from that *xterm* and they will all be displayed on your screen automatically (no -display option is necessary).

In one of the examples in the preceding section, we ran an *xterm* on the remote system *oz*, specifying the local display kansas:0.0 with the -display option. To query the contents of the DISPLAY variable in the resulting *xterm* (under the C shell), use the command:

```
% echo $DISPLAY
```

The system should echo:

```
% kansas:0.0
```

verifying that the display name has been passed to the DISPLAY variable in the new *xterm* window. You can then run any client you want on *oz* by entering the command in this *xterm* window and the window will automatically be displayed on kansas:0.0. The DISPLAY setting will also be passed to any children of *this* process as well, and will be propagated for any number of "generations."

Logging In to a Remote System

If you log in to a remote UNIX system using *rlogin* (or *telnet*) in an *xterm* window, it's a good idea to set the DISPLAY variable in the new shell to reflect your local display. Then if you run a client process from this window, the new window will be placed on your local display and the DISPLAY setting will be passed on to all child processes.

When you set the DISPLAY variable from the command line, the syntax varies depending on the UNIX shell running. The following command sets the variable under the C shell.

```
% setenv DISPLAY kansas:0.0
```

To set the DISPLAY variable under the Bourne shell, use:

```
$ DISPLAY=kansas:0.0; export DISPLAY
```

Monitoring the Load on a Remote System

A client you may wish to run on another machine is *xload*, which is used to keep track of the system load average. By default, *xload* polls the system for the load average at five-second intervals and displays the results in a simple histogram.

If you are running processes on more than one machine, it's useful to gauge the level of activity on the systems in question. This information should help you judge when to start processes and monitor how your processes are impacting system resources.

Say you're running clients both on the local machine *kansas* and on the remote machine *oz*. On the local display, you can have two *xload* windows, one showing activity on *kansas* and another showing activity on *oz*.

To create an *xload* window monitoring activity on *kansas*, use the command:

```
% xload &
```

Once the *xload* window is created, move it to a convenient location on the screen.

Then run an *xload* process on *oz* using a remote shell and display the results in a window on *kansas*:

```
% rsh oz xload -display kansas:0.0 &
```

The display option tells *xload* to create its window on the local display (*kansas*). Again, move the window using the pointer.

Figure 3-11 shows the resulting *kansas* display: two *xload* windows—the top window monitoring activity on the local system and the bottom one monitoring activity on the remote system.

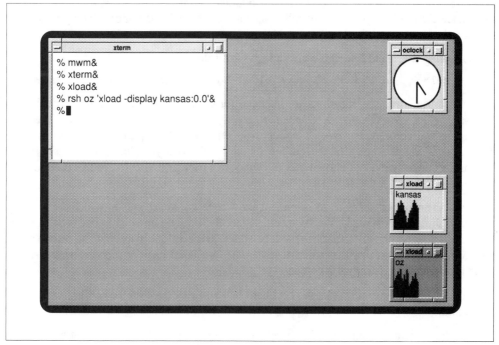

Figure 3-11. Monitoring activity on two systems with xload

Other Command Line Options

We've already seen how to use the -geometry and -display options, which are accepted by most clients. Chapter 9, *Command Line Options*, describes some of the other options accepted by most of the standard clients. These options set window features such as:

- The font in which text is displayed.

- The background color.

- The foreground color (such as the color of text).

- The text displayed in the title area.

- The text of an icon label.

Many clients also accept a large number of application-specific options (listed on the reference page for each client in Part Three of this guide). Using a combination of standard and application-specific options, you can tailor a client to look and behave in ways that better suit your needs.

Like most clients, *xclock* accepts a variety of options. Some of *xclock*'s options are intended to enhance the clock display aesthetically and some to affect its operation. Taking a look at a few of *xclock*'s options should give you a better idea of the flexibility of X.

The following command line runs a custom *xclock* display:

```
% xclock -hd green -hl royalblue -bg lightblue -update 1 -chime &
```

As you can see, these specifications are intended for a color monitor. (X is highly flexible in the use of color. See Chapter 9, *Command Line Options*, for more information.) The -hd option sets the color of the clock's hands to green. The -hl option provides even more detail, specifying the color of the outline of the hands as royal blue. -bg is one of the options accepted by most clients; it sets the window's background color, in this case to light blue.

The -update option takes as its argument the frequency in seconds at which the time on the clock should be updated. We've specified that the time be updated at one second intervals. Thus a second hand (also green) will be added to the *xclock* display. (The *xclock* reference page in Part Three of this guide specifies that a second hand is added if -update is given an argument of less than 30 seconds.)

The -chime option specifies that the keyboard bell will ring once on the half hour and twice on the hour.

These options create a somewhat fancy *xclock* display. You might or might not want to use so many options, but these and several more are available.

By default, *xclock* displays a traditional clock face (an analog clock). You can create a digital *xclock* using the following option:

```
% xclock -digital &
```

The digital *xclock* is pictured in Figure 3-12.

```
Wed Nov 14  13:25:13  1990
```

Figure 3-12. Digital xclock display

Logically, the −hd and −hl options, which set the color of the clock hands, are only valid with the analog (default) *xclock*. For a complete list of options, see the *xclock* reference page in Part Three of this guide.

Command line options override the default characteristics of a client for the *single* client process. Traditional UNIX applications rely on command line options to allow users to customize the way they work. X also offers many command line options, but these options have some limitations and liabilities.

First, the number of client features that can be controlled by command line options is limited. Most applications have many more customizable features than their command line options indicate. Actually, a client can have so many customizable features that typing a command line to set them all would be impractical. And if you generally use the same options with a client, it is tedious (and a waste of time) to type the options each time you run the program.

X offers an alternative to customizing a single client process on the command line. You can specify default characteristics for a client using variables called *resources*, described later in this chapter.

Putting it All Together

Now that we've learned something about the tools of the display, how to size and position windows, and run remote processes, let's try to set up a useful working display.

Say we're using a Sun 3/60 workstation with the hostname *jersey*. The workstation has a single display with two screens: screen 0 is color and screen 1 is black and white. Once X and the window manager are running, we might set up the display using the following commands.

First, run an *xterm* on a more powerful remote system called *manhattan* and place it on screen 0 of *jersey*.

```
% rsh manhattan xterm -geometry +0-0 -display jersey:0.0 &
```

Run *xload* windows on both *jersey* and *manhattan* to monitor loads on these systems. Again, place the windows on *jersey*'s color screen in convenient locations.

```
% xload -geometry -10-200 &
% rsh manhattan xload -geometry -10-20 -display jersey:0.0 &
```

Run another *xterm* window on *jersey*.

```
% xterm -geometry +50-0 &
```

Then iconify the login *xterm* window so that you don't inadvertently kill it (and shut down X in the bargain). Remember: to iconify a window place the pointer on the Minimize command button on the window's frame and click the first button. (See "Converting a Window to an Icon" earlier in this chapter.)

Run an *oclock*.

```
% oclock &
```

Figure 3-13 shows the *jersey* display, screen 0: a fairly useful layout.

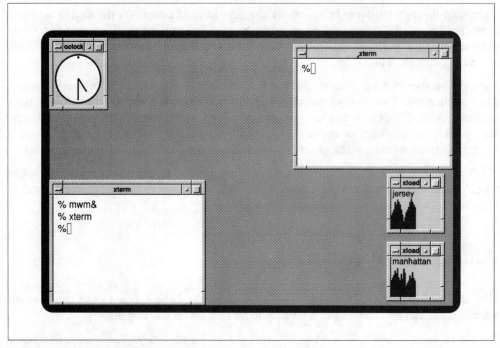

Figure 3-13. A working display, screen 0

You might also place client windows on the workstation's alternate screen, the black and white screen numbered 1. By default, windows are always placed on screen 0 but you can place a client window on screen 1 by specifying the screen number in the -display option when starting the client. For instance, each of the following commands places an *xterm* window on screen 1.

```
% xterm -display jersey:0.1 &
% rsh manhattan xterm -geometry -0-0 -display jersey:0.1 &
```

Figure 3-14 illustrates screen 1.

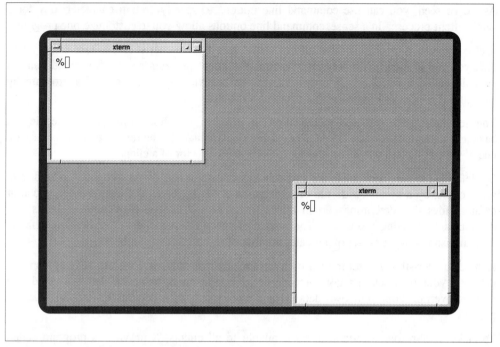

Figure 3-14. A working display, screen 1

As we'll see in Appendix A, *System Management*, on most systems you can place the commands you run to set up your display in a special file that is invoked when you log in. Once this file (usually called either *xinitrc* or *xsession*) is in place, when you log in your display will be set up to your specifications automatically.

Notice that the commands we used to set up *jersey* illustrate the power of the -geometry and -display options to create a working environment that suits individual needs. However, these options barely hint at the number of features you can specify for each client. The following section introduces some principles of client customization. Part Two of this guide examines customization in depth.

Customizing the X Environment: Specifying Resources

As we've seen, you can use command line options to specify certain characteristics for a single client process. In a sense, command line options allow you to customize one program.

X also provides a mechanism that allows you to specify characteristics that take effect *every* time you run a client. Almost every feature of a client program can be controlled using a variable called a *resource*. You can change the behavior or appearance of a program by changing the *value* associated with a resource variable.

You generally place resource specifications in a file in your home directory. (The file can have any name, but is often called *Xresources* or *Xdefaults*.) The resources you specify are one of several factors that affect the appearance and behavior of a client.

By default, the way a client looks and behaves is determined by the program code, and in some cases, by a system-wide file of *application defaults*. Several clients have application defaults files that determine certain client features.* Within an application defaults file, defaults are set using resources. The resources specified in a client's application defaults files are usually just a subset of a greater number of resources that can be set.

If the characteristics you set in your own resources file already have system-wide application defaults, your own settings take precedence. Keep in mind, however, that command line options override both your own defaults and any system-wide defaults for the single client process.

To make your resource specifications available to all clients, X provides a program called *xrdb*, the X resource database manager. *xrdb* stores resources directly in the server where they are accessible to all clients, regardless of the machine the clients are running on.

In some cases, a resource variable controls the same characteristic as a command line option. However, while the option specifies a characteristic for the single client process being invoked, a resource variable makes the characteristic the program default.

The basic syntax of a resource specification is fairly simple. Each client recognizes certain resource variables that can be assigned a value. The variables for each client are listed on its reference page in Part Three of this guide.

A resource definition file is basically a two-column list, where each line specifies a different resource. The simplest resource definition line has the name of the client, followed by an

---

*For *xterm*, the application defaults specify such things as the labels for menu items, the fonts used to display menu items, and the shape of the pointer when it's in an *xterm* window.

Application defaults files generally reside in the directory */usr/lib/X11/app-defaults* and are named for the client application. In describing the appearance and behavior of clients in this guide, we assume all of the standard application defaults files are present on your system and accessible by the client programs. If, by some chance, a client's application defaults file has been edited or removed from your system, the client may not look or behave exactly as we describe it. If a client application appears substantially different than depicted in this guide, you may be using a different version of the program or the application defaults may be different. Consult your system administrator.

asterisk, and the name of the variable, followed by a colon, in the left column. The right column (separated from the left by a tab or whitespace) contains the value of the resource variable.

```
client*variable:    value
```

The following example shows five simple resource specifications for the *xclock* client. These particular resources specify the same characteristics as the command line options we used to create the green and blue *xclock* in the section "Other Command Line Options."

Example 3-1. Resources to create a custom xclock

```
xclock*hands: green
xclock*highlight: royalblue
xclock*background:lightblue
xclock*update:     1
xclock*chime: true
```

To set up your environment so that these characteristics apply each time you run *xclock*, you would perform the following steps:

1. In your home directory, create a file containing the resources listed in Example 3-1. Name the file *Xresources*. (A resource file can actually have any name, but is often called *Xresources* or *Xdefaults*.)

2. Load the resources into the server by entering the following command in an *xterm* window:

    ```
    % xrdb -load .Xresources
    ```

Then each time you run *xclock* without options (for the remainder of that login session), the window will reflect the new defaults.

You should load resources using *xrdb* every time you log in. In Appendix A, *System Management*, we'll describe how to automate this process using a special startup script, which also opens the client windows you want on your display.

If you want to run an application with different characteristics (colors, update frequency, etc.) from the defaults, use the appropriate command line options to override the resource specifications.

Resource specifications can be much more complicated than our samples suggest. For applications written with a toolkit (such as the X Toolkit or the Open Software Foundation's Motif Toolkit), X allows you to specify different characteristics for individual components, or *widgets*, within the application. Typical widgets create graphical features such as menus, command buttons, dialog boxes, and scrollbars. Within most toolkit applications is a fairly complex widget hierarchy—widgets exist within widgets (e.g., a command button within a dialog box).

Resource naming syntax can parallel the widget hierarchy within an application. For instance, you might set different background colors for different command buttons and specify still another background color for the dialog box that encloses them. In such cases, the actual widget names are used within the resource specification. Chapter 10, *Setting Resources* explains the resource naming syntax in greater detail and outlines the rules governing the precedence of resources.

Where to Go From Here

There are many useful client programs supplied with the X Window System. Details of how to use one of the most important clients, the *xterm* terminal emulator, are provided in Chapter 5, *The xterm Terminal Emulator*. Clients to list and display fonts are described in Chapter 6, *Font Specification*. Chapter 7, *Graphics Utilities*, describes several graphics utilities available with X. An overview and tutorial for other standard clients is provided in Chapter 8, *Other Clients*. All clients are described in detail in a reference page format in Part Three of this guide.

We've introduced some basic operations you can perform using the *mwm* window manager. For instructions on performing additional window manager operations, such as resizing a window, read Chapter 4, *More about the mwm Window Manager*. You can then go on to read more about *xterm* in Chapter 5 and about some of the other standard clients in Chapters 6 through 8.

4

More about the
mwm Window Manager

This chapter describes additional functions you can perform using the Motif window manager, mwm.

In This Chapter:

mwm Manager

4
More about the mwm Window Manager

In Chapter 3, we explained the procedures for raising, moving, and iconifying windows using the pointer on the *mwm* window frame. *mwm* allows you to perform many other window management functions, which are described in this chapter. You can:

- Create additional *xterm* windows.

- Change the size of windows.

- Lower windows (move them to the back of others).

- Refresh your screen.

- Remove windows.

The Motif window manager allows you to invoke window management functions in a variety of ways:

- Using the window "frame" and various features available on it: the Minimize (iconify) button, Maximize button, title area, Window Menu, etc.

- Using the Root Menu.

- Using keyboard keys, pointer buttons, and key and button combinations.

In this chapter, we'll review some basics about focusing input to a window or icon and consider how window management functions rely on focus being directed properly. Then we'll consider some additional window management functions you can perform using the *mwm* frame and take a closer look at the Window Menu and Root Menu.

As we'll see, some window management functions can be performed using keyboard shortcuts. These shortcuts involve using special keys, commonly called modifier keys. Before considering window management functions, we'll take a brief look at the special keys significant to X.

Keep in mind that *mwm* is very flexible. In Chapter 11, we'll consider how to customize various features of the window manager. Perhaps the most useful customization that can be performed involves selecting a keyboard focus policy, either pointer focus or click-to-type (also referred to as *explicit*) focus. By default, *mwm* uses click-to-type focus. Keyboard focus is described in Chapter 1.

mwm Manager

This chapter is intended primarily for those using the Release 1.1 version of *mwm*. (Unlike the 1.0 version, *mwm* 1.1 is compatible with Release 4 of X.) If *mwm* has been customized at your site or you are running a different version, the principles should be basically the same, but the window management functions may be invoked in different ways. From time to time, we'll mention how commands or functionality might vary, depending on the version of *mwm*.

Using Special Keys

Undoubtedly you know the basics of using a keyboard. However, X interprets certain keys somewhat differently than the labels on the keys would indicate.

Most workstations have a number of "modifier" keys, so-called because they modify the action of other keys. Generally these keys are used to invoke commands of some sort, such as window manager functions.

Three of these modifier keys should be familiar to any user of a standard ASCII terminal or a personal computer—Shift, Caps Lock, and Control. However, many workstations have additional modifier keys as well. A PC has an "Alt" key, a Macintosh™ has a "fan" key, a Sony workstation has keys named "Nfer" and "Xfer," and certain model Sun workstations have three additional modifier keys, labeled "Left," "Right," and "Alternate."

Because X clients are designed to run on many different workstations, with different keyboards, it is difficult to assign functions to special keys on the keyboard. A developer can't count on the same key always being present!

For this reason, many X clients make use of "logical" modifier keynames, which can be mapped by the user to any actual key on the keyboard.

Up to eight separate modifier keys can be defined. The most commonly used (after Shift, Caps Lock, and Control) has the logical keyname "Meta."

We'll talk at length about this subject in Chapter 12, *Setup Clients*, but we wanted to warn you here. When we talk later in this chapter about pressing the "Meta" key, you should be aware that there is not likely to be a physical key on the keyboard with that name. For example, on one workstation, the Meta key might be labeled "Alt" and, on another, "Funct." And as we'll show in Chapter 12, you can choose any key you want to act as the Meta key.

Unfortunately, X provides no easy way to find out which key on your keyboard has been assigned to be the Meta key. When you need to know, please turn to the discussion of key mapping in Chapter 12, for information on how you can find out.

Input Focus and the Window Manager

As explained in Chapter 3, the default operation of *mwm* is that you select the window to receive input (the active window) by clicking the first pointer button anywhere within the window. This focus policy is called click-to-type, or explicit. Whether *mwm* is started automatically or you started it by typing in an *xterm* window, you must then click in a window in order to enter text.

Once you focus input to a window, all text typed is interpreted by that client, regardless of where you move the pointer. In the case of *xterm* and similar clients, the text appears in the window. Other clients might simply interpret the keystrokes as possible commands. Some clients, such as *xclock*, do not recognize keyboard input at all. Regardless of the client, certain keystrokes might also be interpreted as commands to the window manager to effect changes on the focus window. In order to type in or issue commands to affect another window, you must transfer focus to that window by clicking the first pointer button within it. In Chapter 11, *Customizing mwm*, we'll describe how to make the keyboard focus follow pointer movement.

Also keep in mind that in order to manage a window using the various methods provided by *mwm*, the window must have the input focus. Since most actions you'll perform involve placing the pointer somewhere on the frame and performing some kind of pointer action (such as clicking, pressing, releasing, etc.), controlling a window using the frame selects that window to receive the input focus at the same time.

However, before invoking certain window management functions, you must first select a focus window (or icon). For example, each Window Menu item has a keyboard shortcut. If you want to affect a window using a keyboard shortcut, you must *first* select it as the focus window by clicking on it with the pointer—otherwise the keyboard shortcut will affect the current focus window. This is probably the only circumstance in which you would select a window that doesn't accept keyboard input (such as *xclock*) as the focus window. Keyboard shortcuts for Window Menu functions are described in "Using the Window Menu."

As we've seen, when you focus input on a window, the window frame changes color. The color of the active window's frame depends on the version of *mwm* you are running and the color resources for your system. In some versions, be aware that the black window frame of non-active windows obscures the titlebar text, which also appears in black. Only the title of the active window is visible in these cases.

If you are working with a stack of windows that overlap, selecting a window as the active window automatically raises that window to the top of the stack. This behavior is controlled by an *mwm* resource variable called `focusAutoRaise`, which is true by default when click-to-type focus is in effect. (This resource is described in Chapter 11, *Customizing mwm*.) If the focus window is killed or converted to an icon, the focus switches back to the window that previously had it.

mwm Manager

Focusing Input on an Icon

Though it may not be immediately obvious, you can select an iconified window to receive the input focus. You direct input to an icon by placing the pointer on it and clicking the first button. As illustrated in Chapter 3, *Working in the X Environment*, this action displays an *mwm* menu (the Window Menu) over the icon. (See Figure 3-4.)

The icon label also becomes wider and the label and the frame surrounding the icon are highlighted. These changes indicate that the icon has the input focus. Even after the menu is removed, the label will remain wider and the border highlighted (that is, the icon will retain the focus), until you direct focus to another window or icon.

When an icon has the input focus, the application window the icon represents will not interpret keystrokes. However, the window manager will interpret relevant keystrokes as commands. For instance, you need to focus input to an icon in order to invoke a Window Menu item on it using the item's keyboard shortcut. Keyboard shortcuts for Window Menu functions are described in "Using the Window Menu on Icons" later in this chapter.

Transferring the Focus with Keystrokes

If you are running the default version of *mwm* (which assumes click-to-type focus), you can cause the focus to circulate from window to window (including iconified windows) within the stack using any of the key combinations that appear in Table 4-1.

Table 4-1. Key Combinations to Change Focus Window

Key Combination	Action
Meta-Tab	Move focus to next window in stack.
Meta-Shift-Tab	Move focus to previous window in stack.
Meta-Escape	Move focus to next window in stack.
Meta-Shift-Escape	Move focus to previous window in stack.

The key combinations Meta-Tab and Meta-Escape circulate the focus from the current top of the stack to the bottom. What this means is that the top window in the stack is moved to the bottom; the second highest window becomes the top window and gets the input focus.

The key combinations Meta-Shift-Tab and Meta-Shift-Escape circulate the focus from the current bottom of the stack to the top. In other words, the lowest window in the stack is moved to the top and given the input focus.

As explained previously, there is probably no key labeled "Meta" on your keyboard. Meta is a logical keyname recognized by X which is mapped to a physical key. Also be aware that, in most cases, *mwm* considers the Meta key and the Alt key interchangeable. (Alt is another logical keyname that may be mapped to a key with another label.) Thus, the actions in Table 4-1 should also work if you substitute Alt for Meta. For help in locating the Meta and Alt keys on your keyboard, see the discussion of *xmodmap* in Chapter 12, *Setup Clients*.

mwm's ability to transfer focus from window to window according to keystrokes is important to some Motif applications. The Motif Toolkit supports the building of applications that use several subwindows, each with a different albeit related purpose. (Such applications can be described as *form-based*.) A form-based Motif application can be built that allows users to move among the subwindows using keystrokes.

Some of the more common elements of Motif applications are described in Chapter 8, *Other Clients*.

What to do if mwm Dies and the Focus is Lost

If the *mwm* process dies, the focus policy should revert to pointer focus. To restart the window manager, you should simply be able to move the pointer into an *xterm* window and enter the *mwm* command. However, *mwm* has a bug that makes it possible to lose the focus entirely when the window manager dies. Obviously, restarting the window manager in such a situation is problematic. If *mwm* dies and no window retains the focus, you can restore focus to an *xterm* window using the Secure Keyboard item of the client's Main Options menu. See Chapter 5, *The xterm Terminal Emulator*, for details.

Using the mwm Window Frame

In Chapter 3, *Working in the X Environment*, we introduced some of the basic window management functions you can perform using the pointer on the *mwm* frame, which appears surrounding an *xterm* window in Figure 4-1.

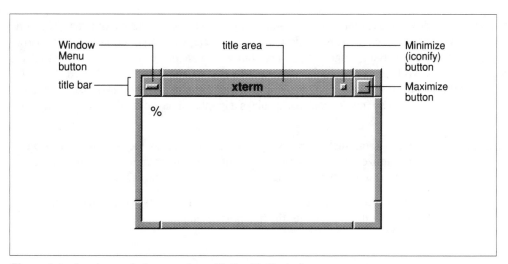

Figure 4-1. An xterm window running with the Motif window manager

Before proceeding, read the section "Raising, Moving, and Iconifying Windows" in Chapter 3. (This section also describes some basic actions you can perform on icons using the pointer: raising and moving an icon and converting an icon back to a window.)

mwm Manager

The following sections describe the features of the *mwm* window frame not covered in Chapter 3 and the functions they perform. Later, we'll take a look at menu items and keyboard shortcuts that also perform window and icon management functions.

Maximizing a Window

The two command buttons on the right side of the titlebar are the Minimize and Maximize buttons. The Minimize command button converts a window to an icon, as described in Chapter 3, *Working in the X Environment*.

Maximizing a window means enlarging it to the size of the root window. This action can be performed using the Maximize command button.

The Maximize Button

To the right of the Minimize command button (in the upper-right corner of the window), the Maximize command button is identified by a larger square in its center. The Maximize button allows you to enlarge the window to the size of the root window, and once it has been enlarged, to convert it back to its original size.

To maximize a window, use the following steps:

1. Place the pointer within the Maximize command button. The pointer simply has to rest within the button's outer border, not within the square identifying it.

2. Click the first pointer button. The window is maximized, as illustrated in Figure 4-2.

The large window should function in the same way it did before it was maximized. Theoretically, you can maximize an *xterm* window to have a single, very large terminal screen. However, be aware that certain programs you may run within an *xterm*, such as the *vi* text editor, do not always work properly within a window of this size (even if you've used the *resize* client, as described in Chapter 5, *The xterm Terminal Emulator*). The Maximize function is more safely used with an application that displays a graphic image or performs a simple function, such as *xclock*.

Also, some client programs that do not support resizing, such as the Release 3 version of *xcalc*, cannot be maximized correctly. In the case of *xcalc*, the frame surrounding the calculator application is maximized, but the actual calculator remains the same size.

The Maximize button is a toggle. To convert a maximized window back to its original size, click on the Maximize button again with the first pointer button.

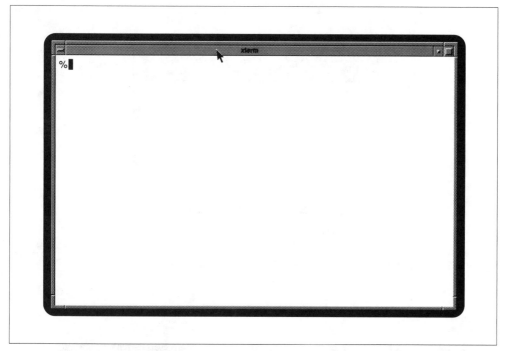

Figure 4-2. Maximizing a window

Resizing a Window

One of the most distinctive and useful features of the *mwm* window frame is not at all obvious. The entire frame (other than the titlebar—i.e., the title area and command buttons) is designed to allow you to resize the window using the pointer. Notice that the frame is divided by small lines into eight sections: four long borders (two horizontal and two vertical) and four corners. Figure 4-3 shows these sections of the window frame.

If you place the pointer within a window and then move it into one of the long horizontal or vertical borders, you'll notice the pointer changes to a new shape: an arrow (pointing toward the window border), with a short line perpendicular to it. This short line represents the window border. Try moving the pointer in this fashion in one of the windows on your display to get a better idea of what the pointer looks like. If you move the pointer from within a window into the outer border at one of the corners, the pointer will become an arrow pointing diagonally at a small corner symbol, as pictured in Figure 4-4. Figure 4-5 shows all of the possible resize pointers.

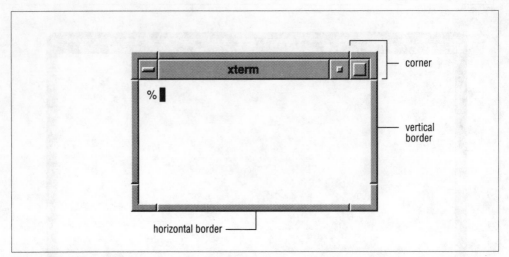

Figure 4-3. *The outer frame is divided into four long borders and four corners*

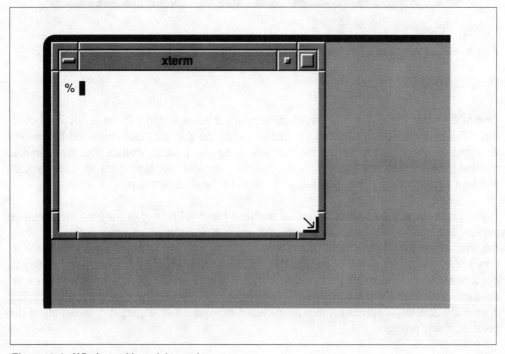

Figure 4-4. *Window with resizing pointer*

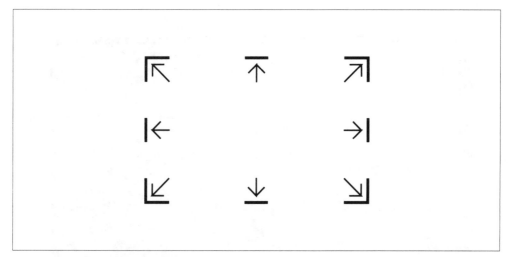

Figure 4-5. Resizing pointer symbols

Once the pointer changes to one of these shapes, you can move the border (or corner) of the window. Resizing from one of the long borders only allows you to change one dimension of the window: a horizontal border can only be moved up or down, changing the height; a vertical border can only be moved left or right, changing the width.

Resizing from a corner offers the most flexibility. You can move a corner in any direction you choose, changing both dimensions of the window if you want. For example, you can drag the lower-right corner of a window down and to the right to enlarge the window in both dimensions.

You determine the size and shape of the window by choosing the border or corner you want to extend (or contract) and moving it the desired amount using the following steps:

1. Move the pointer from within the window to the border or corner you want to move. The pointer changes to one of the symbols pictured in Figure 4-5.

2. Press and hold down the first pointer button and drag the window border or corner in the direction you want. As you resize the window, an image of the moving border(s) tracks the pointer movement. Also, in the center of the display, a small rectangular window shows the dimensions of the window as they change (in characters and lines for *xterm* windows, in pixels for most other clients).

3. Resize the window as desired.

4. Release the first pointer button. The window is redisplayed in the new shape. (The border image and window geometry tracking box disappear.)

Figure 4-6 shows a window being "stretched" from the lower-right corner.

mwm Manager

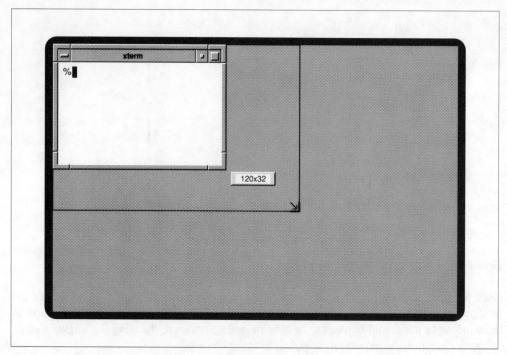

Figure 4-6. Dragging the corner to make a window larger

The Window Menu Button: Display a Menu or Close the Window

The command button on the left side of the titlebar is used to bring up the Window Menu, which provides seven items that can be used to manage the window and its icon. The following sections describe how to bring up the Window Menu and invoke its various functions.

This command button also has another function. Double-clicking the first pointer button on the Window Menu command button kills the client program and closes the window. Be aware that, like other methods of 'killing' a program (such as the *xkill* client), double clicking on the Window Menu button can adversely affect underlying processes. Refer to the section on *xkill* in Chapter 8, *Other Clients*, for a more complete discussion of the hazards of killing a client and a summary of alternatives.

You can customize *mwm* so that double clicking performs no function by setting a resource variable, wMenuButtonClick2, to false. See the sections "Setting mwm Resources" and "mwm-Specific Appearance and Behavior Resources" in Chapter 11, and the *mwm* reference page in Part Three of this guide for details.

Using the Window Menu

The Window Menu can actually be displayed from either a window or an icon. As we'll see, certain menu functions apply only to one or the other. This section describes using the Window Menu to perform various management functions on a window. (The section "Working with Icons," later in this chapter, describes the use of Window Menu items, pointer commands, and other shortcuts on icons.)

The Window Menu command button is in the upper-left corner of the window frame and is identified by a narrow rectangle in its center. You can display the Window Menu from a window by moving the pointer to the command button and either:

* Clicking the first pointer button.

* Pressing and holding down the first pointer button.

(You can also display the menu using keyboard shortcuts described at the end of this section.) If you've clicked the first pointer button to display the menu (the easier method), the first item that is available for selection is highlighted by a box. Figure 4-7 shows the default Window Menu, which has been displayed by clicking the first pointer button in the menu command button.

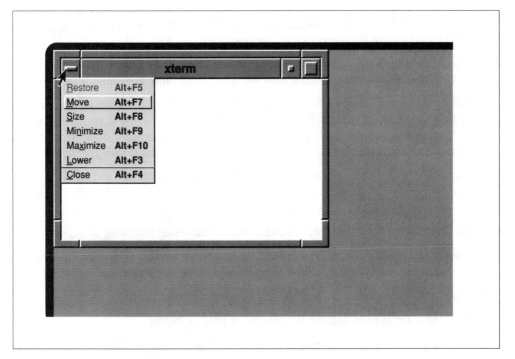

Figure 4-7. The Window Menu

There are also keyboard shortcuts to display the Window Menu on the focus window: Shift-Escape or Meta-space.

The function performed by each of the Window Menu items is fairly obvious. Six of the seven menu items (all but Lower) allow you to perform functions that can also be performed by simple pointer actions on the *mwm* window frame. Since effecting changes on a window using the frame is very simple and accessible, you will probably not use the Window Menu often.

You may want to use the menu to Lower a window (to the bottom of the stack), since this function cannot be performed by a simple pointer action on the frame. (If you learn the keyboard shortcut for this menu item, explained later in this section, you may not need the Window Menu to manage windows at all.) You may find the menu more helpful in managing icons, as described later in this chapter.

In any case, learning how to invoke the Window Menu items is helpful in orienting yourself within the Motif environment.

Invoking Window Menu Items

Let's take another look at the Window Menu in Figure 4-7. Notice that the first item available for selection (indicated by the surrounding box) is Move. The first item on the menu, Restore, is used to change an icon back into a window or a maximized window back to its original size; therefore, it is not useful at this time. The fact that Restore is not selectable is indicated by the fact that it appears in a lighter typeface.

Notice also that one letter of each menu item is underlined. This letter represents a unique abbreviation for the menu item, called a *mnemonic*, and is useful in selecting the item.

A keyboard shortcut follows each command. These shortcuts are known as *accelerators* because they facilitate the action. The keyboard accelerators allow you to perform all of the functions without having to display the menu (though they also work while the menu is displayed). To invoke an action using an accelerator, the window must have the input focus.

All of the keyboard accelerators for the menu items involve the Alt key and a function key. Remember that *mwm* considers the Alt and Meta keys to be equivalent. What this boils down to is that, for any of the shortcuts, you can substitute Meta for Alt.

Once the Window Menu is displayed, you can select an item in the following ways:

- If you displayed the menu by pressing and holding down the first pointer button, drag the pointer down the menu to the desired item and release the first button.

- If you displayed the menu by clicking the first pointer button, either:

  — Move the pointer onto the item and click the first button.

  — Type the unique abbreviation (the underlined letter). (Though several of the abbreviations are capital letters, you should type the lowercase equivalent.)

  — Type the accelerator key combination. (Though these are intended to save you the trouble of displaying the menu, they also work when it is displayed.)

— To select the boxed item (the first available for selection), you can alternatively press either the Return key or the space bar.

To remove the menu without making a selection, move the pointer off of the menu and release or click the first pointer button, as appropriate.

Most items work similarly to the comparable functions performed using the pointer on the frame. The primary difference relates to moving or resizing a window. Using the frame, you press and hold down a pointer button, move the pointer, and release the button to complete the action. Once you invoke the Move or Size item from the Window Menu (by any of the methods described previously), you simply move the pointer (without holding a button down); then click the first pointer button to complete the action.

If you test the various items, you'll find that each item works in a fairly predictable way. When you select Move, for instance, the pointer changes to the cross-arrow cursor, which appears in the center of the window; as you move the pointer, a window outline follows; you place the window in its new location by clicking the first pointer button. When you select Size, the pointer again changes to the cross-arrow cursor in the center of the window; move the pointer into any part of the resize border and the pointer symbol becomes one of the resize cursors; as you drag the border or corner, a window outline follows the pointer; then complete the resizing by clicking the first pointer button.

Pointer Commands to Manage Icons

In addition to managing windows, *mwm* provides several easy methods for managing icons. The following functions can be invoked using simple pointer button actions on an icon:

Move   Hold down the first pointer button and drag the icon to the desired position. Then release the button.

Raise   Click on the obscured icon with the first pointer button. The icon is raised to the top of the stack. (*mwm* does not allow icons to overlap one another; you'll need to raise an icon only when it's obscured by a window.)

Restore (Deiconify)
        To convert an icon back to a window, double click on the icon with the first pointer button.

Each of these icon management function using the pointer is described in greater detail in the section "Raising, Moving, and Iconifying Windows" in Chapter 3, *Working in the X Environment*.

Using the Window Menu on Icons

You can also display the Window Menu from an icon and invoke menu items that affect it. To display the menu, just place the pointer on the icon and click the first button. (You can also press and hold down either the first or third button; or you can use either of these keyboard shortcuts: Shift-Escape or Meta-space.)

The Window Menu displayed from an icon is virtually identical to the menu displayed from a window; it contains all of the same items, but only five of the seven are selectable. (When displayed from a window, six of the seven items are selectable.) The five selectable items are: Restore, Move, Maximize, Lower, and Close. These items perform actions on an icon analogous to those performed on a window (see "Using the Window Menu" earlier in this chapter).

Two menu items, Size and Minimize, appear in a lighter typeface, indicating they are not available for selection. Size cannot be selected because, unlike a window, an icon cannot be resized. Obviously, Minimize cannot be used to iconify an icon.

Table 4-2 summarizes the Window Menu functions when invoked from an icon. For instructions on selecting an item and performing the various functions, read "Using the Window Menu" earlier in this chapter. Note that the keyboard shortcuts (accelerators) for the commands are also the same as those described for windows.

Table 4-2. Window Menu Actions on an Icon

Menu Item	Function	Shortcut
Restore	Converts the icon back to a window.	Alt+F5
Move	Moves the icon on the display.	Alt+F7
Size	Not available for selection.	n/a
Minimize	Not available for selection.	n/a
Maximize	Converts an icon to a window the size of the root window.	Alt+F10
Lower	Sends an icon to the bottom of the window/icon stack.	Alt+F3
Close	Exits the client, removing the icon.	Alt+F4

To invoke a Window Menu action on an icon using the keyboard accelerator, the icon must have the input focus. As explained earlier in this chapter, you can direct focus to an icon by placing the pointer on it and clicking the first button (which also displays the Window Menu). The icon label becomes wider and the border is highlighted.

An icon also retains the input focus when you display the Window Menu and then remove it without selecting an item (by clicking anywhere outside the menu). The icon label will remain wide and the border highlighted until you direct focus to another window or icon. As long as an icon remains highlighted, you can invoke Window Menu commands using their keyboard accelerators.

In Chapter 11, we'll discuss using *mwm* resources to set up an icon box, a window for organizing icons on the display. Using an icon box changes the way you work with the Window Menu from an icon and introduces another menu item, PackIcons, which reorganizes icons in the icon box.

The Root Menu

The Root Menu is *mwm*'s main menu. It provides commands that can be thought of as affecting the entire display. To display the Root Menu, move the pointer to the root window and press and hold down the first pointer button. The default Root Menu appears in Figure 4-8.

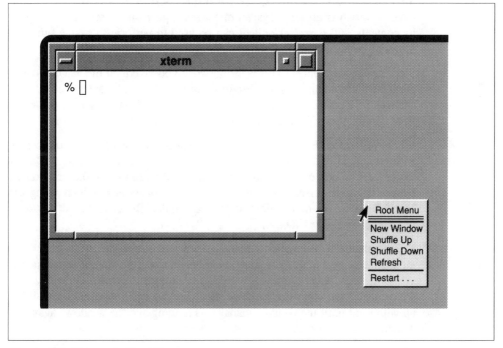

Figure 4-8. The mwm Root Menu

When you display the Root Menu, the pointer changes to the arrow pointer. As you can see, the default Root Menu offers only five items. To select an item, use the following steps:

1. As you continue to hold down the first pointer button, move the pointer onto the desired item name. (If you accidentally move the pointer off the menu, it will still remain displayed, as long as you continue to hold the first button down.) As you move the pointer onto an item, notice that a rectangular box is displayed around the item to highlight it.

2. Once the pointer is positioned on the item you want, release pointer button one. The action is performed.

The functions performed by the default Root Menu are described below.

New Window   By default, this command runs an *xterm* window on the display specified by the DISPLAY environment variable, generally the local display. When you create a new window (by using the menu or typing the command in an *xterm*), the new window automatically becomes the active window.

Shuffle Up   If windows and/or icons are stacked on your display, this command moves the bottom window or icon in the stack to the top (raises it). (It's generally simpler to raise a window or icon by placing the pointer on it and clicking the first button.)

Shuffle Down   If windows and/or icons are stacked on your display, this command moves the top window or icon in the stack to the bottom (lowers it).

Refresh   This command is used to *refresh* the display screen, that is, redraw its contents. Refresh is useful if system messages appear on the screen, overlaying its contents. (The *xrefresh* client can be used to perform the same function. Simply type xrefresh at the system prompt in an *xterm* window.)

Restart ...   Stops and restarts *mwm*. This is useful when you've edited the *.mwmrc* configuration file, which specifies certain *mwm* features, and want to activate the changes. Since this function is potentially more dangerous than the other Root Menu options, it is separated from the other options by a horizontal line.

When you select Restart, a dialog box appears in the center of the screen with command buttons asking you to either OK the restart process or Cancel the request. Click on the appropriate command button using the first pointer button. (Dialog boxes commonly appear in applications written using the Motif Toolkit. For more information, see "Dialog Boxes and Push Buttons" in Chapter 8, *Other Clients*.)

If you select OK, the window manager process is stopped. The screen will momentarily go blank. The new *mwm* process will be started immediately. While the new *mwm* process is starting, an hourglass symbol is displayed in the center of the otherwise blank screen. The hourglass appears to be filling up with sand until the window manager is running and the windows again are displayed on the screen.

Keep in mind that you can add, change, or remove menu items using the *mwm* configuration file, *.mwmrc*, in your home directory. We'll discuss customizing the Root Menu in Chapter 11.

5

The xterm Terminal Emulator

This chapter describes how to use xterm, *the terminal emulator. You use this client to create multiple terminal windows, each of which can run any programs available on the underlying operating system.*

In This Chapter:

5

The xterm Terminal Emulator

xterm provides you with a terminal within a window. Anything you can do using a standard terminal, you can do in an *xterm* window. Once you have an *xterm* window on your screen, you can use it to run other clients.

You can bring up more than one *xterm* window at a time. For example, you might want to list the contents of a directory in one window while you edit a file in another window. Although you can display output simultaneously in several windows, you can type in only one window at a time.

When you start an *xterm* process on the command line in one *xterm* window, the second *xterm* inherits the environment variables of the first (including the DISPLAY setting); the second shell also starts in the working directory of the first shell.

The basic operation of *xterm* should be obvious to anyone familiar with a terminal. You should be able to work productively immediately.

But *xterm* provides much more than basic terminal capabilities. Two of *xterm*'s most useful features are a scrollbar, which allows you to review text in the window, and a "copy and paste" facility, which allows you to select text from one window using the pointer and paste it into another (or even the same) window.

As we'll see, you can create an *xterm* window with a scrollbar using the −sb command line option or specify a scrollbar as a default characteristic of *xterm* using the scrollbar resource variable. You can also add a scrollbar to (or remove one from) an *xterm* window already running on the display by using one of the client's four menus. Without customizing the client in any way, you can cut and paste text between *xterm* windows.

Among the less obvious features of *xterm* is a dual functionality. By default, *xterm* emulates a DEC VT102 terminal, a common alphanumeric terminal type. However, *xterm* can also emulate a Tektronix 4014 terminal, which is used to display graphics. For each *xterm* process, you can switch between these two types of terminal windows. You can display both a VT102 and a Tektronix window at the same time but only one of them can be the "active" window, i.e., the window receiving input and output. Hypothetically, you could be editing in the VT102 window while looking at graphics in the Tektronix window.

You switch between the VT102 window and the Tektronix window using items from certain *xterm* menus. *xterm* has four menus that can be used to control the VT102 and Tek windows, to select many terminal settings, and to run other commands that affect the *xterm* process.

The VT Fonts menu represents a welcome Release 4 innovation. Using this menu, you can change the font used to display text in the VT102 window. You may want to change the font for a number of reasons. Perhaps you need a larger font to read text more easily; or maybe you want to use a smaller font to reduce the size of a window while a program is running and you don't need to monitor it's progress. Prior to Release 4, if you didn't like the display font, you had to start a new *xterm* process, specifying an alternative. The VT Fonts menu makes *xterm* much more flexible.

We'll take a look at some of the more useful items on each menu as well as some alternatives to menu items later in this chapter. For more complete information about menus, see the *xterm* reference page in Part Three of this guide.

We'll also consider how to run a program in a temporary *xterm* window, which goes away when the program finishes.

But first, let's consider some preliminary issues: which terminal type to specify for *xterm* and what to do when resizing an *xterm* window causes problems with its terminal emulation.

Then we'll look at the *xterm* features you'll probably use most frequently: the scrollbar and the text selection mechanism.

Terminal Emulation and the xterm Terminal Type

Anyone who has used a variety of terminals knows that they don't all work the same way. As a terminal emulator, an *xterm* window must be assigned a terminal type that tells the system how the window should operate, that is, what type of terminal it should emulate. When *xterm* is assigned an invalid terminal type, the window does not display properly at all times, particularly when using a text editor such as *vi*. If one of your login files (*.login*, *.profile*, *.cshrc*, etc.) currently specifies a default terminal type, you will need to replace this with a type valid for *xterm*. (If none of your login files specifies a terminal type, *xterm* automatically searches the file of TERMCAP entries for the first valid entry.)

xterm can emulate a variety of terminal types, which are listed on the client reference page in Part Three of this guide. An *xterm* window most successfully emulates a terminal when it has been assigned the terminal type xterm. For the xterm terminal type to be recognized on your system, the system administrator will have had to add it to the file containing valid TERMCAP entries. (The xterm TERMCAP entry is supplied with the standard release of X.) If this has not been done, the system will not recognize the xterm terminal type. In these cases, try the vt100 terminal type, which also generally works well or use one of the other types listed on the client reference page.

See Appendix A, *System Management*, and the *xterm* reference page in Part Three of this guide for information about customizing the *termcap* file.

Resizing an xterm Window

xterm sets the TERMCAP environment variable for the dimensions of the window you create. Clients (including *xterm*) use this TERMCAP information to determine the physical dimensions of input and output to the window.

If you resize an *xterm* window, programs running within the window must be notified so they can adjust the dimensions of input and output to the window. If the underlying operating system supports terminal resizing capabilities (for example, the SIGWINCH signal in systems derived from BSD 4.3), *xterm* will use these facilities to notify programs running in the window whenever it is resized. However, if your operating system does not support terminal resizing capabilities, you may need to request explicitly that TERMCAP be updated to reflect the resized window.

The *resize* client sends a special escape sequence to the *xterm* window and *xterm* sends back the current size of the window. The results of *resize* can be redirected to a file that can then be sourced to update TERMCAP. To update TERMCAP to match a window's changed dimensions, enter:

    % **resize** > *filename*

and then execute the resulting shell command file:

    % **source** *filename*   *C shell syntax*

or:

    $. *filename*   *Bourne shell syntax*

TERMCAP will be updated and the dimensions of the text within the window will be adjusted accordingly.

If your version of UNIX includes the C shell, you can also define this alias for *resize*:

    alias rs 'set noglob; eval 'resize'; unset noglob'

Then use rs to update the TERMCAP entry to reflect a window's new dimensions.

Note that even if your operating system supports terminal resizing capabilities, *xterm* may have trouble notifying programs running in the window that the window has been resized. On some older systems (based on BSD 4.2 or earlier), certain programs, notably the *vi* editor, cannot interpret this information. If you resize a window during a *vi* editing session, *vi* will not know the new size of the window. If you quit out of the editing session and start another one, the editor should know the new window size and operate properly. On newer systems (e.g., BSD 4.3 and later), these problems should not occur.

Using the Scrollbar

When using *xterm*, you are not limited to viewing the 24 lines displayed in the window at one time. By default, *xterm* actually remembers the last 64 lines that have appeared in the window. If the window has a scrollbar, you can scroll up and down through the saved text.

To create a single *xterm* window with a scrollbar, use the −sb command line option:

```
% xterm -sb &
```

To display all *xterm* windows with a scrollbar by default, set scrollBar in your *Xresources* file, as described in Chapter 10. The appropriate resource setting is illustrated below:

```
XTerm*scrollBar: true
```

If an *xterm* window was not created with a scrollbar, you can add one using the Enable Scrollbar item on the VT Options menu. See the section "VT Options Menu" later in this chapter for instructions on selecting a menu item.

Many applications provide horizontal and/or vertical scrollbars that allow you to look at a window's contents that extend beyond the viewing area. You move text (or images in graphics applications) in the window by placing the pointer on the scrollbar and performing some sort of action.

xterm's scrollbar is created by the Athena Scrollbar widget. (As we'll see in subsequent chapters, several of the standard X clients use Athena scrollbars.) An Athena scrollbar looks and operates differently than a scrollbar provided by a Motif application (that is, one created using the Motif widget set), as described in Chapter 8. If you're accustomed to using a Motif (or even a Macintosh) scrollbar, the Athena scrollbar may take some getting used to. While Motif and Mac scrollbars have separate parts to invoke different types of scrolling, the Athena scrollbar moves text according to which pointer button you use and how you use it.

Figure 5-1 shows an *xterm* window with a scrollbar.

The Athena scrollbar has two parts: a *thumb* (the highlighted area within the scrollbar) which moves within the *scroll region*. The thumb displays the position and amount of text currently showing in the window relative to the amount saved. When an *xterm* window with a scrollbar is first created, the thumb fills the entire scrollbar. As more text is saved, the size of the thumb decreases. The number of lines saved is 64 by default but an alternative can be specified with either the −sl command line option or the saveLines value in an *Xresources* file.

You scroll through the saved text using various pointer commands. When the pointer is positioned in the scrollbar, the cursor changes to a two-headed arrow. The scrollbar commands are summarized in Table 5-1.

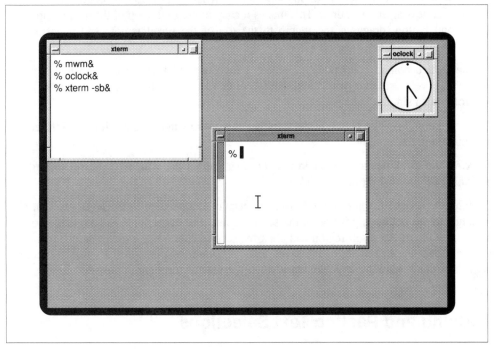

Figure 5-1. An xterm window with a scrollbar

Table 5-1. Athena Scrollbar Commands

To move text in this direction:	Place pointer Bon scrollbar and:	Notes:
Either up or down	Hold down second pointer button and drag thumb.	Text follows pointer movement.
Down	Click first pointer button.	Scrolls towards latest saved text (towards bottom of window).
Up	Click third pointer button.	Scrolls towards earliest saved text (towards top of window).
Either up or down	Click second pointer button.	Scrolls to a position in saved text that corresponds to the pointer's position in scroll region.

The first command in Table 5-1 involves dragging the text in the window using the second pointer button. This command is the simplest and offers the most control over how much scrolling takes place. To drag the text in this manner: first place the pointer on the scrollbar; press and hold down the second pointer button; then drag the thumb up and down. Notice that text moves as you move the thumb. If you drag up, the window scrolls back toward the beginning of information saved in the window. If you drag down, the window scrolls forward toward the end of information in the window. When you release the button, the window displays the text at that location. This makes it easy to get to the top of the data by pressing the second button, dragging the thumb to the top of the scroll region, and releasing the pointer button.

The next three pointer commands in Table 5-1 involve a click that causes the text to scroll However, if you test them, you'll find that it's difficult to judge how much text you're going to scroll with a single click.

Clicking the first pointer button in the scrollbar causes the window to scroll toward the end of information in the window.

Clicking the third pointer button in the scrollbar causes the window to scroll toward the beginning of information in the window.

Clicking the second pointer button moves the display to a position in the saved text that corresponds to the pointer's position in the scroll region. For example, if you move the pointer to the very top of the scroll region and click the second button, the window scrolls to a position very near the beginning of the saved text. As you might imagine, it's very difficult to guess how much scrolling will take place when you use the scrollbar in this way.

Copying and Pasting Text Selections

Once your *xterm* window is created, you can select text to copy and paste within the same or other *xterm* windows using the pointer. You don't need to be in a text editor to copy and paste. You can also copy or paste text to and from the command line.

Text copied into memory using the pointer is saved in a global cut buffer and also becomes what is known as the PRIMARY text "selection."* Both the contents of the cut buffer and the contents of the PRIMARY text selection are globally available to all clients. When you paste text into an *xterm* window, by default the contents of the PRIMARY selection are pasted. If no text is in the PRIMARY selection, the contents of the cut buffer (called CUT_BUFFER0), are pasted. (In most cases, these will be the same.)

Copying and pasting is one way in which clients exchange information, in this case, text. Later in this chapter, we'll consider some of the complications that can arise when copying and pasting between applications that save information differently. For now, however, let's see how to copy and paste text between *xterm* windows.

---

*The PRIMARY selection and the cut buffer are stored as *properties* of the root window. A property is a piece of information associated with a window (or font) and stored in the server, where it can be accessed by any client. The property mechanism permits "cut" text to be stored and later "pasted" into the windows of other clients. See Chapter 1 and Chapter 10 for more about properties and interclient communication.

Selecting Text to Copy

There are several ways to select (copy) text. You can select text by individual words or lines, or you can select a passage of text.

In order to copy text from a window, the window must have the input focus. The click to focus input is not interpreted as an attempt to start a text selection.

There are two methods for selecting a passage of text. First, you can make the selection by dragging the pointer: place the pointer at the beginning of the text you want to select; hold down the first button; move the pointer to the end of the desired text; then release the button. The text is highlighted, copied into the global cut buffer (called CUT_BUFFER0) and also made the PRIMARY selection.

The second way to select a passage is even simpler: mark the beginning of the selection by clicking the first pointer button; then mark the end of the selection by clicking the third pointer button. The text between the marks is highlighted, copied into CUT_BUFFER0, and made the PRIMARY selection.

You can select a single word or line simply by clicking. To select a single word, place the pointer on the word and double-click the first button.* To select a single line, place the pointer on the line and triple-click the first button.

If you hold the button down after double- or triple-clicking (rather than releasing it) and move the pointer, you will select additional text by words or lines at a time. Then release the button to end the selection.

Table 5-2 lists the possible pointer actions and the selections they make. You always begin by placing the pointer on the text you want to select.

Table 5-2. Button Combinations to Select Text for Copying

To select	Do this
Passage	At the beginning of the selection, hold down the first button; move the pointer to the end of the desired text; and release the button. Or:
	Click the first button at the start of the selection and the third button at the end of the selection.
Word	Double-click the first button anywhere on the word.
Line	Triple-click the first button anywhere on the line.

---

*To be more precise, double-clicking selects all characters of the same class (e.g., alphanumeric characters). By default, punctuation characters and whitespace are in a different class from letters or digits—hence, the observed behavior. However, character classes can be changed. For example, if you wanted to double-click to select email addresses, you'd want to include the punctuation characters !, %, @, and . in the same class as letters and digits. However, redefining the character classes is not something you'd do every day. See the *xterm* reference page in Part Three of this guide for details.

Each selection replaces the previous contents of CUT_BUFFER0 and the previous PRIMARY text selection. You can make only one selection at a time. (The *xclipboard* client, described later in this chapter, can be used to store multiple text selections.)

Once you have made a selection with the first button, you can extend that selection with the third button. This example shows how this works:

1. Bring up *vi* (or any other text editor with which you are familiar) in an *xterm* window, and type in this sample sentence:

   The X Window System is a network-based `graphics window system that was developed at MIT in 1984.`

2. Place the pointer on the word *graphics* in the sample sentence and select it by double-clicking the first button.

3. Then press and hold down the third pointer button. Move the pointer away from the word *graphics* to the left or right. A new selection now extends from the last selection (*graphics*) to the pointer's location and looks something like this:

   `The X Window System is a network-based graphics` window system that was developed at MIT in 1984.

   or:

   The X Window System is a network-based graphics window system that was developed at MIT in 1984.

Remember that the extension always begins from the last selection. By moving the pointer up or down, or to the right or left of the last selection, you can use this technique to select part of one line or add or subtract several lines of text.

To select text that fills more than one screen, select the first screenful. Use the scrollbar to view the additional text. Then use the third pointer button to extend the selection. The original selection does not need to be in view; clicking the third button will extend it to the point you choose.

To clear the highlighting, move the pointer off the selection and click the first button anywhere else in the window. Note, however, that the text still remains in memory until you make another selection.

Complications can arise if you're copying text that includes tabs. With the current implementation of the copy and paste feature, tabs are saved as spaces. If you're copying a large amount of text with many tabs from one text file to another, having tabs converted to spaces can create problems. A possible workaround is to change all tabs in the first file to some unique character or string (using a global command provided by your text editor); copy and paste the text into the second file; convert the unique strings back to tabs in both files using your text editor.

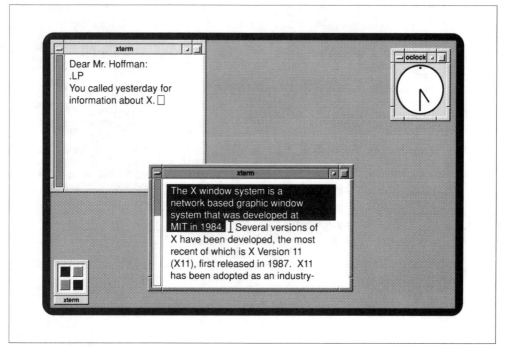

Figure 5-2. Highlighted text saved as the PRIMARY selection

Pasting Text Selections

The second button inserts the text from the PRIMARY selection (or CUT_BUFFER0, if the selection is empty) as if it were keyboard input. You can move data from one *xterm* window to another by selecting the data in one window with the first button, moving the pointer to another window, and clicking the second button.

You can paste text either into an open file or at a command line prompt. To paste text into an open file, as illustrated in Figure 5-3, click the second button within the window containing the file. The text from the memory area will be inserted at the text editor cursor. (Of course, the file must be in a mode where it is expecting text input, such as the insert mode of an editor.) You can paste the same text as often as you like. The contents of the PRIMARY selection remain until you make another selection.

To paste text at a command line prompt, you must first close any open file within the window. Then click the second button anywhere within the window to place the text on the command line at the end of text in the window. (Note that the window will scroll to the bottom on input.) You can make multiple insertions by repeatedly clicking the second button.

Note that you can paste text into a window when click-to-type focus is in effect, even if the window does not have the input focus. The act of pasting does not transfer focus either. (Similarly, if you click on a window to focus input, the click is not interpreted as an attempt to start a text selection.)

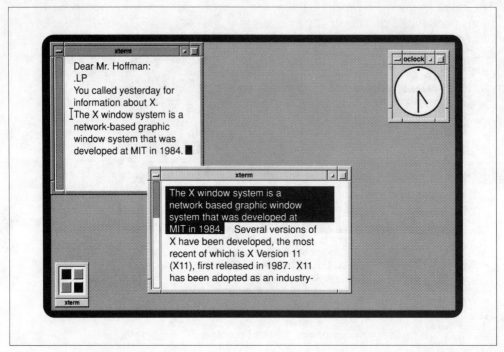

Figure 5-3. Pasting text into an open file

Keep in mind that you can paste *over* existing text in a file with the *vi* change text commands (such as cw, for change word). For example, you can paste over five words by specifying the *vi* command 5cw, and then pasting text by clicking the second pointer button. Note that you can paste over existing text in any editor that has an overwrite mode.

More About Text Selections

Prior to Release 3, many clients exchanged information solely by means of global cut buffers, which are, in effect, owned by the server, and available to all clients. Cut buffers are useful only for copying and pasting information that does not need to be translated to another format, such as ASCII text between two *xterm* windows.

In accordance with the newer interclient communication conventions developed since Release 2, most Release 3 and 4 clients, notably *xterm*, primarily exchange information via selections. The advantage of the selection mechanism is that it allows data from one client to be converted to a different format to be used by another client. Cut buffers do not perform this type of translation.

A selection is globally available but not owned by the server. A selection is owned by a client—initially by the client from which you copy it. Then when the text selection is pasted in another window, that window becomes the owner of the selection.

As we've said, if you are copying text between *xterm* windows, the contents of CUT_BUFFER0 and the PRIMARY selection should be the same. However, while some applications (notably the current version of *xterm*) copy to both the cut buffer and the selection, other applications (generally prior to Release 3) copy only to the cut buffer. If you are using both types of applications together and are trying to transfer text between them, differences between the contents of the cut buffer and the PRIMARY selection may make copying and pasting problematic. If you are only copying text between *xterm* windows (Release 3 or later), problems of this type will never arise.

Because of the rules of precedence governing cut buffers and selections and the nature of selections (particularly the issue of ownership), the following problems can arise in transferring data:

1. If one client communicates via cut buffers while another communicates via selections, copying and pasting between them is inherently problematic. By default, the selection takes precedence. How do you paste the contents of the cut buffer instead?

2. By default, you can save only one selection at a time.

3. For a selection to be transferred to a client, the selection must be owned by a client. If the client that owns the selection no longer exists, the transfer cannot be made.

The *xcutsel* and *xclipboard* clients address the first two of these problems, respectively.

Most users will probably not encounter the third problem. You are probably doing all of your copying and pasting between *xterm* windows. If you've made a selection from an *xterm* window and the window is killed, the *selection* contents are lost. However, the cut buffer contents remain intact and are pasted instead. (Since all *xterm* windows interpret ASCII text, the translation capabilities of the selection mechanism are not needed.)

Problems involving the loss of selections are more likely to happen if you are transferring information between clients that require information to be in different formats. If you are having such problems, you can customize the clients involved to copy information to what is known as the CLIPBOARD selection.

The CLIPBOARD selection is intended to avert problems of selection ownership by providing centralized ownership. Once the CLIPBOARD owns a selection, the selection can be transferred (and translated), even if the client that previously owned the selection goes away.

You can customize a client to send data to the CLIPBOARD selection by using *event translations*, which are discussed in Chapter 10. See the client reference pages in Part Three of this guide for information on the appropriate translations. For more information on selections and translations, see Volume One, *Xlib Programming Manual*.

Copying and Pasting between Release 2 and 3 Clients: xcutsel

The *xcutsel* client is intended to bridge a gap that exists between the ways older and newer clients allow you to copy text. If all the clients you are using are from Release 3 or later, you will probably have no use for *xcutsel* and should skip ahead to the next section.

Since Release 3, when you select text from an *xterm* window with the pointer, the text is copied into the global cut buffer and made the PRIMARY selection. (Thus, generally, the contents of the cut buffer and the PRIMARY selection are the same.) By default, the PRIMARY selection is what gets pasted into a window. If there is no PRIMARY selection, the contents of the cut buffer are pasted.

Prior to Release 3, clients did not use selections. Text was copied into the cut buffer only (and was not equated with a PRIMARY selection). Problems can arise if you run clients that only use cut buffers (many Release 2 clients and *uwm*, any release) with clients that primarily use selections (Release 3 and later) and try to paste text between them.

For instance, say you copy text in a Release 3 *xterm* window using the pointer. The text is copied into the cut buffer and also becomes the PRIMARY selection. If you paste in any window, the PRIMARY selection is what you get. Then, say you copy text in a R2 *xterm* window. The text is stored in the cut buffer, replacing the text in the cut buffer from the R3 window but it does *not* replace the PRIMARY selection. You can paste the text from the R2 window in another R2 window because the window only understands cut buffers but you can't paste it in an R3 window. If you try to, by default you get the PRIMARY selection (from the other R3 window).

xcutsel enables you to switch the text in the *cut* buffer and the PRIMARY *sel*ection so that you can cut and paste between clients that use cut buffers and clients that use selections.

To open an *xcutsel* window, type:

    % xcutsel &

and then position the window on your screen. Figure 5-4 shows an *xcutsel* window.

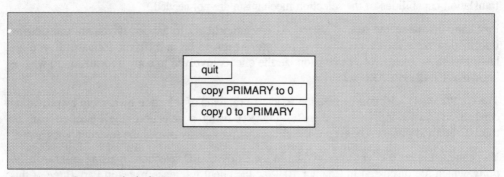

Figure 5-4. An xcutsel window

The window contains three command buttons whose functions are described below:

quit	Exits the *xcutsel* program.
copy PRIMARY to 0	Copies the contents of the PRIMARY selection to CUT_BUFFER0.
copy 0 to PRIMARY	Copies the contents of CUT_BUFFER0 to the PRIMARY selection.

Now let's go back to the problem we set up earlier in this section. If you copy text from an R2 window and want to paste in an R3 window, you merely click on the copy 0 to PRIMARY button. The contents of the cut buffer (from the R2 client) replace the previous PRIMARY selection (from the R3 client). When you paste, you get the text you want (from the R2 window).

Now say you have the same situation but the opposite problem. You made a selection from an R3 window, which filled the cut buffer and the PRIMARY selection. Then you copied text from an R2 window, which merely filled the buffer. (The contents of the buffer and the PRIMARY selection are different.) But now say you want to paste the text from the PRIMARY selection (from the R3 window) in an R2 window. If you paste text in an R2 window, you get the contents of the cut buffer (the text from the other R2 window).

To solve this problem, just click on the copy PRIMARY to 0 button in the *xcutsel* window. The contents of the PRIMARY selection (from the R3 window) replace the contents of the cut buffer (from the R2 window). When you paste in an R2 window, you get still get the contents of the cut buffer but it is now the text you want.

This business of selections versus cut buffers can be pretty confusing. If you have problems pasting the text you want, experiment a little with *xcutsel*.

Saving Multiple Selections: xclipboard

The *xclipboard* client provides a window in which you can paste multiple text selections and from which you can copy text selections to other windows. Similar to the clipboard feature of the Macintosh operating system, the *xclipboard* is basically a storehouse for text you may want to paste into other windows, perhaps multiple times. The *xclipboard* window is shown in Figure 5-5.

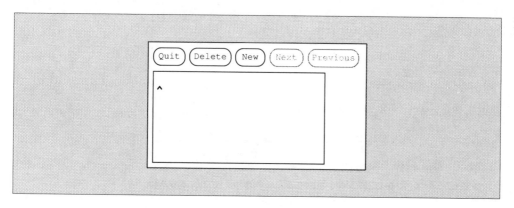

Figure 5-5. An xclipboard window

To open an *xclipboard*, type:

```
% xclipboard &
```

You can paste text into the *xclipboard* window using the pointer in the manner described previously and then copy and paste it elsewhere but this is not its intended use. To use the *xclipboard* most effectively, you must do some customization involving a resource file, such as *.Xresources*. The necessary steps are described in detail in Chapter 10. For now, suffice it to say that you want to set up the *xclipboard* so that you can select text to be made the CLIPBOARD selection and have that text *automatically pasted* in the *xclipboard* window, as illustrated in Figure 5-6.

Since the *xclipboard* client is intended to be coordinated with the CLIPBOARD selection, the X server allows you to run only one *xclipboard* at a time.

In order to illustrate how the clipboard works, let's presume it has been set up according to the guidelines in Chapter 10. According to those guidelines, you make text the CLIPBOARD selection by selecting it with the first pointer button (as usual) and then, while holding down the first button, clicking the third button. (You could specify another button combination or a button and key combination but we've found this one works pretty well.) The first pointer action makes the text the PRIMARY selection (and it is available to be pasted in another window using the pointer); the second pointer action additionally makes the text the CLIPBOARD selection (and it is automatically sent to the *xclipboard* window).

These guidelines still allow you to select text with the first pointer button alone and that text will be made the PRIMARY selection; however, the text will not automatically be sent to the *xclipboard*. This enables you to make many selections but to direct to the *xclipboard* only those selections you consider important (perhaps those you might want to paste several times).

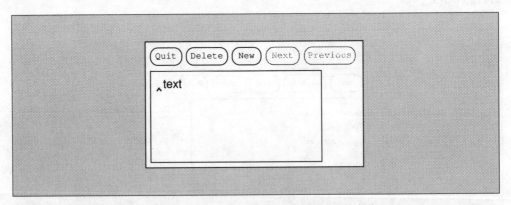

Figure 5-6. Selected text appears automatically in the xclipboard window

In order to allow you to store multiple text selections, the seemingly tiny *xclipboard* actually provides multiple screens, each of which can be thought of as a separate buffer. (However, as we'll see, a single text selection can span more than one screen.) Each time you use the pointer to make text the CLIPBOARD selection, the *xclipboard* advances to a new screen in which it displays and stores the text.

Once you have saved multiple selections, the client's Next and Previous command buttons allow you to move forward and backward among these screens of text. The functionality of the client's command buttons is summarized in Table 5-3. They are all selected by clicking the first pointer button.

Table 5-3. Command Buttons and Functions

Button	Function
Quit	Causes the application to exit.
Delete	Deletes the current *xclipboard* buffer; the current screenful of text is cleared from the window and the next screenful (or previous, if there is no next) is displayed.
New	Opens a new buffer into which you can insert text; the window is cleared.
Next and Previous	Once you have sent multiple selections to the *xclipboard*, Next and Previous allow you to move from one to another (e.g., display them sequentially). Before two or more CLIPBOARD selections are made, these buttons are not available for use. (Their labels will appear in a lighter typeface to indicate this.)

The command buttons you will probably use most frequently are Delete, Next, and Previous.

When you select text using the first and third pointer buttons, the text will automatically be displayed in the *xclipboard* window and will, in effect, be the first screenful of text (or first buffer) saved in the *xclipboard*. Subsequent CLIPBOARD selections will be displayed and saved in subsequent screens.

You select text from the *xclipboard* and paste it where you want it just as you would any text. Just display the text you want in the *xclipboard* window, using Next or Previous as necessary. Then select the text using the first pointer button and paste it using the second pointer button.

You can remove a screenful of text from the *xclipboard* by displaying that screenful and then clicking on the Delete command button. When you delete a screenful of text using this command button, the next screenful (if any) will be displayed in the window. If there is no next screenful, the previous screenful will be displayed.

Certain features (and limitations) of the *xclipboard* become apparent only when you make a very large CLIPBOARD selection. Say you select a full *xterm* window of text with the first and third pointer buttons, as described above. The text extends both horizontally and vertically beyond the bounds of a single *xclipboard* screen. (As we suggested earlier, a CLIPBOARD selection can actually span more than one *xclipboard* screen. Pressing Delete will remove all screensful the selection comprises.) When you make a selection that extends beyond the bounds of the *xclipboard* screen (either horizontally, vertically, or both), scrollbars will be activated in the window to allow you to view the entire selection.

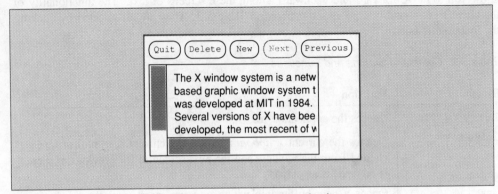

Figure 5-7. xclipboard with scrollbars to view large text selection

If the text extends both horizontally and vertically beyond the bounds of the *xclipboard* screen, as it does in Figure 5-7, the window will display both horizontal and vertical scrollbars. If the text extends beyond the screen in only one of these two ways, the window will display either a horizontal or vertical scrollbar, as needed.* These scrollbars are selection-specific: they are only displayed as long as the current selection cannot be viewed in its entirety without them. If you move to a previous or subsequent selection that *can* be viewed without scrollbars, the scrollbars will be deactivated.

Problems with Large Selections

If you experiment making large selections with *xclipboard*, you may discover what seems to be a bug in the program. Though in most circumstances, making a new selection causes the screen to advance and display the new text, this does not happen reliably after a selection vertically spanning more than one screenful. In these cases, the new selection *is* saved in the *xclipboard*; however, the *xclipboard* window does not automatically advance to show you the new current selection. Instead, the previous long selection is still displayed. This is a bit of *xc ipboard* sleight-of-hand. The new selection has been successfully made but the appearance of the window belies this fact. (The Next button will probably add to your confusion; it will not be available for selection, suggesting that the text in the window is the last selection saved. This is not the case.)

In order to get around this problem and display the actual current selection, press the Previous button. The same long selection (which is, in actuality, the Previous selection) will again be displayed. Then the Next button will be enabled, and you can click on it to display the actual current selection.

---

*An application created using the X Toolkit, which provides horizontal and vertical scrollbars, is described as a *viewport*. See Chapter 8 for more information about viewports and other X Toolkit features.

Editing Text Saved In the xclipboard

You can edit text you send to the *xclipboard* using the same commands recognized by *xedit*. These commands are described in the section "The xedit Text Editor" in Chapter 8. A small caret cursor will be visible in each screenful of text. You can move this cursor by clicking the pointer where you'd like it to appear. Then you can backspace to delete letters or type to insert them. When you edit a screenful of text, the *xclipboard* continues to store the edited version, until you delete it or exit the program.

Be aware that, without performing customization, you can still use *xclipboard* on a very simple level. You can paste text into and copy text from the *xclipboard* window just as you would any other, using the pointer movements described earlier in this chapter. You can also type in the *xclipboard* window and then copy and paste what you've typed. Just move the pointer into the window and try typing. However, keep in mind that this is not the intended use of the *xclipboard*.

If you do choose to use the clipboard in a limited way, it can still be a helpful editing tool. For example, say you wanted to create a paragraph composed of a few lines of text from each of two files. You could copy the text from each file using the pointer and paste it into the *xclipboard* window. (Each time you paste text into the *xclipboard* window, the text is appended to whatever text was already pasted there.) Again using the pointer, you could copy the newly formed paragraph from the *xclipboard* window and paste it into a file in another window.

Running a Program in a Temporary xterm Window

Normally, when you start up an *xterm* window, it automatically runs another instance of the UNIX Bourne or C shell (depending on which is set in your *Xresources* file or the SHELL environment variable). If you want to create an *xterm* window that runs some other program and goes away when that program terminates, you can do so with the *xterm* −e option:

```
% xterm -e command [arguments]
```

For example, if you want to look at the file *temp* in a window that will disappear when you quit out of the file, you can use the UNIX *more* program as follows:

```
% xterm -e more temp
```

When you are using other options to *xterm* on the command line, the −e option must appear last because everything after the −e option is read as a command.

The xterm Menus

xterm has four different menus:

* Main Options menu (formerly called xterm menu).

* VT Options menu (formerly called **Modes** menu).

* VT Fonts menu (available as of Release 4).

* Tek Options menu (formerly called Tektronix menu).

The VT Fonts menu, which allows you to change the *xterm* display font dynamically, was introduced in Release 4. The other three menus are updated versions of menus available in Release 3. As is indicated above, these three menus have been renamed in Release 4. Most of the *items* available on these menus have not changed in functionality since Release 3, though many have been renamed and some have been reorganized.

As shown in Figure 5-8, three of the four *xterm* menus are divided into sections separated by horizontal lines. The top portion of each divided menu contains various modes that can be toggled. (The one exception is the Redraw Window item on the Main Options menu, which is a command.) A check mark appears next to a mode that is currently active. Selecting one of these modes toggles its state.

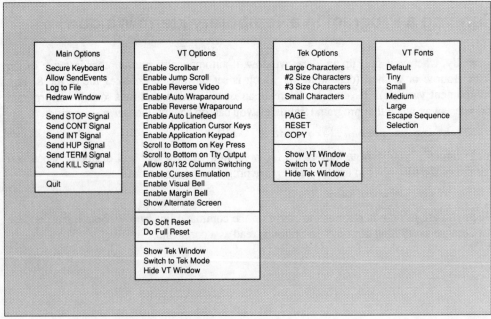

Figure 5-8. The Release 4 xterm menus

The items on the VT Fonts menu change the font in which text is displayed in the *xterm* window. Only one of these fonts can be active at a time. To toggle one off, you must activate another.

Most mode entries can also be set by command line options when invoking *xterm*, or by entries in a resource startup file (such as *Xdefaults* or *Xresources*) as described in Chapter 10. (See the *xterm* reference page in Part Three of this guide for a complete list of command options and resource variables.) The various modes on the menus are very helpful if you've set (or failed to set) a particular mode on the command line and then decide you want the opposite characteristic.

The sections below the modes portion of each menu contain various commands. Selecting one of these commands performs the indicated function. Many of these functions can only be invoked from the *xterm* menus. However, some functions can be invoked in other ways: for example, from an *mwm* menu, on the command line, by a sequence of keystrokes (such as Control-C). This chapter includes alternatives to some of the menu items which, in certain cases, may be more convenient. Of course, the *xterm* menus can be very helpful when other methods to invoke a function fail.

Menus are displayed by placing the pointer on the window and simultaneously pressing a keyboard key and pointer button. (The exact key and button combinations are described below with each menu.) When you're using a window manager, such as *mwm*, that provides a titlebar or frame, the pointer must rest within the window proper—not on any window decoration. (Note that the pointer be within the window, even if click-to-type focus is enabled. See Chapter 1 for a discussion of focus policy.)

When you display an *xterm* menu, the pointer becomes the arrow pointer and initially appears in the menu's title. Once the menu appears, you can release any keyboard key. The menu will remain visible as long as you continue to hold down the appropriate pointer button. (You can move the pointer off the menu without it disappearing.)

If you decide not to select a menu item after the menu has appeared, move the pointer off the menu and release the button. The menu disappears and no action is taken.

In this discussions of the four *xterm* menus, we'll consider some of the more useful items as well as some alternatives to menu items. For more complete information about each menu, see the *xterm* reference page in Part Three of this guide.

The Main Options Menu

The Main Options menu, shown in Figure 5-9, allows you to set certain modes and to send signals (such as SIGHUP) that affect the *xterm* process.

To bring up the Main Options menu, move the pointer to the *xterm* window you want to change, hold down the Control key, and press the first (usually the left) pointer button.* The pointer changes to the menu pointer, and this menu of three modes and eight commands appears. (You can release the Control key but must continue to press the first pointer button to hold the Main Options menu in the window.) Note that Main Options menu items apply only to the *xterm* window the pointer is in when you display the menu. To effect changes in another *xterm*, you must move the pointer to that window, display the menu, and specify the items you want.

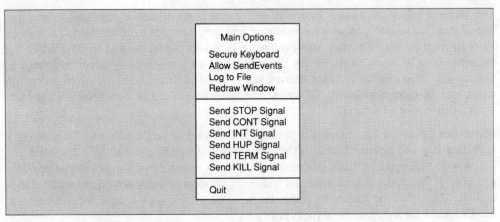

Figure 5-9. The Main Options menu

To select a menu item, move the menu pointer to that item and release the first button. After you have selected a mode (Secure Keyboard, Allow SendEvents, or Log to File), a check mark appears before the item to remind you that it is active. The Log to File mode on the Main Options menu can also be set by a command line option when invoking *xterm*. In addition, both Log to File and Allow SendEvents can be set by entries in a resource startup file such as *.Xresources*. The menu selections enable you to change your mind once *xterm* is running. (See the *xterm* reference page in Part Three for more information on these modes.)

The Secure Keyboard mode toggle was added to the menu (in a Release 3 patch) to help counteract one of the security weaknesses of X. This mode is intended to be activated when you want to type a password or other important text in an *xterm* window. Generally, when you press a keyboard key or move the pointer, the X server generates a packet of information that is available for other clients to interpret. These packets of information are known as *events*. Moving the pointer or pressing a keyboard key causes input events to occur.

There is an inherent security problem in the client-server model. Because events such as the keys you type in an *xterm* window are made available via the server to other clients, hypothetically an adept system hacker could access this information. (Naturally, this is not an issue in every environment.) A fairly serious breach of security could easily occur, for

---

*The right button can be made to function as the "first" button. This is especially useful if you are left-handed. See Chapter 12, *Setup Clients*, for instructions on how to customize the pointer with *xmodmap*.

instance, if someone were able to find out a user's password or the *root* password. Enabling Secure Keyboard mode causes all user input to be directed *only* to the *xterm* window itself.

Of course, in many environments, precaution is probably not necessary: if the nature of the work is in no way sensitive, if the system administrator has taken pains to secure the system in other ways, etc. If your environment might be vulnerable, you can enable Secure Keyboard mode before typing passwords and other important information and then disable it again using the menu.

When you enable Secure Keyboard mode, the foreground and background colors of the *xterm* window will be exchanged (as if you had enabled the Reverse Video mode from the VT Options menu), as shown in Figure 5-10. When you disable Secure Keyboard mode, the colors will be switched back.

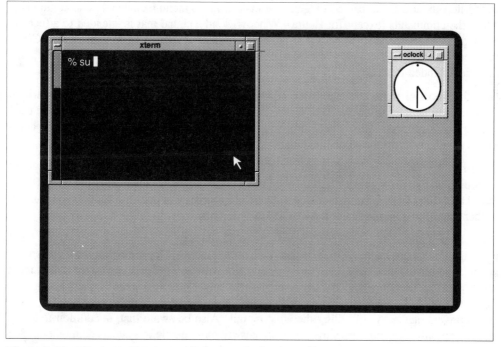

Figure 5-10. Reverse video is enabled when the keyboard is secure

Be aware that only one X client at a time can secure the keyboard. Thus, if you have enabled Secure Keyboard mode in one *xterm*, you will not be allowed to enable it in another *xterm* until you disable it in the first. If Secure Keyboard mode is not available when you request it, the colors will not be switched and a bell will sound.

If you request Secure Keyboard mode and are not refused but the colors are *not* exchanged, be careful: you are not in Secure Keyboard mode. If this happens, there's a good chance that someone has tampered with the system. If the application you're running displays a prompt before asking for a password, it's a good idea to enable Secure Keyboard mode before the prompt is displayed and then verify that the prompt is displayed in the proper colors. Before entering the password, you can also display the Main Options menu again and verify that a check mark appears next to Secure Keyboard mode.

Be aware that Secure Keyboard will be disabled automatically if you iconify the *xterm* window, or start *mwm* or another window manager that provides a titlebar or other window decoration. (You can enable Secure Keyboard mode once *mwm* is running, though.) This limitation is due to the X protocol. When the mode is disabled, the colors will be switched back and the bell will sound to warn you.

Though intended to counteract a security weakness, the Secure Keyboard mode toggle can also be used to get around a weakness of *mwm*. As described in Chapter 4, if *mwm* dies, it's possible that the focus can be lost—i.e., the focus is no longer directed to any application window. Selecting Secure Keyboard mode for any *xterm* should cause that window to grab the focus again.

In addition to modes that can be toggled, the Main Options menu includes several commands. All of the commands (except for Redraw Window) send a signal that is intended to affect the *xterm* process: suspend it (Send STOP Signal), terminate it (Send TERM Signal), etc. Given that your operating system may recognize only certain signals, every menu item may not produce the intended function.

Note that most of these commands are equivalent to common keystroke commands, which are generally simpler to invoke. For example, in most terminal setups Control-C can be used to interrupt a process. This is generally simpler than using the Send INT Signal menu command, which performs the same function.

Similarly, if your system supports job control, you can probably suspend a process by typing Control-Z and start the process again by typing Control-Y, rather than using the Send STOP Signal and Send CONT Signal menu commands. If your system does not support job control, neither the menu commands nor the keystrokes will work.

Four of the commands (Send HUP Signal, Send TERM Signal, Send KILL Signal, and Quit) send signals that are intended to terminate the *xterm* window. Depending on the signals your system recognizes, these commands may or may not work as intended. Be aware that in most cases you can probably end an *xterm* process simply by typing some sequence (such as Control-D or exit) in the window. Of course the menu items may be very helpful if the more conventional ways of killing the window fail. Also be aware that, in addition to being recognized only by certain systems, some signals are more gentle to systems than others. See the *xterm* reference page in Part Three of this guide for information on the signal sent by each of the menu commands and the *signal*(3C) reference page in the *UNIX Programmer's Manual* for more information on what each signal does.

The Quit command sends a SIGHUP to the process group of the process running under *xterm*, usually the shell. (The Send HUP Signal command sends the same signal.) This ends up killing the *xterm* process, and the window disappears from the screen.

Quit is separated from the earlier commands by a horizontal line so it's easier to point at. Sending a SIGHUP with Quit is slightly more gentle to the system than sending a SIGKILL with Send KILL Signal.

The Redraw Window command redraws the contents of the window. As an alternative, you can redraw the entire screen using the *xrefresh* client. See the *xrefresh* reference page in Part Three of this guide for more information about this client.

VT Options Menu

The VT Options menu provides many VT102 setup functions. Some of these mode settings are analogous to those available in a real VT102's setup mode; others, such as *scrollbar*, are *xterm*-only modes.

The VT Options menu items allow you to reset several modes at once, select the Tektronix window to accept input, and hide the VT window.

To bring up the VT Options menu, move the pointer to the *xterm* window, hold down the Control key, and then press and hold down the second pointer button. (You can release the Control key but must continue to press the second button to keep the VT Options menu in the window.) The menu shown in Figure 5-11 appears.

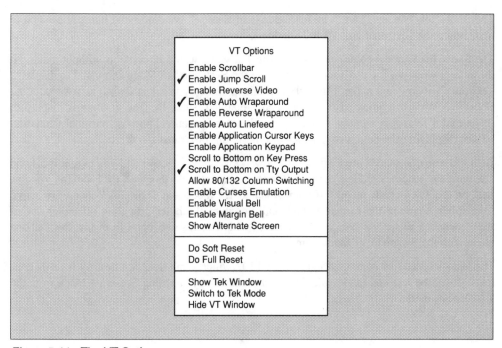

Figure 5-11. The VT Options menu

Check marks indicate the active modes. For example, Jump Scroll, Auto Wraparound, and Scroll to Bottom on Tty Output* are active in the VT Options menu displayed in Figure 5-12. These are the only modes active by default. To turn off one of these modes, move the menu pointer to that mode and release the second button.

Most of these modes can also be set by command line options when invoking *xterm* or by entries in a resource startup file like *Xresources* (see Chapter 10). The menu selections allow you to change your mind once *xterm* is running.

The toggle Allow 80/132 Column Switching warrants a little more explanation. This mode allows *xterm* to recognize the DECCOLM escape sequence, which switches the terminal between 80- and 132-column mode. The DECCOLM escape sequence can be included in a program (such as a spreadsheet) to allow the program to display in 132-column format. See Appendix E, *xterm Control Sequences*, for more information. This mode is off by default.

The VT Options menu commands (in the second and third partitions of the menu) perform two sets of functions, neither of which can be performed from the command line or a resource definition file. The commands Soft Reset and Full Reset reset some of the modes on the menu to their initial states. See the *xterm* reference page in Part Three of this guide for more information.

The Show Tek Window, Switch to Tek Mode, and Hide VT Window menu items allow you to manipulate the Tektronix and VT102 windows.

The Show Tek Window command displays the Tek window and its contents without making it the active window (you can't input to it). Use the Switch to Tek Mode command to display a Tektronix window and make it the active window. When you select Switch to Tek Mode, the Show Tek Window command is automatically enabled, since the Tek window is displayed. (Note that a Tektronix window is not commonly used for general purpose terminal emulation but for displaying the output of graphics or typesetting programs.)

Both of these commands are toggles. If Show Tek Window is active and you toggle it off, the Tek window becomes hidden. (As we'll see, you can also do this with the Hide Tek Window item on the Tek Options menu.) If both Switch to Tek Mode and Show Tek Window are active (remember, enabling the former automatically enables the latter), toggling off either one of them switches the *xterm* back to VT mode. (This can also be done from the Tek Options menu with the Switch to VT Mode item.)

The Hide VT Window command hides the VT102 window but does not destroy it or its contents. It can be restored (and made the active window) by choosing Select VT Mode from the Tek Options menu.

---

*This mode indicates that if you are using the scrollbar and the window receives output (or a key is pressed, if stty echo is enabled), the window scrolls forward so that the cursor is at the current line. (You can use the menu to toggle off this mode but it is generally desirable to have.)

VT Fonts Menu

The VT Fonts menu is a welcome Release 4 innovation. It allows you to change the display font of an *xterm* window while the window is running. To bring up the VT Fonts menu, move the pointer inside the *xterm* window. Press and hold down the Control key on the keyboard and press the third (usually the right) pointer button. The VT Fonts menu is shown in Figure 5-12.

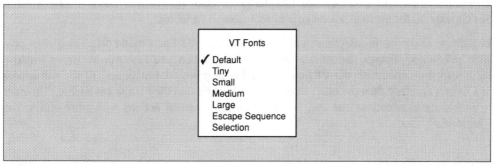

Figure 5-12. VT Fonts menu

If you have not toggled any items on this menu, a check mark will appear before the Default mode setting. The Default is the font specified when the *xterm* window was run. This font could have been specified on the *xterm* command line or in a resource file such as *Xresources*. Whatever the case, this font remains the Default for the duration of the current *xterm* process.

The items Default, Tiny, Small, Medium, and Large can be toggled to set the font displayed in the *xterm* window. The font can be changed any number of times to accommodate a variety of uses. You might choose to use a large font for editing a file (chances are you've chosen a large enough default font, though). You could then change to a smaller font while a process is running since you don't need to be reading or typing in that *xterm*. Changing the font also changes the size of the window.

There are also default settings for the Tiny, Small, Medium, and Large fonts. They are all constant-width fonts from the directory */usr/lib/X11/fonts/misc* and are listed in Table 5-4.

Table 5-4. VT Fonts Menu Defaults

Menu Item	Default Font
Tiny	nil2
Small	6x10
Medium	8x13
Large	9x15

Bring up the VT Fonts menu and toggle some of these fonts to see what they look like. The default Tiny font, *nil2*, is actually too small to be legible. It is not intended to be read. If you select this font, your *xterm* window becomes tiny, almost the size of some application icons. Though you cannot read the actual text in a window this size, the window is still active and you *can* observe if additional output, albeit minuscule, is displayed. An *xterm* window displaying text in such a small font can, in effect, serve as an *active icon*.

Be aware that you can specify your own Tiny, Small, Medium, and Large fonts using entries in a resource startup file such as *Xresources*. The corresponding resource names are font1, font2, font3, and font4. See Chapter 6 for more information about available fonts. See Chapter 10 for instructions on how to set resource variables.

In addition to the menu selections we've discussed, the VT Fonts menu offers two other possible selections: Escape Sequence and Selection. When you first run an *xterm* window, these selections appear on the VT Fonts menu but they are not functional. (They will appear in a lighter typeface than the other selections, indicating that they are not available.) In order to enable these selections for use, you must perform certain actions which are outlined in Chapter 6.

Tek Options Menu

The Tek Options menu controls certain modes and functions of the Tektronix window. The menu can only be displayed from within the Tektronix window. As previously described, you can display the Tek window and make it the active window by using the Switch to Tek Mode command on the VT Options menu.

To display the Tek Options menu, move the pointer inside the Tektronix window. Press and hold down the Control key on the keyboard and press the second pointer button. The Tek Options menu appears. With this menu you set the size of the text in the Tektronix window and select some commands.

Note that these modes (above the first line) can only be set from the Tek Options menu. All of these modes set the point size of the text displayed in the Tektronix window. (Only one of these four modes can be enabled at any time.)

The most important command on the Tek Options menu, shown in Figure 5-13, is Switch to VT Mode. If the Tek window has been made the active window (using the Switch to Tek Mode command from the VT Options menu), you can choose Switch to VT Mode to make the VT window the active window again. (If both windows are showing, you can also toggle Switch to Tek Mode on the VT Options menu to *deactivate* it; that is, switch *from* Tek mode and back to VT mode.) Switch to VT Mode is also a toggle; if you deactivate it, *xterm* will switch back to Tek mode.

Selecting Show VT Window displays the VT window if it has been hidden (using the Hide VT Window command from the VT Options menu) or hides it if it is being displayed. (Again, the command is a toggle.) Remember that you cannot input to the VT window until you make it the active window by using Switch to VT Mode.

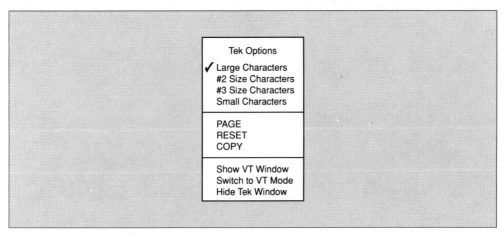

Figure 5-13. The Tek Options menu

6

Font Specification

This chapter describes what you need to know in order to select display fonts for the various client applications. After acquainting you with some of the basic characteristics of a font, this chapter describes the rather complex font naming conventions and how to simplify font specification. This chapter also describes how to use the xlsfonts, xfd, *and* xfontsel *clients to list, display, and select available screen fonts.*

In This Chapter:

6
Font Specification

Many clients allow you to specify the font used to display text in the window, in menus and labels, or in any other text fields. For example, you can choose the font used for the text in *mwm* menus or in *xterm* windows.

Unfortunately, for the most part, there are no simple "font menus" like there are on systems such as the Macintosh.* Instead, X has a fairly complex font naming system (which, like most things about X, is designed for maximum flexibility rather than for simplicity or ease of use). Of course, there will no doubt soon be many applications, such as word processors and publishing packages, that provide a simple interface for selecting fonts. However, for the clients in the X distribution, you are generally limited to selecting fonts via command line options or resource specifications.

This wouldn't be so bad if a typical font name weren't mind-bending at first glance. Imagine typing this command line to create an *xterm* window whose text is to be displayed in 14-point Courier bold:

`% xterm -fn -adobe-courier-bold-r-normal--14-140-75-75-m-90-iso8859-1`

Fortunately, you can use asterisks as wildcards to simplify this name to a somewhat more reasonable one:

`% xterm -fn '*courier-bold-r*140*'`

and you can define even simpler aliases, so that you could end up typing a command line similar to this:

`% xterm -fn courierB14`

In this chapter, we're going to try to make sense out of the sometimes bewildering jungle of information about fonts under X. First, we'll explain the font naming convention in detail. Along the way, we'll acquaint you with the appearance of some of the basic font families (groups of related fonts), and the various permutations (such as weight, slant, and point size) within each family.

---

*An exception is the VT fonts menu in the R4 *xterm*. But even then, you need to know a lot about font naming to change the fonts on the menu.

Then, we'll talk about how to use font name wildcards to simplify font specification. We'll also talk about the font search path (the directories where the font files are stored), and how to define aliases for font names.

Finally, we'll talk about some of the utilities X provides for dealing with fonts:

- *xlsfonts*, which lists the names of the fonts available on your server, as well as any aliases.

- *xfd* (font displayer), which allows you to display the character set for any individual font you specify on the command line.

- *xfontsel* (font selector), which allows you to preview fonts and select the name of the one you want. (This name can then be pasted onto a command line, into a resource file, etc.)

Font Naming Conventions

In Release 2 and earlier, fonts were simply identified by the name of the file in which they were stored, minus the *.snf* ("server natural format") extension. For example, the file *8x13.snf* contained a font named *8x13*. (See Appendix A, *System Management*, for a discussion of font file formats.)

However, starting with Release 3, a new logical font naming convention was adopted. As we'll see in a moment, these logical font names allow for complete specification of all of the characteristics of each font. Unfortunately, this completeness makes them somewhat difficult to work with—at least until you learn what all the parts of the names mean, and get a handle on which parts you need to remember and which you can safely ignore. (By the end of this chapter, you should have that knowledge.)

The *xlsfonts* client can be used to display the names of all the fonts available on your server. When you run *xlsfonts*, you'll get an intimidating list of names similar to the name in Figure 6-1. Upon close examination, this rather verbose name contains a great deal of useful information: the font's developer, or foundry (Adobe); the font family (Courier); weight (bold); slant (oblique); set width (normal); size of the font in pixels (10); size of the font in tenths of a point (100 tenths of a point, thus 10 points); horizontal resolution (75 dpi); vertical resolution (75 dpi); spacing (m, for monospace); average width (60—measured in tenths of a pixel, thus 6 pixels); and character set (iso8859-1).

As mentioned earlier, font name wildcarding can eliminate lots of unnecessary detail. If you are already familiar with font characteristics, skip ahead to the section "Font Name Wildcarding," later in this chapter, for some tips and tricks. If you need a refresher on fonts, read on as we illustrate and explain each of the elements that make up the font name.

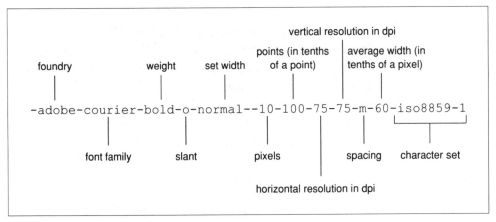

Figure 6-1. Font name, Release 3 and Release 4

Font Families

It has been several years since the advent of desktop publishing and, by now, it is unlikely that anyone in the computer industry is unaware that text can be displayed on the screen and printed on the page using different fonts.

However, the term *font* is used somewhat ambiguously. Does it refer to a family of typefaces (such as Times® Roman or Helvetica®), which comes in different sizes, weights, and orientations? Or should each distinct set of character glyphs be considered a separate font?

X takes the latter approach. When the documentation says that Release 3 includes 157 fonts, and Release 4 more than 400, this sounds either intimidating or impressive, depending on your mood. But, in fact, the R3 X distribution includes only six font families (Courier, Helvetica, New Century Schoolbook®, Symbol, and Times), plus several miscellaneous fonts that are found only in individual sizes and orientations.* R4 includes two more font families: Lucida® and the Clean family of fixed-width fonts, plus many more special purpose fonts.

When you think about it this way, you can quickly reduce the clutter. Figure 6-2 shows the major families of commercial fonts that are available under X. To illustrate the fonts, we've used the simple expedient of printing each font name in the font itself. Font names are truncated to fit on the page.† (For those of you who don't read the Greek alphabet, the fourth line down reads "-adobe-symbol-medium-r-normal--18 . . ." This font is used for mathematical equations and so forth, rather than for normal display purposes.)

---

*By contrast, the Macintosh supports dozens of font families; commercial typesetters support hundreds and, in some cases, even thousands of families. Many of these fonts will doubtless be made commercially available for X.

†To generate the figures in this section and in Appendix B, *Release 4 Standard Fonts*, we wrote a short program called *xshowfonts*, which displays a series of fonts in a scrollable window. Source code for *xshowfonts* is listed in Appendix B, *Release 4 Standard Fonts*. In each case, we used wildcards (discussed later in this chapter) to select the fonts we wanted and then did screendumps of the resulting images. Note that the fonts look better on the screen than they do in the illustration, since the scaling factor used to make the screen dumps exacerbates the "jagged edges" endemic to bitmap fonts.

```
-adobe-courier-medium-r-normal--18-180-75-75-m-1
-adobe-helvetica-medium-r-normal--18-180-75-75-p-98-is
-adobe-new century schoolbook-medium-r-normal--18-180-
-αδοβε-σψμβολ-μεδιυμ-ρ-νορμαλ--18-180-75-75-π-107-αδοβε
-adobe-times-medium-r-normal--18-180-75-75-p-94-iso8859-
-b&h-lucida-medium-r-normal-sans-18-180-75-75-
-b&h-lucidabright-medium-r-normal--18-180-75-75-p-
-b&h-lucidatypewriter-medium-r-normal-sans-18-18
-bitstream-charter-medium-r-normal--19-180-75-75-p-106-iso885
```

Figure 6-2. The major commercial font families available in the standard X distribution

You'll notice that with the exception of Courier and Lucidatypewriter, all of the fonts in the figure are *proportionally spaced*. That is, each character has a separate width. This makes them look good on a printed page but makes them less appropriate for screen display in terminal windows (especially for program editing), since text will not line up properly unless all characters are the same width.

You will most likely use these proportional fonts for labels or menu items, rather than for running text. (Word processing or publishing programs will, of course, use them to represent proportional type destined for the printed page.)

Courier and Lucidatypewriter are *monospaced* fonts: every character has the same width. Monospaced fonts can be used effectively for the text font in *xterm* windows. There are also some special monospaced fonts originally designed for computer displays. You can think of these as *character cell fonts*. They, too, are monospaced but the spacing relates to the size of a cell that contains each character, rather than (necessarily) to the character itself. Some of these fonts were originally available in Release 2 and even in R3 they don't have the same complex names as the proportional fonts. Instead, they have simple names expressing their size in pixels. For example, in the font named 8x13, each character occupies a box 8 pixels wide by 13 pixels high.

In R4 they were renamed to use the logical font naming conventions with a foundry name of "misc," and a font family of "fixed." There are also one or two larger fixed fonts donated by Sony for use with their extra-high resolution monitor, with a foundry name of "sony." Figure 6-3 shows the character cell fonts, using their R3 names, which still exist as aliases in R4. (Not all of these fonts were available in R3.)

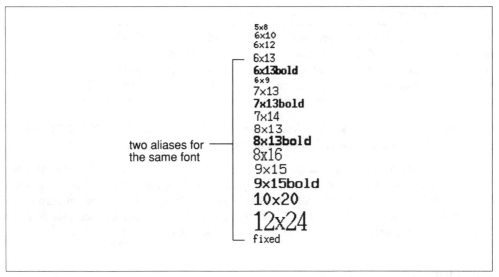

Figure 6-3. Miscellaneous fonts for xterm text

Table 6-1 shows the correspondence between these aliases and full font names. Note that the 6x13 font also has an alias called "fixed" defined for it. The "fixed" alias is used as the default font for *xterm* windows. (Twelve-point Helvetica bold roman has the alias "variable," which several applications use as the default font for labels. *mwm* uses this font for the application name that appears in the title area of the window frame.)

Table 6-1. Fixed Font Aliases and Font Names

Alias	Filename
fixed	-misc-fixed-medium-r-semicondensed--13-120-75-75-c-60-iso8859-1
5x8	-misc-fixed-medium-r-normal--8-80-75-75-c-50-iso8859-1
6x9	-misc-fixed-medium-r-normal--9-90-75-75-c-60-iso8859-1
6x10	-misc-fixed-medium-r-normal--10-100-75-75-c-60-iso8859-1
6x12	-misc-fixed-medium-r-semicondensed--12-110-75-75-c-60-iso8859-1
6x13	-misc-fixed-medium-r-semicondensed--13-120-75-75-c-60-iso8859-1
6x13bold	-misc-fixed-bold-r-semicondensed--13-120-75-75-c-60-iso8859-1
7x13	-misc-fixed-medium-r-normal--13-120-75-75-c-70-iso8859-1
7x13bold	-misc-fixed-bold-r-normal--13-120-75-75-c-70-iso8859-1
7x14	-misc-fixed-medium-r-normal--14-130-75-75-c-70-iso8859-1
8x13	-misc-fixed-medium-r-normal--13-120-75-75-c-80-iso8859-1
8x13bold	-misc-fixed-bold-r-normal--13-120-75-75-c-80-iso8859-1
8x16	-sony-fixed-medium-r-normal--16-120-100-100-c-80-iso8859-1

Table 6-1. Fixed Font Aliases and Font Names (continued)

Alias	Filename
9x15	-misc-fixed-medium-r-normal--15-140-75-75-c-90-iso8859-1
9x15bold	-misc-fixed-bold-r-normal--15-140-75-75-c-90-iso8859-1
10x20	-misc-fixed-medium-r-normal--20-200-75-75-c-100-iso8859-1
12x24	-sony-fixed-medium-r-normal--24-170-100-100-c-120-iso8859-1

R4 also includes the Clean family of fixed-width fonts from Schumacher, and DEC's terminal fonts, both of which are illustrated in Appendix B, *Release 4 Standard Fonts*.

There are also many other special purpose fonts, such as the Greek Symbol font that we already saw, the cursor font, the OPEN LOOK™ cursor and glyph fonts, and Kana and Kanji Japanese fonts. (The Kana and Kanji fonts can only be displayed with special hardware.) See Appendix B, *Release 4 Standard Fonts*, for comprehensive lists and samples of these fonts, as well as pictures of the complete character set in some representative fonts.

Stroke Weight and Slant

The characters in a given font family can be given a radically different appearance by changing the *stroke weight* or the *slant*, or both.

The most common weights are medium and bold. The most common slants are roman (upright), italic, or oblique. (Both italic and oblique are slanted; however, italic versions of a font generally have had the character shape changed to make a more pleasing effect when slanted, while oblique fonts are simply a slanted version of the upright font. In general, *serif* fonts (those with little decorations on the ends and corners of the characters) are slanted via italics, while *sans-serif* fonts are made oblique.)

Figure 6-4 compares the medium and bold weights, and the roman and italic or oblique slants in the Charter® and Helvetica font families.

Release 4 also includes one font that has an in-between weight called *demibold*. Weight names are somewhat arbitrary, since a demibold weight in one family may be almost as dark as a bold weight in another.

The font naming convention also defines two counter-clockwise slants called *reverse italic* (ri) and *reverse oblique* (ro), as well as a catch-all called *other* (ot).

Font Sizes

Font sizes are often given in a traditional printer's measure known as a *point*. A point is approximately one seventy-second of an inch. Most of the font families are provided in the six point sizes shown in Figure 6-5.

```
-adobe-helvetica-medium-o-normal--18-180-75-75-p-98-is
-adobe-helvetica-medium-r-normal--18-180-75-75-p-98-is
-adobe-helvetica-bold-o-normal--18-180-75-75-p-104-is
-adobe-helvetica-bold-r-normal--18-180-75-75-p-103-i
-bitstream-charter-medium-i-normal--19-180-75-75-p-103-iso8859-
-bitstream-charter-medium-r-normal--19-180-75-75-p-106-iso885
-bitstream-charter-bold-i-normal--19-180-75-75-p-117-i
-bitstream-charter-bold-r-normal--19-180-75-75-p-119-
```

Figure 6-4. The same fonts in different weights and slants

```
 8 point   -bitstream-charter-medium-r-normal--8-80-75-75-p-45-iso8859-1
10 point   -bitstream-charter-medium-r-normal--10-100-75-75-p-56-iso8859-1
12 point   -bitstream-charter-medium-r-normal--12-120-75-75-p-67-iso8859-1
14 point   -bitstream-charter-medium-r-normal--15-140-75-75-p-84-iso8859-1
18 point   -bitstream-charter-medium-r-normal--19-180-75-75-p-106-
24 point   -bitstream-charter-medium-r-normal--25-24
```

Figure 6-5. The same font in six different point sizes

However, the size story doesn't end there. Note that some servers (such as Sun's combined X11/NeWS™ server) support scalable outline fonts that are device-independent and, thus, true-to-size regardless of the output device. But the standard X fonts are simply bitmaps. Because of the different resolution of computer monitors, a font with a given nominal point size might actually appear larger or smaller on the screen.

Most monitors on the market today have a resolution between 75 dots per inch (dpi) and 100 dots per inch. Accordingly, there are both 75-dpi and 100-dpi versions of a few of the fonts in R3, and of most of them in R4. These separate versions of each font are stored in different directories. By setting the font search path so that the appropriate directory comes first, you can arrange to get the correct versions without having to specify them in the font name.*

But how do you tell which kind of monitor you have?

---

*We'll talk about how to set the font search path later in this chapter.

If you have the manufacturer's specs on your monitor, they might give you this figure. But they'll more likely give you the overall resolution in rows and columns. After measuring the physical screen, you can do some rough calculations to arrive at the equivalent in dots per inch. For example, the 16-inch monitor on the Sony NEWS workstation has an advertised resolution of 1280 x 1024 pixels. The actual viewing area is approximately 13 inches wide by 10 inches high. Dividing the resolution by the size, you come up with a vertical resolution of 102.4 dpi and a horizontal resolution of 98.5 dpi.

The Sun 19-inch monitor, by contrast, has an advertised resolution of 1152 x 900 pixels. The horizontal and vertical dimensions of the viewing area are approximately 13.75 x 10.75 inches. This yields a resolution of about 84 dpi.

What happens if you select the wrong resolution for your monitor? Given the difference in the pixel size, the same size font will appear larger or smaller than the nominal point size.

For example, consider the 75- and 100-dpi versions of the 24-point charter medium italic font:

```
-bitstream-charter-medium-i-normal--25-240-75-75-p-136-iso8859-1
-bitstream-charter-medium-i-normal--33-240-100-100-p-179-iso8859-1
```

If you look at the pixel size field, you will notice that the height of the 75-dpi version is 25 pixels, while the height of the 100-dpi version is 33 pixels. If you use the 75-dpi version on the Sun, you actually get something closer to 21.5 points (75/84*24); on a 100-dpi monitor, you will actually get something closer to 18 points (75/100*24). We noticed this right away when we first began using the Sony workstation. Because of its higher resolution, the font size we had been using on the Sun appeared much smaller.

If you are working on a lower-resolution monitor, you can take advantage of this artifact to display type as large as 32 points (the size that a 24-point 100-dpi font will appear on a 75-dpi monitor.) Figure 6-6 shows the 75- and 100-dpi versions of the same 24-point font, as displayed on a Sun workstation with a 19-inch monochrome monitor. As shown, neither is actually 24 points. The 75-dpi version is actually 21.5 points, as discussed above; the 100-dpi version is about 28.5 points.*

Note that the logical font-naming convention allows for different horizontal and vertical resolution values. This would allow server manufacturers to support fonts that were "tuned" for their precise screen resolution. However, the fonts shipped with the generic X11 distribution all use the same horizontal and vertical resolution.

As suggested above, this resolution may not exactly match the actual resolution of any particular screen, resulting in characters that are not true to their nominal point size. In the case of the Sony monitors, the actual resolution is quite close to the design of the 100-dpi fonts. However, on the Sun monitor, neither the 75- nor 100-dpi fonts will be right. (Of course, if you are using the X11/NeWS server rather than the MIT sample server, you won't be using bitmapped fonts at all but scalable outline fonts, so this isn't a problem.)

---

*Note that the differences are exaggerated further in printing the screen dump of this display. *xpr* lets you select a scale factor such that each pixel on the screen appears as *scale* pixels in the printout. Since the laser printer has a 300-dpi resolution, a scale factor of 4 would produce a true scale screen dump if the resolution on the Sun monitor were truly 75 dpi by 75 dpi. Since it is actually 84 by 84, the printed image is enlarged by about 10 percent.

```
-adobe-new century schoolbook-medium-r-1
-adobe-new century schoolbook-n
```

Figure 6-6. The 100-dpi version of a 24-point font appears larger on a 75-dpi monitor

Other Information in the Font Name

What we've already shown summarizes the most important information in the font name. The remaining fields are explained below:

Foundry Font manufacturers are still referred to as foundries, from the days when type was cast from lead. The X font naming convention specifies the foundry as the company that digitized or last modified the font, rather than its original creator.

For the fonts contained in the standard X distribution, the foundry is not terribly significant since there are no cases where the same font family is available from different foundries. However, there are numerous commercial font families available from more than one foundry. In general, the appearance of the fonts should be quite similar since the font family defines the design of the typeface. However, there may be some small differences in the quality of some of the characters, and there may be more significant differences in the font metrics (the vertical or horizontal measurements of the characters). This might be significant for a publishing application that was using the bitmapped font for a *wysiwyg** screen display that needed to match the fonts in a particular laser printer or typesetter.

Set width A value describing a font's proportionate width, according to the foundry. Typical set widths include: normal, condensed, semicondensed, narrow, double width. All of the Release 3 fonts and most of the Release 4 fonts have the set width *normal*. A few of the Release 4 fonts have the set width *semicondensed*.

Spacing All standard Release 3 fonts are either m (monospace, i.e., fixed-width) or p (proportional, i.e., variable-width). In Release 4, fonts may also have the spacing characteristic c (character cell, a fixed-width font based on the traditional typewriter model, in which each character can be thought to take up the space of a "box" of the same height and width). As mentioned earlier, the original R2 fonts were this type.

---

*This is an acronym for "what you see is what you get" and describes a type of text editor or word processor that displays the page exactly as it would appear in print. MacWrite® is a *wysiwyg* program.

Average width   Mean width of all characters in the font, measured in tenths of a pixel. You'll notice, if you look back at Figure 6-2, that two fonts with the same point size (such as New Century Schoolbook and Times) can have a very different average character width. This field can sometimes be useful if you are looking for a font that is especially wide or especially narrow.

The Schumacher Clean family of fonts offers several fonts in the same point size but with different average widths.*

Character set   In the initial illustration of the font naming convention, Figure 6-1, we identified the character set as a single field. If you look more closely, you'll realize it is actually two fields, the first of which identifies the organization or standard registering the character set, the second of which identifies the actual character set.

Most fonts in the standard X distribution contain the string "iso8859-1" in their names, which represents the ISO Latin-1 character set. The ISO Latin-1 character set is a superset of the standard ASCII character set, which includes various special characters used in European languages other than English. See Appendix H of Volume Two, *Xlib Reference Manual*, for a complete listing of the characters in the ISO Latin-1 character set.

Note, however, that the symbol font contains the strings "adobe-fontspecific" in this position. This means that Adobe Systems defined the character set in this font, and that it is font-specific. You can see from this example that the use of these fields is somewhat arbitrary.

Style   Not represented in the example or in most R3 or R4 font names. However, according to the logical font convention, the style of a font may be specified in the field between set width and pixels. Some of the possible styles are *i* (informal), *r* (roman), *serif* and *sans* (serif). Note that the *r* for roman may also be used in the slant field.

For a complete technical description of font naming conventions, see the X Consortium Standard, *X Logical Font Description Conventions*. This document is available as part of the standard MIT X distribution, and is reprinted as Appendix M in the second edition of Volume 0, *X Protocol Reference Manual*.

---

*These fonts all (incorrectly to our minds) have a set width of "normal." They should be distinguished by set widths such as condensed, semi-condensed, etc. Since they do not, they can be distinguished by the difference in their average width.

Font Name Wildcarding

Prior to Release 3, the use of wildcards within font names was restricted to specifying fonts to list with *xlsfonts*. If you are running Release 3 or Release 4, wildcarded font names can also be used to specify the display font for a client, either on the command line or in a resource specification.

An asterisk (*) can be used to represent any part of the font name string; a question mark (?) can be used to represent any single character. You can usually get the font you want by specifying only the font family, the weight, the slant, and the point size, and wildcarding the rest. For example, to get Courier bold at 14 points, you could use the command line option:

```
-fn '*courier-bold-r*140*'
```

That's starting to seem a little more intuitive!

However, there are a number of "gotchas."

- First, since the UNIX shell also has a special meaning for the * and ? wildcard characters, wildcarded font names must be quoted. This can be done by enclosing the entire font name in quotes (as in the previous example), or by "quoting" each wildcard character by typing a backslash before it. (If you don't do this, the shell will try to expand the * to match any filenames in the current directory, and will give the message "No match.") Wildcards need not be quoted in resource files.

- Second, if the wildcarded font name matches more than one font, the server will use the first one that matches. And unfortunately, because the names are sorted in simple alphabetical order, the bold weight comes before medium, and italic and oblique slants before roman. As a result, the specification:

```
-fn '*courier*'
```

will give you Courier bold oblique, rather than the Courier medium roman you might intuitively expect.

If you aren't sure whether your wildcarded name is specific enough, try using it as an argument to *xlsfonts*. If you get more than one font name as output, you may not get what you want. Try again with a more specific name string.

The exception to this rule has to do with the *75dpi* and *100dpi* directories. If a wildcard matches otherwise identical fonts in these two directories, the server will actually use the one in the directory that comes first in the font path. This means that you should put the appropriate directory first in the font path. (We'll tell you how to do this in the next section.) Thereafter, you can generally wildcard the resolution fields (unless you specifically want a font from the directory later in the path).*

- Third, the * wildcard expansion is resolved by a simple string comparison. So, for example, if you type:

```
-fn '*courier-bold*r*140*'
```

instead of:

```
-fn '*courier-bold-r*140*'
```

(the difference being the asterisk instead of the hyphen before the "r" in the slant field), the "r" would also match the "r" in the string "normal" in the set width field. The result is that you would select all slants. Since o (oblique) comes before r (roman), and you always get the first font that matches, you'd end up with Courier oblique.

The trick is to be sure to include at least one of the hyphens to set the -r- off as a separate field rather than as part of another string.

Even though a wildcarded name such as:

```
*cour*b*r-*140*
```

should get you 14-point Courier bold roman, we think it is good practice to spell out the font family and weight and use hyphens between adjacent fields. As usual there are exceptions: the Lucida family really has three subfamilies; you can get all three by specifying the family as "Lucida*" rather than "Lucida-"; and you might certainly want to abbreviate "New Century Schoolbook" to "New Century*" or "*Schoolbook."

- Font names are case-insensitive. "Courier" is the same as "courier."

Table 6-2 summarizes the values you can use to specify a unique font name (assuming only the standard fonts are loaded). Choose one element from each column. Don't forget to include the leading and trailing asterisks and the hyphen before the slant.

---

*Unlike *xfontsel*, which displays fonts in the order of wildcard matches, *xlsfonts* will always list fonts in straight-sort order, with the sort done character by character across the line. Since size in pixels comes before point size in the name, and the size in pixels of the 100-dpi fonts is larger than that of the equivalent 75-dpi font, the 75-dpi font will always be listed first for a given point size. But when listing more than one point size, the fonts will be jumbled. For example, the size in pixels of the 8-point Charter font at 100-dpi is 11, so it will come after the 10-point Charter font at 75 dpi, with a size in pixels of 10. The 8-point Charter font at 75 dpi gets sorted to the very end of the list, since to a character-by-character sort, its size in pixels (8) looks larger to the size in pixels of even the largest 100-dpi font (the 24 point, with a height of 33 pixels).

X Window System User's Guide, Motif Edition

Table 6-2. Essential Elements of a Font Name

*	Family	–	Weight	–	Slant	*	Point Size	*
	Charter		Medium		r (roman)		80 (8 pt.)	
	Courier		Bold		i (italic)		100 (10 pt.)	
	Helvetica		Demibold		o (oblique)		120 (12 pt.)	
	New century schoolbook				ri (reverse italic)		140 (14 pt.)	
	Symbol				ro (reverse oblique)		180 (18 pt.)	
	Times				ot (other)		240 (24 pt.)	
	Fixed (R4)							
	Clean (R4)							
	OPEN LOOK (R4)							
	Lucida (R4)							
	Terminal (R4)							

The Font Search Path

In both Release 3 and Release 4, fonts are stored in three directories, as shown in Table 6-3.

Table 6-3. Standard Font Directories, Release 3 and Release 4

Directory	Contents
/usr/lib/X11/fonts/misc	Release 3: Six fixed-width fonts (also available in Release 2), plus the cursor font.
	Release 4: Sixty fixed-width fonts, including the six available in Release 3, the cursor font, several Clean family fonts provided by Schumacher, a Kanji font, Kana fonts, and OPEN LOOK cursor and glyph fonts.
/usr/lib/X11/fonts/75dpi	Fixed- and variable-width fonts, 75 dpi.
/usr/lib/X11/fonts/100dpi	Release 3: The Adobe Charter font family, 100 dpi.
	Release 4: Fixed- and variable-width fonts, 100 dpi (all font families).

These three directories (in this order) constitute X's default font path.

Other directories can be added to the font search path, or its order can be rearranged, using *xset* with the `fp` option. To completely replace the font path, simply specify a comma-separated list of directories. For example, to put the *100dpi* directory before the *75dpi* directory, you might enter:

```
% xset fp= /usr/lib/X11/fonts/misc,/usr/lib/X11/fonts/100dpi,\
           /usr/lib/X11/fonts/75dpi
```

(Note that a space must follow the equal sign (=) and that the example above is broken onto two lines escaped with a backslash (\) only so that it can be printed within the page margins.) To restore the default font path, type:

```
% xset fp default
```

Use the `fp+` option to add a directory or list of directories to the end of the font path, or `+fp` to add them at the start. Use `-fp` and `fp-` to delete directories from the beginning or end of the font path.

For a complete list of the fonts in each directory and samples of each font, refer to Appendix B, *Release 4 Standard Fonts*.

The fonts.dir Files

In addition to font files, each font directory contains a file called *fonts.dir*. The *fonts.dir* files serve, in effect, as databases for the X server. When the X server searches the directories in the default font path, it uses the *fonts.dir* files to locate the font(s) it needs.

Each *fonts.dir* file contains a list of all the font files in the directory with their associated font names in two-column form. (The first column lists the font file name and the second column lists the actual font name associated with the file.) The first line in *fonts.dir* lists the number of entries in the file (i.e., the number of fonts in the directory).

Example 6-1 shows a portion of the *fonts.dir* file from the Release 4 */usr/lib/X11/fonts/100dpi* directory. As the first line indicates, the directory contains 200 fonts. The first group of fonts listed below (up to the second ellipse) are available as of Release 4. They are all Courier family fonts. (These fonts are 100-dpi equivalents of fonts that were only available in 75 dpi in Release 3.) The second group of fonts shown in the list below (a few sizes from the Charter family) are also available in the Release 3 *100dpi* directory.

Example 6-1. Subsection of the Release 4 fonts.dir file in /usr/lib/X11/fonts/100dpi

```
200
  .
  .
  .
courBO08.snf  -adobe-courier-bold-o-normal--11-80-100-100-m-60-iso8859-1
courBO10.snf  -adobe-courier-bold-o-normal--14-100-100-100-m-90-iso8859-1
courBO12.snf  -adobe-courier-bold-o-normal--17-120-100-100-m-100-iso8859-1
courBO14.snf  -adobe-courier-bold-o-normal--20-140-100-100-m-110-iso8859-1
courBO18.snf  -adobe-courier-bold-o-normal--25-180-100-100-m-150-iso8859-1
courBO24.snf  -adobe-courier-bold-o-normal--34-240-100-100-m-200-iso8859-1
courB08.snf  -adobe-courier-bold-r-normal--11-80-100-100-m-60-iso8859-1
courB10.snf  -adobe-courier-bold-r-normal--14-100-100-100-m-90-iso8859-1
courB12.snf  -adobe-courier-bold-r-normal--17-120-100-100-m-100-iso8859-1
courB14.snf  -adobe-courier-bold-r-normal--20-140-100-100-m-110-iso8859-1
```

```
courB18.snf  -adobe-courier-bold-r-normal--25-180-100-100-m-150-iso8859-1
courB24.snf  -adobe-courier-bold-r-normal--34-240-100-100-m-200-iso8859-1
courO08.snf  -adobe-courier-medium-o-normal--11-80-100-100-m-60-iso8859-1
courO10.snf  -adobe-courier-medium-o-normal--14-100-100-100-m-90-iso8859-1
courO12.snf  -adobe-courier-medium-o-normal--17-120-100-100-m-100-iso8859-1
courO14.snf  -adobe-courier-medium-o-normal--20-140-100-100-m-110-iso8859-1
courO18.snf  -adobe-courier-medium-o-normal--25-180-100-100-m-150-iso8859-1
courO24.snf  -adobe-courier-medium-o-normal--34-240-100-100-m-200-iso8859-1
courR08.snf  -adobe-courier-medium-r-normal--11-80-100-100-m-60-iso8859-1
courR10.snf  -adobe-courier-medium-r-normal--14-100-100-100-m-90-iso8859-1
courR12.snf  -adobe-courier-medium-r-normal--17-120-100-100-m-100-iso8859-1
courR14.snf  -adobe-courier-medium-r-normal--20-140-100-100-m-110-iso8859-1
courR18.snf  -adobe-courier-medium-r-normal--25-180-100-100-m-150-iso8859-1
courR24.snf  -adobe-courier-medium-r-normal--34-240-100-100-m-200-iso8859-1
        .
        .
        .

charBI08.snf -bitstream-charter-bold-i-normal--11-80-100-100-p-68-iso8859-1
charBI10.snf -bitstream-charter-bold-i-normal--14-100-100-100-p-86-iso8859-1
charBI12.snf -bitstream-charter-bold-i-normal--17-120-100-100-p-105-iso8859-1
charBI14.snf -bitstream-charter-bold-i-normal--19-140-100-100-p-117-iso8859-1
charBI18.snf -bitstream-charter-bold-i-normal--25-180-100-100-p-154-iso8859-1
charBI24.snf -bitstream-charter-bold-i-normal--33-240-100-100-p-203-iso8859-1
        .
        .
        .
```

The *fonts.dir* files are created by the *mkfontdir* client when X is installed. *mkfontdir* reads the font files in directories in the font path, extracts the font names, and creates a *fonts.dir* file in each directory. If *fonts.dir* files are present on your system, you probably won't have to deal with them or with *mkfontdir* at all. If the files are not present, or if you have to load new fonts or remove existing ones, you will have to create files with *mkfontdir*. Refer to Appendix A, *System Management*, for details.

Font Name Aliasing

Another way to abbreviate font names is by aliasing (that is, by associating fonts with alternative names of your own choosing). You can edit or create a file called *fonts.alias*, in any directory (or multiple directories) in the font search path, to set aliases for existing fonts. The X server uses both *fonts.dir* files and *fonts.alias* files to locate fonts in the font path.

If you are running Release 3, there should already be an alias file in the *misc* directory. Release 4 provides a default *fonts.alias* file for each of the three font directories. Take the time to look at the contents of each of these files, since many of the existing aliases may be easier to type than even wildcarded font names. You can also add aliases to the file, change existing aliases, or even replace the entire file. However, this should be done with caution. To play it safe, it's probably a good idea merely to *add* to existing *fonts.alias* files. If you're working in a multiuser environment, the system administrator should definitely be consulted before aliases are added or changed. Note that when you create or edit a *fonts.alias* file, the server does not *automatically* recognize the aliases in question. You must make the server aware of newly created or edited alias files by resetting the font path with *xset*.

The *fonts.alias* file has a two-column format similar to the *fonts.dir* file: the first column contains aliases, the second contains the actual font names. If you want to specify an alias that contains spaces, enclose the alias in double quotes. If you want to include double quotes (") or other special characters as part of an alias, precede each special symbol with a backslash (\).

When you use an alias to specify a font in a command line, the server searches for the font associated with that alias in every directory in the font path. Therefore, a *fonts.alias* file in one directory can set aliases for fonts in other directories as well. You might choose to create a single aliases file in one directory of the font path to set aliases for the most commonly used fonts in all the directories. Example 6-2 shows three sample entries that could be added to an existing *fonts.alias* file (or constitute a new one).

Example 6-2. Sample fonts.alias file entries

```
xterm12    -adobe-courier-medium-r-normal--12-120-75-75-m-70-iso8859-1
xterm14    -adobe-courier-medium-r-normal--14-140-75-75-m-90-iso8859-1
xterm18    -adobe-courier-medium-r-normal--18-180-75-75-m-110-iso8859-1
```

As the names of the aliases suggest, these sample entries provide aliases for three fonts (of different point sizes) that are easily readable in *xterm* windows. (We also recommend the fixed-width font stored in the file *9x15.snf*,* in the *misc* directory.) You can also use wildcards within the font names in the right column of an alias file. For instance, the alias file entries above might also be written as follows:

```
    xterm12    *courier-medium-r-*-120*
    xterm14    *courier-medium-r-*-140*
    xterm18    *courier-medium-r-*-180*
```

In Release 2 of X, a font name is equivalent to the name of the file in which it is stored without the *.snf* extension. In the previous edition of this book (which dealt primarily with Release 3 of X), we recommended a method for emulating this convention. This involved creating a *fonts.alias* file containing this line in every directory in the font path:

```
    FILE_NAMES_ALIASES
```

You could then use a filename (without the *.snf* extension) to specify a font. Due to changes implemented in the Release 4 server, **X Window System developers are now discouraging this practice.**

---

*In Release 3, the actual name of this font is *9x15*. The Release 4 name is:

```
-misc-fixed-medium-r-normal--15-140-75-75-c-90-iso8859-1
```

but is aliased to *9x15* in the default *fonts.alias* file in the *misc* directory.

If you would still like to emulate Release 2 conventions in Releases 3 or 4, you must explicitly assign every font name an alias corresponding to the name of the file in which it is stored without the *.snf* extension. This could actually be done rather easily by editing a copy of each *fonts.dir* file and appending the copy to the *fonts.alias* file in the same directory. (If you are running Release 3, remember that neither the *75dpi* nor the *100dpi* directory has a default *fonts.alias* file. You may need to create one, rather than append to an existing one. These aliases could also be appended to the *fonts.alias* file in the *misc* directory, since the server searches all directories in the font path.)

Once the server is made aware of aliases, you can specify an alias on the command line. For example, you can use a font name alias as an argument to *xfd*. If you've used an alias file or files to emulate the Release 2 font naming conventions, you can display the font stored in the file *courR12.snf* using the command:

```
% xfd -fn courR12
```

A special note about the *misc* directory: when X was configured for your system, a *fonts.alias* file should have been created in this directory. The first two entries in this file are shown below:

```
fixed     -misc-fixed-medium-r-semicondensed--13-120-75-75-c-60-iso8859-1
variable -*-helvetica-bold-r-normal-*-*-120-*-*-*-*-*-*
```

The default file contains an additional 56 entries but the entries pictured above are particularly important. The aliases called "fixed" and "variable" are invoked as the default fonts for many clients. The "fixed" font can be thought of as a system-wide default. The "variable" font, described in the right column as a 12-point bold Helvetica font, is used as the default font by *bitmap*, as well as by other clients. If this file is removed or replaced, when you run *bitmap*, you'll get an error message that the server cannot open the variable font, and text in the *bitmap* window will display in the smaller, somewhat less readable "fixed" font.

If you do choose to edit the *fonts.alias* file in the *misc* directory, it is important to preserve at least these two aliases. (As we've said, it's probably a better idea to keep all the default entries and merely append any new ones.)

If you're running Release 3, the *fonts.alias* file in the *misc* directory will be somewhat different. The Release 3 version of the *fonts.alias* file in the *misc* directory comprises only these two lines:

```
fixed        6x13
variable     *-helvetica-bold-r-normal-*-*-140-*
```

Regardless of what edits you make to the file, the line specifying the variable alias must not be changed.

The variable font is slightly larger in Release 3 (14-point) than in Release 4 (12-point). If you examine the Release 3 alias file a little more closely, you may notice that the first line contains an *incorrect* alias specification. Remember, in Release 3, *fixed* is actually the name of the default system font—it is not an alias. The first column should contain aliases; the second column should contain proper font names. However, 6x13 is not a proper font name. It is actually the name of the file that contains the font named *fixed*. You can specify *fixed* as a font on the command line and it will work—but as a font name, not an alias.

Making the Server Aware of Aliases

After you create (or update) an alias file, the server does not automatically recognize the aliases in question. You must make the server aware of newly created or edited alias files by "rehashing" the font path with *xset*. Enter:

```
% xset fp rehash
```

on the command line. The *xset* option `fp` (font path) with the `rehash` argument causes the server to reread the *fonts.dir* and *fonts.alias* files in the current font path. You need to do this every time you edit an alias file. (You also need to use *xset* if you add or remove fonts. See Appendix A, *System Management*, for details.)

Utilities for Displaying Information about Fonts

We've already mentioned *xlsfonts*, which simply displays the names and aliases of available fonts. In addition, *xfd* can be used to display the full character set of a particular font, and *xfontsel* can be used to interactively preview and select a font for use in another window.

The Font Displayer: xfd

If you're unfamiliar with the general appearance of a particular font, we've included pictures of some representative fonts in Appendix B, *Release 4 Standard Fonts*.

You can also display the characters in a font using the *xfd* (font displayer) client. Note that since Release 3, *xfd* has taken an option, `-fn`, before the font name. For example, to display the default system font, a 6x13 pixel fixed-width font known as *fixed*,* enter:

```
% xfd -fn fixed &
```

The *xfd* window will display the specified font as shown in Figure 6-7.

This figure depicts the Release 4 version of *xfd*, which has been greatly enhanced since Release 3. The font name is now displayed across the top of the window. (This is the actual font name, which we specified on the command line by the alias *fixed*.) Three command buttons have also been added to the application in Release 4. They appear in the upper-left corner of the window below the font name. If the font being displayed doesn't fit within a single *xfd* screen, Prev Page and Next Page allow you to scroll through multiple screens. (The horizontal and vertical window dimensions can vary slightly to accommodate different fonts but certain fonts will still require multiple screens.) The Quit button causes the application to exit, though this can also be done by typing q or Q while input is focused on the *xfd* window.

---

*In Release 3, *fixed* is a legitimate font name. In Release 4, it is an alias for a longer font name that follows the conventions outlined previously.

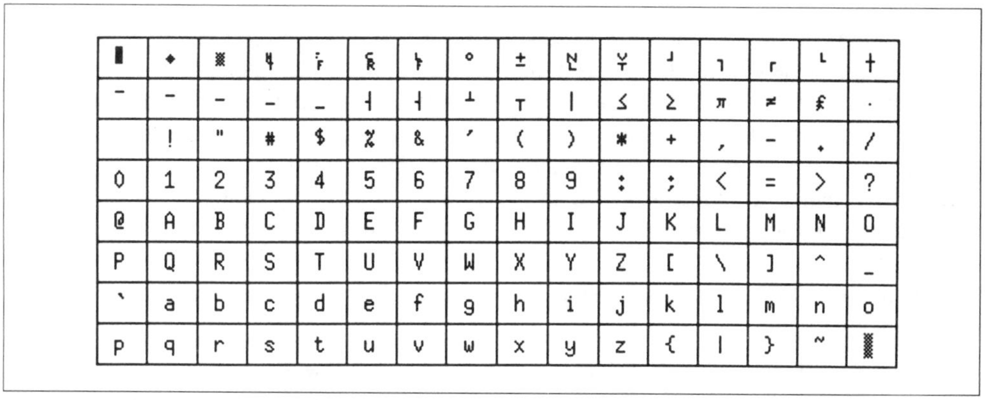

▮	◆	▒	¶	⫶	℞	⊦	°	±	א	⅄	⌐	⌐	⌐	⌐	†
-	-	-	-	_	⊣	⊣	⊥	⊤	|	≤	≥	π	≠	£	·
	!	"	#	$	%	&	′	(	)	*	+	,	-	.	/
0	1	2	3	4	5	6	7	8	9	:	;	<	=	>	?
@	A	B	C	D	E	F	G	H	I	J	K	L	M	N	O
P	Q	R	S	T	U	V	W	X	Y	Z	[	\	]	^	_
`	a	b	c	d	e	f	g	h	i	j	k	l	m	n	o
p	q	r	s	t	u	v	w	x	y	z	{	|	}	~	▒

Figure 6-7. Fixed font, 6x13 pixels

In addition to displaying a font, *xfd* also allows you to display certain information about the individual characters. But before we examine these capabilities, let's take a closer look at the way the characters in a font are identified and how the *xfd* window makes use of this information.

Within a font, each character is considered to be numbered. The *xfd* client displays a font's characters in a grid. By default, the first character of the font appears in the upper-left position; this is character number 0. The two text lines above the grid identify the upper-left character and the range of characters in the window by character numbers both in hexadecimal and in decimal notation (in parentheses following the hex character number).

You can specify a character other than character number 0 to be in the first position in the window using the `-start` option. For example, if you enter this command line:

```
% xfd -start 15 -fn fixed &
```

the *xfd* window begins with character number 15.

Notice the instruction `Select a character` below the command buttons. To display information about a particular character, click any pointer button within the character's grid square. Statistics about the character's width, left bearing, right bearing, ascent, and descent are displayed where the line `Select a character` previously appeared.

The *xfd* client is most useful when you have an idea what font you might want to display. If you don't have a particular font in mind or would like to survey the possibilities, the *xfontsel* client (available as of Release 4) allows you to preview a variety of fonts by specifying each component of the font name using a different menu.

Previewing and Selecting Fonts: xfontsel

The *xfontsel* client, available as of Release 4, provides a font previewer window in which you select the font to view using 14 menus corresponding to the 14 components of a font name. By specifying various font name components, you can take a look at a variety of fonts. This is particularly useful if you are trying to pick good display fonts and you don't have a clear idea what type of font would be best. Rather than running several instances of *xfd*, you can dynamically change the font displayed in the *xfontsel* window by changing the font name components. (Despite the flexibility of *xfontsel*, it's certainly not practical to preview *all* of the available fonts. If you have no idea what a particular font family looks like, see the discussion earlier in this chapter, or refer to Appendix B, *Release 4 Standard Fonts*, for complete listings.)*

Once you've displayed the desired font using the menus, you can make the name of that font the PRIMARY text selection by clicking on the window's select button. You can then paste the font name into another window using the pointer: onto a command line, into a resource file, etc. Making a font name the PRIMARY selection also enables you to choose that font from the *xterm* VT Fonts menu. (Selecting text and using *xterm* menus are described in Chapter 5, *The xterm Terminal Emulator*.

Previewing Fonts with the xfontsel Menus

To run *xfontsel*, enter this command in an *xterm* window:

```
% xfontsel &
```

If your system is using the standard Release 4 fonts, the *xfontsel* window initially displays a bold, constant-width, 7x13 pixel font from the *misc* font directory, as shown in Figure 6-8. This is the first font in the default font search path.

The upper-left corner of the *xfontsel* window features two command buttons: quit and select. As we've explained, clicking on select with the first pointer button makes the font displayed in the window the PRIMARY text selection; obviously, quit causes the application to exit.

Below the command buttons is, in effect, a generic font name or font name template. It is divided into 14 fields corresponding to the 14 parts of a standard font name. Each field is an abbreviation for one part of a font name. Take a look again at the sample font name in Figure 6-1 to refresh your memory as to the components. Each of the fields in the *xfontsel* window is actually the handle to a menu which lets you specify this part of the font name.

---

*To our minds, the major drawback of *xfontsel* is that it shows you only the first font that matches a given wildcarded font name. A far better interface would list all of the matching fonts so that you could compare and choose the one that best suited your needs. There is no way in the standard X distribution to display the appearance of a group of fonts. To produce the figures in this book, we had to write such a program, which we called *xshowfonts*. The program has since been posted to *comp.sources.x*, and a listing appears in Appendix B, *Release 4 Standard Fonts*.

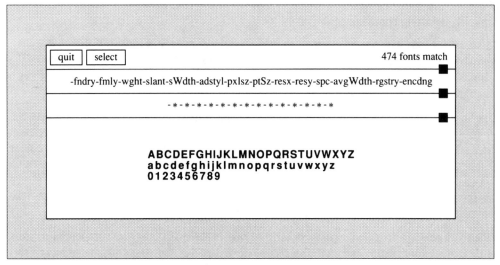

Figure 6-8. xfontsel window displaying 7x13 bold font

To get a clearer idea of how this works, move the pointer onto the generic font name—specifically onto the first field, fndry. (This is an abbreviation for the first part of a font name, the foundry.) When you place the pointer on fndry, the field title should be highlighted by a box. You can then display a menu of foundry names by pressing and holding down the first pointer button, as in Figure 6-9.

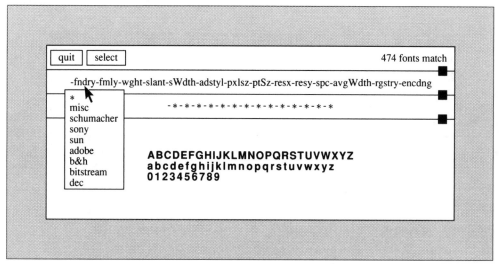

Figure 6-9. xfontsel window with foundry menu displayed

Notice that the first choice is the asterisk (*) wildcard character. This is the first choice on all of the menus, allowing you to include wildcards in the font name you specify rather than explicitly selecting something from all 14 menus.

To specify a font name component (i.e., make a selection from the menu), first display the menu by pressing and holding down the first pointer button. Then move the pointer down the menu. As the pointer rests on each menu item, it is highlighted by reverse video. To select a highlighted menu item, release the first pointer button.

The line below the font name menus represents the actual font name. When you first run *xfontsel*, all of these fields contain wildcard characters because no menu selections have been made. The number of fonts matched by the font name is displayed in the upper-right corner of the window. The number of fonts initially matched depends on the number of fonts with this naming convention available on your system. In this example, 474 fonts match. (Since this line of wildcards can match *any* 14-part font name, the server chooses the first font in the font path that reflects this naming convention.)

When you select a font name component from one of the 14 menus, the component appears in the actual font name, and the *xfontsel* window displays the first font that matches this name. For example, say we select adobe from the fndry menu, the *xfontsel* window would look like Figure 6-10.

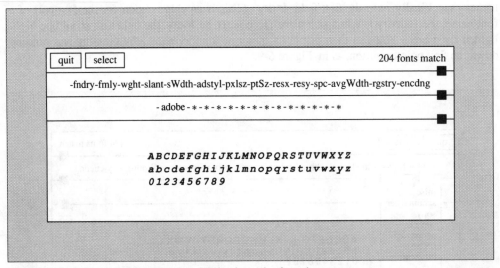

Figure 6-10. xfontsel after choosing Adobe from the foundry menu

The font name is now:

```
-adobe-*-*-*-*-*-*-*-*-*-*-*-*-*
```

and the window displays the first font in the font path that matches this wildcarded name. In this case, the first font to match is a 12-point bold Oblique Courier font, which is stored in the file *courBO10.snf* and has the actual font name:

```
-adobe-courier-bold-o-normal-*-10-100-75-75-m-60-iso8859-1
```

Once you make a selection from one menu, the number of possible fonts matched by the name changes. (Notice the line 204 fonts match in the upper-right corner of the window.) Choosing one font name component also eliminates certain choices on other menus. For example, after you select Adobe as the foundry, the possible choices for font family (the second menu, fmly) are narrowed from 14 to 5 (not counting the asterisk). Again display the fmly menu using the first pointer button. The available choices for font family appear in a regular typeface; the items that are unavailable (i.e., cannot be selected) appear in a lighter typeface. Families such as Clean, Lucida, and Charter are in a lighter typeface because none of the standard X fonts provided by Adobe is from these families. Adobe fonts in the standard X distribution are limited to the five families Courier, Helvetica, New Century Schoolbook, Symbol, and Times; these are the items available on the fmly menu.

In order to display a particular font, you'll probably have to make selections from several of the menus. As described earlier in the section "Font Name Wildcarding," we suggest you explicitly select at least these parts of the font name:

- Font family

- Weight

- Slant

- Point size

Thus, you would make selections from the fmly, wght, slant, and ptSz menus.

You can also use the *-pattern* option with a wildcarded font name to start out with a more limited range of options. For example, if you typed:

```
% xfontsel -pattern '*courier-bold-o-*'
```

you'd start out with the pattern you specified in the filename template part of the *xfontsel* display. You could then simply select from the ptSz menu to compare the various point sizes of Courier bold oblique until you found the one you wanted.

Note that if the pattern you specify to *xfontsel* matches more than one font, the one that is displayed (the first match found) is the one that the server will use. This is in contrast to *xlsfonts*, which sorts the font names. You can always rely on *xfontsel* to show you the actual font that will be chosen, given any wildcard specification.

Selecting a Font Name

Once you make selections from the menus to compose the name of the font you want, the corresponding font is displayed in the *xfontsel* window. Then you can select that font name by clicking on the select command button with the first pointer button. The font name becomes the PRIMARY text selection and thus can be pasted in another window using the second pointer button, as described in Chapter 5, *The xterm Terminal Emulator*.

You might paste the font name on a client command line in an *xterm* window in order to specify it as the client's display font. (See Chapter 9, *Command Line Options*.) You might paste it into a resource file such as *Xresources* to specify it as the default font for a client or some feature of a client (such as a menu). (See Chapter 10, *Setting Resources*, for more information.)

Less obviously, once a font name is made the PRIMARY text selection, it can be toggled as the *xterm* display font using the Selection item of the *xterm* VT Fonts menu. The Selection menu item can only be chosen from the VT Fonts menu when there is a PRIMARY text selection. (Otherwise, the menu item appears in a lighter typeface, indicating that it is not available.) If the PRIMARY text selection is a valid font name (as it is when you've pressed the select button in the *xfontsel* window), the *xterm* window displays in that font. (In cases where the PRIMARY selection is not a valid font name, the *xterm* display font does not change.)

By default, *xfontsel* displays the lowercase and uppercase letters a through z and the digits 0 through 9. You can specify alternative sample text using the -sample option. For more information about this and other options, see the *xfontsel* reference page in Part Three of this guide.

Changing Fonts in xterm Windows

xterm includes a VT Fonts menu that allows you to change fonts on the fly. We discussed most of the menu entries in Chapter 5. However, two of the many items require a greater understanding of font naming than we'd covered by that point. So we've saved them until now.

The Great Escape

Though it is by no means obvious, *xterm* allows you to change the display font by sending an escape sequence, along with the new font name, to the terminal window. Once you change the font in this way, the Escape Sequence item on the *xterm* VT Fonts menu becomes available and choosing it toggles the font you first specified with the escape sequence. (In effect, whatever font you specify using the escape sequence is stored in memory as the menu's Escape Sequence font selection.)

You send an escape sequence to the terminal window by using the UNIX *echo*(1) command. The escape sequence to change the *xterm* display font comprises these keystrokes:

```
Esc ] 50 ; fontname Control-G
```

To clarify, these keystrokes are: the Escape key, the right bracket (]), the number 50, a semi-colon (;), a *fontname*, and the Control-G key combination. We've shown the keystrokes with spaces between them for readability, but when you type the sequence on the command line, there should be no spaces. Note also that to supply this sequence as an argument to *echo*, you must enclose it in quotes:

```
% echo "Esc]50;fontnameControl-G"
```

These are the literal keys you type. However, be aware that when you type these keys as specified, the command line will not look exactly like this. Certain keys, such as Escape, and key combinations, such as Control-G, are represented by other symbols on the command line. When you type the previous key sequence, the command line will actually look like this:

```
% echo "^[]50;fontname^G"
```

Pressing the Escape key generates the ˆ[symbol; typing the Control-G key combination generates ˆG. You can use a full fontname, an alias, or a wildcarded font specification as the font name. You should be aware that if the wildcarded specification matches more than one font, you will get the first font in the search path that matches. For example:

```
% echo "ˆ[]50;*courier*ˆG"
```

will get you a 10-point courier bold oblique. The advantage of being able to change the display font with an escape sequence is that it allows you to add another font to your choices on the fly.*

Changing the fonts associated with the Tiny, Small, Medium, and Large menu items is a more laborious process. It involves specifying other fonts in a resource file, making those resources available to the server, and then running another *xterm* process. (See Chapter 10, *Setting Resources*, for more information.) However, you can change the font specified by the Escape Sequence menu item as often as you want during the current *xterm* process, simply by typing the escape sequence described previously.

Now that we've looked at the mechanics of the escape sequence, let's consider its practical use. Say you want to run a program in an *xterm* window and you want to be able to read the output easily, but you would like the window to be moderately small. You discover that toggling the Medium font, the 8x13 font by default, makes the window a good size, but the typeface is too light to be read easily. (We presume you are using the default menu fonts and have not customized them using a resource file.) You could dynamically change the display font to a bold font of the same size by entering the following command line:

```
% echo "Esc]50;8x13boldControl-G"
```

The *xterm* font becomes the desired 8x13bold, a good choice; in addition, the Escape Sequence item of the VT Fonts menu becomes available for selection. This menu item allows you to toggle the 8x13bold font at any time during the *xterm* process. Thus, you could switch back to any of the other fonts available on the menu (Small, Large, etc.) and then use Escape Sequence to again select 8x13bold.

This font will remain the Escape Sequence font for the duration of the *xterm* process, unless you again change the display font with an escape sequence. If you enter another font name using the escape sequence described above, the window will display in that new font and the Escape Sequence menu item will toggle it.

---

*Specifying a font with an escape sequence affects only the current *xterm* window and enables only that window's Escape Sequence menu selection.

The Selection Menu Item

The Selection menu item allows you to toggle a font whose name you've previously "selected." The font name could be selected with the pointer, for example, from *xlsfonts* output, using the "cut-and-paste" techniques described in Chapter 5, *The xterm Terminal Emulator*. It is far more likely, though, that you would use this menu item after selecting a font with *xfontsel*. This menu item was clearly designed with *xfontsel* in mind. (If no text is currently selected, this menu item appears in a lighter typeface, indicating that it is unavailable.)

The main limitation of this menu item is that it uses the *last text selected* as the font name, regardless of what that text is. If you select a font name, that name is only available through Selection until you use the pointer to select other text. Since cutting and pasting text is one of the most useful features of *xterm*, you will probably be making frequent selections. If the last selected text was not a valid font name, toggling Selection will not change the display font, and a beep will inform you that the toggle failed.

7

Graphics Utilities

*This chapter describes how to use the major graphics clients included with X,
notably the* bitmap *editor.*

In This Chapter:

Graphics Utilities

7
Graphics Utilities

The standard release of X includes four utilities to help you create bitmap images: *bitmap*, *bmtoa*, *atobm*, and *xmag*. The most powerful and useful of these clients is *bitmap*, a program that lets you create and edit bitmap files. This section includes detailed instructions for using the *bitmap* client.

The *bmtoa* and *atobm* clients are programs that convert bitmaps to arrays (of ASCII characters) and arrays to bitmaps. They are used to facilitate printing and file manipulation and can help you convert a font character to a bitmap, as we'll demonstrate.

In a sense, the *xmag* client is a desk accessory for graphics programs. This client is used to magnify a portion of the screen, to assist you in creating images with a graphics editor, such as *bitmap*, or in capturing screen images with the *xwd* window dump utility, described in Chapter 8, *Other Clients*. This chapter provides all the information you need to get started with *xmag*.

In addition to these standard clients, the user-contributed part of the X distribution includes a very useful library of graphic utilities: the Portable Bitmap Toolkit, developed by Jef Poskanzer. The PBM Toolkit is made up of dozens of programs that convert graphic images to and from portable formats. Some of the conversions you can perform are described later in this chapter.

Creating Icons and Other Bitmaps

The *bitmap* program allows you to create and edit small *bitmaps*. A bitmap is a grid of pixels, or picture elements, each of which is white, black, or, in the case of color displays, a color. You can use *bitmap* to create backgrounds, icons, and pointers.

At this point in X Window System development, *bitmap* is primarily a programming tool for application developers. However, several applications allow you to design your own icon or background pattern with *bitmap*, save it in a bitmap file, and specify that filename on the command line.* For example, *xsetroot* (described in Chapter 12, *Setup Clients*) allows you

---

*There are many bitmaps included in the X distribution. These can generally be found in the directory */usr/include/X11/bitmaps*. Samples are shown in Appendix C, *Standard Bitmaps*.

to specify a bitmap that will be used as the background pattern for the root window or as the root window pointer.

To invoke *bitmap*, type:

```
% bitmap filename &
```

The *bitmap* window is shown in Figure 7-1.

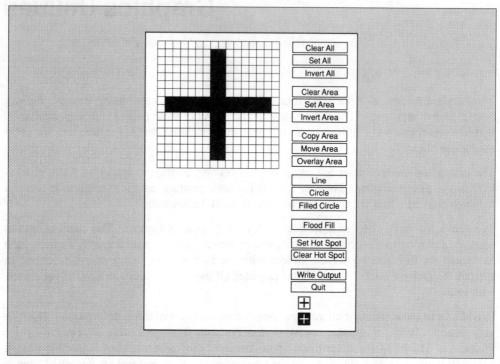

Figure 7-1. Bitmap window

The window that *bitmap* creates has three sections:

1. The largest section is the checkerboard grid, which is a magnified version of the bitmap you are editing. The default size grid for new bitmaps is 16x16. (For existing bitmaps, the size of the grid will be the size of the bitmap. For example, if you open a file containing a bitmap of size 100 pixels by 62 pixels, the grid will be 100 cells wide and 62 cells high.) If the cells in the grid aren't large enough for comfortable editing, resize the window. Each square on the grid will be enlarged proportionally.

2. On the right side of the window is a list of commands in command buttons that you can invoke with any pointer button.

3. Beneath the commands is an actual size picture of the bitmap you are editing; below this is an inverted version of the same bitmap. Each time the grid changes, the same change occurs in the actual size bitmap and its inverse.

If you want to create a new bitmap in a grid of different proportions than the default size 16x16 grid, you can specify *WIDTHxHEIGHT* on the command line after *filename*. For example, to create a grid double the default size, enter:

```
% bitmap filename 32x32 &
```

The *WIDTHxHEIGHT* argument is used only when creating a new bitmap. Existing bitmaps are always edited at their current size.

Keep in mind that there is an interaction between the size of the bitmap being edited and the size of the *bitmap* window. By default, each cell in the *bitmap* editing area is 13 pixels square. If the bitmap being edited is large, this may result in an application window larger than the screen. (Since *bitmap* does not provide a scrollbar, a large window may make it impossible to edit!) Specifying an explicit size for the overall application using the −geometry option (or resizing it with the window manager) will change the size of the editing window because *bitmap* will automatically adjust the size of each editing cell to fit.

However, this type of adjustment has limitations. The *bitmap* application defines a minimum size of 3 pixels for the cells in the bitmap editing area. This means that in the smallest *bitmap* window you can create, each pixel in the bitmap itself will be represented by a cell 3 pixels square. Even if this adjustment creates a window that fits on your screen, it is extremely difficult to edit individual pixels represented by cells 3 pixels square.

Figure 7-2 shows a 40x40 grid with a bitmap we created of Gumby©. We think it makes a fun root window pattern. (See the discussion of *xsetroot* in Chapter 12, *Setup Clients*, for instructions on specifying a bitmap as your root window pattern.)

Figure 7-2 shows our own rendition of Gumby, created using various *bitmap* editing commands. The standard cursor font also contains a Gumby character. (You can specify the Gumby cursor as the *xterm* window pointer, as described in Chapter 10, *Setting Resources*, or as the root window pointer using the *xsetroot* client, as described in Chapter 12, *Setup Clients*.) Later in this chapter, we'll show you how to convert the Gumby character of the cursor font to a bitmap file using the *atobm* client.

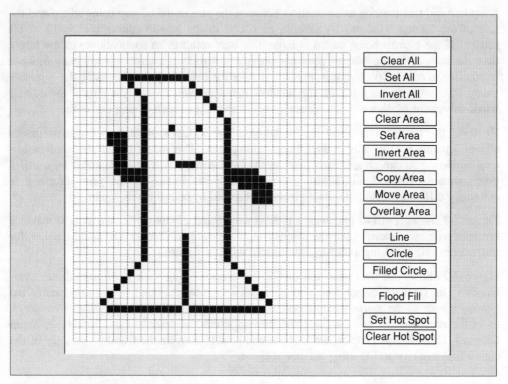

Figure 7-2. Gumby bitmap

Bitmap Editing Commands

You can create and edit a bitmap using a combination of pointer commands and command buttons on the right side of the window. The pointer commands work on one grid square at a time, while the command buttons can work on the entire grid or a specified area.

Pointer Commands

When the pointer is in the checkerboard grid, each pointer button has a different effect on the single square under the pointer. You can hold down a pointer button and drag the pointer to affect several squares in a row.

First button
Changes a grid square to the foreground color and sets the corresponding bitmap bit to 1. (On a monochrome display, background color means white; foreground color means black.)

Second button
Inverts a grid square, changing its color and inverting its bitmap bit.

Third button
Changes a grid square to the background color and sets the corresponding bitmap bit to 0.

Bitmap Command Boxes

To invoke any *bitmap* command, move the pointer to the appropriate command button and click any button. *bitmap* does not have an undo command; once you have made a change, you cannot retrieve the original.

Acting on the Entire Grid: Clear All, Set All, Invert All

To Clear All, Set All, or Invert All, click on the appropriate command button.

Clear All
Changes all the grid squares to the background color and sets all bitmap bits to 0.

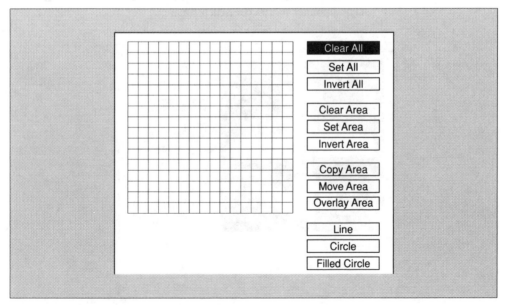

Figure 7-3. Clearing all

Set All   Changes all the grid squares to the foreground color and sets all bit-
                           map bits to 1.

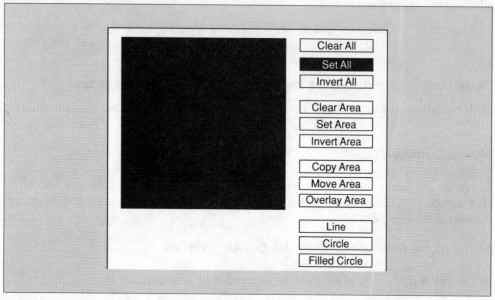

Figure 7-4. Setting all

Invert All   Inverts all the grid squares and bitmap bits, as if you had clicked the
                           second pointer button over each square.

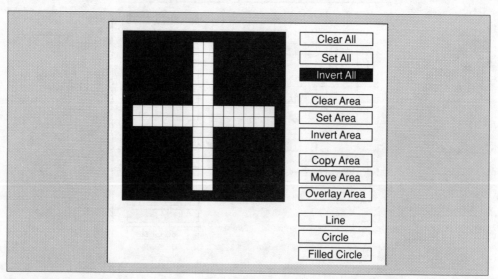

Figure 7-5. Inverting all

Acting on an Area: Clear Area, Set Area, Invert Area

Clear Area

Clears a rectangular area of the grid, i.e., changes it to the background color and sets the corresponding bitmap bits to 0.

Set Area

Changes a rectangular area of the grid to the foreground color and sets the corresponding bitmap bits to 1.

Invert Area

Changes a rectangular area of the grid from the background color to the foreground color or the foreground color to the background color.

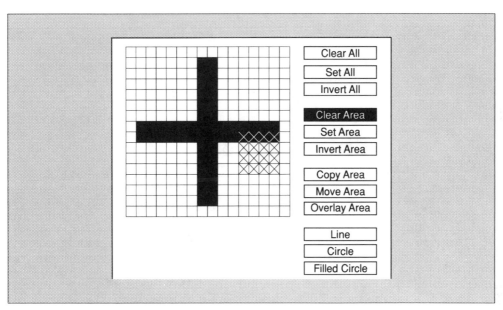

Figure 7-6. Selecting an area to clear, set, or invert

The procedure to act on an area is:

1. Click the pointer over the command (Clear Area, Set Area, or Invert Area). The pointer turns into an upper-left corner.

2. Move the pointer over the upper-left corner of the area you want to clear, set, or invert. Press and hold any button. The pointer changes to a lower-right corner.

3. Move the pointer to the lower-right corner of the area you want to act on. X's cover the rectangular area as you move the pointer. Release the button.

   If the pointer has changed to a lower-right corner and you wish to abort the command without inverting an area, either click another button, move the pointer outside the grid, or move the pointer above or to the left of the upper-left corner.

Copy Area, Move Area, Overlay Area

Copy Area   Copies a rectangular area from one part of the grid to another.

Move Area   Moves a rectangular area from one part of the grid to another.

Overlay Area   Lays a rectangular area from one part of the grid over a rectangular area in another part of the grid. Overlay is not a pixel-for-pixel replacement but those pixels that are clear (bitmap bits set to 0) allow those pixels that are set (bitmap bits set to 1) to show through the overlay.

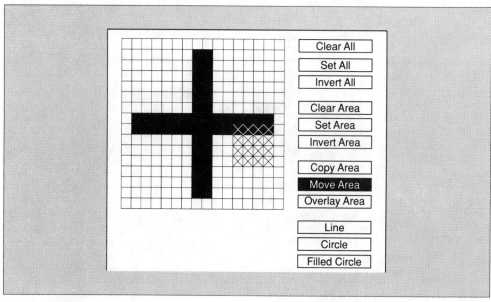

Figure 7-7. Selecting an area to copy, move, or overlay

The procedure to Copy Area, Move Area, or Overlay Area is:

1. Click the pointer over the command (Copy Area, Move Area, or Overlay Area). The pointer turns into an upper-left corner.

2. Move the pointer over the upper-left corner of the area you want to copy, move, or overlay. Press and hold any button. The pointer changes to a lower-right corner.

3. Move the pointer to the lower-right corner of the area you want to act on. Xs cover the rectangular area as you move the pointer. Release the button. The pointer changes to an upper-left corner.

4. Move the pointer to the desired location and click any button.

   OR:

   Press and hold any button to see the outline of the destination rectangle, move the pointer to the desired location, then release the button.

5. To cancel an overlay, copy, or move command, move the pointer outside the grid and release the button.

Drawing: Line, Circle, Filled Circle

When you use a drawing command, the drawing is always done in the foreground color.

Line   Draws a line between any two points you select.

Circle   Draws a circle. You specify the center and the radius.

Filled Circle   Draws a filled circle. You specify the center and the radius.

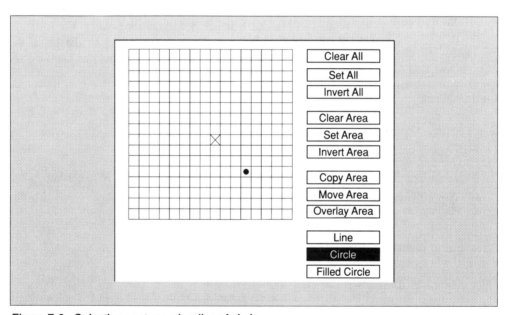

Figure 7-8. Selecting center and radius of circle

To draw a line or circle:

1. Click the pointer over the command Line, Circle, or Filled Circle. The pointer changes to the dot cursor shape (•).

2. Move the pointer to the first point of the line or to the center of the circle. Click any button. An X fills the square which is the starting point of the line or center of the circle.

3. Move the pointer to the end point of the line or to the outside circumference of the circle. Click any button. The graphic is drawn.

Filling In a Shape: Flood Fill

Flood Fill	Fills all clear squares in a closed shape.

To fill a shape:

1. Click the pointer over the command Flood Fill. The pointer changes to the dot cursor shape (•).

2. Move the pointer into the shape you want to fill.

3. Click on any clear square inside the closed shape and all clear squares are filled out to the shape's border. If the shape is not closed, the entire grid will be filled. (A closed shape to be filled can be drawn pixel-by-pixel, or by using the *Line* command.

Hot Spots: Set Hot Spot, Clear Hot Spot

Set Hot Spot	Designates a point on the bitmap as the hot spot. If a program is using your bitmap as a pointer, the hot spot indicates which point on the bitmap will track the actual location of the pointer. For instance, if your pointer is an arrow, the hot spot should be the tip of the arrow; if your pointer is a cross, the hot spot should be the intersection point of the perpendicular lines.
Clear Hot Spot	Removes a hot spot defined on this bitmap.

To set or clear a hot spot:

1. Click the pointer over Set Hot Spot or Clear Hot Spot.

2. Move the pointer to the location of the hot spot. Click any button. When a hot spot is active a diamond (◊) appears in the square.

Saving and Quitting: Write Output, Quit

Write Output	Writes the current bitmap value to the file specified in the command line. If the file already exists, the original file is first renamed to *filename⁻*.
	If either the renaming or the writing causes an error (e.g., permission denied), a dialog box appears, asking whether you want to write the file */tmp/filename* instead. If you click Yes, all future Write Output commands in the current *bitmap* editing session write to */tmp/filename*. See the *bitmap* reference page in Part Three of this guide for information on the format of the output file.

Quit   Terminates *bitmap*. If you have edited the bitmap and have not invoked Write Output or you have edited it since the last time you invoked Write Output, a dialog box appears, asking if you want to save changes before quitting. Yes does a Write Output before terminating; No just terminates, losing the edits. Cancel means you decided not to terminate after all.

You can also terminate *bitmap* by typing Control-C or q anywhere in the window. If you have edited the bitmap and have not invoked Write Output, a dialog box appears, asking if you want to save changes before quitting.

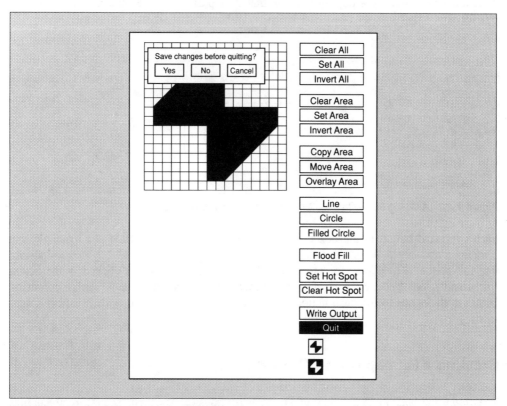

Figure 7-9. Bitmap window with quit dialog box

Dialog Boxes and Command Buttons

Some applications provide a a dialog box when a small piece of information, such as a filename, is required from the user, or when the application simply must notify the user of something. *bitmap* is one of the few standard clients that uses a dialog box. The dialog box provided by *bitmap* is an X Toolkit feature. It differs somewhat from a dialog box created with the Motif Toolkit. See "Dialog Boxes and Push Buttons" in Chapter 8, *Other Clients*, for information about Motif dialogs.

A dialog box created using the X Toolkit typically has three elements: it always has the first element, and may or may not have the second and/or third elements in this list:

- A prompt that identifies the purpose of the widget. In the case of *bitmap*, the string is "Save changes before quitting?" In other applications, the string might be as simple as "Filename:".

- An area in which you can type your response. (*bitmap*'s dialog does not have this feature.)

- Command buttons that allow you to confirm or cancel the dialog input.

A dialog box is usually a pop-up window that disappears after the required information is provided.

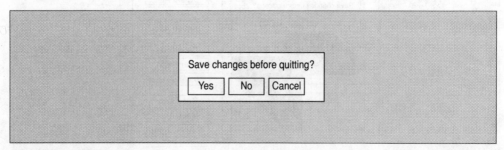

Figure 7-10. A dialog box with Yes, No, and Cancel command buttons

Each command button in the box is itself a widget. A command button is a rectangle that contains a text label. When the pointer is on the button, its border is highlighted to indicate that the button is available for selection. When a pointer button is clicked, some action (presumably indicated by the label) is performed by the program. The X Toolkit command button is analogous to the push button provided by the Motif Toolkit, as described in Chapter 8.

Creating a Bitmap from a Cursor

The *atobm* and *bmtoa* clients allow you to convert *arrays* (of ASCII characters) *to bitmap* files and to convert *bitmap* files *to arrays*. These clients are commonly used to facilitate printing: a bitmap file that is converted to ASCII text can be printed more readily and can also be included in standard ASCII text files. Once converted to ASCII, bitmap files can also be more quickly copied or mailed to other directories or systems, where they can be used in ASCII format or converted back to bitmap format.

Among their uses, the *bmtoa* and *atobm* utilities make it possible to convert a character from a font, such as the cursor font, to the *bitmap* file format. Once converted, the file can be edited using the *bitmap* client and used as you would any other bitmap file: specified as the root window pattern (with *xsetroot*), etc.

When a bitmap file is converted to ASCII text, it is in the form of an array consisting of two types of characters. (An array is a number of elements arranged in rows and columns; it is sometimes called a matrix.) One character represents set or filled squares of the bitmap (bitmap bit 1) and the other character represents empty squares (bitmap bit 0). By default, the number sign character (#) represents filled squares and the hyphen (–) represents empty squares. Figure 7-11 shows the British pound sign character of the 9x15 font (in the *misc* directory) as an array of these ASCII symbols.

```
---###-
--#---#
--#----
####--
--#----
-###--
#-#--##
-#-----
```

Figure 7-11. ASCII array representing the British pound sign

As you can see, the array is a rectangle. In a sense, the array is similar to the *bitmap* grid. (You can edit or create the array using an ASCII text editor, as long as you use the standard two characters and keep the array rectangular.)

To convert the Gumby character of the cursor font to a bitmap, the first thing you must do is display the cursor font as ASCII text. This can be done with the *showsnf* client, which allows you to display the contents of a font file (with a *.snf* extension). The –g option specifies that arrays of all the characters in the font be displayed as well.

To display the cursor font with each character represented as an array, use *showsnf* with the font filename as an argument and redirect output to a file called */tmp/cursor.array*:

```
% showsnf -g /usr/lib/X11/fonts/misc/cursor.snf > /tmp/cursor.array
```

The *cursor.array* file contains information about the font and an array for each character. Using your ASCII text editing program, edit the file, writing the Gumby array to another file called */tmp/gumby.array*. The Gumby array is pictured in Figure 7-12.

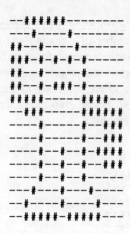

Figure 7-12. /tmp/gumby.array

You can then use the *atobm* client to convert this array to a bitmap. Use the *gumby.array* file as an argument and redirect the output to a bitmap file:

```
% atobm /tmp/gumby.array > /tmp/gumby.bitmap
```

Figure 7-13 shows the Gumby bitmap. As you can see from the bitmap, the Gumby character of the cursor font is considerably smaller than the Gumby we created (Figure 7-3) with *bitmap*.

If you want, you can then edit the *gumby.bitmap* file using the *bitmap* client.

If you specify the unedited bitmap as the root window pattern, you'll notice that there is virtually no space between the Gumby figures. This is because the array file had no extra hyphens (representing empty *bitmap* squares) padding it. If you want, you can add some hyphens to the *gumby.array* file (keeping the image symmetrical) and then use *atobm* to create a more padded version of the bitmap. Figure 7-14 shows the *gumby.array* file after it was padded with hyphens.

See the *bitmap* reference page in Part Three of this guide for more information on the *atobm* and *bmtoa* conversion clients.

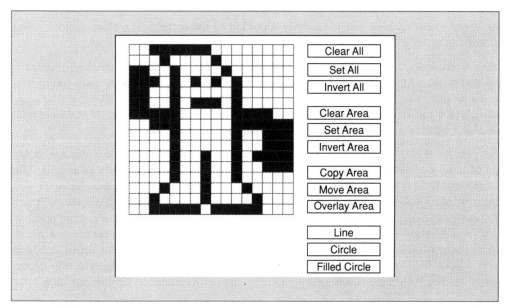

Figure 7-13. Bitmap of the Gumby cursor

```
--------------------------------
--------------------------------
----------#####-----------------
----------#----#----------------
--------##--#----#--------------
--------###-#-#-#-#-------------
--------##--#-----#-------------
--------##--#-###-#-------------
--------#####----####-----------
----------###-----######--------
------------#-----#--###--------
------------#-----#--###--------
------------#--#--#-####--------
------------#--#--#--###--------
------------#--#--#-------------
------------#---#---#-----------
----------#----#----#-----------
----------#####-#####-----------
--------------------------------
--------------------------------
```

Figure 7-14. gumby.array padded by hyphens

Magnifying Portions of the Screen: xmag

The *xmag* client enables you to magnify a portion of the screen. The close-up look *xmag* affords can assist you in creating and editing bitmaps and other graphic images.

xmag is primarily a tool for application developers using sophisticated graphics programs. But you could also use *xmag* in concert with the *bitmap* client. For instance, say you're running a program that creates a special image on the root window and you'd like to create a *bitmap* file of a part of that image. You can display a magnification of the image you want with *xmag* and try to recreate the image by editing in an open *bitmap* window.

xmag is also useful for capturing a screen image that can then be saved as a window dump file with the *xwd* client (described in Chapter 8, *Other Clients*). *xwd* makes a dump file of a single window at a time (though that window may be the root). In some cases, however, you might want to make a dump file of a portion of a window or of multiple windows. *xmag* allows you to magnify any portion of the screen; thus the *xmag* window can capture portions of several windows at once. You can then use *xwd* to make a dump file of the *xmag* window. (Since *xmag* is intended to magnify, if you want the window image to be the actual size, you must specify that no magnification is performed. To do this, run *xmag* with the option −mag 1. See the *xmag* reference page in Part Three of this guide for more information.)

If you invoke *xmag* without options, you can interactively choose the area to be magnified (the *source* area) and position the magnified image on your screen. At the command line, type:

```
% xmag &
```

The pointer changes to a small cross (the crosshair cursor) in the center of a small, hollow square with a wavering border. (By default, the square is 64 pixels on each side.) Move the crosshair cursor, placing the square over the area you want to magnify, and click the first pointer button.

The hollow square becomes enlarged to the size of the magnified image. (By default, the image is magnified five times.) By default, *mwm* places the *xmag* window containing the magnified image in the upper-left quadrant of the display. A magnified bitmap image is shown in Figure 7-15.

If you are using a window manager that provides titlebars, such as *mwm*, the title string "Magnifying Glass" will be displayed in the *xmag* window titlebar. This is the default title string of the application.*

The default size *xmag* window shows an area 64 pixels square, magnified five times. This magnification enables you to see the individual pixels, which are represented by squares of the same color as the corresponding pixels in the source image.

Rather than use the default source area and magnification, you can specify other values on the command line. See the *xmag* reference page in Part Three of this guide for a complete list of options.

---

*Applications written using the X Toolkit allow you to change the title string. See the section "Title and Name" in Chapter 9, *Command Line Options*, for details. The *xmag* client was not written using the X Toolkit and provides no method for changing the title string.

Figure 7-15. xmag window displaying magnified screen area

Quitting xmag

To exit the program, type q, Q, or Control-C in the *xmag* window.

What xmag Shows You

xmag enables you to determine the x and y coordinates, bitmap bit setting, and RGB color value of every pixel in the *xmag* window. (See Chapter 9, *Command Line Options*, for a discussion of the RGB color model.) If you move the pointer into the *xmag* window, the cursor becomes an arrow. Point the arrow at one of the magnified pixels and press and hold down the first pointer button. A banner across the top edge of the window displays information about the pixel, as shown in Figure 7-16.

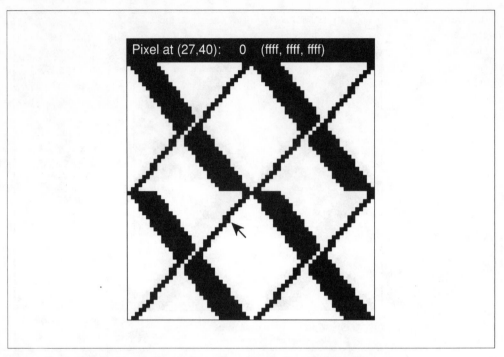

Figure 7-16. Displaying pixel statistics with pointer in xmag window

The banner displays the following information about the specified pixel:

- The x and y coordinates relative to the window. The default *xmag* window is, in effect, a grid of 64 squares on each side. Therefore, each pixel has x,y coordinates between 0,0 and 63,63.

- The bitmap bit setting. This is either 0 if the pixel is in the background color or 1 if the pixel is in the foreground color.

- The RGB value. This is a 16-bit value. The RGB specification is in three parts (of four hexadecimal digits each), corresponding to the three primaries in the RGB color model.

If you are trying to create a graphic image on a grid (such as the *bitmap* client provides), the x and y coordinates of each pixel can be especially useful. Also, the 16-bit RGB value specifies the color of each pixel with incredible precision. Depending on the number of colors available on your display, you can learn to use RGB values to specify an enormous range of colors.

xmag provides these pixel statistics dynamically. If you continue to hold down the first pointer button and drag the pointer across the window, the banner will display values for each pixel as the pointer indicates it.

Note that if you select a pixel near the top edge of the window, the banner will appear across the bottom edge. Otherwise, the banner would obscure the pixel you are pointing at.

Dynamically Choosing a Different Source Area

If you want to magnify another portion of the screen using the same source area size and magnification, you do not have to start *xmag* again. Simply move the pointer into the *xmag* window and click the second or third pointer button, or press the space bar. The magnified image disappears and the cursor again becomes a crosshair surrounded by a hollow square. Move the crosshair cursor, placing the square over the new source area you want to magnify, and click any pointer button. The magnified image is immediately displayed in the same location as the first image.

You can select any number of source areas during a single *xmag* session.

The Portable Bitmap Toolkit

The Portable Bitmap Toolkit (in the user-contributed distribution) provides dozens of utilities for converting graphics files to and from portable formats. Developed by Jef Poskanzer, the Toolkit is composed of four parts, three of which correspond to a particular portable format:

- PBM: utilities to convert files to and from portable bitmap format.

- PGM: utilities to convert files to and from portable graymap format (grayscale images).

- PPM: utilities to convert files to and from portable pixmap format (color images).

The fourth part of the toolkit, PNM, provides utilities to manipulate images in any of the three formats. For example, the program *pnmenlarge* enlarges a portable "anymap" by a factor you supply. *pnminvert* inverts an image in any of the three portable formats.

The available utilities and the conversions they perform are summarized in the *README* file in the source directory. Table 7-1 lists some representative conversion utilities and their functions.

Table 7-1. Some PBM Toolkit Conversion Utilities

Utility	Converts
giftoppm	GIF to portable pixmap.
ppmtogif	Portable pixmap to GIF.
ppmtoxwd	Portable pixmap to X11 window dump.
xwdtoppm	X10 or X11 window dump to portable pixmap.
ppmtopgm	Portable pixmap to portable graymap.
fstopgm	Usenix FaceSaver file to portable graymap.
pgmtops	Portable graymap to Encapsulated PostScript.
pgmtopbm	Portable graymap to portable bitmap.
pbmtomacp	Portable bitmap to MacPaint.
macptopbm	MacPaint to portable bitmap.
pbmtoxbm	Portable bitmap to X11 bitmap.
pbmtox10bm	Portable bitmap to X10 bitmap.

Graphics Utilities

Table 7-1. Some PBM Toolkit Conversion Utilities (continued)

Utility	Converts
xbmtopbm	X10 or X11 bitmap to portable bitmap.
pbmtoxwd	portable bitmap to X11 window dump.
xwdtopbm	X10 or X11 window dump to portable bitmap.

As the table indicates, some of the available utilities come in pairs—they can be used to convert a file to a portable format and back to its original format again. (The table also includes a group of three related utilities to convert X10 and X11 bitmaps to portable bitmaps and back again.)

Certain conversions can only be performed in one direction. For example, you can convert a portable graymap to a portable bitmap (using *pgmtopbm*), but you can't convert a bitmap to a graymap. The one-way conversions generally involve changing a file to a simpler format.

You'll probably be most interested in converting graphics files to formats suitable for use with X: X bitmaps or window dump files. Keep in mind that a portable bitmap has a different format than an X bitmap. The program *pbmtoxbm* converts a portable bitmap to a bitmap compatible with X11.

The conversions you may want to perform can be simple (directly from one format to another) or complex (through several intermediate formats). An example of a simple conversion is changing a portable pixmap to a portable graymap using *ppmtopgm*:

```
% ppmtopgm pixmap > graymap
```

The PBM Toolkit source directory includes a file called *TIPS* that provides helpful hints on using the utilities. Based on these suggestions, we performed a fairly complex conversion: a Usenix FaceSaver image to a bitmap suitable for use with X. The following command performed the conversion on the file *myface* to create *myface.bitmap*:

```
fstopgm myface | pnmenlarge 3 | ppmscale -yscale 1.125 | ppmtopgm |\
         pgmnorm | pgmtopbm | pbmtoxbm > myface.bitmap
```

Notice that this particular conversion requires seven utilities! This procedure is by no means intuitive. We relied heavily on the *TIPS* provided.

The seven conversions performed are:

• Convert FaceSaver image to portable graymap (`fstopgm`).

• Enlarge a portable anymap three times (`pnmenlarge 3`).

• Scale pixels in y dimension; x dimension is adjusted accordingly (`ppmscale -yscale 1.125`). This program produces portable pixmap output.

• Convert portable pixmap to portable graymap (`ppmtopgm`).

• Normalize contrast of portable graymap (`pgmnorm`).

- Convert portable graymap to portable bitmap (pgmtopbm).

- Convert portable bitmap to X11 bitmap (pbmtoxbm).

Be aware that the command:

```
ppmscale -yscale 1.125
```

may not be necessary on all systems or the necessary arguments may vary. If you omit *ppmscale* and the command is necessary, the system should return a message to that effect and also tell you what arguments to use.

The possible uses of the PBM Toolkit programs and the ways in which they can be combined are extremely varied. You'll have to do some experimenting. To orient yourself, read the files *README*, *TIPS*, and *FORMATS* in the source directory. The source directory also includes reference pages for each utility.

Graphics Utilities

8

Other Clients

This chapter gives an overview of other clients available with X, including window and display information clients, printing utilities, the xkill *program, and several "desk accessories." It also examines some of the features common to applications written with the Motif Toolkit.*

In This Chapter:

Other Clients

8
Other Clients

In addition to *xterm*, the MIT distribution includes many other clients. This chapter discusses some of the more useful clients, grouped according to basic functionality:

- Desk accessories: *xclock*, *oclock*, *xcalc*, *xbiff*, *xload*, and *xman*.

- Text editor: *xedit*.

- Printing utilities: *xwd*, *xpr*, and *xdpr*.

- Program to remove a client window: *xkill*.

- Window and display information programs: *xwininfo*, *xlswins*, *xlsclients*, and *xdpyinfo*.

- Alternative window managers and other user-contributed clients, including a program to display available colors and change color preferences: *xcol*.

Most sections in this chapter are intended to acquaint you with the major features of some of the available clients. Additional detailed information is provided on the reference pages for each client in Part Three of this guide.

Many of the standard clients have been written (or rewritten) with a programming library called the X Toolkit. As explained in Chapter 1, the X Toolkit includes a set of predefined components (or widgets), known as the Athena widget set. Widgets make it easier to create complex applications; they also ensure a consistent user interface between applications.

Although most of the standard clients described in this guide were originally written before the X Toolkit was fully developed, many have since been rewritten to use the Toolkit. In discussing various clients in this chapter, we'll point out some of the features attributable to the X Toolkit.

For a comprehensive treatment of the X Toolkit, see Volume Four, *X Toolkit Intrinsics Programming Manual*, and Volume Five, *X Toolkit Intrinsics Reference Manual*.

Later in this chapter we'll also take a look at some of the features common to applications written with the Motif Toolkit.

Other Clients

Desk Accessories

The clients *xclock*, *oclock*, *xcalc*, *xload*, *xbiff*, and *xman* can be thought of as *desk accessories*. (Desk accessories is a term we've borrowed from the Macintosh environment, meaning small applications available—and useful—at any time.)

You can start these clients from the command line in any *xterm* window or, if you like, you can add them to an *mwm* menu. (See Chapter 11, *Customizing mwm*.)

Clock Programs: xclock and oclock

The standard release of X includes two clients that display the time: *xclock* and *oclock* (the *oclock* client was added to the standard distribution of X in Release 4). The time displayed by both *xclock* and *oclock* is the system time set and displayed with the UNIX *date*(1) command.

xclock continuously displays the time, either in analog or digital form, in a standard window. The analog *xclock* shows a round 12-hour clock face with tick marks representing the minutes. The digital *xclock* shows the 24-hour time (2:30 PM would be represented as 14:30) as well as the day, month, and year. You can run more than one clock at a time. The analog clock is the default. Figure 8-1 shows two *xclock* applications being run: an analog clock above a digital clock.

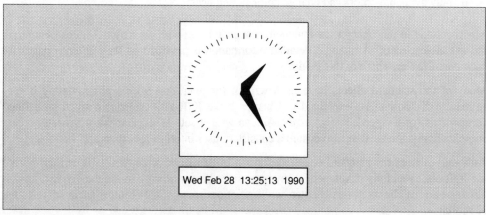

Figure 8-1. Two xclock displays: analog clock above digital clock

The *oclock* client (available as of Release 4) displays the time in analog form on a round 12-hour clock face without tick marks. The only features of an *oclock* display are the round clock outline, hour and minute hands, and the "jewel" marking 12 o'clock.

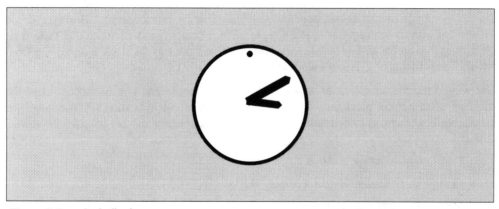

Figure 8-2. oclock display

Though it is somewhat more difficult to read the precise time on the simple *oclock* display, the *oclock* is perhaps a little more aesthetic than the analog *xclock*.

oclock also makes use of the X Shape extension, which supports non-rectangular windows. If you try to resize the round *oclock*, you'll discover that it's possible to "stretch" it into various oblong shapes, as shown in Figure 8-3.

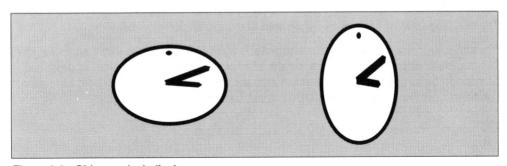

Figure 8-3. Oblong oclock displays

Though the default colors for *oclock* are black and white, it was designed to be run in color. The minute hand, hour hand, jewel, clock border, and background can all be set to a color, using either command line options (as described in Chapter 9) or by specifying client resources (as described in Chapter 10). See the *oclock* reference page in Part Three of this guide for the necessary command line options and color suggestions.

Removing an xclock or oclock

Usually when you invoke *xclock* or *oclock* you will leave the clock running. However, if you experiment with these programs to test size, location, or color, you will notice that there is no obvious way to delete an unwanted clock. (Moving the cursor to the clock and pressing Control-C, Control-D, q, or Q doesn't work with *xclock* or *oclock*.)

One way to remove an *xclock* or *oclock* window is to identify and kill the process using the standard UNIX control mechanisms. First, find the process identification (PID) number for the client. For example, to determine the process ID number for *xclock*, go to an *xterm* window and type:

    % ps -aux | grep xclock

at a system prompt. Under System V, type:

    % ps -e | grep xclock

at a system prompt. The resulting display should look something like this:

    128 p0 0:00 xclock
    142 p0 0:00 grep xclock

The number in the first column is the process ID. Type:

    % kill process_id

The *xclock* display will be removed, and you will get the message:

    Terminated   xclock

The same sequence of commands can be used to remove an *oclock* window.

You can also remove either an *xclock* or *oclock* window by using the Close item of *mwm*'s Window Menu or by double clicking on the Window Menu command button, as described in Chapter 4. Be aware, however, that these and other methods of "killing" a client have certain liabilities. See "Problems with Killing a Client" later in this chapter.

A Scientific Calculator: xcalc

xcalc is a scientific calculator that can emulate a Texas Instruments TI-30 or a Hewlett Packard HP-10C. Once you place the pointer within the *xcalc* window, the calculator can be operated in two ways: with the pointer, by clicking the first pointer button on the buttons in the calculator window, or with the keyboard, by typing the same numbers and symbols that are displayed in the calculator window. When using the first method, notice that the pointer appears as a small hand, enabling you to "press" the buttons. Figure 8-4 shows *xcalc* on the screen.

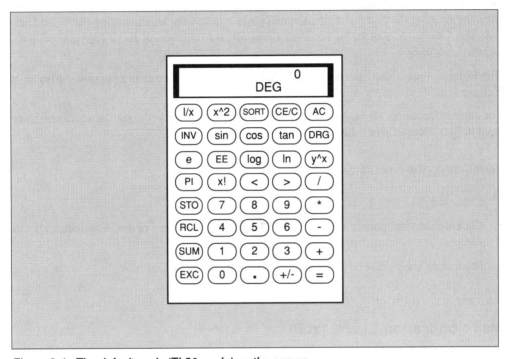

Figure 8-4. The default xcalc (TI-30 mode) on the screen

Figure 8-4 depicts the version of the calculator provided with Release 4 of X. As you can see, it features oval buttons. If you are running an earlier release, the calculator will have rectangular buttons and may also have a darker background color. These differences do not affect functionality. However, the Release 3 and Release 4 versions of *xcalc* do work somewhat differently. We describe some of those differences later. For additional information, see the *xcalc* reference page in Part Three of this guide.

The values punched on the calculator and the results of calculations are displayed in the long horizontal window along the top of the *xcalc*. You can enter values either by clicking on the calculator keys with the pointer, or by pressing equivalent keys on the keyboard. Most of the calculator keys have keyboard equivalents. The not-so-obvious equivalents are described on the *xcalc* reference page in Part Three of this guide.

By default, *xcalc* works like a TI-30 calculator. To run *xcalc* in this mode, enter:

    % xcalc &

You can also operate the calculator in Reverse Polish Notation (as an HP-10C calculator operates), by entering:

    % xcalc -rpn &

In Reverse Polish Notation the operands are entered first, then the operator. For example, 5 * 4 = would be entered as 5 Enter 4 *. This entry sequence is designed to minimize keystrokes for complex calculations.

As of Release 4, *xcalc* allows you to select the number in the calculator display. You select the number using the first pointer button and paste it in another window using the second button. See Chapter 5, *The xterm Terminal Emulator*, for information about copying and pasting text selections.

The Release 4 *xcalc* can also be resized. In prior releases, this was not possible. Also as of Release 4, *xcalc* no longer emulates a slide rule.*

For more information on the function of each of the calculator keys, see the *xcalc* reference page in Part Three of this guide.

Terminating the calculator

Terminate the calculator by either:

- Clicking the third pointer button on the TI calculator's AC key or the HP calculator's ON key, or:

- Positioning the pointer on the calculator and typing q, Q, or Control-C.

Mail Notification Client: xbiff

xbiff is a simple program that notifies you when you have mail. It puts up a window showing a picture of a mailbox. When you receive new mail, the keyboard emits a beep, the flag on the mailbox goes up, and the image changes to reverse video. Figure 8-5 shows the *xbiff* mailbox before and after mail is received.

After you read your mail (and the mail file is empty), the image changes back to its original state; or you can click on the full mailbox icon with any pointer button to change it back to empty. Regardless of the number of mail messages when you do this, *xbiff* remembers the current size of your mail file to be the *empty* size.

---

*If you are running an earlier release of X, you can operate *xcalc* as a slide rule by using the -analog option. Drag the slide using the first pointer button. Be aware that the slide rule mode doesn't work very well. To terminate the slide rule, use *kill*(1), as described in Chapter 8 for *oclock*. The slide rule emulation was eliminated in Release 4.

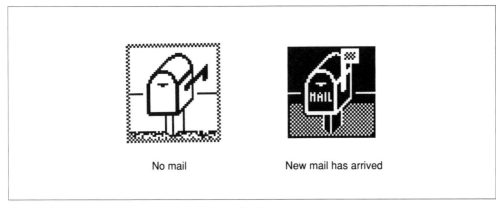

No mail

New mail has arrived

Figure 8-5. xbiff before and after mail is received

This feature of *xbiff* has two implications, one obvious and the other not so obvious: when additional mail arrives (and the mail file becomes larger), *xbiff* notifies you; but when you delete messages from the current mail file (and the file becomes smaller), *xbiff* also notifies you—when you exit the mail program and the file is saved. This can be a little confusing until you get used to it.

While *xbiff* is intended to monitor a mail file, it can actually be set up to watch any file whose size changes using the −file option (followed by the name of the file to be monitored). For instance, if you're running a program that produces output intermittently, you can start *xbiff* with −file followed by the name of the output file; then *xbiff* will notify you when output is returned. (You can even specify an image other than the mailbox using resource variables—even for a single *xbiff* process.) See the *xbiff* reference page in Part Three of this guide for a list of options and resources. See Chapter 10, *Setting Resources*, for the syntax of resource specifications.

Monitoring System Load Average: xload

xload periodically polls the system for the load average and graphically displays that load using a simple histogram. By default, *xload* polls the system every five seconds. You can change this frequency with the −update option. For example, if you enter this command in an *xterm* window:

```
% xload -update 3 &
```

the resulting *xload* window will poll the system every three seconds, as in Figure 8-6.

Other Clients

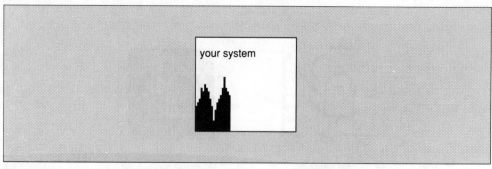

Figure 8-6. A sample xload window

If you are using both the local machine and remote machines, you can display loads for all systems and do your processing on the system that is fastest at the time.

Like *xclock* and *oclock*, *xload* provides no exit command. To remove an *xload* window, you need to kill the client process. See "Removing an xclock or oclock" earlier in this chapter.

Browsing Reference Pages: xman

The *xman* client allows you to display and browse through formatted versions of reference pages. By default, *xman* lets you look at the standard UNIX manpages found in subdirectories of the directory */usr/man*. The standard version of X assumes there are 10 subdirectories: *man1* through *man8*, corresponding to the eight sections of reference pages in the UNIX documentation set; *manl* (man local) and *mann* (man new). You can specify other directories by setting the MANPATH system variable. (The individual directory names should be separated by colons.)

This section describes the version of *xman* provided with Release 4 of X. From a user's viewpoint, the general operation of the client has not changed much since prior releases but the organization of menus and options has changed.

Regardless of the version of X, you run *xman* by typing:

```
% xman &
```

in an *xterm* window.

The initial *xman* window, shown in Figure 8-7, is a small window containing only a few commands.

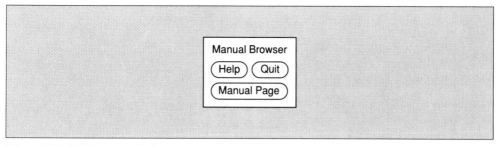

Figure 8-7. Initial xman window

This window is small enough to be displayed for prolonged periods during which you might have need to examine UNIX manual pages. You select a command by clicking on it with the first pointer button.

The Manual Page command brings up a larger window in which you can display a formatted version of any manual page in the MANPATH. By default, the first page displayed contains general help information about *xman*. Use this information to acquaint yourself with the client's features.* (The actual *xman* reference page in Part Three of this guide primarily describes how to customize the client.)

Once you've opened this larger window, you can display formatted manual pages in it. Notice the horizontal bar spanning the top edge of the window. (If you're running *mwm* or a similar window manager, this bar appears beneath the titlebar provided by the window manager.) The bar is divided into three parts labeled Options, Sections, and Xman Help. The part currently labeled Xman Help is merely informational and the text displayed in it will change depending on the contents of the window. The parts labeled Options and Sections are actually handles to two *xman* menus.

If you place the pointer on the Options box and press and hold down the first button, a menu called Xman Options will be displayed below. The menu is pictured in Figure 8-8.

---

*Selecting the Help command also opens a large window in which the same help information is displayed. The Help command is something of a dead end, however; you cannot display any other text in this window.

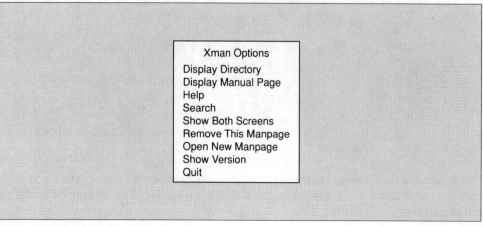

Xman Options
Display Directory
Display Manual Page
Help
Search
Show Both Screens
Remove This Manpage
Open New Manpage
Show Version
Quit

Figure 8-8. Xman Options menu

The functionality of these options is described in the online *xman* help page. To select an option, move the pointer down the menu and release the first button on the option you want. The option you will probably use most frequently is the first one, Display Directory.

Display Directory lists the reference pages in the current reference page directory (also called a *section*). By default, this is *man1*, the user commands. When you list the contents of *man1* in this way, the informational section of the horizontal bar reads Directory of: (1) User Commands.

xman displays each manpage directory in a window known as a *viewport*, created with the Athena Viewport widget from the X Toolkit. A viewport is a composite widget that provides a main window and horizontal and/or vertical scrollbars. The Athena Viewport widget is analogous to the Motif Toolkit's ScrolledWindow, described later in this chapter.

xman's scrollbar is also an Athena widget. (See Chapter 5, *The xterm Terminal Emulator*, for instructions on using an Athena scrollbar.) The Motif Toolkit also provides a scrollbar widget, described later in this chapter, which looks and operates somewhat differently than the Athena scrollbar.

For a list of the Athena widgets, see Appendix G, *Athena Widget Resources*. For complete information about the X Toolkit, see Volume Four, *X Toolkit Intrinsics Programming Manual*, and Volume Five, *X Toolkit Intrinsics Reference Manual*.

Once you've listed a reference page directory in the *xman* window, you can display a formatted version of any page in the list simply by clicking on the name with the first pointer button. Figure 8-9 shows the formatted reference page for the UNIX *cd*(1) command.

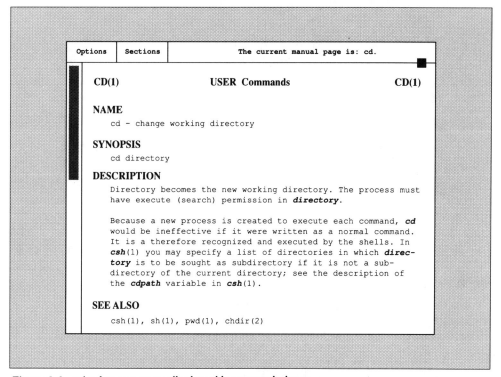

```
 ┌─────────┬──────────┬──────────────────────────────────────┐
 │ Options │ Sections │    The current manual page is: cd.   │ ■
 ├─────────┴──────────┴──────────────────────────────────────┤
 │                                                            │
 │█  CD(1)                   USER Commands              CD(1) │
 │█                                                           │
 │█  NAME                                                     │
 │█     cd - change working directory                        │
 │█                                                           │
 │█  SYNOPSIS                                                 │
 │█     cd directory                                          │
 │█                                                           │
 │   DESCRIPTION                                              │
 │      Directory becomes the new working directory. The process must │
 │      have execute (search) permission in directory.        │
 │                                                            │
 │      Because a new process is created to execute each command, cd │
 │      would be ineffective if it were written as a normal command. │
 │      It is a therefore recognized and executed by the shells. In │
 │      csh(1) you may specify a list of directories in which direc- │
 │      tory is to be sought as subdirectory if it is not a sub- │
 │      directory of the current directory; see the description of │
 │      the cdpath variable in csh(1).                        │
 │                                                            │
 │   SEE ALSO                                                 │
 │      csh(1), sh(1), pwd(1), chdir(2)                       │
 │                                                            │
 └────────────────────────────────────────────────────────────┘
```

Figure 8-9. cd reference page displayed in xman window

To display another manual page from the same directory, display the Xman Options menu again. Select Display Directory and the directory listing is again displayed in the window. Then click on another command name to display its manual page in the window. (If you decide not to display another reference page, you can remove the directory listing and go back to the reference page previously displayed by using the second Xman Options menu selection, Display Manual Page. Display Directory and Display Manual Page are toggles of one another.)

To display a manual page from another directory in the MANPATH, you must first change to that directory using the second *xman* menu, Xman Sections. Bring up the menu by placing the pointer in the Sections box in the application's titlebar and holding down the first button. The Xman Sections menu lists the default directories of UNIX manual pages, as shown in Figure 8-10.

Other Clients

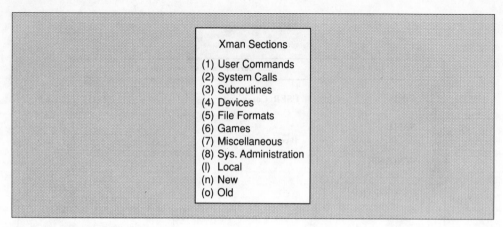

Figure 8-10. Xman Sections menu

Click on the first pointer button to select another directory of reference pages from which to choose. Once you select a directory, the files in that directory are listed in the window. Again, you display a page by clicking on its name with the first pointer button.

You can display more than one "browsing" window simultaneously by selecting the Open New Manpage option from the Xman Options menu. An additional reference page window will be opened again starting with the help information.

The various windows *xman* creates can all be iconified and each is represented by a different icon symbol. The icon symbols for the initial *xman* window, the help window, and the browsing window appear in Figure 8-11. When the *mwm* window manager is running, the icons appear as in Figure 8-12. Keep in mind that if you've displayed several browsing windows simultaneously, you can iconify each of them.

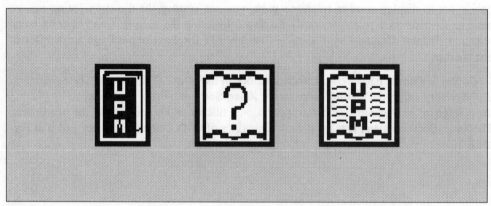

Figure 8-11. Icons for xman's initial window, help window, and browsing window

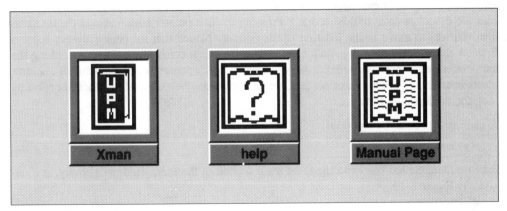

Figure 8-12. xman icons under mwm

You can remove a browsing window by selecting the Remove This Manpage option from the Xman Options menu. (Prior to Release 4, selecting this option resulted in an error and caused the *xman* program to exit.)

Selecting Quit from the Xman Options menu or from the initial *xman* window causes the client to exit.

The xedit Text Editor

The *xedit* client provides a window in which you can create and edit text files. The editing commands *xedit* recognizes are provided by the Athena Text widget. Many other standard and user-contributed clients also include areas in which you can enter text. Several of these clients, including *xclipboard* and *xmh*, also use the Text widget, and thus recognize the same editing commands as *xedit*.

The *xedit* client is valuable to illustrate the use of the Athena Text widget. (*xedit* can also be used to illustrate several other widgets.) However, we do not recommend using *xedit* as your primary text editor. The program is somewhat buggy and its behavior can be erratic. For example, it's fairly easy to overwrite files inadvertently, as explained in the discussion of the Load button later in this section. The redraw command (Control-L) causes text in the window to scroll so as to reposition the cursor in the center of the editing window—not a welcome surprise. Some of the commands to create a new paragraph may also inadvertently copy preceding text. These are just a few of *xedit*'s inconvenient features.

Still, it is necessary to know something about the Athena Text widget in order to be able to enter and edit text in windows provided by many clients.

xedit recognizes various Control and Meta keystroke combinations that are bound to a set of commands similar to those provided by the *emacs* text editor.* In addition, you can use the

---

*The commands may be bound to keys different from the defaults described below through the standard X Toolkit key translation mechanisms. See Chapter 10, *Setting Resources*, for more information.

pointer to move the cursor in the text or to select a portion of text. The *xedit* cursor is a caret symbol (ˆ). A caret cursor appears in each of the three areas that accept text entry. (These areas are described later in this section.) Pressing the first pointer button causes the insertion point (cursor) to move to the location of the pointer. Notice that the cursor always appears between characters, rather than on a character as the *xterm* cursor does. Double-clicking the first pointer button selects a word, triple-clicking selects a paragraph, and quadruple-clicking selects everything. After you select text, the selection may be extended in either direction by using the third pointer button.

You can invoke *xedit* by entering:

```
% xedit &
```

Since no filename has been specified, the main section of the *xedit* window is empty, as illustrated by Figure 8-13.

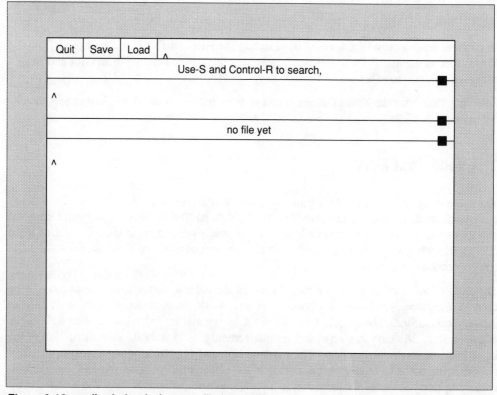

Figure 8-13. *xedit window before text file is read in*

Notice that the *xedit* window is divided into four parts:

- A commands section, which features three command push buttons (Quit, Save, and Load) and an area to their right in which a filename can be entered.

- A message window, which displays messages from the client and can also be used as a scratch pad.

- The filename display, which shows the name of the file being edited and the read/write permissions for the file.

- The edit window, in which the text of the file is displayed and in which you issue the editing commands.

The *xedit* application uses the Athena VPaned widget (of the X Toolkit), which arranges subwindows one above the other without overlapping. The subwindows are also known as *vertical panes* and the non-overlapping, top-to-bottom arrangement is commonly described as *vertical tiling*.

The individual panes organized by a VPaned widget can be any other type of widget. In the case of *xedit*, for example, the commands section is one pane that contains three command buttons (another widget) and a small window to the right of the buttons (a Text widget) in which a filename can be entered.

Notice the three small black rectangles on the borders between the panes. These features are called *grips* and they serve as handles to allow you to resize the subwindows. When the pointer is positioned on the grip and a button pressed, an arrow is displayed that indicates the direction in which the border between the two windows can be moved. If you move the pointer in the direction of the arrow (while pressing the button), one subwindow will grow while the other will shrink.

You can enter text in three areas of the *xedit* window: the message window, the edit window, and the small window immediately to the right of the command buttons in which you can enter a filename. (Thus all three use a Text widget.) Note that the small filename window to the right of the command buttons is different from the filename display (lower in the *xedit* window). The filename display is simply that—a display of the filename; the window does not support editing.

All three areas that permit editing display the caret text cursor. In order to focus keyboard input to a particular area, the pointer must rest in that area—regardless of whether *mwm* is operating with the default click-to-type focus. (If click-to-type focus is in effect, the *xedit* window must also be selected as the focus window.) This is extremely important to remember. Both the message window and the edit window will display a vertical scrollbar if the text is too large to fit. (Be aware also that a scrollbar technically is not part of the text entry window it borders. If the pointer is resting in a scrollbar, keyboard input will be lost—it will not be directed to the corresponding text area!)

The three push buttons in the commands section have the following functions:

Quit   Exits the current editing session and closes the window. If changes have not been saved, *xedit* displays a warning in the message window, and does not exit, thus allowing the user to save the file.

Save   Writes the file. If file backups are enabled (using the `enableBackups` resource), *xedit* first stores a copy of the unedited file as *filename.BAK* and then overwrites *filename* with the contents of the edit window. The *filename* used is the text that appears in the area immediately to the right of the Load button.

Load   Loads the file displayed immediately to the right of the button into the edit window. If a file is currently being displayed and has been modified, a warning message will ask the user to save the changes, or to press Load again.

This interface has at least two serious pitfalls. First, if you're working on a file that has unsaved changes and you try to load a second file, it's possible to overwrite the second file. This is how it happens. In order to load a second file, you must enter the name of the file in the area next to the Load button; then press Load. If you try to load a second file while editing a file with unsaved changes, *xedit* warns you to save or press Load again. If you press Save the current file will be saved—but as the name to the right, the second file you intended to load.

If backups are not enabled, this action will overwrite the file you wanted to load. If backups are enabled, the first file will be saved under the name of the second file with a *.BAK* extension and the second file will not be overwritten. Because of this potential problem, we recommend that you set the resource `enable-Backups` to on (and load the resources using *xrdb*) before using *xedit*.

A second problem can occur after you've loaded a file by entering the name in the window next to the Load button. Say you've been editing the file for some time, but haven't saved the changes. If you go to save the changes and accidentally double-click on Load (not that difficult to do), you'll reload the version of the file before you made the edits. The changes are lost!

Now, after considering some of the possible pitfalls, let's load a file into the empty *xedit* window as shown in Figure 8-13. (Obviously, in this case, there's no danger of overwriting an existing file.) To load a file called *test*:

1. Place the pointer in the area to the right of the Load button.

2. Type *test*. Notice that the caret cursor moves as you type.

3. Place the pointer on the Load command button and press the first pointer button.

The file called *test* is displayed in the edit window, as shown in Figure 8-14.

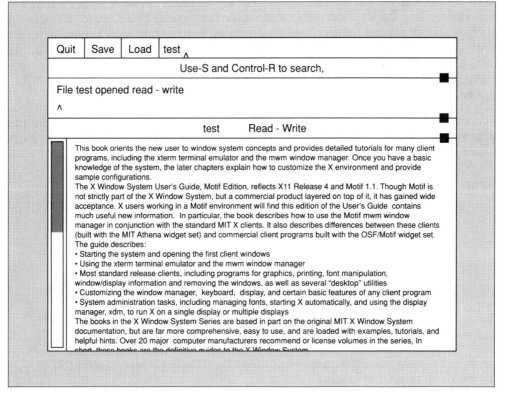

Figure 8-14. test file displayed in edit window

The simpler commands to edit or append text are intuitive. A backspace deletes the character to the left of the cursor. Typing enters characters immediately before the cursor point, causing the cursor to advance to the right. When you first load a file, the cursor appears at the beginning of the text in the edit window. If you want to append text to the end of the file, move the pointer to the end of the text and click the first button. The caret cursor appears where the pointer is and any text you type is added to the end of the file, moving the cursor to the right.

The list at the end of this section summarizes all of the editing command recognized by *xedit*. In this list of commands, a *line* refers to one row of characters displayed in the window. A *paragraph* refers to the text between manually inserted carriage returns or blank lines. Text within a paragraph is automatically broken into lines based on the current width of the window.

The keystroke combinations are defined as indicated. (Note that "Control" and "Meta" are two of the "soft" keynames X recognizes. They are mapped to particular physical keys which may vary from keyboard to keyboard. See the "xmodmap" section in Chapter 12, *Setup Clients*, for a discussion of modifier key mapping.) If you are using an earlier release of X, a few of these keystroke combinations may produce slightly different results.

Keep in mind that you can redefine any of these key combinations using what are known as *translations*. Translations allow you to assign actions recognized by a client to particular key combinations, or key and pointer button combinations. For example, *xedit* recognizes actions to delete text, to copy text, to move the cursor, etc. *xedit* defines key combinations to invoke these actions. (The key/action mappings appear in the list at the end of this section.) For information on specifying alternate mappings, see "Event Translations" in Chapter 10, *Setting Resources*.

Note that the function assigned to the Return key in the following list applies only to the edit window and message window. In the filename window (next to the command buttons), Return simply moves the cursor to the end of the line.

Control-A	Move to the beginning of the current line.
Control-B	Move backward one character.
Control-D	Delete the next character.
Control-E	Move to the end of the current line.
Control-F	Move forward one character.
Control-H or Backspace	Delete the previous character.
Return Control-J, Control-M, or LineFeed	New paragraph. (Linefeed, Control-J, and Control-M may be unreliable on some terminals.)
Control-K	Kill the rest of this line. (Does not kill the carriage return at the end of the line. To do so, use Control-K twice. However, be aware that the second kill overwrites the text line in the kill buffer.)
Control-L	Redraw the window. (Also scrolls text so that cursor is positioned in the middle of the window.)
Control-N	Move down to the next line.
Control-O	Divide this line into two lines at this point.
Control-P	Move up to the previous line.
Control-V	Move down to the next screenful of text.
Control-W	Kill the selected text.
Control-Y	Insert the last killed text. (If the last killed text is a carriage return—see Control-K above—a blank line is inserted.)
Control-Z	Scroll up the text one line.
Meta-<	Move to the beginning of the file.

Meta->	Move to the end of the file.
Meta-[	Move backward one paragraph.
Meta-]	Move forward one paragraph.
Meta-B	Move backward one word.
Meta-D	Kill the next word.
Meta-F	Move forward one word.
Meta-H or Meta-Delete	Kill the previous word.
Meta-I	Insert a file. If any text is selected, use the selected text as the filename. Otherwise, a dialog box will appear in which you can type the desired filename.
Meta-V	Move up to the previous screenful of text.
Meta-Y	Insert the last selected text here. Note that this can be text selected in some other text subwindow. Also, if you select some text in an *xterm* window, it may be inserted in an *xmh* window with this command. Pressing pointer button 2 is equivalent to this command.
Meta-Z	Scroll down the text one line.
Delete	Delete the previous character.

Printing Utilities: xwd, xpr, xdpr

xwd stores window images in a formatted window dump file. This file can be read by various other X utilities for redisplay, printing, editing, formatting, archiving, image processing, etc.

To create a window dump file, type:

```
% xwd > file
```

The pointer will change to a small crosshair symbol. Move the crosshair pointer to the desired window and click any button. The keyboard bell rings once when the dump starts and twice in rapid succession when the dump is finished.

To make a dump of the entire root window (and all windows on it), use the −root option:

```
% xwd -root > file
```

When you select a single window, by default *xwd* takes an image of the window proper. As of Release 4, to include a window manager frame or titlebar, use the −frame option.

xwd allows you to capture a single window or the entire root window. But what if you want an image that includes more than one window or parts of multiple windows? You can use *xmag* (described in Chapter 7) to capture an image of multiple windows and then use *xwd* on the *xmag* window! Since *xmag* is intended to magnify, if you want the window image to be the actual size, you must specify that no magnification is performed. To do this, you run *xmag* with the option −mag 1. See Chapter 7, *Graphics Utilities*, and the *xmag* reference page in Part Three of this guide for more information.

To redisplay a file created with *xwd* in a window on the screen, use the *xwud* client, an undumping utility. Specify the dump file to display as an argument to the −in option:

```
% xwud -in file
```

Then remove the image by typing Control-C in the *xterm* from which you started *xwud*.

xpr takes as input an X Window System dump file produced by *xwd* and converts it to a printer-specific format that can be printed on the DEC LN03 or LA100 printer, a PostScript printer such as the Apple LaserWriter, the IBM PP3812 page printer, and as of Release 4, the HP LaserJet (or other PCL printers) or the HP PaintJet. By default, output is formatted for the DEC LN03 printer. Use the −device option to format for another printer. For example, to format a window dump file for a PostScript printer, type:

```
% xpr -device ps file > file.ps
```

Other options allow you to change the size, add headers or footers, and so on. See the *xpr* reference page in Part Three of this guide for details.

You can use *xwd* and *xpr* together, using the standard UNIX pipe mechanism. For example:

```
% xwd | xpr -device ps | lpr
```

The *xdpr* command rolls these three separate commands into one. *xdpr* accepts most of the options accepted by *xwd*, *xpr*, and *lpr*(1). Thus, you could use the command:

```
% xdpr -device ps
```

to take a window dump (xwd), convert that file to PostScript (xpr -device ps), and print the output (lpr). See the *xdpr* reference page in Part Three of this guide for more information.

Note that when you start piping together the output of X clients, you run into some ambiguities. For example, if you pipe the output of *xwd* to *xpr* and for some reason the *xpr* command fails, *xwd* will still be there waiting for pointer input. The original UNIX pipe mechanism doesn't have the concept of data dependent on pointer input! The integration of the UNIX model of computing (in which standard input and output are always recognized) and the window model is not always complete, sometimes leading to unexpected behavior.

As an even more flagrant example, you can create a pipe between two programs, the first of which doesn't produce standard output and the second of which doesn't recognize standard input. The shell doesn't know any better and the programs themselves go on their merry way with pointer and windows.

However, it is nice to know that you can pipe together program output, even when some of those programs may not produce output until you intervene with the pointer.

Even without pipes, you should start thinking about how these programs could work together. For example, the pictures of fonts in Appendix B, *Release 4 Standard Fonts*, were created by these steps:

1. Display a font with *xfd*. (See Chapter 6, *Font Specification*, for instructions on how to use *xfd*.)

2. Resize the window to improve readability, using the *mwm* resize handles or the Resize item of the Window Menu.

3. Create a window dump file with the command `xwd > file`.

4. Create a PostScript file from the dump with the command:

   ```
   xpr -device ps file> file.ps
   ```

5. Print the PostScript file on an Apple LaserWriter with the standard print command *lpr*(1).

Even though the UNIX shell will accept a pipe between *xfd*, *xwd*, and *xpr*, what actually happens is that *xwd* starts up faster than *xfd*, and is ready to dump a window before the *xfd* window appears.

Killing a Client Window with xkill

The *xkill* program allows you to kill a client window or, more specifically, to force the server to end the connection to the client. The process exits and the associated window is removed.

xkill is a fairly drastic method of terminating a client and should *not* be used as the method of choice. In most cases, clients can be terminated in other ways. The possible repercussions of using *xkill* and some of the alternatives are discussed in the next section.

xkill is intended primarily to be used in cases where more conventional methods of removing a client window do not work. It is especially useful when programs have displayed undesired windows on the screen. To remove a stubborn client window, type:

```
% xkill
```

on the command line of an *xterm* window. The pointer changes to a "draped box" pointer and you are instructed to:

```
Select the window whose client you wish to kill with button 1 . . .
```

Move the draped box pointer to the window you want to remove, as shown in Figure 8-15, and click the first pointer button. The window is removed. (*xkill* does not allow you to select the root window.)

Other Clients

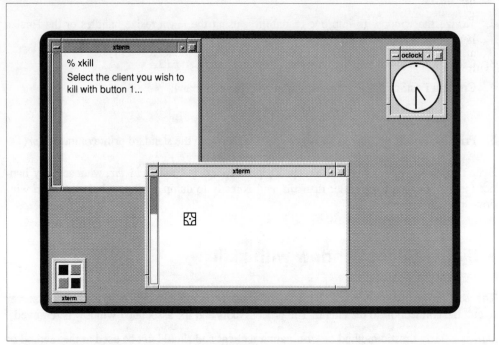

% xkill
Select the client you wish to
kill with button 1...

Figure 8-15. Selecting the window to be removed

You can also specify the window to be killed by its *window ID* (also called the *resource ID*). Every window has an identification number associated with it. The *xwininfo* client can be used to display a window's window/resource ID (see the section "Window and Display Information" later in this chapter).

To remove a window using its ID number, type:

    % **xkill -id** *number*

The window with the ID *number* is removed. Killing a window by its ID number is more cumbersome but it's somewhat safer than choosing the window to be killed with the pointer. It's too easy to click in the wrong place. (Of course, it's less treacherous to use the pointer on an isolated window than a window in a stack.)

Problems with Killing a Client

The most obvious problem with *xkill* is that it's possible to kill the wrong window inadvertently. Perhaps less obvious is a problem inherent in "killing" a program. As a general rule, a command that "kills" a program does not give the program time to save or complete processes that are still running—in effect, to clean up after itself. The processes that can be adversely affected may be visible to the user, such as an editing session, or they may be underlying system processes, such as writing to or reading from a socket.

Most clients can be terminated in ways that allow them to finish all relevant processes and then exit cleanly. These methods should be attempted *before* you use *xkill*, or some other program that kills the client.

For example, you can generally remove an *xterm* window by typing in the window the same command you use to log off the system. You should also be able to remove an *xterm* window with various Main Options menu commands, depending on the signals that can be interpreted by your system. (Some of these signals, such as SIGHUP and SIGTERM, are more gentle to the system. See the *xterm* reference page in Part Three of this guide for a list of menu commands and the signals they send.) An *xcalc* window can generally be removed by typing q, Q, or Control-C in the window. A *bitmap* window has a Quit command button, etc.

A few clients, such as *oclock*, cannot be removed *except* by killing. You must use *xkill* or a similar method to remove an *oclock* window.

Generally, however, you should exhaust the safer alternatives before you use *xkill* and other commands that kill a client.

When you want to remove a window, depending on the client and what commands it recognizes, try these methods (roughly) in this order:

1. Methods that cause the client to exit after finishing relevant processes:

    a. Special commands (e.g., `exit`) or key sequences (e.g., Control-D, Control-C, q, Q) recommended to stop a client.

    b. Certain application-specific menu items (e.g., for *xterm*, the Main Options menu commands Send HUP Signal, Send TERM Signal, and Quit; the *bitmap* Quit button).

2. When these methods don't work or don't apply (as in the case of *oclock*), *then* use commands or menu items that kill the client:

    a. The Send KILL Signal item on the *xterm* Main Options menu, for removing *xterm* windows only. (See Chapter 5, *The xterm Terminal Emulator*.)

    b. The Close item on the *mwm* Window Menu; or a double click on the Window Menu command button. (See Chapter 4, *More about the mwm Window Manager*.)

    c. The UNIX *kill* command with the client's process ID number, which is determined using *ps*. (This method of removing a window is described for *xclock* earlier in this chapter.*)

    d. The *xkill* client.

---

*This method is powerful but in practice has limitations. Many versions of UNIX only allow you to kill a process if you are the owner of the process or if you are root. Thus, if a client has been started on your display from a remote system and you don't know the root password, you may not be in a position to use the UNIX *kill* command.

Window and Display Information Clients

The standard release of X includes four clients that provide information about windows on the display and about the display itself. Much of the information is probably more relevant to a programmer than to the typical user. However, these clients also provide certain pieces of information, such as window geometry, window ID numbers, and the number and nature of screens on the display, that can assist you in using other clients.

Displaying Information about a Window: xwininfo

The *xwininfo* client displays information about a particular window. Some of this information can be useful in determining or setting window geometry (described in Chapter 3). *xwininfo* also provides you with the *window ID* (also called the resource ID). Each window has a unique identification number associated with it. This number can be used as a command line argument with several clients. Most notably, the window ID can be supplied to the *xkill* client to specify the window be killed.

You can also use the window ID as an argument to the *xprop* client, which displays various window properties. As described in Chapter 1, a property is a piece of information associated with a window or a font and stored in the server. Properties facilitate interclient communication; they are used by clients to store information that other clients might need to know. Storing properties in the server makes the information they contain accessible to all clients. See Chapter 1, the *xprop* reference page in Part Three of this guide, and Volume One, *Xlib Programming Manual*, for more information about properties and the *xprop* client.

To display information about a window, type this command in an *xterm* window:

```
% xwininfo
```

The pointer changes to the crosshair pointer and you are directed to select the window about which you want information:

```
xwininfo ==> Please select the window about which you
         ==> would like information by clicking the
         ==> mouse in that window.
```

You can select any window on the display, including the window in which you've typed the command and the root window. (Rather than using the pointer, you can specify a window on the command line by supplying its title, or name if it has no title, as an argument to *xwininfo*'s own -name option. See Chapter 9 for information about setting a client's title and name. See the *xwininfo* reference page in Part Three of this guide for a list of its options.)

Figure 8-16 shows the statistics of *xwininfo* supplies with some typical readings.

```
xwininfo ==> Window id: 0x70000e (xterm)
         ==> Absolute upper-left X: 12
         ==> Absolute upper-left Y: 29
         ==> Relative upper-left X: 0
         ==> Relative upper-left Y: 0
         ==> Width: 818
         ==> Height: 484
         ==> Depth: 8
         ==> Border width: 0
         ==> Window class: InputOutput
         ==> Colormap: 0x8006b (installed)
         ==> Window Bit Gravity State: NorthWestGravity
         ==> Window Window Gravity State: NorthWestGravity
         ==> Window Backing Store State: NotUseful
         ==> Window Save Under State: no
         ==> Window Map State: IsViewable
         ==> Window Override Redirect State: no
         ==> Corners:  +12+29  -322+29  -322-387  +12-387
```

Figure 8-16. Window information displayed by xwininfo

These readings are for a login *xterm* window displayed using a 12-point Roman Courier font. All numerical information is in pixels, except depth, which is in bits per pixel. The *mwm* window manager is also running. The statistics from Figure 8-16 that are most significant for the average user are:

```
xwininfo ==> Window id: 0x70000e (xterm)
         ==> Absolute upper-left X: 12
         ==> Absolute upper-left Y: 29
         ==> Relative upper-left X: 0
         ==> Relative upper-left Y: 0
         ==> Width: 818
         ==> Height: 484
         ==> Depth: 8
         ==> Border width: 0
         ==> Colormap: 0x8006b (installed)
         ==> Corners:  +12+29  -322+29  -322-387  +12-387
```

The first piece of information is the window ID, which can be used as an argument to *xkill*. Specifying the window to be killed by its ID number is somewhat less risky than choosing it with the pointer.

With many window managers, you can use some of the other statistics to gauge the window's geometry (size and position). Generally, the absolute upper-left X and Y correspond to the positive x and y offsets that can be supplied to the -geometry option used to place a client window. (The use of the -geometry option is discussed in Chapter 3.)

The *mwm* frame complicates matters. When *mwm* is running, the absolute upper-left X and Y correspond to the x and y coordinates of the application window—but not the framed window!

Other Clients

Let's take another look at the sample *xwininfo* output. The absolute upper-left X and Y suggest that the window is located at coordinates 12,29. However, the output is actually for an *xterm* located at coordinates 0,0! The 12,29 are the coordinates of the *xterm* window itself; the coordinates represent the distance of the window from 0,0 *including the dimensions of the frame*. The default frame is actually 12 pixels in the x dimension and 29 pixels in the y dimension (because of the titlebar).

If you're using the default configuration of *mwm*, you can determine the positive x and y offsets of a window by subtracting 12 and 29 from the absolute upper-left X and Y provided by *xwininfo*. These figures can be supplied as arguments to the −geometry option on the command line to specify window placement, as described in Chapter 3. (Chapter 3 also describes a somewhat simpler method of gauging x and y offsets.)

The relative upper-left X and Y are not meaningful if you're running *mwm*. Regardless of a window's location, the relative upper-left X and Y are 0 and 0.

The four corners (again, including the frame) are listed with the upper-left corner first and the other three clockwise around the window (i.e., upper-right, lower-right, lower-left). The coordinates of the upper-left corner are, of course, the absolute upper-left X and Y. The width and height in pixels are somewhat less useful, since the geometry option to *xterm* requires that these figures be specified in characters and lines.

The values for window depth and colormap relate to how color is specified. See the discussion of color in Chapter 9 for more information.

The other statistics provided by *xwininfo* are listed below:

```
==> Window class: InputOutput
==> Window Bit Gravity State: NorthWestGravity
==> Window Window Gravity State: NorthWestGravity
==> Window Backing Store State: NotUseful
==> Window Save Under State: no
==> Window Map State: IsViewable
==> Window Override Redirect State: no
```

These statistics have to do with the underlying mechanics of how a window is resized, moved, obscured, unobscured, and otherwise manipulated. They are inherent in the client program and you cannot specify alternatives. For more information on these and other window attributes, see Chapter 4 in Volume One, *Xlib Programming Manual*.

You can also use *xwininfo* with various options to display other window attributes. See the reference page in Part Three of this guide for details.

Listing the Window Tree: xlswins

Windows are arranged in a hierarchy, much like a family tree, with the root window at the top. The *xlswins* client displays the window tree starting with the root window, listing each window by its resource ID and title (or name), if it has one. (See Chapter 9 for a discussion of setting a client's title and name with command line options.)

A resource ID can be supplied to *xkill* to specify the window to kill. You can also supply a resource ID to *xwininfo* to specify the window you want information about, or to *xprop* to get the window's properties. Being able to display the ID numbers of all windows on the screen simultaneously is especially helpful if one or more windows is obscured in the stack. The *xwininfo* client is virtually useless in situations in which one window is hidden behind another. *xlswins* allows you to determine by process of elimination which window is hidden—without having to circulate all the windows on your screen. You can then use *xwininfo* with the ID number (displayed by *xlswins*) to get information about the obscured window.

Figure 8-17 shows the results of *xlswins* for a simple window arrangement: a single *xterm* (login) window on a root window. (The *mwm* window manager is not running.)

```
0x8006e  ()
  0x30000e  (xterm)
    0x300015  ()
      0x300016  ()
```

Figure 8-17. Window tree displayed by xlswins

The *xterm* window is easily identified. Any client that displays an application window, such as *xterm*, *xclock*, *xfd*, *bitmap*, etc., will be listed by name (in parentheses) following the ID number.* The root window is listed above the *xterm* in the window hierarchy. Client (and other) windows displayed on the root window are called *children* of the root window, in keeping with the family tree analogy; thus, the root window is the parent of the *xterm* window. In the *xlswins* listing, a child window is indented once under its parent.

But what are the other windows listed in Figure 8-18? A superficial examination of these other windows provides a brief introduction to the inner workings of X. An underlying feature of X is that menus, boxes, icons, and even *features* of client windows, such as scrollbars, are actually windows in their own right. What's more, these windows (and client window icons) may still exist, even when they are not displayed.

The two remaining windows are unnamed. From the relative indents of the windows, we can tell certain information. The first unnamed window is a child of the *xterm*, the second is a child of the child.

If we again run *xlswins*, this time requesting a long listing (with the −1 option), we get geometry information that helps identify each window. This is shown in Figure 8-18.

```
0:  0x8006e  (); ()()       1152x900+0+0   +0+0
1:    0x30000e  (xterm); (xterm)(XTerm)     818x484+0+0   +0+0
2:      0x300015  (); ()()      818x484+0+0   +1+1
3:        0x300016  (); ()()     14x484+-1+-1   +0+0
```

Figure 8-18. Window tree with geometry specifications

The first number on each line refers to the level of the window in the hierarchy, the root window being at level 0, client windows at 1, etc. Following the *xterm* application window are

---

*Most likely, you will not have to deal with the ID numbers for windows other than the explicitly named client windows. You can use the IDs of the client windows in all of the ways we've discussed: with *xkill*, *xwininfo*, *xprop*, etc.

what are known as the instance and class resource names for the client (in this case, `xterm`, `XTerm`). You use the instance and class resource names to specify default window characteristics, generally by placing them in a file in your home directory. This is described in detail in Chapter 10, *Setting Resources*.

The first geometry string is the complete specification relative to the *parent* window. The second geometry string is the current position relative to the *root* window. Since *mwm* is not running, frames are not an issue. Thus, a window at coordinates 0,0 would have the position +0+0 relative to the root.

The two unnamed windows under *xterm* are the VT102 window and the window's scrollbar, respectively. (The first *xterm* listing is the application shell window, which can be displayed both as a VT102 and a Tektronix window.)

The listing in Figure 8-18 was generated when the *mwm* window manager was not running. If *mwm* is running, the *xlswins* output is considerably more complicated. Many of the features provided by *mwm*, such as the window frame and its command buttons, and the Root Menu and Window Menu, are actually all windows. This *greatly* complicates the window hierarchy. If you run *xlswins* while *mwm* is running, even if the display has only a single application window, the output will be dozens of lines long; you can assume that most of the mysterious windows in the hierarchy are features provided by the window manager.

You may also notice that application windows, such as *xterm*, are now at level 3 in the hierarchy. This is because *mwm reparents* all client windows; that is, the window manager creates another window that is the parent window of the application window and is itself the child of the root window. (The frame is actually a window in its own right; think of the window manager as creating a window that contains the application window.)

The geometry strings for application windows will also be different when *mwm* is running because of this reparenting and because of the presence of the frame. The first geometry string, which gives the position relative to the parent window, will always end with the x,y coordinates +0+0, since the parent is the window manager. The second geometry string, which gives the position relative to the root window, will include the dimensions of the frame. A window located at coordinates 0,0 will have the string +12,+29 because the x and y dimensions of the default frame are 12 and 29 pixels, respectively. See the preceding discussion of *xwininfo* for more information.

For more information on the window hierarchy, see Volume One, *Xlib Programming Manual*.

Listing the Currently Running Clients: xlsclients

You can get a listing of the client applications running on a particular display by using *xlsclients*. Without any options, *xlsclients* displays a two-column list, similar to:

```
colorful   xterm -geometry 80x24+10+10 -ls
colorful   xclock -geometry -0-0
```

The first column shows the name of the display (machine) and the second the client running on it. The client is represented by the command line used to initiate the process.

This sample listing indicates that there is one *xterm* window and one *xclock* window running on the display `colorful`. (The option `-ls` following the *xterm* command reveals that the shell running in this window is a login shell.)

You can use *xlsclients* to create an *.xsession* or *.xinitrc* file, which specifies the clients you want to be run automatically when you log in. In order to do this, you must have set up client windows in an arrangement you like using command line options alone (that is, without having moved or resized windows via the window manager). You can then run *xlsclients* to print a summary of the command lines you used to set up the display and include those command lines in your *.xsession* or *.xinitrc* file. See Appendix A, *System Management*, for information on setting up a user session.

By default, *xlsclients* lists the clients running on the display corresponding to the DISPLAY environment variable, almost always the local display. You can list the clients running on another display by using the `-display` command line option. See Chapter 3, *Working in the X Environment*, for more information about the `-display` option.

With the option `-l` (indicating long), *xlsclients* generates a more detailed listing. Figure 8-19 shows the long version of the listing on the previous page.

```
Window 0x30000e:
  Machine:  colorful
  Name:  xterm
  Icon Name:  xterm
  Command:  xterm -geometry 80x24+10+10 -ls
  Instance/Class:  xterm/XTerm
Window 0x40000b:
  Machine:  colorful
  Name:  xclock
  Icon Name:  xclock
  Command:  xclock -geometry -0-0
  Instance/Class:  xclock/XClock
```

Figure 8-19. Long xlsclients listing

For each client, *xlsclients* displays six items of information: the window ID number, machine name, client name, icon name, command line used to run the client, and the instance and class resource names associated with the client.

As we'll see in Chapter 9, many clients, including *xterm*, allow you to specify an alternate name for a client and a title for the client's window. If you've specified a title, it will appear in the *xlsclients* Name field. If you haven't specified a title but have specified a name for the application, the name will appear in this field. Neither of the clients in the sample display has been given an alternate name or title.

You use the instance and class resource names to specify default window characteristics, generally by placing them in a file in your home directory. This is described in detail in Chapter 10, *Setting Resources*.

Generating Information about the Display: xdpyinfo

The *xdpyinfo* client gives information about the X display, including the name of the display (contents of the DISPLAY variable), version and release of X, number of screens, current screen, and statistics relating to the color, resolution, input, and storage capabilities of each screen. The *xdpyinfo* reference page in Part Three of this guide shows a listing for a display that supports both a color and monochrome screen.

Much of the information provided by *xdpyinfo* has to do with how clients communicate information to one another and is more relevant to a programmer than to the typical user. However, the basic statistics about the name of the display, the version and release of X, and the number and nature of screens might be very helpful to a user, particularly one who is using a display for the first time.

In addition, the detailed information about each screen's color capabilities can also be very valuable in learning how to use color more effectively. This information includes the default number of colormap cells: the number of colors you can use on the display at any one time. See Chapter 9, *Command Line Options*, for more information on the use of color and how to specify colors for many clients.

See Volume One, *Xlib Programming Manual*, for insights into some of the other information provided by *xdpyinfo*.

User-contributed Clients

In addition to the clients in the standard MIT X distribution, there are many user-contributed clients available in the X source tree, distributed over Usenet, and perhaps included with various commercial distributions. If you have access to Usenet, the newsgroup *comp.windows.x* contains voluminous discussions of X programming and the newsgroup *comp.sources.x* contains sources.

Prior to Release 4, *uwm* (the *u*niversal *w*indow *m*anager) was the official window manager shipped with the standard X Window System. As of Release 4, *uwm* is no longer supported but is still available as a user-contributed client. However, be aware that *uwm* does not comply with accepted interclient communication conventions and thus, should probably not be the window manager of choice.

Several other window managers are widely used and have been tailored to reflect the interclient communication conventions proposed in Release 3. Some of the more popular window managers that reflect these conventions are:

awm   Ardent window manager (written by Jordan Hubbard of Ardent Computer Corporation).

rtl   Tiled window manager (written by Ellis Cohen at Siemens Research & Technology Laboratories, RTL).

olwm OPEN LOOK window manager (developed by AT&T).

A version of the OPEN LOOK window manager is available as a user-contributed client.

Commercial products (such as spreadsheets, word processors, and graphics or publishing applications) based on the X Window System are also becoming available.

Previewing Colors for Your Monitor: xcol

Among the more useful user-contributed clients is *xcol*, developed by Helmut Hoenig. Most X applications allow you to specify colors for a window's background, foreground, and border. In addition, the *mwm* window manager allows you to specify the color of the frame it places around all windows on the display. The standard colors recognized by the X server are listed in a file called *rgb.txt* which is generally stored in */usr/lib/X11*. See Chapter 9 for a discussion of the color options accepted by most clients and an overview of X's color capabilities and the standard colors provided.

Colors can look different on different monitors, perhaps much different than a color name suggests. Hypothetically, you could spend a lot of time experimenting with color specifications. The *xcol* client allows you to see how colors appear on your display before you specify the colors for a client. Once you've selected certain colors, *xcol* can also assist you in editing the color specifications in your *.Xresources* file. (See Chapter 3, *Working in the X Environment*, for an introduction to resources, and Chapter 10, *Setting Resources*, for more detailed instructions.)

To run the *xcol* program, simply enter:

```
% xcol&
```

A window titled ColorView will be placed on your screen. The ColorView window displays the outline of a cube containing scattered pixels of the available colors, almost like a universe of colored stars. The position of each of the colored pixels in the cube represents its RGB value (see Chapter 9).

In many cases, a primary shade is associated with several subshades, which are distinguished from the primary shade by a number appended to its name. For example, you can specify the color dark sea green, and also DarkSeaGreen1 through DarkSeaGreen4. Within *xcol*'s ColorView window, colors with the same name but different RGB values (signaling different intensities) are represented by a single pixel.

The pixels are not labeled but you should be able to distinguish basic colors on a good quality color monitor. If you place the pointer on any of the pixels, a small box containing the color name will be displayed. The color name appears in white and the border of the box appears in the color specified. If the pixel represents several associated colors of differing intensities, the box will also contain a spectrum of those colors (though the individual shades are lumped under the primary name). By moving the pointer onto various pixels, you should be able to get an idea of how certain colors look on your display.

Some areas of the window are more cluttered with pixels than others. In these areas, you may not be able to distinguish individual pixels. However, if you move the pointer slowly over these "bunches," the individual color names will be displayed, outlined in the color.

Other Clients

While the pointer is in the ColorView window, you may notice the rest of the display becomes slightly darkened. This darkening happens because *xcol* provides its own colormap, different from the default. It is a normal effect and will stop when you move the pointer out of the window.

In addition to letting you preview colors, *xcol* can also be used to edit color resource specifications. If you want to edit the color specifications in your *Xresources* file, start the client using the command line:

```
% xcol ~/.Xresources &
```

This time two windows will be displayed: the ColorView window and a second window titled TextView, which contains the specifications pertaining to color from the *Xresources* file, as in Figure 8-20.

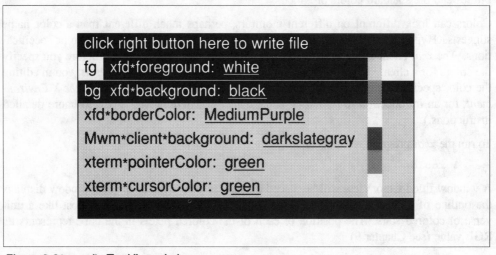

Figure 8-20. *xcol's TextView window*

The size of the TextView window depends on the number of color specifications in the *Xresources* file. Though you can't tell from our black and white illustration, each specification in the TextView window appears in the color it names (the color is the foreground color of the text line). If you click the second pointer button on a specification line, a reverse video effect takes place: the named color becomes the background and the previous background color (gray by default) becomes the foreground (text) color. An "R" appears to the left of the text line, indicating that reverse video is enabled. Although reverse video is not necessary, it sometimes provides a better look at a color than the default display—and also a better look than the boxes surrounding color names in the ColorView window. Reverse video display is a toggle: if you want to return to the default display, click the second pointer button on the text line again.

By using the pointer on both the TextView and ColorView windows, you can change the colors specified in the *Xresources* file. To select the resource to change, place the pointer on the corresponding line in the TextView window and click the first button. The selected line will be outlined in the current foreground color.

Once you've selected a resource, you can change the corresponding color value:

1. Place the pointer on a pixel in the ColorView window; wait until the color name box is displayed.

2. While the pointer rests on the pixel, click the first button.

The color value of the resource in the TextView window is changed to the color you select. The named color is also displayed as either the foreground or background color of the text line—background if reverse video was active. You can change the color any number of times without saving changes to the text file—just to take a look at some colors.

Now let's consider a practical example. Say we want to change the following specification in our sample resource file:

```
Mwm*client*background: darkslategray
```

which makes client window frames dark slate gray. First we select the resource by clicking on it with the first pointer button. Then we move the pointer to the ColorView window and search for an alternative color that would be good for the *mwm* frame. Moving the pointer among the colored pixels in the ColorView window, we settle on medium orchid. While the pointer rests on the medium orchid pixel and the box enclosing the color name is displayed, we click the first pointer button. The resource in the TextView window changes to reflect our choice:

```
Mwm*client*background: mediumorchid
```

and the color in which the line is displayed also changes from dark slate gray to medium orchid.

If the file displayed in the TextView window includes background and foreground specifications for the same resource, those resources are grouped together, and the letters "fg" and "bg" appear to the left of the foreground and background resources, respectively. These associated resources are displayed using the foreground and background color specifications they name. In our sample TextView window, the following resources are grouped:

```
xfd*foreground: white
xfd*background: black
```

These resources set the foreground and background colors for the *xfd* font displayed, described in Chapter 6, to white and black respectively. Thus, in the TextView window these specification lines appear in white with a black background.

To switch the colors specified by a foreground/background pair, place the pointer on either resource line and click the second button. Our sample resources would be changed to:

```
xfd*foreground: black
xfd*background: white
```

and the resources in the TextView window would also switch to black on white.

Keep in mind that you can change only one of the associated resources if you want, by using the method described previously.

Once you've selected colors you like, you can save the changes to the text file by placing the pointer in the horizontal bar at the top of the TextView window right below the frame and clicking the third button. The bar contains the message:

```
click right button here to write file.
```

When you click the third pointer button on this bar, *xcol* beeps and asks you to confirm the choice by displaying:

```
confirm writing with right button!
```

To write the file, click the third button on the bar again. The *Xresources* file is saved and the following message is displayed in the horizontal bar:

```
file written with backup.
```

The previous version of the *Xresources* file is saved as a backup and given the filename *Xresources˜*. To restore the old settings, simply rename the backup file *Xresources*.

To quit the application, place the pointer on either the TextView or ColorView window and type q. Be aware that *xcol* will allow you to quit without saving changes and will not inform you.

Working with Motif Applications

The Athena widget set provides X Toolkit applications with certain common features, many of which have been described in this chapter. As explained in Chapter 1, an application coded using the Motif widget set has a slightly different look and feel.

In the remainder of this chapter, we'll look at some of the features you're liable to encounter in a Motif application and learn how to use them. Some of these features are provided in a slightly different flavor by the Athena widget set; others are unique to Motif.

Most of the sample components we're using are taken from the *mre* demo program introduced in Chapter 1. The Motif resource editor assists you in editing your own resource specification file, but it is primarily intended to demonstrate many of the Motif widgets.

The following sections mention the comparable Athena widgets where appropriate. Some of the Athena widgets are illustrated using the standard MIT clients earlier in this chapter, as well as in Chapter 5, *The xterm Terminal Emulator*, and Chapter 7, *Graphics Utilities*.

Dialog Boxes and Push Buttons

If you've tried to restart *mwm* from the window manager's Root Menu, you've already encountered a Motif dialog box. When you select the Restart menu item, the dialog box pictured in Figure 8-21 is displayed.

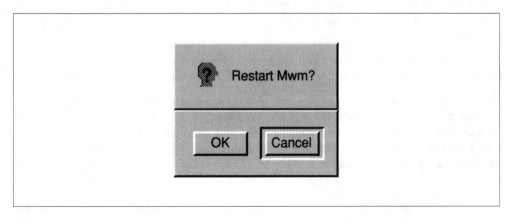

Figure 8-21. Typical Motif dialog box with two push buttons

A dialog box generally displays a message relevant to the application and requires a response from the user. In this case, the dialog box queries whether you really want to Restart mwm?.

A Motif dialog box contains one or more *push buttons* that allow you to respond to the message. (Many applications use push buttons; they are not confined to dialog boxes.) When a dialog is displayed and the default click-to-type focus is in effect, the input focus is usually switched to the dialog window. Until you respond to the dialog box, the application cannot continue. Once you respond to the dialog, the focus should switch back to the main application window.

Whether the dialog box contains one push button or multiple buttons, one button is always highlighted, generally by outlining. You can push the highlighted push button simply by pressing the Return key on your keyboard. To push another button, you must place the pointer on it and click the first pointer button.

A response might be a simple acknowledgment that you've seen the message: some dialogs feature only one button that reads OK. For instance, when you start the *mre* resource editor demo without a filename argument, the program looks for a file called *Xdefaults* in your home directory. If *mre* cannot find the file, it displays a dialog box containing a message similar to:

```
Couldn't open /home/pat/.Xdefaults.
```

with an OK button. When a dialog has only one button, the button is always highlighted. Pressing Return or clicking the first pointer button on the OK button informs the client that you've seen the message and removes the dialog window.

Some responses request an action, such as proceeding with a previously invoked process, cancelling the process, or even exiting the program. The dialog box in Figure 8-21 contains two push buttons labeled OK and Cancel. Pushing the OK button tells *mwm* to proceed with the restart process. The Cancel button gives you a chance to avert the restart process in case you invoked the command by mistake or have changed your mind. Since Cancel is highlighted, you can push it either by pressing Return or by using the pointer.

Whatever the message or potential responses, you react to a dialog box either by pressing Return (to push the highlighted push button) or by placing the pointer on one of the push buttons and clicking the first pointer button. Action will be taken if requested and the dialog box will be removed.

As we'll see, some Motif applications support another kind of push button called a *drawn button*. A drawn button is basically a push button decorated with a bitmap rather than text.

The Athena widget set provides comparable widgets to the Motif dialog box and push button. An Athena dialog box provides virtually the same functionality as a Motif dialog. The most obvious difference is that, in an Athena dialog, you must click on a command button to invoke it. The Return key shortcut only works with a Motif push button. See "Dialog Boxes and Command Buttons" in Chapter 7, *Graphics Utilities*, for more information about Athena dialogs.

Menu Bars and Pull-down Menus

Figure 8-22 illustrates the *menu bar* on the *mre* window.

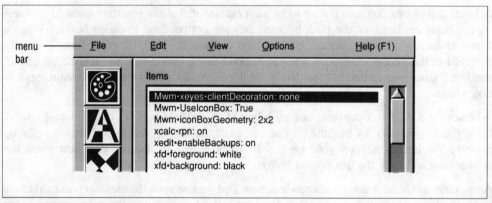

Figure 8-22. mre menu bar

A menu bar is a horizontal bar from which pull-down menus can be displayed. Each word on the bar is a menu title; you display the menu by placing the pointer on its title and clicking the first pointer button. The title becomes raised and highlighted by a box, the menu is displayed and the first selectable item is also raised and boxed. Figure 8-23 shows *mre*'s File pull-down menu.

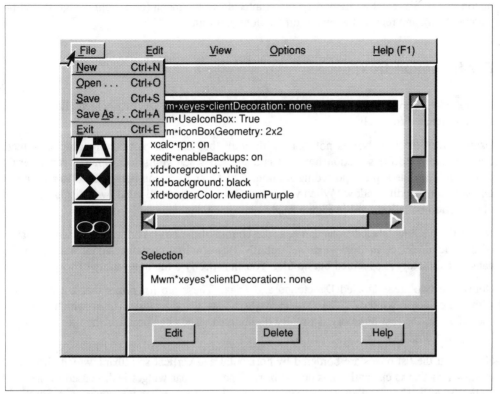

Figure 8-23. mre File menu

Notice that one letter of each menu item is underlined. As explained in Chapter 4, that letter represents a unique abbreviation, or mnemonic, for the menu item, which can be used to select the item.

Notice also that each menu item has a keyboard shortcut, or *accelerator*, that appears in the right hand column of the menu. An accelerator can be used to invoke the action without displaying the menu at all (though they also work while the menu is displayed).

When you've displayed a menu by placing the pointer on the title and clicking the first button, you can select an item by:

- Placing the pointer on the item and clicking the first button.

- typing the mnemonic abbreviation for the menu item.

- Typing the accelerator key combination. (Though these are intended to save you the trouble of displaying the menu, they also work when it is displayed.)

- To select the boxed item (the first available for selection), you can alternatively press either the Return key or the space bar.

You can also display a menu from a menu bar by placing the pointer on the title and pressing the first pointer button. The menu is displayed as long as you continue to hold the pointer button down. To select an item, drag the pointer down the menu (each item is highlighted by a box in turn), and release the button on the item you want.

File Selection Box

Several Motif applications feature something called a *file selection box*, which allows you to select a filename from a list.

Using a file selection box is not exactly difficult, but it's not particularly obvious either. Let's consider the file selection box that is displayed when you select Open... from *mre*'s File menu illustrated in the preceding section. The Open... menu item is used to read a file into *mre*'s main edit window. When you select Open..., a second window is displayed—the file selection box illustrated in Figure 8-24.

Notice the window labeled Selection near the bottom of the box. You want to place the name of the file to select in this window. Initially this window contains an incomplete pathname—a directory is specified but no file. You can specify a file in a variety of ways.

Notice the two areas labeled Directories and Files. These are *list boxes* that are contained within the larger window. The Directories box lists the directories from which you can choose a file; the first directory is usually highlighted. The Files box lists the files within the highlighted directory.

Notice that the list boxes are bordered by horizontal and vertical scrollbars, which allow you to view text that is currently outside the box. (The Scrollbar widget is discussed in the next section.) A list box and its accompanying scrollbars form what is known as a Scrolled-Window. The Motif ScrolledWindow is comparable to the Athena Viewport widget, discussed in the section "Browsing Reference Pages: xman" earlier in this chapter.

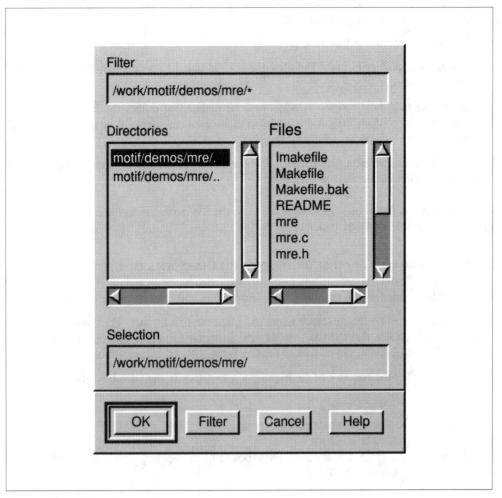

Figure 8-24. A file selection box

The file selection box allows you to select a file from any directory on the system, using various procedures. You can select a file from the list currently in the Files box; you can list the files in another directory currently displayed in the the Directories box and select one of those files; or you can list the contents of an entirely different directory and select a file from that directory.

Selecting a File from the Files Box

To select a file currently in the Files box:

1. Place the pointer on the filename.

2. Click the first pointer button. The filename is highlighted by a dark bar; the letters appear in reverse video.

   Notice also that the Selection window will be updated to reflect the filename; and the push button to confirm the selection (OK in many applications) will be highlighted, indicating that you can select the file by pressing Return.

3. Select the filename either by pressing Return or by placing the pointer on the OK push button and clicking the first pointer button.

When you select a file in *mre*'s file selection box, the file is read in to the initial *mre* editing window and the selection box disappears.

Choosing a File from another Directory in the Directories Box

To list the files in another directory in the Directories box and select one of those files:

1. Place the pointer on the directory name and click the first button. The directory name is highlighted. Notice that the box labeled Filter is updated to reflect the new pathname and the Filter push button at the bottom of the box is highlighted for selection.

2. Then, to display the contents of the highlighted directory in the Files box either:

   • Press Return; or

   • Click on the Filter push button.

3. To select a file from the updated Files box, follow the steps outlined previously in "Selecting a File from the Files Box."

Choosing a File from Another Directory on the System

You can specify an alternative directory from which a file can be selected by changing the filter, that is, the path in the Filter window (near the top of the file selection box). Initially the Filter window reflects the current working directory. In Figure 8-24, the filter is */work/motif/demos/mre/** and the Directories box lists two directories:

```
/work/motif/demos/mre/.          \"the current directory
/work/motif/demos/mre/..         \"previous directory in the tree
```

To specify another filter, place the pointer within the Filter window and double click the first pointer button. The window becomes highlighted with a black bar (the text is visible in reverse video); now whatever you type will replace the current text.

When you type a pathname and hit Return (or click on the Filter push button at the bottom of the file selection box), the Directories box will be updated to reflect the filter you've specified. For example, if you enter the following pathname in the Filter window:

```
/home/pat/*
```

and hit Return or click on the Filter push button, the Directories box will be updated to reflect the directory */home/pat*, its subdirectories, and the directory above it in the tree, as shown in Figure 8-25.

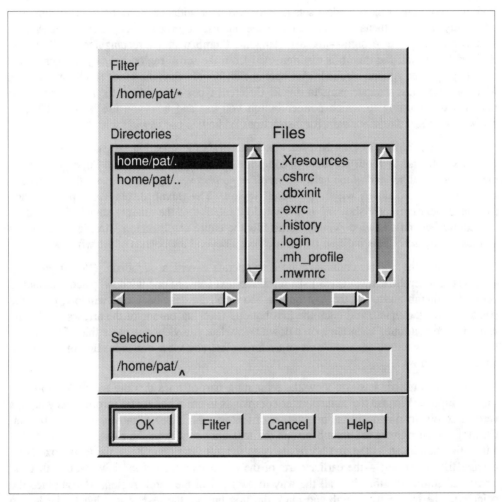

Figure 8-25. Directories and Files boxes updated by changing filter

Notice that the first directory in the Directories box, */home/pat/.*, is highlighted and the files in that directory are listed in the Files box.

You can then choose any of the files in the Files box using the steps outlined previously in "Selecting a File from the Files Box."

The Motif Scrollbar

Each of the list boxes in the File Selection Box features both a horizontal and a vertical scrollbar. A vertical scrollbar is commonly used review text that has scrolled off the top of a window or extends past the bottom. In the case of *mre*'s Files box, the vertical scrollbar is used to scan a list of files too long to fit in the window at one time. A horizontal scrollbar is commonly used to view text or graphics that are too wide to fit in the viewing area. You'll probably encounter vertical scrollbars most often.

Both the Motif and Athena widget sets provide scrollbar widgets. A Motif scrollbar operates differently than an Athena scrollbar, such as the one used by *xterm*. As you know, an Athena scrollbar is simple in design—just a rectangular thumb within a rectangular scroll region. Both parts are flat; the thumb is distinguished from the scroll region only by its (generally) darker color. The Athena scrollbar also operates differently than the Motif scrollbar. While a Motif scrollbar has separate parts to invoke different types of scrolling, the Athena scrollbar moves text according to which pointer button you use and how you use it. (See Chapter 5, *The xterm Terminal Emulator*, for instructions on how to use *xterm*'s scrollbar.)

Now let's take another look at the Files box from *mre*'s file selection box, which is bordered by two scrollbars. A Motif scrollbar is comprised of four parts, labeled in Figure 8-24: two *arrows* (one at either end of the bar), the *scroll region* between the arrows, and the *thumb*, the raised area which moves within the scroll region. The thumb displays the position and amount of text currently showing in the window relative to the amount saved. If text does not extend beyond the window, the thumb fills the entire scroll region. In Figure 8-24, the thumbs in both scrollbars indicate that text extends beyond the bounds of the window.

Let's consider the pointer commands used to operate a vertical scrollbar. (You'll probably use a vertical scrollbar most often.) To scroll the text forward one window, place the pointer below the thumb and click the first button. To scroll the text back one window, place the pointer above the thumb and click the first button. Clicking on one of the arrows scrolls the text one line at a time: each click on a down arrow lets you view one more line of text at the bottom of the window; each click on an up arrow lets you view one more line of text at the top of the window.

A horizontal scrollbar lets you view the remaining part of lines that are too wide to fit in a single window. You use the same pointer commands to use a horizontal scrollbar as you do a vertical scrollbar; obviously the orientation of text and directions of movement are different. Clicking to the right of the thumb scrolls the text horizontally to the right. Clicking to the left of the thumb scrolls the text horizontally to the left. In Figure 8-24, the Files box is displaying filenames only—the earlier parts of the pathnames are not in view. Notice that the horizontal scrollbar's thumb is all the way to the right of the scroll region. If you place the pointer to the left of the thumb and click the first button, the text is scrolled to the left to reveal the earlier parts of the pathname. Clicking on either arrow of the horizontal scrollbar moves the text one character to the left or right, depending on the direction of the arrow.

The unit scrolled when you click on an arrow depends on the application. Scrollbars are also sometimes featured on application windows that contain graphic elements rather than text. Obviously, such a window cannot be scrolled by text characters or lines. The *mwm* icon box, described in Chapter 11, *Customizing mwm*, can be scrolled the height or width of one icon.

Drawn Buttons

A *drawn button* is a push button decorated with a pixmap rather than a text label. Figure 8-26 shows four drawn buttons from *mre*'s main window.

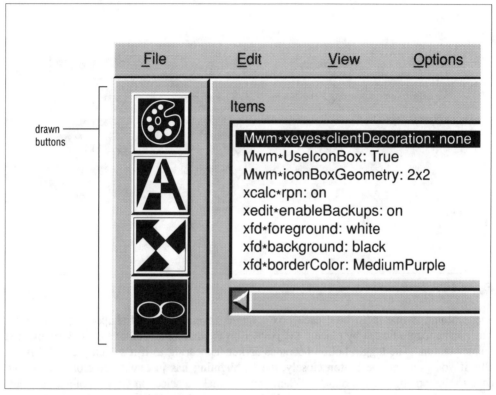

Figure 8-26. Four drawn buttons

The image on a drawn button should signal its function. If a program uses drawn buttons effectively, they can enhance an application's aesthetics.

mre uses drawn buttons well. The button decorated with an artist's palette tells *mre* to place resource specifications relating to color in the application's editing window. The button showing the letter "A" places resources specifying fonts in the editing window. The button featuring the mirror image of the arrows in reverse colors is a rather clever graphical representation of a difficult concept. The image is a sort of technical yin-yang symbol: it tells *mre* to place resources that can be toggled (turned on or off; set to be true or false, yes or no, etc.) in the editing window. Finally, the button featuring the eternity symbol tells *mre* to put all of the resources in the user's resource file in the editing window.

Radio Boxes and Toggle Buttons

A *radio box* is made up of a column of toggles (mutually exclusive choices). Figure 8-27 shows four radio boxes in *mre*'s Font Selection window.

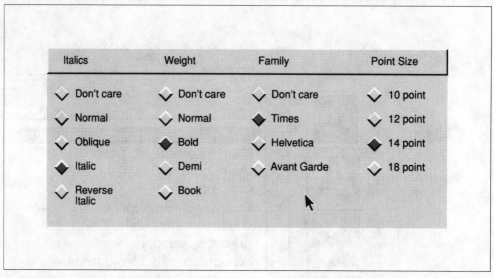

Figure 8-27. Four radio boxes

Each column is one radio box; each box contains several diamond shaped *toggle buttons*. You push a toggle button by placing the pointer on the diamond symbol and clicking the first pointer button. The toggle button becomes darker (appearing as if it's been pressed). Actually, if you examine the button closely, the highlighting has just switched from the bottom edge to the top edge of the button. When you first make a selection from a column, the button and the accompanying text label are highlighted by a box. When you make a selection in another column, the highlighting box appears in that column (and disappears from the previous one).

Toggles in the same column are mutually exclusive. If you select one and then select another from the same column, the first one is toggled off. (The button appears to pop up—i.e., the highlighting switches back to the bottom edge of the button; also the highlighting box appears around the latest selection.)

Part Two:

Customizing X

X has been designed to put the user in the driver's seat. Everything from the colors and sizes of windows to the contents of mwm *menus can be customized by the user. This part of the book tells you how to reshape X to your liking.*

9

Command Line Options

This chapter describes command line options that are common to most clients. Some arguments to command line options can also be specified as the values of resource variables, described in Chapter 10, Setting Resources. For example, the format of a geometry string or a color specification is the same whether it is specified as an argument to an option or as the value of a resource definition.

In This Chapter:

9
Command Line Options

As explained in Chapter 3, *Working in the X Environment*, X allows the user to specify numerous (very numerous!) command line options when starting most clients. The command line options for each client are detailed on the reference pages in Part Three of this guide.

As a general rule, all options can be shortened to the shortest unique abbreviation. For example, `-display` can be shortened to `-d` if there is no other option beginning with "d." (Note that while this is true for all the standard MIT clients, it may not be true of any random client taken off the net.)

In addition to certain client-specific options, all applications built with the X Toolkit (or a toolkit based on the Xt Intrinsics, such as the Motif Toolkit) accept certain standard options, which are listed in Table 9-1. (Some non-Toolkit applications may also recognize these options.) The first column contains the name of the option, the second the name of the resource to which it corresponds (see Chapter 10, *Setting Resources*), and the third a brief description of what the option does.

This chapter discusses some of the more commonly used Toolkit options and demonstrates how to use them. (For the syntax of the other Toolkit options, see the *X* reference page in Part Three of this guide.)

The options `-selectionTimeout` and `-xnllanguage` are available as of Release 4.

Table 9-1. Standard Options

Option	Resource	Description
`-bg`	`background`	Background color of window.
`-background`	`background`	Background color of window.
`-bd`	`borderColor`	Color of window border.
`-bordercolor`	`borderColor`	Color of window border.
`-bw`	`borderWidth`	Border width of window in pixels.
`-borderwidth`	`borderWidth`	Border width of window in pixels.
`-display`	`display`	Display on which client can run.
`-fn`	`font`	Font for text display.
`-font`	`font`	Font for text display.

Table 9-1. Standard Options (continued)

Option	Resource	Description
-fg	foreground	Foreground (drawing or text) color of window.
-foreground	foreground	Foreground (drawing or text) color of window.
-geometry	geometry	Geometry string for window size and placement.
-iconic		Start the application in iconified form.
-name	name	Specify a name for the application being run.
-rv	reverseVideo	Reverse foreground and background colors.
-reverse	reverseVideo	Reverse foreground and background colors.
+rv	reverseVideo	Don't reverse foreground and background.
-selectionTimeout	selectionTimeout	Timeout in milliseconds within which two communicating applications must respond to one another for a selection request.
-synchronous	synchronous	Enable synchronous debug mode.
+synchronous	synchronous	Disable synchronous debug mode.
-title	title	Specify a window title (e.g., to be displayed in a titlebar).
-xnllanguage	xnlLanguage	The language, territory, and codeset for National Language Support; this information helps resolve resource and other filenames.
-xrm	value of next arg	Next argument is a quoted string containing a resource manager specification, as described in Chapter 10, *Setting Resources*.

Though all Toolkit options are preceded by a minus sign, client-specific options may or may not require it. See the reference page for each client in Part Three of this guide for the syntax of all options.

Perhaps the most useful of the Toolkit options are -display and -geometry, which allow you to specify the display on which a client window should appear, and the size and position of that window, respectively. See Chapter 3, *Working in the X Environment*, for detailed instructions on using these options. In the remainder of this chapter we'll discuss some of the other useful Toolkit options.

Window Title and Application Name

The name of the program (as known to the server) and the title of the window can be specified on the command line. The -title option allows you to specify a text string as the title of the application's window. If your application has a titlebar or if the window manager you are using puts titlebars on windows, this string will appear in the titlebar. Window titles can be useful in distinguishing multiple instances of the same application.

The -name option actually changes the name by which the server identifies the program. Changing the name of the application itself (with the -name option) affects the way the application interprets resource files. This option is discussed further in Chapter 10, *Setting Resources*. If a name string is defined for an application, that string will appear as the application name in its icon.

If you display information about currently running windows using the *xwininfo* or *xlswins* client, title strings will appear in parentheses after the associated window ID numbers. (If there is no title string but there is a name string, the name string will be displayed.)

You can also use the *xwininfo* client to request information about a particular window by title, or name, if no title string is defined, using that application's own -name option. See the *xlswins* and *xwininfo* reference pages in Part Three of this guide and the section "Window and Display Information Clients" in Chapter 8, *Other Clients*, to learn more about these clients.

Starting a Client Window as an Icon

The -iconic command line option starts the client window in iconified form. To start an *xterm* window as an icon, type:

```
% xterm -iconic &
```

This can be especially useful for starting the login *xterm* window. As described in Chapter 3, *Working in the X Environment*, terminating the login *xterm* window kills the X server and all other clients that are running. It's always possible to terminate a window inadvertently by selecting the wrong menu option or typing the wrong key sequence. If your login *xterm* window is automatically iconified at startup, you are far less likely to terminate the window inadvertently and end your X session.

For most clients, the size and position of the icon can be set using resource variables in an *Xdefaults* or other resource file. (Setting the icon geometry in a resource file is highly recommended if you are starting the login *xterm* window as an icon.) See the appropriate client reference pages in Part Three of this guide for a complete list of available resources. Refer to Chapter 10, *Setting Resources*, for instructions on how to set resources.

Specifying Fonts on the Command Line

Many clients allow you to specify the font to be used when displaying text in the window. (These are known as *screen fonts* and are not to be confused with *printer fonts*.) For clients written with the X Toolkit, the option to set the display font is −fn. For example, the command line:

```
% xterm -fn fontname &
```

creates an *xterm* window in which text will be displayed with the font named *fontname*.

Chapter 6, *Font Specification*, describes the available screen fonts and font naming conventions.

Reverse Video

There are three options to control whether the application will display in reverse video—that is, with the foreground and background colors reversed. The −rv or −reverse option is used to request reverse video.

The +rv option is used to override any reverse video request that might be specified in a resource file. (See Chapter 10, *Setting Resources*.) This is important, because not all clients handle reverse video correctly, and even those that do usually do so only on black and white displays.

Specifying Color

Many clients have options that allow you to specify the color of the window background, foreground (the color in which text or graphic elements will be displayed), and border. These options generally have the form:

−bg *color*   Sets the background color.

−fg *color*   Sets the foreground color.

−bd *color*   Sets the border color.

By default, the background of an application window is usually white and the foreground black, even on color workstations. You can specify a new color using either the color names listed in a system file called *rgb.txt* or hexadecimal values representing colors.

Many clients accept a −bd option that is intended to specify the color of the window border. However, if you're using the *mwm* window manager, this customization is generally useless: the *mwm* frame effectively replaces most window borders. As an alternative, you can change the color of the frame by specifying resources for *mwm* in a *Xresources* or *Xdefaults* file in your home directory. For more information, see Chapter 10, *Setting Resources*, and the *mwm* reference page in Part Three of this guide.

In the next section, we'll take a look at some of the color names you can use. For now, let's consider the syntax of a command line specifying an *xterm* to be displayed in three colors:

```
% xterm -bg lightblue -fg darkslategrey -bd plum &
```

This command creates an *xterm* window with a background of light blue, foreground of dark slate gray, and window border of plum (all colors are available in both Releases 3 and 4).

At the command line, a color name should be typed as a single word (for example, `dark-slategray`). However, you can type the words that make up a color name separately if you enclose them in quotes, as in the command line:

```
% xterm -bg "light blue" -fg "dark slate grey" -bd plum &
```

As we'll see, the *rgb.txt* file contains variants of the same color name (for example, "navy blue" and "NavyBlue," or "grey" and "gray") to allow a range of spelling, spacing, and capitalization on the command line.

Some clients allow additional options to specify color for other elements, such as the cursor, highlighting, and so on. See the appropriate client reference pages in Part Three of this guide for details.

The rgb.txt File

The *rgb.txt* file, usually located in */usr/lib/X11*, is supplied with the standard distribution of X and consists of predefined colors assigned to specific text names.

A corresponding compiled file called *rgb.dir* contains the definitions used by the server; this machine-readable file serves as a color name database and is discussed more fully in Appendix A, *System Management.* The *rgb.txt* file is the human-readable equivalent.

Release 4 Color Names

The default *rgb.txt* file shipped with Release 4 of X contains 738 color name definitions. This number is slightly deceptive, since a number of the color names are merely variants of another color name (differing only in spelling, spacing, and capitalization).

Still, the number of colors available in Release 4 is more than double the number available in Release 3. Some of the Release 4 colors are entirely new (such as snow and misty rose) but many are just slightly different shades of colors available in prior releases.

For example, the Release 3 *rgb.txt* file includes the color sea green. The Release 4 *rgb.txt* file offers several shades of that color:

```
light sea green
sea green
medium sea green
dark sea green
SeaGreen1
SeaGreen2
SeaGreen3
```

```
SeaGreen4
DarkSeaGreen1
DarkSeaGreen2
DarkSeaGreen3
DarkSeaGreen4
```

Each of these names corresponds to a color definition. (This list does not include the variants SeaGreen, LightSeaGreen, MediumSeaGreen, and DarkSeaGreen, which also appear in the file.) As you can see, some of these shades are distinguished in the fairly traditional way of being called "light," "medium," and "dark." The light, medium, and dark shades of a color can probably be distinguished from one another on virtually any monitor.

Beyond this distinction, there are what might be termed "sub-shades": gradations of a particular shade identified by number (SeaGreen1, SeaGreen2, etc.). Numerically adjacent sub-shades of a color may not be clearly distinguishable on all monitors. For example, Sea-Green1 and 2 may look very much the same. (You certainly would not choose to create a window with a SeaGreen1 background and SeaGreen2 foreground! On the other hand, sub-shades a couple of numbers apart are probably sufficiently different to be used on the same window.)

By supplying many different shades of a single, already fairly precise color like sea green, X developers have tried to provide definitions that work well on a variety of commonly used monitors.* You may have to experiment to determine which colors (or shades) display best on your monitor.

The color names in the Release 4 *rgb.txt* file are too numerous to list here. Although there are no literal dividers within the file, it can roughly be considered to fall into three sections:

Section 1:   A standard spectrum of colors, many available in or similar to colors in Release 3 (such as sea green). These colors seem to be ordered roughly as: off-whites and other pale colors, greys, blues, greens, yellows, browns, oranges, pinks, reds, and purples.

Section 2:   Sub-shades of Section 1 colors (such as SeaGreen 1 through 4). These sub-shades make up the largest part of the file.

Section 3:   One hundred and one additional shades of grey, numbered 0 through 100 (also available in Release 3). This large number of precisely graduated grays provides a wide variety of shading for monochrome screens.

Rather than list every color in the *rgb.txt* file, we've compiled this table of representative colors. We've chosen some of the more esoteric color names. Naturally all of the primary and secondary colors are also available.

Section 1:

ghost white	peach puff	lavender blush	lemon chiffon
slate grey	midnight blue	cornflower blue	medium slate blue
dodger blue	powder blue	turquoise	pale green
lawn green	chartreuse	olive drab	lime green

---

*The color database shipped with prior releases of X was originally designed to display optimally on the vt240 series terminals manufactured by Digital Equipment Corporation.

khaki	light yellow	goldenrod	indian red
sienna	sandy brown	salmon	coral
tomato	hot pink	maroon	violet red
magenta	medium orchid	blue violet	purple

Section 2:

snow1 - 4	bisque1 - 4	cornsilk1 - 4	honeydew1 -4
azure1 - 4	SteelBlue1 - 4	DeepSkyBlue1 - 4	LightCyan1 - 4
PaleTurquoise1 - 4	aquamarine1 - 4	PaleGreen1 - 4	DarkOliveGreen1 - 4
SpringGreen1 -4	gold1 - 4	RosyBrown1 - 4	burlywood1 - 4
chocolate1 - 4	firebrick1 - 4	DarkOrange1 - 4	OrangeRed1 - 4
DeepPink1 - 4	PaleVioletRed1 - 4	plum1 - 4	DarkOrchid1 - 4

Section 3:

```
grey0 (gray0) through grey100 (gray100)
```

If you want to look more closely at the *rgb.txt* file, you can open it with any text editor. As an alternative, you can display the contents of the file using the *showrgb* client. *showrgb* seems to do nothing more than *cat*(1) the file to your terminal window. Given the size of the file, it's necessary to pipe the command's output to a paging program, such as *pg*(1) or *more*(1).

```
% showrgb | more
```

See Appendix A, *System Management*, for information on customizing color name definitions.

Keep in mind that colors look different on different monitors. The *xcol* client, from the user-contributed distribution, allows you to display the colors defined in the *rgb.txt* file. *xcol* can also be used to edit the color specifications in a resource file. See Chapter 8, *Other Clients*, and the *xcol* client reference page in Part Three of this guide.

Alternative Release 4 Color Databases

In addition to the standard color database described previously, Release 4 also includes three other databases your system administrator can compile. These files can be found in the general release in the directory *./rgb/others*.

raveling.txt   Designed by Paul Raveling, this database rivals the default database in size and scope but was tuned to display optimally on Hewlett-Packard monitors.

thomas.txt   Based on the Release 3 database, this file has been modified by John Thomas of Tektronix to approximate the colors in a box of Crayola Crayons.

old-rgb.txt   This is nothing more than the Release 3 database.

Hexadecimal Color Specification

You can specify colors more exactly than is possible with the names in the *rgb.txt* file by using a hexadecimal color string. You probably won't use this method unless you require a color not available by using a color name. In order to understand how this works, you may need a little background on how color is implemented on most workstations.

The RGB Color Model

Most color displays on the market today are based on the RGB color model. Each pixel on the screen is actually made up of three phosphors: one red, one green, and one blue. Each of these three phosphors is excited by a separate electron beam. When all three phosphors are fully illuminated, the pixel appears white to the human eye. When all three are dark, the pixel appears black. When the illumination of each primary color varies, the three phosphors generate a subtractive color. For example, equal portions of red and green, with no admixture of blue, makes yellow.

As you might guess, the intensity of each primary color is controlled by a three-part digital value—and it is the exact makeup of this value that the hexadecimal specification allows you to set.

Depending on the underlying hardware, different servers may use a larger or smaller number of bits (from 4 to 16) to describe the intensity of each primary. To insulate you from this variation, most clients are designed to take color values containing anywhere from 4 to 16 bits (1 to 4 hex digits), and the server then scales them to the hardware. As a result, you can specify hexadecimal values in any one of these formats:

```
#RGB
#RRGGBB
#RRRGGGBBB
#RRRRGGGGBBBB
```

where R, G, and B represent single hexadecimal digits and determine the intensity of the red, green, and blue primaries that make up each color.

When fewer than four digits are used, they represent the most significant bits of the value. For example, #3a6 is the same as #3000a0006000.*

What this means concretely is perhaps best illustrated by looking at the values that correspond to some colors in the color name database. We'll use 8-bit values—two hexadecimal digits for each primary. These definitions are the hexadecimal equivalents of the decimal values for some of the colors found in the *rgb.txt* file:

```
#000000      black
#FFFFFF      white
#FF0000      red
#00FF00      green
#0000FF      blue
```

---

*If you are unfamiliar with hexadecimal numbering, see the Glossary for a brief explanation, or a basic computer textbook for a more extended discussion.

```
#FFFF00        yellow
#00FFFF        cyan
#FF00FF        magenta
#5F9EA0        cadet blue
#6495ED        cornflower blue
#ADD8E6        light blue
#B0C4DE        light steel blue
#0000CD        medium blue
#000080        navy blue
#87CEED        sky blue
#6A5ACE        slate blue
#4682B4        steel blue
```

As you can see from the colors previously given, pure red, green, and blue result from the corresponding bits being turned on fully. All primaries off yields black, while all nearly full on gives white. Yellow, cyan, and magenta can be created by pairing two of the other primaries at full intensity. The various shades of blue shown previously are created by varying the intensity of each primary—sometimes in unexpected ways.

The bottom line here is that if you don't intimately know the physics of color, the best you can do is look up existing colors from the color name database and experiment with them by varying one or more of the primaries till you find a color you like. Unless you need precise colors, you are probably better off using color names.

How Many Colors are Available?

The number of distinct colors available on the screen at any one time depends on the amount of memory available for color specification. (The *xdpyinfo* client provides information about a display, including the number of colors available at one time. See Chapter 8, *Other Clients*, and the *xdpyinfo* reference page in Part Three of this guide for details.)

A color display uses multiple bits per pixel (also referred to as multiple planes or the *depth* of the display) to select colors. Programs that draw in color use the value of these bits as a pointer to a lookup table called a *colormap*, in which each entry (or *colorcell*) contains the RGB values for a particular color.* As shown in Figure 9-1, any given pixel value is used as an index into this table—for example, a pixel value of 16 will select the 16th colorcell.

Why is this technical detail important? Because it explains several issues that you might encounter in working with color displays.

First, the range of colors possible on the display is a function of the number of bits available in the colormap for RGB specification. If 8 bits are available for each primary, then the range of possible colors is 256^3 (more than 16 million colors). This means that you can create incredibly precise differences between colors.

---

*There is a type of high-end display in which pixel values are used directly to control the illumination of the red, green, and blue phosphors. But far more commonly the bits per pixel are used indirectly with the actual color values specified independently.

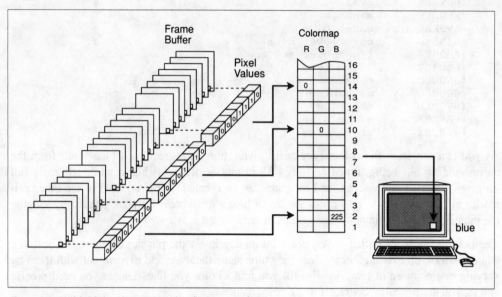

Figure 9-1. Multiple planes used to index a colormap

However, the number of different colors that can be displayed on the screen at any one time is a function of the number of planes. A four-plane system can index 2^4 colorcells (16 distinct colors); an 8-plane system can index 2^8 colorcells (256 distinct colors); and a 24-plane system can index 2^{24} colorcells (more than 16 million distinct colors).

If you are using a 4-plane workstation, the fact that you can precisely define hundreds of different shades of blue is far less significant than the fact that you can't use them all at the same time. There isn't space for all of them to be stored in the colormap at one time or any mechanism for them to be selected even if they could be stored.

This limitation is made more significant by the fact that X is a multi-client environment. When X starts up, usually no colors are loaded into the colormap. As clients are invoked, certain of these cells are allocated. But when all of the free colorcells are used up, it is no longer possible to request new colors. When this happens, you will usually be given the closest possible color from those already allocated. However, you may instead be given an error message and told that there are no free colorcells.

In order to minimize the chance of running out of colorcells, many programs use *shared* colorcells. Shared colorcells can be used by any number of applications but they can't be changed by any of them. They can only be deallocated by each application that uses them, and when all applications have deallocated the cell, it is available for setting one again. Shared cells are most often used for background, border, and cursor colors.

Alternately, some clients have to be able to change the color of graphics they have already drawn. This requires another kind of cell, called *private*, which can't be shared. A typical use of a private cell would be for the palette of a color-mixing application. Such a program might have three bars of each primary color and a box that shows the mixed color. The primary bars would use shared cells, while the mixed color box would use a private cell.

In summary, some programs define colorcells to be read-only and sharable, while others define colorcells to be read/write and private.

To top it off, there are even clients that may temporarily swap in a private colormap of their own. If this happens, all other applications will be displayed in unexpected colors because of the way color is implemented.

In order to minimize such conflicts, you should request precise colors only when necessary. By preference, use color names or hexadecimal specifications that you specified for other applications.

Border Width

Many clients accept a −bw option that is intended to specify the width of the window border in pixels. However, as in the case of the −bd (border color) option, if you're using the *mwm* window manager, this customization is generally useless because the *mwm* frame effectively replaces most window borders.

As an alternative, you *can* change the width of the frame by specifying resources for *mwm* in a *Xresources* or *Xdefaults* file in your home directory. For more information, see Chapter 10, *Setting Resources*, and the `frameBorderWidth` and `resizeBorderWidth` resources on the *mwm* reference page in Part Three of this guide.

10

Setting Resources

This chapter describes how to set resource variables that determine application features such as color, geometry, fonts, and so on. It describes the syntax of resource definition files such as .Xresources, as well as the operation of xrdb, a client that can be used to change resource definitions dynamically and make resources available to clients running on other machines.

In This Chapter:

10
Setting Resources

Virtually all X clients are customizable. You can specify how a client looks on the screen—its size and placement, its border and background color or pattern, whether the window has a scrollbar, and so on. Some applications even allow you to redefine the keystrokes or pointer actions used to control the application.

Traditional UNIX applications rely on command line options to allow users to customize the way they work. As we've already discussed in Chapter 9, *Command Line Options*, X applications support command line options too, but often not for all features. Also, there can be so many customizable features in an application that entering a command line to set them all would be completely impractical. (Imagine the aggravation of misspelling an option in a command that was three lines long!)

X offers an alternative to customizing an application on the command line. Almost every feature of a program can be controlled by a variable called a *resource*; you can change the behavior or appearance of a program by changing the *value* associated with a resource variable. (All of the standard X Toolkit *Command Line Options* described in Chapter 9 have corresponding resource variable names. See Table 9-1 for more information.)

Resource variables may be Boolean (such as `scrollBar: True`) or take a numeric or string value (`borderWidth: 2` or `foreground: blue`). What's more, in applications written with the X Toolkit (or an Xt-based toolkit such as the Motif toolkit), resources may be associated with separate *objects* (or "widgets") within an application. There is a syntax that allows for separate control over both a *class* of objects in the application and an individual *instance* of an object. This is illustrated by these resource specifications for a hypothetical application called *xclient*:

```
xclient*Buttons.foreground:    blue
xclient*help.foreground:       red
```

The first resource specification makes the foreground color of all buttons in the *xclient* application (in the class `Buttons`) blue; the second resource specification makes the foreground color of the `help` button in this application (an instance of the class `Buttons`) red.

The values of resources can be set as application defaults using a number of different mechanisms, including resource files in your home directory and a program called *xrdb* (X resource database manager). As we'll see, the *xrdb* program stores resources directly in the server, making them available to all clients, regardless of the machine the clients are running on.

Placing resources in files allows you to set many resources at once, without the restrictions encountered when using command line options. In addition to a primary resource file (often called *Xdefaults* or *Xresources*) in your home directory, which determines defaults for the clients you yourself run, the system administrator can create system-wide resource files to set defaults for all instances of the application run on this machine. It is also possible to create resource files to set some resources only for the local machine, some for all machines in a network, and some for one or more specific machines.

The various resource files are automatically read in and processed in a certain order within an application by a set of routines called the *resource manager*. The syntax for resource specifications and the rules of precedence by which the resource manager processes them are intended to give you the maximum flexibility in setting resources with the minimum amount of text. You can specify a resource that controls only one feature of a single application, such as the red `help` button in the hypothetical *xclient* settings above. You can also specify a resource that controls one feature of multiple objects within multiple applications with a single line.

It is important to note that command line options normally take precedence over any prior resource settings; so you can set up the files to control the way you *normally* want your application to work and then use command line options to specify changes you need for only one or two instances of the application.

In this chapter, we'll first look at the syntax of resource specifications. Then we'll consider some methods of setting resources, primarily some special command line options and the *xrdb* program. Finally, we'll take a brief look at other sources of resource definition, additional files that can be created or edited to set application resources.

Resource Naming Syntax

The basic syntax of a resource definition file is fairly simple. Each client recognizes certain resource variables that can be assigned a value. The variables for each client are documented on its reference page in Part Three of this guide.

Most of the common clients are written to use the X Toolkit. As described in Chapter 8, *Other Clients*, toolkits are a mechanism for simplifying the design and coding of applications, and making them operate in a consistent way. Toolkits provide a standard set of objects, or widgets, such as menus, command buttons, dialog boxes, scrollbars, and so on. As we'll see, the naming syntax for certain resources parallels the object hierarchy that is built into X Toolkit programs.*

---

*If a client was built with the X Toolkit, this should be noted on the reference page. In addition to certain application-specific resource variables, most clients that use the X Toolkit recognize a common set of resource variables, listed in Table 10-1.

In addition, X Toolkit clients recognize a set of Core resource variables, listed in Table G-1. However, though all Toolkit applications recognize these variables, not all applications make use of them. This fine distinction is addressed in Appendix G, *Athena Widget Resources*, which gives a more technical discussion of how widgets use resources, and how applications use widgets. Appendix G also gives a detailed listing of the resources defined by each of the Athena widgets.

The most basic line you can have in a resource definition file consists of the name of a client, followed by a period or an asterisk, and the name of a variable. A colon and whitespace separate the client and variable names from the actual value of the resource variable. The following line specifies that all instances of the *xterm* application have a scrollbar:

```
xterm*scrollBar:    True
```

If the name of the client is omitted, the variable applies to all instances of all clients (in this case, all clients that can have a scrollbar). If the same variable is specified as a global variable and a client-specific variable, the value of the client-specific variable takes precedence for that client. Note, however, that if the name of the client is omitted, the line should generally begin with an asterisk.

Be sure not to inadvertently omit the colon at the end of a resource specification. This is an easy mistake to make and the resource manager provides no error messages. If there is an error in a resource specification (including a syntax error such as the omission of the colon or a misspelling), the specification is ignored. The value you set will simply not take effect. To include a comment in a resource file or comment out one of the resource specifications, begin the line in question with an exclamation point (!). If the last character on a line is a backslash (\), the resource definition on that line is assumed to continue on the next line.

Syntax of Toolkit Client Resources

As mentioned above, X Toolkit applications (and Xt-based toolkit applications) are made up of predefined components called widgets. There can be widgets within widgets (e.g., a command button within a dialog box). The syntax of resource specifications for Toolkit clients parallels the levels of the widget hierarchy. Accordingly, you should think of a resource specification as having this format:

```
object.subobject[.subobject...].attribute:  value
```

where:

object   is the client program or a specific instance of the program. (See "The –name Option" later in this chapter.)

subobjects   correspond to levels of the widget hierarchy (usually the major structures within an application, such as windows, menus, scrollbars, etc.).

attribute   is a feature of the last *subobject* (perhaps a command button), such as background color or a label that appears on it.

value   is the actual setting of the resource *attribute*, i.e., the label text, color, or other feature.

The type of `value` to supply is often evident from the name of the resource or from the description of the resource variable on the reference page. Most of these values are similar to those used with the command line options described in Chapter 9.

For example, various resources, such as `borderColor` or `background`, take color specifications; `geometry` takes a geometry string, `font` takes a font name, and so on. Logical values, such as the values taken by `scrollBar`, can generally be specified as: `on` or `off`; `yes` or `no`; or `True` or `False`.

Tight Bindings and Loose Bindings

Binding refers to the way in which components of a resource specification are linked together. Resource components can be linked in two ways:

- By a *tight* binding, represented by a dot (.).

- By a *loose* binding, represented by an asterisk (*).

A tight binding means that the components on either side of the dot must be next to one another in the widget hierarchy. A loose binding is signaled by an asterisk, a wildcard character which means there can be any number of levels in the hierarchy between the two surrounding components.

If you want to specify tight bindings, you must be very familiar with the widget hierarchy: it's easy to use tight bindings incorrectly.

For example, this resource specification to request that *xterm* windows be created with a scrollbar doesn't work:

```
xterm.scrollBar:   True
```

The previous specification ignores the widget hierarchy of *xterm*, in which the VT102 window is considered to be one widget, the Tektronix window another, and the menus a third. This means that if you want to use tight bindings to request that *xterm* windows be created with a scrollbar, you should specify:

```
xterm.vt100.scrollBar: True
```

Of course rather than decipher the widget hierarchy (which may even change with subsequent versions of an application), it is far simpler just to use the asterisk connector in the first place:

```
xterm*scrollBar:   True
```

In an application that supports multiple levels of widgets, you can mix asterisks and periods. In general, though, the developers of X recommend always using the asterisk rather than the dot as the connector even with simple applications, since this gives application developers the freedom to insert new levels in the hierarchy as they produce new releases of an application.

Instances and Classes

Each component of a resource specification has an associated *class*. Several different widgets, or widget attributes, may have the same class. For example, in the case of *xterm*, the color of text (`foreground`), the pointer color, and the text cursor color are all defined as *instances* of the class `Foreground`. This makes it possible to set the value of all three with a single resource specification. That is, if you wanted to make the text, the pointer, and the cursor dark blue, you could specify either:

```
xterm*foreground:     darkblue
xterm*cursorColor:    darkblue
xterm*pointerColor:   darkblue
```

or:

```
xterm*Foreground:     darkblue
```

Initial capitalization is used to distinguish class names from instance names. By convention, class names always begin with an uppercase letter, while instance names always begin with a lowercase letter. Note, however, that if an instance name is a compound word (such as cursorColor), the second word is usually capitalized.

The real power of class and instance naming is not apparent in applications such as *xterm* that have a simple widget hierarchy. In complex applications written with the X Toolkit or the Motif Toolkit, class and instance naming allows you to do such things as specify that all buttons in dialog box be blue but that one particular button be red. For example, in the hypothetical *xclient* application, you might have a resource file that reads:

```
xclient*buttonbox*Buttons*foreground:   blue
xclient*buttonbox*delete*foreground:    red
```

where Buttons is a class name and the delete button is an instance of the Buttons class. This type of specification works because an instance name always overrides the corresponding class name for that instance. Class names thus allow default values to be specified for all instances of a given type of object. Instance names can be used to specify exceptions to the rules outlined by the class names. Note that a class name can be used with a loose binding to specify a resource for all clients. For example, this specification would say that the foreground colors for all clients should be blue:

```
*Foreground:     blue
```

The reference page for a given program should always give you both instance and class names for every resource variable you can set. You'll notice that in many cases the class name is identical to the instance name, with the exception of the initial capital letter. Often (but not always) this means that there is only one instance of that class. In other cases, the instance with the same name is simply the primary or most obvious instance of the class.

Precedence Rules for Resource Specification

Even within a single resource file, such as *Xresources*, resource specifications often conflict. For instance, recall the example from the first page of the chapter involving the hypothetical *xclient* application:

```
xclient*Buttons.foreground:    blue
xclient*help.foreground:       red
```

The first resource specification makes the foreground color of all buttons (in the class Buttons) blue. The second resource specification overrides the first in one instance: it makes the foreground color of the help button (an instance of the class Buttons) red. In the event of conflicting specifications, there are a number of rules that the resource manager follows in deciding which resource specification should take effect.

We've already seen two of these rules, which are observable in the way the resource manager interprets definitions in a user-created resource file. (The first rule applies in the previous *xclient* example.)

- Instance names take precedence over class names.

- Tight bindings take precedence over loose bindings.

From just these two rules, we can deduce a general principle: the more specific a resource definition is, the more likely it is to be honored in the case of a conflict.

However, for cases in which you want to set things up very carefully, you should know a bit more about how programs interpret resource specifications.

For each resource, the program has both a complete, fully specified, tightly bound instance name and class name. In evaluating ambiguous specifications, the program compares the specification against both the full instance name and the full class name. If a component in the resource specification matches either name, it is accepted. If it matches more than one element in either name, it is evaluated according to these precedence rules:

1. The levels in the hierarchy specified by the user must match the program's expectations or the entry will be ignored. For example, if the program expects either:

   ```
   xterm.vt100.scrollBar:        value        instance name
   ```

   or:

   ```
   XTerm.VT100.ScrollBar:        value        class name
   ```

   the resource specification:

   ```
   xterm.scrollBar:    True
   ```

   won't work, because the tight binding is incorrect. The objects `xterm` and `scroll-Bar` are not adjacent in the widget hierarchy: there is another widget, `vt100`, between them. The specification would work if you used a loose binding, however:

   ```
   xterm*scrollBar:    True
   ```

   (Note that the class name of *xterm* is `XTerm`, not `Xterm` as you might expect.)

2. Tight bindings take precedence over loose bindings. That is, entries with instance or class names prefixed by a dot are more specific than entries with names prefixed by an asterisk, and more specific entries take precedence. For example, the entry `xterm.vt100.geometry` will take precedence over the entry `xterm*geometry`.

3. Similarly, instances take precedence over classes. For example, the entry `*scroll-Bar` will take precedence over the entry `*Scrollbar`.

4. An instance or class name that is explicitly stated takes precedence over one that is omitted. For example, the entry `xterm*scrollbar` is more specific than the entry `*scrollBar`.

5. Left components carry more weight than right components. For example, the entry `xterm*background` will take precedence over `*background`.

To illustrate these rules, let's consider the following resource specifications for the hypothetical Toolkit application *xclient*, shown in Example 10-1.

Example 10-1. Sample resources

```
xclient.toc*Command.activeForeground:    black
*Command.Foreground:    green
```

The program would try to match these specifications against these complete tightly bound instance and class specifications:

```
xclient.toc.messageFunctions.include.activeForeground        instance name
Xclient.Box.SubBox.Command.Foreground                        class name
```

Note that these specifications are the instance and class names for the same resource. Each component of the instance name belongs to the class in the corresponding component of the class name. Thus, the instance `toc` occurs in the class `Box`, the `messageFunctions` instance name is from the class `SubBox`, etc.

Both resource specifications in Example 10-2 match these instance and class names. However, with its tight bindings and instance names, `xclient.toc*Command.active-Foreground` matches more explicitly (i.e., with higher precedence). The resource is set: the `foreground` color of the `include` button in its `active` state is set to `black`.

The specification `*Command.Foreground` also matches the instance and class names but is composed entirely of class names which are less specific; thus, it takes lower precedence than the first line in Example 10-2 (which sets the `include` button to `black`).

However, since the second line is an acceptable specification, hypothetically it would set the foreground color of other objects in the `Command` class. This resource would be set for *xclient*, as well as any other application, since the line begins with the asterisk wildcard. So if there were other *xclient* command buttons comparable to the `include` button in the hierarchy, this second line would set the foreground color of these buttons to `green`. If you want a more detailed description of how resource precedence works, see Section 9.2.3 of Volume Four, *X Toolkit Intrinsics Programming Manual*.

Some Common Resources

Each Toolkit command line option (listed in Table 9-1) has a corresponding resource variable. Most X Toolkit (and Motif Toolkit) applicatons recognize some subset of these resources.

Table 10-1 lists the resource variables recognized by most Toolkit clients.

Table 10-1. Common Toolkit Resources

Instance Name	Class Name	Default	Description
background	Background	White	Background color.
foreground	Foreground	Black	Foreground color.
borderColor	BorderColor	Black	Border color.
borderWidth	BorderWidth	1 pixel	Border width.

Note that in a complex Toolkit application these values can occur at every level in a widget hierarchy. For example, our hypothetical *xclient* application might support these complete instance names:

```
xclient.background
xclient.buttonBox.background
xclient.buttonBox.commandButton.background
xclient.buttonBox.quit.background
```

These resources would specify the background color for the application window, the button-box area, any command buttons, and the quit command button, respectively.

Of course, the specification:

```
xclient*background
```

would match any and all of them.

Appendix G lists resources for each of the Athena widgets.

Event Translations

We've discussed the basics of resource naming syntax. From the sample resource settings, it appears that what many resource variables do is self-evident or nearly so. Among the less obvious resource variables, there is one type of specification, an event translation, that can be used with many clients and warrants somewhat closer examination.

User input and several other types of information pass from the server to a client in the form of *events*. An event is a packet of information that tells the client something it needs to act on, such as keyboard input. As mentioned in Chapter 1, *An Introduction to the X Window System*, moving the pointer or pressing a key, etc., causes *input* events to occur. When a program receives a meaningful event, it responds with some sort of action.

For many clients, the resource manager recognizes mappings between certain input events (such as a pointer button click) and some sort of action by the client program (such as selecting text). A mapping between one or more events and an action is called a *translation*. A resource containing a list of translations is called a *translation table*.

Many event translations are programmed into an application and are invisible to the user.* For our purposes we are only concerned with very visible translations of certain input events, primarily the translation of keystrokes and pointer button clicks to particular actions by a client program.

The Syntax of Event Translations

The operation of many clients, notably *xterm*, is partly determined by default input event translations. For example, as explained in Chapter 5, *The xterm Terminal Emulator*, selecting text with the first pointer button (an event) saves that text into memory (an action).

In this case, the input "event" is actually three separate X events:

1. Pressing the first pointer button.

2. Moving the pointer while holding down the first button.

3. Releasing the button.

Each of these input events performs a part of the action of selecting text:

1. Unselects any previously selected text and begins selecting new text.

2. Extends the selection.

3. Ends the selection, saving the text into memory (both as the PRIMARY selection and CUT_BUFFER0).

The event and action mappings would be expressed in a translation table as:

```
<Btn1Down>: select-start()\n\
<Btn1Motion>: select-extend()\n\
<Btn1Up>: select-end(PRIMARY,CUT_BUFFER0)
```

where each event is enclosed in angle brackets (< >) and produces the action that follows the colon (:). A space or tab generally precedes the action, though this is not mandatory:

```
<event>: action
```

A translation table must be a continuous string. In order to link multiple mappings as a continuous string, each event-action line should be terminated by a newline character (\n), which is in turn followed by a backslash (\) to escape the actual newline.

These are default translations for *xterm*.† All of the events are simple, comprised of a single button motion. As we'll see, events can also have modifiers: i.e., additional button motions or keystrokes (often Control or Meta) that must be performed with the primary event to pro-

---

*For more information on events and translations, see Volume Four, *X Toolkit Programming Manual*.

†They are actually slightly simplified versions of default translations. Before you can understand the actual translations listed on the *xterm* reference page in Part Three of this guide, you must learn more about the syntax of translations. In addition to the current chapter, read Appendix F, *Translation Table Syntax*.

duce the action. (Events can also have modifiers that *must not* accompany the primary event if the action is to take place.)

As you can see, the default actions listed in the table are hardly intuitive. The event-action mappings that can be modified using translation resources are usually described on the reference page for the particular client.

You can specify non-default translations using a translation table (a resource containing a list of translations). Since actions are part of the client application and cannot be modified, what you are actually doing is specifying alternative events to perform an action.* Keep in mind that only applications written with the X Toolkit (or an Xt-based toolkit such as the Motif Toolkit) recognize translation table syntax.

The basic syntax for specifying a translation table as a resource is:

```
[object*[subobject...]]*translations:   #override\
    [modifier]<event>:   action
```

The first line is basically like any other resource specification with a few exceptions. First, the final `argument` is always `translations`, indicating that one (or more) of the event-action bindings associated with the `[object*[subobject...]]` are being modified.

Second, note that `#override` is not the `value` of the resource; it is literal and indicates that what follows should override any default translations. In effect, `#override` is no more than a pointer to the true `value` of the resource: a new event-action mapping (on the following line), where the event may take a modifier.†

A not-so-obvious principle behind overriding translations is that you only literally "override" a default translation when the event(s) of the new translation match the event(s) of a default translation *exactly*. If the new translation does not conflict with any existing translation, it is merely appended to the defaults.

In order to be specified as a resource, a translation table must be a single string. The `#override` is followed by a backslash (\) to indicate that the subsequent line should be a continuation of the first.

In the previous basic syntax example, the `value` is a single event-action mapping. The `value` could also be a list of several mappings, linked by the characters "\n\" to make the resource a continuous string.

The following *xterm* translation table shows multiple event-action mappings linked in this manner:

```
*VT100.Translations:   #override\
    <Btn1Down>:      select-start()\n\
    <Btn1Motion>:    select-extend()\n\
    <Btn1Up>:        select-end(PRIMARY,CUT_BUFFER0)
```

---

*As we'll see, in certain cases you may be able to supply an alternative *argument* (such as a selection name) to an action. These changes *are* interpreted by the resource manager.

†The use of modifiers can actually become quite complicated, sometimes involving multiple modifiers. For our purposes, we'll deal only with simple modifiers. For more information on modifiers, see Appendix F in this guide and Volume Four, *X Toolkit Programming Manual*.

xterm Translations to Use xclipboard

As explained in Chapter 5, the *xclipboard* client provides a window in which you can store text selected from other windows. You can also paste text from the *xclipboard* window into other windows. See the discussion of *xclipboard* in Chapter 5 before proceeding.

You can specify translations for *xterm* so that text you copy with the pointer is made the CLIPBOARD selection. The CLIPBOARD selection is the property of the *xclipboard* client. If you are running *xclipboard* and you copy text to be made the CLIPBOARD selection, this text automatically appears in the *xclipboard* window.

Some sample translations that would allow you to use the *xclipboard* in this way are:

```
*VT100.Translations:    #override\
        Button1 <Btn3Down>:    select-end(CLIPBOARD)\n\
        ~Ctrl ~Meta <Btn2Up>: insert-selection(PRIMARY,CLIPBOARD)
```

According to this translation table, while selecting text with `Button1` (the modifier), the event of pressing the third pointer button (`Btn3Down`), while continuing to hold down the first button, produces the action of making the text the CLIPBOARD selection. (Notice that we've taken the `select-end` action and combined it with the argument CLIPBOARD. The default translation uses the arguments `PRIMARY,CUT_BUFFER0`.)

The second line modifies the way selected text is pasted into a window so that the CLIPBOARD selection can be pasted. As described in Chapter 5, pressing the second pointer button pasted the contents of the PRIMARY selection, by default. If there is no PRIMARY selection, the contents of the cut buffer are pasted. The default translation that sets this behavior is the following:

```
        ~Ctrl ~Meta <Btn2Up>:    insert-selection(PRIMARY,CUT_BUFFER0)
```

This translation specifies that releasing pointer button 2, while pressing any modifier button or key other than Control or Meta, inserts text from the PRIMARY selection or, if the selection is empty, from cut buffer 0. In the second line of our translation table, we've replaced `CUT_BUFFER0` with the CLIPBOARD selection. The new behavior is that releasing the second pointer button pastes the PRIMARY selection, or if there is none, the CLIPBOARD selection.

Thus, according to the translations in the example, if you select text as usual with the first pointer button, and then additionally press the third button (while continuing to hold down the first button), the text becomes the CLIPBOARD selection and appears automatically in the *xclipboard* window, as shown in Figure 10-1.

Since our first translation specifies a different event/action mapping than the default translation for selecting text (discussed in the previous section), the default translation still applies. If you select text with the first pointer button alone, that text is still made the PRIMARY selection and fills CUT_BUFFER0. To send text to the *xclipboard*, you would need to press the third pointer button as well; thus, not all selected text needs to be made the CLIPBOARD selection (and sent automatically to the *xclipboard*).

There are advantages to making only certain selections CLIPBOARD selections. You can keep *xclipboard* running and make many text selections by the default method (first pointer button), without filling up the *xclipboard* window. And chances are you don't want to save every piece of text you copy for an extended period of time, anyway.

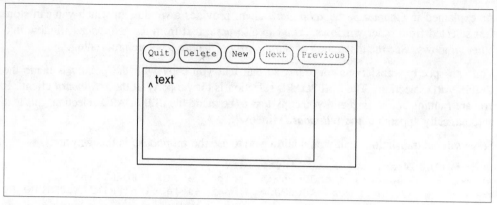

Figure 10-1. Selected text appears automatically in the xclipboard window

The CLIPBOARD selection and the *xclipboard* client also get around the potential problems of selection ownership discussed in Chapter 5. Once text becomes the CLIPBOARD selection, it is owned by the *xclipboard* client. Thus, if the client from which text was copied (the original owner) goes away, the selection is still available, owned by the *xclipboard*, and can be transferred to another window (and translated to another format if necessary).

Entering Frequently Used Commands with Function Keys

The sample *xterm* translations to use the *xclipboard* client involve just a few of the actions *xterm* recognizes. Among the more useful translations you can specify for *xterm* are function key mappings that allow you to enter frequently used commands with a single keystroke. This sort of mapping involves an action called `string`, which passes a text string to the shell running in the *xterm* window.

The translation table syntax for such a function key mapping is fairly simple. The following line maps the text string "lpq -Pprinter1" (the BSD 4.3 command to check the queue for the printer named printer1) to the F1 function key:

```
<Key>F1:        string("lpq -Pprinter1")
```

Notice the quotes surrounding the text string. If the argument to `string` includes spaces or non-alphanumeric characters, the whole argument must be enclosed in one pair of double quotes. (Don't make the mistake of quoting individual words.)

The translation table would be:

```
*VT100.Translations:    #override\
        <Key>F1:        string("lpq -Pprinter1")
```

This sample translation causes `lpq -Pprinter1` to be passed to the command line in the active *xterm* window when you press the F1 function key, as in Figure 10-2.

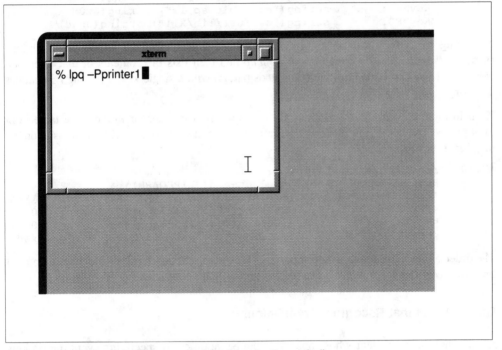

Figure 10-2. Pushing F1 passes command text to xterm shell

Notice, however, that the command is not invoked because there has been no carriage return. The sample translation does not specify a return. You can add a return as the argument to another `string` action within the same translation.

To specify the Return (or any) key, use the hexadecimal code for that key as the argument to `string`. Keycodes and the procedure for determining them are explained in Chapter 12, *Setup Clients*. The letters "0x" signal a hexadecimal key code. If you want to enter a key as an argument to `string`, use "0x" followed by the specific code. The code for the Return key is "d" or "0d."* The following translation table specifies that pressing F1 passes the line `lpq -Pprinter1` followed by a carriage return to an *xterm* window:

```
*VT100.Translations:    #override\
       <Key>F1:         string("lpq -Pprinter1") string(0x0d)
```

Remember, you can list several translations in a single table. The following table maps function keys F1 through F3:

---

*As explained in Chapter 12, *Setup Clients*, the command `xmodmap -pk` returns a long listing of all keycodes. The codes have the either of the following forms:

> 0xff*ab*
> 0x00*ab*

where *ab* represents two alphanumeric characters. To specify a key as an argument to `string`, you can omit the "ff" or "00" in the *xmodmap* listing.

```
*VT100.Translations:      #override\
      <Key>F1:            string("lpq -Pprinter1") string(0x0d)\n\
      <Key>F2:            string("cd ~/bitmap;ls") string(0x0d)\n\
      <Key>F3:            string("cd /usr/lib/X11") string(0x0d)
```

According to these translations, pressing F2 inserts the command string cd ~/bit-map;ls, which changes directory to ~/bitmap and then lists the contents of that directory. Notice that you can issue multiple commands (cd, ls) with a single key. Pressing F3 changes directory to /usr/lib/X11.

Keep in mind that all the translations for an application can appear in the same table. For example, we can combine the xterm translations to use the xclipboard with the translations to map function keys.

```
*VT100.Translations:      #override\
      Button1 <Btn3Down>:      select-end(CLIPBOARD)\n\
      ~Ctrl ~Meta <Btn2Up>:   insert-selection(PRIMARY,CLIPBOARD)\n\
      <Key>F1:                string("lpq -Pprinter1") string(0x0d)\n\
      <Key>F2:                string("cd ~/bitmap;ls") string(0x0d)\n\
      <Key>F3:                string("cd /usr/lib/X11") string(0x0d)
```

The order of the translations is not important. However, it is necessary to end all but the final line with the sequence "\n\" to make the resource a continuous string.

Other Clients that Recognize Translations

xterm is not the only client whose operation can be modified by specifying event translations as resources (though it is probably the client you'll be most interested in modifying). Among the standard clients, xbiff, xcalc, xdm, xman, and xmh all recognize certain actions that can be mapped to particular keys or key combinations using the translation mechanism. See the relevant client reference pages in Part Three of this guide for complete lists of actions.

You can also modify the operation of the Text widget used by xedit, xmh, and other X Toolkit applications. See Appendix G, Athena Widget Resources, for a list of actions recognized by the Text widget. Keep in mind, however, that the default Text widget recognizes dozens of commands, which are summarized in the discussion of xedit in Chapter 8, Other Clients. It may not be practical or desirable to modify them all.

If you choose to modify the Text widget, you can do so for all relevant clients by introducing the translations with the line:

```
*Text*Translations: #override\
```

You can also specify different translations for different clients that use the widget by prepending the client's name. To affect the operation of the Text widget only under xedit, introduce the translation table with the line:

```
Xedit*Text*Translations: #override\
```

In modifying the operation of the Text widget, keep in mind that insert mode is the default. In other words, like emacs, most of the individual keystrokes you type are added to the text file; an exception is Backspace, which predictably deletes the preceding character. The commands to move around in a file, copy and delete text, etc., involve a combination of keys, one of which is generally a modifier key. If you want to modify a command, you should use an alternative key combination, rather than a single key.

For example, the following table offers two suitable translations:

```
*Text*Translations:  #override\
    Meta<Key>f:   next-page()\n\
    Meta<Key>b:   previous-page()
```

The first translation specifies that pressing the key combination Meta-f moves the cursor ahead one page in the file (scrolls the file forward one window); the second translation specifies that Meta-b moves the cursor back one page. The actions performed are fairly obvious from their names. For a complete list of actions recognized by the Text widget, see Appendix G.

For more information about events, actions, and translation table syntax, see Appendix F, *Translation Table Syntax*, and Volume Four, *X Toolkit Programming Manual*.

Though *mwm* does not provide actions that can be modified using a translation table, you can change the key and pointer button events used to invoke window manager functions by editing a special file called *.mwmrc* in your home directory. See Chapter 11, *Customizing mwm*, for details.

How to Set Resources

Learning to write resource specifications is a fairly manageable task, once you understand the basic rules of syntax and precedence. In contrast, the multiple ways you can set resources—for a single system, for multiple systems, for a single user, for all users—can be confusing. For our purposes, we are primarily concerned with specifying resources for a single user running applications both on the local system and on remote systems in a network.

As we've said, resources are generally specified in files. A resource file can have any name you like. Resources are generally "loaded" into the X server by the *xrdb* client, which is normally run from your startup file or run automatically by *xdm* when you log in. (See Appendix A, *System Management*, for information about startup files and *xdm*.) Prior to Release 2 of X, there was only one resource file called *Xdefaults*, placed in the user's home directory. If no resource file is loaded into the server by *xrdb*, the *Xdefaults* file will still be read.

Remember that X allows clients to run on different machines across a network, not just on the machine that supports the X server. The problem with the older *Xdefaults* mechanism was that users who were running clients on multiple machines had to maintain multiple *Xdefaults* files, one on each machine. By contrast, *xrdb* stores the application resources directly in the server, thus making them available to all clients, regardless of the machine on which the clients are running. As we'll see, *xrdb* also allows you to change resources without editing files.

Of course, you may want certain resources to be set on all machines and others to be set only on particular machines. See the section "Other Sources of Resource Definition" later in this chapter for information on setting machine-specific resources. This section gives an overview of additional ways to specify resources using a variety of system files.

In addition to loading resource files, you can specify defaults for a particular instance of an application from the command line using two options: -xrm and -name.

First we'll consider a sample resources file. Then we'll take a look at the use of the -xrm and -name command line options. Finally, we'll discuss various ways you can load resources using the *xrdb* program and consider other sources of resource definition, later in this chapter.

A Sample Resources File

Figure 10-3 shows a sample resources file. This file sets the border width for all clients to a default value of two pixels, and sets other specific variables for *xclock* and *xterm*. The meaning of each variable is obvious from its name (for example, xterm*scrollBar: True means that *xterm* windows should be created with a scrollbar.

Note that comments are preceded by an exclamation point (!).

For a detailed description of each possible variable, see the appropriate client reference pages in Part Three of this guide.

```
*borderWidth:           2
!
! xclock resources
!
xclock*borderWidth:     5
xclock*geometry:        64x64
!
! xterm resources
!
xterm*curses:           on
xterm*cursorColor:      skyblue
xterm*pointerShape:     pirate
xterm*jumpScroll:       on
xterm*saveLines:        300
xterm*scrollBar:        True
xterm*scrollKey:        on
xterm*background:       black
xterm*borderColor:      blue
xterm*borderWidth:      3
xterm*foreground:       white
xterm*font:             8x13
```

Figure 10-3. A sample resources file

Specifying Resources from the Command Line

Two command line options supported by all clients written with the X Toolkit can be useful in specifying resources.

The –xrm Option

The -xrm option allows you to set on the command line any specification that you would otherwise put into a resources file. For example:

```
% xterm -xrm 'xterm*Foreground: blue' &
```

Note that a resource specification on the command line must be quoted using the single quotes in the line above.

The -xrm option only specifies the resource(s) for the current instance of the application. Resources specified in this way do not become part of the resource database.

The -xrm option is most useful for setting classes, since most clients have command line options that correspond to instance variable names. For example, the -fg command line option sets the foreground attribute of a window, but -xrm must be used to set Foreground.

Note also that a resource specified with the -xrm option will not take effect if a resource that takes precedence has already been loaded with *xrdb*. For example, say you've loaded a resource file that includes the specification:

```
xterm*pointerShape:    pirate
```

These command line specification of another cursor will fail:

```
% xterm -xrm '*pointerShape:    gumby' &
```

because the resource xterm*pointerShape is more specific than the resource *pointerShape. Instead, you'll get an *xterm* with the previously specified pirate cursor.

To override the resource database (and get the Gumby cursor), you'd need to use a resource equally (or more) specific, such as the following:

```
% xterm -xrm 'xterm*pointerShape:    gumby' &
```

The –name Option

The -name option lets you name one instance of an application; the server identifies the single instance of the application by this name. The name of an application affects how resources are interpreted.

For example, the following command sets the *xterm* instance name to bigxterm:

```
% xterm -name bigxterm &
```

When this command is run, the client uses any resources specified for bigxterm rather than for xterm.

The −name option allows you to create different instances of the same application, each using different resources. For example, you could put the following entries into a resource file such as *Xresources*:

```
XTerm*Font:         8x13
smallxterm*Font:    6x10
smallxterm*Geometry: 80x10
bigxterm*Font:      9x15
bigxterm*Geometry:  80x55
```

You could then use these commands to create *xterm*s of different specifications:

    % xterm &

would create an *xterm* with the default specifications, while:

    % xterm −name bigxterm &

would create a big *xterm*, 80 characters across by 55 lines down, displaying in the font 9x15. The command:

    % xterm −name smallxterm &

would create a small *xterm*, 80 characters across by 10 lines down, displaying in the font 6x10.

Setting Resources with xrdb

The *xrdb* program saves you from the difficulty of maintaining multiple resource files if you run clients on multiple machines. It stores resources in the X server, where they are accessible to all clients using that server. (Technically speaking, the values of variables are stored in a data structure referred to as the RESOURCE_MANAGER property of the root window of screen 0 for that server. From time to time, we may refer to this property colloquially simply as the resource database.)

The appropriate *xrdb* command line should normally be placed in your *xinitrc* file or *xsession* file to initialize resources at login, although it can also be invoked interactively. It has the following syntax:

    xrdb [options] [filename]

The *xrdb* client takes several options, all of which are documented on the reference page in Part Three of this guide. Several of the most useful options are discussed in subsequent sections. (Those that are not discussed here have to do with *xrdb*'s ability to interpret C preprocessor-style defined symbols; this is an advanced topic. For more information, see the *xrdb* reference page in Part Three of this guide, and the *cpp*(1) reference page in your *UNIX Reference Manual*.)

The optional *filename* argument specifies the name of a file from which the values of client variables (resources) will be read. If no filename is specified, *xrdb* will expect to read its data from standard input. That is, the program will appear to hang, until you type some data, followed by an end-of-file (Control-D on many UNIX systems). Note that whatever you type will override the previous contents of the RESOURCE_MANAGER property, so if you inadvertently type *xrdb* without a filename argument, and then quit with Control-D, you will delete any previous values. (You can append new settings to current ones using the −merge option discussed later in this chapter.)

The resource `filename` can be anything you want. Two commonly used names are *Xresources* and *Xdefaults*.

You should load a resource file with the *xrdb* −load option. For example, to load the contents of your *Xresources* file into the RESOURCE_MANAGER, you would type:

```
% xrdb -load .Xresources
```

Querying the Resource Database

You can find out what options are currently set by using the −query option. For example:

```
% xrdb -query
XTerm*ScrollBar:        True
bigxterm*font:          9x15
bigxterm*Geometry:      80x55
smallxterm*Font:        6x10
smallxterm*Geometry:    80x10
xterm*borderWidth:      3
```

If *xrdb* has not been run, this command will produce no output.

Loading New Values into the Resource Database

By default, *xrdb* reads its input (either a file or standard input) and stores the results into the resource database, replacing the previous values. If you simply want to merge new values with the currently active ones (perhaps by specifying a single value from standard input), you can use the −merge option. Only the new values will be changed; variables that were already set will be preserved rather than overwritten with empty values.

For example, let's say you wanted to add new resources listed in the file *new.values*. You could say:

```
% xrdb -merge new.values
```

As another example, if you wanted all subsequently run *xterm* windows to have scrollbars, you could use standard input, and enter:

```
% xrdb -merge
xterm*scrollBar:    True
```

and then press Control-D to end the standard input. Note that because of precedence rules for resource naming, you may not automatically get what you want. For example, if you specify:

```
xterm*scrollBar:   True
```

and the more specific value:

```
xterm*vt100.scrollBar: False
```

has already been set, your new, less specific setting will be ignored. The problem isn't that you used the −merge option incorrectly—you just got caught by the rules of precedence.

If your specifications don't seem to work, use the −query option to list the values in the RESOURCE_MANAGER property and look for conflicting specifications.

Note also that when you add new specifications, they won't affect any programs already running, but only programs started after the new resource specifications are in effect. (This is also true even if you overwrite the existing specifications by loading a new resource file. Only programs run after this point will reflect the new specifications.)

Saving Active Resource Definitions in a File

Assume that you've loaded the RESOURCE_MANAGER property from an *Xresources* or other file. However, you've dynamically loaded a different value using the −merge option and you'd like to make the new value your default.

You don't need to edit the file manually (although you certainly could.) The −edit option allows you to write the current value of the RESOURCE_MANAGER property to a file. If the file already exists, it is overwritten with the new values. However, *xrdb* is smart enough to preserve any comments and preprocessor declarations in the file being overwritten, replacing only the resource definitions.

For example:

```
% xrdb -edit ~/.Xresources
```

will save the current contents of the RESOURCE_MANAGER property in the file *Xresources* in your home directory.

If you want to save a backup copy of an existing file, use the −backup option:

```
% xrdb -edit .mydefaults -backup old
```

The string following the −backup option is used as an extension to be appended to the old filename. In the prior example, the previous copy of *.mydefaults* would be saved as *.mydefaults.old*.

Removing Resource Definitions

You can delete the definition of the RESOURCE_MANAGER property from the server by calling *xrdb* with the -remove option.

There is no way to delete a single resource definition other than to read the current *xrdb* values into a file. For example:

```
% xrdb -query > filename
```

Use an editor to edit the file, deleting the resource definitions you no longer want and save the file:

```
% vi filename
```

Then read the edited values back into the RESOURCE_MANAGER with *xrdb*:

```
% xrdb -load filename
```

Listing the Current Resources for a Client: appres

The *appres* (*app*lication *res*ource) program, available as of Release 4, lists the resources that currently might apply to a client. These resources may be derived from several sources, including the user's *.Xresources* file and a system-wide application defaults file. The directory */usr/lib/X11/app-defaults* contains application default files for several clients. The function of these files is discussed in the next section. For now, be aware that all of the resources contained in these files begin with the class name of the application.

Also be aware that *appres* has one serious limitation: it cannot distinguish between valid and invalid resource specifications. It lists all resources that might apply to a client, whether or not the resources are correctly specified.

appres lists the resources that apply to a client having the `class_name` and/or `instance_name` you specify. Typically, you would use *appres* before running a client program to find out what resources the client program will access.

For example, say you want to run *xterm* but you can't remember the latest resources you've specified for it, whether you've loaded them, or perhaps what some of the application defaults are, etc. You can use the *appres* client to check the current *xterm* resources. If you specify only a class name, as in this command line:

```
% appres XTerm
```

appres lists the resources that any *xterm* would load. In the case of *xterm*, this is an extensive list, encompassing all of the system-wide application defaults as well as any other defaults you have specified in a resource file.

You can additionally specify an instance name to list the resources applying to a particular instance of the client, as in:

```
% appres XTerm bigxterm
```

If you omit the class name, *xappres* assumes the class -NoSuchClass-, which has no defaults, and returns only the resources that would be loaded by the particular instance of the client.

Note that the instance can simply be the client name, for example, xterm. In that case none of the system-wide application defaults would be listed, since all begin with the class name XTerm. For example, the command:

```
% appres xterm
```

might return resources settings similar to these:

```
xterm.vt100.scrollBar:  True
xterm*PhonyResource:    youbet
xterm*pointerShape:     gumby
xterm*iconGeometry:     +50+50
*VT100.Translations:    #override\
   Button1 <Btn3Down>:    select-end(CLIPBOARD)\n\
   ~Ctrl ~Meta <Btn2Up>: insert-selection(PRIMARY,CLIPBOARD)
```

Most of these resources set obvious features of *xterm*. The translation table sets up *xterm* to use the *xclipboard*. Notice also that *appres* has returned an invalid resource called Phony-Resource that we created for demonstration purposes. You can't rely on *appres* to tell you what resources a client will actually load because the *appres* program cannot distinguish a valid resource specification from an invalid one. Still, it can be fairly useful to jog your memory as to the defaults you've specified in your *Xresources* file, as well as the system-wide application defaults.

Other Sources of Resource Definition

If *xrdb* has not been run, the RESOURCE_MANAGER property will not be set. Instead, the resource manager looks for a file called *Xdefaults* in the user's home directory. As we discussed earlier, resources found in this way are only available to clients running on the local machine.

Whether or not resources have been loaded with *xrdb*, when a client is run these sources of resource definition are consulted in this order:

1. A file with the same name as the client application, in the directory */usr/lib/X11/app-defaults* will be loaded into the resource manager.

2. Files in the directory named by the environment variable XAPPLRESDIR or, if the variable is not set, in the user's home directory, with the name *Class*, where *Class* is the class name of a client program.

3. Resources loaded into the RESOURCE_MANAGER property of the root window with *xrdb*; these resources are accessible regardless of the machine on which the client is running.

   If no resources are loaded in this way, the resource manager looks for a *Xdefaults* file in the user's home directory; these resources are only available on the local machine.

4. Next, the contents of any file specified by the shell environment variable XENVIRON-MENT will be loaded.

    If this variable is not defined, the resource manager looks for a file named *Xdefaults-hostname* in the user's home directory, where ***hostname*** is the name of the host where the client is running. These methods are used to set machine-specific resources.

5. Any values specified on the command line with the −xrm option will be loaded for that instance of the program.

All of these various sources of defaults will be loaded and merged according to the precedence rules described earlier in the section "Precedence Rules for Resource Specification."

The client will then merge these various defaults specified by the user with its own internal defaults, if any.

Finally, if the user has specified any options on the command line (other than with the −xrm option), these values will override those specified by resource defaults, regardless of their source.

11

Customizing mwm

This chapter describes the syntax of the .mwmrc *startup file that can be used to customize the operation of the* mwm *window manager. It describes how to bind functions to keys and how to define your own* mwm *menus. This chapter also explains how to set up* mwm *to use an icon box, a window in which icons on the display can be organized.*

In This Chapter:

11
Customizing mwm

The Motif window manager is one of the more flexible window managers available in the X market today. As we saw in Chapter 3 and Chapter 4, *mwm* provides a wide variety of methods for managing windows (i.e., moving, resizing, iconifying, etc.). In addition, virtually every feature of *mwm* can be customized. You can change the appearance of window frames, icons, and menus, the functions available on the Root Menu and the Window Menu, the keyboard focus policy, how icons are arranged on the display, as well as the appearance of client applications running with *mwm*. As we'll see, you can also create additional menus, displayed from the root window, to perform actions on the display as a whole.

Customization of *mwm* is controlled in two ways:

- Through a special file, called *.mwmrc*, in your home directory.

- Through *mwm* resources you can enter in your *Xresources* file (or other sources of resource specification).

The default operation of *mwm* is largely controlled by a system-wide file, called *system.mwmrc*, which establishes the contents of the Root Menu and Window Menu, how menu functions are invoked, and what key and button combinations can be used to manage windows. To modify the behavior of *mwm*, you can edit a copy of this file in your home directory. The version of this file in your home directory should be called *.mwmrc*. We'll take a look at the *system.mwmrc* and ways to edit your own *.mwmrc* file to make the window manager work more effectively for you.

In addition to the flexibility provided by the *.mwmrc* file, *mwm* provides dozens of application resources that you can set! It's neither practical nor necessary to discuss all of those resources here. (You could spend quite a long time customizing *mwm*, if you had the time and inclination.) We'll just consider some basic categories into which *mwm* resources can be divided and also look at some of the more useful resources. See Chapter 10 for syntax rules and information about loading resources into the server so that they will be accessible to client programs. See the *mwm* reference page in Part Three of this guide for descriptions of all available resources.

In the remainder of this chapter, we're going to demonstrate the *basics* of customizing *mwm* and suggest what we think are helpful modifications. (This is still quite a lot to absorb.) To illustrate, we'll discuss how to customize the following features of *mwm*:

- The menus and how menu functions are invoked.

- The keyboard focus policy.

- How icons are organized (namely, how to set up a window known as an *icon box*, in which icons on the display can be organized).

Before we can customize the *mwm* menus or the ways in which their functions are invoked, we need to take a closer look at the *system.mwmrc* file. First, however, let's consider an important topic: how to make the window manager aware of customizations.

Activating Changes to the Window Manager

Be aware that if you edit your *.mwmrc* or *.Xresources* file to change the way *mwm* works, the changes will not take effect automatically. Whether you change resource settings, edit your *.mwmrc* file, or both, you must restart *mwm* for the changes to take effect.

If you edit your resources file, you must first make the server aware of the new resource specifications by using the *xrdb* client. Generally, you will enter the following command at the prompt in an *xterm* window:

```
% xrdb -load .Xresources
```

The settings in the current version of your *.Xresources* file will replace the resource settings previously stored in the resource database. You can merely append new settings to the old ones using the *xrdb* -merge option. See Chapter 10, *Setting Resources*, for more information.

Once you've loaded the new resource settings, you can restart *mwm*. This can be done using the Restart item of the Root Menu, as described in Chapter 4. When *mwm* has been restarted, it should reflect any changes made to the *.mwmrc* and *.Xresources* files.

The system.mwmrc File

Example 11-1 shows the *system.mwmrc* file shipped with OSF/Motif Release 1.1. If you've used other window managers, this file may seem a bit more complicated than other configuration files, but the complexity is deceptive. Note that comment lines are introduced by the number sign (#).

If you wish to change the operation of *mwm*, you shouldn't change the *system.mwmrc* file. Instead, copy it to your home directory, under the name *.mwmrc*, and make changes to that copy.

Example 11-1. The system.mwmrc file, Release 1.1

```
#
#   DEFAULT mwm RESOURCE DESCRIPTION FILE (system.mwmrc and .mwmrc)
#
#
```

Example 11-1. The system.mwmrc file, Release 1.1 (continued)

```
# menu pane descriptions
#

# Root Menu Description
Menu RootMenu
{
    "Root Menu"          f.title
    "New Window"         f.exec "xterm &"
    "Shuffle Up"         f.circle_up
    "Shuffle Down"       f.circle_down
    "Refresh"            f.refresh
    no-label             f.separator
    "Restart..."         f.restart
}


# Default Window Menu Description
Menu DefaultWindowMenu
{
    Restore      _R      Alt<Key>F5      f.normalize
    Move         _M      Alt<Key>F7      f.move
    Size         _S      Alt<Key>F8      f.resize
    Minimize     _n      Alt<Key>F9      f.minimize
    Maximize     _x      Alt<Key>F10     f.maximize
    Lower        _L      Alt<Key>F3      f.lower
    no-label                             f.separator
    Close        _C      Alt<Key>F4      f.kill
}


#
# key binding descriptions
#

Keys DefaultKeyBindings
{
  Shift<Key>Escape           window|icon         f.post_wmenu
  Meta<Key>space             window|icon         f.post_wmenu
  Meta<Key>Tab               root|icon|window    f.next_key
  Meta Shift<Key>Tab         root|icon|window    f.prev_key
  Meta<Key>Escape            root|icon|window    f.next_key
  Meta Shift<Key>Escape      root|icon|window    f.prev_key
  Meta Shift Ctrl<Key>exclam root|icon|window    f.set_behavior
  Meta<Key>F6                window              f.next_key transient
  Meta Shift<Key>F6          window              f.prev_keytransient
  <Key>F4                    icon                f.post_wmenu
}

#
# button binding descriptions
#

Buttons DefaultButtonBindings
{
    <Btn1Down>        icon|frame      f.raise
    <Btn3Down>        icon            f.post_wmenu
    <Btn1Down>        root            f.menu      RootMenu
}
```

Example 11-1. The system.mwmrc file, Release 1.1 (continued)

```
Buttons ExplicitButtonBindings
{
    <Btn1Down>              frame|icon          f.raise
    <Btn3Down>              frame|icon          f.post_wmenu
    <Btn1Down>              root                f.menu        RootMenu
    Meta<Btn1Down>          window|icon         f.lower
    Meta<Btn2Down>          window|icon         f.resize
    Meta<Btn3Down>          window|icon         f.move
}

Buttons PointerButtonBindings
{
    <Btn1Down>              frame|icon          f.raise
    <Btn3Down>              frame|icon          f.post_wmenu
    <Btn1Down>              root                f.menu        RootMenu
    <Btn1Down>              window              f.raise
    Meta<Btn1Down>          window|icon         f.lower
    Meta<Btn2Down>          window|icon         f.resize
    Meta<Btn3Down>          window|icon         f.move
}

#
#   END OF mwm RESOURCE DESCRIPTION FILE
#
```

The *system.mwmrc* file can be divided into three sections:

- Menu specifications.

- Key bindings.

- Button bindings.

The menu section of the *system.mwmrc* file defines the contents of the Root Menu and the Window Menu. Menu item labels are paired with predefined *mwm* functions.

A *binding* is a mapping between a user action (such as a keystroke) and a function, in this case a window manager function. The key bindings section specifies keyboard keys that can be used to invoke some of the predefined window manager functions. The button bindings section specifies pointer buttons or key/button combinations that can be used to invoke various functions.

Each section of the *system.mwmrc* file matches the following basic template:

```
Section_Type  Section_Title
{
definitions
}
```

For example, the basic syntax of a menu specification is as follows:

```
Menu menu_name . . .
{
menu items defined
}
```

Menu is the *Section_Type*. The other possible section types are Keys and Buttons. The *Section_Title* is somewhat arbitrary. In this case, it corresponds to the title of a menu. In the key and button sections, it is simply a title assigned to a group of bindings.

However, the *Section_Title* can be very significant. As we'll see, a section title can be used as the value of a resource variable in your *Xresources* file. Menu titles are often referenced elsewhere in the *.mwmrc* file. The *menu_name* is generally paired with a pointer button action (in the button bindings section of the *.mwmrc* file) to allow you to use a particular button to display the menu.

The syntax of the actual menu items, key bindings, and button bindings requires further explanation. But first, let's take a look at some of the predefined window manager functions.

mwm Functions

mwm has a number of predefined functions. Each of these functions has a name beginning with "f.". Several functions appear in the *system.mwmrc* file, paired with the method by which the function can be invoked: by menu item, pointer button action, keystroke(s), or key and pointer button combinations.

The meaning of most of these functions should be fairly obvious to you from the name, if not from your experience using the window manager. For example, f.resize is used to resize a window, f.move to move a window, or f.minimize to change a window to an icon.

Others are less obvious. The function f.post_wmenu is used to display (or post) the Window Menu. Notice the function f.separator, which appears in the menu definition coupled with the instruction no-label rather than with a menu item. This line in the *.mwmrc* creates a divider line on a menu. For example, such a divider line is used to isolate the Restart... item from the other items on the Root Menu.

As we'll see, the function f.menu is used to associate a menu with the key or button binding that is used to display it. The f.menu function takes a required argument: the menu name. This function can also be used to define a submenu.

Each of the functions is described in detail on the reference page for *mwm* in Part Three of this guide.

Menu Specifications

The first section of the *system.mwmrc* file contains specifications for the Root Menu and Window Menu. As we've said, the basic syntax of a menu specification is as follows:

```
Menu menu_name . . .
{
menu items defined
}
```

Menu items are defined in slightly different ways for the Root Menu and the Window Menu. The following text in the *system.mwmrc* file creates the Root Menu:

```
# Root Menu Description
Menu RootMenu
{
        "Root Menu"         f.title
        "New Window"        f.exec "xterm &"
        "Shuffle Up"        f.circle_up
        "Shuffle Down"      f.circle_down
        "Refresh"           f.refresh
        no-label            f.separator
        "Restart..."        f.restart
}
```

The syntax for defining Root Menu items is very simple. Each item is defined by a line of this format:

"label" function

When you pair a label with a menu function, that label appears as a menu item. You can invoke the function by selecting the item from the menu using the pointer. For example, the line:

```
        "Refresh"       f.refresh
```

sets up the Refresh menu item, which can be selected from the Root Menu as discussed in Chapter 4. (Again, the function performed is obvious from the function name.) As we'll see later, it's easy to add items to the Root Menu by adding lines of label/function pairs.

Because Window Menu items can be invoked in a variety of ways, the syntax for defining items is more complicated. The following text defines the Window Menu:

```
# Default Window Menu Description

Menu DefaultWindowMenu
{
        Restore       _R      Alt<Key>F5      f.normalize
        Move          _M      Alt<Key>F7      f.move
        Size          _S      Alt<Key>F8      f.resize
        Minimize      _n      Alt<Key>F9      f.minimize
        Maximize      _x      Alt<Key>F10     f.maximize
        Lower         _L      Alt<Key>F3      f.lower
        no-label                              f.separator
        Close         _C      Alt<Key>F4      f.kill
}
```

The syntax of each menu item is as follows:

"label"   mnemonic   accelerator   function

(The *mnemonic* and *accelerator* fields are optional.) Like the Root Menu, each item on the Window Menu can be invoked by selecting its label with the pointer. In addition, there are two shortcuts defined for invoking the function: a mnemonic and an accelerator. As you may recall, a mnemonic is a unique letter abbreviation for the menu item label. On the menu, mnemonic abbreviations are underlined; thus an underscore precedes each mnemonic definition in the *system.mwmrc* file. Once the Window Menu is displayed, you can select an item by typing its mnemonic abbreviation. Similarly, you can invoke the function without displaying the menu, simply by typing the accelerator keys (by default, the Alt key plus a function key).*

Now let's see how one of the Window Menu definition lines fits this template:

```
Move _M    Alt<Key>F7     f.move
```

The menu item label is **Move**. Selecting the item invokes the `f.move` function. The mnemonic "m" or the accelerator key combination Alt-F7 can also be used to invoke the function.

Key Bindings

The second section of the *system.mwmrc* file binds keystroke combinations to window manager functions.

Like the menu definition section, the key bindings section of the file is titled and bracketed:

```
Keys Section_Title
{

key bindings defined

}
```

The section type is `Keys`. The section title in the *system.mwmrc* file is `DefaultKey-Bindings`. This title can also be specified as the value of the *mwm* resource `key-Bindings` in your *Xresources* file. However, since these bindings are used by default, this is not necessary.

Using the section title as a resource becomes significant when you want to create an alternative set of bindings. Hypothetically, you could add another set of bindings with a different title to your *.mwmrc* file. Then specify this title as the value of the `keyBindings` resource in your *Xresources* file. If you add the following resource specification to your *Xresources* file, `MyButtonBindings` replace `DefaultButtonBindings` for all client applications running with *mwm*:

```
Mwm*keyBindings:    MyButtonBindings
```

If you want to use different sets of bindings for different applications, you can add an application name between the parts of the resource specification. For example, if you want `My-ButtonBindings` to apply only to *xterm* windows running with *mwm*, you could enter the following resource line:

```
Mwm*xterm*keyBindings:    MyButtonBindings
```

Then `DefaultButtonBindings` would still apply to all applications other than *xterm*.

---

*If you're keyboard does not have an F10 function key, you cannot use the accelerator for the Maximize item without doing some customization. A possible workaround is to edit the line defining the Maximize menu item in your *.mwmrc* file. Changing F10 to F2 will suffice in most cases.

A non-obvious principle behind a key/function (or button/function) binding is that in order for the keys (or buttons) to invoke the function, the pointer must be in a certain location. This location is known as the *context*. For key bindings, the useful contexts are: `root`, `window`, and `icon`. The `window` context refers to the entire window, including the frame. (There are other more specific contexts, such as `border`, explained under "Button Bindings," but when specifying key bindings, these contexts are all equivalent to `window`.)

Some functions can be invoked if the pointer is in more than one context. For example, as we saw in Chapter 4, you can display the Window Menu from either a window or an icon using the keyboard shortcuts Meta-space or Shift-Escape. The action involved is `f.post_wmenu` and the window and the icon are the pointer contexts from which this action can be performed. These keyboard shortcuts are defined in the key bindings section of the *system.mwmrc* file as follows:

```
Shift<Key>Escape    window|icon    f.post_wmenu
Meta<Key>space      window|icon    f.post_wmenu
```

Upon examining these lines, we can discern the template for a key binding:

```
[modifier_keys]<Key>key_name        context            function
```

Each binding can have one or more modifier keys (modifiers are optional) and *must* have a single primary key (signaled by the word <Key> in angle brackets) to invoke the function. In the first specification, Shift is the modifier and Escape is the primary key. In the second specification, Meta is the modifier and space is the primary key. Both specifications have two acceptable pointer contexts: either a window or an icon. And both bindings are mapped to the same action, `f.post_wmenu`, which displays the Window Menu.

Button Bindings

The key bindings section of the file is also titled and bracketed:

```
Buttons Section_Title
{
button bindings defined

}
```

The section type is `Buttons`. The *system.mwmrc* file contains three sets of button bindings with the section titles:

```
DefaultButtonBindings
ExplicitButtonBindings
PointerButtonBindings
```

Button bindings clearly illustrate the need to coordinate your *Xresources* and *.mwmrc* files. The three sets of button bindings correspond to three possible settings for the resource `buttonBindings`. The default setting for the resource is:

```
Mwm*buttonBindings:    DefaultButtonBindings
```

specifying that the `DefaultButtonBindings` are used.

You can specify that one of the other sets of button bindings is to be used by setting this resource in your *Xresources* file. For example, if you add the following specification to your resource file:

```
Mwm*buttonBindings:     ExplicitButtonBindings
```

mwm will use those bindings that come under the heading `ExplicitButtonBindings` in the *.mwmrc* file.

Be aware that if you do specify different button bindings, the value of the resource must exactly match the title associated with the bindings, or the bindings will not take effect.

The syntax for a button binding specification is very similar to that of a key binding:

[modifier_key]<button_event>　　　　*context*　　　　*function*

Each button binding can have one or more modifier keys (modifiers are optional) and *must* have a single button event (enclosed in angle brackets) to invoke the function. The motion that comprises each button event should be fairly obvious. (Lists of acceptable button events and modifier keys appear on the *mwm* reference page in Part Three of this guide.)

For button bindings. the valid contexts are `root`, `window`, `icon`, `title`, `border`, `frame`, and `app`. The `title` context refers to the title area of the frame. `border` refers to the frame exclusive of the titlebar. `frame` refers to the entire frame (thus it encompasses `title` and `border`). The `app` context refers to the application window proper (i.e., exclusive of the frame). The `window` context includes the application window and the frame (thus it encompasses `app`, `frame`, `border`, and `title`).

Now let's see how the button binding syntax relates to the default button bindings in the *system.mwmrc* file:

```
Buttons DefaultButtonBindings
{
    <Btn1Down>          icon|frame      f.raise
    <Btn3Down>          icon            f.post_wmenu
    <Btn1Down>          root            f.menu      RootMenu
}
```

The first specification is familiar. It indicates that the event of pressing down the first pointer button while the pointer is in a window frame or an icon performs the action of raising the window or icon, respectively.

The second binding reveals *still another* way to display the Window Menu, by pressing the third pointer button on an icon.

The third binding is also familiar and illustrates the use of the `f.menu` function. As previously mentioned, the `f.menu` function is used to associate a menu with the key or button binding that is used to display it. The following binding specifies that the Root Menu is displayed by pressing and holding down the first pointer button on the root window:

```
    <Btn1Down>          root            f.menu      RootMenu
```

Notice that the function requires an argument, the menu name (RootMenu), which also appears in the first line of the menu definition. This correspondence is required—`f.menu` needs to know which menu to display.

Customizing the Root Menu

You can add items to the Root Menu simply by adding lines of the format:

"label"   function

within the menu definition section of your *.mwmrc* file.

The f.exec function allows you to execute system commands from a menu. In the default Root Menu, the New Window command uses the f.exec function to execute the system command xterm &, as shown below:

```
# Root Menu Description
Menu RootMenu
{
        "Root Menu"          f.title
        "New Window"         f.exec "xterm &"
        "Shuffle Up"         f.circle_up
        "Shuffle Down"       f.circle_down
        "Refresh"            f.refresh
        no-label             f.separator
        "Restart..."         f.restart
}
```

To create a menu item labeled Clock that opens an *xclock* window on your display, simply add a line to your *.mwmrc* file, as shown here:

```
# Root Menu Description
Menu RootMenu
{
        "Root Menu"          f.title
        "New Window"         f.exec "xterm &"
        "Clock"              f.exec "xclock &"
        "Shuffle Up"         f.circle_up
        "Shuffle Down"       f.circle_down
        "Refresh"            f.refresh
        no-label             f.separator
        "Restart..."         f.restart
}
```

You can also edit (or remove) existing menu items. For example, if you want to run a terminal emulator program other than *xterm*, you can edit the menu item definition in your *.mwmrc* file. Say you want to run the *hpterm* terminal emulator (developed by Hewlett-Packard), you would edit your menu specification to look like this:

```
# Root Menu Description
Menu RootMenu
{
        "Root Menu"          f.title
        "New Window"         f.exec "hpterm &"
        "Shuffle Up"         f.circle_up
        "Shuffle Down"       f.circle_down
        "Refresh"            f.refresh
        no-label             f.separator
        "Restart..."         f.restart
}
```

Creating New Menus

Keep in mind that *mwm* also allows you to specify entirely new menus in your *.mwmrc* file. A new menu can be separate from all existing menus, or it can be a submenu of an existing menu. (Submenus are described in the following section, "Cascading Menus.")

If you want to create a new, independent menu, it must conform to the menu specification syntax discussed earlier. Items must invoke predefined window manager functions.

The *.mwmrc* file must also specify how the menu will be displayed and in what context. This involves associating a key or button with the f.menu function. Say you've specified a new menu, titled GamesMenu, that runs various game programs, each in its own window. (The f.exec function would be used to define each item.) The following button binding specifies that pressing the second pointer button on the root window displays the Games Menu:

```
<Btn2Down>        root       f.menu     GamesMenu
```

Cascading Menus

mwm also allows you to create submenus, generally known as *cascading* menus because they are displayed to the right side of (and slightly lower than) another menu. You define a submenu just as you would any other, using the syntax rules discussed earlier. The following lines create a Utilities Menu that invokes several "desktop" clients and one game:

```
Menu UtilitiesMenu
{
        "Utilities Menu"    f.title
        "Clock"             f.exec "xclock &"
        "System Load"       f.exec "xload &"
        "Calculator"        f.exec "xcalc &"
        "Manpage Browser"   f.exec "xman &"
        "Tetris"            f.exec "xtetris &"
}
```

In order to make the Utilities Menu a submenu of the Root Menu, you need to add an f.menu function to the Root Menu. This f.menu function must be coupled with the correct submenu title:

```
# Root Menu Description
Menu RootMenu
{
        "Root Menu"         f.title
        "New Window"        f.exec "xterm &"
        "Shuffle Up"        f.circle_up
        "Shuffle Down"      f.circle_down
        "Refresh"           f.refresh
        "Utilities"         f.menu            UtilitiesMenu
        no-label            f.separator
        "Restart..."        f.restart
}
```

After you specify the preceding menus in your *.mwmrc* file (and restart *mwm*), display the Root Menu. It will feature a new item, labeled Utilities. Since this item is actually a pointer to a submenu, it will be followed by an arrow pointing to the right, as in Figure 11-1.

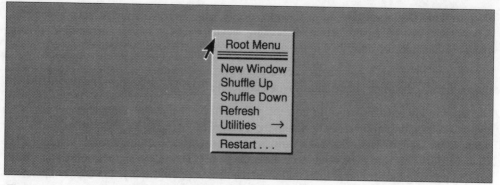

Figure 11-1. An arrow pointing to the right indicates a submenu

If you drag the pointer down the Root Menu to the Utilities item, the submenu will appear to cascade to the right. Figure 11-2 shows it appearing.

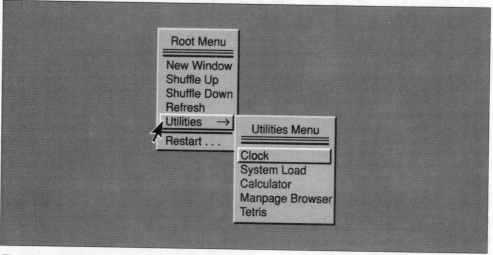

Figure 11-2. Utilities submenu of the Root Menu

If you release the pointer button, both menus will remain displayed and the Utilities item and the first item on the Utilities Menu will be highlighted by a box. You can then select an item from the Utilities Menu by moving the pointer to the item and clicking the first button.

Keep in mind that you can create several submenus beneath a single menu and that menus can cascade several levels, though such complexity is not necessarily desirable.

Note also that if you pair a label with an invalid function (or with f.nop, which specifies no operation), or with a function that doesn't work in the current context, the label appears in a lighter typeface. This "graying out" indicates that the menu item is not available for selection.

Setting mwm Resources

The Motif window manager provides dozens of resources that control the appearance and functionality of the window manager, its component features, and other clients running with it. *mwm* resources should be entered in your *.Xresources* file and will take effect when the resources have been loaded into the server and *mwm* has been started or restarted. See Chapter 10, *Setting Resources*, for syntax information and instructions on how to load resources using the *xrdb* client. See "Activating Changes to the Window Manager" earlier in this chapter for information about running *mwm* with the new resource settings.

mwm resources are considered to fall into three categories:

1. *mwm* component appearance resources. These resources set the characteristics of *mwm*'s component features, such as the window frame, menus, and icons.

2. *mwm-specific* appearance and behavior resources. These resources set characteristics of the window manager client, such as focus policy, key and button bindings, and so forth.

3. *Client-specific* resources. These *mwm* resources can be used to set the appearance and behavior of a particular client or class of clients.

Under these categories fall dozens of *mwm* resources. The sheer number of resources makes it impractical for all of them to be discussed here. In the following sections, we discuss the three categories of resources in somewhat greater detail. We'll then take a look at two of the more powerful and useful resources, `keyboardFocusPolicy` and `useIconBox`, which set the focus policy and set up *mwm* to use an icon box, respectively. For a comprehensive list of available resources, see the *mwm* reference page in Part Three of this guide.

Component Appearance Resources

The Motif window manager can be considered to be made up of components: client window frames, menus, icons, and what are known as *feedback* or *dialog boxes*. An example of a feedback box is the box that appears so that you can confirm or cancel a Restart command from the Root Menu. (See "The Root Menu" section in Chapter 4, *More about the mwm Window Manager*.)

Certain resources allow you to specify the appearance of one or all of these *mwm* component features. In specifying the resource setting, you can use the name of one of the features as part of the resource name. For example, one of the most useful component appearance resources is `background`, which, as we know from Chapter 10, specifies the background color. You can specify a resource that sets the background color of any of the *mwm* components. The following resource specification sets the background color of all client window frames to light blue:

```
Mwm*client*background:    lightblue
```

Table 11-1 summarizes the resource name that corresponds to each of the *mwm* components.

Table 11-1. Resource Names Corresponding to mwm Components

Component	Resource name
Menu	menu
Icon	icon
Client window frame	client
Feedback/dialog box	feedback

Thus, to set the background color of feedback boxes to sea green, you'd use the following resource:

```
Mwm*feedback*background:    seagreen
```

Of course, if you omit any specific component from the resource specification, it applies to *all* components. Thus, the following specification sets the background color of all window frames, feedback boxes, icons, and menus to light grey:

```
Mwm*background:    lightgrey
```

mwm-specific Appearance and Behavior Resources

The *mwm*-specific resources control aspects of what you probably think of as the window manager application itself, features such as the focus policy, whether windows are placed on the display automatically or interactively, which set(s) of button and key bindings are used, whether an icon box is used, and so forth.

The syntax of *mwm*-specific resource specifications is very simple—the *mwm* class name connected by a loose binding to the resource variable name, as shown here:

```
Mwm*clientAutoPlace:    false
```

This resource establishes the behavior that the user will interactively place client windows on the display. (The default is true, meaning *mwm* places them automatically.)

Two of the *mwm*-specific resources bring up an issue of coordination between the *.Xresources* and *.mwmrc* files. Remember, the default *.mwmrc* file contains three sets of button bindings:

```
DefaultButtonBindings
ExplicitButtonBindings
PointerButtonBindings
```

These three sets of button bindings correspond to three possible settings for the resource variable buttonBindings. If your resource file contains the following setting:

```
Mwm*buttonBindings:    ExplicitButtonBindings
```

mwm will use those bindings that come under the heading ExplicitButtonBindings in the *.mwmrc* file.

Similarly, the resource variable `keyBindings` should be coordinated to match the key bindings in the *.mwmrc* file. Since the default *.mwmrc* file has only one set of key bindings, named `DefaultKeyBindings`, and the `keyBindings` resource also sets this by default, coordination should not be an issue unless you create a new set of key bindings with a different name.

Two of the most useful and powerful *mwm*-specific resources set the keyboard focus policy and specify that icons be stored in an icon box. We'll discuss the use and advantages of these resources later in this chapter.

Client-specific Resources

Some *mwm* resources can be set to apply to certain client applications or classes of applications. These resources generally have the form:

```
Mwm*application*resource_variable:
```

where `application` can be an instance name or a class name. Be aware that the application name is optional. If you omit an application name, the resource applies to all clients.

Many of the client-specific resources provide what might be considered advanced customization. For example, a combination of resources allows you to specify your own bitmap as the image for a client icon. Other resources allow you to suppress certain features of the window frame for particular clients. For instance, you may choose to omit the Maximize button from the frame surrounding *xterm* windows. The average user will probably not need most of these resources.

One client-specific resource users might be interested in is called `focusAutoRaise`. This resource causes a window to be raised to the top of the stack when it is selected as the focus window. When the focus policy is explicit (click-to-type), `focusAutoRaise` is true for all clients by default. When the focus policy is pointer (real-estate-driven), `focusAutoRaise` is false for all clients by default.

These defaults are very sensible. If you are using the default click-to-type focus, `focusAutoRaise` is clearly very desirable. You click on a window to focus input and the window is raised to the top of the stack so that you can work with it easily. However, if you change the focus policy to pointer focus (as we'll describe in the following section), turning `focusAutoRaise` on can make the display seem chaotic.

When pointer focus is active as you move the pointer across the display, the focus changes from window to window based on the location of the pointer, often a desirable feature. However, if `focusAutoRaise` is set to be true, each time the pointer moves into a window, the window will be moved to the front of the display. Simply moving the pointer across a screenful of windows can create a distracting shuffling effect! If you set the focus policy to pointer, we suggest you leave `focusAutoRaise` set to false.

Of course, using pointer focus without `focusAutoRaise` is just our preference. You may want to experiment awhile to see how you like working with it.

Hypothetically, you *can* turn `autoFocusRaise` behavior on or off only for particular clients, but this is not necessarily desirable, with either focus policy. For instance, say you're using the default *mwm* settings so that explicit focus is in effect and `focusAutoRaise` is true for all clients. You can suppress the auto-raise feature only for the class of *xterm* windows by specifying:

```
Mwm*XTerm*focusAutoRaise:   false
```

But what is the point? In most cases, you want to raise the focus window so that you can work with it more easily.*

When pointer focus is in effect, setting `focusAutoRaise` differently for different clients can have tedious and unnecessary complications. It becomes fairly easy to "bury" one window beneath another inadvertently. For example, say `focusAutoRaise` is turned on for *xterm* windows only, and turned off for *xbiff*. If an *xbiff* window appears on top of an *xterm* and you move the pointer into the *xterm*, the *xterm* is raised automatically, covering the *xbiff* window.

You can send the *xterm* to the back using the Lower item of the Window Menu. Although the *xterm* retains the focus, it is not raised. `focusAutoRaise` specifies that a window is raised when the focus is moved to a window (retaining the focus is a different matter). However, if you move the pointer to another window and back to the *xterm*, the *xbiff* window will be buried again. In order to avoid such a situation, you would have to arrange all windows so that a part of the frame is exposed at all times. No window should ever appear entirely on top of another.

Given the limitations and potential problems, **we discourage setting** `focusAutoRaise` **differently for different applications, regardless of the focus policy.**

Setting the Focus Policy

The most common resource users will probably want to set controls *mwm*'s keyboard focus policy. By default, *mwm* has explicit (or click-to-type) focus, which is set using the following resource:

```
Mwm*keyboardFocusPolicy:    explicit
```

To change the keyboard focus policy from explicit to pointer focus (that is, focus follows the movement of the pointer), enter the following line in your *Xresources* file:

```
Mwm*keyboardFocusPolicy:    pointer
```

---

*Note that even if you turn off the auto-raise feature for *xterm*, it is still possible to raise an *xterm* and select it to receive input simultaneously, but in a more restricted way. Clicking anywhere on a window selects that window to receive the focus. Clicking on the frame, exclusive of the command buttons, raises a window. Thus, by clicking this part of the frame, you can perform both actions simultaneously. However, why restrict yourself to using only a part of the frame, when you can use the entire window?

Using an Icon Box

One of the most interesting (and desirable) features *mwm* can provide is a window in which icons can be organized on the display. This window is known as an *icon box*, and is pictured in Figure 11-3.

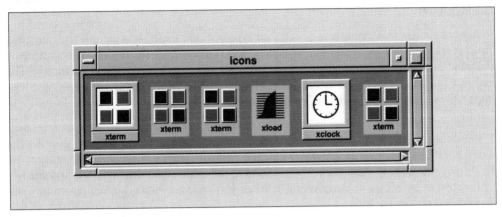

Figure 11-3. An icon box

As we'll see, in addition to organizing icons neatly on the display, the icon box also provides a few window management functions.

You can set up *mwm* to provide an icon box automatically by specifying the following resource in your *Xresources* file:

```
Mwm*useIconBox:     true
```

If this resource is included in your *Xresources* file (and the resources have been loaded as described in Chapter 10) *mwm* will provide an icon box when it is started (or restarted). Other resources can be used to customize the size, appearance and location of the icon box, as well as the window's title. By default, the icon box is six icons wide by one icon high and is located in the lower-left corner of the display.

The horizontal and vertical scrollbars within the icon box suggest a significant, albeit not an obvious, feature. Icons can extend beyond the visible bounds of the icon box. If more than six icons are present in the default size box, you can view them using the scrollbars. (See Chapter 8, *Other Clients*, for instructions on using a Motif scrollbar.) Keep in mind that if icons do extend beyond the visible bounds of the box, the appearance of the scrollbars will indicate it.

The presence of an icon box changes the way icons are used on the display. If you are using *mwm* without an icon box, only those windows that have been iconified are represented by icons on the display. If you are using *mwm* with an icon box, *all* windows on the display are represented by icons that are stored in the box, whether or not the windows are in an iconified state.

When a client window is started, the window appears on the display *and* a corresponding icon appears in the icon box. However, an icon that represents a window currently visible on the display has a different appearance than an actual icon (that is, an iconified window). An icon corresponding to a window currently on the display appears flatter and less defined than the image of an iconified window. The former probably has fewer lines in its outer border. If you set up *mwm* to use an icon box, the differing appearance of these two types of icons should be obvious.

Somewhat similar to a menu item in a lighter typeface, the flatter, less defined icon suggests that it is not available to be chosen. In a sense, this is true. Since the flat icon is not an iconified window, but merely an image, it is not available to be converted back to a window. The icon box in Figure 11-3 contains two iconified windows (*xclock* and the first *xterm*) and four icons representing windows currently visible on the display.

You can perform some window management functions by clicking on icons in the icon box. If you double click on an iconified window using the first pointer button, the icon is converted back to a window. If you double click on an icon representing an active window on the display, the corresponding window is raised to the front of the display. (We find this latter function to be not particularly useful.) When you raise a window by clicking on its icon, the icon box retains the focus.

When performing either function, between the first and second clicks you'll probably notice that the Window Menu is displayed for an instant above the icon. If you pause too long between the two clicks in either of these functions, the action you intend (either deiconifying or raising) will fail and the Window Menu will remain on the screen.

If you get stuck on the Window Menu when trying to convert an icon to a window, place the pointer on the Restore menu item and click the first pointer button.

If you get stuck on the Window Menu when trying to raise a window on the display (by clicking on its icon), the menu affords no item to complete the action. Instead you should move the pointer onto the root window and click the first button—the menu will be removed. Then try double clicking again. Or raise the window simply by clicking the first pointer button on the window's frame (exclusive of the frame's command buttons).

As these actions suggest, you can display the Window Menu from any of the icons in the box by clicking the first pointer button on the icon image.* (You can also display the Window Menu from and manage the icon box itself, as we discuss later on.) Depending on whether you click on an iconified window or an icon representing an active window on the display, different Window Menu items are available for selection.

When you display the Window Menu from an iconified window within the icon box, the items Restore, Move, Maximize, and Close are available for selection. Be aware that the Move menu item only allows you to move the icon itself—to another location within the icon box. The other available items perform their standard functions, which are described in the section "Using the Window Menu on Icons" in Chapter 4.

---

*The 1.0 version of *mwm* was documented to display the Window Menu from an icon within the icon box, but the program did not seem to work according to the specifications. The 1.1 version of *mwm* does provide this functionality.

Displaying the Window Menu from an icon representing an active window on the display is not particularly useful: only the items Move and Close are available for selection. And again the Move menu item only allows you to move the icon within the icon box.

When you display the Window Menu from the icon box, the menu commands apply to the box itself (which is actually a window). You can display the menu from the icon box using any of the methods described in the section "Using the Window Menu" in Chapter 4. For example, if you use the keyboard shortcut Meta-space, the menu is displayed above the Window Menu command button in the upper-left corner of the icon box frame.

When displayed from the icon box, the Window Menu Close item is replaced by an item called PackIcons (mnemonic "p", accelerator Shift+Alt+F7). PackIcons rearranges the icons in the box to fill in empty slots. This is useful when icons are removed from the box or the box is resized.

When you remove a window, the corresponding icon is removed from the box, leaving an empty slot. PackIcons will move any icons that are to the right of the slot one space to the left to fill the hole. If you resize the icon box, PackIcons will arrange the icons to fit the new window in an optimal way. For instance, say we resize the icon box in Figure 11-3 so that it is only three icons wide, but twice as high, as in Figure 11-4. The first three icons from the box appear; the second three are obscured.* Notice the horizontal scrollbar at the bottom of the window, indicating that the other three icons are still to the right of these and thus not viewable in the resized box. If you place the pointer on the scrollbar, hold down the first button and drag the scrollbar to the right, the hidden icons will be revealed.

In order to rearrange the icons to better fill the new shape box, use the PackIcons menu item. Figure 11-5 shows the icon box after you've selected PackIcons.

---

*When you resize the icon box, you'll notice the resize action has a tendency to jump the width or height of an icon at a time. *mwm* only allows the box to be resized exactly to fit a number of icons wide and a number high, though there are no obvious limitations as to the numbers. Basically, you can have an icon box of any size, even one icon high and wide, and display the other icons using the scrollbars. As you resize the box, the small rectangular window in the center of the screen assists you: it shows the dimensions in the number of icons wide by the number of icons high.

Figure 11-4. In the resized icon box, only three icons are visible

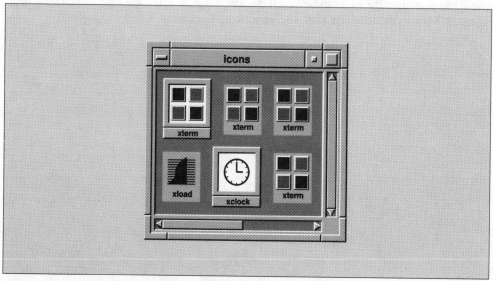

Figure 11-5. PackIcons menu item rearranges icons in resized box

If you want to reorganize icons in the box yourself, without PackIcons, this is also possible. You can actually move icons into adjacent empty slots using the pointer. Just hold down the first pointer button on the icon and drag it into the next slot. If you first make the icon box larger, so that there are several empty spaces, you'll find you can radically reorganize icons. Once you've arranged them as you like, you resize the box to fit the icons—or perhaps make it even smaller and view the obscured icons using the scrollbars.

Keep in mind that the next time you log in, the icon box will be brought up at its default size. To specify alternate dimensions, set the variable `iconBoxGeometry` in your *Xresources* file. For example, if you want an icon box three icons wide by two icons high, use the specification:

```
Mwm*iconBoxGeometry:   3x2+0-0
```

which creates a box of the desired size in the lower-left corner of the display. (This is the default location; you could omit the +0-0 from the geometry string and get the same result.)

The following specification creates an icon box four icons wide by three icons high in the lower-right corner of the display:

```
Mwm*iconBoxGeometry:   4x3-0-0
```

12

Setup Clients

This chapter describes three useful setup clients that can be used to customize the appearance of your display, and the operation of your keyboard and pointer.

In This Chapter:

12
Setup Clients

This chapter discusses how to set up certain features of your working environment, using these clients:

xset   To set certain characteristics of the keyboard, pointer, and display.

xsetroot   To set root window characteristics.

xmodmap   To change pointer and modifier key mappings.

xset: Setting Display and Keyboard Preferences

The *xset* client allows you to set an assortment of user preference options for the display and keyboard. Some of these are followed by on or off to set or unset the option. Note that *xset* is inconsistent with other UNIX and X programs in its use of a dash (–) as an option flag. Some options use a preceding dash to indicate that a feature be disabled; this can be confusing at first to users accustomed to seeing a dash as an introductory symbol on all options.

Although *xset* can be run any time, it is suggested that you run it at startup. These settings reset to the default values when you log out. Not all X implementations are guaranteed to honor all of these options.

Keyboard Bell

The b option controls bell volume (as a percentage of its maximum), pitch (in hertz), and duration (in milliseconds). It accepts up to three numerical parameters:

    b volume pitch duration

If no parameters are given, the system defaults are used. If only one parameter is given, the bell volume is set to that value. If two values are listed, the second parameter specifies the bell pitch. If three values are listed, the third one specifies the duration.

For example, the command:

    % xset b 70 1000 100

sets the volume of the keyboard bell to 70 percent of the maximum, the pitch to 1000 hertz, and the duration to 100 milliseconds.

Note that bell characteristics vary with different hardware. The X server sets the characteristics of the bell as closely as it can to the user's specifications.

The b option also accepts the parameters on or off. If you specify xset b on, system defaults for volume, pitch and duration are used.

The bell can also be turned off with the option -b, or by setting the volume parameter to 0 (xset b 0).

Bug Compatibility Mode

Some Release 3 clients were written to work with "features" of the Release 3 server, which could more accurately be called bugs. Many of these bugs have been eliminated in Release 4. In order to allow certain Release 3 clients to work under the Release 4 server, the Release 4 server has a bug compatibility mode that can be enabled using *xset*. In this mode, the Release 4 server is compatible with Release 3 clients that depended on bugs in the Release 3 server to work properly (most notably the Release 3 version of *xterm*).

To enable bug compatibility mode, use the command xset bc; to disable it, use the command xset -bc.

Keyclick Volume

The c option sets the volume of the keyboard's keyclick and takes the form:

    c volume

volume can be a value from 0 to 100, indicating a percentage of the maximum volume. For example:

    % xset c 75

sets a moderately loud keyclick. The X server sets the volume to the nearest value that the hardware can support.

The c option also accepts the parameters on or off. If you specify xset c on, the system default for volume is used.

The keyclick can also be turned off with the option -c, or by setting the volume parameter to 0 (xset c 0).

On some hardware, a volume of 0 to 50 turns the keyclick off, and a volume of 51 to 100 turns the keyclick on.

Enabling or Disabling Auto-repeat

The r option controls the keyboard's auto-repeat feature. (Auto-repeat causes a keystroke to be repeated over and over when the key is held down.) Use xset r or xset r on to enable key repeat. Use xset -r or xset r off to disable key repeat. On some keyboards (notably Apollo) only some keys repeat regardless of the state of this option.

Changing or Rehashing the Font Path

As discussed in Chapter 6, *Font Specification*, when a client is to be displayed in a particular font, the server by default looks for the font in three subdirectories of */usr/lib/X11/fonts*: *misc*, *75dpi*, and *100dpi*.

The fp (font path) option of *xset* can be used to change the font path, i.e., to direct the X server to search other directories for fonts called by a client. The option must be followed by a directory or a comma-separated list of directories, as in this example:

```
% xset fp /work/andy/fonts,/usr/lib/X11/newfonts
```

To restore the default font path, type:

```
% xset fp default
```

As discussed in Chapter 6, the fp option with the rehash parameter causes the server to reread the *fonts.dir* and *fonts.alias* files in the current font path. You need to do this every time you edit an alias file to make the server aware of the changes.

To make the server aware of aliases, type:

```
% xset fp rehash
```

You also have to do this if you add or remove fonts. See Appendix A, *System Management* for more information.

Keyboard LEDs

The led option controls the enabling or disabling of one or all of the keyboard's LEDs. It accepts the parameters on or off to enable or disable all of the LEDs. A preceding dash also disables all of the LEDs (-led).

You can also enable or disable individual LEDs by supplying a numerical parameter (a value between 1 and 32) that corresponds to a particular LED. The led option followed by a numerical parameter enables that LED. The led option preceded by a dash and followed by a numerical parameter disables that LED. For example:

```
% xset led 3
```

would enable LED #3, while:

```
% xset -led 3
```

would disable LED #3.

Note that the particular LED values may refer to different LEDs on different hardware.

Pointer Acceleration

The m (mouse) option controls the rate at which the mouse or pointer moves across the screen. This option takes two parameters: *acceleration* and *threshold*. They must be positive integers. (The acceleration can also be written as a numerator/denominator combination separated by a slash, for example, 5/4.)

The mouse or pointer moves *acceleration* times as fast when it travels more than the *threshold* number of pixels in a short time. This way, the pointer can be used for precise alignment when it is moved slowly, yet it can be set to travel across the screen by a flick of the wrist when desired. If only one parameter is given, it is interpreted as the acceleration.

For example, the command:

    % xset m 5 10

sets the pointer movement so that if you move the pointer more than 10 pixels, the pointer cursor moves five times as many pixels on the screen as you moved the pointer on the pad.

If no parameter or the value default is used, the system defaults will be set.

If you want to change the threshold and leave the acceleration unchanged, enter the value default for acceleration.

Screen Saver

X supports a screen saver to blank or randomly change the screen when the system is left unattended for an extended period. This avoids the "burn in" that can occur when the same image is displayed on the screen for a long time. The s (screen saver) option to *xset* determines how long the server must be inactive before the screen saver is started.

The s option takes two parameters: *time* and *cycle*. The screen goes blank if the server has not received any input for the time interval specified by the *time* parameter. The contents of the screen reappear upon receipt of any input. If the display is not capable of blanking the screen, then the screen is shifted a pixel in a random direction at time intervals set by the *cycle* parameter. The parameters are specified in seconds.

For example, the command:

    % xset s 600

sets the length of time before the screen saver is invoked to 600 seconds (10 minutes).

For a display not capable of blanking the screen, the command:

    % xset s 600 10

sets the length of time before the screen saver is invoked to 10 minutes and shifts the screen every 10 seconds thereafter, until input is received.

The s option also takes the parameters:

default   Resets the screen save option to the default.

blank   Turns on blanking and overrides any previous settings.

noblank   Displays a background pattern rather than blanking the screen; overrides any previous settings.

off   Turns off the screen saver option and overrides any previous settings.

expose   Allows window exposures (the server can discard window contents).

noexpose   Disables screen saver unless the server can regenerate the screens without causing exposure events (i.e., without forcing the applications to regenerate their own windows).

Color Definition

On color displays, every time a client requests a private read/write colorcell, a new color definition is entered in the display's colormap. The p option sets one of these colormap entries even though they are supposed to be private. The parameters are a positive integer identifying a cell in the colormap to be changed and a color name:

```
p entry_number color_name
```

The root window colors can be changed on some servers using *xsetroot*. An error results if the map entry is a read-only color.

For example, the command:

```
% xset p 3 blue
```

sets the third cell in the colormap to the color blue but only if some client has allocated this cell read/write.

The client that allocated the cell is likely to change it again sometime after you try to set it, since this is the usual procedure for allocating a read/write cell.

Help with xset Options

The q option lists the current values of all *xset* preferences.

xsetroot: Setting Root Window Characteristics

You can use the *xsetroot* client to tailor the appearance of the background (root) window on a display running X.

The *xsetroot* client is primarily used to specify the root window pattern: as a plaid-like grid, tiled gray pattern, solid color, or a bitmap. You can also specify foreground and background colors (defaults are black and white), reverse video, and set the shape of the pointer when it's in the root window.

If no options are specified, or the -def option is specified, *xsetroot* resets the root window to its default state, a gray mesh pattern, and resets the pointer to the hollow X pointer. The -def option can also be specified with other options; those characteristics that are not set by other options are reset to the defaults.

Although *xsetroot* can be run at any time, it is suggested that you run it from a startup shell script, as described at the end of this chapter. All settings reset to the default values when you log out.

For a complete list of options, see the *xsetroot* reference page in Part Three of this guide. Not all X implementations are guaranteed to support all of these options. Some of the options may not work on certain hardware devices.

The -help option prints all the *xsetroot* options to standard output. The options you'll probably use most frequently are explained in the next section. Since only one type of background pattern can be specified at a time, the -solid, -gray, -grey, -bitmap and -mod options are mutually exclusive.

Setting Root Window Patterns

The default root window pattern is called a "gray mesh." On most displays, it is fairly dark.

The *xsetroot* client allows you to specify an alternative gray background with the -grey (or -gray) option. This tiled gray pattern is slightly lighter than the default gray mesh pattern.

The *xsetroot* client also allows you to create a root window made up of repeated "tiles" of a particular bitmap, using the option:

    -bitmap filename

where *filename* is the bitmap file to be used as the window pattern.

You can choose any of the bitmaps in the directory */usr/include/X11/bitmaps* or make your own bitmap files using the *bitmap* client (see Chapter 7, *Graphics Utilities*).

For example, the command:

    % xsetroot -bitmap /usr/andy/gumby -fg red -bg blue

fills the root window with a tiling of the bitmap */usr/andy/gumby* (a virtual army of Gumbys!), using the colors red and blue.

The −mod option sets a plaid-like grid pattern on the root window. You specify the horizontal (x) and vertical (y) dimensions in pixels of each square in the grid. The syntax of the option is:

```
−mod x y
```

where the parameters *x* and *y* are integers ranging from 1 to 16 (pixels). (Zero and negative numbers are taken as 1.)

The larger the x and y values you specify, the larger (and more visible) each square on the root window grid pattern. Try the command:

```
% xsetroot −mod 16 16
```

for the largest possible grid squares. Then test different x and y specifications.

The *xsetroot* option:

```
−solid color
```

sets the color of the root window to a solid color. This can be a color from the color name database or a more exact color name specified by its RGB value.

The command:

```
% xsetroot −solid lightblue
```

sets the color of the root window to light blue.* See Chapter 9, *Command Line Options*, for more information on how to specify colors.

Foreground Color, Background Color, and Reverse Video

In addition to specifying a solid color for the root window pattern, *xsetroot* allows you to specify foreground and background colors if you set the pattern with −bitmap or −mod. The standard Toolkit options are used to set foreground and background colors: −fg and −bg. The defaults are black and white.

Colors can be specified as names from the color name database, or as RGB values. See Chapter 9, *Command Line Options* for more instructions on how to specify color.

If you specify reverse video (−rv), the foreground and background colors are reversed.

---

*For technical reasons, colors set with xsetroot −solid may change unexpectedly. When you set a color with the −solid option to *xsetroot*, the client allocates a colorcell, sets the color, and deallocates the colorcell. The root window changes to that color. If another client is started that sets a new color, it allocates the next available colorcell—which may be the same one *xsetroot* just deallocated. This results in that color changing to the new color. The root window also changes to the new color. If this happens, you can run *xsetroot* again and if there are other colorcells available, the root window changes to the new color. If all colorcells are allocated, any call to change a colorcell results in an error message.

While this behavior may seem to be a serious bug, it is actually an optimization designed to ensure applications don't run out of colors unnecessarily. Free colormap cells can be a scarce resource. See Volume One, *Xlib Programming Manual*, for more information.

Foreground and background colors also take effect when you set the root window pointer, as described in the next section.

Changing the Root Window Pointer

By default, the pointer is an X when it's in the root window. You can change the shape of the root window pointer to one of the standard X cursor shapes or to any bitmap, using these options:

```
-cursor_name standard_cursor_name

-cursor cursorfile maskfile
```

Available as of Release 4, the first option allows you to set the root window pointer to one of the standard cursor symbols, which are generally listed in the file */usr/include/X11/cursorfont.h*. We've provided a list of the standard cursors in Appendix D, *Standard Cursors*. To specify a standard cursor on a command line or in a resource file, strip the XC_ prefix from the name. Thus, to set the root window pointer to the pirate cursor symbol, you would enter:

```
% xsetroot -cursor_name pirate
```

The Release 3 version of *xsetroot* requires you to use a more roundabout method to set the root window pointer to one of the standard cursor shapes. You first convert the cursor character you want to a bitmap, using the *atobm* client, described in Chapter 7, *Graphics Utilities*. Then you can specify the bitmap as the root window cursor shape using the *xsetroot* option described in the following paragraphs.

This second option is intended to allow you to set the root window pointer to a bitmap, perhaps one you create. The parameters `cursorfile` and `maskfile` are bitmaps. The `cursorfile` sets the bitmap for the pointer shape. In effect, the `maskfile` is placed behind the `cursorfile` bitmap to set it off from the root window. The `maskfile` should be the same shape as the `cursorfile` but should generally be at least one pixel wider in all directions.*

For the `cursorfile`, you can use any of the standard bitmaps in */usr/include/X11/bitmaps* or you can make your own with the *bitmap* client (see Chapter 7, *Graphics Utilities*).

Every standard cursor has an associated mask. Pictures of the cursors appear in Appendix D, *Standard Cursors*. To get an idea of what masks look like, display the cursor font using the command:

```
% xfd -fn cursor.
```

If you are using your own bitmap as the `cursorfile`, until you get used to the way masks work, create a `maskfile` that is a copy of the `cursorfile` with all bits set, i.e., the

---

*Technically speaking, the mask determines the pixels on the screen that are disturbed by the cursor. It functions as a sort of outliner or highlighter for the cursor shape. The mask appears as a white (or background color) border around the cursor (black or another foreground color), making it visible over any root window pattern. This is especially important when a black cursor appears on a black root window.

With the *xsetroot* defaults, you can observe the effect of a mask. When you move the X pointer onto the dark gray root window, the X should have a very thin white border, which enables you to see it more clearly.

maskfile should be all black* (or the foreground color). Then edit the `maskfile` to make it wider than the `cursorfile` by at least one pixel in all directions.

To specify a root window pointer made from the smiling Gumby bitmap we created for Figure 7-2, first copy the bitmap to make a mask file:

```
% cp gumby gumby.mask
```

Then edit the *gumby.mask* file using the *bitmap* client, setting all squares inside the Gumby. (You can use the *bitmap* command box Flood Fill to set all the empty squares at once.) Continue to edit the bitmap, making it one pixel wider in all directions.

Then specify the new pointer with *xsetroot*:

```
% xsetroot -cursor gumby gumby.mask
```

See Chapter 7, *Graphics Utilities*, for more information on using *bitmap*.

xmodmap: Modifier Key and Pointer Customization

The *xmodmap* client is used to assign (or map) key functions to physical keys on the keyboard. Primarily, *xmodmap* is used to assign so-called "modifier" key functions to physical keys but it can also change the way other keys (and even pointer buttons) function.

As described in Chapter 3, *Working in the X Environment*, keys with labels such as Shift, Control, Caps Lock, etc. are called "modifier" keys because they modify the action of other keys. The number and names of modifier keys differ from workstation to workstation. Every keyboard is likely to have a Shift, Caps Lock, and Control key but after that, the babble begins. One workstation might have an Alt key, another might have a Funct key, and yet another a Gold key. On the Sun-3 keyboard, there are no less than three additional modifier keys, labeled Alternate, Right, and Left.

Because of the differences between keyboards, X programs are designed to work with *logical* modifier keynames. The logical keynames represent functions recognized by X programs. These modifier keynames can be mapped by the user to any physical key on the keyboard with the *xmodmap* client.

The logical keynames that X recognizes are:

- Shift
- Lock
- Control
- Mod1 (Meta in *mwm*)
- Mod2

---

*Don't be confused by the idea of a black cursor with a black mask on a black root window. Remember, the mask determines the pixels that are disturbed by the cursor—in effect creating an outline around the cursor. The outline appears in white (or specified background color), regardless of the color of the `maskfile`.

- Mod3
- Mod4
- Mod5

These keynames are case-insensitive.

Of these X modifier keys, only Shift, Caps Lock, Control, and Meta are in common use. Note that *uwm* also recognizes the mod keys simply by number alone (1-5) and recognizes mod1 as Meta (i.e., mod1, Meta and 1 are equivalent).

The primary function of *xmodmap* is to allow you to assign these important modifier keyname functions (Shift, Control, Meta, etc.) to convenient keys on the keyboard. For example, you could choose to map the Shift function to a single key called "Shift," to two "Shift" keys (one on either side of the keypad), to an "Alt" key, or to any other convenient key or keys on the physical keyboard. A left-handed person might choose to map modifier keys that more often are found on the left side, such as Control, on the right side of the keyboard.

In practical terms, each server will have a default keyboard configuration. The Shift, Caps Lock, and Control modifier keynames will be mapped to obvious keys. The assignment of the Meta key might be less obvious.

The *xmodmap* client allows you to print out the current assignments of modifier keyname functions to physical keys and/or to change the assignments.

xmodmap also has two other functions that you will probably use less frequently. In addition to mapping modifier keyname functions to physical keys, *xmodmap* also allows you to assign the function of *any* key on the keyboard to any other key. For instance, you can make the Backspace key and the Delete key both function as Delete keys. (This may be helpful if the Backspace key is easier to reach.)

Also, in addition to keyboard mappings, *xmodmap* can be used to display or change the pointer button assignments. Many X clients recognize logical pointer button commands. For example, holding down and dragging the first logical pointer button in an *xterm* window copies the text into memory. (In many default pointer maps, the first logical button is the leftmost button, designed to be pressed by the right index finger.) Each logical button is associated with a *button code*. The first logical button generates button code 1, the second logical button generates button code 2, etc. *xmodmap* allows you to reassign logical buttons to different physical buttons on the pointer.

Thus, basically, *xmodmap* can perform three types of mappings:

1. Assign modifier keyname functions (such as Shift, Control, Meta) recognized by X to physical keys.

2. Make any key on the keyboard function as any other key (for example, making Backspace function like Delete).

3. Reassign logical pointer button functions to other physical buttons (for example, making the rightmost physical button function as the first logical button).

In the following sections, we discuss key mapping, with an emphasis on the first type of mapping, of modifier keyname functions. Chances are, you'll have relatively little call to map other key functions (such as Backspace), though we have included an example of one such mapping, just in case.

After considering key mapping, we'll take a look at the much simpler issues involved in mapping pointer button functions. As you might expect, when you're changing the functionality of (up to) three pointer buttons, it's fairly simple to keep track of what you're doing.

On the other hand, mapping modifier key functions to physical keys can be more than a little confusing. In order to understand the mechanics of mapping keys, we first need to take a look at some terms used to describe keyboard keys.

Keycodes and Keysyms

Each key on a physical keyboard can be identified by a number known as a *keycode*. (Technically speaking, a keycode is the actual value that the key generates.) Keycodes cannot be mapped to other keys. No matter what functions you assign to various keys with *xmodmap*, the keycode associated with each physical key remains the same.

In addition to a keycode, each physical key is associated with a name known as a keysym. A *keysym* (*key sym*bol name) is a name that represents the label on a key (theoretically) and corresponds to its function.

Alphanumeric keys generally have obvious keysyms, corresponding to the label on the key: for example, the keysym for the key labeled "H" is *h*. Unfortunately, a keysym does not always correspond to the key label. For example, on a Sun-3 workstation, though the keysym for the key labeled "Return" is *Return*, the keysym for the key labeled "Alternate" is *Break*, and the keysym for the key labeled "Right" is *Meta_R*.

While each keycode is tied to a physical key, each keysym corresponds to a *function*—and the keysym/function is mapped to a particular physical key (keycode). Every keyboard has a default assignment of keysyms to keycodes. In most cases, each physical key on the keyboard will be associated with a different keysym. As we'll see, however, the keysym (function) associated with a particular physical key (keycode) can be changed. This is done by assigning the keysym of one key to the keycode of another.

The modifier keynames recognized by X are not to be confused with keysyms. The X modifier keys are limited to the eight keynames discussed previously and are assigned *in addition* to the regular keysym/keycode pairings. In other words, when a physical key is mapped to function as the X Control key, it already has a default functionality (keysym) and keycode.

By default, most modifier keyname functions are mapped to keys having keysyms representing the same function. For example, the X Control keyname is probably mapped to the key labeled Control, and having the keysym Control.

The Meta modifier keyname is probably also assigned to a key having the keysym Meta. However, determining which physical key has the keysym Meta can be something of a puzzle. Later in this chapter, we'll consider a program called *xev*, which can be used to determine the keysym and keycode of any physical key.

With this background information in mind, we can now tackle a procedure to map modifier keynames.

Procedure to Map Modifier Keys

In order to change modifier key mappings with a minimum of confusion, you should perform these steps:

1. Display the current *modifier* key mappings using *xmodmap*.

2. Then print out the default assignments of keysyms to keycodes for *all* keys, using *xmodmap* with the −pk option. Save this list of the default key assignments in a file as a reference.

3. Experiment with the *xev* client to determine the keysyms associated with certain physical keys. This will help you find the key(s) assigned as the Meta modifier key (which probably also has the keysym Meta).

4. Once you're familiar with the current assignments, you can remap modifier keys using *xmodmap*.

Displaying the Current Modifier Key Map

Before mapping any modifier keynames, you should take a look at the current assignments. With no options, *xmodmap* displays the current map of X modifier keynames to actual keys. Type *xmodmap* and you get a display similar to this:

```
xmodmap: up to 2 keys per modifier, (keycodes in parentheses):

shift       Shift_L (0x6a), Shift_R (0x75)
lock        Caps_Lock (0x7e)
control     Control_L (0x53)
mod1        Meta_L (0x7f),  Meta_R (0x81)
mod2
mod3
mod4
mod5
```

For each logical keyname (on the left), *xmodmap* lists one or more keysyms, each followed in parentheses by an actual hardware keycode. The keycodes displayed by *xmodmap* are represented in hex. As we'll see, the equivalent decimal and octal keycodes are also accepted as arguments to *xmodmap*.

Logical modifier keyname recognized by X	Keysym	Keycode (hex version)
Shift	Shift_L	(0x6a)
	Shift_R	(0x75)
Lock	Caps_Lock	(0x7e)
Control	Control_L	(0x53)
Mod1	Meta_L	(0x7f)
	Meta_R	(0x81)

In this mapping, two keys are assigned as Meta (mod1) keys: keys having the keysyms Meta_L and Meta_R (for left and right, apparently one on each side of the keyboard). Unfortunately, as you can see, this doesn't really tell you which keys these are on the physical keyboard. You still need to know which physical keys (keycodes) have the keysyms Meta_L and Meta_R. You can determine this using the *xev* client, described later in this chapter.

Determining the Default Key Mappings

Before you start mapping keys, you should display and save a map of the default assignments of keysyms to keycodes. Running *xmodmap* with the −pk option prints a current map of all keyboard keys to standard output. This map, called a keymap table, lists the decimal keycode on the left and the associated keysym(s) on the right. Figure 12-1 shows a portion of a typical keymap table, for a Sun-3 keyboard.

Notice that each keysym is listed by a keysym name (comma, Caps_Lock, etc.) and a keysym value (0x002c, 0xffe5, etc). For our purposes, this value is irrelevant. It cannot be supplied as a keysym argument to *xmodmap*.

As you can see, the keymap table lists regular keyboard keys (C, V, comma, slash, space, etc.), and function/numeric keypad keys (R13, F35, etc.) as well as modifier keys (Caps_Lock, Meta_L and Meta_R). If you map several keys, you may get confused as to the original assignments. Before you map any keys, we suggest you redirect the keymap table to a file to save and use as a reference:

```
% xmodmap −pk > keytable
```

The keysyms recognized by your server are a subset of a far greater number of keysyms recognized internationally. The file */usr/include/X11/keysym.h* lists the keysym *families* that are enabled for your server. The file */usr/include/X11/keysymdef.h* lists the keysyms in each of the families enabled for your server, as well as the keysyms in several other families. See Appendix H, *Keysyms*, of Volume Two, *Xlib Reference Manual*, for more information on keysyms and tables of the most common ones.

```
Keycode        Keysym
               value (name)
109            0x0043 (C)
110            0x0056 (V)
111            0x0042 (B)
112            0x004e (N)
113            0x004d (M)
114            0x002c (comma)   0x003c (less)
115            0x002e (period)  0x003e (greater)
116            0x002f (slash)   0x003f (question)
117            0xffe2 (Shift_R)
118            0xff0a (Linefeed)
119            0xffde (R13)
120            0xff54 (Down)     0xffdf (F34)
121            0xffe0 (F35)
                   .
                   .
                   .
126            0xffe5 (Caps_Lock)
127            0xffe7 (Meta_L)
128            0x0020 (space)
129            0xffe8 (Meta_R)
```

Figure 12-1. Partial keymap table

Matching Keysyms with Physical Keys Using xev

The keysym and keycode for any key can be determined with the *xev* client.* This is particularly useful for finding the Meta key(s). The *xev* client is used to keep track of *events*, packets of information that are generated by the server when actions occur and are interpreted by other clients. Moving the pointer or pressing a keyboard key cause input events to occur. (For more information about events, see Volume One, *Xlib Programming Manual*.)

To use *xev*, enter the command:

    % xev

in an *xterm* window, and then use the pointer to place the *xev* window, as in Figure 12-2.

Within the *xev* window is a small box. Move the pointer inside this box. When you type a key inside the box, information about the key, including its keysym and keycode, will be displayed in the *xterm* window from which you started *xev*. The relevant information will look like this:

---

*xev is a Release 3 standard client. In Release 4, it has been moved to the *demos* directory. If an executable version does not exist on your system, ask your system administrator.

If you cannot use *xev*, you must rely on the keymap table and a little deductive reasoning. Since certain *mwm* functions have keyboard shortcuts involving the Meta key, testing these shortcuts should help you locate this key. See Chapter 4, *More about the mwm Window Manager*, for more information.

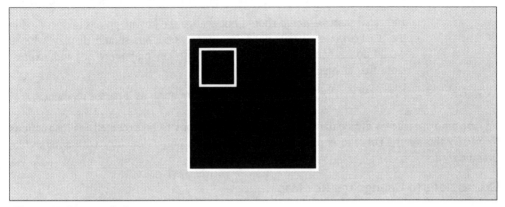

Figure 12-2. xev window

```
. . . keycode 127 (keysym 0xffe7, Meta_L) . . .
```

Notice that the keycode is given as a decimal number. You can use the decimal keycode as an argument to *xmodmap*. The keysym is listed by name, Meta_L, and value, 0xffe7. Again, this value cannot be supplied as a keysym argument to *xmodmap*. (See the *xev* reference page in Part Three of this guide for more information.)

To find the Meta key, type a few likely keys in the *xev* window. Type Control-C in the window from which you invoked *xev* to terminate the program. (If you ran *xev* in the background, you'll have to kill the *xev* window. See Chapter 8, *Other Clients*, for ways to kill a client window.)

Changing the Map with xmodmap

xmodmap executes an expression or list of expressions that is interpreted as instructions to modify the key (or pointer) map. The expressions that can be interpreted by *xmodmap* are described in the next section.

xmodmap has this syntax:

xmodmap [*options*] [*filename*]

An expression can be executed in either one of two ways:

- From the command line, using the −e *expression* option. This option specifies an expression to be executed (as an instruction to modify the map). Any number of expressions may be specified from the command line. An *expression* should be enclosed in quotes.

- Entered in a file that is used as an argument to *xmodmap*. Several expressions can be entered in one file.

See the *xmodmap* reference page in Part Three of this guide for a complete list of options. Other than `-e expression`, the most important options for our purposes are listed below.

`-n` Indicates that *xmodmap* should not change the key mappings as specified in the `filename` or command line expression but should display what it would do. A handy test. (Only works with key mappings, not with expressions that change the pointer map.)

`-verbose` Indicates that *xmodmap* should print information as it parses its input.

`filename` specifies a file containing *xmodmap* expressions to be executed (as instructions to modify the map). This file is usually kept in the user's home directory with a name like *.xmodmaprc*.

Expressions to Change the Key Map

The expressions interpreted by *xmodmap* can be used to perform these types of key mappings:*

1. Assign and remove keysyms as modifier keynames recognized by X.

2. Map any keysym (function) to any physical key (keycode).

This list shows allowable expressions, divided by function. (Using *xmodmap* with the `-grammar` option returns a help message with much of this information.) Those expressions that include an equal sign require a space before and after the sign.

1. To assign and remove keysyms as modifier keynames:

`clear MODIFIERNAME`

Removes all entries in the modifier map for the given modifier, where valid modifier names are: shift, lock, control, mod1, mod2, mod3, mod4, and mod5 (case does not matter in modifier names, although it does matter for all other names). For example, the expression `clear Lock` will remove all keys that were bound to the lock modifier.

`add MODIFIERNAME = KEYSYMNAME`

Adds the given keysym to the indicated modifier map. For example, you could make the Alt key an additional shift modifier key. The keysym name is evaluated after all input expressions are read to make it easy to write expressions to swap keys.

---

*Expressions to change the pointer map are discussed in the section "Displaying and Changing the Pointer Map," later in this chapter.

```
remove MODIFIERNAME = KEYSYMNAME
```

> Removes the given keysym from the indicated modifier map (unmaps it). For
> example, remove Caps_Lock as the lock modifier key. Unlike with the add
> expression, the keysym names are evaluated as the line is read in. This allows
> you to remove keys from a modifier without having to worry about whether they
> have been reassigned.

2. To map any keysym(s) to any physical key (keycode):

```
keycode NUMBER = KEYSYMNAME
```

> Assigns the keysym to the indicated keycode (which may be specified in deci-
> mal, hex or octal). Usually only one keysym is assigned to a given code.

```
keysym KEYSYMNAME = KEYSYMNAME
```

> Assigns the keysym on the right to the keycode of the keysym on the left. Note
> that if you have the same keysym bound to multiple keys, this might not work.

Key Mapping Examples

Expressions can be used on the *xmodmap* command line or entered in a file that is then used
as an argument to *xmodmap*. Note that *xmodmap* should be run from your startup script (discussed in Appendix A, *System Management*) to take effect for all clients in the login session.
This section includes three examples, corresponding to the three types of mappings you can
perform.

Remember that including the −n option on the *xmodmap* command line allows you to see
what the new mappings *would* be, without actually performing them. This can be very useful, particularly while you're learning to use *xmodmap* and getting used to the syntax of
expressions. (Note, however, that −n cannot be used with expressions to change the pointer
mapping.)

First, the *xmodmap* client also allows you to assign logical modifier keynames to physical
keys. A not so obvious feature of *xmodmap* is that to change the mapping of a modifier key,
you must first remove that key from the current modifier map. For example, to swap the left
Control and (Caps) Lock keys, you would first need to unmap both physical keys
(Caps_Lock, Control_L) from their respective modifier keynames (lock, control):

```
remove lock = Caps_Lock
remove control = Control_L
```

And then reverse the mappings:

```
add lock = Control_L
add control = Caps_Lock
```

If you then type *xmodmap* without options, you see the new map:

```
xmodmap: up to 2 keys per modifier, (keycodes in parentheses):

shift      Shift_L (0x6a), Shift_R (0x75)
lock       Control_L (0x53)
control    Caps_Lock (0x7e)
```

```
mod1          Meta_L (0x7f), Meta_R (0x81)
mod2
mod3
mod4
mod5
```

The key with the keysym Control_L functions as a Lock key and the key with the keysym Caps_Lock functions as a Control key.

Second, *xmodmap* allows you to assign any keysym to any other key. For example, you might make the Backspace key function as a Delete key:

```
% xmodmap -e 'keysym BackSpace = Delete'
```

Then when you display the keymap table and grep for the Delete keysym, you'll see that it is assigned twice. On the command line of an *xterm* window, type:

```
% xmodmap -pk | grep Delete
```

and you'll get two lines from the current keymap table, similar to these:

```
50            0xffff (Delete)
73            0xffff (Delete)
```

The 50 and 73 are keycodes representing two physical keys. As you can see, both of these keys now function as Delete keys.

This example suggests some of the confusion you can experience using *xmodmap*. We know that one of these keys previously functioned as the Backspace key. But how can we tell which one? Here is an instance when our default keymap table comes in handy. If you've run xmodmap -pk and redirected it to a file before changing any mappings, you can check the file for the keysyms originally associated with the keycodes 50 and 73. In this case, the file tells us 50 originally was Backspace and 73 was Delete.

Of course, you could also figure out the original assignments by remapping one of the key-codes to Backspace. Then, if the key marked Backspace functions as marked, you know you've mapped the keysym to the original keycode. But, as you can see, the default keymap table can greatly simplify matters.

This example also implies that there are advantages to using expressions of the form:

```
keycode number = keysymname
```

This expression syntax requires you to be aware of default keycode/keysym assignments. Also, if you explicitly assign a keysym to a particular keycode, it's much easier to keep track of what you're doing and retrace your steps if necessary. On the down side, though keysyms are portable, keycodes may vary from server to server. Thus, expressions using this syntax cannot be ported to other systems.

Displaying and Changing the Pointer Map

If you want to change the assignment of logical pointer buttons to physical buttons, you should first display the current pointer map with the −pp option to *xmodmap*. A typical pointer map appears in Figure 12-3.

```
There are 3 pointer buttons defined.
      Physical         Button
       Button           Code
         1                1
         2                2
         3                3
```

Figure 12-3. Pointer map

This is a fairly simple map: the physical buttons are listed on the left and the corresponding logical functions (button codes) are listed on the right.

These are typical assignments for a right-handed person: the first logical button is the left-most button, designed to be pressed by the right index finger. The *xmodmap* client allows you to reassign logical buttons so that the pointer can be more easily used with the left hand.

The *xmodmap* client allows you to change the pointer map.* There are two *xmodmap* expressions: one to assign logical pointer buttons (button codes) to physical buttons; and another to restore the default assignments. The syntax of the expressions is:

`pointer = x y z`

> Sets the first, second, and third physical buttons to the button codes *x*, *y*, and *z*.

`pointer = default`

> Sets the pointer map back to its default settings (button 1 generates a code of 1, button 2 generates a code of 2, etc.).

Being able to change the pointer button assignments is very useful if you happen to be left-handed and would like the rightmost physical button to function as the first logical button (i.e., generate button code 1). To configure the pointer for a southpaw:

`% xmodmap -e 'pointer = 3 2 1'`

---

*Remember that the −n option, which allows you to see what *xmodmap* *would* do without performing the changes cannot be used with expressions to change the pointer mapping.

Then if you display the pointer mappings with xmodmap -pp, you get this:

```
There are 3 pointer buttons defined.
     Physical      Button
     Button        Code
       1             3
       2             2
       3             1
```

You can then push the first logical button (button code 1) with the index finger of your left hand.

You can return to the default pointer button assignments by entering:

```
% xmodmap -e 'pointer = default'
```

Part Three:

Client Reference Pages

This part of the guide provides UNIX-style "man-pages" for each of the standard X programs, as well as the mwm window manager. These pages are arranged alphabetically for ease of reference, and they contain detailed information (such as all options to a program) that is not covered in other parts of this guide.

The following reference pages appear in this section:

Reference Pages

Name

Intro – overview of reference page format.

Syntax

This section describes the command line syntax for invoking the client. Anything in **bold** type should be typed exactly as shown. Items in *italics* are parameters that should be replaced by actual values when you enter the command. Anything enclosed in brackets is optional. For example:

bitmap [*options*] *filename*

means to type the command **bitmap** followed by zero or more options (from the list of options on the reference page), followed by the name of the file containing the bitmap to be edited.

Description

This section explains the operation of the client. In some cases, additional descriptive sections appear later on in the reference page.

Options

This section lists available command line options. In some cases, reference is made to "all of the standard X Toolkit command line options." These X Toolkit options are listed in Chapter 9 of this guide, as well as in the first reference page in this section, which is simply labled *X*.

Resources

This section lists the resource variable names that can be specified in an *Xresources* or other resource file. In some cases, reference is made to "all the core resource names and classes." A list of the core names and classes appears in Appendix G, *Athena Widget Resources*. Syntax rules and examples appear in Chapter 10, *Setting Resources*. For complete information, see Volume Four, *X Toolkit Intrinsics Programming Manual*.

Widget Hierarchy

Applications written with the X Toolkit are comprised of widgets, which are pre-defined user interface components or objects. Typical widgets create graphical features such as menus, command buttons, dialog boxes, and scrollbars. Applications composed of widgets are always window-based (such as *xterm*, *xclock*, and *xman*). X also provides clients that are not window-based (such as *xlsfonts*, *xwininfo*, and *xlsclients*) and thus do not use widgets.

If present on a reference page, the section "Widget Hierarchy" diagrams the relationship of the widgets within the application. The widget hierarchy is significant in specifying client resources. Most Toolkit clients accept both application-specific resources (listed in the "Resources" section) and resources for the component widgets. Appendix G lists the user-settable resources for the Athena widgets and explains the somewhat complicated mechanisms by which resources are interpreted.

Reference Pages

Files

If present, this section lists the system and/or application-specific files relevant to the application.

Environment

If present, this section lists shell environment variables used by the client. This section does not list the DISPLAY and XENVIRONMENT variables, which are used by all clients. These variables are used as follows:

DISPLAY

> To get the default display name (specifically, the host, server/display, and screen). The DISPLAY variable typically has the form:
>
> `hostname:server.screen`
>
> (for example, `isla:0.0`). See *X* for more information about display name syntax.

XENVIRONMENT

> To get the name of a resource file containing host-specific resources. If this variable is not set, the resource manager will look for a file called *Xdefaults-hostname* (where ***hostname*** is the name of a particular host) in the user's home directory. See the *X* reference page for more information.

See Also

This section lists other reference pages in Part Three of this guide that may also be of interest. Note that versions of these pages may have been installed in the usual online manual hierarchy, and may be available via the UNIX *man*(1) command. References such as *stat*(2) can be found in the standard UNIX documentation. This section may also include references to documentation on Xlib, the X Toolkit, various widgets, etc.

Bugs

If present, this section lists areas in which the author of the program thinks it could be improved.

Author

The authors of the program and (generally) of the reference page as well. Most of the reference pages are subject to the copyright provisions in the "Copyright" section of the X reference page. Where appropriate, additional copyrights are noted on individual pages.

Note, however, that those portions of this document that are based on the original X11 documentation and other source materials have been revised and that all such revisions are copyright © 1987, 1988, 1989 O'Reilly & Associates, Inc. Inasmuch as the proprietary revisions can't be separated from the freely copyable MIT source material, the net result is that copying of this document is not allowed. Sorry for the doublespeak!

Name

X – a portable, network-transparent window system.

Description

X is a network-transparent window system developed at MIT that runs on a wide range of computing and graphics machines. The Release 4 core distribution from MIT supports the following operating systems:

Ultrix 3.1 (Digital)
SunOS 4.0.3 (Sun)
HP-UX 6.5 (Hewlett-Packard)
Domain/OS 10.1 (HP/Apollo)
A/UX 1.1 (Apple)
AIX RT-2.2 and PS/2-1.1 (IBM)
AOS-4.3 (IBM)
UTEK 4.0 (Tektronix)
NEWS-OS 3.2 (Sony; client only)
UNICOS 5.0.1 (Cray; client only)
UNIX™ System V, Release 3.2 (AT&T 6386 WGS; client only)

It should be relatively easy to build the client-side software on a variety of other systems. Commercial implementations are also available for a much wider range of platforms.

The X Consortium requests that the following names be used when referring to this software:

X
X Window System
X Version 11
X Window System, Version 11
X11

The name "X Windows" should not be used. *X Window System* is a trademark of the Massachusetts Institute of Technology.

X window system servers run on computers with bitmap displays. The server distributes user input to and accepts output requests from various client programs through a variety of different interprocess communication channels. Although the most common case is for the client programs to be running on the same machine as the server, clients can also be run transparently from other machines, including machines with different architectures and operating systems).

X supports overlapping hierarchical subwindows and text and graphics operations, on both monochrome and color displays. For a full explanation of the functions that are available, see Volume One, *Xlib Programming Manual*, and Volume Two, *Xlib Reference Manual*.

The number of programs that use X is growing rapidly. Of particular interest are: a terminal emulator (*xterm*), a window manager (*twm*), a display manager (*xdm*), mail managing utilities (*xmh* and *xbiff*), a manual page browser (*xman*), a bitmap editor (*bitmap*), access control programs (*xauth* and *xhost*), user preference setting programs (*xrdb*, *xset*, *xsetroot*, and *xmodmap*), a load monitor (*xload*), clocks (*oclock* and *xclock*), a font displayer (*xfd*), utilities for listing information about fonts, windows, and displays (*xlsfonts*, *xfontsel*, *xlswins*, *xwininfo*, *xdpyinfo*, *xlsclients*, and *xprop*), a diagnostic for seeing what events are generated and when (*xev*), screen image manipulation utilities (*xwd*, *xwud*, *xpr*, and *xmag*), and various demos (*xeyes*, *ico*, *muncher*, *puzzle*, *xgc*, etc.).

Many other utilities, window managers, games, toolkits, and so on are available from the user-contributed distribution. See your site administrator for details.

Starting Up

There are two ways of starting the X server and an initial set of client applications. The particular method used depends on which operating system you are running and on whether or not you use other window systems in addition to X. The methods are:

xdm (the X Display Manager)

> If you want to have X running on your display at all times, your site administrator can set up your machine to use the X Display Manager *xdm*. This program is typically started by the system at boot time and takes care of keeping the server running and getting users logged in. If you are running *xdm*, you will see a window on the screen welcoming you to the system and asking for your username and password. Simply type them in as you would at a normal terminal, pressing the Return key after each. If you make a mistake, *xdm* will display an error message and ask you to try again. After you have successfully logged in, *xdm* will start up your X environment. By default, if you have an executable file named *.xsession* in your home directory, *xdm* will treat it as a program (or shell script) to be run to start up your initial clients (such as terminal emulators, clocks, a window manager, user settings for things like the background, the speed of the pointer, etc.). Your site administrator can provide details.

xinit (run manually from the shell)

> Sites that support more than one window system might choose to use the *xinit* program for starting X manually. If this is true for your machine, your site administrator will probably have provided a program named "x11", "startx", or "xstart" that will do site-specific initialization in a nice way (such as loading convenient default resources, running a window manager, displaying a clock, and starting several terminal emulators). If not, you can build such a script using the *xinit* program. This utility simply runs one user-specified program to start the server, runs another to start up any desired clients, and then waits for either to finish. Since either or both of the user-specified programs may be a shell script, this gives substantial flexibility at the expense of a nice interface. For this reason, *xinit* is not intended for end users.

Display Names

From the user's perspective, every X server has a *displayname* of the form:

    host:display.screen

This information is used by the application to determine how it should connect to the server and which screen it should use by default (on displays with multiple monitors):

host   The name of the machine to which the display is physically connected. If the *host* name is not given, the most efficient way of communicating to a server on the same machine will be used.

display

The *display* number. The phrase "display" is usually used to refer to a collection of monitors that share a common keyboard and pointer (mouse, tablet, etc.). Most workstations tend to have only one keyboard, and therefore only one display. Larger, multiuser systems, however, will frequently have several displays so that more than one person can be doing graphics work at once. To avoid confusion, each display on a machine is assigned a *display* number (beginning at 0) when the X server for that display is started. The *display* number must always be given in a display name. In this guide, the *display* number is also referred to as the *server* number (referring to the phrase *display server*).

screen

The *screen* number. Some displays share a single keyboard and pointer among two or more monitors. Since each monitor has its own set of windows, each screen is assigned a *screen* number (beginning at 0) when the X server for that display is started. If the *screen* number is not given, then screen 0 will be used.

On POSIX systems, the default display name is stored in your DISPLAY environment variable. This variable is set automatically by the *xterm* terminal emulator. However, when you log into another machine on a network, you'll need to set DISPLAY by hand to point to your display. For example:

```
% setenv DISPLAY myws:0          (C Shell)
$ DISPLAY=myws:0; export DISPLAY   (Bourne Shell)
```

Finally, most X programs accept a command line option of -display *displayname* to temporarily override the contents of DISPLAY. This is most commonly used to pop windows on another person's screen or as part of a "remote shell" command to start an xterm pointing back to your display. For example:

```
% xeyes -display joesws:0 -geometry 1000x1000+0+0
% rsh big xterm -display myws:0 -ls </dev/null &
```

X servers listen for connections on a variety of different communications channels (network byte streams, shared memory, etc.). Since there can be more than one way of contacting a given server, the *host* name part of the display name is used to determine the type of channel (also called a transport layer) to be used. The sample servers from MIT support the following types of connections:

local   The *host* part of the display name should be the empty string. For example: :0, :1, and :0.1. The most efficient local transport will be chosen.

TCP/IP The *host* part of the display name should be the server machine's IP address name. Full Internet names, abbreviated names, and IP addresses are all allowed. For example: `expo.lcs.mit.edu:0`, `expo:0`, `18.30.0.212:0`, `bigmachine:1`, and `hydra:0.1`.

DECnet

The *host* part of the display name should be the server machine's nodename followed by two colons instead of one. For example: `myws::0`, `big::1`, and `hydra::0.1`.

Access Control

The sample server provides two types of access control: an authorization protocol that provides a list of "magic cookies" that clients can send to request access (available as of Release 4); and a list of hosts from which connections are always accepted. *xdm* initializes magic cookies in the server, and also places them in a file accessible to the user. Normally, the list of hosts from which connections are always accepted should be empty, so that only clients that are explicitly authorized can connect to the display. When you add entries to the host list (with *xhost*), the server no longer performs any authorization on connections from those machines. Be careful with this.

The file for authorization used by both *xdm* and Xlib can be specified with the environment variable XAUTHORITY, and defaults to the file *.Xauthority* in the home directory. *xdm* uses *$HOME/.Xauthority* and will create it or merge in authorization records if it already exists when a user logs in.

To manage a collection of authorization files containing a collection of authorization records, use *xauth*. This program allows you to extract records and insert them into other files. Using this, you can send authorization to remote machines when you log in. As the files are machine-independent, you can also simply copy the files or use NFS to share them. If you use several machines, and share a common home directory with NFS, then you never really have to worry about authorization files—the system should work correctly by default. Note that magic cookies transmitted "in the clear" over NFS or using *ftp* or *rcp* can be "stolen" by a network eavesdropper, and as such may enable unauthorized access. In many environments this level of security is not a concern, but if it is, you need to know the exact semantics of the particular magic cookie to know if this is actually a problem.

Geometry Specifications

One of the advantages of using window systems instead of hardwired terminals is that applications don't have to be restricted to a particular size or location on the screen. Although the layout of windows on a display is controlled by the window manager that the user is running (described below), most X programs accept a command line argument of the form `-geometry` *widthxheight±xoff±yoff* (where *width*, *height*, *xoff*, and *yoff* are numbers) for specifying a preferred size and location for this application's main window.

The *width* and *height* parts of the geometry specification are usually measured in either pixels or characters, depending on the application. The *xoff* and *yoff* parts are measured in pixels and are used to specify the distance of the window from the left or right and top and bottom edges of the screen, respectively. Both types of offsets are measured from the indicated edge of the screen to the corresponding edge of the window. The x offset may be specified in the following ways:

+xoff The left edge of the window is to be placed *xoff* pixels in from the left edge of the screen (i.e., the x coordinate of the window's origin will be *xoff*). *xoff* may be negative, in which case the window's left edge will be off the screen.

-xoff The right edge of the window is to be placed *xoff* pixels in from the right edge of the screen. *xoff* may be negative, in which case the window's right edge will be off the screen.

The y offset has similar meanings:

+yoff The top edge of the window is to be *yoff* pixels below the top edge of the screen (i.e., the y coordinate of the window's origin will be *yoff*). *yoff* may be negative, in which case the window's top edge will be off the screen.

-yoff The bottom edge of the window is to be *yoff* pixels above the bottom edge of the screen. *yoff* may be negative, in which case the window's bottom edge will be off the screen.

Offsets must be given as pairs; in other words, in order to specify either *xoff* or *yoff* both must be present. Windows can be placed in the four corners of the screen using the following specifications:

+0+0   The upper-left corner.

−0+0   The upper-right corner.

−0−0   The lower-right corner.

+0−0   The lower-left corner.

In the following examples, a terminal emulator will be placed in roughly the center of the screen and a load average monitor, mailbox, and clock will be placed in the upper-right corner:

```
% xterm -fn 6x10 -geometry 80x24+30+200 &
% xclock -geometry 48x48-0+0 &
% xload -geometry 48x48-96+0 &
% xbiff -geometry 48x48-48+0 &
```

Window Managers

The layout of windows on the screen is controlled by special programs called *window managers*. Although many window managers will honor geometry specifications as given, others may choose to ignore them (requiring the user to explicitly draw the window's region on the screen with the pointer, for example).

Since window managers are regular (albeit complex) client programs, a variety of different user interfaces can be built. The core distribution comes with a window manager named *twm*, which supports overlapping windows, popup menus, point-and-click or click-to-type input models, titlebars, nice icons (and an icon manager for those who don't like separate icon windows).

Several other window managers are available in the user-contributed distribution: *uwm*, *gwm*, *m_swm*, *olwm*, and *tekwm*.

Font Names

Collections of characters for displaying text and symbols in X are known as *fonts*. A font typically contains images that share a common appearance and look nice together (for example, a single size, boldness, slant, and character set). Similarly, collections of fonts that are based on a common type face (the variations are usually called roman, bold, italic, bold italic, oblique, and bold oblique) are called *families*.

Sets of font families of the same resolution (usually measured in dots-per-inch) are further grouped into *directories* (so named because they were initially stored in file system directories). Each directory contains a database that lists the name of the font and information on how to find the font. The server uses these databases to translate *font names* (which have nothing to do with filenames) into font data.

The list of font directories in which the server looks when trying to find a font is controlled by the *font path*. Although most installations will choose to have the server start up with all of the commonly used font directories, the font path can be changed at any time with the *xset* program. However, it is important to remember that the directory names are on the *server's* machine, not on the application's.

The default font path for the sample server contains three directories:

/usr/lib/X11/fonts/misc

This directory contains several miscellaneous fonts that are useful on all systems. It contains a small family of fixed-width fonts in pixel heights 5 through 10, a family of fixed-width fonts from Dale Schumacher in similar pixel heights, several Kana fonts from Sony Corporation, a Kanji font, the standard cursor font, two cursor fonts from Digital Equipment Corporation, and OPEN LOOK cursor and glyph fonts from Sun Microsystems, Inc. It also has font name aliases for the fonts *fixed* and *variable*.

/usr/lib/X11/fonts/75dpi

This directory contains fonts contributed by Adobe Systems, Inc., Digital Equipment Corporation, Bitstream, Inc., Bigelow and Holmes, and Sun Microsystems, Inc. for 75 dots-per-inch displays. An integrated selection of sizes, styles, and weights is provided for each family.

/usr/lib/X11/fonts/100dpi

This directory contains 100 dots per inch versions of the fonts in the *75dpi* directory.

Font databases are created by running the *mkfontdir* program in the directory containing the source or compiled versions of the fonts (in both compressed and uncompressed formats). Whenever fonts are added to a directory, *mkfontdir* should be rerun so that the server can find the new fonts. To make the server reread the font database, reset the font path with the *xset* program. For example, to add a font to a private directory, the following commands could be used:

```
% cp newfont.snf ~/myfonts
% mkfontdir ~/myfonts
```

```
% xset fp rehash
```

The *xlsfonts* program can be used to list all of the fonts that are found in font databases in the current font path. Font names tend to be fairly long as they contain all of the information needed to uniquely identify individual fonts. However, the sample server supports wildcarding of font names, so the full specification:

```
-adobe-courier-medium-r-normal--10-100-75-75-m-60-iso8859-1
```

could be abbreviated as:

```
*-courier-medium-r-normal--*-100-*
```

Because the shell also has special meanings for * and ?, wildcarded font names should be quoted:

```
% xlsfonts -fn '*-courier-medium-r-normal--*-100-*'
```

If more than one font in a given directory in the font path matches a wildcarded font name, the choice of which particular font to return is left to the server. However, if fonts from more than one directory match a name, the returned font will always be from the first such directory in the font path. The example given above will match fonts in both the *75dpi* and *100dpi* directories; if the *75dpi* directory is ahead of the *100dpi* directory in the font path, the smaller version of the font will be used.

Color Names

Most applications provide ways of tailoring (usually through resources or command line arguments) the colors of various elements in the text and graphics they display. Although black and white displays don't provide much of a choice, color displays frequently allow anywhere between 16 and 16 million different colors.

Colors are usually specified by their commonly-used names (for example, *red*, *white*, or *medium slate blue*). The server translates these names into appropriate screen colors using a color database that can usually be found in */usr/lib/X11/rgb.txt*. Color names are case-insensitive, meaning that *red*, *Red*, and *RED* all refer to the same color.

Many applications also accept color specifications of the following form:

```
#rgb
#rrggbb
#rrrgggbbb
#rrrrggggbbbb
```

where *r*, *g*, and *b* are hexidecimal numbers indicating how much *red*, *green*, and *blue* should be displayed (zero being none and ffff being on full). Each field in the specification must have the same number of digits (e.g., #rrgb or #gbb are not allowed). Fields that have fewer than four digits (e.g., #rgb) are padded out with zeros following each digit (i.e., #r000g000b000). The eight primary colors can be represented as:

black	#000000000000 (no color at all)
red	#ffff00000000

Reference Pages

green	#0000ffff0000
blue	#00000000ffff
yellow	#ffffffff0000 (full red and green, no blue)
magenta	#ffff0000ffff (full red and blue, no green)
cyan	#0000ffffffff (full green and blue, no red)
white	#ffffffffffff (full red, green, and blue)

Unfortunately, RGB color specifications are highly unportable since different monitors produce different shades when given the same inputs. Similarly, color names aren't portable because there is no standard naming scheme and because the color database needs to be tuned for each monitor. Application developers should take care to make their colors tailorable.

Keys

The X keyboard model is broken into two layers: server-specific codes (called *keycodes*), which represent the physical keys, and server-independent symbols (called *keysyms*), which represent the letters or words that appear on the keys. Two tables are kept in the server for converting keycodes to keysyms:

modifier list

Some keys (such as Shift, Control, and Caps Lock) are known as *modifier keys* and are used to select different symbols that are attached to a single key (such as Shift-a generates a capital A, and Control-L generates a formfeed character ^L). The server keeps a list of keycodes corresponding to the various modifier keys. Whenever a key is pressed or released, the server generates an *event* that contains the keycode of the indicated key as well as a mask that specifies which of the modifer keys are currently pressed. Most servers set up this list to initially contain the various shift, control, and shift lock keys on the keyboard.

keymap table

Applications translate event keycodes and modifier masks into keysyms using a *keymap table* which contains one row for each keycode and one column for each of the modifiers. This table is initialized by the server to correspond to normal typewriter conventions, but is used only by client programs.

Although most programs deal with keysyms directly (such as those written with the X Toolkit Intrinsics), most programming libraries provide routines for converting keysyms into the appropriate type of string (such as ISO Latin-1).

Options

Most X programs attempt to use the same names for command line options and arguments. All applications written with the X Toolkit Intrinsics automatically accept the following options:

-display [*host*]:*server*[.*screen*]

Specifies the name of the display to use. *host* specifies the machine, *server* specifies the display server number, and *screen* specifies the screen number. Either or both of the *host* and *screen* elements to the display specification can be omitted. If *host* is omitted, the local machine is assumed. If *screen* is omitted, screen 0 is assumed (and the period is unnecessary). The colon and (display) *server* are necessary in all cases.

For example, the following command creates an *xclock* window on screen 1 on server 0 on the machine *your_node*.

xclock -display *your_node***:0.1**

The -display option can be abbreviated as -d, unless the client accepts another option that begins with "d."

-geometry *geometry*
>Specifies the initial size and location of the application window. The -geometry option can be (and often is) abbreviated to -g, unless there is a conflicting option that begins with "g." The argument (*geometry*) is referred to as a "standard geometry string," and has the form *widthxheight±xoff±yoff*.

>The -geometry option can be abbreviated as -g, unless the client accepts another option that begins with "g."

-bg *color*, -background *color*
>Either option specifies the color to use for the window background.

-bd *color*, -bordercolor *color*
>Either option specifies the color to use for the window border.

-bw *pixels*, -borderwidth *pixels*
>Either option specifies the width in pixels of the window border.

-fg *color*, -foreground *color*
>Either option specifies the color to use for text or graphics.

-fn *font*, -font *font*
>Either option specifies the font to use for displaying text.

-iconic
>Indicates that the user would prefer that the application's windows initially not be visible, as if the windows had been immediately iconified by the user. Window managers may choose not to honor the application's request.

-name *app_name*
>Specifies the name under which resources for the application should be found. This option is useful in shell aliases to distinguish between invocations of an application, without resorting to creating links to alter the executable filename.

-rv, -reverse
>Either option indicates that the program should simulate reverse video if possible, often by swapping the foreground and background colors. Not all programs honor this or implement it correctly. It is usually used only on monochrome displays.

+rv
>Indicates that the program should not simulate reverse video. This is used to override any defaults since reverse video doesn't always work properly.

Reference Pages

-selectionTimeout *milliseconds*

> Specifies the timeout in milliseconds within which two communicating applications must respond to one another for a selection request.

-synchronous

> Indicates that requests to the X server should be sent synchronously, instead of asynchronously. Since Xlib normally buffers requests to the server, errors are not necessarily reported immediately after they occur. This option turns off the buffering so that the application can be debugged. It should never be used with a working program.

-title *string*

> Specifies the title to be used for this window. This information is sometimes used by a window manager to provide some sort of header identifying the window.

-xnllanguage *language[_territory][.codeset]*

> Specifies the language, territory, and codeset for use in resolving resource and other filenames.

-xrm *resourcestring*

> Specifies a resource name and value to override any defaults. It is very useful for setting resources that don't have explicit command line arguments.

Resources

To make the tailoring of applications to personal preferences easier, X supports several mechanisms for storing default values for program resources (e.g., background color, window title, etc.). Resources are specified as strings of the form:

*appname*appname**subname**subsubname* ...: *value*

that are read in from various places when an application is run.

By convention, the application class name is the same as the program name, but with the first letter capitalized (e.g., *Bitmap* or *Emacs*) although some programs that begin with the letter "x" also capitalize the second letter for historical reasons. The precise syntax for resources is:

```
ResourceLine   =  Comment | ResourceSpec
Comment        =  "!" string | <empty line>
ResourceSpec   =  WhiteSpace ResourceName WhiteSpace ":" WhiteSpace value
ResourceName   =  [Binding] ComponentName {Binding ComponentName}
Binding        =  "." | "*"
WhiteSpace     =  {" " | "\t"}
ComponentName  =  {"a"-"z" | "A"-"Z" | "0"-"9" | "_" | "-"}
value          =  string
string         =  {<any character not including "\n">}
```

Note that elements enclosed in curly braces ({...}) indicate zero or more occurrences of the enclosed elements.

To allow values to contain arbitrary octets, the 4-character sequence *nnn*, where *n* is a digit in the range of "0"–"7", is recognized and replaced with a single byte that contains this sequence interpreted as an octal number. For example, a value containing a NULL byte can be stored by specifying "\\000".

The Xlib routine `XGetDefault(3X)` and the resource utilities within the X Toolkit obtain resources from the following sources:

RESOURCE_MANAGER root window property

> Any global resources that should be available to clients on all machines should be stored in the RESOURCE_MANAGER property on the root window using the *xrdb* program. This is frequently taken care of when the user starts up X through the display manager or *xinit*.

application-specific files

> Programs that use the X Toolkit Intrinsics will also look in the directories named by the environment variable XUSERFILESEARCHPATH or the environment variable XAPPLRESDIR, plus directories in a standard place (usually under */usr/lib/X11/*, but this can be overriden with the XFILESEARCHPATH environment variable) for application-specific resource files. Files are generally named *Class*—for the class name of the application.

> XAPPLRESDIR configuration files are actually loaded *before* the RESOURCE_MANAGER property, so that the property can override the values. See Volume Four, *X Toolkit Intrinsics Programming Manual*, for details.

XENVIRONMENT

> Any user- and machine-specific resources may be specified by setting the XENVIRONMENT environment variable to the name of a resource file to be loaded by all applications. If this variable is not defined, a file named *$HOME/.Xdefaults-hostname* is looked for instead, where **hostname** is the name of the host where the application is executing.

`-xrm` *resourcestring*

> Applications that use the X Toolkit can have resources specified from the command line. The *resourcestring* is a single resource name and value as shown above. Note that if the string contains characters interpreted by the shell (e.g., asterisk), they must be quoted. Any number of `-xrm` arguments may be given on the command line.

Program resources are organized into groups called *classes*, so that collections of individual resources (each of which is called *instances*) can be set all at once. By convention, the instance name of a resource begins with a lowercase letter and class name with an uppercase letter. Multiple word resources are concatentated with the first letter of the succeeding words capitalized. Applications written with the X Toolkit Intrinsics will have at least the following resources:

`background` (class `Background`)

> Specifies the color to use for the window background.

`borderWidth` (class `BorderWidth`)
> Specifies the width in pixels of the window border.

`borderColor` (class `BorderColor`)
> Specifies the color to use for the window border.

Most applications using the X Toolkit Intrinsics also have the resource `foreground` (class `Foreground`), specifying the color to use for text and graphics within the window.

By combining class and instance specifications, application preferences can be set quickly and easily. Users of color displays will frequently want to set `Background` and `Foreground` classes to particular defaults. Specific color instances such as text cursors can then be overridden without having to define all of the related resources. For example,

```
bitmap*Dashed:  off
XTerm*cursorColor:  gold
XTerm*multiScroll:  on
XTerm*jumpScroll:  on
XTerm*reverseWrap:  on
XTerm*curses:  on
XTerm*Font:  6x10
XTerm*scrollBar: on
XTerm*scrollbar*thickness: 5
XTerm*multiClickTime: 500
XTerm*charClass:  33:48,37:48,45-47:48,64:48
XTerm*cutNewline: off
XTerm*cutToBeginningOfLine: off
XTerm*titeInhibit:  on
XTerm*ttyModes:  intr ^c erase ^? kill ^u
XLoad*Background: gold
XLoad*Foreground: red
XLoad*highlight: black
XLoad*borderWidth: 0
emacs*Geometry:  80x65-0-0
emacs*Background:  #5b7686
emacs*Foreground:  white
emacs*Cursor:  white
emacs*BorderColor:  white
emacs*Font:  6x10
xmag*geometry:  -0-0
xmag*borderColor:  white
```

If these resources were stored in a file called *Xresources* in your home directory, they could be added to any existing resources in the server with the following command:

`% xrdb -merge $HOME/.Xresources`

This is frequently how user-friendly startup scripts merge user-specific defaults into any site-wide defaults. All sites are encouraged to set up convenient ways of automatically loading resources.

Examples

The following is a collection of sample command lines for some of the more frequently used commands. For more information on a particular command, please refer to that command's reference page.

```
% xrdb -load $HOME/.Xresources
% xmodmap -e 'keysym BackSpace = Delete'
% mkfontdir /usr/local/lib/X11/otherfonts
% xset fp+ /usr/local/lib/X11/otherfonts
% xmodmap $HOME/.keymap.km
% xsetroot -solid '#888'
% xset b 100 400 c 50 s 1800 r on
% xset q
% twm
% xmag
% xclock -geometry 48x48-0+0 -bg blue -fg white
% xeyes -geometry 48x48-48+0
% xbiff -update 20
% xlsfonts '*helvetica*'
% xlswins -l
% xwininfo -root
% xdpyinfo -display joesworkstation:0
% xhost -joesworkstation
% xrefresh
% xwd | xwud
% bitmap companylogo.bm 32x32
% xcalc -bg blue -fg magenta
% xterm -geometry 80x66-0-0 -name myxterm
```

Diagnostics

A wide variety of error messages are generated from various programs. Various toolkits are encouraged to provide a common mechanism for locating error text so that applications can be tailored easily. Programs written to interface directly to the Xlib C language library are expected to do their own error checking.

The default error handler in Xlib (also used by many toolkits) uses standard resources to construct diagnostic messages when errors occur. The defaults for these messages are usually stored in */usr/lib/X11/XErrorDB*. If this file is not present, error messages will be rather terse and cryptic.

When the X Toolkit Intrinsics encounter errors converting resource strings to the appropriate internal format, no error messages are printed. This is convenient when it is desirable to have one set of resources across a variety of displays (e.g., color versus monochrome, lots of fonts versus very few, etc.), although it can pose problems in trying to determine why an application might be failing. This behavior can be overridden by setting the `StringConversion-Warning` resource.

To force the X Toolkit Intrinsics to always print string conversion error messages, the following resource should be placed at the top of the file that is loaded onto the RESOURCE_MANAGER property using the *xrdb* program (frequently called *Xresources* or *Xres* in the user's home directory):

```
*StringConversionWarnings: on
```

To have conversion messages printed for just a particular application, the appropriate instance name can be placed before the asterisk:

```
xterm*StringConversionWarnings: on
```

Bugs

If you encounter a *repeatable* bug, please contact your site administrator for instructions on how to submit an X Bug Report.

See Also

XConsortium(1), XStandards(1), Xserver, mkfontdir, bdftosnf, bitmap, bsdtosnf, oclock, showsnf, twm, uwm, x10tox11, xauth, xbiff, xcalc, xclock, resize, xdpyinfo, xedit, xev, xfd, xfontsel, xhost, xinit, xkill, xload, xlogo, xlsclients, xlsfonts, xlswins, xmag, xman, xmh, xmodmap, xpr, xprop, xrdb, xrefresh, xset, xsetroot, biff(1), mh(1), init(8), ttys(5); Volume One, *Xlib Programming Manual*; Volume Two, *Xlib Reference Manual*; Volume Four, *X Toolkit Intrinsics Programming Manual*; Volume Five, *X Toolkit Intrinsics Reference Manual*.

Copyright

The following copyright and permission notice outlines the rights and restrictions covering most parts of the standard distribution of the X Window System from MIT. Other parts have additional or different copyrights and permissions; see the individual source files.

Copyright 1984, 1985, 1986, 1987, 1988, 1989 Massachusetts Institute of Technology.

Permission to use, copy, modify, and distribute this software and its documentation for any purpose and without fee is hereby granted, provided that the above copyright notice appear in all copies and that both that copyright notice and this permission notice appear in supporting documentation, and that the name of M.I.T. not be used in advertising or publicity pertaining to distribution of the software without specific, written prior permission. M.I.T. makes no representations about the suitability of this software for any purpose. It is provided "as is" without express or implied warranty.

This software is not subject to any license of the American Telephone and Telegraph Company or of the Regents of the University of California.

Trademarks

UNIX and OPEN LOOK are trademarks of AT&T. X Window System is a trademark of MIT.

Authors

A cast of thousands. See the file *doc/contributors* in the standard sources for some of the names.

Name

X – X Window System server.

Syntax

X [: *displaynumber*] [*options*] [*ttyname*]

Description

X is the generic name for the X Window System server. It is frequently a link to or a copy of the appropriate server binary for driving the most frequently used server on a given machine. The sample server from MIT supports the following platforms:

Xqvss	Digital monochrome vaxstationII or II
Xqdss	Digital color vaxstationII or II
Xsun	Sun monochrome or color Sun 2, 3, or 4
Xhp	HP Topcat 9000s300
Xibm	IBM AED, APA and megapel PC/RT, 8514 and VGA PS/2 model 80
Xapollo	Apollo monochrome or color (Domain/OS SR10.1 or SR10.2)
XmacII	Apple monochrome Macintosh II
Xcfbpmax	Digital color DECstation 3100
Xmfbpmax	Digital monochrome DECstation 3100
Xtek	Tektronix 4319 (this is the only tested configuration)

Starting the Server

The server is usually started from the X Display Manager program, *xdm*. This utility is run from the system boot files and takes care of keeping the server running, prompting for user-names and passwords, and starting up user sessions. It is easily configured for sites that wish to provide consistent interfaces for novice users (loading convenient sets of resources, starting up a window manager, clock, and a wide selection of terminal emulator windows).

Since *xdm* now handles automatic starting of the server in a portable way, the –L option to *xterm* is now considered obsolete. As of Release 4, support for starting a login window from BSD 4.3-derived */etc/ttys* files is no longer included.

Installations that run more than one window system will still need to use the *xinit* utility. However, *xinit* is to be considered a tool for building startup scripts and is not intended for use by end users. Site adminstrators are strongly urged to build more friendly interfaces for novice users.

When the sample server starts up, it takes over the display. If you are running on a workstation whose console is the display, you cannot log into the console while the server is running.

Network Connections

The sample server supports connections made using the following reliable byte-streams:

TCP/IP The server listens on port htons(6000+*n*), where *n* is the display number.

UNIX Domain

The sample server uses */tmp/.X11-unix/Xn* as the filename for the socket, where **n** is the display number.

DECnet

The server responds to connections to object *X$Xn*, where **n** is the display number.

Options

All of the sample servers accept the following command line options:

-a *number*

Sets pointer acceleration (i.e., the ratio of how much is reported to how much the user actually moved the pointer).

-auth *authorization_file*

Specifies a file that contains a collection of authorization records used to authenticate access. (Available as of Release 4.)

bc

Disables certain kinds of error checking, for bug compatibility with previous releases (e.g., to work around bugs in Release 2 and Release 3 versions of *xterm* and the toolkits). Use of this option is discouraged. (Available as of Release 4.)

-bs

Disables backing store support on all screens.

-c

Turns off key-click.

c *volume*

Sets key-click volume (allowable range: 0-8).

-cc *class*

Sets the visual class for the root window of color screens. The class numbers are as specified in the X protocol. Not obeyed by all servers. (Available as of Release 4.)

-dpi *resolution*

Sets the resolution of the screen, in dots-per-inch. To be used when the server cannot determine the screen size from the hardware.

-f *volume*

Sets beep (bell) volume (allowable range: 0-7).

-I

Causes all remaining command line arguments to be ignored. (Available as of Release 4.)

-ld *kilobytes*

Sets the data space limit of the server to the specified number of kilobytes. The default value is zero, making the data size as large as possible. A value of –1 leaves the data space limit unchanged. (Available as of Release 4. Not available in all operating systems.)

-ls *kilobytes*
> Sets the stack space limit of the server to the specified number of kilobytes. The default value is zero, making the stack size as large as possible. A value of –1 leaves the stack space limit unchanged. (Available as of Release 4. Not available in all operating systems.)

-logo Turns on the X Window System logo display in the screen saver. There is currently no way to change this from a client.

nologo
> Turns off the X Window System logo display in the screen saver. There is currently no way to change this from a client.

-p *minutes*
> Sets screen saver pattern cycle time, in minutes.

-r Turns off auto-repeat.

r Turns on auto-repeat.

-s *minutes*
> Sets screen saver timeout, in minutes.

-su Disables save under support on all screens.

-t *numbers*
> Sets pointer acceleration threshold, in pixels (i.e., after how many pixels pointer acceleration should take effect).

-to *seconds*
> Sets default screen saver timeout, in seconds.

v Sets video-on screen saver preference.

-v Sets video-off screen saver preference.

-co *filename*
> Sets the name of the RGB color database.

-help Prints a usage message.

-fp *font_path*
> Sets the search path for fonts. This path is a comma-separated list of directories that the server searches for font databases.

-fc *cursor_font*
> Sets the default cursor font.

-fn *font*
> Sets the default font.

-wm Forces the default backing-store of all windows to be WhenMapped; a cheap-trick way of getting backing-store to apply to all windows.

-x *extension*

> Loads the specified extension at init. (Available as of Release 4; not supported in most implementations.)

XDMCP-specific Options (Release 4)

You can also have the X server connect to *xdm* using XDMCP. Although this is not typically useful, because it doesn't allow *xdm* to manage the server process, it can be used to debug XDMCP implementations, and servers as a sample implementation of the server side of XDMCP. For more information on this protocol, see the XDMCP specification in the MIT X distribution under the filename *docs/XDMCP/xdmcp.ms*. The following options control the behavior of XDMCP:

-query *host_name*

> Enables XDMCP and sends Query packets to the specified host.

-broadcast

> Enables XDMCP and broadcasts BroadcastQuery packets to the network. The first responding display manager will be chosen for the session.

-indirect *host_name*

> Enables XDMCP and sends IndirectQuery packets to the specified host.

-port *port_num*

> Specifies an alternate port number for XDMCP packets. Must be specified before any -query, -broadcast, or -indirect options.

-once Makes the server exit after the first session is over. Normally, the server keeps starting sessions, one after the other.

-class *display_class*

> XDMCP has an additional display qualifier used in resource lookup for display-specific options. This option sets that value; by default, it is "MIT-Unspecified" (not a very useful value).

-cookie *xdm_auth_bits*

> When testing XDM-AUTHENTICATION-1, a private key is shared between the server and the manager. This option sets the value of that private data (not that it's very private, being on the command line).

-displayID *display_id*

> Yet another XDMCP-specific value, this one allows the display manager to identify each display so that it can locate the shared key.

Many servers also have device-specific command line options. For more details, see the manual pages for the individual servers.

Security

As of Release 4, the sample server implements a simplistic authorization protocol, MIT-MAGIC-COOKIE-1, which uses data private to authorized clients and the server. This is a rather trivial scheme; if the client passes authorization data which is the same as the data the server has, it is allowed access. This scheme is worse than the host-based access control

Reference Pages

mechanisms in environments with unsecure networks because it allows any host to connect, given that it has discovered the private key. But in many environments, this level of security is better than the host-based scheme, because it allows access to be controlled per-user instead of per-host.

In addition, the server provides support for a DES-based authorization scheme, XDM-AUTHORIZATION-1, which is more secure (given a secure key distribution mechanism), but as DES is not generally distributable, the implementation is missing routines to encrypt and decrypt the authorization data. This authorization scheme can be used in conjunction with XDMCP's authentication scheme, XDM-AUTHENTICATION-1, or in isolation.

The authorization data is passed to the server in a private file named with the −auth command line option. Each time the server is about to accept the first connection after a reset (or when the server is starting), it reads this file. If this file contains any authorization records, the local host is not automatically allowed access to the server, and only clients which send one of the authorization records contained in the file in the connection setup information will be allowed access. See the *Xau* manual page for a description of the binary format of this file. Maintenance of this file, and distribution of its contents to remote sites for use there, is left as an exercise for the reader.

The sample server also uses a host-based access control list for deciding whether or not to accept connections from clients on a particular machine. This list initially consists of the host on which the server is running as well as any machines listed in the file */etc/Xn.hosts*, where *n* is the display number of the server. Each line of the file should contain either an Internet hostname (e.g., expo.lcs.mit.edu) or a DECnet hostname in double colon format (e.g., hydra::). There should be no leading or trailing spaces on any lines. For example:

```
joesworkstation
corporate.company.com
star::
bigcpu::
```

Users can add or remove hosts from this list and enable or disable access control using the *xhost* command from the same machine as the server. For example:

```
% xhost +janesworkstation      janesworkstation added to access control list
% xhost -star::                star:: removed from access control list
% xhost +                      all hosts allowed (access control disabled)
% xhost -                      all hosts restricted (access control enabled)
% xhost
access control enabled (only the following hosts are allowed)
joesworkstation
janesworkstation
corporate.company.com
bigcpu::
```

Unlike some window systems, X does not have any notion of window operation permissions or place any restrictions on what a client can do; if a program can connect to a display, it has full run of the screen. Sites that have authentication and authorization systems (such as Kerberos) might wish to make use of the hooks in the libraries and the server to provide additional security.

Signals

The sample server attaches special meaning to the following signals:

SIGHUP   Causes the server to close all existing connections, free all resources, and restore all defaults. It is sent by the display manager whenever the main user's primary application (usually an *xterm* or window manager) exits to force the server to clean up and prepare for the next user.

SIGTERM   Causes the server to exit cleanly.

SIGUSR1   This signal is used quite differently from either of the above. When the server starts, it checks to see if it has inherited SIGUSR1 as SIG_IGN instead of the usual SIG_DFL. In this case, the server sends a SIGUSR1 to its parent process, after it has set up the various connection schemes. *xdm* uses this feature to recognize when it is possible to connect to the server.

Fonts

Fonts are usually stored as individual files in directories. The list of directories in which the server looks when trying to open a font is controlled by the *font path*. Although most sites will choose to have the server start up with the appropriate font path (using the −fp option mentioned above), it can be overridden using the *xset* program.

The default font path for the sample server contains three directories:

/usr/lib/X11/fonts/misc

This directory contains several miscellaneous fonts that are useful on all systems. It contains a small family of fixed-width fonts in pixel heights 5 through 10, a family of fixed-width fonts from Dale Schumacher in similar pixel heights, several Kana fonts from Sony Corporation, a Kanji font, the standard cursor font, two cursor fonts from Digital Equipment Corporation, and OPEN LOOK cursor and glyph fonts from Sun Microsystems, Inc. It also has font name aliases for the fonts fixed and variable.

/usr/lib/X11/fonts/75dpi

This directory contains fonts contributed by Adobe Systems, Inc., Digital Equipment Corporation, Bitstream, Inc., Bigelow and Holmes, and Sun Microsystems, Inc. for 75 dots per inch displays. An integrated selection of sizes, styles, and weights is provided for each family.

/usr/lib/X11/fonts/100dpi

This directory contains versions of the fonts in the *75dpi* directory for 100 dots-per-inch displays.

Font databases are created by running the *mkfontdir* program in the directory containing the compiled versions of the fonts (the *.snf* files). Whenever fonts are added to a directory, *mkfontdir* should be rerun so that the server can find the new fonts. If *mkfontdir* is not run, the server will not be able to find any fonts in the directory.

Reference Pages

Diagnostics

Too numerous to list them all. If run from *init*(8), errors are logged in the file */usr/adm/Xnmsgs*.

Files

/etc/Xn.hosts	Initial access control list.
/usr/lib/X11/fonts/misc, /usr/lib/X11/fonts/75dpi, /usr/lib/X11/fonts/100dpi	Font directories.
/usr/lib/X11/rgb.txt	Color database.
/tmp/X11-unix/Xn	UNIX domain socket.
/usr/adm/Xnmsgs	Error log file.

See Also

X, mkfontdir, twm, uwm, xauth, xdm, xhost, xinit, xset, xsetroot, xterm, ttys(5), init(8); *X Window System Protocol; Definition of the Porting Layer for the X v11 Sample Server; Strategies for Porting the X v11 Sample Server; Godzilla's Guide to Porting the X V11 Sample Server.*

Bugs

The option syntax is inconsistent with itself and *xset*.

The acceleration option should take a numerator and a denominator like the protocol.

If *X* dies before its clients, new clients won't be able to connect until all existing connections have their TCP TIME_WAIT timers expire.

The color database is missing a large number of colors. However, there doesn't seem to be a better one available that can generate RGB values tailorable to particular displays.

Authors

The sample server was originally written by Susan Angebranndt, Raymond Drewry, Philip Karlton, and Todd Newman, of Digital Equipment Corporation, with support from a large cast. It has since been extensively rewritten by Keith Packard and Bob Scheifler of MIT.

Name

appres – list application resource database.

Syntax

appres [[*classname*][*instancename*]] [**-xrm** *resource*]

Description

Available as of Release 4, the *appres* client prints the resources seen by an application of the specified `classname` and `instancename`. It is used to help determine which resources a particular program would load from the various sources of resource specifications.

Note that *appres* doesn't really know anything about classes and instances as they may be defined by the client itself. As a result, it takes no account of conflicts between different resource settings, or their correctness. It simply loads the resource database into a temporary file and does a string comparison on the strings:

```
[*.]
classname[*.]
instancename[*.]
```

(where [*.] means either * or .) and then prints out the lines that match. Basically, *appres* searches for occurrences of any class and/or instance name supplied to it. In addition, *appres* searches for resources not assigned to a particular client—i.e., resources beginning with an asterisk or a dot. (These resources may or may not apply to the client whose class and instance names you supply.)

For example:

% appres XTerm

would list the resources that include the classname `XTerm`, as well as any resources beginning with an asterisk or dot.

To also match particular instance names, you can enter both an instance and a class name, as in the following:

% appres XTerm myxterm

In this case, *appres* would list the resources that include any of the following terms: the classname `XTerm`; the instance name `myxterm`; or an initial asterisk or dot.

If no application class is specified, the class `-NoSuchClass-` (which should have no defaults) is used.

Keep in mind the limitations of supplying only one argument (either a class name or an instance name). For example, if resources are specified in the database for the instance name `xterm`, typing `appres XTerm` will not list them; and if they are specified for class name `XTerm`, typing `appres xterm` will not list them. To be safe, you should specify both the class name and the instance name.

Options

appres supports the following command line option:

-xrm *resource*

> Specifies that, in addition to the current application resources, *appres* should return the *resource* specified as an argument to −xrm, if that resource would apply to the *classname* or *instancename*. You must specify both a *classname* and an *instancename* in order to use the −xrm option. (Note that −xrm does not actually load any resources.)

Without any arguments, *appres* returns those resources that might apply to any application (for example, those beginning with an asterisk in your *Xresources* file).

See Also

X, xrdb, listres.

Author

Jim Fulton, MIT X Consortium.

Name

bdftosnf – BDF to SNF font compiler for X11.

Syntax

bdftosnf [*options*] *bdf_file*

Description

bdftosnf reads a Bitmap Distribution Format (BDF) font from the specified file (or from standard input if no file is specified) and writes an X11 Server Natural Format (SNF) font to standard output.

Options

bdftosnf accepts the following options:

-p*number*
> Forces the glyph padding to a specific *number*. The legal values are 1, 2, 4, and 8.

-u*number*
> Forces the scanline unit padding to a specific *number*. The legal values are 1, 2, and 4.

-m   Forces the bit order to most significant bit first.

-l   Forces the bit order to least significant bit first.

-M   Forces the byte order to most significant byte first.

-L   Forces the byte order to least significant byte first.

-w   Prints warnings if the character bitmaps have bits set to one outside of their defined widths.

-W   Prints warnings for characters with an encoding of –1; the default is to silently ignore such characters.

-t   Expands glyphs in "terminal-emulator" fonts to fill the bounding box.

-i   Suppresses computation of correct ink metrics for "terminal-emulator" fonts.

See Also

X, Xserver, Appendix F, *Logical Font Description Conventions*, in Volume 0, *X Protocol Reference Manual*. Also see the document *Bitmap Distribution Format*, in the MIT distribution.

Reference Pages

Name

bitmap, bmtoa, atobm – system bitmap editor and conversion utilities.

Syntax

```
bitmap [options] filename [WIDTHxHEIGHT]

bmtoa [options] filename

atobm [options] filename
```

Description

bitmap allows you to create and edit small bitmaps that you can use to create backgrounds, icons, and pointers. A bitmap is a grid of pixels, or picture elements, each of which is white, black, or, in the case of color displays, a color.

The *bmtoa* and *atobm* filters convert *bitmap* files to and from ASCII strings. They are most commonly used to quickly print out bitmaps and to generate versions for inclusion in text.

The window that *bitmap* creates has three sections (see Figure 7-1 in Part One of this guide). The largest section is the checkerboard grid, which is a magnified version of the bitmap you are editing. Squares on the grid can be set, cleared, or inverted directly with the buttons on the pointer. A menu of higher-level operations, such as drawing lines and circles, is provided to the right of the grid. You can invoke these menu commands by clicking with any mouse button. Beneath the menu commands is an actual size picture of the bitmap you are editing; below this is an inverted version of the same bitmap. Each time the grid changes, the same change occurs in the actual-size bitmap and its inverse. If the specified filename is new (i.e., the file is empty), bitmap will display a blank image area, suitable for you to begin editing.

If the bitmap is to be used for defining a cursor, one of the squares in the image may be designated as the *hot spot*. This determines where the cursor is actually pointing. For cursors with sharp tips (such as arrows or fingers), this is usually at the end of the tip; for symmetric cursors (such as crosses or bullseyes), this is usually at the center.

Bitmaps are stored as small C code fragments suitable for including in applications. They provide an array of bits as well as symbolic constants giving the width, height, and hot spot (if specified) that may be used in creating cursors, icons, and tiles. A selection of commonly-used bitmaps is stored in */usr/include/x11/bitmaps* on UNIX systems.

The *WIDTHxHEIGHT* argument is used only when creating a new bitmap. It gives the size in pixels of the bitmap to be created (and consequently, the number of cells in the bitmap editing area). Existing bitmaps are always edited at their current size. The default size for new bitmaps is 16x16. (This is a little small—an icon such as the mailbox displayed by *xbiff* is 48x48 pixels.)

Note that there is an interaction between the size of the bitmap being edited and the size of the *bitmap* window. By default, each cell in the *bitmap* editing area is 13 pixels square. If the bitmap being edited is large, this may result in an application window larger than the screen. Specifying an explicit size for the overall application using the -geometry option (or resizing it with the window manager) will work because *bitmap* will automatically adjust the size of each editing cell to fit. But this adjustment is useful only up to a point. The minimum size defined in the code for the cells in the *bitmap* editing area is 3 pixels (that is, each pixel in the bitmap itself will be represented by a cell 3 pixels square in the editing area). And even at that size, it is extremely difficult to edit individual pixels. At any rate, beyond a certain bitmap size, the constraint on the size of the cells will override your geometry specification; the editing area will be three times the dimensions of the actual bitmap, with the rest of the application sized to match.

bitmap should really be implemented with a scrollable editing area, so that the size of the application can be completely independent of the size of the bitmap being edited.

Options: bitmap

bitmap accepts all of the standard X Toolkit command line options, which are listed on the *X* reference page. (We've included some of the more commonly used Toolkit options later in this section.) In addition, *bitmap* accepts the following application-specific options:

−help Prints a brief description of the allowable options.

−hl *color*
Specifies the color to be used for highlighting.

−ms *color*
Specifies the color to be used for the pointer (mouse). Default is black.

−name *variable*
Specifies the variable name to be used when writing out the bitmap file. The default is to use the basename of the *filename* command line argument.

−nodashed
Specifies that the grid lines in the *bitmap* window are drawn as solid lines, not as dashed lines. Default is dashed lines. On some servers, dashed lines are significantly slower.

WIDTHxHEIGHT
Two numbers, separated by the letter "x", which specify the size of the checkerboard grid within the *bitmap* window (e.g., 9x13). The first number is the grid's width; the second number is its height. Default is 16x16.

The following standard X Toolkit options are commonly used with *bitmap*:

−display [*host*]:*server*[.*screen*]
Allows you to specify the host, server, and screen on which to create the *bitmap* window. *host* specifies the machine, *server* specifies the server number, and *screen* specifies the screen number. For example:

bitmap −display *your_node***:0.1**

creates a *bitmap* window on screen 1 of server 0 on the machine *your_node*. If the host is omitted, the local machine is assumed. If the screen is omitted, screen 0 is assumed; the server and colon (:) are necessary in all cases.

−geometry *geometry*
The bitmap is created with the specified size and location determined by the supplied geometry specification. The −geometry option can be (and often is) abbreviated to

Reference Pages

-g, unless there is a conflicting option that begins with "g." The argument to the geometry option (*geometry*) has the form `widthxheight±xoff±yoff`, where both the size (*width* and *height*) and position on the screen (± *xoff* ± *yoff*) are given in pixels. If you do not specify the geometry, the window manager may place the window automatically; if not, *bitmap* will ask you for window placement when it starts up. See "Window Geometry: Specifying Size and Location" in Chapter 3 of this guide for details.

-fg *color*
Specifies the color to be used for the foreground. Default is black.

-bg *color*
Specifies the color to be used for the background. Default is white.

-bd *color*
Specifies the color to be used for the window border.

-bw *number*
Specifies the border width in pixels of the *bitmap* window. Default is 3 pixels.

-fn *font*
Specifies the font to be used in the command buttons (refer to the "Menu Commands" section below). Default is *fixed*, a 6x13 pixel, monospaced font.

Options: bmtoa

The *bmtoa* conversion program accepts the following option:

-chars *cc*
Specifies the pair of characters to use in the string version of the bitmap. The first character is used for 0 bits and the second character is used for 1 bits. The default is to use dashes (–) for 0s and number signs (#) for 1s.

Options: atobm

The *atobm* conversion program accepts the following options:

-chars *cc*
Specifies the pair of characters to use when converting string bitmaps into arrays of numbers. The first character represents a 0 bit and the second character represents a 1 bit. The default is to use dashes (–) for 0s and number signs (#) for 1s.

-name *variable*
Specifies the variable name to be used when writing out the bitmap file. The default is to use the basename of the `filename` command line argument or leave it blank if the standard input is read.

-xhot *number*
Specifies the X coordinate of the hot spot. Only positive values are allowed. By default, no hot spot information is included.

-yhot *number*
>Specifies the Y coordinate of the hot spot. Only positive values are allowed. By default, no hot spot information is included.

Resources

The *bitmap* program accepts the following resources. The foreground, background, and highlight colors are ignored unless you specify new values for all three options.

Background
>Determines the window's background color. Bits which are 0 in the bitmap are displayed in this color. Default is white.

BodyFont
>Determines the text font. Default is *fixed*, a 6x13 pixel, monospaced font.

BorderColor
>Determines the color of the border. Default is black.

BorderWidth
>Determines the border width. Default is 2 pixels.

Dashed
>Determines whether dashed or solid lines are used for the *bitmap* grid. (On specifies dashed lines, off specifies solid.) Default is on. (Available as of Release 4.)

Foreground
>Determines the foreground color. Bits which are 1 in the bitmap are displayed in this color. Default is black.

Highlight
>Determines the highlight color. *bitmap* uses this color to show the hot spot and to indicate rectangular areas that are affected by the Move Area, Copy Area, Set Area, Clear Area, and Invert Area commands. If a highlight color is not given, then *bitmap* highlights by inverting. For example, if you have a black rectangular area selected for a move, white Xs appear in the rectangle.

Mouse Determines the pointer's color. Default is black.

Geometry
>Determines the size and location of the *bitmap* window.

Dimensions
>Determines the *WIDTHxHEIGHT* of the checkerboard grid within the *bitmap* window. Default is 16x16.

Changing Grid Squares

Grid squares may be set, cleared, or inverted by pointing to them and clicking one of the buttons indicated below. Multiple squares can be changed at once by holding the button down and dragging the cursor across them. Set squares are filled and represent 1s in the bitmap; clear squares are empty and represent 0s.

Reference Pages

Button 1 (usually the left)
>   Changes one or more grid squares to the foreground color and sets the corresponding bits in the bitmap to 1.

Button 2 (usually the middle)
>   Inverts one or more grid squares. The corresponding bit or bits in the bitmap are inverted (1s become 0s and 0s become 1s).

Button 3 (usually the right)
>   Changes one or more grid squares to the background color and sets the corresponding bits in the bitmap to 0.

Menu Commands

To make defining shapes easier, *bitmap* provides 13 commands for drawing whole sections of the grid at once, two commands for manipulating the hot spot, and two commands for updating the bitmap file and exiting. A command button for each of these operations is located to the right of the grid.

Several of the commands operate on rectangular portions of the grid. These areas are selected after the command button is pressed by moving the cursor to the upper-left square of the desired area, pressing a pointer button, dragging the cursor to the lower right-hand corner (with the button still pressed), and then releasing the button. The command may be aborted by pressing any other button while dragging or by releasing outside the grid.

To invoke a command, move the pointer over that command and click any button.

The following command descriptions assume that black is the foreground color and white is the background color (the defaults).

Clear All
>   Turns all the grid squares white and sets all bitmap bits to 0. This is irreversible, so invoke it with caution.

Set All   Turns all the grid squares black and sets all bitmap bits to 1. This is also irreversible, so invoke it with caution.

Clear Area
>   Clears a rectangular area of the grid, turning it white and setting the corresponding bitmap to 0. After you click on this command, the cursor turns into a corner cursor representing the upper-left corner of the area you want to clear. Press and hold down any mouse button while moving the mouse to the lower-right corner of the area you want to clear, then release the button.
>
>   While you are holding down the button, the selected area is covered with Xs, and the cursor changes to a lower-right corner cursor. If you now wish to abort the command without clearing an area, either press another mouse button, move the cursor outside the grid, or move the cursor to the left of or above the left corner.

Set Area
>   Turns a rectangular area of the grid black and sets the corresponding bitmap bits to 1. It works the same way as the Clear Area command.

Invert Area

Inverts rectangular area of the grid. It works the same way as the Clear Area command.

Copy Area

Copies a rectangular area from one part of the grid to another. First, you select the rectangle to be copied, in the manner described under Clear Area above.

Once you have selected the area to copy, the cursor changes to an upper-left corner cursor. When you press a mouse button, a destination rectangle overlays the grid; moving the mouse while holding down the button moves this destination rectangle. The copy occurs when you release the button. To cancel the copy, move the mouse outside the grid and then release the button.

Move Area

Works identically to Copy Area, *except* it clears the source rectangle after copying to the destination.

Overlay Area

Lays a rectangular area from one part of the grid over a rectangular area in another part of the grid. Select the area as described under Clear Area. Overlay is not a pixel for pixel replacement: those pixels that are clear (bitmap bits set to 0) allow those pixels that are set (bitmap bits set to 1) to show through the overlay.

Line   Draws a line between two points. When you select this menu option, the cursor changes to a dot shape. Position the cursor over the first point of the line you want to draw and click any mouse button. Then position the cursor over the end point of the line and click any mouse button. A black line is drawn between the two points.

Circle   Draws a circle. When you select this menu option, the cursor changes to a dot shape. First, position the cursor over the point you want to specify as the center and click any mouse button. Then position the cursor over a point you want to specify as the radius and click any mouse button. A black circle is drawn.

Filled Circle

Draws a filled circle when you specify the center and radius of the circle as with Circle.

Flood Fill

Fills all clear squares in a closed shape you specify. When you select this menu option, the cursor changes to a dot shape. Click on any clear square inside the shape you want to fill and all clear squares are filled out to the border of the closed shape. If the shape is not closed, the entire grid will be filled. (Closed shapes to be filled may be drawn by setting individual pixels or using the Line command.)

Set Hot Spot

Designates a point on the bitmap as the "hot spot." If a program is using your bitmap as a cursor, the hot spot indicates which point on the bitmap is the "actual" location of

Reference Pages

the cursor. For instance, if your cursor is an arrow, the hot spot could be the tip of the arrow; if your cursor is a cross, the hot spot should be where the perpendicular lines intersect.

Clear Hot Spot

Removes any hot spot that was defined for this bitmap.

Write Output

Writes the current bitmap value to the file specified in the command line. If the file already exists, the original file is first renamed to *filename˜* (in the manner of *emacs*(1) and other text editors).

If either the renaming or the writing causes an error, a dialog box will appear asking if you want to write the file */tmp/filename* instead. If you say yes, all future Write Output commands are written to */tmp/filename* as well. See *File Format* below for the format of the output file.

Quit   Exits the *bitmap* program. If you have edited the bitmap and have not invoked Write Output, or you have edited since the last time you invoked Write Output, a dialog window appears, asking if you want to save changes before quitting. "Yes" does a Write Output before exiting. "No" just exits, losing the edits. "Cancel" means you decided not to quit after all and you can continue with your editing.

You can also terminate *bitmap* by typing Control-C or q anywhere in the window. If you have edited the bitmap and have not invoked Write Output, a dialog window appears, asking if you want to save changes before quitting.

File Format

The Write Output command stores bitmaps as simple C program fragments that can be compiled into programs, referred to by X Toolkit pixmap resources, manipulated by other programs (such as *xsetroot*), or read in using utility routines in the various programming libraries. The width and height of the bitmap as well as the hot spot, if specified, are written as preprocessor symbols at the start of the file. The bitmap image is then written out as an array of characters:

```
#define name_width 11
#define name_height 5
#define name_x_hot 5
#define name_y_hot 2

static char name_bits[] = {
    0x91, 0x04, 0xca, 0x06, 0x84,
    0x04, 0x8a, 0x04, 0x91, 0x04
};
```

The variables ending with *_x_hot* and *_y_hot* are optional; they must be present only if a hot spot has been defined for this bitmap. The other variables must be present.

In place of *name*, the five variables are prefixed with a string derived from the name of the file specified on the original command line. Any directories are stripped off the front of the *filename* and any suffix (including the preceding period) is stripped off the end. Any remaining non-alphabetic characters are replaced with underscores.

For example, invoking *bitmap* with filename */usr/include/bitmaps/cross.bitmap* produces a file with variable names `cross_width`, `cross_height`, and `cross_bits` (and `cross_x_hot` and `cross_y_hot`, if a hot spot is defined).

Each character in the the array contains 8 bits from one row of the image (rows are padded out at the end to a multiple of 8 to make this possible). Rows are written out from left to right and top to bottom. The first character of the array holds the leftmost 8 bits of top line, and the last character holds the rightmost 8 bits (including padding) of the bottom line. Within each character, the leftmost bit in the bitmap is the least significant bit in the character.

This process can be demonstrated visually by splitting a row into words containing 8 bits each, reversing the bits in each word (since Arabic numbers have the significant digit on the right and images have the least significant bit on the left), and translating each word from binary to hexadecimal.

In the following example, the array of 1s and 0s on the left represents a bitmap containing 5 rows and 11 columns that spells *X11*. To its right is the same array split into 8-bit words with each row padded with 0s so that it is a multiple of 8 in length (16):

```
10001001001          10001001 00100000
01010011011          01010011 01100000
00100001001          00100001 00100000
01010001001          01010001 00100000
10001001001          10001001 00100000
```

Reversing the bits in each word of the padded, split version of the bitmap yields the left-hand figure below. Interpreting each word as hexadecimal number yields the array of numbers on the right:

```
10010001 00000100          0x91 0x04
11001010 00000110          0xca 0x06
10000100 00000100          0x84 0x04
10001010 00000100          0x8a 0x04
10010001 00000100          0x91 0x04
```

The character array can then be generated by reading each row from left to right, top to bottom:

```
static char name_bits[] = {
    0x91, 0x04, 0xca, 0x06, 0x84,
    0x04, 0x8a, 0x04, 0x91, 0x04
};
```

The *bmtoa* program may be used to convert bitmap files into arrays of characters for printing or including in text files. The *atobm* program can be used to convert strings back to bitmap format.

Using Bitmaps in Programs

To define a bitmap or pointer in an X program, include (*#include*) a bitmap file and refer to its variables. For instance, to use a pointer defined in the files *this.cursor* and *this_mask.cursor*, write:

```
#include "this.cursor"
#include "this_mask.cursor"
XColor foreground background;
Pixmap source = XCreateBitmapFromData (display, drawable, this_bits,
    this_width, this_height);
Pixmap mask = XCreateBitmapFromData (display, drawable, this_mask_bits,
    this_mask_width, this_mask_height);
Cursor cursor = XCreatePixmapCursor (display, source, mask, foreground,
    background, this_x_hot, this_y_hot);
```

where `foreground` and `background` are `XColor` values.

Additional routines are available for reading in bitmap files and returning the data in the file in bitmap (single-plane pixmap for use with routines that require stipples) or full depth Pixmaps (often used for window backgrounds and borders). Applications writers should be careful to understand the difference between bitmaps and pixmaps so that their programs function correctly on color and monochrome displays.

For backward compatibility, *bitmap* will also accept X10 format bitmap files. However, when the file is written out again it will be in X11 format.

Files

Many standard bitmaps can be found in the directory */usr/include/X11/bitmaps*.

Bugs

The old command line arguments aren't consistent with other X programs.

If you move the pointer too fast while holding a pointer button down, some squares may be missed. This is caused by limitations in how frequently the X server can sample the pointer location.

There is no way to write to a file other than the one specified on the command line.

There is no way to change the size of the bitmap once the program has started.

There is no Undo command.

See Also

Chapter 7 of this guide; Volume One, *Xlib Programming Manual*; `XmuReadBitmapData-FromFile`.

Author

bitmap by Ron Newman, MIT Project Athena; *bmtoa* and *atobm* by Jim Fulton, MIT X Consortium.

Name
listres – list resources in widgets.

Syntax
listres [*options*] [*widget . . .*]

Description
Available as of Release 4, the *listres* program generates a list of each specified widget's resource database. The list includes the class in which each resource is first defined, the instance and class name, and the type of each resource.

If no specific widgets are given, a two-column list of known widget names and their class hierarchies is printed. In the MIT distribution, this includes the intrinsics-defined widget classes Core, Composite, Constraint, and Shell (and Shell's six subclasses), plus the Athena widgets.

Case is not significant when specifying the name of the widget or widgets whose resources are to be printed. For example:

% **listres Core**

is equivalent to:

% **listres CORE**

Options
listres accepts the following application-specific options:

-all   Indicates that *listres* should print information for all known widgets and objects.

-nosuper
     Indicates that resources that are inherited from a superclass should not be listed. This is useful for determining which resources are new to a subclass.

-variable
     Indicates that widgets should be identified by the names of the class record variables rather than the class name given in the variable. This is useful for distinguishing subclasses that have the same class name as their superclasses.

-top *name*
     Specifies the name of the widget to be treated as the top of the hierarchy. Case is not significant, and the name may match either the class variable name or the class name. The default is Core.

-format *printf_string*
     Specifies the printf-style format string to be used to print out the name, instance, class, and type of each resource.

listres also *recognizes* all of the standard X Toolkit options (i.e., the program will run); however, since *listres* is not a window-based application, it does not *use* them.

Reference Pages

See Also

X, xrdb; Volume Four, *X Toolkit Intrinsics Programming Manual*; Volume Five, *X Toolkit Intrinsics Reference Manual*; Appendix G, *Athena Widget Resources*, in this guide.

Bugs

On operating systems that do not support dynamic linking of run-time routines, this program must have all of its known widgets compiled in. The sources provide several tools for automating this process for various widget sets.

Author

Jim Fulton, MIT X Consortium.

Name

mkfontdir – creates a *fonts.dir* file for each specified directory of font files.

Syntax

`mkfontdir` [*directory-names*]

Description

For each directory argument, *mkfontdir* reads all of the font files in the directory and searches for properties named "FONT", or (failing that) the name of the file stripped of its suffix. These are used as font names, which are written out to the file *fonts.dir* in the directory, along with the name of the font file.

The kinds of font files read by *mkfontdir* depend on configuration parameters, but typically include SNF (suffix *.snf*), compressed SNF (suffix *.snf.Z*), BDF (suffix *.bdf*), and compressed BDF (suffix *.bdf.Z*). If a font exists in multiple formats, the most efficient format will be used.

Font Name Aliases

The file *fonts.alias*, which can be put in any directory of the font path, is used to map new names to existing fonts, and should be edited by hand. The format is straightforward enough: two white-space separated columns, the first containing aliases and the second containing font-name patterns.

When a font alias is used, the name it references is searched for in the normal manner, looking through each font directory in turn. This means that the aliases need not mention fonts in the same directory as the alias file.

To embed white space in either name, simply enclose the name in double-quote marks. To embed double-quote marks (or any other special character), precede it with a backslash:

```
"magic-alias with spaces"    "\"fontname\" with quotes"
regular alias                fontname
```

Usage

Xserver looks for both *fonts.dir* and *fonts.alias* in each directory in the font path each time the font path is set (see *xset*).

See Also

X, Xserver, xset, Chapter 6, *Font Specification*, Appendix M, *Logical Font Description Conventions*, in Volume 0, *X Protocol Reference Manual*.

Reference Pages

mwm

Motif window manager —

Name

mwm – the Motif window manager.

Syntax

mwm [*options*]

Description

The Motif window manager, *mwm*, provides all of the standard window management functions. It allows you to move, resize, iconify/deiconify, maximize, and close windows and icons, focus input to a window or icon, refresh the display, etc. *mwm* provides much of its functionality via a frame that (by default) is placed around every window on the display. The *mwm* frame has the three-dimensional appearance characteristic of the OSF/Motif graphical user interface.

Chapters 3 and 4 of this guide discuss input focus, the components of the *mwm* frame, and the various window management functions you can perform using the pointer on the frame. In addition, Chapter 4 describes how to perform window/icon management functions using *mwm*'s Window Menu (as well as keyboard shortcuts for menu functions). Chapter 4 also describes the Root Menu, which provides commands that can be thought of as affecting the display as a whole.

By default, *mwm* manages only screen 0. (You can specify an alternate screen by setting the DISPLAY environment variable or using the `-display` option.) If you want *mwm* to manage all screens on the display, use the `-multiscreen` option or set the `multiScreen` resource to `True`. (See "mwm-specific Appearance and Behavior Resources.")

You can customize dozens of *mwm* features by editing a startup file (*.mwmrc*) and/or by specifying resources for the *mwm* client. You can place *mwm* resources in your regular resource file (often called *.Xresources*) in your home directory; or you can create a file called *Mwm* (also in your home directory) for *mwm* resources only. If you place conflicting specifications in both files, the resources in *.Xresources* (presuming they are loaded into the RESOURCE_MANAGER) take precedence. (These files are generally kept in the user's home directory. Note, however, that the actual location of resource files may depend on certain environment variables. See the section "Environment Variables" for more information.)

Chapter 11 of this guide describes the syntax of the *.mwmrc* file and of *mwm* resource specifications. Chapter 11 also describes how to use an icon box, which can be set up to organize icons on the display.

The current reference page primarily describes the actions and resources by *mwm*. This reference page should assist you in customizing *mwm*, according to the guidelines specified in Chapter 11.

Options
-display [*host*]:*server*[*.screen*]

Specifies the name of the display on which to run *mwm*. *host* specifies the machine, *server* specifies the display server number, and *screen* specifies the screen number. Either or both of the *host* and *screen* elements can be omitted. If *host* is omitted, the local machine is assumed. If *screen* is omitted, screen 0 is assumed (and the period is unnecessary). The colon and (display) *server* are necessary in all cases.

For example, the following command runs *mwm* on screen 1 on server 0 on the machine *your_node*.

mwm -display *your_node***:0.1**

-multiscreen

Specifies that *mwm* should manage all screens on the display. The default is to manage only screen 0. You can specify an alternate screen by setting the DISPLAY environment variable or using the -display option.

You can also specify that *mwm* manage all screen by assigning a value of True to the multiScreen resource variable. See "mwm-specific Appearance and Behavior Resources."

-name *app_name*

Specifies the name under which resources for the window manager should be found.

-screens *screen_name* [*screen_name*]...

Assigns resource names to the screens *mwm* is managing. If *mwm* is managing a single screen, only the first name in the list is used. If *mwm* is managing multiple screens, the names are assigned to the screens in order, starting with screen 0. If there are more screens than names, resources for the remaining screens will be retrieved using the first *screen_name*.

-xrm *resourcestring*

Specifies a resource name and value to override any defaults. This option is very useful for setting resources that don't have explicit command line arguments.

.mwmrc Startup File
The default operation of *mwm* is largely controlled by a system-wide file, called *system.mwmrc*, which establishes the contents of the Root Menu and Window Menu, how menu functions are invoked, and what key and button combinations can be used to manage windows. To modify the behavior of *mwm*, you can edit a copy of this file in your home directory. The version of this file in your home directory should be called *.mwmrc*. (You can specify an alternate startup file using the configFile resource variable.)

The syntax of the *system.mwmrc* file is described in Chapter 11 of this guide. Chapter 11 also examines how to create menus, how to modify existing menus, and how to bind window manager functions to keystrokes, pointer button actions, or a combination of keys and buttons.

Reference Pages

In describing the syntax of button and key bindings, Chapter 11 refers to the variables *modifier_key* and *button_event*. Acceptable values for *modifier_key* are: Ctrl, Shift, Alt, Meta, Lock, Mod1, Mod2, Mod3, Mod4, and Mod5. *mwm* considers Alt and Meta to be equivalent. See Chapter 12, *Setup Clients*, for a discussion of modifier keys and key mapping.

The acceptable values for *button_event* are:

```
Btn1Down
Btn1Up
Btn1Click
Btn1Click2
Btn2Down
Btn2Up
Btn2Click
Btn2Click2
   .
   .
   .
Btn5Down
Btn5Up
Btn5Click
Btn5Click2
```

Most of these button actions are obvious. (A specification ending in Click2 refers to a double click. Thus, Button1Click2 means to double click button 1.) Note that the list indicates a range between button 1 and button 5 (i.e., the same button events can be specified for buttons 2, 3, and 4).

mwm Functions

This section describes the functions you can specify in an *mwm* startup file.

Unless otherwise noted, you can specify that each action is invoked:

* In any of the following contexts: root, window, and icon;
* Using button bindings, key binding, or menu items.

When a function is specified with the context icon | window and you invoke the function from the icon box, the function applies to the icon box itself (rather than to any of the icons it contains).

A function is treated as f.nop when it is:

* Not a valid function name.
* Specified inappropriately (e.g., mapped to a button when the function cannot be invoked using button bindings).
* Invoked in an invalid context; (For example, you cannot invoke f.minimize on a window that is already iconified).

See Chapter 11 for a discussion of context, bindings, and menus.

mwm recognizes the following functions:

`f.beep`

>   Causes a beep from the keyboard.

`f.circle_down [icon | window]`

>   Causes the window or icon on the top of the stack to be lowered to the bottom of the stack. If the `icon` argument is specified, the function applies only to icons. If the `window` argument is specified, the function applies only to windows.
>
>   This function is invoked by the Shuffle Down item on the default Root Menu.

`f.circle_up [icon | window]`

>   Causes the window or icon on the bottom of the stack to be raised to the top. If the `icon` argument is specified, the function applies only to icons. If the `window` argument is specified, the function applies only to windows.
>
>   This function is invoked by the Shuffle Up item on the default Root Menu.

`f.exec [command]`

or:

`! [command]`

>   Executes *command* using the shell specified by the MWMSHELL environment variable. (If MWMSHELL isn't set, the command is executed using the shell specified by the SHELL environment variable; otherwise, using */bin/sh*).

`f.focus_color`

>   Sets the colormap focus to a client window. If this function is invoked in the `root` context, the default colormap (specified by X for the screen where *mwm* is running) is installed and there is no specific client window colormap focus. For the `f.focus_color` function to work, the `colormapFocusPolicy` should be specified as `explicit`; otherwise the function is treated as `f.nop`.

`f.focus_key`

>   Sets the input focus to a window or icon. For the `f.focus_key` function to work, the `keyboardFocusPolicy` should be specified as `explicit`. If `keyboard-FocusPolicy` is not `explicit`, or if the function is invoked in the `root` context, it is treated as `f.nop`.

`f.kill`

>   Terminates a client. Specifically, sends the WM_DELETE_WINDOW message to the selected window if the client application has requested it through the WM_PROTO-COLS property. The application is supposed to respond to the message by removing the indicated window. If the WM_SAVE_YOURSELF protocol is set up and the WM_DELETE_WINDOW protocol is not, the client is sent a message, indicating that the client needs to prepare to be terminated. If the client does not have the WM_DELETE_WINDOW or WM_SAVE_YOURSELF protocol set, the `f.kill` function causes a client's X connection to be terminated (usually resulting in termination of the client).

This function is invoked by the Close item on the default Window Menu. The f.kill function can only be invoked in the contexts window and icon.

See also the quitTimeout resource.

f.lower [-*client*]
> Lowers a window or icon to the bottom of the stack. By default, the context in which the function is invoked indicates the window or icon to lower. This function is invoked by the Lower item on the default Window Menu.
>
> If the -*client* argument is specified, the function is invoked on the named client. (*client* must be the instance or class name of a program.)

f.maximize
> Causes a window to be redisplayed at its maximum size. The f.maximize function is invoked by the Maximize item on the default Window Menu. This function cannot be invoked in the context root or on a window that is already maximized.

f.menu *menu_name*
> Associates a cascading (i.e., pull-right) menu with a menu item (from which the cascading menu is displayed); or associates a menu with a button or key binding. The *menu_name* argument specifies the menu.

f.minimize
> Causes a window to be minimized (i.e., iconified). When no icon box is being used, icons are placed on the bottom of the stack (generally in the lower-left corner of the screen; see also iconPlacement in "mwm-specific Appearance and Behavior Resources"). If an icon box is being used, icons are placed inside the box.
>
> The f.minimize function is invoked by the Minimize item on the default Window Menu. This function cannot be invoked in the context root or on an iconified window.

f.move
> Allows you to move a window interactively, using the pointer. This function is invoked by the Move item on the default Window Menu.

f.next_cmap
> Installs the next colormap in the list of colormaps for the window with the colormap focus. (See f.focus_color.)

f.next_key [icon | window | transient]
> Without any arguments, this function advances the input focus to the next window or icon in the stack. You can specify only icon or window to make the function apply only to icons or windows, respectively.
>
> Generally, the focus is moved only to windows that do not have an associated secondary window that is application modal. (An active dialog box is application modal.) If the transient argument is specified, transient (secondary) windows are also traversed. Otherwise, if only window is specified, focus is moved only to the last window in a transient group to have the focus.

For this function to work, `keyboardFocusPolicy` must be `explicit`; otherwise, the function is treated as `f.nop`. See Chapter 4 for the default key combinations to move the focus.

`f.nop`   Specifies no operation. (In other words, it does nothing.)

`f.normalize`
Causes a client window to be displayed at its normal size. The `f.normalize` function is invoked by the Restore item on the default Window Menu. This function cannot be invoked in the context `root` or on a window that is already at its normal size.

`f.normalize_and_raise`
Causes the client window to be displayed at its normal size and raised to the top of the stack. This function cannot be invoked in the context `root`.

`f.pack_icons`
Rearranges icons in an optimal fashion (based on the layout policy being used), either on the root window or in the icon box. See `iconPlacement` in "mwm-specific Appearance and Behavior Resources." (See Chapter 11 for instructions on using an icon box.)

`f.pass_keys`
Toggles processing of key bindings for window manager functions. When key binding processing is disabled, all keys are passed to the window with the keyboard input focus and no window manager functions are invoked. If the `f.pass_keys` function is set up to be invoked with a key binding, the binding can be used to toggle (enable/disable) key binding processing.

`f.post_wmenu`
Displays the Window Menu. If a key is used to display the menu and a Window Menu command button is present, the upper-left corner of the menu is placed at the lower-left corner of the command button. If no Window Menu command button is present, the menu is placed in the upper-left corner of the window.

`f.prev_cmap`
This function installs the previous colormap in the list of colormaps for the window with the colormap focus. (See `f.focus_color`.)

`f.prev_key` [icon | window | transient]
Without any arguments, this function moves the input focus to the previous window or icon in the stack. You can specify only `icon` or `window` to make the function apply only to icons or windows, respectively.

Generally, the focus is moved only to windows that do not have an associated secondary window that is application modal. (An active dialog box is application modal.) If the `transient` argument is specified, transient (secondary) windows are also traversed. Otherwise, if only `window` is specified, focus is moved only to the last window in a transient group to have the focus.

Reference Pages

For this function to work, keyboardFocusPolicy must be explicit; otherwise, the function is treated as f.nop. See Chapter 4 for the default key combinations to move the focus.

f.quit_mwm
Stops the *mwm* window manager. Note that this function does not stop the X server.

f.raise [-client]
Raises a window or icon to the top of the stack. By default, the context in which the function is invoked indicates the window or icon to raise. If the -client argument is specified, the function is invoked on the named client. (client must be the instance or class name of a program.)

f.raise_lower
Raises a window to the top of the stack or lowers a window to the bottom of the stack, as appropriate to the context.

f.refresh
Redraws all windows. This function is invoked by the Refresh item on the default Root Menu.

f.refresh_win
Redraws a single window.

f.resize
Allows you to resize a window interactively, using the pointer. This function is invoked by the Size item on the default Window Menu.

f.restart
Restarts the *mwm* window manager. (Specifically, this function causes the current *mwm* process to be stopped and a new *mwm* process to be started.) This function is invoked by the Restart... item on the default Root Menu.

f.send_msg *message_number*
Sends a message of the type _MOTIF_WM_MESSAGES to a client; the message type is indicated by the *message_number* argument. The message is sent only if the client's _MOTIF_WM_MESSAGES property includes *message_number*.

If a menu item is set up to invoke f.send_msg and the *message_number* is not included in the client's _MOTIF_WM_MESSAGES property, the menu item label is greyed out (indicating that it is not available for selection).

f.separator
Creates a divider line in a menu. Any associated label is ignored.

```
f.set_behavior
```
> Restarts *mwm* with the default behavior for the particular system. By default this function is invoked using the following key sequence: `Shift Ctrl Meta !`.

```
f.title
```
> Specifies the title of a menu. The title string is separated from the menu items by a double divider line.

Resources

mwm resources are considered to fall into three categories:

- *mwm* component appearance resources. These resources set the characteristics of *mwm*'s component features, such as the window frame, menus, and icons.

- *mwm*-specific appearance and behavior resources. These resources set characteristics of the window manager client, such as focus policy, key and button bindings, and so forth.

- Client-specific resources. These *mwm* resources can be used to set the appearance and behavior of a particular client or class of clients.

The following sections simply describe the valid resources. For a discussion of *mwm* resource syntax, see Chapter 11 in this guide. (For more information about basic resource syntax and the precedence of resource specifications, see Chapter 10.)

Note that you can specify resources for multiple screens using the names supplied to the `-screens` command line option in place of mwm or Mwm in the resource line. (See "Options.")

mwm Component Appearance Resources

The Motif window manager can be considered to be made up of components: client window frames, menus, icons, and feedback (dialog) boxes. Some component appearance resources can be set for all of these components; others can be set only for the frame and icons.

Unless a default is specified, the default varies based on system specifics (such as screen type, color resources, etc.).

The following component appearance resources apply to all window manager components:

`background` (class `Background`)
> Specifies the background color.

`backgroundPixmap` (class `BackgroundPixmap`)
> Specifies the background pixmap of the *mwm* decoration when the window does not have the input focus (i.e., is inactive).

`bottomShadowColor` (class `Foreground`)
> Specifies the color to be used for the lower and right bevels of the window manager decoration.

`bottomShadowPixmap` (class `BottomShadowPixmap`)
> Specifies the pixmap to be used for the lower and right bevels of the window manager decoration.

Reference Pages

`fontList` (class `FontList`)
>   Specifies the font to be used in the window manager decoration. The default is `fixed`.

`foreground` (class `Foreground`)
>   Specifies the foreground color.

`saveUnder` (class `SaveUnder`)
>   Specifies whether save unders are used for *mwm* components. By default (`False`), save unders will not be used on any window manager frames.
>
>   Save unders must be implemented by the X server for this function to to take effect. When save unders are implemented, the X server saves the contents of windows obscured by other windows that have the save under attribute set. If the `saveUnder` resource is `True`, *mwm* will set the save under attribute on the frame of any client that has it set.

`topShadowColor` (class `Background`)
>   Specifies the color to be used for the upper and left bevels of the window manager decoration.

`topShadowPixmap` (class `TopShadowPixmap`)
>   Specifies the pixmap to be used for the upper and left bevels of the window manager decoration.

The following component appearance resources apply to the window frame and icons:

`activeBackground` (class `Background`)
>   Specifies the background color of the *mwm* decoration when the window has the input focus (i.e., is active).

`activeBackgroundPixmap` (class `ActiveBackgroundPixmap`)
>   Specifies the background pixmap of the *mwm* decoration when the window has the input focus (i.e., is active).

`activeBottomShadowColor` (class `Foreground`)
>   Specifies the bottom shadow color of the *mwm* decoration when the window has the input focus (i.e., is active).

`activeBottomShadowPixmap` (class `BottomShadowPixmap`)
>   Specifies the bottom shadow pixmap of the *mwm* decoration when the window has the input focus (i.e., is active).

`activeForeground` (class `Foreground`)
>   Specifies the foreground color of the *mwm* decoration when the window has the input focus (i.e., is active).

`activeTopShadowColor` (class `Background`)
>   Specifies the top shadow color of the *mwm* decoration when the window has the input focus (i.e., is active).

activeTopShadowPixmap (class TopShadowPixmap)
> Specifies the top shadow Pixmap of the *mwm* decoration when the window has the input focus (i.e., is active).

mwm-specific Appearance and Behavior Resources

The *mwm*-specific resources control aspects of what you probably think of as the window manager application itself, features such as the focus policy, whether windows are placed on the display automatically or interactively, which set(s) of button and key bindings are used, whether an icon box is used, and so forth.

The following *mwm*-specific appearance and behavior resources can be specified:

autoKeyFocus (class AutoKeyFocus)
> If True (the default), when the focus window is withdrawn from window management or is iconified, the focus bounces back to the window that previously had the focus. This resource is available only when keyboardFocusPolicy is explicit. If False, the input focus is not set automatically.

autoRaiseDelay (class AutoRaiseDelay)
> Specifies the amount of time (in milliseconds) that *mwm* will wait before raising a window after it receives the input focus. The default is 500. This resource is available only when focusAutoRaise is True and the keyboardFocusPolicy is pointer.

bitmapDirectory (class BitmapDirectory)
> Identifies the directory to be searched for bitmaps referenced by *mwm* resources (if an absolute pathname to the bitmap file is not given). The default is */usr/include/X11/bitmaps*, the standard location of the system bitmap directory.

buttonBindings (class ButtonBindings)
> Identifies the set of button bindings to be used for window management functions; must correspond to a set of button bindings specified in the *mwm* startup file. Button bindings specified in the startup file are merged with built-in default bindings. The default is DefaultButtonBindings.

cleanText (class CleanText)
> Specifies whether text that appears in *mwm* title and feedback windows is displayed over the existing background pattern. If True (the default), text is drawn with a clear (no stipple) background. (Only the stippling in the area immediately around the text is cleared.) This enhances readability, especially on monochrome systems where a backgroundPixmap is specified. If False, text is drawn on top of the existing background.

clientAutoPlace (class ClientAutoPlace)
> Specifies the location of a window when the user has not specified a location. If True (the default), windows are positioned with the upper-left corners of the frames offset horizontally and vertically (so that no two windows completely overlap).
>
> If False, the currently configured position of the window is used.
>
> In either case, *mwm* will attempt to place the windows totally on screen.

Reference Pages

`colormapFocusPolicy` (class `ColormapFocusPolicy`)
> Specifies the colormap focus policy. Takes three possible values: `keyboard`, `pointer`, and `explicit`. If `keyboard` (the default) is specified, the input focus window has the colormap focus. If `explicit` is specified, a colormap selection action is done on a client window to set the colormap focus to that window. If `pointer` is specified, the client window containing the pointer has the colormap focus.

`configFile` (class `ConfigFile`)
> Specifies the pathname for the *mwm* startup file. The default startup file is *.mwmrc*.

> *mwm* searches for the configuration file in the user's home directory. If the `config-File` resource is not specified or the file does not exist, *mwm* defaults to */usr/lib/X11/system.mwmrc*.

> If the LANG environment variable is set, *mwm* looks for the configuration file in a *$LANG* subdirectory first. For example, if the LANG environment variable is set to Fr (for French), *mwm* searches for the configuration file in the directory *$HOME/Fr* before it looks in *$HOME*. Similarly, if the `configFile` resource is not specified or the file does not exist, *mwm* defaults to */usr/lib/X11/$LANG/system.mwmrc* before it reads */usr/lib/X11/system.mwmrc*.

> If the `configFile` pathname does not begin with "~/", *mwm* considers it to be relative to the current working directory.

`configFile` (class `ConfigFile`)
> Specifies the pathname for the *mwm* startup file.

> If the LANG environment variable is set, *mwm* looks for *$HOME/$LANG/config-File*. If that file does not exist or if LANG is not set, *mwm* looks for *$HOME/configFile*.

> If the `configFile` pathname does not begin with "~/", *mwm* considers it to be relative to the current working directory.

> If the `configFile` resource is not specified or if that file does not exist, *mwm* uses several default paths to find a configuration file. If the LANG environment variable is set, *mwm* looks for the configuration file first in *$HOME/$LANG/.mwmrc*. If that file does not exist or if LANG is not set, *mwm* looks for *$HOME/.mwmrc*. If that file does not exist and if LANG is set, *mwm* next looks for */usr/lib/X11/$LANG/system.mwmrc*. If that file does not exist or if LANG is not set, *mwm* looks for */usr/lib/X11/system.mwmrc*.

`deiconifyKeyFocus` (class `DeiconifyKeyFocus`)
> If `True` (the default), a window receives the input focus when it is normalized (deiconified). This resource applies only when the `keyboardFocusPolicy` is `explicit`.

`doubleClickTime` (class `DoubleClickTime`)
> Specifies the maximum time (in milliseconds) between the two clicks of a double click. The default is the display's multi-click time.

`enableWarp` (class `EnableWarp`)
> If `True` (the default), causes *mwm* to *warp* the pointer to the center of the selected window during resize and move operations invoked using keyboard accelerators. (The cursor symbol disappears from its current location and reappears at the center of the window.) If `False`, *mwm* leaves the pointer at its original place on the screen, unless the user explicitly moves it.

`enforceKeyFocus` (class `EnforceKeyFocus`)
> If `True` (the default), the input focus is always explicitly set to selected windows even if there is an indication that they are "globally active" input windows. (An example of a globally active window is a scrollbar that can be operated without setting the focus to that client.) If the resource is `False`, the keyboard input focus is not explicitly set to globally active windows.

`fadeNormalIcon` (class `FadeNormalIcon`)
> If `True`, an icon is greyed out when it has been normalized. The default is `False`.

`frameBorderWidth` (class `FrameBorderWidth`)
> Specifies the width in pixels of a window frame border, without resize handles. (The border width includes the three-dimensional shadows.) The default is 5.

`iconAutoPlace` (class `IconAutoPlace`)
> Specifies whether the window manager arranges icons in a particular area of the screen or places each icon where the window was when it was iconified. If `True` (the default), icons are arranged in a particular area of the screen, determined by the `iconPlacement` resource. If `False`, an icon is placed at the location of the window when it is iconified.

`iconBoxGeometry` (class `IconBoxGeometry`)
> Specifies the initial position and size of the icon box. Takes as its argument the standard geometry string:
>
> *widthxheight±xoff±yoff*
>
> where *width* and *height* are measured in icons. The default geometry string is `6x1+0-0`, which places an icon box six icons wide by one icon high in the lower-left corner of the screen.
>
> You can omit either the dimensions or the x and y offsets from the geometry string and the defaults apply. If the offsets are not provided, the `iconPlacement` resource is used to determine the initial placement.
>
> The actual screen size of the icon box depends on the `iconImageMaximum` and `iconDecoration` resources, which specify icon size and padding. The default value for size is (6 x *icon_width* + padding) wide by (1 x *icon_height* + padding) high.

Reference Pages

`iconBoxName` (class `IconBoxName`)
> Specifies the name under which icon box resources are to be found. The default is `iconbox`.

`iconBoxSBDisplayPolicy` (class `IconBoxSBDisplayPolicy`)
> Specifies what scrollbars are displayed in the icon box. The resource has three possible values: `all`, `vertical`, and `horizontal`. If `all` is specified (the default), both vertical and horizontal scrollbars are displayed at all times. `vertical` specifies that a single vertical scrollbar is displayed (this also sets the orientation of the icon box to horizontal—regardless of the `iconBoxGeometry` specification). `horizontal` specifies that a single horizontal scrollbar is displayed in the icon box (this also sets the orientation of the icon box to vertical—regardless of the `iconBoxGeometry` specification).

`iconBoxTitle` (class `IconBoxTitle`)
> Specifies the name to be used in the title area of the icon box. The default is `Icons`.

`iconClick` (class `IconClick`)
> If `True` (the default), the Window Menu is displayed and displayed when the pointer is clicked on an icon.

`iconDecoration` (class `IconDecoration`)
> Specifies how much icon decoration is used. The resource value takes four possible values (multiple values can also be supplied): `label`, which specifies that only the label is displayed; `image`, which specifies that only the image is displayed; and `activelabel`, which specifies that a label (not truncated to the width of the icon) is used when the icon has the focus.
>
> The default decoration for icons in an icon box is `label image`, which specifies that both the label and image parts are displayed. The default decoration for individual icons on the screen proper is `activelabel label image`.

`iconImageMaximum` (class `IconImageMaximum`)
> Specifies the maximum size of the icon image. Takes a value of *widthxheight* (e.g., `80x80`). The maximum size supported is 128x128. The default is `50x50`.

`iconImageMinimum` (class `IconImageMinimum`)
> Specifies the minimum size of the icon image. Takes a value of *widthxheight* (e.g., `36x48`). The minimum size supported is 16x16 (which is also the default).

`iconPlacement` (class `IconPlacement`)
> Specifies an icon placement scheme. The resource takes a value of the syntax:
>
> *primary_layout   secondary_layout*
>
> There are four possible layout policies:
>
> `top`, which specifies that icons are placed from the top of the screen to the bottom; `bottom`, which specifies a bottom to top arrangement; `left`, which specifies that icons are placed from the left to the right; `right`, which specifies a right to left arrangement.

The *primary_layout* specifies whether icons are placed in a row or a column and the direction of placement. The *secondary_layout* specifies where to place new rows or columns. For example, a value of top right specifies that icons should be placed from top to bottom on the screen and that columns should be added from right to left on the screen.

A horizontal (vertical) layout value should not be used for both the *primary_layout* and the *secondary_layout*. For example, don't use top for the *primary_layout* and bottom for the *secondary_layout*.

The default placement is left bottom (i.e., icons are placed left to right on the screen, with the first row on the bottom of the screen, and new rows added from the bottom of the screen to the top of the screen).

iconPlacementMargin (class IconPlacementMargin)
  Sets the distance from the edge of the screen at which icons are placed. (The value should be greater than or equal to 0. A default value is used if an invalid distance is specified.) The default value is equal to the space between icons as they are placed on the screen (which is is based on maximizing the number of icons in each row and column).

interactivePlacement (class InteractivePlacement)
  If True, specifies that new windows are to be placed interactively on the screen using the pointer. When a client is run, the pointer shape changes to an upper-left corner cursor; move the pointer to the location you want the window to appear and click the first button; the window is displayed in the selected location. If False (the default), windows are placed according to the initial window configuration attributes.

keyBindings (class KeyBindings)
  Identifies the set of key bindings to be used for window management functions; must correspond to a set of key bindings specified in the *mwm* startup file. Note that key bindings specified in the startup file replace the built-in default bindings. The default is DefaultKeyBindings.

keyboardFocusPolicy (class KeyboardFocusPolicy)
  If explicit focus is specified (the default), placing the pointer on a window (including the frame) or icon and pressing the first pointer button focuses keyboard input on the client. If pointer is specified, the keyboard input focus is directed to the client window on which the pointer rests (the pointer can also rest on the frame).

limitResize (class LimitResize)
  If True (the default), the user is not allowed to resize a window to greater than the maximum size.

Reference Pages

lowerOnIconify (class LowerOnIconify)
> If True (the default), a window's icon is placed on the bottom of the stack when the window is iconified. If False, the icon is placed in the stacking order at the same place as its associated window.

maximumMaximumSize (class MaximumMaximumSize)
> Specifies the maximum size of a client window (as set by the user or client). Takes a value of *widthxheight* (e.g., 1024x1024) where *width* and *height* are in pixels. The default is twice the screen width and height.

moveThreshold (class MoveThreshold)
> Controls the sensitivity of dragging operations (such as those used to move windows and icons on the display). Takes a value of the number of pixels that the pointing device is moved while a button is held down before the move operation is initiated. The default is 4. This resource helps prevent a window or icon from moving when you click or double click and inadvertently jostle the pointer while a button is down.

multiScreen (class MultiScreen)
> If False (the default), *mwm* manages only a single screen. If True, *mwm* manages all screens on the display. (See "Options.")

passButtons (class PassButtons)
> Specifies whether button press events are passed to clients after the events are used to invoke a window manager function (in the client context). If False (the default), button presses are not passed to the client. If True, button presses are passed to the client. (Note that the window manager function is done in either case.)

passSelectButton (class PassSelectButton)
> Specifies whether select button press events are passed to clients after the events are used to invoke a window manager function (in the client context). If True (the default), button presses are passed to the client window. If False, button presses are not passed to the client. (Note that the window manager function is done in either case.)

positionIsFrame (class PositionIsFrame)
> Specifies how *mwm* should interpret window position information (from the WM_NORMAL_HINTS property and from configuration requests). If True (the default), the information is interpreted as the position of the *mwm* client window frame. If False, it is interpreted as being the position of the client area of the window.

positionOnScreen (class PositionOnScreen)
> If True (the default), specifies that windows should initially be placed (if possible) so that they are not clipped by the edge of the screen. (If a window is larger than the size of the screen, at least the upper-left corner of the window is placed is on the screen.) If False, windows are placed in the requested position even if totally off the screen.

quitTimeout (class QuitTimeout)
> Specifies the amount of time (in milliseconds) that *mwm* will wait for a client to update the WM_COMMAND property after *mwm* has sent the WM_SAVE_YOURSELF message. This protocol is used only for those clients that have a

WM_SAVE_YOURSELF atom and no WM_DELETE_WINDOW atom in the WM_PROTO-COLS client window property. The default is `1000`. (See the `f.kill` function for additional information.)

raiseKeyFocus (class RaiseKeyFocus)
> If `True`, specifies that a window raised by means of the `f.normal-ize_and_raise` function also receives the input focus. This function is available only when the `keyboardFocusPolicy` is `explicit`. The default is `False`.

resizeBorderWidth (class ResizeBorderWidth)
> Specifies the width in pixels of a window frame border, with resize handles. (The border width includes the three-dimensional shadows.) The default is `10`.

resizeCursors (class ResizeCursors)
> If `True` (the default), the resize cursors are always displayed when the pointer is in the window resize border.

screens (class Screens)
> Assigns resource names to the screens *mwm* is managing. If *mwm* is managing a single screen, only the first name in the list is used. If *mwm* is managing multiple screens, the names are assigned to the screens in order, starting with screen 0. (See also "Options.")

showFeedback (class ShowFeedback)
> Specifies when *mwm* feedback information is displayed. You can use this resource to control the display of *mwm*: dialog boxes; feedback boxes that relate the position and/or size of a window—during move and resize operations and during initial window placement (if interactive placement is specified).
>
> `showFeedback` accepts a list of options, each of which corresponds to the type of feedback given in a particular circumstance. Depending on the syntax in which the options are entered, you can either enable or disable a feedback option (as explained later).
>
> The possible feedback options are: `all`, which specifies that *mwm* show all types of feedback (this is the default); `behavior`, which specifies that feedback is displayed to confirm a behavior switch; `kill`, which specifies that feedback is displayed on receipt of a KILL signal; `move`, which specifies that a box containing the coordinates of a window or icon is displayed during a move operation; `placement`, which specifies that a box containing the position and size of a window is displayed during initial (interactive) placement; `quit`, which specifies that a dialog box is displayed so that the user can confirm (or cancel) the procedure to quit *mwm*; `resize`, which specifies that a box containing the window size is displayed during a resize operation; `restart`, which displays a dialog box so that the user can confirm (or cancel) an *mwm* restart procedure; the `none` option specifies that no feedback is shown.
>
> By default, *mwm* supplies feedback in `all` cases. (`all` encompasses all of the other options—with the exception of the `none` option.)

Reference Pages

To limit feedback to particular cases, you can use one of two syntaxes: with the first syntax, you disable feedback in specified cases (all other default feedback is still used); with the second syntax, you enable feedback only in specified cases.

Initially, the syntax may be confusing, but it is actually quite simple. You supply this resource with a list of options to be enabled or disabled. If the first item is preceded by a minus sign, feedback is disabled for all options in the list. (Any option not listed remains enabled.)

If the first item is preceded by a plus sign (or no sign is used), feedback is enabled only for options in the list.

For example, the following resource specification:

```
Mwm*showFeedback: resize placement restart
```

enables the feedback options `resize`, `placement`, and `restart`. What this means is that: size information is displayed when a window is resized; coordinates are displayed when a window is placed interactively on the screen; a dialog box is displayed so that the user can confirm or cancel a window manager restart request. Feedback is supplied in these circumstances only, overriding the default `all` option.

The following line specifies the same characteristics using the alternate syntax:

```
Mwm*showFeedback: -move kill behavior quit
```

This line disables the feedback options `move`, `kill`, `behavior`, and `quit`. The other options encompassed by the default `all` (`resize`, `placement`, and `restart`) remain enabled.

startupKeyFocus (class **StartupKeyFocus**)
If `True` (the default), the input focus is transferred to a window when the window is mapped (i.e., initially managed by the window manager). This function is available only when `keyboardFocusPolicy` is `explicit`.

transientDecoration (class **TransientDecoration**)
Specifies the amount of decoration *mwm* puts on transient windows. The decoration specification is exactly the same as for the `clientDecoration` (client-specific) resource. Transient windows are identified by the WM_TRANSIENT_FOR property, which is added by the client to indicate a relatively temporary window. The default is `menu title`, which specifies that transient windows have resize borders and a titlebar with a Window Menu command button.

transientFunctions (class **TransientFunctions**)
Specifies which window management functions are applicable (or not applicable) to transient windows. The function specification is exactly the same as for the `client-Functions` (client-specific) resource. The default is `-minimize maximize`.

useIconBox (class UseIconBox)
> If True, icons are placed in an icon box. By default, the individual icons are placed on the root window.

wMenuButtonClick (class WMenuButtonClick)
> If True (the default), a pointer button click on the Window Menu button displays the Window Menu and leaves it displayed.

wMenuButtonClick2 (class WMenuButtonClick2)
> If True, double clicking on the Window Menu command button removes the client window (actually invokes the f.kill function).

Client-specific Resources

Some *mwm* resources can be set to apply to certain client applications or classes of applications. Many of the client-specific resources provide what might be considered advanced customization.

The following client-specific resources can be specified:

clientDecoration (class ClientDecoration)
> Specifies the amount of window frame decoration. The default frame is composed of several component parts: the titlebar, resize handles, border, and three command buttons (Minimize, Maximize, and Window Menu). You can limit the frame decoration for a client using the clientDecoration resource.
>
> clientDecoration accepts a list of options, each of which corresponds to a part of the client frame. Depending on the syntax in which the options are entered, you can either enable or disable an option (as explained later).
>
> The options are: maximize (button); minimize (button); menu (the Window Menu button); border; title (titlebar); resizeh (resize handles); all, which encompasses all decorations previously listed (this is the default); and none, which specifies that no decorations are used.
>
> Some decorations require the presence of others; if you specify such a decoration, any decoration required with it will be used automatically. Specifically: if any of the command buttons is specified, a titlebar is also used; if resize handles or a titlebar is specified, a border is also used.
>
> By default, a client window has all decoration. To specify only certain parts of the default frame, you can use one of two syntaxes: with the first syntax, you disable certain frame features (all other default features are still used); with the second syntax, you enable only certain features. (The syntax is virtually the same as that described for showFeedback.)
>
> You supply clientDecoration with a list of options to be enabled or disabled. If the first item is preceded by a minus sign, the features in the list are disabled. (Any option not listed remains enabled.)
>
> If the first item is preceded by a plus sign (or no sign is used), only those features listed are enabled.

Reference Pages

For example, the following resource specification:

```
Mwm*XCalc*clientDecoration: -minimize maximize menu
```

removes the three command buttons from *xcalc* window frames. (The window will still have the titlebar, resize handles, and border.)

The following line specifies the same characteristics using the alternate syntax:

```
Mwm*XCalc*clientDecoration: title resizeh border
```

clientFunctions (class ClientFunctions)

Specifies whether certain *mwm* functions can be invoked on a client window. (See "mwm Functions" earlier in this reference page.) The only functions that can be controlled are those that are executable using the pointer on the default window frame.

`clientFunctions` accepts a list of options, each of which corresponds to an *mwm* function. Depending on the syntax in which the options are entered, you can either allow or disallow a function (as explained later).

The options (and the functions to which they correspond) are: `resize` (`f.resize`); `move` (`f.move`); `minimize` (`f.minimize`); `maximize` (`f.maximize`); `close` (`f.kill`); `all` (encompasses all of the previously listed functions); `none` (none of the default functions is allowed).

By default, a client recognizes `all` functions. To limit the functions a client recognizes, you can use one of two syntaxes: with the first syntax, you disallow certain functions (all other default functions are still allowed); with the second syntax, you allow only *certain* functions. (The syntax is virtually the same as that described for `clientDecoration`.)

You supply `clientFunctions` with a list of options (corresponding to functions) to be allowed or disallowed. If the first item is preceded by a minus sign, the functions in the list are disallowed. (Any option not listed remains allowed.)

If the first option is preceded by a plus sign (or no sign is used), only those functions listed are allowed.

A less than obvious reprecussion of disallowing a particular function is that the client window frame will be altered to prevent your invoking that function. For instance, if you disallow the `f.resize` function for a client, the client's frame will not include resize borders. (Features of the frame can also be suppressed using the `client-Decoration` resource.) In addition, the Window Menu Size item, which invokes the `f.resize` function, will no longer appear on the menu. (You cannot affect the Window Menu using `clientDecoration`.)

For example, the following resource line:

```
Mwm*xfd*clientFunctions: -resize maximize
```

specifies that you cannot invoke the `f.resize` and `f.maximize` functions on an *xfd* window. As a result, the resize borders and Maximize command button will not appear on the frame, and the Size and Maximize items will not appear on the Window Menu.

The following line specifies the same characteristics using the alternate syntax:

```
Mwm*xfd*clientFunctions: minimize move close
```

focusAutoRaise (class FocusAutoRaise)

If True, a window is raised when it receives the input focus. Otherwise, directing focus to a window does not affect the stacking order.

The default depends on the value assigned to the keyboardFocusPolicy resource. If the keyboardFocusPolicy is explicit, the default for focus-AutoRaise is True. If the keyboardFocusPolicy is pointer, the default for focusAutoRaise is False.

iconImage (class IconImage)

Specifies the pathname of a bitmap file to be used as an icon image for a client. (For example, you might specify: Mwm*xclock*iconImage: ~/bitmaps/big-ben.) The default is to display an icon image supplied by the window manager.

If the useClientIcon resource is set to True, an icon image supplied by the client takes precedence over an icon image supplied by the user.

iconImageBackground (class Background)

Specifies the background color of the icon image. The default is the color specified by Mwm*background or Mwm*icon*background.

iconImageBottomShadowColor (class Foreground)

Specifies the bottom shadow color of the icon image. The default is the color specified by Mwm*icon*bottomShadowColor.

iconImageBottomShadowPixmap (class BottomShadowPixmap)

Specifies the bottom shadow pixmap of the icon image. The default is the pixmap specified by Mwm*icon*bottomShadowPixmap.

iconImageForeground (class Foreground)

Specifies the foreground color of the icon image. The default varies based on the icon background.

iconImageTopShadowColor (class Background)

Specifies the top shadow color of the icon image. The default is the color specified by Mwm*icon*topShadowColor.

iconImageTopShadowPixmap (class TopShadowPixmap)

Specifies the top shadow Pixmap of the icon image. The default is the pixmap specified by Mwm*icon*topShadowPixmap.

matteBackground (class Background)

Specifies the background color of the matte. The default is the color specified by Mwm*background or Mwm*client*background. This resource is only relevant if matteWidth is positive.

Reference Pages

matteBottomShadowColor (class Foreground)
> Specifies the bottom shadow color of the matte. The default is the color specified by Mwm*bottomShadowColor or Mwm*client*bottomShadowColor. This resource is only relevant if matteWidth is positive.

matteBottomShadowPixmap (class BottomShadowPixmap)
> Specifies the bottom shadow pixmap of the matte. The default is the pixmap specified by Mwm*bottomShadowPixmap or Mwm*client*bottomShadowPixmap. This resource is only relevant if matteWidth is positive.

matteForeground (class Foreground)
> Specifies the foreground color of the matte. The default is the color specified by Mwm*foreground or Mwm*client*foreground. This resource is only relevant if matteWidth is positive.

matteTopShadowColor (class Background)
> Specifies the top shadow color of the matte. The default is the color specified by Mwm*topShadowColor or Mwm*client*topShadowColor. This resource is only relevant if matteWidth is positive.

matteTopShadowPixmap (class TopShadowPixmap)
> Specifies the top shadow pixmap of the matte. The default is the pixmap specified by Mwm*topShadowPixmap or Mwm*client*topShadowPixmap. This resource is only relevant if matteWidth is positive.

matteWidth (class MatteWidth)
> Specifies the width of the matte. The default is 0 (thus, no matte is used).

maximumClientSize (class MaximumClientSize)
> Specifies the size for a maximized window as *widthxheight*. If the WM_NORMAL_HINTS property is set, the default is obtained from it. If WM_NORMAL_HINTS is not set, the default is the size (including borders) that fills the screen.

> Note that the width and height are interpreted in the units used by the client. For example, icon box geometry is measured in the width and height of an icon, so the size of a maximized icon box might be 8x4, which specifies a box eight icons wide and four icons high. Similarly, *xterm* measures width and height in font characters and lines.

> If maximumClientSize is not specified, *mwm* uses any value supplied to maximumMaximumSize.

useClientIcon (class UseClientIcon)
> If True, an icon image supplied by the client takes precedence over an icon image supplied by the user. The default is False.

windowMenu (class WindowMenu)
> Specifies a name for the Window Menu (which must be defined in the startup file). The default is DefaultWindowMenu. See the section ".mwmrc Startup File" earlier in this reference page and Chapter 11 of this guide.

Environment Variables

The following environment variables are used by *mwm*:

HOME   The user's home directory.

LANG   The language to be used for the *mwm* message catalog and the *mwm* startup file.

XFILESEARCHPATH

Used to determine the location of system-wide class resource files. If the LANG variable is set, the *$LANG* subdirectory is also searched.

XUSERFILESEARCHPATH, XAPPLRESDIR

Used to determine the location of user-specific class resource files. If the LANG variable is set, the *$LANG* subdirectory is also searched.

MWMSHELL, SHELL

MWMSHELL specifies the shell to use when executing a command supplied as an argument to the f.exec function. (See "mwm Functions" earlier in this reference page.) If MWMSHELL is not set, SHELL is used.

Files

/usr/lib/X11/$LANG/system.mwmrc
/usr/lib/X11/system.mwmrc
/usr/lib/X11/app-defaults/Mwm
$HOME/Mwm
$HOME/$LANG/.mwmrc
$HOME/.mwmrc

See Also

X, Xserver, xdm, xrdb.

oclock

Name

oclock – display time of day in analog form.

Syntax

oclock [*options*]

Description

Available as of Release 4, *oclock* displays the current time on an analog display. The clock face is smaller and more stylized than that for *xclock*. For example, there are no tick-marks, save for a "jewel" at the 12 o'clock position. The chief virtue of *oclock*, and the one thing that has made it popular, is that it makes use of the X shape extension, which supports non-rectangular windows. The default *oclock* window is round, but it can be resized into all kinds of interesting ovals.

Options

oclock accepts all of the standard X Toolkit command line options, which are listed on the *X* reference page. (We've included some of the more commonly used Toolkit options later in this section.) In addition, *oclock* accepts the following application-specific options:

-jewel *color*
> Specifies a color for the jewel on the clock.

-minute *color*
> Specifies a color for the minute hand of the clock.

-hour *color*
> Specifies a color for the hour hand of the clock.

-backing *level*
> Selects an appropriate level of backing store.

-noshape
> Causes the clock not to use the shape extension for non-rectangular windows; in short, with -noshape, you get a square or rectangular clock. Note that the behavior is still different from *xclock -analog*. If you resize *xclock* so that its window is rectangular, the round clockface image is centered in the rectangle. With *oclock*, the border of the window is always the shape of the clock.

The following standard X Toolkit options are commonly used with *oclock*:

-bw *pixels*
> Specifies a width in pixels for the window border. As the Clock widget changes its border around quite a bit, this is most usefully set to zero.

-fg *color*
> Specifies a color for both the hands and the jewel of the clock.

-bg *color*
> Specifies a color for the background.

Colors

Although the default colors for the Clock widget are black and white, the widget was designed in color; unfortunately, the toolkit makes specifying these colors in a device-independent manner difficult. If you want to see the correct colors, add the following lines to your resource file:

```
Clock*Background: grey
Clock*BorderColor: light blue
Clock*hour: yellow
Clock*jewel: yellow
Clock*minute: yellow
```

See Also

X; Volume Four, *X Toolkit Intrinsics Programming Manual*; Volume Five, *X Toolkit Intrinsics Reference Manual*.

Author

Keith Packard, MIT X Consortium.

Reference Pages

resize

Name

resize – utility to set TERMCAP and terminal settings to the current window size.

Syntax

```
resize [options]
```

Description

The *resize* client is provided for use with systems that lack the ability to automatically notify processes of window size changes. Normally, on operating systems that support this feature, *xterm* sends a signal (e.g., SIGWINCH on BSD 4.3-derived UNIX systems) to notify processes running in the window that the window size has changed. These programs can adjust their behavior if necessary.

resize prints a shell command for setting the TERM and TERMCAP environment variables to indicate the current size of the *xterm* window from which the command is run. For this output to take effect, *resize* must either be evaluated as part of the command line (usually done with a shell alias or function) or else redirected to a file which can then be read in. From the C shell (usually known as */bin/csh*), the following alias could be defined in the user's *.cshrc*:

```
%  alias rs 'set noglob; eval `resize`; unset noglob'
```

After resizing the window, the user would type:

```
%  rs
```

Users of versions of the Bourne shell (usually known as */bin/sh*) that don't have command functions will need to send the output to a temporary file and then read it back in with the "." command:

```
$  resize >/tmp/out
$  . /tmp/out
```

Options

resize accepts the following options:

-u   Indicates that Bourne shell commands should be generated even if the user's current shell isn't */bin/sh*.

-c   Indicates that C shell commands should be generated even if the user's current shell isn't */bin/csh*.

-s [*rows columns*]
      Indicates that Sun console escape sequences will be used instead of the special *xterm* escape code. If *rows* and *columns* are given, *resize* will ask the *xterm* to resize itself. However, the window manager may choose to disallow the change.

The -u or -c must appear to the left of -s if both are specified.

Files

/etc/termcap
> For the base termcap entry to modify.

˜/.cshrc User's alias for the command.

See Also

csh(1), tset(1), xterm.

Bugs

There should be some global notion of display size; *termcap* and *terminfo* need to be rethought in the context of window systems. (Fixed in BSD 4.3 and Ultrix-32 1.2.)

Authors

Mark Vandevoorde, MIT Project Athena, and Edward Moy Berkeley.
Copyright (c) 1984, 1985 by Massachusetts Institute of Technology.
See *X* for a complete copyright notice.

Reference Pages

showsnf

Name

showsnf – print contents of an SNF file to standard output.

Syntax

```
showsnf [options] snf_file
```

Description

showsnf displays the contents of font files in the Server Natural Format produced by *bdftosnf*. The information displayed includes the value of each of the font properties (see Appendix M, *Logical Font Description Conventions*, in Volume 0, *X Protocol Reference Manual*), as well as information on font metrics (see section 6.2.3, *Character Metrics*, in Volume 1, *Xlib Programming Manual*).

showsnf is usually used only to verify that a font file hasn't been corrupted or to convert the individual glyphs into arrays of characters for proofreading or for conversion to some other format.

Options

showsnf accepts the following options:

- `-v` Indicates that bearings and sizes should be printed for each character in the font. (These are in an ASCII format similar to that produced by *bmtoa*. They can be converted to standard X bitmaps using *atobm*, and then edited with *bitmap*.)

- `-g` Indicates that character glyph bitmaps should be printed.

- `-m` Indicates that the bit order of the font is most significant bit first.

- `-l` Indicates that the bit order of the font is least significant bit first.

- `-M` Indicates that the byte order of the font is most significant byte first.

- `-L` Indicates that the byte order of the font is least significant byte first.

- `-pnumber`
  Specifies the glyph padding of the font.

- `-unumber`
  Specifies the scanline unit of the font.

See Also

X, Xserver, bdftosnf, bitmap.

Bugs

There is no way to print out only a single glyph.

Name
xauth – X authority file utility.

Syntax
xauth [*options*] [*command arguments*]

Description
Available as of Release 4, the *xauth* program is used to edit and display authorization information used when connecting to the X server. This program is generally used to extract authorization records from one machine and merge them in on another (as is the case when using remote logins or to grant access to other users). Note that this program does *not* contact the X server.

Options
The following options may be used with *xauth*. They may be given individually (for example, -q -i) or may be combined (for example, -qi).

-f *authfile*
> Specifies the name of the authority file to use. By default, *xauth* will use the file specified by the XAUTHORITY environment variable or *.Xauthority* in the user's home directory.

-q
> Indicates that *xauth* should operate quietly and not print unsolicited status messages. This is the default if an *xauth* command is given on the command line or if the standard output is not directed to a terminal.

-v
> Indicates that *xauth* should operate verbosely and print status messages indicating the results of various operations (for example, how many records have been read in or written out). This is the default if *xauth* is reading commands from its standard input and its standard output is directed to a terminal.

-i
> Indicates that *xauth* should ignore any authority file locks. Normally, *xauth* will refuse to read or edit any authority files that have been locked by other programs (usually *xdm* or another *xauth*).

-b
> Indicates that *xauth* should attempt to break any authority file locks before proceeding and should only be used to clean up stale locks.

Commands
Commands may be entered interactively, on the *xauth* command line, or in scripts. The following commands may be used to manipulate authority files:

add *displayname protocolname hexkey*
> An authorization entry for the indicated *displayname* using the given *protocolname* and *hexkey* data is added to the authorization file.

> The *hexkey* data is specified as an even-lengthed string of hexadecimal digits, each pair representing one octet. The first digit gives the most significant 4 bits of the octet and the second digit gives the least significant 4 bits. At present, only the *protocolname* MIT-MAGIC-COOKIE-1 is supported in the MIT distribution. The use of

more secure protocols is limited by export limits on DES encryption. A protocol name consisting of just a single period is treated as an abbreviation for MIT-MAGIC-COOKIE-1. Note that *xauth* will not give you an error if you specify an invalid protocol name.

[n]extract *filename displayname* . . .
Authorization entries for each of the specified displays are written to the indicated file. If the nextract command is used, the entries are written in a numeric format suitable for non-binary transmission (such as secure electronic mail). The extracted entries can be read back in using the merge and nmerge commands. If the filename consists of just a single dash, the entries will be written to the standard output.

[n]list [*displayname*...]
Authorization entries for each of the specified displays (or all, if no displays are named) are printed on the standard output. If the nlist command is used, entries will be shown in the numeric format used by the nextract command; otherwise, they are shown in a textual format. Key data is always displayed in the hexadecimal format given in the description of the add command.

[n]merge [*filename*...]
Authorization entries are read from the specified files and are merged into the authorization database, superceding any matching existing entries. If the nmerge command is used, the numeric format given in the description of the extract command is used. If a filename consists of just a single dash, the standard input will be read if it hasn't been read before.

remove *displayname*...
Authorization entries matching the specified displays are removed from the authority file.

source *filename*
The specified *filename* is treated as a script containing *xauth* commands to execute. In such a file, blank lines and lines beginning with a sharp sign (#) are ignored. A single dash may be used to indicate the standard input, if it hasn't already been read.

info   Information describing the authorization file, whether or not any changes have been made, and from where *xauth* commands are being read is printed on the standard output.

exit   If any modifications have been made, the authority file is written out (if allowed), and the program exits. An end-of-file is treated as an implicit exit command.

quit   The program exits, ignoring any modifications. This may also be accomplished by pressing the interrupt character.

help [*string*]
A description of all commands that begin with the given *string* (or all commands, if no string is given) is printed on the standard output.

? A short list of the valid commands is printed on the standard output.

Display Names

Display names for the add, [n]extract, [n]list, [n]merge, and remove commands use the same format as the DISPLAY environment variable and the common -display command line option. Display-specific information (such as the screen number) is unnecessary and will be ignored. Same-machine connections (such as local-host sockets, shared memory, and the Internet Protocol hostname *localhost*) are referred to as *hostname*/unix:*displaynumber* so that local entries for different machines may be stored in one authority file.

Example

The most common use for *xauth* is to extract the entry for the current display, copy it to another machine, and merge it into the user's authority file on the remote machine:

```
% xauth extract - $DISPLAY | rsh other xauth merge -
```

Environment Variables

This *xauth* program uses the following environment variables:

XAUTHORITY
 To get the name of the authority file to use if the -f option isn't used. If this variable is not set, *xauth* will use *Xauthority* in the user's home directory.

HOME To get the user's home directory if XAUTHORITY isn't defined.

Bugs

Users that have unsecure networks should take care to use encrypted file transfer mechanisms to copy authorization entries between machines. Similarly, the MIT-MAGIC-COOKIE-1 protocol is not very useful in unsecure environments. Sites that are interested in additional security may need to use encrypted authorization mechanisms such as Kerberos.

Spaces are currently not allowed in the protocol name. Quoting could be added for the truly perverse.

See Also

X, Xserver, xdm.

Author

Jim Fulton, MIT X Consortium.

Reference Pages

Name

xbiff – mail notification program for X.

Syntax

xbiff [*options*]

Description

The *xbiff* program displays a little image of a mailbox. When there is no mail in the user's mailbox, the flag on the mailbox is down. When mail arrives, the flag goes up and the mailbox beeps. By default, pressing any mouse button in the image forces *xbiff* to remember the current size of the mail file as being the "empty" size and to lower the flag.

This program is nothing more than a wrapper around the Athena Mailbox widget.

Options

xbiff accepts all of the standard X Toolkit command line options, which are listed on the *X* reference page. (We've included some of the more commonly used Toolkit options later in this section.) In addition, *xbiff* accepts the following application-specific options:

−help   Indicates that a brief summary of the allowed options should be printed on the standard error.

−update *seconds*
  Specifies the frequency in seconds at which *xbiff* should update its display. If the mailbox is obscured and then exposed, it will be updated immediately. The default is 60 seconds.

−file *filename*
  Specifies the name of the file that should be monitored. By default, *xbiff* watches */usr/spool/mail/username*, where **username** is your login name.

−shape
  Indicates that the mailbox window should be shaped if masks for the empty or full images are given. (Available as of Release 4.)

−volume *percentage*
  Specifies how loud the bell should be rung when new mail comes in.

The following standard X Toolkit options are commonly used with *xbiff*:

−geometry *geometry*
  Specifies the size and location of the mailbox window. The −geometry option can be (and often is) abbreviated to −g, unless there is a conflicting option that begins with "g." The argument to the geometry option (*geometry*) is referred to as a "standard geometry string," and has the form *width*x*height*±*xoff*±*yoff*. If you do not specify the geometry, the window manager may place the window automatically; if not, *xbiff* will ask you for window placement when it starts up. See "Window Geometry: Specifying Size and Location" in Chapter 3 of this guide for details. The default mailbox is 48 pixels on each side and is centered in the window.

`-xrm` `resourcestring`
> Specifies a resource string to be used. This is especially useful for setting resources that do not have separate command line options.

Resources

xbiff is implemented using a simple widget, the Mailbox widget from the Athena Widget Set. It understands all of the core resource names and classes as well as those from the Mailbox widget. The resources you might want to set are listed below:

`checkCommand` (class `CheckCommand`)
> Specifies a shell command to be executed to check for new mail rather than examining the size of `file`. The specified string value is used as the argument to a *system*(3) call and may therefore contain I/O redirection. An exit status of 0 indicates that new mail is waiting, 1 indicates that there has been no change in size, and 2 indicates that the mail has been cleared.

`file` (class `File`)
> Specifies the name of the file to monitor. The default is to watch */usr/spool/mail/ user-name*, where ***username*** is your login name.

`flip` (class `Flip`)
> Specifies whether or not the image that is shown when mail has arrived should be inverted. The default is true. (Available as of Release 4.)

`fullPixmap` (class `Pixmap`)
> Specifies a bitmap to be shown when new mail has arrived. (Available as of Release 4.)

`fullPixmapMask` (class `PixmapMask`)
> Specifies a mask for the bitmap to be shown when new mail has arrived. (Available as of Release 4.)

`emptyPixmap` (class `Pixmap`)
> Specifies a bitmap to be shown when no new mail is present. (Available as of Release 4.)

`emptyPixmapMask` (class `PixmapMask`)
> Specifies a mask for the bitmap to be shown when no new mail is present. (Available as of Release 4.)

`width` (class `Width`)
> Specifies the width of the mailbox. The default is 48 pixels.

`height` (class `Height`)
> Specifies the height of the mailbox. The default is 48 pixels.

`onceOnly` (class `Boolean`)
> Specifies that the bell is rung only the first time new mail is found and is not rung again until at least one interval has passed with no mail waiting. The window will continue to indicate the presence of new mail until it has been retrieved.

Reference Pages

shapeWindow (class ShapeWindow)
>   Specifies whether or not the mailbox window should be shaped to the given full-PixmapMask and emptyPixmapMask. (Available as of Release 4.)

update (class Interval)
>   Specifies the frequency in seconds at which the mail should be checked.

volume (class Volume)
>   Specifies how loud the bell should be rung. The default is 33 percent.

foreground (class Foreground)
>   Specifies the color for the foreground. The default is black since the core default for background is white.

reverseVideo (class ReverseVideo)
>   Specifies that the foreground and background should be reversed.

Widget Hierarchy

xbiff is implemented using a single widget, the Athena Mailbox widget. All applicable resources of the widget are listed above. The class and instance hierarchy is shown below:

```
Xbiff   xbiff
     Mailbox   mailbox
```

See Appendix G, *Athena Widget Resources* for a list of resources that can be set for the Athena widgets.

Actions

The Mailbox widget provides the following actions for use in event translations:

check()
>   Causes the widget to check for new mail and display the flag appropriately.

unset()
>   Causes the widget to lower the flag until new mail comes in.

set()   Causes the widget to raise the flag until the user resets it.

The default translation is:

```
<ButtonPress>:unset()
```

See Also

X, xrdb, stat(2).

Author

Jim Fulton, MIT X Consortium; Additional hacks by Ralph Swick, DEC/MIT Project Athena.

Name

xcalc – scientific calculator for X.

Syntax

xcalc [*options*]

Description

xcalc is a scientific calculator desktop accessory that can emulate a TI-30 or an HP-10C. The Release 4 version of *xcalc* has been rewritten to use the X Toolkit. Also as of Release 4, the number in the calculator display can be selected, allowing you to paste the result of a calculation into text.

In Release 4, the *xcalc* buttons have been changed to an oval shape (they are rectangular in the Release 3 version) and the window is somewhat smaller overall than it is in the Release 3 version. For those of you who like the size of the calculator under R3, try a geometry specification of approximately 167x222 (under *mwm*) and specify rectangular buttons using the resource setting:

```
xcalc*shapeStyle: rectangular
```

As of Release 4, *xcalc* no longer emulates a slide rule. (The −analog option has been eliminated.)

Options

xcalc accepts all of the standard X Toolkit command line options, which are listed on the *X* reference page. In addition, *xcalc* accepts the following application-specific options:

−rpn   Indicates that Reverse Polish Notation should be used. In this mode, the calculator will look and behave like an HP-10C. Without this flag, it will emulate a TI-30.

−stip, −stipple
        Indicates that the background of the calculator should be drawn using a stipple of the foreground and background colors. On monochrome displays, this improves the appearance. The −stipple version of this option is available as of Release 4. The −stip option can also still be used.

Calculator Operations

Pointer Usage

Operations may be performed with pointer button 1 (usually the leftmost button), or in many cases, with the keyboard. Many common calculator operations have keyboard equivalents, which are called accelerators, because they facilitate data entry. There are several ways to cause *xcalc* to exit: pressing the AC key of the TI calculator or the ON key of the HP calculator with pointer button 3 (usually the rightmost button); typing q, Q, or Control-C while the pointer is in the *xcalc* window.

Calculator Key Usage (TI Mode)

The number keys, the +/– key, and the +, −, *, /, and = keys all do exactly what you would expect them to. It should be noted that the operators obey the standard rules of precedence.

Thus, entering "3+4*5=" results in 23, not 35. Parentheses can be used to override this. For example, " (1+2+3) * (4+5+6) =" is evaluated as "6*15=" which results in 90.

The action associated with each function is given below. These are useful if you are interested in defining a custom calculator. The action used for all digit keys is digit(n), where n is the corresponding digit, 0-9. (The actions are available as of Release 4).

The keys are described below:

1/x　　　　　Replaces the number in the display with its reciprocal. The corresponding action is reciprocal().

x^2　　　　　Squares the number in the display. The corresponding action is square().

SQRT　　　　Evaluates the square root of the number in the display. The corresponding action is squareRoot().

CE/C　　　　When pressed once, clears the number in the display without clearing the state of the machine. Allows you to re-enter a number if you make a mistake. Pressing it twice clears the state also. The corresponding action is clear().

AC　　　　　Clears everything: the display, the state, and the memory. Pressing it with the third (usually the right) button "turns off" the calculator, in that it exits the program. The corresponding action to clear the state is off(); to quit, the action is quit().

INV　　　　　Inverts the meaning of the function keys. See the individual function keys for details. The corresponding action is inverse().

sin　　　　　Computes the sine of the number in the display, as interpreted by the current DRG mode (see DRG, below). If inverted, it computes the arcsine. The corresponding action is sine().

cos　　　　　Computes the cosine, or arccosine when inverted. The corresponding action is cosine().

tan　　　　　Computes the tangent, or arctangent when inverted. The corresponding action is tangent().

DRG　　　　Changes the DRG mode, as indicated by DEG, RAD, or GRAD at the bottom of the calculator "liquid crystal" display. When in DEG mode, numbers in the display are taken as being degrees. In RAD mode, numbers are in radians, and in GRAD mode, numbers are in gradians. When inverted, the DRG key has the handy feature of converting degrees to radians to gradians and vice versa. For example, put the calculator into DEG mode and type "45 INV DRG". The calculator should display approximately .785398, which is 45 degrees converted to radians. The corresponding action is degree().

e　　　　　　Is the constant "e" (2.7182818 . . .). The corresponding action is e().

EE	Is used for entering exponential numbers. For example, to enter "-2.3E-4" you would type "2 . 3 +/- EE 4 +/-". The corresponding action is scientific().
log	Calculates the log (base 10) of the number in the display. When inverted, it raises 10.0 to the number in the display. For example, entering "3 INV log" should result in 1000. The corresponding action is logarithm().
ln	Calculates the log (base e) of the number in the display. When inverted, it raises "e" to the number in the display. For example, entering "e ln" should result in 1. The corresponding action is naturalLog().
y^x	Raises the number on the left to the power of the number on the right. For example, "2 y^x 3 =" results in 8, which is 2^3. Also, "(1+2+3) y^x (1+2) =" is evaluated as "6 y^x 3=" which results in 216. The corresponding action is power().
PI	The constant "pi". (3.1415927 ....) The corresponding action is pi().
x!	Computes the factorial of the number in the display. The number in the display must be an integer in the range 0-500, though depending on your math library, it might overflow long before that. The corresponding action is factorial().
(	Left parenthesis. The corresponding action for TI calculators is leftParen().
)	Right parenthesis. The corresponding action for TI calculators is rightParen().
/	Division. The corresponding action is divide().
*	Multiplication. The corresponding action is multiply().
−	Subtraction. The corresponding action is subtract().
+	Addition. The corresponding action is add().
=	Perform calculation. The TI-specific action is equal().
STO	Copies the number in the display to the memory location. The corresponding action is store().
RCL	Copies the number from the memory location to the display. The corresponding action is recall().
SUM	Adds the number in the display to the number in the memory location. The corresponding action is sum().
EXC	Swaps the number in the display with the number in the memory location. The corresponding action is exchange().
+/−	Negate (change sign). The corresponding action is negate().
.	Decimal point. The corresponding action is decimal().

Reference Pages

Calculator Key Usage (RPN mode)

The number keys, CHS (change sign), +, −, *, /, and ENTR keys all do exactly what you would expect them to. Many of the remaining keys are the same as in TI (default) mode. The differences are detailed below. The action for the ENTR key is `enter()`.

<-	Is a backspace key that can be used while entering a number. It will erase digits from the display. (See "Bugs.") Inverse backspace clears the X register. The corresponding action is `back()`.
ON	Clears everything: the display, the state, and the memory. Pressing it with the third (usually the right) pointer button "turns off" the calculator, in that it exits the program. The corresponding action to clear the state is `off()`; to quit, the action is `quit()`.
INV	Inverts the meaning of the function keys. This would be the "f" key on an HP calculator, but *xcalc* does not display multiple legends on each key. See the individual function keys for details.
10ˆx	Raises 10.0 to the number in the top of the stack. When inverted, it calculates the log (base 10) of the number in the display. The corresponding action is `tenpower()`.
eˆx	Raises "e" to the number in the top of the stack. When inverted, it calculates the log (base e) of the number in the display. The corresponding action is `epower()`.
STO	Copies the number in the top of the stack to one of ten memory locations. The desired memory is specified by pressing this key and then pressing a digit key.
RCL	Pushes the number from the specified memory location onto the stack.
SUM	Adds the number on top of the stack to the number in the specified memory location.
x:y	Exchanges the numbers in the top two stack positions, the X and Y registers. The corresponding action is `XexchangeY()`.
R v	Rolls the stack downward. When inverted, it rolls the stack upward. The corresponding action is `roll()`.

Blank keys were used for programming functions on the HP-10C. Their functionality has not been duplicated in *xcalc*.

Keyboard Equivalents (Accelerators)

If you have the pointer in the *xcalc* window, you can use the keyboard to enter numbers and other keys. Almost all of the calculator keys have keyboard equivalents, which are known as *accelerators* because they speed entry. The number keys, the operator keys, and the parentheses all have the obvious equivalents. The accelerators defined by *xcalc* are listed in the following table:

TI Key	HP Key	Keyboard Accelerator	TI Function	HP Function
SQRT	SQRT	r	squareRoot()	squareRoot()
AC	ON	space	clear()	clear()
AC	<-	Delete	clear()	back()
AC	<-	Backspace	clear()	back()
AC	<-	Control-H	clear()	back()
AC		Clear	clear()	
AC	ON	q	quit()	quit()
AC	ON	Control-C	quit()	quit()
INV	i	i	inverse()	inverse()
sin	s	s	sine()	sine()
cos	c	c	cosine()	cosine()
tan	t	t	tangent()	tangent()
DRG	DRG	d	degree()	degree()
e		e	e()	
ln	ln	l	naturalLog()	naturalLog()
y^x	y^x	^	power()	power()
PI	PI	p	pi()	pi()
x!	x!	!	factorial()	factorial()
(		(	leftParen()	
)		)	rightParen()	
/	/	/	divide()	divide()
*	*	*	multiply()	multiply()
−	−	−	subtract()	subtract()
+	+	+	add()	add()
=		=	equal()	
0...9	0...9	0...9	digit()	digit()
.	.	.	decimal()	decimal()
+/-	CHS	n	negate()	negate()
	x:y	x		XexchangeY()
	ENTR	Return		enter()
	ENTR	Linefeed		enter()

Note that the use of the "e" keyboard accelerator to invoke the "e" calculator key is new as of Release 4. In the Release 3 version of *xcalc*, the "e" keyboard accelerator corresponds to the EE calculator key.

Reference Pages

Resources

xcalc defines the following application resources:

rpn (class Rpn)

A Boolean value that specifies whether or not the rpn mode should be used. The default is off—that is, the calculator will be used in TI mode.

stipple (class Stipple)

A Boolean value that indicates whether or not the background should be stippled. The default is on for monochrome displays, and off for color displays.

cursor (class Cursor)

The name of the symbol used to represent the pointer. The default is hand2. See Appendix D for a list of cursor names.

Widget Hierarchy

In addition, you can specify resources for each of the widgets that make up *xcalc*. In the notation below, indentation indicates the hierarchical structure of the widgets. The widget class name is given first, followed by the widget instance name.

```
XCalc xcalc
            Form   ti  or  rpn          (the name depends on the mode)
              Form   bevel
                Form   screen
                    Label   M           (the memory indicator on the screen)
                    Toggle  LCD         (where the data is displayed)
                    Label   INV         (the inverted indicator on the display)
                    Label   DEG         (the degrees indicator on the display)
                    Label   RAD         (the radians indicator on the display)
                    Label   GRAD        (the gradians indicator on the display)
                    Label   P           (the Parenthesis indicator on the display)
                Command   button1       (the actual calculator buttons)
                Command   button2       (buttons are numbered from right to left)
                Command   button3       (See the app-defaults file for associations
                                            and so on...)
                Command   button38      (between widget names and default labels)
                Command   button39
                Command   button40      (Only 39 buttons in HP mode)
```

See Appendix G, *Athena Widget Resources* for a list of resources that can be set for the Athena widgets.

Customization

The application class name is XCalc.

As of Release 4, *xcalc* has an enormous application defaults file, which specifies the position, label, and function of each key on the calculator. It also gives translations to serve as keyboard accelerators. Because these resources are not specified in the source code, you can create a customized calculator by writing a private application defaults file, using the Athena Command and Form widget resources to specify the size and position of buttons, the label for each button, and the function of each button.

The foreground and background colors of each calculator key can be individually specified. For the TI calculator, a classical color resource specification might be:

```
XCalc.ti.Command.background:       grey50
XCalc.ti.Command.foreground:       white
```

For each of buttons 20, 25, 30, 35, and 40, specify:

```
XCalc.ti.button20.background:      black
XCalc.ti.button20.foreground:      white
```

For each of buttons 22, 23, 24, 27, 28, 29, 32, 33, 34, 37, 38, and 39:

```
XCalc.ti.button22.background:      white
XCalc.ti.button22.foreground:      black
```

Bugs

In HP mode, a bug report claims that the sequence of keys 5, ENTR, and <— should clear the display, but it doesn't.

See Also

X, xrdb, and Appendix G, *Athena Widget Resources*.

Authors

John Bradley, University of Pennsylvania;
Mark Rosenstein, MIT Project Athena.

Reference Pages

xclipboard

Name

xclipboard – X clipboard client.

Syntax

xclipboard [*options*]

Description

The *xclipboard* program is used to collect and display text selections that are sent to the CLIP-BOARD by other clients. It is typically used to save CLIPBOARD selections for later use.

Since *xclipboard* uses a Text widget to display the contents of the clipboard, text sent to the CLIPBOARD may be re-selected for use in other applications. The contents may also be edited, using any of the editing commands built into the Text widget. (See the reference page for *xedit* for details.)

xclipboard stores each CLIPBOARD selection as a separate string, each of which can be selected. Each time CLIPBOARD is asserted by another application, *xclipboard* transfers the contents of that selection to a new buffer and displays it in the text window. Buffers are never automatically deleted, so you'll want to use the delete button to get rid of useless items.

xclipboard also responds to requests for the CLIPBOARD selection from other clients by sending the entire contents of the currently displayed buffer.

An *xclipboard* window has the following buttons across the top:

quit   When this button is pressed, *xclipboard* exits.

delete   When this button is pressed, the current buffer is deleted and the next one displayed.

new   Creates a new buffer with no contents. Useful in constructing a new CLIPBOARD selection by hand.

next   Displays the next buffer in the list.

previous   Displays the previous buffer.

Options

xclipboard accepts all of the standard X Toolkit command line options, which are listed on the *X* reference page. In addition, *bitmap* accepts the following application-specific options:

-w   Indicates that lines of text that are too long to be displayed on one line in the clipboard should wrap around to the following lines.

-nw   Indicates that long lines of text should not wrap around. This is the default behavior.

Sending and Retrieving Clipboard Contents

Text is copied *to* the clipboard whenever a client asserts ownership of the CLIPBOARD selection. Text is copied *from* the clipboard whenever a client requests the contents of the CLIP-BOARD selection. This doesn't necessarily happen automatically; you must add translations for each application that you want to have work with *xclipboard*. Examples of event bindings that a user may wish to include in a resource configuration file to use the clipboard from *xterm* are:

```
*VT100.Translations: #override \n\
    Button1 <Btn3Up>:  select-end(CLIPBOARD) \n\
    ~Ctrl ~Meta <Btn2Up>:    insert-selection(PRIMARY,CLIPBOARD) \n\
    <Btn2Down>:ignore()
```

The first translation, `Button1 <Btn3Up>:  select-end(CLIPBOARD)`, specifies that if button 3 is clicked while button 1 is held down, the selection will be added to the CLIPBOARD. If button 3 isn't clicked while button 1 is held down, the default *xterm* translation, namely to add the selection to the PRIMARY selection and CUT_BUFFER0 on any key up, takes effect instead.

On paste, the translation `~Ctrl ~Meta <Btn2Up>: insert-selection (PRIMARY, CLIPBOARD)` will paste the PRIMARY selection if one is available (that is, if it is still highlighted in a window); otherwise, it will paste the current contents of the *xclipboard* window. (Note that this is a small change in the normal *xterm* selection behavior, in that usually, the PRIMARY selection would stay asserted until another selection was made, even if the selected text was no longer highlighted.) `~Ctrl` and `~Meta` are specified to keep this translation from conflicting with the translations that invoke the *xterm* menus. The `ignore()` action is provided to keep the `<Btn2Down>` event from invoking any other action.

In the notation below, indentation indicates the hierarchical structure of the widgets. The widget class name is given first, followed by the widget instance name. The first line shows the application class and instance names:

```
XClipboard  xclipboard
        Form  form
                Command  quit
                Command  delete
                Command  new
                Command  next
                Command  prev
                Text     text
```

For information on the resources available in each of the Athena widgets, see Appendix G, *Athena Widget Resources*.

Files

/usr/lib/X11/app-defaults/XClipboard
        Specifies required resources (as of Release 4).

See Also

X, xcutsel, xterm, individual client documentation for how to make a selection and send it to the CLIPBOARD.

Reference Pages

Author

Ralph R. Swick, DEC/MIT Project Athena;
Chris Peterson, MIT X Consortium;
Keith Packard, MIT X Consortium.

Name

xclock – continuously display the time in either analog or digital form.

Syntax

xclock [*options*]

Description

xclock continuously displays the time of day, either in digital or analog form. In digital form, *xclock* displays the time using a 24-hour clock. It also displays the day, month, and year. In analog form, *xclock* displays a standard 12-hour clock face. You can set up more than one clock simultaneously.

The default clock is an analog clock with a black foreground on a white background. If you want to change the clock's appearance, type in the appropriate options. For example,

xclock -bd slateblue -fg navyblue -hl darkslategrey &

sets up a conventional 12-hour clock with a slate blue window border, navy blue tick marks, and dark slate grey hands.

By default, the clock is positioned in the upper-left corner of your background window. If you are running the default version of *mwm*, the window manager will place the clock in the upper-left quadrant of the screen, offset from the corner.

Options

xclock accepts all of the standard X Toolkit command line options, which are listed on the *X* reference page. (We've included some of the more commonly used Toolkit options later in this section.) In addition, *xclock* accepts the following application-specific options:

−help Displays a brief summary of *xclock*'s calling syntax and options.

−analog
    Draws a conventional 12-hour clock face with tick marks for each minute and stroke marks for each hour. This is the default.

−digital or −d
    Displays the date and time in digital format. Note that −display must be used to specify a display.

−chime
    Indicates that the clock should chime once on the half hour and twice on the hour.

−hd *color*
    Specifies the color of the hands on an analog clock. The default is black.

−hl *color*
    Specifies the color of the edges of the hands on an analog clock. Only useful on color displays. The default is black.

Reference Pages

-padding *pixels*

> Specifies the width in pixels of the space between the window border and any portion of the *xclock* display. The default is 10 pixels in digital mode and 8 pixels in analog mode.

-update *seconds*

> Specifies the frequency in seconds with which *xclock* updates its display. If the *xclock* window is obscured and then exposed, *xclock* overrides this setting and redisplays immediately. A value of less than 30 seconds will enable a second hand on an analog clock. The default is 60 seconds.

The following standard X Toolkit options are commonly used with *xclock*:

-bw *pixels*

> Specifies the width in pixels of the border around the *xclock* window. The default is 2 pixels.

-fg *color*

> Determines the color of the text in digital mode, and the color of the tick and stroke marks in analog mode. The default is black.

-fn *font*

> Specifies the font to be used in digital mode. Any fixed-width font may be used. The default is 6x10.

-geometry *geometry*

> Sets *xclock* window size and location according to the geometry specification. The -geometry option can be (and often is) abbreviated to -g, unless there is a conflicting option that begins with "g." The argument to the geometry option (*geometry*) is referred to as a "standard geometry string," and has the form *widthx-height±xoff±yoff*.

> In digital mode, height and width are determined by the font in use, unless otherwise specified. In analog mode, width and height defaults are 164 pixels, unless otherwise specified. The default value for any unspecified x or y offset is –0. All values are in pixels. If you do not specify the geometry, the window manager may place the window; if not, *xclock* will ask you for placement when it starts up.

-display [*host*]:*server*[.*screen*]

> Allows you to specify the host, server, and screen on which to create the *xclock* window. See "Options" on the *X* reference page for an example of usage.

> Note that -display cannot be abbreviated to -d, which is shorthand for *xclock*'s -digital option.

-xrm *resourcestring*

> Specifies a resource string to be used. This is especially useful for setting resources that do not have separate command line options.

Resources

xclock uses the Athena Clock widget. It understands all of the core resource names and classes as well as the new resources defined by the Clock widget. Resources you may want to set in user resource files include:

update (class Interval)
> Specifies the frequency in seconds at which the time should be redisplayed.

hands (class Foreground)
> Specifies the color of the insides of the clock's hands. The default is the foreground color.

highlight (class Foreground)
> Specifies the color used to highlight the clock's hands. The default is the foreground color.

analog (class Boolean)
> Specifies whether or not an analog clock should be used instead of a digital one. The default is true.

chime (class Boolean)
> Specifies whether or not a bell should be rung on the half hour and on the hour. The default is false.

padding (class Margin)
> Specifies the amount of internal padding in pixels to be used. The default is 8.

You may also want to set the following core resources:

width (class Width)
> Specifies the width of the clock.

height (class Height)
> Specifies the height of the clock.

background (class Background)
> Determines the background color. The default is white.

foreground (class Foreground)
> Specifies the color for the tick marks and stroke marks. Using the class specifies the color for all things that normally would appear in the foreground color. The default is black since the core default for background is white.

font (class Font)
> Specifies the font to be used for the digital clock. Note that variable-width fonts currently will not always display correctly.

reverseVideo (class ReverseVideo)
> Specifies that the foreground and background colors should be reversed.

Reference Pages

Widget Hierarchy

In order to specify resources, it is useful to know the hierarchy of the widgets which compose *xclock*. In the notation below, indentation indicates hierarchical structure. The widget class name is given first, followed by the widget instance name.

```
XClock  xclock
    Clock  clock
```

Files

/usr/lib/X11/app-defaults/XClock   Specifies default resources (as of Release 4).

Bugs

xclock believes the system clock.

When in digital mode, the string should be centered automatically.

No way to exit the program.

See Also

X, oclock, xrdb, time(3C), Athena Clock widget.

Authors

Tony Della Fera (MIT-Athena, DEC);
Dave Mankins (MIT-Athena, BBN);
Ed Moy (UC Berkeley).

Name

xcol – display colors and change color entries in resource files.

Syntax

xcol [*options*] [*filename*]

Description

xcol displays the colors defined in the *rgb.txt* file of the X server. The colors are sorted by their names and their RGB-values and shown in a cube in the ColorView window (The positions represent the RGB-values). Since there usually are more colors defined in the file than cells in the colormap, entries with the same name, but different RGB-values for different intensities, are grouped together.

If a filename is given as a parameter, all occurrences of color names in that file are shown in a second window, called the TextView window. To change the colors specified in the file, a text line has to be made active. Then a new color can be selected in the ColorView window.

To get a better impression of the color, a help (highlight/background) color can be selected for each text line. If two lines define a foreground and a background color, an association can be made and the colors of both lines can be selected together.

Pointer Commands

In the ColorView window, pointer clicks have the following effects:

First button: Selects color for the active resource line in the TextView window.

Second button: Selects help (i.e., highlight) color for the active resource line in the TextView window.

Third button: Moves pointer to the pixel of the color specified by the active resource line in the TextView window.

In the TextView window, pointer clicks have the following effects:

First button: Selects the text line as the active line.

Second button: Toggles reverse video mode or connects/disconnects two associated lines (e.g., background and foreground color specifications for the same resource).

Third button: Highlights the line in the text file.

Options

−rv

Color positions are reversed in the cube. Some new colors can become visible in the area of the very bright colors.

−b*number*

The size of color blocks is set to the constant *number*. By default, it depends on the size of the ColorView window.

-grann*number*

     Sets the maximum number of associated colors to *number*. By default, this value is 11. (You can see the effect when reaching the grey field, where 101 associated entries are possibly available.)

-dark*number*

     Sets the percentage of the intensity of other colors. The default is 50. It's easier to select a color if the screen is darkened a little bit.

+*char_list*

     Adds characters in *char_list* to list of 'space' characters. A color string in the text file must occur between 2 'space' characters to be recognized. By default, these characters are " ", "\t", "\n", ":", """".

-strings

     Specifies that names of colors in the file are only recognized when used in a string (useful for C source code). This means that the list of "space" characters is set to """" only.

-case

     Specifies that all occurrences of color names in the wrong case are replaced by the appropriate color names from the *rgb.txt* file.

-help

     Prints some instructions (e.g., on the usage of buttons).

-file *filename*

     Specifies an alternative file to the *rgb.txt* file.

Files

/usr/lib/X11/rgb.txt

See Also

X; Chapter 8, *Other Clients*; Chapter 9, *Command Line Options*.

Bugs

The author wanted the program to work with the selection mechanism used in *xterm* (when no text file is given), but it seems to be too complicated. So, the current version always stores the string of the color in CUT_BUFFER0. If anyone has an easy way to use the correct selection mechanism, please contact the author.

Copyright

Copyright 1990, University of Kaiserslautern.

Permission to use, copy, modify, and distribute this software for any purpose and without fee is hereby granted, provided that the above copyright notice appear in all copies.

Author

Helmut Hoenig (hoenig@informatik.uni-kl.de).

Name

xcutsel – interchange between cut buffer and selection.

Syntax

xcutsel [*options*]

Description

xcutsel is used to copy the current selection into a cut buffer and to make a selection that contains the current contents of the cut buffer. It acts as a bridge between applications that don't support selections and those that do.

By default, *xcutsel* will use the selection named PRIMARY and the cut buffer CUT_BUFFER0. Either or both of these can be overridden by command line arguments or by resources.

An *xcutsel* window has the following buttons:

quit When this button is pressed, *xcutsel* exits. Any selections held by *xcutsel* are automatically released.

copy PRIMARY to 0
When this button is pressed, *xcutsel* copies the current selection into the cut buffer.

copy 0 to PRIMARY
When this button is pressed, *xcutsel* converts the current contents of the cut buffer into the selection.

The button labels reflect the selection and cut buffer selected by command line options or through the resource database.

When the copy 0 to PRIMARY button is activated, the button will remain inverted as long as *xcutsel* remains the owner of the selection. This serves to remind you which client owns the current selection. Note that the value of the selection remains constant; if the cut buffer is changed, you must again activate the copy button to retrieve the new value when desired.

Options

xcutsel accepts all of the standard X Toolkit command line options, which are listed on the *X* reference page. In addition, *xcutsel* accepts the following application-specific options:

-selection *name*
Specifies the name of the selection to use. The default is PRIMARY. The only supported abbreviations for this option are -select, -sel, and -s, since the standard Toolkit option -selectionTimeout has a similar name.

-cutbuffer *number*
Specifies the cut buffer to use. The default is cut buffer 0.

Resources

This program accepts all of the standard X Toolkit resource names and classes as well as:

selection (class Selection)
This resource specifies the name of the selection to use. The default is PRIMARY.

Reference Pages

cutBuffer (class CutBuffer)

>This resource specifies the number of the cut buffer to use. The default is 0.

Widgets

xcutsel is made up of the following widgets.

```
xcutsel xcutsel
    Box box
    Command sel-cut
    Command cut-sel
    Command quit
```

If you specify a different selection or cut buffer to use, you will probably also want to customize the labels of the buttons. Unfortunately, it isn't obvious which button widget name corresponds to the current labels. Here's the correspondence, in case you need to change the labels:

sel-cut

>This is the button normally labeled copy PRIMARY to 0.

cut-sel

>This is the button normally labeled copy 0 to PRIMARY.

quit   This is the quit button.

Bugs

There is no way to change the name of the selection or the number of the cut buffer while the program is running.

See Also

X, xterm, xclipboard; Chapter 5, *The xterm Terminal Emulator*; Text widget information in Chapter 8, *Other Clients*, and Appendix G, *Athena Widget Resources*.

Author

Ralph R. Swick, DEC/MIT Project Athena.

Name

xditview – display *ditroff* DVI files.

Syntax

xditview [*options*]

Description

The *xditview* program displays *ditroff* output on an X display. It uses special font metrics that match the font set distributed with X11 Release 3, so it does not require access to the server machine for font loading.

Options

xditview accepts all of the standard X Toolkit command line options, which are listed on the *X* reference page. (We've included one of the more commonly used Toolkit options later in this section.) In addition, *xditview* accepts the following application-specific options:

−help Indicates that a brief summary of the allowed options should be printed.

-page Specifies the page number of the document to be displayed.

-backingStore *backing_store_type*
> Redisplay of the DVI window can take up to a second or so. This option causes the server to save the window contents so that when it is scrolled around the viewport, the window is painted from contents saved in backing store. *backing_store_type* can be one of Always, WhenMapped, or NotUseful.

The following standard X Toolkit option is commonly used with *xditview*:

−fn *font*
> Specifies the font to be used for displaying widget text. The default is *fixed*.

Resources

This program uses the Dvi widget in the Athena Widget Set. It understands all of the core resource names and classes as well as:

width (class Width)
> Specifies the width of the window.

height (class Height)
> Specifies the height of the window.

foreground (class Foreground)
> Specifies the default foreground color.

font (class Font)
> Specifies the font to be used for error messages.

Reference Pages

Using xditview with ditroff

To build a DVI file suitable for use with *xditview*, use the device description in the subdirectory *devX75* (under *xditroff* in the MIT source tree). *ditroff* looks for the font files in the directory */usr/lib/font*, so the appropriate font files must be installed, and referenced by *ditroff*'s −T option, as shown in the following example:

```
$ cd devX75
$ makedev DESC
$ mkdir /usr/lib/font/devX75
$ cp *.out /usr/lib/font/devX75
$ ditroff -TX75 ditroff_input | xditview
```

See Also

X, xrdb, ditroff(1).

Bugs

xditview can be easily confused by attempting to display a DVI file constructed for the wrong device. Support for *pic* is not yet implemented.

Authors

Portions of this program originated in *xtroff* which was derived from *suntroff*.

Keith Packard (MIT X Consortium);
Richard L. Hyde (Purdue);
David Slattengren (Berkeley);
Malcom Slaney (Schlumberger Palo Alto Research);
Mark Moraes (University of Toronto).

Name

xdm – X display manager.

Syntax

xdm [*options*]

Description

xdm manages a collection of X displays, both local and possibly remote—the emergence of X terminals guided the design of several parts of this system, along with the development of the X Consortium standard XDMCP, the X Display Manager Control Protocol (introduced in Release 4). It is designed to provide services similar to that provided by *init*, *getty*, and *login* on character terminals: prompting for login/password, authenticating the user, and running a "session."

A *session* is defined by the lifetime of a particular process; in the traditional character-based terminal world, it is the user's login shell process. In the *xdm* context, it is an arbitrary session manager. This is because, in a windowing environment, a user's login shell process would not necessarily have any terminal-like interface with which to connect.

Until real session managers become widely available, the typical *xdm* substitute would be either a window manager with an exit option, or a terminal emulator running a shell—with the condition that the lifetime of the terminal emulator is the lifetime of the shell process that it is running—thus degenerating the X session to an emulation of the character-based terminal session.

When the session is terminated, *xdm* resets the X server and (optionally) restarts the whole process.

Because *xdm* provides the first interface that users will see, it is designed to be simple to use and easy to customize to the needs of a particular site. *xdm* has many options, most of which have reasonable defaults. Browse through the various sections, picking and choosing the things you want to change. Pay particular attention to *The Xsession File*, which will describe how to set up the style of session desired.

Options

First, note that all of these options, except `-config`, specify values that can also be specified in the configuration file as resources.

`-config` *configuration_file*

Specifies a resource file which specifies the remaining configuration parameters. If no file is specified and the file */usr/lib/X11/xdm/xdm-config* exists, *xdm* will use it.

`-daemon`

Specifies `true` as the value for the `DisplayManager.daemonMode` resource. This makes *xdm* close all file descriptors, disassociate the controlling terminal, and put itself in the background when it first starts up (just like the host of other daemons). It is the default behavior.

`-debug` *debug_level*

Specifies the numeric value for the `DisplayManager.debugLevel` resource. A non-zero value causes *xdm* to print piles of debugging statements to the terminal; it

also disables the `DisplayManager.daemonMode` resource, forcing *xdm* to run
synchronously. To interpret these debugging messages, a copy of the source code for
xdm is almost a necessity. No attempt has been made to rationalize or standardize the
output.

`-error error_log_file`
> Specifies the value for the `DisplayManager.errorLogFile` resource. This file
> contains errors from *xdm* as well as anything written to standard error by the various
> scripts and programs run during the progress of the session.

`-nodaemon`
> Specifies `false` as the value for the `DisplayManager.daemonMode` resource.

`-resources resource_file`
> Specifies the value for the `DisplayManager*resources` resource. This file is
> loaded using *xrdb* to specify configuration parameters for the authentication widget.

`-server server_entry`
> Specifies the value for the `DisplayManager.servers` resource. (See
> "Resources" below.)

`-udpPort port_number`
> Specifies the value for the `DisplayManager.requestPort` resource. This sets
> the port number which XDM will monitor for XDMCP requests. As XDMCP uses the
> registered well-known udp port 177, this resource should probably not be changed
> except for debugging. (Available as of Release 4.)

`-session session_program`
> Specifies the value for the `DisplayManager*session` resource. This indicates
> the program to run when the user has logged in as the session. (Available as of
> Release 4.)

`-xrm resource_specification`
> Allows an arbitrary resource to be specified, just as most toolkit applications.

Resources

At many stages the actions of *xdm* can be controlled through the use of the configuration file,
which is in the familiar X resource format. See Chapter 10 for a description of the resource file
format. Some resources modify the behavior of *xdm* on all displays, while others modify its
behavior on a single display. Where actions relate to a specific display, the display name is
inserted into the resource name between "DisplayManager" and the final resource name seg-
ment. For example, `DisplayManager.expo_0.startup` is the name of the resource that
defines the startup shell file on the "expo:0" display. Because the resource manager uses colons
to separate the name of the resource from its value and dots to separate resource name parts,
xdm substitutes underscores for the dots and colons when generating the resource name. (The
use of underscores to separate the parts of the display name is new in Release 4. In Release 3,
`DisplayManager.expo.0.startup` is the resource. The Release 3 *xdm* substitutes dots
for the colons when generating the resource name.)

DisplayManager.servers

> Specifies either a filename full of server entries, one per line, or a single server entry. Each entry indicates a display that should constantly be managed and that is not using XDMCP. (If the resource value begins with a slash, it is assumed to be the name of a file containing the list.) Each entry consists of at least three parts: a display name, a display class (new as of Release 4), and a display type. Local servers will also have a command line to start the server. (The program name should be an absolute UNIX pathname, since *xdm* does not search through the directories of the PATH environment variable.) Foreign servers can have a comment in place of the command line. A typical entry for local display number 0 would be:

        :0 Digital-QV local /usr/bin/X11/X :0

The display types are:

local   A local display, i.e., one that has a server program to run.

foreign   A remote display, i.e., one that has no server program to run.

The display name must be something that can be passed in the −display option to any X program. This string is used in the display-specific resources to specify the particular display, so be careful to match the names (e.g., use :0 local /usr/bin/X11/X :0 instead of *localhost*:0 local /usr/bin/X11/X :0 if your other resources are specified as DisplayManager._0.session).

The display class portion can also be used in display-specific resources, as the class name of the resource. This is useful if you have a large collection of similar displays (perhaps several X terminals) and would like to set resources for groups of them. When using XDMCP, the display is required to specify the display class. Your X terminal documentation should describe a reasonably standard display class string for your device.

DisplayManager.requestPort

> Indicates the UDP port number which *xdm* uses to listen for incoming XDMCP requests. Unless you need to debug the system, leave this with its default value of 177. (Available as of Release 4.)

DisplayManager.errorLogFile

> Error output is normally directed at the system console. To redirect, it simply set this resource to any filename. A method to send these messages to syslog should be developed for systems that support it; however the wide variety of "standard" interfaces precludes any system-independent implementation. This file also contains any output directed to standard error by *Xstartup*, *Xsession*, and *Xreset*, so it will contain descriptions of problems in those scripts as well.

DisplayManager.debugLevel

> A non-zero value specified for this integer resource will enable reams of debugging information to be printed. It also disables daemon mode, which would redirect the information into the bit-bucket. Specifying a non-zero debug level also allows non-

root users to run *xdm*, which would normally not be useful. (Available as of Release 4.)

`DisplayManager.daemonMode`

Normally, *xdm* attempts to make itself into an unassociated daemon process. This is accomplished by forking and leaving the parent process to exit, then closing file descriptors and mangling the controlling terminal. When attempting to debug *xdm*, this is quite bothersome. Setting this resource to `false` will disable this feature. (Available as of Release 4.)

`DisplayManager.pidFile`

The filename specified will be created to contain an ASCII representation of the process ID of the main *xdm* process. This is quite useful when reinitializing the system. *xdm* also uses file locking to attempt to eliminate multiple daemons running on the same machine, which would cause quite a bit of havoc. (Available as of Release 4.)

`DisplayManager.lockPidFile`

Controls whether *xdm* uses file locking to keep multiple *xdm* processes from running amok. On System V, this uses the *lockf* library call, while on BSD it uses *flock*. The default value is `true`. (Available as of Release 4.)

`DisplayManager.remoteAuthDir`

This is a directory name that *xdm* uses to temporarily store authorization files for displays using XDMCP. The default value is */usr/lib/X11/xdm*. (Available as of Release 4.)

`DisplayManager.autoRescan`

This Boolean controls whether *xdm* rescans the configuration file and servers file after a session terminates and the files have changed. By default it is `true`. You can force *xdm* to reread these files by sending a SIGHUP to the main process. (Available as of Release 4.)

`DisplayManager.removeDomainname`

When computing the display name for XDMCP clients, the resolver will typically create a fully qualified host name for the terminal. Since this is sometimes confusing, *xdm* will remove the domain name portion of the host name if it is the same as the domain name for the local host when this variable is set. By default the value is `true`. (Available as of Release 4.)

`DisplayManager.keyFile`

XDM-AUTHENTICATION-1 style XDMCP authentication requires that a private key be shared between *xdm* and the terminal. This resource specifies the file containing those values. Each entry in the file consists of a display name and the shared key. By default, *xdm* does not include support for XDM-AUTHENTICATION-1 as it requires DES, which is not generally distributable. (Available as of Release 4.)

`DisplayManager.DISPLAY.resources`

Specifies the name of the file to be loaded by *xrdb* as the resource database onto the root window of screen 0 of the display. This resource database is loaded just before the authentication procedure is started, so it can control the appearance of the "login" window. See "Authentication Widget Resources," which describes the various resources which are appropriate to place in this file. There is no default value for this resource, but the conventional name is */usr/lib/X11/xdm/Xresources*.

`DisplayManager.`*`DISPLAY`*`.xrdb`
Specifies the program used to load the resources. By default, *xdm* uses */usr/bin/X11/xrdb*.

`DisplayManager.`*`DISPLAY`*`.cpp`
Specifies the name of the C preprocessor used by *xrdb*. (Available as of Release 4.)

`DisplayManager.`*`DISPLAY`*`.startup`
Specifies a program which is run (as root) after the authentication process succeeds. By default, no program is run. The conventional name for a file used here is *Xstartup*. See "The Xstartup File" below.

`DisplayManager.`*`DISPLAY`*`.session`
Specifies the session to be executed (not running as root). By default, */usr/bin/X11/xterm* is run. The conventional name is *Xsession*. See "The Xsession File" below.

`DisplayManager.`*`DISPLAY`*`.reset`
Specifies a program which is run (as root) after the session terminates. Again, by default no program is run. The conventional name is *Xreset*. See "The Xreset File" below.

`DisplayManager.`*`DISPLAY`*`.openDelay,`
`DisplayManager.`*`DISPLAY`*`.openRepeat,`
`DisplayManager.`*`DISPLAY`*`.openTimeout,`
`DisplayManager.`*`DISPLAY`*`.startAttempts`
Numeric resources control the behavior of *xdm* when attempting to open intransigent servers. `openDelay` is the length of the pause (in seconds) between successive attempts. `openRepeat` is the number of attempts to make. `openTimeout` is the amount of time to wait while actually attempting the open (i.e., the maximum time spent in the *connect* syscall). `startAttempts` (available as of Release 4) is the number of times this entire process is done before giving up on the server. After `openRepeat` attempts have been made, or if `openTimeout` seconds elapse in any particular attempt, *xdm* terminates and restarts the server, attempting to connect again. This process is repeated `startAttempts` times, at which point the display is declared dead and disabled. Although this behaviour may seem arbitrary, it has been empirically developed and works quite well on most systems. The default values are 5 for `openDelay`, 5 for `openRepeat`, 30 for `openTimeout`, and 4 for `start-Attempts`.

`DisplayManager.`*`DISPLAY`*`.pingInterval,`
`DisplayManager.`*`DISPLAY`*`.pingTimeout`
To discover when remote displays disappear, *xdm* occasionally "pings" them, using an X connection and sending XSync requests. `pingInterval` specifies the time (in minutes) between each ping attempt, `pingTimeout` specifies the maximum amount

Reference Pages

of time (in minutes) to wait for the terminal to respond to the request. If the terminal does not respond, the session is declared dead and terminated. By default, both are set to 5 minutes. *xdm* will not ping local displays. Although it would seem harmless, it is unpleasant when the workstation session is terminated as a result of the server hanging for NFS service and not responding to the ping. (Available as of Release 4.)

DisplayManager.*DISPLAY*.terminateServer
Specifies whether the X server should be terminated when a session terminates (instead of resetting it). This option can be used when the server tends to grow without bound over time in order to limit the amount of time the server is run. The default value is false.

DisplayManager.*DISPLAY*.userPath
xdm sets the PATH environment variable for the session to this value. It should be a colon separated list of directories; see *sh*(1) for a full description. The default value can be specified in the X system configuration file with DefUserPath; frequently it is set to *:/bin:/usr/bin:/usr/bin/X11:/usr/ucb*.

DisplayManager.*DISPLAY*.systemPath
xdm sets the PATH environment variable for the startup and reset scripts to the value of this resource. The default for this resource is specified with the DefaultSystem-Path entry in the system configuration file, but it is frequently */etc:/bin:/usr/bin:/usr/bin/X11:/usr/ucb*. Note the conspicuous absence of "." from this entry. This is a good practice to follow for root; it avoids many common trojan horse system penetration schemes.

DisplayManager.*DISPLAY*.systemShell
xdm sets the SHELL environment variable for the startup and reset scripts to the value of this resource. By default, it is */bin/sh*.

DisplayManager.*DISPLAY*.failsafeClient
If the default session fails to execute, *xdm* will fall back to this program. This program is executed with no arguments, but executes using the same environment variables as the session would have had. See "The Xsession File" below. By default, */usr/bin/X11/xterm* is used.

DisplayManager.*DISPLAY*.grabServer
DisplayManager.*DISPLAY*.grabTimeout
To eliminate obvious security shortcomings in the X protocol, *xdm* grabs the server and keyboard while reading the name and password. The grabServer resource specifies if the server should be held for the duration of the name and password reading; when false, the server is ungrabbed after the keyboard grab succeeds, otherwise the server is grabbed until just before the session begins. The grabTimeout resource specifies the maximum time *xdm* will wait for the grab to succeed. The grab may fail if some other client has the server grabbed, or possibly if the network laten-

cies are very high. This resource has a default value of 3 seconds; you should be cautious when raising it, as a user can be spoofed by a look-alike window on the display. If the grab fails, *xdm* kills and restarts the server (if possible) and session. (Available as of Release 4.)

`DisplayManager.`*DISPLAY*`.authorize`
`DisplayManager.`*DISPLAY*`.authName`

> `authorize` is a Boolean resource that controls whether *xdm* generates and uses authorization for the server connections. If authorization is used, `authName` specifies the type to use. Currently, *xdm* supports only MIT-MAGIC-COOKIE-1 authorization; XDM-AUTHORIZATION-1 could be supported as well, but DES is not generally distributable. XDMCP connections specify which authorization types are supported dynamically, so `authName` is ignored in this case. When `authorize` is set for a display and authorization is not available, the user is informed by having a different message displayed in the login widget. By default, `authorize` is `true` and `authName` is MIT-MAGIC-COOKIE-1. (Available as of Release 4.)

`DisplayManager.`*DISPLAY*`.authFile`

> This file is used to communicate the authorization data from *xdm* to the server, using the `-auth` server command line option. It should be kept in a directory which is not world-writable, as it could easily be removed, disabling the authorization mechanism in the server. (Available as of Release 4.)

`DisplayManager.`*DISPLAY*`.resetForAuth`

> The original implementation of authorization in the sample server reread the authorization file at server reset time, instead of when checking the initial connection. As *xdm* generates the authorization information just before connecting to the display, an old server would not get up-to-date authorization information. This resource causes *xdm* to send SIGHUP to the server after setting up the file, causing an additional server reset to occur, during which time the new authorization information will be read. (Available as of Release 4.)

`DisplayManager.`*DISPLAY*`.userAuthDir`

> When *xdm* is unable to write to the usual user authorization file (*$HOME/Xauthority*), it creates a unique file name in this directory and points the environment variable XAUTHORITY at the created file. By default, it uses */tmp*. (Available as of Release 4.)

Controlling The Server

xdm controls local servers using POSIX signals. SIGHUP is expected to reset the server, closing all client connections and performing other clean up duties. SIGTERM is expected to terminate the server. If these signals do not perform the expected actions, *xdm* will not perform properly.

To control remote servers not using XDMCP, *xdm* searches the window hierarchy on the display and uses the protocol request `KillClient` in an attempt to clean up the terminal for the next session. This may not actually kill all of the clients, as only those which have created windows will be noticed. XDMCP provides a more certain mechanism; when *xdm* closes its initial connection, the session is over and the terminal is required to close all other connections.

Reference Pages

Controlling xdm

xdm responds to two signals: SIGHUP and SIGTERM. When sent a SIGHUP, *xdm* rereads the file specified by the `DisplayManager.servers` resource and notices if entries have been added or removed. If a new entry has been added, *xdm* starts a session on the associated display. Entries that have been removed are disabled immediately, meaning that any session in progress will be terminated without notice, and no new session will be started.

When sent a SIGTERM, *xdm* terminates all sessions in progress and exits. This can be used when shutting down the system.

xdm attempts to mark the various subprocesses for *ps*(1) by editing the command line argument list in place. Because *xdm* can't allocate additional space for this task, it is useful to start *xdm* with a reasonably long command line (15 to 20 characters should be enough). Each process that is servicing a display is marked *-<Display_Name>*.

Authentication Widget Resources

The authentication widget reads a name/password pair from the keyboard. As this is a toolkit client, nearly every imaginable parameter can be controlled with a resource. Resources for this widget should be put into the file named by `DisplayManager.DISPLAY.resources`. All of these resources have reasonable default values, so it is not necessary to specify any of them.

`xlogin.Login.width, xlogin.Login.height, xlogin.Login.x,`
`xlogin.Login.y`
> The geometry of the login widget is normally computed automatically. If you wish to position it elsewhere, specify each of these resources.

`xlogin.Login.foreground`
> The color used to display the typed-in user name.

`xlogin.Login.font`
> The font used to display the typed-in user name.

`xlogin.Login.greeting`
> A string which identifies this window. The default is "Welcome to the X Window System".

`xlogin.Login.unsecureGreeting`
> When X authorization is requested in the configuration file for this display and none is in use, this greeting replaces the standard greeting. Its default value is "This is an unsecure session". (Available as of Release 4.)

`xlogin.Login.greetFont`
> The font used to display the greeting.

`xlogin.Login.greetColor`
> The color used to display the greeting.

`xlogin.Login.namePrompt`
> The string displayed to prompt for a user name. *xrdb* strips trailing white space from resource values, so to add spaces at the end of the prompt (usually a nice thing), add spaces escaped with backslashes. (In Release 3, Control-A should work.) The default is "Login:".

`xlogin.Login.passwdPrompt`
> The string displayed to prompt for a password. The default is "Password:".

`xlogin.Login.promptFont`
> The font used to display both prompts.

`xlogin.Login.promptColor`
> The color used to display both prompts.

`xlogin.Login.fail`
> A message which is displayed when the authentication fails. The default is "Login Failed, please try again".

`xlogin.Login.failFont`
> The font used to display the failure message.

`xlogin.Login.failColor`
> The color used to display the failure message.

`xlogin.Login.failTimeout`
> The time (in seconds) that the fail message is displayed. The default is 30 seconds.

`xlogin.Login.translations`
> This specifies the translations used for the login widget. See Chapter 10, *Setting Resources*, and Appendix F, *Translation Table Syntax*, for more information on translations. The default translation table for *xdm* is:

```
Ctrl<Key>H:          delete-previous-character() \n\
Ctrl<Key>D:          delete-character() \n\
Ctrl<Key>B:          move-backward-character() \n\
Ctrl<Key>F:          move-forward-character() \n\
Ctrl<Key>A:          move-to-begining() \n\
Ctrl<Key>E:          move-to-end() \n\
Ctrl<Key>K:          erase-to-end-of-line() \n\
Ctrl<Key>U:          erase-line() \n\
Ctrl<Key>X:          erase-line() \n\
Ctrl<Key>C:          restart-session() \n\
Ctrl<Key>\\:         abort-session() \n\
<Key>BackSpace:      delete-previous-character() \n\
<Key>Delete:         delete-previous-character() \n\
<Key>Return:         finish-field() \n\
<Key>:               insert-char() \
```

Reference Pages

The actions that are supported by the widget are:

delete-previous-character
>   Erases the character before the cursor.

delete-character
>   Erases the character after the cursor.

move-backward-character
>   Moves the cursor backward one character.

move-forward-character
>   Moves the cursor forward one character.

move-to-beginning
>   Moves the cursor to the beginning of the editable text.

move-to-end
>   Moves the cursor to the end of the editable text.

erase-to-end-of-line
>   Erases all text after the cursor.

erase-line
>   Erases the entire text.

finish-field
>   If the cursor is in the name field, proceeds to the password field; if the cursor is in
>   the password field, check the current name/password pair. If the name/password
>   pair is valid, *xdm* starts the session. Otherwise, the failure message is displayed and
>   the user is prompted to try again.

abort-session
>   Terminates and restarts the server.

abort-display
>   Terminates the server, disabling it. This is a rash action and is not accessible in the
>   default configuration. It can be used to stop *xdm* when shutting the system down, or
>   when using *xdmshell*.

restart-session
>   Resets the X server and starts a new session. This can be used when the resources
>   have been changed and you want to test them, or when the screen has been overwritten
>   with system messages.

insert-char
>   Inserts the character typed.

set-session-argument
>   Specifies a single word argument which is passed to the session at startup. See "The
>   Xsession File" and "Typical Usage" below.

allow-all-access

> Disables access control in the server, this can be used when the *Xauthority* file cannot be created by *xdm*. Be very careful when using this; it might be better to disconnect the machine from the network first. (Available as of Release 4.)

The Xstartup File

This file is typically a shell script. It is run as root and should be very careful about security. This is the place to put commands which make fake entries in */etc/utmp*, mount users' home directories from file servers, display the message of the day, or abort the session if logins are not allowed. Various environment variables are set for the use of this script:

DISPLAY   is set to the associated display name.

HOME   is set to the home directory of the user.

USER   is set to the user name.

PATH   is set to the value of `DisplayManager.DISPLAY.systemPath`.

SHELL   is set to the value of `DisplayManager.DISPLAY.systemShell`.

XAUTHORITY   may be set to a non-standard authority file (Release 4).

No arguments of any kind are passed to the script. *xdm* waits until this script exits before starting the user session. If the exit value of this script is non-zero, *xdm* discontinues the session immediately and starts another authentication cycle.

The Xsession File

This is the script that is run as the user's session. It is run with the permissions of the authorized user, and has several environment variables specified:

DISPLAY   is set to the associated display name.

HOME   is set to the home directory of the user.

USER   is set to the user name.

PATH   is set to the value of `DisplayManager.DISPLAY.userPath`.

SHELL   is set to the user's default shell (from */etc/passwd*).

XAUTHORITY   may be set to a non-standard authority file (Release 4).

At most installations, *Xsession* should look in $HOME for a file *.xsession*, which would contain commands that each user would like to use as a session. This would replace the system default session. *Xsession* should also implement the system default session if no user-specified session exists. See "Typical Usage" below.

An argument may be passed to this program from the authentication widget using the "set-session-argument" action. This can be used to select different styles of session. One very good use of this feature is to allow the user to escape from the ordinary session when it fails. This would allow users to repair their own *.xsession* if it fails, without requiring administrative intervention. The section "Typical Usage" demonstrates this feature.

Reference Pages

The Xreset File

Symmetrical with *Xstartup*, this script is run after the user session has terminated. Run as root, it should probably contain commands that undo the effects of commands in *Xstartup*, removing fake entries from */etc/utmp* or unmounting directories from file servers. The collection of environment variables that were passed to *Xstartup* is also given to *Xreset*.

Typical Usage

Actually, *xdm* is designed to operate in such a wide variety of environments that "typical" is probably a misnomer. However, this section will focus on making *xdm* a superior solution to traditional means of starting X from */etc/ttys* or manually.

First off, the *xdm* configuration file should be set up. A good thing to do is to make a directory (*/usr/lib/X11/xdm* comes immediately to mind) that will contain all of the relevant files. Here is a reasonable configuration file for Release 4, which could be named *xdm-config*:

```
DisplayManager.servers:            /usr/lib/X11/xdm/Xservers
DisplayManager.errorLogFile:       /usr/lib/X11/xdm/xdm-errors
DisplayManager.pidFile:            /usr/lib/X11/xdm/xdm-pid
DisplayManager*resources:          /usr/lib/X11/xdm/Xresources
DisplayManager*session:            /usr/lib/X11/xdm/Xsession
DisplayManager._0.authorize:       true
DisplayManager*authorize:          false
```

As you can see, the *xdm-config* file primarily contains references to other files. Note that some of the resources are specified with "*" separating the components. These resources can be made unique for each different display by replacing the "*" with the display name, but normally this is not very useful. See the "Resources" section for a complete discussion.

The first file, */usr/lib/X11/xdm/Xservers*, contains the list of displays to manage. Most workstations have only one display, numbered 0, so the file will look like this:

```
:0 display_class local /usr/bin/X11/X :0
```

This will keep */usr/bin/X11/X* running on this display and manage a continuous cycle of sessions.

The file */usr/lib/X11/xdm/xdm-errors* will contain error messages from *xdm* and anything output to standard error by *Xstartup, Xsession* or *Xreset*. When you have trouble getting *xdm* working, check this file to see if *xdm* has any clues to the trouble.

The next configuration entry, */usr/lib/X11/xdm/Xresources*, is loaded onto the display as a resource database using *xrdb*. As the authentication widget reads this database before starting up, it usually contains parameters for that widget:

```
xlogin*login.translations: #override\\e
  <Key>F1: set-session-argument(failsafe) finish-field()\\en\\e
  <Key>Return: set-session-argument() finish-field()
xlogin*borderWidth: 3
#ifdef COLOR
xlogin*greetColor: #f63
xlogin*failColor: red
```

```
xlogin*Foreground: black
xlogin*Background: #fdc
#else
xlogin*Foreground: black
xlogin*Background: white
#endif
```

The various colors specified here look reasonable on several of the displays we have, but may look awful on other monitors. As X does not currently have any standard color naming scheme, you might need to tune these entries to avoid disgusting results. Please note the translations entry; it specifies a few new translations for the widget which allow users to escape from the default session (and avoid troubles that may occur in it). Note that if #override is not specified, the default translations are removed and replaced by the new value, not a very useful result as some of the default translations are quite useful (like *<Key>:* insert-char(), which responds to normal typing).

The *Xstartup* file used here simply prevents login while the file */etc/nologin* exists. As there is no provision for displaying any messages here (there isn't any core X client which displays files), the user will probably be baffled by this behavior. I don't offer this as a complete example, but simply a demonstration of the available functionality.

Here is a sample *Xstartup* script:

```
#!/bin/sh
#
# Xstartup
#
# This program is run as root after the user is verified
#
if [ -f /etc/nologin ]; then
        exit 1
fi
exit 0
```

The most interesting script is *Xsession*. This version recognizes the special "failsafe" mode, specified in the translations in the *Xresources* file above, to provide an escape from the ordinary session:

```
#!/bin/sh
#
# Xsession
#

# This is the program that is run as the client
# for the display manager.  This example is
# quite friendly as it attempts to run a per-user
# .xsession file instead of forcing a particular
# session layout
```

Reference Pages

```
case $# in
1)
        case $1 in
        failsafe)
                exec xterm -geometry 80x24-0-0 -ls
                ;;
        esac
esac

startup=$HOME/.xsession
resources=$HOME/.Xresources

#
# check for a user-specific session and execute it
#
# Note: the -x flag to test is not supported in all versions of
#       unix, check with local authorities before proceeding...
#
if [ -f $startup ]; then
        if [ -x $startup ]; then
                exec $startup
        else
                exec /bin/sh $startup
        fi
else
        #
        # a simple default session.  Check to see
        # if the user has created a default resource file
        # and load it, start the universal window manager
        # and use xterm as the session control process.
        #
        if [ -f $resources ]; then
                xrdb -load $resources
        fi
        twm &
        exec xterm -geometry 80x24+10+10 -ls
fi
```

No *Xreset* script is necessary, so none is provided in Release 4.

Some Other Possibilities

You can also use *xdm* to run a single session at a time, using the 4.3 *init* options or other suitable daemon by specifying the server on the command line:

```
% xdm -server ":0 SUN-3/60CG4 local /usr/bin/X :0"
```

Or, you might have a file server and a collection of X terminals. The configuration for this could look identical to the sample above, except the *Xservers* file might look like:

```
extol:0 VISUAL-19 foreign
exalt:0 NCD-19 foreign
explode:0 NCR-TOWERVIEW3000 foreign
```

This would direct *xdm* to manage sessions on all three of these terminals. See "Controlling xdm" above for a description of using signals to enable and disable these terminals in a manner reminiscent of *init*.

One thing that *xdm* isn't very good at doing is coexisting with other window systems. To use multiple window systems on the same hardware, you'll probably be more interested in *xinit*.

See Also

X, xinit, XDMCP.

Author

Keith Packard, MIT X Consortium.

Name

xdpr – dump an X window directly to the printer.

Syntax

xdpr [*filename*] [*options*]

Description

xdpr runs the commands *xwd*, *xpr*, and *lpr*(1) to dump an X window, process it for a laser printer, and print it out. This is the easiest way to get a printout of a window. *xdpr* by default will print the largest possible representation of the window on the output page.

Options

The options for *xdpr* are the same as those for *xpr*, *xwd*, and *lpr*(1). The most commonly used options are described below; see the reference pages for these commands for detailed descriptions of the many other options available.

filename
> Specifies an existing file containing a window dump (created by *xwd*) to be printed instead of selecting an X window.

-P*printer*
> Specifies the name of the printer to be used. If a printer name is not specified here, *xdpr* (really, *lpr*(1)) will send your output to the printer specified by the PRINTER environment variable. Be sure that the type of the printer matches the type specified with the -device option.

-device *printer_device*
> Specifies the device on which the file is to be printed. Currently the following printers are supported:

> ln03   Digital LN03.

> la100 Digital LA100.

> ljet   HP LaserJet series and other monochrome PCL devices, such as ThinkJet, QuietJet, RuggedWriter, HP2560 series, and HP2930 series printers. (Available as of Release 4.)

> pjet   HP PaintJet (color mode). (Available as of Release 4.)

> pjetxl
> HP PaintJet XL Color Graphics Printer (color mode). (Available as of Release 4.)

> pp   IBM PP3812.

> ps   PostScript printer.

-help Displays the list of options known to *xdpr*.

```
-display [host]:server[.screen]
```
Allows you to specify the server to connect to. *host* specifies the machine, *server* specifies the server number, and *screen* specifies the screen number. For example,

xdpr -display *your_node***:0.1**

prints a dump of an X window from screen 1 of server 0 on the machine *your_node*. If the host is omitted, the local machine is assumed. If the screen is omitted, screen 0 is assumed; the server and colon (:) are necessary in all cases.

Any other arguments will be passed to the *xwd*, *xpr*, and *lpr*(1) commands as appropriate for each.

Environment Variables
PRINTER   Specifies which printer to use by default.

See Also
X, xwd, xpr, xwud, lpr(1).

Authors
Paul Boutin, MIT Project Athena;
Michael R. Gretzinger, MIT Project Athena;
Jim Gettys, MIT Project Athena.

Reference Pages

xdpyinfo

Name

xdpyinfo – display information utility for X.

Syntax

xdpyinfo [*option*]

Description

xdpyinfo is a utility for displaying information about an X server. It is used to examine the capabilities of a server, the predefined values for various parameters used in communicating between clients and the server, and the different types of screens and visuals that are available.

Option

xdpyinfo accepts the following option:

-display [*host*]:*server*[.*screen*]

> Specifies the display about which *xdpyinfo* should display information. *host* specifies the machine, *server* specifies the server number, and *screen* specifies the screen number. By default, *xdpyinfo* displays information about all screens on the display. For example,
>
> **xdpyinfo -display** *your_node*:**0.0**
>
> displays information about all screens of server 0 of the machine *your_node*. If the hostname is omitted, the local node is assumed. If the screen is omitted, screen 0 is assumed. The server and colon (:) are necessary in all cases.

Sample Output

The following example shows the output produced by *xdpyinfo* when connected to a display that supports an 8-plane screen and a 1-plane screen.

```
name of display:      :0.0
version number:    11.0
vendor string:     MIT X Consortium
vendor release number:    4
maximum request size:  16384 longwords (65536 bytes)
motion buffer size:  0
bitmap unit, bit order, padding:    32, MSBFirst, 32
image byte order:     MSBFirst
number of supported pixmap formats:    2
supported pixmap formats:
    depth 1, bits_per_pixel 1, scanline_pad 32
    depth 8, bits_per_pixel 8, scanline_pad 32
keycode range:    minimum 8, maximum 129
number of extensions:    4
    SHAPE
    MIT-SHM
    Multi-Buffering
    MIT-SUNDRY-NONSTANDARD
default screen number:    0
```

```
number of screens:      2

screen #0:
  dimensions:      1152x900 pixels (325x254 millimeters)
  resolution:      90x90 dots per inch
  depths (2):      1, 8
  root window id:      0x8006e
  depth of root window:      8 planes
  number of colormaps:      minimum 1, maximum 1
  default colormap:      0x8006b
  default number of colormap cells:      256
  preallocated pixels:      black 1, white 0
  options:      backing-store YES, save-unders YES
  current input event mask:      0xd0801d
    KeyPressMask          ButtonPressMask          ButtonReleaseMask
    EnterWindowMask       ExposureMask             SubstructureRedirectMask
    PropertyChangeMask    ColormapChangeMask
  number of visuals:      6
  default visual id:  0x80065
  visual:
    visual id:      0x80065
    class:      PseudoColor
    depth:      8 planes
    size of colormap:      256 entries
    red, green, blue masks:      0x0, 0x0, 0x0
    significant bits in color specification:      8 bits
  visual:
    visual id:      0x80066
    class:      DirectColor
    depth:      8 planes
    size of colormap:      8 entries
    red, green, blue masks:      0x7, 0x38, 0xc0
    significant bits in color specification:      8 bits
  visual:
    visual id:      0x80067
    class:      GrayScale
    depth:      8 planes
    size of colormap:      256 entries
    red, green, blue masks:      0x0, 0x0, 0x0
    significant bits in color specification:      8 bits
  visual:
    visual id:      0x80068
    class:      StaticGray
    depth:      8 planes
    size of colormap:      256 entries
    red, green, blue masks:      0x0, 0x0, 0x0
    significant bits in color specification:      8 bits
  visual:
    visual id:      0x80069
    class:      StaticColor
```

Reference Pages

```
      depth:    8 planes
      size of colormap:    256 entries
      red, green, blue masks:    0x7, 0x38, 0xc0
      significant bits in color specification:    8 bits
   visual:
      visual id:    0x8006a
      class:    TrueColor
      depth:    8 planes
      size of colormap:    8 entries
      red, green, blue masks:    0x7, 0x38, 0xc0
      significant bits in color specification:    8 bits
   number of mono multibuffer types:    6
      visual id, max buffers, depth:    0x80065, 0, 8
      visual id, max buffers, depth:    0x80066, 0, 8
      visual id, max buffers, depth:    0x80067, 0, 8
      visual id, max buffers, depth:    0x80068, 0, 8
      visual id, max buffers, depth:    0x80069, 0, 8
      visual id, max buffers, depth:    0x8006a, 0, 8
   number of stereo multibuffer types:    0

screen #1:
   dimensions:    1152x900 pixels (325x254 millimeters)
   resolution:    90x90 dots per inch
   depths (1):    1
   root window id:    0x80070
   depth of root window:    1 plane
   number of colormaps:    minimum 1, maximum 1
   default colormap:    0x8006c
   default number of colormap cells:    2
   preallocated pixels:    black 1, white 0
   options:    backing-store YES, save-unders YES
   current input event mask:    0xd0801d
      KeyPressMask          ButtonPressMask        ButtonReleaseMask
      EnterWindowMask       ExposureMask           SubstructureRedirectMask
      PropertyChangeMask    ColormapChangeMask
   number of visuals:    1
   default visual id: 0x80064
   visual:
      visual id:    0x80064
      class:    StaticGray
      depth:    1 plane
      size of colormap:    2 entries
      red, green, blue masks:    0x0, 0x0, 0x0
      significant bits in color specification:    1 bits
   number of mono multibuffer types:    1
      visual id, max buffers, depth:    0x80064, 0, 1
   number of stereo multibuffer types:    0
```

See Also

X, xwininfo, xprop, xrdb.

Author

Jim Fulton, MIT X Consortium.

Name

xedit – simple text editor for X.

Syntax

xedit [*options*] [*filename*]

Description

xedit provides a window consisting of the following four areas:

Commands Section

A set of commands that allow you to exit *xedit*, save the file, or load a new file into the edit window.

Message Window

Displays *xedit* messages. In addition, this window can be used as a scratch pad.

Filename Display

Displays the name of the file currently being edited, and whether this file is *Read–Write* or *Read Only*.

Edit Window

Displays the text of the file that you are editing or creating.

The *xedit* window appears in Figure 8-13 in Part Two of this guide.

Command Buttons

Quit   Quits the current editing session. If any changes have not been saved, *xedit* displays a warning message, allowing the user to save the file.

Save   If file backups are enabled (see "Resources"), *xedit* stores a copy of the original, unedited file in <prefix>*filename*<suffix>, then overwrites the *filename* with the contents of the edit window. The *filename* is retrieved from the Text widget directly to the right of the Load button.

Load   Loads the file named in the Text widget immediately to the right of this button and displays it in the Edit Window. If the currently displayed file has been modified, a warning message will ask the user to save the changes or to press Load again.

Editing

The Athena Text widget is used for the three sections of this application that allow text input, namely the Message Window, the the Edit Window, and the window to the right of the command buttons, in which a filename can be entered.

The characters typed will go to the Text widget that the pointer is currently over. If the pointer is not over a Text widget, then the keypresses will have no effect on the application. This is also true for the special key sequences that pop-up dialog widgets; so, for example, typing Control-S in the filename widget (next to the command buttons) will enable searching in that widget, not the Edit Window (edit widget).

Both the Message Window and the Edit Window will create a scrollbar if the text to display is too large to fit in that window. Horizontal scrolling is not allowed by default, but can be turned on through the Text widget's resources. See Appendix G, *Athena Widget Resources*, for more information.

The following list summarizes the editing commands recognized by *xedit* (i.e., by the Text widget).

Control-A	Move to the beginning of the current line.
Control-B	Move backward one character.
Control-D	Delete the next character.
Control-E	Move to the end of the current line.
Control-F	Move forward one character.
Control-H or Backspace	Delete the previous character.
Return Control-J, Control-M, or LineFeed	New paragraph. (Linefeed, Control-J, and Control-M may be unreliable on some terminals.)
Control-K	Kill the rest of this line. (Does not kill the carriage return at the end of the line. To do so, use Control-K twice. However, be aware that the second kill overwrites the text line in the kill buffer.)
Control-L	Redraw the window. (Also scrolls text so that cursor is positioned in the middle of the window.)
Control-N	Move down to the next line.
Control-O	Divide this line into two lines at this point.
Control-P	Move up to the previous line.
Control-V	Move down to the next screenful of text.
Control-W	Kill the selected text.
Control-Y	Insert the last killed text. (If the last killed text is a carriage return—see Control-K above—a blank line is inserted.)
Control-Z	Scroll up the text one line.
Meta-<	Move to the beginning of the file.
Meta->	Move to the end of the file.
Meta-[	Move backward one paragraph.
Meta-]	Move forward one paragraph.

Reference Pages

Meta-B	Move backward one word.
Meta-D	Kill the next word.
Meta-F	Move forward one word.
Meta-H, or	Kill the previous word.
Meta-Delete	
Meta-I	Insert a file. If any text is selected, use the selected text as the filename. Otherwise, a dialog box will appear in which you can type the desired filename.
Meta-V	Move up to the previous screenful of text.
Meta-Y	Insert the last selected text here. Note that this can be text selected in some other text subwindow. Also, if you select some text in an *xterm* window, it may be inserted in an *xmh* window with this command. Pressing pointer button 2 is equivalent to this command.
Meta-Z	Scroll down the text one line.
Delete	Delete the previous character.

Note that a translation in the `app-defaults` file overrides the translation for the Return key for the text window in which a filename can be entered (next to the command buttons); in this window only, instead of starting a new line, Return moves the editing cursor to the end of the current line.

Options

xedit accepts all of the standard X Toolkit command line options, which are listed on the *X* reference page. In addition, *xedit* accepts the following argument:

filename
> Specifies the file that is to be loaded during start up. This is the file that will be edited. If a file is not specified, *xedit* lets you load a file or create a new file after it has started up.

Widget Hierarchy

In order to specify resources, it is useful to know the hierarchy of the widgets which compose *xedit*. In the notation below, indentation indicates hierarchical structure. The widget class name is given first, followed by the widget instance name.

```
Xedit   xedit
        Paned   paned
                Paned   buttons
                        Command   quit
                        Command   save
                        Command   load
                        Text      filename
                Label   bc_label
                Text    messageWindow
```

```
Label    labelWindow
Text     editWindow
```

See Appendix G, *Athena Widget Resources* for a list of resources that can be set for the Athena widgets.

Application Resources

The available application resources are:

enableBackups (class EnableBackups)
> Specifies that, when edits made to an existing file are saved, *xedit* is to copy the original version of that file to <prefix>*filename*<suffix> before it saves the changes. The default value for this resource is "off," stating that no backups should be created.

backupNamePrefix (class BackupNamePrefix)
> Specifies a string that is to be prepended to the backup filename. The default is that no string shall be prepended.

backupNameSuffix (class BackupNameSuffix)
> Specifies a string that is to be appended to the backup filename. The default is to append the string ".BAK".

Files

/usr/lib/X11/app-defaults/Xedit —Specifies required resources (Release 4).

Restrictions

There is no undo function.

See Also

X, xrdb, Appendix G, *Athena Widget Resources*.

Copyright

Copyright © 1988, Digital Equipment Corporation. Copyright © 1989, Massachusetts Institute of Technology.

Author

Chris D. Peterson, MIT X Consortium.

Reference Pages

Name

xev – print contents of X events.

Syntax

xev [*options*]

Description

xev creates a window and then asks the X server to send it notices, called *events*, whenever anything happens to the window (such as being moved, resized, typed in, clicked in, etc.). It is useful for seeing what causes events to occur and to display the information that they contain.

xev was included in the Release 3 standard distribution; in Release 4, it has been moved to *demos*. We feel it is sufficiently useful that we continue to document it here.

Options

xev accepts the following options:

-display [*host*]:*server*[.*screen*]

Allows you to specify the host, server, and screen to connect to. *host* specifies the machine, *server* specifies the server number, and *screen* specifies the screen number. For example,

xev -display *your_node*:**0.1**

specifies screen 1 of server 0 on the machine *your_node*. Either or both the *host* and *screen* elements can be omitted. If *host* is omitted, the local machine is assumed. If *screen* is omitted, screen 0 is assumed (and the period is unnecessary). The colon and *server* are necessary in all cases.

-geometry *geometry*

The *xev* window is created with the specified size and location determined by the supplied geometry specification. The -geometry option can be (and often is) abbreviated to -g, unless there is a conflicting option that begins with "g." The argument to the geometry option (*geometry*) is referred to as a "standard geometry string," and has the form *widthxheight±xoff±yoff*.

-bw *pixels*

Specifies the width of the window border in pixels.

See Also

X, xwininfo, xdpyinfo; Volume One, *Xlib Programming Manual*; Volume Zero, *X Protocol Reference Manual*.

Author

Jim Fulton, MIT X Consortium.

Name

xfd – X window font displayer.

Syntax

xfd [*options*] **-fn** *fontname*

Description

xfd creates a window containing the name of the font being displayed, a row of command buttons, several lines of text for displaying character metrics, and a grid containing one glyph per cell. The characters are shown in increasing order from left to right, top to bottom. The first character displayed at the top left will be character number 0 unless the -start option has been supplied, in which case the character with the number given in the -start option will be used.

The characters are displayed in a grid of boxes, each large enough to hold any single character in the font. Each character glyph is drawn using the PolyText16 request (used by the Xlib routine XDrawString16). If the -box option is given, a rectangle will be drawn around each character, showing where an ImageText16 request (used by the Xlib routine XDraw-ImageString16) would cause background color to be displayed.

The origin of each glyph is normally set so that the character is drawn in the upper left corner of the grid cell. However, if a glyph has a negative left bearing or an unusually large ascent, descent, or right bearing (as is the case with the cursor font), some characters may not appear in their own grid cells. The -center option may be used to force all glyphs to be centered in their respective cells.

All the characters in the font may not fit in the window at once. To see the next page of glyphs, press the Next button at the top of the window. To see the previous page, press Prev. To exit *xfd*, press Quit.

Individual character metrics (index, width, bearings, ascent, and descent) can be displayed at the top of the window by pressing on the desired character.

The font name displayed at the top of the window is the full name of the font, as determined by the server. See *xlsfonts* for ways to generate lists of fonts, as well as more detailed summaries of their metrics and properties.

Options

xfd accepts all of the standard X Toolkit command line options, which are listed on the *X* reference page. In addition, *xfd* accepts the following application-specific options. (Note that the option -fn *font* is required.)

-fn *font*
   Specifies the font to be displayed.

-box   Indicates that a box outlining the area that would be filled with background color by an ImageText request should be displayed.

-center
   Indicates that each glyph should be centered in its grid.

`-start` *char_num*

> Specifies that character number *char_num* should be the first character displayed. (It appears in the upper left-hand corner of the grid.) This option is used to view characters at arbitrary locations in the font. The default is 0.

`-bc` *color*

> Specifies the color to be used if `ImageText` boxes are drawn.

Resources

The Release 4 version of *xfd* was written with the X Toolkit Intrinsics. *xfd* accepts the following resources, which are accepted by most applications written with the Toolkit:

`background` (class `Background`)

> Specifies the color to use for the window background.

`borderWidth` (class `BorderWidth`)

> Specifies the width in pixels of the window border.

`borderColor` (class `BorderColor`)

> Specifies the color to use for the window border.

`foreground` (class `Foreground`)

> Specifies the color to use for text and graphics within the window.

Bugs

xfd should skip over pages full of non-existent characters.

See Also

X, xfontsel, xlsfonts, xrdb.

Author

Jim Fulton, MIT X Consortium.

Name

xfontsel – point-and-click interface for selecting display font names.

Syntax

xfontsel [*options*]

Description

Available as of Release 4, *xfontsel* provides a simple way to display the fonts known to your X server, examine samples of each, and retrieve the X Logical Font Description (XLFD) full name for a font.

If –pattern is not specified, all fonts with XLFD 14-part names will be selectable. To work with only a subset of the fonts, specify -pattern followed by a partially or fully qualified font name. For example,

    % xfontsel -pattern *medium*

will select the subset of fonts that contain the string medium somewhere in their font name. Be careful about escaping wildcard characters in your shell.

If –print is specified on the command line, the selected font specifier will be written to standard output when the quit button is activated. Regardless of whether or not –print was specified, the font specifier may be made the (text) selection by activating the select button.

Clicking any pointer button in one of the XLFD field names will pop up a menu of the currently-known possibilities for that field. If previous choices of other fields were made, only values for fonts which matched the previously selected fields will be selectable; to make other values selectable, you must deselect some other field(s) by choosing the "*" entry in that field. Unselectable values may be omitted from the menu entirely as a configuration option; see the ShowUnselectable resource, below. Whenever any change is made to a field value, *xfontsel* will assert ownership of the PRIMARY_FONT selection. Other applications (such as *xterm*) may then retrieve the selected font specification.

Clicking the left pointer button in the select widget will cause the currently selected font name to become the PRIMARY text selection as well as the PRIMARY_FONT selection. Then you can paste the string into other applications. The select button remains highlighted to remind you of this fact, and de-highlights when some other application takes the PRIMARY selection away. The select widget is a toggle; pressing it when it is highlighted will cause *xfontsel* to release the selection ownership and de-highlight the widget. Activating the select widget twice is the only way to cause *xfontsel* to release the PRIMARY_FONT selection.

Options

xfontsel accepts all of the standard X Toolkit command line options, which are listed on the *X* reference page. In addition, *xfontsel* accepts the following application-specific options:

pattern *fontname*)

> Specifies a subset of the available fonts, those with names that contain *fontname*, which can be a partial or full name.

print)

> Specifies that the selected font will be written to standard output when the quit button is activated.

sample *text*)

> Specifies the sample *text* to be used to display the selected font, overriding the default (the lowercase and uppercase alphabets and the digits 0 through 9).

Resources

The application class is XFontSel. Most of the user-interface is configured in the app-defaults file; if this file is missing, a warning message will be printed to standard output and the resulting window will be nearly incomprehensible.

Most of the significant parts of the widget hierarchy are documented in the app-defaults file (normally */usr/lib/X11/app-defaults/XFontSel*).

Application specific resources: Specifies the cursor for the application window.

pattern (class Pattern)

> Specifies the font name pattern for selecting a subset of available fonts. Equivalent to the -pattern option. Most useful patterns will contain at least one field delimiter, for example, *-m-* for monospaced fonts.

printOnQuit (class PrintOnQuit)

> If True, the currently selected font name is printed to standard output when the quit button is activated. Equivalent to the -print option.

Widget-specific resources:

showUnselectable (class ShowUnselectable)

> For each field menu, specifies whether or not to show values that are not currently selectable, based upon previous field selections. If shown, the unselectable values are clearly identified as such and do not highlight when the pointer is moved down the menu. The full instance name of this resource is fieldN.menu.options.show-Unselectable, class MenuButton.SimpleMenu.Options.Show-Unselectable; where N is replaced with the field number (starting with the left-

most field numbered 0). The default is `True` for all but field 11 (average width of characters in font) and `False` for field 11. If you never want to see unselectable entries, `*menu.options.showUnselectable: False` is a reasonable thing to specify in a resource file.

Files

/usr/lib/X11/app-defaults/XFontSel—Specifies default resources.

See Also

xrdb.

Bugs

Sufficiently ambiguous patterns can be misinterpreted and can lead to an initial selection string which may not correspond to what the user intended and which may cause the initial sample text output to fail to match the proffered string. Selecting any new field value will correct the sample output, though possibly resulting in no matching font.

Should be able to return a font for the PRIMARY selection, not just a string.

Any change in a field value will cause *xfontsel* to assert ownership of the PRIMARY_FONT selection. Perhaps this should be parameterized.

When running on a slow machine, it is possible for the user to request a field menu before the font names have been completely parsed. An error message indicating a missing menu is printed to standard error, but otherwise nothing happens.

Author

Ralph R. Swick, Digital Equipment Corporation/MIT Project Athena.

Reference Pages

xhost

Name

xhost – server access control program for X.

Syntax

xhost [*options*]

Description

The *xhost* program is used to add and delete hosts to and from the list of machines that are allowed to make connections to the X server. This provides a rudimentary form of privacy control and security. It is only sufficient for a workstation (single user) environment, although it does limit the worst abuses. Environments that require more sophisticated measures should use the hooks in the protocol for passing authentication data to the server.

The server initially allows network connections only from programs running on the same machine or from machines listed in the file */etc/Xn.hosts* (where *n* is the display number of the server). The *xhost* program is usually run either from a startup file or interactively to give access to other users.

Hostnames that are followed by two colons (::) are used in checking DECnet connections; all other hostnames are used for TCP/IP connections.

If no command line options are given, the list of hosts that are allowed to connect is printed on the standard output along with a message indicating whether or not access control is currently enabled. This is the only option that may be used from machines other than the one on which the server is running.

Options

xhost accepts the command line options described below. For security, the options that affect access control may only be run from the same machine as the server.

[+]*hostname*

> The given *hostname* (the plus sign is optional) is added to the list of machines that are allowed to connect to the X server.

-*hostname*

> The given *hostname* is removed from the list of machines that are allowed to connect to the server. Existing connections are not broken, but new connection attempts will be denied. Note that the current machine is allowed to be removed; however, further connections (including attempts to add it back) will not be permitted. Resetting the server (thereby breaking all connections) is the only way to allow local connections again.

+

> Access is granted to everyone, even if they aren't on the list of allowed hosts (i.e., access control is turned off).

−

> Access is restricted to only those machines on the list of allowed hosts (i.e., access control is turned on).

X Window System User's Guide Copyright © 1990 O'Reilly & Associates

Files

*/etc/X**n**.hosts*

Bugs

You can't specify a display on the command line because `-display` indicates that you want to remove the machine named `display` from the access list.

See Also

X, Xserver, xauth.

Authors

Bob Scheifler, MIT Laboratory for Computer Science;
Jim Gettys, MIT Project Athena (DEC).

Name

xinit – X Window System initializer.

Syntax

xinit [[_client_] _options_] [-- [_server_program_]
     [-display [_host_]: _server_[. _screen_]] _options_]

Description

The _xinit_ program is used to start the X Window System server program and a first client program (usually a terminal emulator) on systems that cannot start X directly from _/etc/init_ or in environments that use multiple window systems. When this first client exits, _xinit_ will kill the X server program and then terminate.

If no specific client program is given on the command line, _xinit_ will look in the user's home directory for a file called _.xinitrc_ to run as a shell script to start up other client programs. If no such file exists, _xinit_ will use the following _xterm_ command line as a default:

```
xterm -geometry +1+1 -n login -display :0
```

If no specific server program is given on the command line, _xinit_ will look in the user's home directory for a file called _.xserverrc_ to run as a shell script to start up the server. If no such file exists, _xinit_ will use the following as a default server specification:

```
X :0
```

Note that this assumes that there is a server program called _X_ in the current search path. However, servers are usually named _Xdisplaytype_, where _displaytype_ is the type of graphics display which is driven by the server (for example, _Xsun_). The site administrator should therefore make a link to the appropriate type of server on the machine (see Chapter 2, _Getting Started_, in Part One of this guide for details), or create a shell script that runs _xinit_ with the appropriate server.

Note that programs run by _.xinitrc_ and by _.xserverrc_ should be run in the background if they do not exit right away, so that they don't prevent other programs from starting up. However, the last long-lived program started (usually a window manager or terminal emulator) should be left in the foreground so that the script won't exit (which indicates that the user is done and that _xinit_ should exit).

An alternate client and/or server may also be specified on the command line. The desired client program and its arguments should be given as the first command line arguments to _xinit_. To specify a particular server program, append a double dash (--) to the _xinit_ command line (after any client and arguments) followed by the desired server program.

Both the client program name and the server program name must begin with a slash (/) or a period (.); otherwise, they are treated as arguments to be appended to their respective startup lines. This makes it possible to add arguments (for example, foreground and background colors) without having to retype the whole command line.

If an explicit server name is not given and the first argument following the double dash (--) is a colon followed by a digit, _xinit_ will use that number as the display number instead of zero. All remaining arguments are appended to the server command line.

Note that you can start X manually by running *xinit* from the command line or start it automatically by adding the *xinit* command line to your *.login* or *.profile* file. (See Appendix A, *System Management*, for more information.)

Options

xinit accepts the following options:

client
> Specifies the client to be started with the server.

server_program
> Specifies the server program to be used.

-display [*host*]:*server*[.*screen*]
> Specifies the host, server and screen on which you are initializing the X Window System. For example,
>
> > **xinit -display** *your_node*:**0.1**
>
> specifies screen 1 on server 0 on the machine *your_node*. If the host is omitted, the local machine is assumed. If the screen is omitted, the screen 0 is assumed; the server and colon (:) are necessary in any case.

Examples

xinit Will start up a server named *X* and run the user's *xinitrc*, if it exists, or else start an *xterm*.

xinit -- /usr/bin/X11/Xqdss :1
> Is how one could start a specific type of server on an alternate display.

xinit -geometry 80x65+10+10 -fn 8x13 -j -fg white -bg navy
> Will start up a server named *X*, and will append the given arguments to the default *xterm* command. It will ignore *xinitrc*.

xinit -e widgets -- Xsun -l -c
> Will use the command *./Xsun -l -c* to start the server and will append the arguments *-e widgets* to the default *xterm* command.

xinit rsh fasthost cpupig -display workstation:1 -- -l -a 2 -t 5
> Will start a server named *X* on display 1 with the arguments -a 2 -t 5. It will then start a remote shell on the machine fasthost in which it will run the command *cpupig*, telling it to display back on the local workstation.

Below is a sample *xinitrc* that starts a clock, several terminals, and leaves the window manager running as the "last" application. Assuming that the window manager has been configured properly, the user then chooses the Exit menu item to shut down X.

```
xrdb -load $HOME/.Xres
xsetroot -solid grey &
xclock -g 50x50-0+0 -bw 0 &
xload -g 50x50-50+0 -bw 0 &
xterm -g 80x24+0+0 &
```

Reference Pages

```
xterm -g 80x24+0-0 &
twm
```

Sites that want to create a common startup environment could simply create a default *xinitrc* that references a site-wide startup file:

```
#!/bin/sh
./usr/local/lib/site.xinitrc
```

Another approach is to write a script that starts *xinit* with a specific shell script. Such scripts are usually named *x11*, *xstart*, or *startx* and are a convenient way to provide a simple interface for novice users:

```
#!/bin/sh
./xinit/usr/local/bin/startx -- /usr/bin/X11/Xhp :1
```

Environment Variables

XINITRC

Specifies an init file containing shell commands to start up the initial windows. By default, *xinitrc* in the home directory will be used.

See Also

X, Xserver, xterm.

Author

Bob Scheifler, MIT Laboratory for Computer Science.

Name

xkill – kill a client by its X resource.

Syntax

xkill [*options*]

Description

xkill is a utility for forcing the X server to close connections to clients. This program is very dangerous, but is useful for aborting programs that have displayed undesired windows on a user's screen. If no resource identifier is given with −id, *xkill* will display a special cursor as a prompt for the user to select a window to be killed. If a pointer button is pressed over a non-root window, the server will close its connection to the client that created the window.

Options

xkill accepts the following specific options:

−id *resource*

> Specifies the X identifier for the resource whose creator is to be aborted. If no resource is specified, *xkill* will display a special cursor with which you should select a window to be killed.

−button *number*
−button any

> Specifies the number of the pointer button that should be used to select the window to kill. If the word any is specified, any button on the pointer can be used. By default, the first button in the pointer map (which is usually the leftmost button) is used.

−all   Indicates that all clients with top-level windows on the screen should be killed. *xkill* will ask you to select the root window with each of the currently defined buttons to give you several chances to abort. Use of this option is highly discouraged.

−frame

> Indicates that *xkill* should ignore the standard conventions for finding top-level client windows (which are typically nested inside a window manager window), and simply believe that you want to kill direct children of the root. (Available as of Release 4.)

−display [*host*]:*server*[.*screen*]

> Allows you to specify the host, server, and screen to connect to. *host* specifies the machine, *server* specifies the server number, and *screen* specifies the screen number. For example,

> **xkill −display** *your_node*:**0.1**

specifies screen 1 of server 0 on the machine *your_node*. Either or both the *host* and *screen* elements to the display specification can be omitted. If *host* is omitted, the local machine is assumed. If *screen* is omitted, screen 0 is assumed (and the period is unnecessary). The colon and *server* are necessary in all cases.

Reference Pages

Resources

xkill defines the following application resource:

Button

> Specifies a pointer button number to use when selecting the window to be removed. If the word any is specified, any button on the pointer can be used.

ee Also

X, xwininfo; Volume One, *Xlib Programming Manual*.

Author

Jim Fulton, MIT X Consortium;
Dana Chee, Bellcore.

Name

xload – display system load average.

Syntax

xload [*options*]

Description

The *xload* program displays a periodically updating histogram of the system load average.

Options

xload accepts all of the standard X Toolkit command line options, which are listed on the *X* reference page. (We've included some of the more commonly used Toolkit options later in this section.) In addition, *xload* accepts the following application-specific options:

-scale *integer*

> Specifies the minimum number of tick marks in the histogram, where one division represents one load average point. If the load goes above this number, *xload* will create more divisions, but it will never use fewer than this number. The default is 1.

-update *seconds*

> Specifies the frequency in seconds at which *xload* updates its display. If the load average window is uncovered (by moving windows with a window manager or by the *xrefresh* program), the graph will also be updated. In Release 4, the minimum amount of time allowed between updates is 1 second (the default is 5 seconds). In Release 3, the minimum amount of time allowed between updates is 5 seconds (which is also the default).

-hl *color* or
-highlight *color*

> Specifies the color of the scale lines in Release 4. (Specifies the color of the label and scale lines in Release 3.)

-jumpscroll *pixels*

> Specifies the number of pixels to shift the graph to the left when the graph reaches the right edge of the window. The default value is 1/2 the width of the current window. Smooth scrolling can be achieved by setting it to 1. (Available as of Release 4.)

-label *string*

> Specifies the text string for the label above the load average. (Available as of Release 4.)

-nolabel

> Specifies that no label be displayed above the load graph. (Available as of Release 4.)

The following standard X Toolkit options are commonly used with *xload*:

-bd *color*

> Specifies the border color. The default is black.

-bg *color*

> Specifies the background color. The default is white.

Reference Pages

-bw *pixels*
> Specifies the width in pixels of the border around the window. The default is 2.

-fg *color*
> Specifies the graph color. The default is black.

-fn *fontname*
> Specifies the font to be used in displaying the name of the host whose load is being monitored. The default is the 6x10 pixel, fixed-width font "fixed".

-rv
> Indicates that reverse video should be simulated by swapping the foreground and background colors.

-geometry *geometry*
> Specifies the size and location of the window. The -geometry option can be (and often is) abbreviated to -g, unless there is a conflicting option that begins with "g." The argument to the geometry option (*geometry*) is referred to as a "standard geometry string," and has the form *widthxheight±xoff±yoff*.

-display [*host*]:*server*[*.screen*]
> Allows you to specify the host, server, and screen on which to create the *xload* window. See "Options" on the *X* reference page for an example of usage.

-xrm *resourcestring*
> Specifies a resource string to be used. This is especially useful for setting resources that do not have separate command line options.

Resources

In addition to the resources available to each of the widgets used by *xload*, there is one resource defined by the application itself.

showLabel (class Boolean)
> If False, then no label will be displayed.

Widget Hierarchy

In order to specify resources, it is useful to know the hierarchy of the widgets that compose *xload*. In the notation below, indentation indicates hierarchical structure. The widget class name is given first, followed by the widget instance name.

```
XLoad  xload
       Paned  paned
              Label  label
              StripChart  load
```

See Appendix G, *Athena Widget Resources* for a list of resources that can be set for the Athena widgets.

See Also

X, xrdb, mem(4), Appendix G, *Athena Widget Resources*.

Diagnostics

Unable to open display or create window. Unable to open */dev/kmem*. Unable to query window for dimensions. Various X errors.

Bugs

This program requires the ability to open and read */dev/kmem*. Sites that do not allow general access to this file should make *xload* belong to the same group as */dev/kmem* and turn on the *set group id* permission flag.

Reading */dev/kmem* is inherently non-portable. Therefore, the routine used to read it (get_load.c) must be ported to each new operating system.

Border color has to be explicitly specified when reverse video is used.

Authors

K. Shane Hartman (MIT-LCS) and Stuart A. Malone (MIT-LCS);
with features added by Jim Gettys (MIT-Athena), Bob Scheifler (MIT-LCS), Tony Della Fera (MIT-Athena), and Chris Peterson (MIT-LCS).

Reference Pages

Name

xlogo – X Window System logo.

Synopsis

xlogo [*options*]

Description

The *xlogo* program displays the X Window System logo. This program is nothing more than a wrapper around the *undocumented* Athena Logo widget.

Options

xlogo accepts all of the standard X Toolkit command line options, which are listed on the *X* reference page. The following Toolkit options are commonly used:

-bg *color*

Specifies the color to use for the background of the window. The default is white. A correct color for the background is something like maroon.

-bd *color*

Specifies the color to use for the border of the window. The default is black.

-bw *pixels*

Specifies the width in pixels of the border surrounding the window.

-fg *color*

Specifies the color to use for displaying the logo. The default is black. A correct color for the foreground is something like silver, which you can approximate with a shade of grey.

-rv

Indicates that reverse video should be simulated by swapping the foreground and background colors.

-geometry *geometry*

The *xlogo* window is created with the specified size and location determined by the supplied geometry specification. The -geometry option can be (and often is) abbreviated to -g, unless there is a conflicting option that begins with "g." The argument to the geometry option (*geometry*) is referred to as a "standard geometry string," and has the form *width*x*height*±*xoff*±*yoff*.

-display [*host*]:*server*[.*screen*]

Allows you to specify the host, server and screen on which to create the *xlogo* window. See "Options" on the *X* reference page for an example of usage.

-xrm *resourcestring*

Specifies a resource string to be used. This is especially useful for setting resources that do not have separate command line options.

Resources

This program uses the Logo widget in the Athena Widget Set. It understands all of the Core resource names and classes. The following resources are commonly used:

`width` (class `Width`)
Specifies the width of the logo.

`height` (class `Height`)
Specifies the height of the logo.

`foreground` (class `Foreground`)
Specifies the foreground color for the logo. The default depends on whether `reverseVideo` is specified. If `reverseVideo` is specified, the default is white; otherwise, the default is black.

`reverseVideo` (class `ReverseVideo`)
Specifies that the foreground and background should be reversed.

Widget Hierarchy

In order to specify resources, it is useful to know the hierarchy of the widgets that compose *xlogo*. In the notation below, indentation indicates hierarchical structure. The widget class name is given first, followed by the widget instance name.

```
XLogo  xlogo
    Logo  xlogo
```

Files

/usr/lib/X11/app-defaults/XLogo—specifies required resources (as of Release 4).

See Also

X, xrdb.

Authors

Ollie Jones of Apollo Computer and Jim Fulton of the X Consortium wrote the logo graphics routine, based on a graphic design by Danny Chong and Ross Chapman of Apollo Computer.

Reference Pages

xlsatoms

Name

xlsatoms – list interned atoms defined on the server.

Syntax

`xlsatoms` [*options*]

Description

Available as of Release 4, *xlsatoms* lists the interned atoms. By default, all atoms starting from 1 (the lowest atom value defined by the protocol) are listed until an unknown atom is found. If an explicit range is given, *xlsatoms* will try all atoms in the range, regardless of whether or not any are undefined.

Options

xlsatoms accepts the following options:

-format *printf_string*

Specifies a printf-style string used to list each atom *<value, name>* pair, printed in that order (*value* is an *unsigned long* and *name* is a *char **). *xlsatoms* will supply a newline at the end of each line. The default is `%ld\t%s`.

-range [*low*]-[*high*]

Specifies the range of atom values to check. If *low* is not given, a value of 1 assumed. If *high* is not given, *xlsatoms* will stop at the first undefined atom at or above *low*.

-name *string*

Specifies the name of an atom to list. If the atom does not exist, a message will be printed on the standard error.

-display [*host*]:*server*[.*screen*]

Allows you to specify the host, server, and screen to connect to. *host* specifies the machine, *server* specifies the server number, and *screen* specifies the screen number. For example,

xlsatoms -display *your_node*:0.1

specifies screen 1 of server 0 on the machine *your_node*. Either or both the *host* and *screen* elements can be omitted. If *host* is omitted, the local machine is assumed. If *screen* is omitted, screen 0 is assumed (and the period is unnecessary). The colon and *server* are necessary in all cases.

See Also

X, Xserver, xprop.

Author

Jim Fulton, MIT X Consortium.

Name

xlsclients – list client applications running on a display.

Syntax

xlsclients [*options*]

Description

Available as of Release 4, *xlsclients* is a utility for listing information about the client applications running on a display. It may be used to generate scripts representing a snapshot of the user's current session.

Options

xlsclients accepts the following options:

-a   Specifies that clients on all screens should be listed. By default, only those clients on the default screen are listed.

-l   Requests a long listing showing the window name, icon name, and class hints in addition to the machine name and command string in the default listing.

-m *maxcmdlength*
     Specifies the maximum number of characters in a command to list. The default is 1000.

-display [*host*]:*server*[.*screen*]
     Allows you to specify the host, server, and screen to connect to. *host* specifies the machine, *server* specifies the server number, and *screen* specifies the screen number. For example,

         xlsclients -display *your_node*:**0.1**

     specifies screen 1 of server 0 on the machine *your_node*. Either or both the *host* and *screen* can be omitted. If *host* is omitted, the local machine is assumed. If *screen* is omitted, screen 0 is assumed (and the period is unnecessary). The colon and *server* are necessary in all cases.

See Also

X, xprop, xwininfo.

Author

Jim Fulton, MIT X Consortium.

xlsfonts

Name

xlsfonts – list available fonts.

Syntax

xlsfonts [*options*] [**-fn** *pattern*]

Description

xlsfonts lists the fonts that match the given *pattern*. The wildcard character "*" may be used to match any sequence of characters (including none), and "?" to match any single character. If no pattern is given, "*" is assumed.

The "*" and "?" characters must be quoted to prevent them from being expanded by the shell.

Options

xlsfonts accepts the following options:

-fn *pattern*
Indicates that only fonts matching the specified *pattern* be listed.

-l[l[l]]
Indicates that medium, long, and very long listings, respectively, should be generated for each font.

-m
Indicates that long listings should also print the minimum and maximum bounds of each font.

-C
Indicates that listings should use multiple columns. This is the same as -n 0.

-1
Indicates that listings should use a single column. This is the same as -n 1.

-w *width*
Specifies the width in characters that should be used in figuring out how many columns to print. The default is 79.

-n *columns*
Specifies the number of columns to use in displaying the output. By default, it will attempt to fit as many columns of font names as possible into the number of characters specified by -w *width*.

-display [*host*]:*server*[.*screen*]
Allows you to specify the host, server, and screen. For example,

    xlsfonts -display *your_node***:0.1**

specifies screen 1 on server 0 on the machine *your_node*. If the host is omitted, the local machine is assumed. If the screen is omitted, the screen 0 is assumed; the server and colon are necessary in all cases.

See Also

X, Xserver, xset, xfd, xfontsel.

Bugs

Doing `xlsfonts -l` can tie up your server for a very long time. This is really a bug with single-threaded, non-preemptable servers, not with this program.

Author

Mark Lillibridge, MIT Project Athena;
Jim Fulton, MIT X Consortium;
Phil Karlton, SGI.

Name

xlswins – server window list displayer for X.

Syntax

xlswins [*options*][*window_id*]

Description

xlswins lists the window tree. By default, the root window is used as the starting point, although another window may be specified using the *window_id* option.

Options

xlswins accepts the following options:

-l   Indicates that a long listing should be generated for each window. This includes a number indicating the depth, the geometry relative to the parent, and the location relative to the root window.

-format *radix*
        Specifies the radix to use when printing out window IDs. Allowable values are: hex, octal, and decimal. The default is hex.

-indent *number*
        Specifies the number of spaces that should be indented for each level in the window tree. The default is 2.

window_id
        Specifies that the starting point for the window tree listing is the window *window_id*.

-display [*host*]:*server*[.*screen*]
        Allows you to specify the host, server, and screen to connect to. *host* specifies the machine, *server* specifies the server number, and *screen* specifies the screen number. For example,

   xlswins -display *your_node*:**0.1**

specifies screen 1 of server 0 on the machine *your_node*. Either or both the *host* and *screen* elements can be omitted. If *host* is omitted, the local machine is assumed. If *screen* is omitted, screen 0 is assumed (and the period is unnecessary). The colon and *server* are necessary in all cases.

See Also

X, Xserver, xwininfo, xprop.

Bugs

This should be integrated with *xwininfo* somehow.

Author

Jim Fulton, MIT X Consortium.

Name

xmag – magnify parts of the screen.

Syntax

xmag [*options*]

Description

The *xmag* program allows you to magnify portions of the screen. If no explicit region is specified, a square centered around the pointer is displayed indicating the area to be enlarged. Once a region has been selected, a window is popped up showing a blown up version of the region in which each pixel in the source image is represented by a small square of the same color. Pressing Button1 on the pointer in the enlargement window pops up a small window displaying the position, number, and RGB value of the pixel under the pointer until the button is released, Pressing the space bar or any other pointer button removes the enlarged image so that another region may be selected. Pressing Q, or Control-C in the enlargement window exits the program.

Options

xmag accepts all of the standard X Toolkit command line options, which are listed on the *X* reference page. (We've included some of the more commonly used Toolkit options later in this section.) In addition, *xmag* accepts the following application-specific options:

-source *geometry*

> This option specifies the size and/or location of the source region on the screen. By default, a 64x64 square centered about the pointer is provided for the user to select an area of the screen. The size of the source is used with the desired magnification to compute the default enlargement window size. Therefore, only one of -geometry *size* and -mag *magfactor* options may be specified if a source size is given with this option.

-mag *magfactor*

> This option specifies an integral factor by which the source region should be enlarged. The default magnification is 5. This is used with the size of the source to compute the default enlargement window size. Therefore, only one of -geometry *size* and -source *geometry* options may be specified if a magnification factor is given with this option.

-z

> This option indicates that the server should be grabbed during the dynamics and the call to XGetImage. This is useful for ensuring that clients don't change their state as a result of entering or leaving them with the pointer.

The following standard X Toolkit options are commonly used with *xmag*:

-display [*host*]:*server*[.*screen*]

> Allows you to specify the host, server and screen to use for both reading the screen and displaying the enlarged version of the image. *host* specifies the machine, *server* specifies the server number, and *screen* specifies the screen number. For example:

Reference Pages

> **xmag -display** *your_node*:**0.1**

specifies screen 1 of server 0 on the machine *your_node*. Either or both the *host* and *screen* elements to the display specification can be omitted. If *host* is omitted, the local machine is assumed. If *screen* is omitted, screen 0 is assumed (and the period is unnecessary). The colon and *server* are necessary in all cases.

-geometry *geometry*

The enlargement window is created with the specified size and location determined by the supplied geometry specification. The -geometry option can be (and often is) abbreviated to -g, unless there is a conflicting option that begins with "g." The argument to the geometry option (*geometry*) is referred to as a "standard geometry string," and has the form *widthxheight±xoff±yoff*.

By default, the size is computed from the size of the source region and the desired magnification. Therefore, only one of -source *size* and -mag *magfactor* options may be specified if a window size is given with the -geometry option.

-bw *pixels*

This option specifies the width in pixels of the border surrounding the enlargement window.

-bd *color*

This option specifies the color to use for the border surrounding the enlargement window.

-bg *color_or_pixel_value*

This option specifies the name of the color to be used as the background of the enlargement window. If the name begins with a percent size (%), it is interpreted to be an absolute pixel value. This is useful when displaying large areas, since pixels that are the same color as the background do not need to be painted in the enlargement. The default is to use the BlackPixel of the screen.

-fn *fontname*

This option specifies the name of a font to use when displaying pixel values (used when button 1 is pressed in the enlargement window).

Resources

The *xmag* program defines the following application resources:

source (class Source)

Specifies the size and/or location of the source region on the screen.

magnification (class Magnification)

Specifies the enlargement factor.

xmag also understands the Core X Toolkit resources, of which the following are commonly used:

geometry (class Geometry)

Specifies the size and/or location of the enlargement window.

`borderWidth` (class `BorderWidth`)
> Specifies the border width in pixels.

`borderColor` (class `BorderColor`)
> Specifies the color of the border.

`background` (class `Background`)
> Specifies the color or pixel value to be used for the background of the enlargement window.

`font` (class `Font`)
> Specifies the name of the font to use when displaying pixel values when the user presses button 1 in the enlargement window.

See Also

X, xwd.

Bugs

This program will behave strangely on displays that support windows of different depths.

Because the window size equals the source size times the magnification, you need to specify only two of the three parameters. This can be confusing.

Being able to drag the pointer around and see a dynamic display would be very nice.

Another possible interface would be for the user to drag out the desired area to be enlarged.

Author

Jim Fulton, MIT X Consortium.

xman

Name

xman – display manual pages.

Syntax

xman [*options*]

Description

xman is a manual page browser. The default size of the initial *xman* window is small so that you can leave it running throughout your entire login session. In the initial window there are three options: Help will pop up a window with online help, Quit will exit, and Manual Page will pop up a window with a manual page browser in it. You may pop up more than one manual page browser window from a single execution of *xman*.

For further information on using *xman*, please read the online help information. The rest of this manual page will discuss customization of *xman*.

Customization

xman allows customization of both the directories to be searched for manual pages, and the name that each directory will map to in the Sections menu. *xman* determines which directories it will search by reading the MANPATH environment variable. If no MANPATH is found then the directory */usr/man* is searched on POSIX systems. This environment is expected to be a colon-separated list of directories for *xman* to search.

```
setenv MANPATH /mit/kit/man:/usr/man
```

By default, *xman* will search each of the following directories (in each of the directories specified in the users MANPATH) for manual pages. If manual pages exist in that directory, then they are added to the list of manual pages for the corresponding menu item. A menu item is only displayed only for those sections that actually contain manual pages.

Directory	Section Name
man1	(1) User Commands
man2	(2) System Calls
man3	(3) Subroutines
man4	(4) Devices
man5	(5) File Formats
man6	(6) Games
man7	(7) Miscellaneous
man8	(8) Sys. Administration
manl	(l) Local
mann	(n) New
mano	(o) Old

For instance, a user has three directories in her manual path and each contains a directory called *man3*. All these manual pages will appear, alphabetically sorted, when the user selects the menu item called (3) Subroutines. If there is no directory called *mano* in any of the directories in her MANPATH, or there are no manual pages in any of the directories called *mano*, then no menu item will be displayed for the section called (o) Old.

By using the *mandesc* file, a user or system manager is able to more closely control which manual pages will appear in each of the sections represented by menu items in the Sections menu. This functionality is available only on a section-by-section basis, and individual manual pages may not be handled in this manner (although generous use of symbolic links, *ln*(1), will allow almost any configuration you can imagine).

The format of the *mandesc* file is a character followed by a label. The character determines which of the sections will be added under this label. For instance, suppose that you would like to create an extra menu item that contains all programmer subroutines. This label should contain all manual pages in both sections two and three. The *mandesc* file would look like this:

```
2Programmer Subroutines
3Programmer Subroutines
```

This will add a menu item to the Sections menu that would bring up a listing of all manual pages in sections two and three of the *UNIX Programmer's Manual*. Since the label names are *exactly* the same, they will be added to the same section. Note, however, that the original sections still exist.

If you want to completely ignore the default sections in a manual directory, then add the line:

```
no default sections
```

anywhere in your *mandesc* file. This keeps *xman* from searching the default manual sections *in that directory only*. As an example, suppose you want to do the same thing as above, but you don't think that it is useful to have the System Calls or Subroutines sections any longer. You would need to duplicate the default entries, as well as adding your new one.

```
no default sections
1(1) User Commands
2Programmer Subroutines
3Programmer Subroutines
4(4) Devices
5(5) File Formats
6(6) Games
7(7) Miscellaneous
8(8) Sys. Administration
1(1) Local
n(n) New
o(o) Old
```

xman will read any section that is of the form *man\<character\>*, where *\<character\>* is an uppercase or lowercase letter (they are treated distinctly) or a numeral (0-9). Be warned, however, that *man*(1) and *catman*(8) will not search directories that are non-standard.

Reference Pages

Options

xman accepts all of the standard X Toolkit command line options, which are listed on the *X* reference page. (We've included some of the more commonly used Toolkit options later in this section.) In addition, *xman* accepts the following application-specific options:

-helpfile *filename*
> Specifies a helpfile to use other than the default.

-bothshown
> Allows both the manual page and manual directory to be on the screen at the same time.

-notopbox
> Starts without the top menu with the three buttons in it.

-pagesize *geometry*
> Sets the size and location of all the manual pages.

The following X Toolkit options are commonly used with *xman*:

-geometry *geometry*
> Sets the size and location of the top menu with the three buttons in it. This menu is created with the specified size and location determined by the supplied geometry specification. The -geometry option can be (and often is) abbreviated to -g, unless there is a conflicting option that begins with "g." The argument to the geometry option (*geometry*) is referred to as a "standard geometry string," and has the form *width*x*height*±*xoff*±*yoff*.

-display [*host*]:*server*[.*screen*]
> Allows you to specify the host, server, and screen on which to display the *xman* window. See "Options" on the *X* reference page for an example of usage.

-bw *pixels* or -borderwidth *pixels*
> Specifies the width of the border for all windows in *xman*.

-bd *color* or -bordercolor *color*
> Specifies the color of the borders of all windows in *xman*.

-fg *color* or -foreground *color*
> Specifies the foreground color to be used.

-bg *color* or -background *color*
> Specifies the background color to be used.

-fn *font* or -font *font*
> Specifies the font to use for all buttons and labels.

-name *name*
> Specifies the name to use when retrieving resources.

-title *title*
> Specifies the title of this application.

`-xrm` *resources*
>   Allows a resource to be specified on the command line.

Resources

The *xman* program uses the following X Toolkit resources: `foreground`, `background`, `width`, `height`, `borderWidth`, and `borderColor`.

In addition, *xman* has application-specific resources that allow unique *xman* customizations.

`manualFontNormal` (class `Font`)
>   The font to use for normal text in the manual pages.

`manualFontBold` (class `Font`)
>   The font to use for bold text in the manual pages.

`manualFontItalic` (class `Font`)
>   The font to use for italic text in the manual pages.

`directoryFontNormal` (class `Font`)
>   The font to use for the directory text.

`bothShown` (class `Boolean`)
>   Either `True` or `False`, specifies whether or not you want both the directory and the manual page shown at startup.

`directoryHeight` (class `DirectoryHeight`)
>   The height in pixels of the directory, when the directory and the manual page are shown simultaneously.

`topCursor` (class `Cursor`)
>   The cursor to use in the top box.

`helpCursor` (class `Cursor`)
>   The cursor to use in the help window.

`manpageCursor` (class `Cursor`)
>   The cursor to use in the manual page window.

`searchEntryCursor` (class `Cursor`)
>   The cursor to use in the search entry text widget.

`pointerColor` (class `Foreground`)
>   The color of all the cursors (pointers) listed above. The name was chosen to be compatible with *xterm*. (Available as of Release 4.)

`helpFile` (class `File`)
>   Use this rather than the system default helpfile.

`topBox` (class `Boolean`)
>   Either `True` or `False`, determines whether the top box (containing the Help, Quit, and Manual Page buttons) or a manual page is put on the screen at startup. The default is `True`.

`verticalList` (class `Boolean`)

    Either `True` or `False`, determines whether the directory listing is vertically or horizontally organized. The default is horizontal (`False`).

Widget Hierarchy

In order to specify resources, it is useful to know the hierarchy of the widgets that compose *xman*. In the notation below, indentation indicates hierarchical structure. The widget class name is given first, followed by the widget instance name.

```
Xman xman        (This widget is never used)
    TopLevelShell  topbox
        Form  form
                Label  topLabel
                Command  helpButton
                Command  quitButton
                Command  manpageButton
        TransientShell  search
                DialogWidgetClass  dialog
                    Label  label
                    Text  value
                    Command  manualPage
                    Command  apropos
                    Command  cancel
        TransientShell  pleaseStandBy
            Label  label
    TopLevelShell  manualBrowser
        Paned  Manpage_Vpane
            Paned  horizPane
                MenuButton  options
                MenuButton  sections
                Label  manualBrowser
            Viewport  directory
                List  directory
                List  directory
                .
                .  (one for each section,
                .   created "on the fly")
                .
            ScrollByLine  manualPage
        SimpleMenu  optionMenu
            SmeBSB  displayDirectory
            SmeBSB  displayManualPage
            SmeBSB  help
            SmeBSB  search
            SmeBSB  showBothScreens
            SmeBSB  removeThisManpage
            SmeBSB  openNewManpage
            SmeBSB  showVersion
            SmeBSB  quit
        SimpleMenu  sectionMenu
```

```
                        SmeBSB   <name of section>
                             .
                             .  (one for each section)
                             .

                TransientShell  search
                        DialogWidgetClass  dialog
                                Label   label
                                Text   value
                                Command   manualPage
                                Command   apropos
                                Command   cancel
                TransientShell  pleaseStandBy
                        Label  label
                TransientShell  likeToSave
                        Dialog  dialog
                                Label   label
                                Text   value
                                Command   yes
                                Command   no
        TopLevelShell  help
        Paned  Manpage_Vpane
                Paned  horizPane
                        MenuButton   options
                        MenuButton   sections
                        Label  manualBrowser
                ScrollByLine  manualPage
        SimpleMenu  optionMenu
                SmeBSB  displayDirectory
                SmeBSB  displayManualPage
                SmeBSB  help
                SmeBSB  search
                SmeBSB  showBothScreens
                SmeBSB  removeThisManpage
                SmeBSB  openNewManpage
                SmeBSB  showVersion
                SmeBSB  quit
```

See Appendix G, *Athena Widget Resources*, for a list of resources that can be set for the Athena widgets.

Global Actions

xman defines all user interaction through global actions. This allows the user to modify the translation table of any widget, and bind any event to the new user action. The list of actions supported by *xman* are:

GotoPage (*page*)

> When used in a manual page display window, this action allows the user to move between a directory and manual page display. The *page* argument can be either Directory or ManualPage.

Quit()
>   Can be used anywhere; exits *xman*.

Search(*type, action*)
>   Useful only when used in a search pop-up, this action will cause the search widget to perform the named search type on the string in the search popup's value widget. This action will also pop down the search widget. The *type* argument can be either Apropos, Manpage, or Cancel. If an *action* of Open is specified, then *xman* will open a new manual page to display the results of the search; otherwise, *xman* will attempt to display the results in the parent of the search popup.

PopupHelp()
>   Can be used anywhere; pops up the help widget.

PopupSearch()
>   Can be used anywhere, except in a help window. It will cause the search popup to become active and visible on the screen, allowing the user to search for a manual page.

CreateNewManpage()
>   Can be used anywhere; creates a new manual page display window.

RemoveThisManpage()
>   Can be used in any manual page or help display window. When called, it will remove the window and clean up all resources associated with it.

SaveFormattedPage(*action*)
>   Can be used only in the likeToSave popup widget, and tells *xman* whether to Save or Cancel a save of the manual page that has just been formatted.

ShowVersion()
>   May be called from any manual page or help display window, and will cause the informational display line to show the current version of *xman*.

Files

>   *<manpath directory>/man<character>*
>   *<manpath directory>/cat<character>*
>   *<manpath directory>/mandesc*
>   */usr/lib/X11/app-defaults/Xman*—Specifies required resources (as of Release 4).
>   */tmp*—*xman* creates temporary files in */tmp* for all unformatted man pages and all apropos searches.

Environment Variables

>   MANPATH
>   >   The search path for manual pages. Directories are separated by colons (e.g., */usr/man:/mit/kit/man:/foo/bar/man*).

XAPPLRESDIR

A string that will have "Xman" appended to it. This string will be the full path name of a user *app-defaults* file to be merged into the resource database after the system *app-defaults* file, and before the resources that are attached to the display. (Available as of Release 4.)

See Also

X, apropos(1), catman(8), man(1), Appendix G, *Athena Widget Resources.*

Authors

Chris Peterson, MIT X Consortium, from the V10 version written by Barry Shein, formerly of Boston University.

Reference Pages

xmh

Name
xmh – X window interface to the *mh* message handling system.

Syntax
xmh [**-path** *mailpath*] [**-initial** *foldername*][**-flag**][*-toolkitoption*]

Description
xmh is a window-oriented user interface to the Rand *mh* Message Handling System. To actually do things with your mail, *xmh* makes calls to the *mh* package. Electronic mail messages may be composed, sent, received, replied to, forwarded, sorted, and stored in folders.

Please don't be misled by the size of this document. It introduces many aspects of the Athena widget set, and provides extensive mechanism for customization of the user interface. *xmh* really is easy to use.

Options
xmh accepts all of the standard X Toolkit command line options, which are listed on the *X* reference page. In addition, *xmh* accepts the following application-specific options:

-path *mailpath*
> To specify an alternate collection of mail folders in which to process mail, use –path followed by the pathname of the alternate mail directory. The default mail path is the value of the Path component in *$HOME/.mh_profile*, or *$HOME/Mail* if the MH Path is not given.

-initial *foldername*
> Specifies an alternate folder that may receive new mail and is initially opened by *xmh*. The default initial folder is inbox.

-flag Causes *xmh* to attempt to change the appearance of its icon when new mail arrives.

These three options have corresponding application-specific resources, named MailPath, InitialFolder, and MailWaitingFlag, which can be used in a resource file.

Installation
The current version of *xmh* requires that the user is already set up to use *mh*, version 6. First, see if there is a file called *.mh_profile* in your home directory. If it exists, check to see if it contains a line that starts with Current-Folder. If it does, you've been using version 4 or earlier of *mh*; to convert to version 6, you must remove that line. (Failure to do so causes spurious output to standard error, which, depending on your setup, can hang *xmh*.)

If you do not already have an *.mh_profile*, you can create one (and everything else you need) by typing inc to the shell. You should do this before using *xmh* to incorporate new mail.

For more information, refer to the *mh*(1) documentation.

Basic Screen Layout

xmh starts out with a single window, divided into four main areas: Six buttons with pull-down command menus. A collection of buttons, one for each top level folder. New users of mh will have two folders, "drafts" and "inbox". A listing, or Table of Contents, of the messages in the open folder. Initially, this will show the messages in "inbox". A view of one of your messages. Initially this is blank.

xmh and the Athena Widget Set

xmh uses the X Toolkit Intrinsics and the Athena widget set. Many of the features described below (scrollbars, buttonboxes, etc.) are actually part of the Athena widget set, and are described here only for completeness. For more information, see Appendix G, *Athena Widget Resources.*

Scrollbars

Some parts of the main window will have a vertical area on the left containing a grey bar. This area is a *scrollbar.* They are used whenever the data in a window takes up more space than can be displayed. The grey bar indicates what portion of your data is visible. Thus, if the entire length of the area is grey, then you are looking at all your data. If only the first half is grey, then you are looking at the top half of your data. The message viewing area will have a horizontal scrollbar if the text of the message is wider than the viewing area.

You can use the pointer in the scrollbar to change what part of the data is visible. If you click with the middle button, then the top of the grey area will move to where the pointer is, and the corresponding portion of data will be displayed. If you hold down the middle button, you can drag around the grey area. This makes it easy to get to the top of the data: just press with the middle, drag off the top of the scrollbar, and release.

If you click with button 1, then the data to the right of the pointer will scroll to the top of the window. If you click with pointer button 3, then the data at the top of the window will scroll down to where the pointer is.

Buttonboxes, Buttons, and Menus

Any area containing many words or short phrases, each enclosed in a rectangle or rounded boundary, is called a *buttonbox.* Each rectangle or rounded area is actually a button that you can press by moving the pointer onto it and pressing pointer button 1. If a given buttonbox has more buttons in it than can fit, it will be displayed with a scrollbar, so you can always scroll to the button you want.

Some buttons have pull-down menus. Pressing the pointer button while the pointer is over one of these buttons will pull down a menu. Holding the button down while moving the pointer over the menu, called dragging the pointer, will highlight each selectable item on the menu as the pointer passes over it. To select an item in the menu, release the pointer button while the item is highlighted.

Adjusting the Relative Sizes of Areas

If you're not satisfied with the sizes of the various areas of the main window, they can easily be changed. Near the right edge of the border between each region is a black box, called a *grip.* Simply point to that grip with the pointer, press a pointer button, drag up or down, and release. Exactly what happens depends on which pointer button you press:

Reference Pages

If you drag with the middle button, then only that border will move. This mode is simplest to understand, but is the least useful.

If you drag with pointer button 1, then you are adjusting the size of the window above. *xmh* will attempt to compensate by adjusting some window below it.

If you drag with pointer button 3, then you are adjusting the size of the window below. *xmh* will attempt to compensate by adjusting some window above it.

All windows have a minimum and maximum size; you will never be allowed to move a border past the point where it would make a window have an invalid size.

Processing Your Mail

This section will define the concepts of the selected folder, current folder, selected message(s), current message, selected sequence, and current sequence. Each *xmh* command is introduced.

For use in customization, action procedures corresponding to each command are given; these action procedures can be used to customize the user interface, particularly the keyboard accelerators and the functionality of the buttons in the optional buttonbox created by the application resource CommandButtonCount.

Selected Folder

A folder contains a collection of mail messages, or is empty.

The selected folder is whichever folder name appears in the bar above the folder buttons. Note that this is not necessarily the same folder that is being viewed. To change the selected folder, just press on the desired folder button; if that folder has subfolders, select a folder from the pull down menu.

The Table of Contents, or toc, lists the messages in the viewed folder. The title bar above the Table of Contents displays the name of the viewed folder.

The toc title bar also displays the name of the viewed sequence of messages within the viewed folder. Every folder has an "all" sequence, which contains all the messages in the folder, and initially the toc title bar will show "inbox:all".

Folder Commands

The Folder command menu contains commands of a global nature:

Open Folder

       Displays the data in the selected folder. Thus, the selected folder also becomes the viewed folder. The action procedure corresponding to this command is XmhOpen-Folder([*foldername*]). It takes an optional argument as the name of a folder to select and open; if no folder is specified, the selected folder is opened. It may be specified as part of an event translation from a folder menu button or from a folder menu, or as a binding of a keyboard accelerator to any widget other than the folder menu buttons or the folder menus.

Open Folder in New Window

> Displays the selected folder in an additional main window. Note, however, that you may not reliably display the same folder in more than one window at a time, although *xmh* will not prevent you from trying. The corresponding action is XmhOpen-FolderInNewWindow().

Create Folder

> Creates a new folder. You will be prompted for a name for the new folder; to enter the name, move the pointer to the blank box provided and type. Subfolders are created by specifying the parent folder, a slash, and the subfolder name. For example, to create a folder named "xmh" which is a subfolder of an existing folder named "clients", type "clients/xmh". Click on the Okay button when finished, or just press Return; click on Cancel to cancel this operation. The action corresponding to Create Folder is Xmh-CreateFolder().

Delete Folder

> Destroys the selected folder. You will be asked to confirm this action (see "Confirmation Windows"). Destroying a folder will also destroy any subfolders of that folder. The corresponding action is XmhDeleteFolder().

Close Window

> Exits *xmh*, after first confirming that you won't lose any changes; or, if selected from any additional *xmh* window, simply closes that window. The corresponding action is XmhClose().

Highlighted and Selected Messages and the Current Message

It is possible to highlight a set of adjacent messages in the area of the Table of Contents. To highlight a message, click on it with pointer button 1. To highlight a range of messages, click on the first one with pointer button 1 and on the last one with pointer button 3; or press pointer button 1, drag, and release. To extend a range of selected messages, use pointer button 3. To highlight all messages in the table of contents, click rapidly three times with pointer button 1. To cancel any selection in the table of contents, click rapidly twice.

The selected messages are the same as the highlighted messages, if any. If no messages are highlighted, then the selected messages are considered the same as the current message.

The current message is indicated by a "+" next to the message number. It usually corresponds to the message currently being viewed. When a message is viewed, the title bar above the view will identify the message.

Table of Contents Commands

The Table of Contents command menu contains commands which operate on the open, or viewed, folder.

Incorporate New Mail

> Adds any new mail received to your inbox folder, and sets the current message to be the first new message. (This command is selectable only if "inbox" is the folder being viewed.) The corresponding action is XmhIncorporateNewMail().

Commit Changes

Executes all deletions, moves, and copies that have been marked in this folder. The corresponding action is XmhCommitChanges().

Pack Folder

Renumbers the messages in this folder so they start with 1 and increment by 1. The corresponding action is XmhPackFolder().

Sort Folder

Sorts the messages in this folder in chronological order. As a side effect, this also packs the folder. The corresponding action is XmhSortFolder().

Rescan Folder

Rebuilds the list of messages. This can be used whenever you suspect that *xmh*'s idea of what messages you have is wrong. (In particular, this is necessary if you change things using straight *mh* commands without using *xmh*.) The corresponding action is XmhForceRescan().

Message Commands

The Message command menu contains commands that operate on the selected message(s), or if there are no selected messages, the current message.

Compose Message

Composes a new message. A new window will be brought up for composition; a description of it is given in the "Composition Windows" section below. This command does not affect the current message. The corresponding action is Xmh-ComposeMessage().

View Next Message

Views the first selected message. If no messages are highlighted, views the current message. If the current message is already being viewed, views the first unmarked message after the current message. The corresponding action is XmhViewNext-Message().

View Previous

Views the last selected message. If no messages are highlighted, views the current message. If current message is already being viewed, views the first unmarked message before the current message. The corresponding action is XmhView-Previous().

Mark Deleted

Marks the selected messages for deletion. If no messages are highlighted, then this marks the current message for deletion and automatically displays the next unmarked message. The corresponding action is XmhMarkDeleted().

Mark Move

Marks the selected messages to be moved into the current (selected) folder. (If the current folder is the same as the viewed folder, this command will just beep.) If no messages are highlighted, this will mark the current message to be moved and display the next unmarked message. The corresponding action is XmhMarkMove().

Mark Copy
>   Marks the selected messages to be copied into the current folder. (If the current folder
>   is the same as the viewed folder, this command will just beep.) If no messages are
>   highlighted, marks the current message to be copied. The corresponding action is
>   `XmhMarkCopy()`.

Unmark Removes any of the above three marks from the selected messages, or the current mes-
>   sage, if none is highlighted. The corresponding action is `XmhUnmark()`.

View in New Window
>   Creates a new window containing only a view of the first selected message, or the cur-
>   rent message, if none is highlighted. The corresponding action is `XmhViewInNew-`
>   `Window()`.

Reply Creates a composition window in reply to the first selected message, or the current
>   message, if none is highlighted. The corresponding action is `XmhReply()`.

Forward Creates a composition window whose body is initialized to be the contents of the
>   selected messages, or the current message if none is highlighted. The corresponding
>   action is `XmhForward()`.

Use as Composition
>   Creates a composition window whose body is initialized to be the contents of the first
>   selected message, or the current message if none is selected. Any changes you make
>   in the composition will be saved in a new message in the "drafts" folder, and will not
>   change the original message. However, this command was designed to be used within
>   the "drafts" folder to compose message drafts, and there is an exception to this rule. If
>   the message to be used as composition was selected from the "drafts" folder, the
>   changes will be reflected in the original message (see "Composition Windows"). The
>   action procedure corresponding to this command is `XmhUseAsComposition()`.

Print Prints the selected messages, or the current message if none is selected. *xmh* normally
>   prints by invoking the *enscript*(1) command, but this can be customized with the appli-
>   cation-specific resource `PrintCommand`. The action procedure corresponding to
>   this command is `XmhPrint()`.

Sequence Commands

The Sequence command menu contains commands pertaining to message sequences (See
"Message Sequences"), and a list of the message sequences defined for the currently viewed
folder. The selected message sequence is indicated by a check mark in its entry in the margin
of the menu. To change the selected message sequence, select a new message sequence from
the sequence menu.

Pick Messages
>   Defines a new message sequence. The corresponding action is `XmhPick-`
>   `Messages()`.

The following menu entries will be sensitive only if the current folder has any message
sequences other than the "all" message sequence.

Reference Pages

Open Sequence

>   Changes the viewed sequence to be the same as the selected sequence. The corre-
>   sponding action is XmhOpenSequence().

Add to Sequence

>   Adds the selected messages to the selected sequence. The corresponding action is
>   XmhAddToSequence().

Remove from Sequence

>   Removes the selected messages from the selected sequence. The corresponding action
>   is XmhRemoveFromSequence().

Delete Sequence

>   Removes the selected sequence entirely. The messages themselves are not affected;
>   they are simply no longer grouped together to define a message sequence. The corre-
>   sponding action is XmhDeleteSequence().

View Commands

Commands in the View menu and in the buttonboxes of view windows (which result from the
Message command View in New Window) correspond in functionality to commands of the
same name in the Message menu, but they operate on the viewed message rather than the
selected messages or current message.

Close Window

>   When the viewed message is in a separate view window, this command will close the
>   view, after confirming the status of any unsaved edits. The corresponding action pro-
>   cedure is XmhCloseView().

Reply   Creates a composition window in reply to the viewed message. The related action
>   procedure is XmhViewReply().

Forward Creates a composition window whose body is initialized to be the contents of the
>   viewed message. The corresponding action is XmhViewForward().

Use As Composition

>   Creates a composition window whose body is initialized to be the contents of the
>   viewed message. Any changes made in the composition window will be saved in a
>   new message in the "drafts" folder, and will not change the original message. An
>   exception: if the viewed message was selected from the "drafts" folder, the original
>   message is edited. The action procedure corresponding to this command is Xmh-
>   ViewUseAsComposition().

Edit Message

>   Enables the direct editing of the viewed message. The action procedure is XmhEdit-
>   View().

Save Message

>   This command is insensitive until the message has been edited; when activated, edits
>   will be saved to the original message in the view. The corresponding action is Xmh-
>   SaveView().

Print   Prints the viewed message. *xmh* prints by invoking the *enscript*(1) command, but this
             can be customized with the application-specific resource `PrintCommand`. The cor-
             responding action procedure is `XmhPrintView()`.

Options Menu

The Options menu contains one entry.

Read in Reverse

When selected, a check mark appears in the margin of this menu entry. Read in
Reverse will switch the meaning of the next and previous messages, and will increment in the opposite direction. This is useful if you want to read your messages in the
order of most recent first. The option acts as a toggle; select it from the menu a second
time to undo the effect. The check mark appears when the option is selected.

Composition Windows

Aside from the normal text editing functions, there are six command buttons associated with
composition windows:

Close Window

Closes this composition window. If changes have been made since the most recent
Save or Send, you will be asked to confirm losing them. The corresponding action is
`XmhCloseView()`.

Send   Sends this composition. The corresponding action is `XmhSend()`.

New Headers

Replaces the current composition with an empty message. If changes have been made
since the most recent Send or Save, you will be asked to confirm losing them. The
corresponding action is `XmhResetCompose()`.

Compose Message

Brings up another new composition window. The corresponding action is `Xmh-
ComposeMessage()`.

Save Message

Saves this composition in your drafts folder. Then you can safely close the composition. At some future date, you can continue working on the composition by opening
the drafts folder, selecting the message, and using the Use as Composition command.
The corresponding action is `XmhSave()`.

Insert   Inserts a related message into the composition. If the composition window was
             created with a Reply command, the related message is the message being replied to;
             otherwise, no related message is defined and this button is insensitive. The message
             may be filtered before being inserted; see `ReplyInsertFilter` under "Applica-
             tion-specific Resources" for more information. The corresponding action is `Xmh-
             Insert()`.

Reference Pages

Accelerators

Accelerators are shortcuts. They allow you to invoke commands without using the menus, either from the keyboard or by using the pointer.

xmh defines pointer accelerators for common actions: to select and view a message with a single click, use pointer button 2 on the message's entry in the table of contents; to select and open a folder or a sequence in a single action, make the folder or sequence selection with pointer button 2.

To mark the highlighted messages to be moved in a single action, or current message if none has been highlighted, use pointer button 3 to select the target folder. Similarly, selecting a sequence with pointer button 3 will add the highlighted or current message(s) to that sequence. In both of these operations, the selected folder or sequence and the viewed folder or sequence are not changed.

xmh defines the following keyboard accelerators over the surface of the main window, except in the view area while editing a message:

Meta-I	Incorporate new mail.
Meta-C	Commit changes.
Meta-R	Rescan folder.
Meta-P	Pack folder.
Meta-S	Sort folder.
Meta-space	View next message.
Meta-c	Mark copy.
Meta-d	Mark deleted.
Meta-f	Forward the selected or current message.
Meta-m	Mark move.
Meta-n	View next message.
Meta-p	View previous message.
Meta-r	Reply to the selected or current message.
Meta-u	Unmark.
Control-V	Scroll the table of contents forward.
Meta-V	Scroll the table of contents backward.
Control-v	Scroll the view forward.
Meta-v	Scroll the view backward.

Text Editing Commands

All of the text editing commands are actually defined by the Text widget in the Athena widget set. The commands may be bound to different keys than the defaults described below through the X Toolkit Intrinsics key re-binding mechanisms. See Chapter 10, *Setting Resources*, and Appendix G, *Athena Widget Resources*, for more details.

Whenever you are asked to enter any text, you will be using a standard text editing interface. Various control and meta keystroke combinations are bound to a somewhat Emacs-like set of commands. In addition, the pointer buttons may be used to select a portion of text or to move the insertion point in the text. Pressing pointer button 1 causes the insertion point to move to the pointer. Double-clicking button 1 selects a word, triple-clicking selects a line, quadruple-clicking selects a paragraph, and quintuple-clicking selects everything. Any selection may be extended in either direction by using pointer button 3.

In the following, a *line* refers to one displayed row of characters in the window, while a *paragraph* refers to the text between carriage returns. Text within a paragraph is broken into lines for display based on the current width of the window. When a message is sent, text is broken into lines based upon the values of the SendBreakWidth and SendWidth application-specific resources.

The following keystroke combinations are defined:

Control-a	Move to the beginning of the current line.
Control-b	Move backward one character.
Control-d	Delete the next character.
Control-e	Move to the end of the current line.
Control-f	Move forward one character.
Control-g	Multiply reset.
Control-h	Delete previous character.
Control-j	Create a new paragraph with the same indentation as the previous one.
Control-k	Kill the rest of the current line.
Control-l	Refresh the window.
Control-m	New paragraph.
Control-n	Move down to the next line.
Control-o	Break this paragraph into two.
Control-p	Move up to the previous line.
Control-r	Search/replace backward.
Control-s	Search/replace forward.
Control-t	Transpose characters.

Reference Pages

Control-u	Multiply by 4.
Control-v	Move down to the next screenful of text.
Control-w	Kill the selected text.
Control-y	Insert the last killed text.
Control-z	Scroll the text up one line.
Meta-B	Move backward one word.
Meta-d	Delete the next word.
Meta-D	Kill the next word.
Meta-f	Move forward one word.
Meta-h	Delete the previous word.
Meta-H	Kill the previous word.
Meta-i	Insert file.
Meta-k	Kill to end of paragraph.
Meta-q	Form paragraph.
Meta-v	Move up to the previous screenful of text.
Meta-y	Insert current text selection.
Meta-z	Scroll one line down.
Meta-<	Move to the beginning of the file.
Meta->	Move to the end of the file.
Meta-]	Move forward one paragraph.
Meta-[	Move backward one paragraph.
Meta-Delete	Delete previous word.

Meta-Shift Delete
         Kill previous word.

Meta-Backspace
         Delete previous word.

Meta-Shift Backspace
         Kill previous word.

In addition, the pointer may be used to cut and paste text:

Button 1 Down
         Start selection.

Button 1 Motion
         Adjust selection.

Button 1 Up   End selection (cut).

Button 2 Down

>Insert current selection (paste).

Button 3 Down

>Extend current selection.

Button 3 Motion

>Adjust selection.

Button 3 Up   End selection (cut).

Confirmation Dialog Boxes

Whenever you press a button that may cause you to lose some work or is otherwise dangerous, a popup dialog box will appear asking you to confirm the action. This window will contain an Abort or No button and a Confirm or Yes button. Pressing the No button cancels the operation, and pressing Yes will proceed with the operation.

Some dialog boxes contain messages from *mh*. Clicking on the message field will cause the dialog box to resize so that you can read the entire message.

Message Sequences

An *mh* message sequence is just a set of messages associated with some name. They are local to a particular folder; two different folders can have sequences with the same name. In all folders, the sequence "all" is predefined; it consists of the set of all messages in that folder. As many as nine sequences may be defined for each folder, including the predefined "all" sequence. (The sequence "cur" is also usually defined for every folder; it consists of only the current message. *xmh* hides "cur" from the user, instead placing a "+" by the current message. Also, *xmh* does not support the "unseen" sequence, so that one is also hidden from the user.)

The message sequences for a folder (including one for "all") are displayed in the Sequence menu, below the sequence commands. The table of contents (also known as the "toc") is at any one time displaying one message sequence. This is called the "viewed sequence," and its name will be displayed in the toc title bar just after the folder name. Also, at any time one of the sequences in the menu will have a check mark next to it. This is called the "selected sequence." Note that the viewed sequence and the selected sequence are not necessarily the same. (This all pretty much corresponds to the way the folders work.)

The Open Sequence, Add to Sequence, Remove from Sequence, and Delete Sequence commands are active only if the viewed folder contains message-sequences.

Note that none of the above actually affect whether a message is in the folder. Remember that a sequence is a set of messages within the folder; the above operations just affect what messages are in that set.

To create a new sequence, select the Pick menu entry. A new window will appear, with lots of places to enter text. Basically, you can describe the sequence's initial set of messages based on characteristics of the message. Thus, you can define a sequence to be all the messages that were from a particular person, or with a particular subject, and so on. You can also connect

Reference Pages

things up with boolean operators, so you can select all things from "weissman" with the subject "xmh."

Hopefully, the layout is fairly obvious. The simplest cases are the easiest: just point to the proper field and type. If you enter in more than one field, it will only select messages which match all non-empty fields.

The more complicated cases arise when you want things that match one field or another one, but not necessarily both. That's what all the or buttons are for. If you want all things with the subject "xmh" or "xterm," just press the or button next to the Subject: field. Another box will appear where you can enter another subject.

If you want all things either from "weissman" or with subject "xmh," but not necessarily both, select the -Or- button. This will essentially double the size of the form. You can then enter weissman in a from: box on the top half, and "xmh" in a subject: box on the lower part.

If you select the Skip button, then only those messages that *don't* match the fields on that row are included.

Finally, several more boxes will appear in the bottom part of the window. One is the name of the sequence you're defining. (It defaults to the name of the selected sequence when Pick was pressed, or to "temp" if "all" was the selected sequence.) Another box defines which sequence to look through for potential members of this sequence; it defaults to the viewed sequence when Pick was pressed.

Two more boxes define a date range; only messages within that date range will be considered. These dates must be entered in 822-style format: each date is of the form dd mmm yy hh:mm:ss zzz, where dd is a one or two digit day of the month, mmm is the three-letter abbreviation for a month, and yy is a year. The remaining fields are optional: hh, mm, and ss specify a time of day, and zzz selects a time zone. Note that if the time is left out, it defaults to midnight; thus if you select a range of "7 nov 86" - "8 nov 86", you will get only messages from the 7th, as all messages on the 8th will have arrived after midnight.

Date field specifies which date field in the header to look at for this date range; it probably won't be useful to anyone. If the sequence you're defining already exists, you can optionally merge the old set with the new; that's what the Yes and No buttons are all about. Finally, you can OK the whole thing, or Cancel it.

In general, most people will rarely use these features. However, it's nice to occasionally use Pick to find some messages, look through them, and then hit Delete Sequence to put things back in their original state.

Widget Hierarchy

In order to specify resources, it is useful to know the hierarchy of widgets which compose *xmh*. In the notation below, indentation indicates hierarchical structure. The widget class name is given first, followed by the widget instance name. The application class name is Xmh.

The hierarchy of the main toc and view window is identical for additional toc and view windows, except that a topLevelShell widget is inserted in the hierarchy between the application shell and the Paned widget.

```
Xmh  xmh
    Paned  xmh
        SimpleMenu  folderMenu
                SmeBSB  open
                SmeBSB  openInNew
                SmeBSB  create
                SmeBSB  delete
                SmeLine  line
                SmeBSB  close
        SimpleMenu  tocMenu
                SmeBSB  inc
                SmeBSB  commit
                SmeBSB  pack
                SmeBSB  sort
                SmeBSB  rescan
        SimpleMenu  messageMenu
                SmeBSB  compose
                SmeBSB  next
                SmeBSB  prev
                SmeBSB  delete
                SmeBSB  move
                SmeBSB  copy
                SmeBSB  unmark
                SmeBSB  viewNew
                SmeBSB  reply
                SmeBSB  forward
                SmeBSB  useAsComp
                SmeBSB  print
        SimpleMenu  sequenceMenu
                SmeBSB  pick
                SmeBSB  openSeq
                SmeBSB  addToSeq
                SmeBSB  removeFromSeq
                SmeBSB  deleteSeq
                SmeLine  line
                SmeBSB  all
        SimpleMenu  viewMenu
                SmeBSB  reply
                SmeBSB  forward
                SmeBSB  useAsComp
                SmeBSB  edit
                SmeBSB  save
                SmeBSB  print
        SimpleMenu  optionMenu
                SmeBSB  reverse
        Viewport.Core  menuBox.clip
            Box  menuBox
                    MenuButton  folderButton
                    MenuButton  tocButton
                    MenuButton  messageButton
```

```
                              MenuButton   sequenceButton
                              MenuButton   viewButton
                              MenuButton   optionButton
            Grip  grip
            Label folderTitlebar
            Grip  grip
            Viewport.Core  folders.clip
                    Box  folders
                              MenuButton   inbox
                              MenuButton   drafts
                                    SimpleMenu   menu
                                        SmeBSB <folder_name>
                                              .
                                              .
                                              .

            Grip  grip
            Label  tocTitlebar
            Grip  grip
            Text toc
                    Scrollbar  vScrollbar
            Grip  grip
            Label  viewTitlebar
            Grip  grip
            Text  view
                    Scrollbar  vScrollbar
                    Scrollbar  hScrollbar
```

The hierarchy of the Create Folder popup dialog box:

```
            transientShell  prompt
                    Dialog  dialog
                            Label  label
                            Text  value
                            Command  okay
                            Command  cancel
```

The hierarchy of the Notice dialog box, which reports messages from mh:

```
            transientShell  notice
                    Dialog  dialog
                            Label  label
                            Text  value
                            Command  confirm
```

The hierarchy of the Confirmation dialog box:

```
            transientShell  confirm
                    Dialog  dialog
                            Label  label
```

```
                        Command  yes
                        Command  no
```

The hierarchy of the dialog box which reports errors:

```
        transientShell  error
                Dialog  dialog
                        Label  label
                        Command  OK
```

The hierarchy of the composition window:

```
        topLevelShell  xmh
                Paned  xmh
                        Label  composeTitlebar
                        Text  comp
                        Viewport.Core  compButtons.clip
                                Box  compButtons
                                        Command  close
                                        Command  send
                                        Command  reset
                                        Command  compose
                                        Command  save
                                        Command  insert
```

The hierarchy of the view window:

```
        topLevelShell  xmh
                Paned  xmh
                        Label  viewTitlebar
                        Text  view
                        Viewport.Core  viewButtons.clip
                                Box  viewButtons
                                        Command  close
                                        Command  reply
                                        Command  forward
                                        Command  useAsComp
                                        Command  edit
                                        Command  save
                                        Command  print
```

The hierarchy of the pick window:
(Unnamed widgets have no name.)

```
        topLevelShell  xmh
                Paned  xmh
                        Label  pickTitlebar
                        Viewport.core  pick.clip
                                Form  form
                                        Form
```

The first 6 rows of the pick window have identical structure:

```
                              Form
                                   Toggle
                                   Toggle
                                   Label
                                   Text
                                   Command
                              Form
                                   Toggle
                                   Toggle
                                   Text
                                   Text
                                   Command
                              Form
                                   Command
            Viewport.core  pick.clip
                  Form  form
                        From
                              Form
                                   Label
                                   Text
                                   Label
                                   Text
                              Form
                                   Label
                                   Text
                                   Label
                                   Text
                                   Label
                                   Text
                              Form
                                   Label
                                   Toggle
                                   Toggle
                              Form
                                   Command
                                   Command
```

See Appendix G, *Athena Widget Resources* for a list of resources that can be set for the Athena widgets.

Application-specific Resources

Resource instance names begin with a lowercase letter but are otherwise identical to the class name.

If `TocGeometry`, `ViewGeometry`, `CompGeometry`, or `PickGeometry` are not specified, then the value of `Geometry` is used instead. If the resulting height is not specified (e.g., "", "=500", "+0-0"), then the default height of windows is calculated from fonts and line counts. If the width is not specified (e.g., "", "=x300", "-0+0), then half of the display width is used. If unspecified, the height of a pick window defaults to half the height of the display.

Any of these options may also be specified on the command line by using the X Toolkit Intrinsics resource specification mechanism. Thus, to run *xmh* showing all message headers,

```
% xmh -xrm '*HideBoringHeaders:off'
```

The following resources are defined:

Banner

> A short string that is the default label of the folder, Table of Contents, and view. The default is:
>
> ```
> xmh    MIT X Consortium    R4
> ```

BlockEventsOnBusy

> Whether to disallow user input and show a busy cursor while *xmh* is busy processing a command. Default is True.

BusyCursor

> The name of the symbol used to represent the position of the pointer, displayed if BlockEventsOnBusy is True, when *xmh* is processing a time-consuming command. The default is watch.

BusyPointerColor

> The foreground color of the busy cursor. Default is XtDefaultForeground.

CheckFrequency

> How often to check for new mail, make checkpoints, and rescan the Table of Contents, in minutes. If CheckNewMail is True, *xmh* checks to see if you have new mail each interval. If MakeCheckpoints is True, checkpoints are made every fifth interval. Also every fifth interval, the Table of Contents is checked for inconsistencies with the file system, and rescanned. To prevent all of these checks from occurring, set CheckFrequency to 0. The default is 1.

CheckNewMail

> If True, *xmh* will check at regular intervals to see if new mail has arrived for any of the folders. A visual indication will be given if new mail is waiting to be retrieved. Default is True. (See "Bugs.") The interval can be adjusted with the CheckFrequency resource.

CommandButtonCount

> The number of command buttons to create in a buttonbox in between the toc and the view areas of the main window. *xmh* will create these buttons with the names *button1*, *button2* and so on, in a box with the name *commandBox*. The user can specify labels and actions for the buttons in a private resource file; see the section on "Actions." The default is 0.

CompGeometry

> Initial geometry for windows containing compositions.

Cursor
> The name of the symbol used to represent the pointer. Default is `left_ptr`.

DraftsFolder
> The folder used for message drafts. Default is `drafts`.

Geometry
> Default geometry to use. Default is none.

HideBoringHeaders
> If "on", then *xmh* will attempt to skip uninteresting header lines within messages by scrolling them off. Default is on.

InitialFolder
> Which folder to display on startup. Can also be set with the command-line option `-initial`. Default is `inbox`.

InitialIncFile
> The file name of your incoming mail drop. *xmh* tries to construct a filename for the `inc -file` command, but in some installations (e.g., those using the Post Office Protocol) no file is appropriate. In this case, `InitialIncFile` should be specified as the empty string, and *inc* will be invoked without a `-file` argument. The default is to use the value of the environment variable MAIL, or if that is not set, to append the value of the environment variable USER to */usr/spool/mail/*.

MailPath
> The full path prefix for locating your mail folders. May also be set with the command-line option, `-path`. The default is the Path component in *$HOME/.mh_profile*, or *$HOME/Mail* if none.

MailWaitingFlag
> If `True`, *xmh* will attempt to set an indication in its icon when new mail is waiting to be retrieved. If this option is `True`, then `CheckNewMail` is assumed to be `True` as well. The `-flag` command line option is a quick way to turn `MailWaitingFlag` on.

MakeCheckpoints
> If `True`, *xmh* will attempt to save checkpoints of volatile information. The frequency of checkpointing is controlled by the resource `CheckFrequency`.

MhPath
> The directory in which to find the *mh* commands. If a command isn't found here, then the directories in the user's path are searched. Default is */usr/local/mh6*.

PickGeometry
> Initial geometry for pick windows.

PointerColor
> The foreground color of the pointer. Default is `XtDefaultForeground`.

PrefixWmAndIconName
> Whether to prefix the window and icon name with "xmh:". Default is `True`.

PrintCommand

>The *sh* command to execute to print a message. Note that standard output and standard error must be specifically redirected! If a message or range of messages is selected for printing, the full file path of each message file is appended to the specified print command. The default is `enscript >/dev/null 2>/dev/null`.

ReplyInsertFilter

>A shell command to be executed when the Insert button is activated in a composition window. The full path and filename of the source message is added to the end of the command before being passed to *sh*(1). The default filter is *cat*; i.e., it inserts the entire message into the composition. Interesting filters are: *awk -e* '{print " " $0}' or *<mh directory>/lib/mhl -form mhl.body*.

ReverseReadOrder

>When `True`, the next message will be the message prior to the current message in the Table of Contents, and the previous message will be the message after the current message in the Table of Contents. The default is `False`.

SendBreakWidth

>When a message is sent from *xmh*, lines longer than this value will be split into multiple lines, each of which is no longer than `SendWidth`. This value may be overridden for a single message by inserting an additional line in the message header of the form `SendBreakWidth: value`. This line will be removed from the header before the message is sent. The default is 85.

SendWidth

>When a message is sent from *xmh*, lines longer than `SendBreakWidth` characters will be split into multiple lines, each of which is no longer than this value. This value may be overridden for a single message by inserting an additional line in the message header of the form `SendWidth: value`. This line will be removed from the header before the message is sent. The default is 72.

SkipCopied

>Whether to skip over messages marked for copying when using View Next Message and View Previous Message. Default is `True`.

SkipDeleted

>Whether to skip over messages marked for deletion when using View Next Message and View Previous Message. Default is `True`.

SkipMoved

>Whether to skip over messages marked for moving to other folders when using View Next Message and View Previous Message. Default is `True`.

StickyMenu

>If `True`, when popup command menus are used, the most recently selected entry will be under the cursor when the menu pops up. Default is `False`. See the file *clients/xmh/Xmh.sample* for an example of how to specify resources for pop up command menus.

TempDir

Directory for *xmh* to store temporary directories. For privacy, a user might want to change this to a private directory. Default is */tmp*.

TocGeometry

Initial geometry for master *xmh* windows.

TocPercentage

The percentage of the main window that is used to display the Table of Contents. Default is 33.

TocWidth

How many characters to generate for each message in a folder's Table of Contents. Default is 100. Use 80 if you plan to use *mhl* a lot, because it will be faster, and the extra 20 characters may not be useful.

ViewGeometry

Initial geometry for windows showing only a view of a message.

Actions

Because *xmh* provides action procedures which correspond to command functionality and installs accelerators, users can customize accelerators in a private resource file. *xmh* provides action procedures which correspond to entries in the command menus; these are given in the sections describing menu commmands. For examples of specifying customized resources, see the file *clients/xmh/Xmh.sample*. Unpredictable results can occur if actions are bound to events or widgets for which they were not designed.

In addition to the actions corresponding to commands, these action routines are defined:

XmhPushFolder([*foldername*, ...])

Pushes each of its argument(s) onto a stack of folder names. If no arguments are given, the selected folder is pushed onto the stack.

XmhPopFolder()

Pops one folder name from the stack and sets the selected folder.

XmhPopupFolderMenu()

Should always be taken when the user selects a folder button. A folder button represents a folder and zero or more subfolders. The menu of subfolders is built upon the first reference, by this routine. If there are no subfolders, this routine will mark the folder as having no subfolders, and no menu will be built. In that case, the menu button emulates a toggle button. When subfolders exist, the menu will popup, using the menu button action PopupMenu().

XmhSetCurrentFolder()

Allows menu buttons to emulate toggle buttons in the function of selecting a folder. This action is for Menubutton widgets only, and sets the selected folder.

XmhLeaveFolderButton()

Ensures that the menu button behaves properly when the user moves the pointer out of the menu button window.

```
XmhPushSequence([sequencename, ...])
```
Pushes each of its arguments onto the stack of sequence names. If no arguments are given, the selected sequence is pushed onto the stack.

```
XmhPopSequence()
```
Pops one sequence name from the stack of sequence names, which then becomes the selected sequence.

```
XmhPromptOkayAction()
```
Equivalent to pressing the Okay *button in the* Create Folder popup.

```
XmhCancelPick()
```
Equivalent to pressing the Cancel button in the Pick window.

Customization Using mh

The initial text displayed in a composition window is generated by executing the corresponding *mh* command; i.e., *comp*, *repl*, or *forw*, and therefore message components may be customized as specified for those commands. *comp* is executed only once per invocation of *xmh* and the message template is re-used for each successive new composition.

Files

⁻/Mail
⁻/.mh_profile—mh profile.
/usr/local/mh6—mh commands.
⁻/Mail/<folder>/.xmhcache—Scan folder.
⁻/Mail/<folder>/.mh_sequences—Sequence definitions.
/tmp—Temporary files.

See Also

X, xrdb, mh(1), enscript(1); Appendix G, *Athena Widget Resources*; Volume Four, *X Toolkit Intrinsics Programming Manual*; Volume Five, *X Toolkit Intrinsics Reference Manual*, and the Nutshell Handbook *MH and xmh: Email for Users and Programmers*.

Bugs

Printing support is minimal.

Should handle the "unseen" message sequence.

Should determine by itself if the user hasn't used *mh* before, and offer to create the *.mh_profile*, instead of hanging on *inc*.

Still a few commands missing (rename folder, remail message).

A bug in *mh* limits the number of characters in *.mh_sequences* to BUFSIZ. When the limit is reached, the *.mh_sequences* file often becomes corrupted, and sequence definitions may be lost.

Except for the icon, there isn't an indication that you have new mail.

There should be a resource, ShowOnInc, which when True, would show the current message in the view after incorporating new mail.

Reference Pages

The CheckFrequency resource should be split into two separate resources.

WM_SAVE_YOURSELF protocol is ignored.

WM_DELETE_WINDOW protocol doesn't work right when requesting deletion of the first toc and view, while trying to keep other *xmh* windows around.

Doesn't support annotations when replying to messages.

Copyright

Copyright 1988, 1989, Digital Equipment Corporation.
Copyright 1989, Massachusetts Institute of Technology.
See *X* for a full statement of rights and permissions.

Author

Terry Weissman, Digital Western Research Laboratory;
Modified by Donna Converse, MIT X Consortium.

xmodmap

Name

xmodmap – keyboard and pointer modifier utility.

Syntax

xmodmap [*options*] [*filename*]

Description

xmodmap is a utility for displaying and altering the X keyboard *modifier map* and *keymap table* on the specified server and host. It is intended to be run from a user's X startup script to set up the keyboard according to personal tastes.

The *filename* specifies a file containing *xmodmap* expressions to be executed. This file is usually kept in the user's home directory and has a name like *xmodmaprc*.

With no arguments, *xmodmap* displays the current map.

The *filename* argument specifies a file containing *xmodmap* expressions to be executed. This file is usually kept in the user's home directory and has a name like *xmodmaprc*.

Options

xmodmap accepts the following options:

-help   Indicates that a brief description of the command line arguments should be printed on the standard error. This will be done whenever an unhandled argument is given to *xmodmap*.

-grammar
    Indicates that a help message describing the expression grammar used in files and with -e expressions should be printed on the standard error.

-verbose
    Indicates that *xmodmap* should print logging information as it parses its input.

-quiet
    Turns off the verbose logging. This is the default.

-n   Indicates that *xmodmap* should not change the mappings, but should display what it would do, as *make*(1) does when given this option. (Cannot be used with expressions to change the pointer mapping.)

-e *expression*
    Specifies an expression to be executed. Any number of expressions may be specified from the command line.

-pm   Indicates that the current modifier map should be printed on the standard output.

-pk   Indicates that the current keymap table should be printed on the standard output.

-pp   Indicates that the current pointer map should be printed on the standard output.

–   A lone dash means that the standard input should be used as the input file.

Reference Pages

-display [*host*]:*server*[.*screen*]
> Allows you to specify the host, server, and screen to use. For example,

> > **xmodmap -display** *your_node***:0.0**

> specifies the screen 0 on server 0 on the machine *your_node*. If the host is omitted, the local machine is assumed. If the screen is omitted, the screen 0 is assumed; the server and colon (:) are necessary in all cases.

For compatibility with an older version, *xmodmap* also accepts the following obsolete single letter options:

-[SLC12345]
> These options indicate that all current keys for the Shift, Lock, Control, or Mod modifier sets should be removed from the modifier map. These are equivalent to clear expressions.

-[slc] *keysym*
> These options specify a *keysym* to be removed from the Shift, Lock, or Control modifier sets. These are equivalent to remove expressions.

+[slc12345] *keysym*
> These options specify a *keysym* to be added to the Shift, Lock, or Control modifier sets. These are equivalent to add expressions.

Expression Grammar

The *xmodmap* program reads a list of expressions and parses them all before attempting to execute any of them. This makes it possible to refer to keysyms that are being redefined in a natural way without having to worry as much about name conflicts. Allowable expressions include:

keycode *NUMBER* = *KEYSYMNAME* . . .
> The list of keysyms is assigned to the indicated keycode (which may be specified in decimal, hex, or octal and can be determined by running the *xev* program in the examples directory). Usually only one keysym is assigned to a given code.

keysym *KEYSYMNAME* = *KEYSYMNAME* . . .
> The *KEYSYMNAME* on the left-hand side is looked up to find its current keycode and the line is replaced with the appropriate keycode expression. Note that if you have the same keysym bound to multiple keys, this might not work.

clear *MODIFIERNAME*
> This removes all entries in the modifier map for the given modifier, where valid name are: Shift, Lock, Control, Mod1, Mod2, Mod3, Mod4, and Mod5 (case does not matter in modifier names, although it does matter for all other names). For example, clear Lock will remove any keys that were bound to the lock modifier.

add *MODIFIERNAME = KEYSYMNAME* . . .

> This adds the given keysyms to the indicated modifier map. The keysym names are evaluated after all input expressions are read to make it easy to write expressions to swap keys.

remove *MODIFIERNAME = KEYSYMNAME* . . .

> This removes the given keysyms from the indicated modifier map. Unlike add, the keysym names are evaluated as the line is read in. This allows you to remove keys from a modifier without having to worry about whether or not they have been reassigned.

pointer = default

> This sets the pointer map back to its default settings (button 1 generates a code of 1, button 2 generates a 2, etc.).

pointer = *X Y Z*

> This sets the pointer map to contain the button codes *X*, *Y*, and *Z*, where *X*, *Y* and *Z* are numbers. The list always starts with the first physical button.

Lines that begin with an exclamation mark (!) are taken as comments.

If you want to change the binding of a modifier key, you must also remove it from the appropriate modifier map.

Examples

Many pointers are designed such that the first button is pressed using the index finger of the right hand. People who are left handed frequently find that it is more comfortable to reverse the button codes that get generated so that the primary button is pressed using the index finger of the left hand. This could be done on a 3-button pointer as follows:

> % **xmodmap -e "pointer = 3 2 1"**

Many editor applications support the notion of Meta keys (similar to Control keys except that Meta is held down instead of Control). However, some servers do not have a Meta keysym in the default keymap table, so one needs to be added by hand. The following command will attach Meta to the Multi-language key (sometimes labeled Compose Character). It also takes advantage of the fact that applications that need a Meta key need simply to get the keycode and don't require the keysym to be in the first column of the keymap table. This means that applications that are looking for a Multi_key (including the default modifier map) won't notice any change.

> % **keysym Multi_key = Multi_key Meta_L**

One of the more simple, yet convenient, uses of *xmodmap* is to set the keyboard's "rubout" key to generate an alternate keysym. This frequently involves exchanging Backspace with Delete to be more comfortable to the user. If the ttymodes resource in *xterm* is set as well, all terminal emulator windows will use the same key for erasing characters:

> % **xmodmap -e "keysym BackSpace = Delete"**
> % **echo "XTerm*ttyModes: erase ^?" | xrdb -merge**

Reference Pages

Some keyboards do not automatically generate less than and greater than characters when the comma and period keys are shifted. This can be remedied with *xmodmap* by resetting the bindings for the comma and period with the following scripts:

```
!
! make shift-, be < and shift-. be >
!
keysym comma = comma less
keysym period = period greater
```

One of the more irritating differences between keyboards is the location of the Control and Shift Lock keys. A common use of *xmodmap* is to swap these two keys as follows:

```
!
! Swap Caps_Lock and Control_L
!
remove Lock = Caps_Lock
remove Control = Control_L
keysym Control_L = Caps_Lock
keysym Caps_Lock = Control_L
add Lock = Caps_Lock
add Control = Control_L
```

The *keycode* command is useful for assigning the same keysym to multiple keycodes. Although unportable, it also makes it possible to write scripts that can reset the keyboard to a known state. The following script sets the backspace key to generate Delete (as shown above), flushes all existing caps lock bindings, makes the CapsLock key a control key, makes F5 generate Escape, and makes Break/Reset be a shift lock.

```
!
! On the HP, the following keycodes have key caps as listed:
!
!     101   Backspace
!      55   Caps
!      14   Ctrl
!      15   Break/Reset
!      86   Stop
!      89   F5
!

keycode 101 = Delete
keycode 55 = Control_R
clear Lock
add Control = Control_R
keycode 89 = Escape
keycode 15 = Caps_Lock
add Lock = Caps_Lock
```

See Also
X.

Bugs
Every time a `keycode` expression is evaluated, the server generates a `MappingNotify` event on every client. This can cause some thrashing. All of the changes should be batched together and done at once. Clients that receive keyboard input and ignore `MappingNotify` events will not notice any changes made to keyboard mappings.

xmodmap should generate `add` and `remove` expressions automatically whenever a keycode that is already bound to a modifier is changed.

There should be a way to have the `remove` expression accept keycodes as well as keysyms for those times when you really mess up your mappings.

Authors
Rewritten by Jim Fulton, MIT X Consortium, from an earlier version by David Rosenthal of Sun Microsystems.

Name

xpr – print an X window dump.

Syntax

xpr [*options*] [*filename*]

Description

xpr takes as input a window dump file produced by *xwd* and formats it for output on PostScript printers, the DEC LN03 or LA100, the IBM PP3812 page printer, or, as of Release 4, the HP LaserJet (or other PCL printers), or the HP PaintJet. If you do not give a file option, standard input is used. By default, *xpr* prints the largest possible representation of the window on the output page. Options allow you to add headers and trailers, specify margins, adjust the scale and orientation, and append multiple window dumps to a single output file. Output is sent to standard output unless you specify –output *filename*.

Options

xpr accepts the following options:

–device *printer_device*

Specifies the device on which the file is to be printed. Currently the following printers are supported:

ln03   Digital LN03.

la100   Digital LA100.

ljet   HP LaserJet series and other monochrome PCL devices, such as ThinkJet, QuietJet, RuggedWriter, HP2560 series, and HP2930 series printers. (Available as of Release 4.)

pjet   HP PaintJet (color mode). (Available as of Release 4.)

pjetxl   HP PaintJet XL Color Graphics Printer (color mode). (Available as of Release 4.)

pp   IBM PP3812.

ps   PostScript printer.

The default printer, for historical reasons, is the LN03. –device lw (Apple Laser-Writer) is equivalent to –device pp and is provided only for backwards compatibility.

–scale *scale*

Affects the size of the window on the page. The PostScript, LN03, and HP printers are able to translate each bit in a window pixel map into a grid of a specified size. For example, each bit might translate into a 3x3 grid. This is specified by –scale 3. By default, a window is printed with the largest scale that fits onto the page for the specified orientation.

–height *inches*

Specifies the maximum height of the page.

`-width` *inches*
> Specifies the maximum width of the page.

`-left` *inches*
> Specifies the left margin in inches. Fractions are allowed. By default, the window is centered on the page.

`-top` *inches*
> Specifies the top margin for the picture in inches. Fractions are allowed. By default, the window is centered on the page.

`-header` *header*
> Specifies a header string to be printed above the window. Default is no header.

`-trailer` *trailer*
> Specifies a trailer string to be printed below the window. Default is no trailer.

`-landscape`
> Prints the window in landscape mode. By default, a window is printed such that its longest side follows the long side of the paper.

`-portrait`
> Prints the window in portrait mode. By default, a window is printed such that its longest side follows the long side of the paper.

`-rv` Reverses the foreground and background colors.

`-compact`
> Compresses white pixels on PostScript printers.

`-output` *filename*
> Specifies an output filename. If this option is not specified, standard output is used.

`-append` *filename*
> Specifies a filename previously produced by *xpr* to which the window contents are to be appended.

`-noff` When specified in conjunction with `-append`, the window appears on the same page as the previous window.

`-split` *n*
> Allows you to split a window onto several pages. This might be necessary for large windows that would otherwise cause the printer to overload and print the page in an obscure manner.

`-plane` *number*
> Specifies which bit plane to use in an image. The default is to use the entire image and map values into black and white based on color intensities. (Available as of Release 4.)

Reference Pages

-grey 2 | 3 | 4

>   Uses a simple 2x2, 3x3, or 4x4 grey scale conversion on a color image, rather than mapping to strictly black and white. This doubles, triples, or quadruples the effective width and height of the image. (Available as of Release 4.)

-psfig

>   Suppress translation of the PostScript picture to the center of the page. (Available as of Release 4.)

-density *dpi*

>   Indicates what dot-per-inch density should be used by the HP printer. (Available as of Release 4.)

-cutoff *level*

>   Changes the intensity level where colors are mapped to either black or white for monochrome output on a LaserJet printer. (Available as of Release 4.) The *level* is expressed as a percentage of full brightness. Fractions are allowed. (Available as of Release 4.)

-noposition

>   Causes header, trailer, and image positioning command generation to be bypassed for LaserJet, PaintJet, and PaintJet XL printers. (Available as of Release 4.)

-gamma *correction*

>   Changes the intensity of the colors printed by PaintJet XL printers. The *correction* is a floating point value in the range 0.00 to 3.00. Consult the operator's manual to determine the correct value for the specific printer. (Available as of Release 4.)

-render *algorithm*

>   Allows PaintJet XL printers to render the image with the best quality versus performance tradeoff. Consult the operator's manual to determine which *algorithm*s are available. (Available as of Release 4.)

-slide

>   Allows overhead transparencies to be printed using the PaintJet and PaintJet XL printers. (Available as of Release 4.)

Limitations

The current version of *xpr* can generally print out on the LN03 most X windows that are not larger than two-thirds of the screen. For example, it will be able to print out a large *emacs* window, but it will usually fail when trying to print out the entire screen. The LN03 has memory limitations that can cause it to incorrectly print very large or complex windows. The two most common errors encountered are "band too complex" and "page memory exceeded." In the first case, a window may have a particular band (a row six pixels deep) that contains too many changes (from black to white to black). This will cause the printer to drop part of the line and, possibly, parts of the rest of the page. The printer will flash the number '1' on its front panel when this problem occurs. A possible solution to this problem is to increase the scale of the picture, or to split the picture onto two or more pages. The second problem, "page memory exceeded," will occur if the picture contains too much black, or if the picture contains complex half-tones such as the background color of a display. When this problem occurs the printer will automatically split the picture into two or more pages. It may flash the number '5' on its front panel. There is no easy solution to this problem. It will probably be necessary to either cut and paste, or rework the application to produce a less complex picture.

There are several limitations on the use of *xpr* with the LA100: the picture will always be printed in portrait mode, there is no scaling, and the aspect ratio will be slightly off.

Support for PostScript output currently cannot handle the `-append`, `-noff`, or `-split` options.

The `-compact` option is supported *only* for PostScript output. It compresses white space but not black space, so it is not useful for reverse-video windows.

For color images, should map directly to PostScript image support.

HP Printer Specifics

If no `-density` is specified on the command line, 300 dots per inch will be assumed for `ljet` and 90 dots per inch for `pjet`. Allowable *density* values for a LaserJet printer are 300, 150, 100, and 75 dots per inch. Consult the operator's manual to determine densities supported by other printers.

If no `-scale` is specified, the image will be expanded to fit the printable page area.

The default printable page area is 8x10.5 inches. Other paper sizes can be accommodated using the `-height` and `-width` options.

Note that a 1024x768 image fits the default printable area when processed at 100 dpi with scale=1; the same image can also be printed using 300 dpi with scale=3, but will require that considerably more data be transferred to the printer.

xpr may be tailored for use with monochrome PCL printers other than the LaserJet. To print on a ThinkJet (HP2225A), *xpr* could be invoked as:

```
% xpr -density 96 -width 6.667 filename
```

or for black-and-white output to a PaintJet:

```
% xpr -density 180 filename
```

The monochrome intensity of a pixel is computed as $0.30*R + 0.59*G + 0.11*B$. If a pixel's computed intensity is less than the `-cutoff` level, it will print as white. This maps light-on-dark display images to black-on-white hardcopy. The default cutoff intensity is 50% of full brightness. Example: specifying `-cutoff 87.5` moves the white/black intensity point to 87.5% of full brightness.

A LaserJet printer must be configured with sufficient memory to handle the image. For a full page at 300 dots per inch, approximately 2MB of printer memory is required.

Color images are produced on the PaintJet at 90 dots per inch. The PaintJet is limited to 16

Reference Pages

colors from its 330 color palette on each horizontal print line. *xpr* will issue a warning message if more than 16 colors are encountered on a line. *xpr* will program the PaintJet for the first 16 colors encountered on each line and use the nearest matching programmed value for other colors present on the line.

Specifying the −rv (reverse video) option for the PaintJet will cause black and white to be interchanged on the output image. No other colors are changed.

Multiplane images must be recorded by *xwd* in ZPixmap format. Single plane (monochrome) images may be in either XYPixmap or ZPixmap format.

Some PCL printers do not recognize image positioning commands. Output for these printers will not be centered on the page and header and trailer strings may not appear where expected.

The −gamma and −render options are supported only on the PaintJet XL printers.

The −slide option is not supported for LaserJet printers.

The −split option is not supported for HP printers.

See Also
xwd, xdpr, xwud, X.

Copyright
Copyright 1988, Massachusetts Institute of Technology.

Copyright 1986, Marvin Solomon and the University of Wisconsin.

Copyright 1988, Hewlett-Packard Company.

See *X* for a full statement of rights and permissions.

Authors
Michael R. Gretzinger, MIT Project Athena;
Jose Capo, MIT Project Athena (PP3812 support);
Marvin Solomon, University of Wisconsin;
Bob Scheifler, MIT;
Angela Bock and E. Mike Durbin, Rich Inc. (greyscale);
Larry Rupp, Hewlett-Packard (HP printer support).

Name

xprop – display window and font properties for X.

Syntax

xprop [*options*]

Description

The *xprop* utility displays window and font properties in an X server. One window or font is selected using the command line arguments or, in the case of a window, by clicking on the desired window. A list of properties is then given, possibly with formatting information.

For each of these properties, its value on the selected window or font is printed using the supplied formatting information, if any. If no formatting information is supplied, internal defaults are used. If a property is not defined on the selected window or font, "not defined" is printed as the value for that property. If no property list is given, all the properties possessed by the selected window or font are printed.

A window may be selected in one of four ways. First, if the desired window is the root window, the -root option may be used. If the desired window is not the root window, it may be selected in two ways on the command line, either by id number such as might be obtained from *xwininfo*, or by name if the window possesses a name. The -id option selects a window by id number in either decimal or hex (must start with 0x) while the -name option selects a window by name.

The last way to select a window does not involve the command line at all. If none of -font, -id, -name, and -root is specified, a crosshair cursor is displayed and the user is allowed to choose any visible window by pressing any pointer button in the desired window. If it is desired to display properties of a font as opposed to a window, the -font option must be used.

Other than the above four options, the -help option for obtaining help, and the -grammar option for listing the full grammar for the command line, all the other command line options are used in specifing both the format of the properties to be displayed and how to display them. The -len *n* option specifies that at most *n* bytes of any given property will be read and displayed. This is useful, for example, when displaying the cut buffer on the root window, which could run to several pages if displayed in full.

Normally each property name is displayed by printing first the property name, then its type (if it has one) in parentheses, followed by its value. The -notype option specifies that property types should not be displayed. The -fs option is used to specify a file containing a list of formats for properties, while the -f option is used to specify the format for one property.

The formatting information for a property actually consists of two parts, a *format* and a *dformat*. The *format* specifies the actual formatting of the property (i.e., is it made up of words, bytes, or longs, etc.), while the *dformat* specifies how the property should be displayed.

The following paragraphs describe how to construct *formats* and *dformats*. However, for the vast majority of users and uses, this should not be necessary as the built-in defaults contain the *formats* and *dformats* necessary to display all the standard properties. It should be necessary to specify *formats* and *dformats* only if a new property is being dealt with or the user dislikes the standard display format. New users especially are encouraged to skip this part.

A *format* consists of one of 0, 8, 16, or 32 followed by a sequence of one or more format characters. The 0, 8, 16, or 32 specifies how many bits per field there are in the property. Zero is a special case, meaning use the field size information associated with the property itself. (This is needed only for special cases like type INTEGER, which is actually three different types depending on the size of the fields of the property.)

A value of 8 means that the property is a sequence of bytes, while a value of 16 means that the property is a sequence of words. The difference between these two lies in the fact that the sequence of words will be byte swapped, while the sequence of bytes will not be, when read by a machine of the opposite byte order of the machine that orginally wrote the property. For more information on how properties are formatted and stored, consult Volume One, *Xlib Programming Manual*.

Once the size of the fields has been specified, it is necessary to specify the type of each field (i.e., is it an integer, a string, an atom, or what?). This is done using one format character per field. If there are more fields in the property than format characters supplied, the last character will be repeated as many times as necessary for the extra fields. The format characters and their meanings are as follows:

a   The field holds an atom number. A field of this type should be of size 32.

b   The field is a Boolean. A 0 means `False` while anything else means `True`.

c   The field is an unsigned number, a cardinal.

i   The field is a signed integer.

m   The field is a set of bit flags, 1 meaning on.

s   This field and the next ones, until either a 0 or the end of the property, represent a sequence of bytes. This format character is usable only with a field size of 8 and is most often used to represent a string.

x   The field is a hex number (like 'c' but displayed in hex—most useful for displaying window ids and the like).

An example *format* is 32ica, which is the format for a property of three fields of 32 bits each, the first holding a signed integer, the second an unsigned integer, and the third an atom.

The format of a *dformat* (unlike that of a *format*) is not so rigid. The only limitations on a *dformat* is that it may not start with a letter or a dash. This is so that it can be distinguished from a property name or an option. A *dformat* is a text string containing special characters instructing that various fields be printed at various points in a manner similar to the formatting string used by *printf*. For example, the *dformat* " is ($0, $1 \)\n" would render the POINT 3, -4 which has a *format* of 32ii as " is (3, -4)\n".

Any character other than a $, ?, \, or a (in a *dformat* prints as itself. To print out one of $, ?, \, or (, preceed it by a \. For example, to print out a $, use \$. Several special backslash sequences are provided as shortcuts. \n will cause a newline to be displayed while \t will cause a tab to be displayed. \o, where o is an octal number, will display character number o.

A $ followed by a number *n* causes field number *n* to be displayed. The format of the displayed field depends on the formatting character used to describe it in the corresponding *format*. For example, if a cardinal is described by "c", it will print in decimal while if it is described by a "x" it will be displayed in hex.

If the field is not present in the property (this is possible with some properties), <field not available> is displayed instead. $*n*+ will display field number *n*, then a comma, then field number *n*+1, then another comma, then ... until the last field defined. If field *n* is not defined, nothing is displayed. This is useful for a property that is a list of values.

A ? is used to start a conditional expression, a kind of if-then statement. ?*exp*(*text*) will display *text* if and only if *exp* evaluates to non-zero. This is useful for two things. First, it allows fields to be displayed if and only if a flag is set. And second, it allows a value such as a state number to be displayed as a name rather than just as a number. The syntax of *exp* is as follows:

```
exp ::= term | term=exp | !exp
term::= n | $n | mn
```

The ! operator is a logical "not," changing 0 to 1 and any non-zero value to 0. = is an equality operator. Note that internally all expressions are evaluated as 32-bit numbers, so -1 is not equal to 65535. = returns 1 if the two values are equal and 0 if not. *n* represents the constant value *n*, while $*n* represents the value of field number *n*. m*n* is 1 if flag number *n* in the first field having format character "m" in the corresponding *format* is 1, 0 otherwise.

Examples: ?m3(count: $3\n) displays field 3 with a label of count if and only if flag number 3 (count starts at 0!) is on. ?$2=0(True)?!$2=0(False) displays the inverted value of field 2 as a Boolean.

In order to display a property, *xprop* needs both a *format* and a *dformat*. Before *xprop* uses its default values of a *format* of 32x and a *dformat* of " = { $0+ }\n", it searches several places in an attempt to find more specific formats. First, a search is made using the name of the property. If this fails, a search is made using the type of the property. This allows type STRING to be defined with one set of formats while allowing property WM_NAME, which is of type STRING, to be defined with a different format. In this way, the display formats for a given type can be overridden for specific properties.

The locations searched are in order: the format, if any, specified with the property name (as in 8x WM_NAME), the formats defined by -f options in last to first order, the contents of the file specified by the -fs option, if any, the contents of the file specified by the environment variable XPROPFORMATS, if any, and finally *xprop*'s built-in file of formats.

The format of the files referred to by the -fs option and the XPROPFORMATS variable is one or more lines of the following form:

```
name format [dformat]
```

Where *name* is either the name of a property or the name of a type, *format* is the *format* to be used with *name*, and *dformat* is the *dformat* to be used with *name*. If *dformat* is not present, " = $0+\n" is assumed.

Reference Pages

Options

xprop accepts the following options:

-help Prints out a summary of command line options.

-grammar

Prints out a detailed grammar for all command line options.

-id *id*

Allows the user to select window *id* on the command line rather than using the pointer to select the target window. This is very useful in debugging X applications where the target window is not mapped to the screen or where the use of the pointer might be impossible or interfere with the application.

-name *name*

Allows the user to specify on the command line that the window named *name* is the target window, rather than using the pointer to select the target window.

-font *font*

Allows the user to specify that the properties of font *font* should be displayed.

-root Specifies that X's root window is the target window. This is useful in situations where the root window is completely obscured.

-display [*host*]:*server*[.*screen*]

Allows you to specify the server to connect to. For example,

> **xprop -display** *your_node***:0.1**

specifies screen 1 on server 0 on the machine *your_node*. If the host is omitted, the local machine is assumed. If the screen is omitted, the screen 0 is assumed; the server and colon (:) are necessary in any case.

-len *n*

Specifies that at most *n* bytes of any property should be read or displayed.

-notype

Specifies that the type of each property should not be displayed.

-fs *file*

Specifies that file *file* should be used as a source of more formats for properties.

-remove *propname*

Specifies the name of a property to be removed from the indicated window.

-f *name format* [*dformat*]

Specifies that the format for *name* should be *format* and that the dformat for *name* should be *dformat*. If *dformat* is missing, " = $0+\n" is assumed.

-frame

Specifies that, when selecting a window by hand (i.e., if none of -name, -root, or -id are given), *xprop* should look at the window manager frame (if any) instead of looking for the client window. (Available as of Release 4.)

-spy   Indicates that *xprop* should examine window properties forever, looking for property
         change events. (Available as of Release 4.)

Examples

To display the name of the root window: prop -root WM_NAME

To display the window manager hints for the clock: xprop -name xclock WM_HINTS

To display the start of the cut buffer: xprop -root -len 100 CUT_BUFFER0

To display the point size of the fixed font: xprop -font fixed POINT_SIZE

To display all the properties of window # 0x200007: xprop -id 0x200007

Environment Variables

XPROPFORMATS

         Specifies the name of a file from which additional formats are to be obtained.

See Also

X, xwininfo.

Author

Mark Lillibridge, MIT Project Athena.

Reference Pages

xdrb

Name

xrdb – X server resource database utility.

Syntax

xrdb [*options*] [*filename* | -]

Description

xrdb is used to get or set the contents of the RESOURCE_MANAGER property on the root window of screen 0. You would normally run this program from your X startup file.

The resource manager (used by the Xlib routine *XGetDefault*(3X) and the X Toolkit) uses the RESOURCE_MANAGER property to get user preferences about color, fonts, and so on for applications. Having this information in the server (where it is available to all clients) instead of on disk solves the problem in previous versions of X that required you to maintain *defaults* files on every machine that you might use. It also allows for dynamic changing of defaults without editing files.

For compatibility, if there is no RESOURCE_MANAGER property defined (either because *xrdb* was not run or the property was removed), the resource manager will look for a file called *.Xdefaults* in your home directory.

The *filename* (or the standard input if – or no input file is given) is optionally passed through the C preprocessor with the following symbols defined, based on the capabilities of the server being used:

SERVERHOST=*hostname*
HOST=*hostname*
> The hostname portion of the display to which you are connected.

WIDTH=*number*
> The width of the default screen in pixels.

HEIGHT=*number*
> The height of the default screen in pixels.

X_RESOLUTION=*number*
> The x resolution of the default screen in pixels per meter.

Y_RESOLUTION=*number*
> The y resolution of the default screen in pixels per meter.

PLANES=*number*
> The number of bit planes (the depth) of the root window of the default screen.

CLASS=*visualclass*
> One of StaticGray, GrayScale, StaticColor, PseudoColor, True-Color, or DirectColor. This is the visual class of the root window of the default screen.

COLOR Defined only if CLASS is one of StaticColor, PseudoColor, TrueColor, or DirectColor.

BITS_PER_RGB=*number*
>   The number of significant bits in an RGB color specification. This is the log base 2 of the number of distinct shades of each primary that the hardware can generate. Note that it is usually not related to the number of PLANES.

CLIENTHOST=*hostname*
>   The name of the host on which *xrdb* is running. (Available as of Release 4.)

RELEASE=*number*
>   The vendor release number for the server. The interpretation of this number will vary depending on VENDOR. (Available as of Release 4.)

REVISION=*number*
>   The X protocol minor version supported by this server (currently 0).

VERSION=*number*
>   The X protocol major version supported by this server (should always be 11).

VENDOR=*number*
>   A string specifying the vendor of the server. (Available as of Release 4.)

Lines that begin with an exclamation mark (!) are ignored and may be used as comments.

Options

xrdb accepts the following options:

-help   This option (or any unsupported option) will cause a brief description of the allowable options and parameters to be printed.

-cpp *filename*
>   Specifies the pathname of the C preprocessor program to be used. Although *xrdb* was designed to use *cpp*, any program that acts as a filter and accepts the -D, -I, and -U options may be used.

-nocpp
>   Indicates that *xrdb* should not run the input file through a preprocessor before loading it into the RESOURCE_MANAGER property.

-symbols
>   Indicates that the symbols that are defined for the preprocessor should be printed onto the standard output. This option can be used in conjunction with -query, but not with the options that change the RESOURCE_MANAGER property.

-query
>   Indicates that the current contents of the RESOURCE_MANAGER property should be printed onto the standard output. Note that since preprocessor commands in the input resource file are part of the input file, not part of the property, they won't appear in the output from this option. The -edit option can be used to merge the contents of the property back into the input resource file without damaging preprocessor commands.

Reference Pages

-load   Indicates that the input should be loaded as the new value of the RESOURCE_MAN-
         AGER property, replacing whatever was there (i.e., the old contents are removed).
         This is the default action.

-merge
         Indicates that the input should be merged with, instead of replacing, the current con-
         tents of the RESOURCE_MANAGER property. Since *xrdb* can read the standard input,
         this option can be used to the change the contents of the RESOURCE_MANAGER prop-
         erty directly from a terminal or from a shell script. Note that this option does a lexico-
         graphic sorted merge of the two inputs, which is almost certainly not what you want,
         but remains for backward compatibility.

-n   Indicates that changes to the property (when used with -load) or to the resource file
         (when used with -edit) should be shown on the standard output, but should not be
         performed. (Available as of Release 4.)

-quiet
         Indicates that warning about duplicate entries should not be displayed. (Available as
         of Release 4.)

-remove
         Indicates that the RESOURCE_MANAGER property should be removed.

-retain
         Indicates that the server should be instructed not to reset if *xrdb* is the first client.
         (Available as of Release 4.)

-edit *filename*
         Indicates that the contents of the RESOURCE_MANAGER property should be edited
         into the given file, replacing any values already listed there. This allows you to put
         changes that you have made to your defaults back into your resource file, preserving
         any comments or preprocessor·lines.

-backup *string*
         Specifies a suffix to be appended to the filename used with -edit to generate a
         backup file.

-D*name*[=*value*]
         Is passed through to the preprocessor and is used to define symbols for use with condi-
         tionals such as *#ifdef*.

-U*name*
         Is passed through to the preprocessor and is used to remove any definitions of this
         symbol.

-I*directory*
         Is passed through to the preprocessor and is used to specify a directory to search for
         files that are referenced with *#include*.

-display [*host*]:*server*[.*screen*]

> Allows you to specify the host, server, and screen to connect to. *host* specifies the machine, *server* specifies the server number, and *screen* specifies the screen number. For example:

> **xrdb -display** *your_node*:**0.0**

> specifies screen 0 of server 0 on the machine *your_node*. If the host is omitted, the local machine is assumed. If the screen is omitted, screen 0 is assumed; the server and colon (:) are necessary in all cases.

Files

Generalizes ~/.*Xdefaults* files.

See Also

X, XGetDefault(3X), Xlib Resource Manager.

Bugs

The default for no arguments should be to query, not to overwrite, so that it is consistent with other programs.

Authors

Phil Karlton, rewritten from the original by Jim Gettys. Copyright 1988, Digital Equipment Corporation.

Reference Pages

xrefresh

Name

xrefresh – refresh all or part of an X screen.

Syntax

xrefresh [*options*]

Description

xrefresh is a simple X program that causes all or part of your screen to be repainted. This is useful when system messages have displayed on your screen. *xrefresh* maps a window on top of the desired area of the screen and then immediately unmaps it, causing refresh events to be sent to all applications. By default, a window with no background is used, causing all applications to repaint "smoothly." However, the various options can be used to indicate that a solid background (of any color) or the root window background should be used instead.

Options

xrefresh accepts the following options:

-white
: Use a white background. The screen just appears to flash quickly, and then repaints.

-black
: Use a black background (in effect, turning off all of the electron guns to the tube). This can be somewhat disorienting as everything goes black for a moment.

-solid *color*
: Use a solid background of the specified color. Try green.

-root Use the root window background.

-none This is the default. All of the windows simply repaint.

-geometry *geometry*
: Specifies the portion of the screen to be repainted. The -geometry option can be (and often is) abbreviated to -g, unless there is a conflicting option that begins with "g." The argument to the geometry option (*geometry*) is referred to as a "standard geometry string," and has the form *width*x*height*±*xoff*±*yoff*.

-display [*host*]:*server*[.*screen*]
: Allows you to specify the server and screen to refresh. For example, *host* specifies the machine, *server* specifies the server number, and *screen* specifies the screen number. For example,

> **xrefresh -display** *your_node*:0.1

specifies screen 1 of server 0 on the machine *your_node*. If the host is omitted, the local machine is assumed. If the screen is omitted, screen 0 is assumed; the server and colon (:) are necessary in all cases.

Resources

The *xrefresh* program uses the routine *XGetDefault*(3X) to read defaults, so its resource names are all capitalized.

```
Black, White, Solid, None, Root
```
Determines what sort of window background to use.

```
Geometry
```
Determines the area to refresh. Not very useful.

See Also

X.

Bugs

It should have just one default type for the background.

Author

Jim Gettys, Digital Equipment Corp., MIT Project Athena.

Name
xset – user preference utility for X.

Syntax
xset [*options*]

Description
xset is used to set various user preference options of the display and keyboard.

Options
xset accepts the following options. (Note that not all X implementations are guaranteed to honor all of these options.)

b

Controls bell volume, pitch, and duration. The b option accepts up to three numerical parameters (*volume*, *pitch*, and *duration*), a preceding dash (–), or an on/off flag. If no parameters are given, or the on flag is used, the system defaults will be used. If the dash or off are given, the bell will be turned off. If only one numerical parameter is given, the bell *volume* will be set to that value, as a percentage of its maximum. Likewise, the second numerical parameter specifies the bell *pitch*, in hertz, and the third numerical parameter specifies the *duration* in milliseconds. Note that not all hardware can vary the bell characteristics. The X server will set the characteristics of the bell as closely as it can to the user's specifications.

-bc, bc

Controls *bug compatibility* mode in the server, if possible. The option with a preceding dash (-) disables the mode; the option alone enables the mode. (Available as of Release 4.)

The need for this option is determined by the following circumstances. Various pre-R4 clients pass illegal values in some protocol requests, and pre-R4 servers do not correctly generate errors in these cases. Such clients, when run with an R4 server, will terminate abnormally or otherwise fail to operate correctly. Bug compatibility mode explicitly reintroduces certain bugs into the X server, so that many such clients can still be run.

This mode should be used with care; new application development should be done with this mode disabled. Be aware that the server must support the MIT-SUNDRY-NONSTANDARD protocol extension in order for this option to work.

c

Controls key click. The c option can take an optional value, a preceding dash (–), or an on/off flag. If no parameter or the on flag is given, the system defaults will be used. If the dash or off flag is used, the keyclick will be disabled. If a value from 0 to 100 is given, it is used to indicate volume, as a percentage of the maximum. The X server will set the volume to the nearest value that the hardware can support.

fp= *path*

Sets the font path used by the server. *path* must be a directory or a comma-separated list of directories. The directories are interpreted by the server, not the client, and are server-dependent. (Directories that do not contain font databases created by *mkfontdir* will be ignored by the server.)

`fp default`

Restores the default font path.

`fp rehash`

Causes the server to reread the font databases in the current font path. This is generally used only when adding new fonts to a font directory (after running *mkfontdir* to recreate the font database).

`-fp` *path* or `fp-` *path*

The `-fp` and `fp-` options remove elements from the current font path. *path* must be a directory or comma-separated list of directories.

`+fp` *path* or `fp+` *path*

The `+fp` and `fp+` options prepend and append, respectively, elements to the current font path. *path* must be a directory or a comma-separated list of directories.

`led`   Controls the turning on or off of one or all of the LEDs. The `led` option accepts an optional integer, a preceding dash (–) or an `on`/`off` flag. If no parameter or the on flag is given, all LEDs are enabled. If a preceding dash or the flag `off` is given, all LEDs are disabled. If a value between 1 and 32 is given, that LED will be enabled or disabled, depending on the existence of a preceding dash. A common LED that can be controlled is the Caps Lock LED. `xset led 3` enables LED #3. `xset -led 3` disables it. The particular LED values may refer to different LEDs on different hardware.

`m`   Controls the mouse parameters. The parameters for the mouse are *acceleration* and *threshold*. The mouse, or whatever pointer the machine is connected to, will go *acceleration* times as fast when it travels more than *threshold* pixels in a short time. This way, the mouse can be used for precise alignment when it is moved slowly, yet it can be set to travel across the screen in a flick of the wrist when desired. One or both parameters for the m option can be omitted, but if only one is given, it will be interpreted as the acceleration. If no parameters or the flag `default` is used, the system defaults will be set.

`p`   Controls pixel color values. The parameters are the color map entry number in decimal, and a color specification. The root background colors may be changed on some servers by altering the entries for `BlackPixel` and `WhitePixel`. Although these are often 0 and 1, they need not be. Also, a server may choose to allocate those colors privately, in which case an error will be generated. The map entry must not be a read-only color, or an error will result.

`r`   Controls the autorepeat. If a preceding dash or the `off` flag is used, autorepeat will be disabled. If no parameters or the `on` flag is used, autorepeat will be enabled.

`s`   Controls the screen saver parameters. The s option accepts up to two numerical parameters (*time* and *cycle*), a `blank`/`noblank` flag, an `expose`/`noexpose` flag, an `on`/`off` flag, or the `default` flag. If no parameters or the `default` flag is

Reference Pages

used, the system will be set to its default screen saver characteristics. The `on/off` flags simply turn the screen saver functions on or off. The `blank` flag sets the preference to blank the video (if the hardware can do so) rather than display a background pattern, while `noblank` sets the preference to display a pattern rather than blank the video. The `expose` flag sets the preference to allow window exposures (the server can freely discard window contents), while `noexpose` sets the preference to disable the screen saver unless the server can regenerate the screens without causing exposure events. The `time` and `cycle` parameters for the screen saver function determine how long the server must be inactive for screen saving to activate, and the period to change the background pattern to avoid burn in, respectively. The arguments are specified in seconds. If only one numerical parameter is given, it will be used for the `time`.

q   Gives you information on the current settings. (In Release 3, the `query` option can also be used.)

These settings will be reset to default values when you log out.

`-display [host]:server[.screen]`
Allows you to specify the host, server, and screen for which to set preferences. `host` specifies the machine, `server` specifies the server number, and `screen` specifies the screen number. For example,

     xset -display *your_node*:**0.1**

specifies screen 1 of server 0 on the machine `your_node`. If the host is omitted, the local machine is assumed. If the screen is omitted, screen 0 is assumed; the server and colon (:) are necessary in all cases.

See Also
X, Xserver, xmodmap, xrdb, xsetroot.

Authors
Bob Scheifler, MIT Laboratory for Computer Science;
David Krikorian, MIT Project Athena (X11 version).

Name

xsetroot – root window parameter setting utility.

Syntax

xsetroot [*options*]

Description

xsetroot allows you to tailor the appearance of the root (background) window on a display. You can experiment with *xsetroot* until you find a look that you like, then put the *xsetroot* command that produces it into your X startup file. If you do not specify any options or you specify –def, the window is reset to its defaults. The –def option can be specified along with other options and only the non-specified characteristics will be reset to the default state.

Options

xsetroot accepts the following options. Note that only one of the background color/tile changing options (-solid, -grey, -gray, -bitmap, or -mod) can be specified at a time. *color* can be specified as a color name or an RGB value.

-help   Displays a brief description of the allowable options.

-def   Resets unspecified attributes to the default values; the background to the grey mesh background and the pointer to the hollow X pointer. If you specify –def and other options, only the non-specified options are reset to their defaults.

-cursor *cursorfile maskfile*
    Specifies the cursor shape to use as the root window pointer. The *cursorfile* and *maskfile* are bitmaps made with the *bitmap* client. Refer to Chapter 7, *Graphics Utilities*, for more information on creating bitmaps. The mask file may need to be all black until you are accustomed to the way masks work. The default root window pointer is an X cursor.

-cursor_name *standard_cursor_name*
    Changes the root window cursor to one of the standard cursors from the cursor font. See Appendix D for a list and pictures of the standard cursors. To specify a cursor name as an argument to a command line option, the XC_ prefix must be stripped from the name. (This option is available as of Release 4.)

-bitmap *filename*
    Uses the bitmap specified in the file to set the window pattern. The entire background is made up of repeated tiles of the bitmap. You can make your own bitmap files using the *bitmap* client or you can use those available with X, in the directory */usr/include/X11/bitmaps*. The default is grey mesh.

-mod *x y*
    Makes a plaid-like grid pattern on your screen. *x* and *y* are integers ranging from 1 to 16. Zero and negative numbers are taken as 1.

-grey or -grey
    Creates a grey background.

-fg *color*

Sets the foreground color of the root window. Foreground and background colors are only meaningful in combination with -cursor, -bitmap, or -mod. The default is black.

-bg *color*

Sets the background color of the root window. Foreground and background colors are meaningful only in combination with -cursor, -bitmap, or -mod. The default is white.

-rv   Reverses the foreground color and the background color when used with another option such as -mod. -rv without another specified option returns the root (background) window to the default state.

-solid *color*

Sets the root window color. The default is grey mesh.

-name *string*

Sets the name of the background window to *string*. There is no default value. Usually, a name is assigned to a window so that the window manager can use a text representation when the window is converted to an icon. This option also allows a client to refer to the root window by name.

-display [*host*]:*server*[.*screen*]

Allows you to specify the host, server, and screen of the root window. *host* specifies the machine, *server* specifies the server number, and *screen* specifies the screen number. For example,

    % **xsetroot -display** *your_node*:**0.1**

specifies screen 1 of server 0 on the machine *your_node*. If the host is omitted, the local machine is assumed. If the screen is omitted, screen 0 is assumed; the server and colon (:) are necessary in all cases.

See Also

X, xset, xrdb.

Author

Mark Lillibridge, MIT Project Athena.

xstdcmap

Name

xstdcmap – X standard colormap utility.

Syntax

xstdcmap [*options*]

Description

Available as of Release 4, the *xstdcmap* utility can be used to selectively define standard colormap properties. It is intended to be run from a user's X startup script to create standard colormap definitions in order to facilitate sharing of scarce colormap resources among clients. Where at all possible, colormaps are created with read-only allocations.

Options

xstdcmap accepts the following options:

-all   Specifies that all six standard colormap properties should be defined on each screen of the display. Not all screens will support visuals under which all six standard colormap properties are meaningful. *xstdcmap* will determine the best allocations and visuals for the colormap properties of a screen. Any previously existing standard colormap properties will be replaced.

-best   Specifies that the RGB_BEST_MAP should be defined.

-blue   Specifies that the RGB_BLUE_MAP should be defined.

-default
        Specifies that the RGB_DEFAULT_MAP should be defined.

-delete *map*
        Specifies that a standard colormap property should be removed. *map* may be one of: default, best, red, green, blue, or grey.

-grey   Specifies that the RGB_GRAY_MAP should be defined.

-green
        Specifies that the RGB_GREEN_MAP should be defined.

-help   Specifies that a brief description of the command line arguments should be printed on the standard error. This will be done whenever an unhandled argument is given to *xstdcmap*.

-red   Specifies that the RGB_RED_MAP should be defined.

-verbose
        Specifies that *xstdcmap* should print logging information as it parses its input and defines the standard colormap properties.

Reference Pages

-display [*host*]:*server*[.*screen*]

    Allows you to specify the host, server, and screen to connect to. *host* specifies the machine, *server* specifies the server number, and *screen* specifies the screen number. For example,

    xstdcmap -display *your_node***:0.1**

    specifies screen 1 of server 0 on the machine *your_node*. Either or both the *host* and *screen* elements can be omitted. If *host* is omitted, the local machine is assumed. If *screen* is omitted, screen 0 is assumed (and the period is unnecessary). The colon and *server* are necessary in all cases.

See Also

X

Author

Donna Converse, MIT X Consortium.

Name

xterm – window terminal emulator.

Syntax

xterm [*options*]

Description

The *xterm* program is a terminal emulator for the X Window System. It provides DEC VT102 and Tektronix 4014 compatible terminals for programs that can't use the window system directly. If the underlying operating system supports terminal resizing capabilities (for example, the SIGWINCH signal in systems derived from BSD 4.3), *xterm* will use the facilities to notify programs running in the window whenever it is resized.

The VT102 and Tektronix 4014 terminals each have their own window so that you can edit text in one and look at graphics in the other at the same time. To maintain the correct aspect ratio (height/width), Tektronix graphics will be restricted to the largest box with a 4014's aspect ratio that will fit in the window. This box is located in the upper-left area of the window.

Although both windows can be displayed at the same time, one of them is considered the *active* window for receiving keyboard input and terminal output. This is the window that contains the text cursor and whose border highlights whenever the pointer is in either window. The active window can be chosen through escape sequences, the VT Options menu in the VT102 window, and the Tek Options menu in the 4014 window.

The Release 4 version of *xterm* provides four menus that allow you to manipulate the VT102 and Tektronix windows: Main Options, VT Options, Tek Options, and VT Fonts. The first three menus are available (with slight variations) in Release 3, but have the names xterm, Modes, and Tektronix. The VT Fonts menu is available as of Release 4.

Options

xterm accepts all of the standard X Toolkit command line options, which are listed on the *X* reference page. (We've included some of the more commonly used Toolkit options later in this section.)

In addition, *xterm* accepts the following application-specific options. Note that if the option begins with a + instead of a –, the option is restored to its default value. (Specifying the default with +*option* can be useful for overriding the opposite value in an *Xresources* file or other prior resource specification.)

-help

    Causes *xterm* to print out a verbose message describing its options.

-132   Causes the VT102 DECCOLM escape sequence, which switches between 80- and 132-column mode, to be recognized, enabling the *xterm* window to resize properly. By default, the DECCOLM escape sequence is ignored. (See Appendix C for more information on *xterm* escape sequences.)

    (This option can be turned on and off from the *xterm* VT Options menu, described below.)

-ah/+ah

-ah specifies that *xterm* should *always* highlight the text cursor and window borders. By default, *xterm* will display a hollow text cursor whenever the focus is lost or the pointer leaves the window. +ah sets the default.

-b *innerborder*

Specifies the width of the inner border (the distance between the outer edge of the characters and the window border) in pixels. The default is two pixels.

-C Specifies that the *xterm* window should receive console output. This is not supported on all systems.

-cc *characterclassrange:value[,...]*

Sets classes indicated by the given ranges for use in selecting by words. See "Specifying Character Classes" below.

-cn, +cn

-cn indicates that newlines should not be cut in line mode selections; +cn indicates that newlines should be cut in line mode selections. Available as of Release 4.)

-cr *color*

Specifies the color to use for the text cursor. The default is to use the same foreground color that is used for text.

-cu, +cu

-cu enables the *curses* fix. Several programs that use the *curses*(3x) cursor motion package have some difficulties with VT102-compatible terminals. The bug occurs when you run the more program on a file containing a line that is exactly the width of the window and that is followed by a line beginning with a tab. The leading tabs are not displayed. This option causes the tabs to be displayed correctly.

+cu indicates that *xterm* should not work around this *curses* bug.

(This option can also be turned on and off from the VT Options menu, described below.)

-e *command* [*arguments*]

Specifies the command (and its arguments) to be run in the *xterm* window. It also sets the window title and icon name to be the name of the program being executed if neither −T or −n are given on the command line. The −e option, command, and the arguments must appear last on the *xterm* command line, for example, xterm -rv -e more bigfile &.

-fb *font*

Uses the specified font as the bold font. This font must be the same height and width as the normal font. If only one of the normal or bold fonts is specified, it is used as the normal font and the bold font is produced by overstriking this font. The default is to overstrike the normal font.

-j,+j

-j indicates that *xterm* should do jump scrolling. Normally, text is scrolled one line at a time; this option allows *xterm* to move multiple lines at a time so that it doesn't fall as far behind. The use of jump scrolling is strongly recommended since it makes *xterm* much faster when scanning through large amounts of text. The VT100 escape sequences for enabling and disabling smooth scroll and the Enable Jump Scroll item of the VT Options menu can also be used to toggle this feature.

The +j option specifies that *xterm* not do jump scrolling.

(This option can be turned on and off from the VT Options menu, described below.)

-l,+l

-l logs *xterm* input/output into a file called *XtermLog.xxxx*, where *xxxx* represents the process ID number. To display your data, turn off logging using the *xterm* menu, then type cat XtermLog.*xxxx* at the *xterm* window prompt and the output file is sent to your *xterm* window. Logging allows you to keep track of the sequence of data and is particularly helpful while debugging code.

+l specifies that *xterm* not do logging.

(This option can also be turned on and off from the VT Options menu, described below.)

-lf *file*

Specifies the file to which the data is written rather than the default *XtermLog.xxxx*, where *xxxx* is the process identification of *xterm* (the file is created in the directory in which *xterm* is started in or the home directory for a login *xterm*). If *file* begins with a "|," then the rest of the string is assumed to be a command to be executed by the shell and a pipe is opened to the process.

-ls,+ls

-ls indicates that the shell that is started in the *xterm* window be a login shell (i.e., the first character of argv[0] will be a dash, indicating to the shell that it should read the user's *.login* or *.profile*).

+ls indicates that the shell that is started should not be a login shell (i.e., it will be a normal "subshell").

-mb, +mb

-mb turns on the margin bell; the default is bell off. +mb indicates that the margin bell should not be rung.

(This option can also be turned on and off from the VT Options menu, described below.)

-mc *milliseconds*

Specifies the maximum time between multi-click selections. (Available as of Release 4.)

-ms *color*
> Sets the color of the pointer. The default is to use the foreground color.

-nb *number*
> Sets the distance at which the margin bell rings for the right margin. Default is 10 characters.

-rw, +rw
> -rw turns on the reverse-wraparound mode that allows the cursor to wrap around from the leftmost column to the rightmost column of the previous line. Allows you to back-space to the previous line and overstrike data or erase data with the spacebar.
>
> +rw indicates that reverse-wraparound should not be enabled.
>
> (This option can also be turned on and off from the VT Options menu, described below.)

-S*ccn* Specifies the last two letters of the name of a pseudo-terminal to use in slave mode, plus the number of the inherited file descriptor. The option is parsed "%c%c%d". This allows *xterm* to be used as an input and output channel for an existing program and is sometimes used in specialized applications.

-s   Allows *xterm* to scroll asynchronously with the display, meaning that the screen does not have to be kept completely up to date while scrolling. *xterm* saves data in memory which is displayed later. This allows *xterm* to run faster when network latencies are high and is useful when running *xterm* across a large internet or many gateways.

> +s indicates that *xterm* should scroll synchronously.

-sb, +sb
> -sb indicates that some number of lines that are scrolled off the top of the window should be saved and that a scrollbar should be displayed at startup so those lines can be viewed.
>
> +sb indicates that a scrollbar should not be displayed at startup.
>
> (This option can also be turned on and off from the VT Options menu, described below.)

-sf, +sf
> -sf indicates that the Sun function key escape codes should be generated for function keys; +sb indicates that the standard escape codes should be generated for function keys. This is the default.

-si, +si
> -si disables repositioning the cursor at the bottom of the scroll region when the process sends output; +si indicates that the cursor should be repositioned at the bottom of the scroll region on output.
>
> (This option can also be turned on and off from the VT Options menu, described below.)

-sk,+sk
> -sk causes the cursor to be repositioned at the bottom of the scroll region when a key is pressed; +sk indicates that pressing a key while using the scrollbar should not cause the cursor to be repositioned at the bottom of the scroll region.
>
> (This option can also be turned on and off from the VT Options menu, described below.)

-sl *number*
> Specifies the maximum number of lines to be saved that are scrolled off the top of the window. Default is 64 lines.

-t, +t
> -t causes the startup *xterm* window to be the Tektronix window rather than the VT102 window; +t causes the startup window to be the VT102 window. This is the default.

-tm *string*
> Specifies a series of terminal-setting keywords followed by the characters that should be bound to those functions, similar to the *stty* program. (In Release 3, this is ignored when −L is given since *getty* resets the terminal. The −L option is not supported in Release 4.) Allowable keywords include: intr, quit, erase, kill, eof, eol, swtch, start, stop, brk, susp, dsusp, rprnt, flush, weras, and lnext. Control characters may be specified as ^Ichar (e.g., ^c or ^u), and ^? may be used to indicate delete.

-tn *name*
> Specifies the name of the terminal type to be set in the TERM environment variable. This terminal type must exist in the *termcap*(5) database and should have *li#* and *co#* entries.

-ut/+ub
> -ut indicates that *xterm* shouldn't write a record into the the system log file */etc/utmp*.
>
> +ut indicates that *xterm* should write a record into the system log file */etc/utmp*.

-vb/+vb
> -vb causes your terminal window to flash whenever an event occurs that would ordinarily cause your terminal bell to ring.
>
> +vb indicates that a visual bell should not be used.
>
> (This option can be turned on and off from the Main Options menu, described below.)

-wf/+wf
> -wf indicates that *xterm* should wait for the window to be mapped the first time before starting the subprocess so that the initial terminal size settings and environment variables are correct. It is the application's responsibility to catch subsequent terminal size changes.
>
> +wf indicates that *xterm* should not wait before starting the subprocess.

Reference Pages

The following X Toolkit options are commonly used with *xterm*:

-bd *color*

    Sets the color of the border. Default of the highlighted border is black. Default of the unhighlighted border is grey.

-bg *color*

    Sets the background color of the *xterm* window. Default is white.

-bw *pixels*

    Specifies the width of the *xterm* window border in pixels. Default is one pixel.

-display [*host*]:*server*[.*screen*]

    By default, *xterm* obtains the host, server, and screen to use from the environment variable DISPLAY. However, you can also specify them usi ng the -display option. *host* specifies which machine to create the window on, *server* specifies the server number, and *screen* specifies the screen number. For example,

        xterm -display *your_node*:**0.1**

    specifies that an *xterm* be created on screen 1 of server 0 on the machine *your_node*. If the host is omitted, the local machine is assumed. If the screen is omitted, screen 0 is assumed; the server and colon (:) are necessary in all cases.

-fg *color*

    Sets the color of the text (foreground). Default is black.

-fn *font*

    Uses the specified font instead of the default font (*fixed*). You can use any fixed-width font.

-geometry *geometry*

    xterm takes this geometry specification for the VT102 window. The -geometry option can be (and often is) abbreviated to -g, unless there is a conflicting option that begins with "g." The argument to the geometry option (*geometry*) is referred to as a "standard geometry string," and has the form *widthxheight±xoff±yoff*.

-iconic

    Causes *xterm* to display an *xterm* icon rather than an *xterm* window when it starts up.

-name *app_name*

    Specifies the application name under which resources are to be obtained, rather than the default executable filename. *app_name* should not contain "." or "*" characters.

-title *string*

    Specifies the window title string, which may be displayed by window managers if the user so chooses. The default title is the command line specified after the -e option, if any, otherwise the application name.

-rv   Reverses the foreground and background colors.

    (This option can be turned on and off from the VT Options menu, described below.)

`-xrm` *resourcestring*

> Specifies a resource string to be used with this instance of the application. This is especially useful for setting resources that do not have command line option equivalents.

The following command line arguments are provided for compatibility with older versions (prior to Release 3). They may not be supported in the next release as the X Toolkit provides standard options that accomplish most of the same tasks. The `-L` option has been eliminated in Release 4.

`-L`   Indicates that *xterm* is being started by *init*. In this mode, *xterm* does not try to allocate a new pseudo-terminal as *init* has already done so. (`xterm` presumes that its file descriptors are already open on a slave pseudo-terminal.) In addition, the system program *getty* is run rather than the user's shell. This option is only used by *init*.

> This option has been superseded by the *xdm* program. Furthermore, `-L` should never be specified by users when starting terminal windows. This option has been eliminated in Release 4.

`%`*geometry*

> Specifies the preferred size and location of the Tektronix window. It is shorthand for specifying the `tekGeometry` resource.

`#`*geometry*

> Specifies the preferred position of the icon. It is shorthand for specifying the `icon-Geometry` resource. The width and height values of the geometry string are optional.

`-n` *string*

> Specifies the icon name for the *xterm* window. It is shorthand for specifying the `*iconName` resource. Note that this is not equivalent to the Toolkit option `-name`. The default icon name is the name of a program run with the `-e` option, if any, otherwise the application name.

`-r`   Indicates that reverse video should be simulated by swapping the foreground and background colors. It is equivalent to `-rv`.

`-w` *pixels*

> Specifies the width in pixels of the border surrounding the window. It is equivalent to `-bw`.

`-T` *string*

> Specifies the title for the *xterm* window. It is equivalent to `-title`.

Resources

The program understands all of the core X Toolkit resource names and classes as well as:

`iconGeometry` (class `IconGeometry`)

> Specifies the preferred size and position of the application when iconified. It is not necessarily obeyed by all window managers.

Reference Pages

termName (class TermName)
>   Specifies the terminal type name to be set in the TERM environment variable.

title (class Title)
>   Specifies a string that may be used by the window manager when displaying this application.

ttyModes (class TtyModes)
>   Specifies a string containing terminal setting keywords and the characters to which they may be bound. (In Release 3, this resource is ignored when −L is given since *getty* resets the terminal. The −L option has been eliminated in Release 4.) Allowable keywords include: intr, quit, erase, kill, eof, eol, swtch, start, stop, brk, susp, dsusp, rprnt, flush, weras, and lnext. Control characters may be specified as ^*char* (e.g., ^c or ^u), and ^? may be used to indicate delete. This is very useful for overriding the default terminal settings without having to do an *stty* every time an *xterm* is started.

utmpInhibit (class UtmpInhibit)
>   Specifies whether or not *xterm* should try to record the user's terminal in */etc/utmp*.

sunFunctionKeys (class SunFunctionKeys)
>   Specifies whether or not Sun Function Key escape codes, instead of standard escape sequences, should be generated for function keys.

The following resources are specified as part of the vt100 widget (class VT100):

allowSendEvents (class AllowSendEvents)
>   Specifies whether or not synthetic key and button events (generated using the X protocol SendEvent request) should be interpreted or discarded. The default is False meaning they are discarded. Note that allowing such events creates a very large security hole. (Available as of Release 4.)

alwaysHighlight (class AlwaysHighlight)
>   Specifies whether or not *xterm* should always display a highlighted text cursor. By default, a hollow text cursor is displayed whenever the pointer moves out of the window or the window loses the input focus.

boldFont (class Font)
>   Specifies the name of the bold font to use instead of overstriking the normal font.

c132 (class C132)
>   Specifies whether or not the VT102 DECCOLM escape sequence should be honored. The default is False.

charClass (class CharClass)
>   Specifies comma-separated lists of character class bindings of the form [*low–*]*high*:*value*. These are used in determining which sets of characters should be treated the same when doing cut and paste. See "Character Classes" below.

curses (class Curses)
>   Specifies whether or not the last column bug in the cursor should be worked around. The default is False.

background (class Background)
> Specifies the color to use for the background of the window. The default is white.

foreground (class Foreground)
> Specifies the color to use for displaying text in the window. Setting the class name instead of the instance name is an easy way to have everything that would normally appear in the "text" color change color. The default is black.

cursorColor (class Foreground)
> Specifies the color to use for the text cursor. The default is black.

eightBitInput (class EightBitInput)
> Specifies whether or not 8-bit characters should be accepted. The default is True. (Available as of Release 4.)

font (class Font)
> Specifies the name of the normal font.

font1 (class Font1)
> Specifies the name of the first alternate font. This font is toggled using the Tiny menu item on the VT Fonts menu. (Available as of Release 4.)

font2 (class Font2)
> Specifies the name of the second alternate font. This font is toggled using the Small menu item on the VT Fonts menu. (Available as of Release 4.)

font3 (class Font3)
> Specifies the name of the third alternate font. This font is toggled using the Medium menu item on the VT Fonts menu. (Available as of Release 4.)

font4 (class Font4)
> Specifies the name of the fourth alternate font. This font is toggled using the Large menu item on the VT Fonts menu. (Available as of Release 4.)

geometry (class Geometry)
> Specifies the preferred size and position of the VT102 window.

internalBorder (class BorderWidth)
> Specifies the number of pixels between the characters and the window border. The default is 2.

jumpScroll (class JumpScroll)
> Specifies whether or not jump scroll should be used. The default is True.

logFile (class Logfile)
> Specifies the name of the file to which a terminal session is logged. The default is XtermLog.*xxxx* (where *xxxx* is the process ID of *xterm*).

logging (class Logging)
> Specifies whether or not a terminal session should be logged. The default is False.

Reference Pages

`logInhibit` (class `LogInhibit`)
> Specifies whether or not terminal session logging should be inhibited. The default is `False`.

`loginShell` (class `LoginShell`)
> Specifies whether or not the shell to be run in the window should be started as a login shell. The default is `False`.

`marginBell` (class `MarginBell`)
> Specifies whether or not the bell should be run when the user types near the right margin. The default is `False`.

`multiClickTime` (class `MultiClickTime`)
> Specifies the maximum time in milliseconds between multi-clock select events. The default is 250 milliseconds. (Available as of Release 4.)

`multiScroll` (class `MultiScroll`)
> Specifies whether or not scrolling should be done asynchronously. The default is `False`.

`nMarginBell` (class `Column`)
> Specifies the number of characters from the right margin at which the margin bell should be run, when enabled.

`pointerColor` (class `Foreground`)
> Specifies the color of the pointer. The default is `XtDefaultForeground` color.

`pointerColorBackground` (class `Background`)
> Specifies the background color of the pointer. The default is `XtDefault-Background` color. (Available as of Release 4.)

`pointerShape` (class `Cursor`)
> Specifies the name of the shape of the pointer. The default is "xterm."

`reverseVideo` (class `ReverseVideo`)
> Specifies whether or not reverse video should be simulated. The default is `False`.

`reverseWrap` (class `ReverseWrap`)
> Specifies whether or not reverse-wraparound should be enabled. The default is `False`.

`saveLines` (class `SaveLines`)
> Specifies the number of lines to save beyond the top of the screen when a scrollbar is turned on. The default is 64.

`scrollBar` (class `ScrollBar`)
> Specifies whether or not the scrollbar should be displayed. The default is `False`.

`scrollInput` (class `ScrollCond`)
> Specifies whether or not output to the terminal should automatically cause the scrollbar to go to the bottom of the scrolling region. The default is `True`.

`scrollKey` (class `ScrollCond`)
> Specifies whether or not pressing a key should automatically cause the scrollbar to go to the bottom of the scrolling region. The default is `False`.

`scrollLines` (class `ScrollLines`)
> Specifies the number of lines that the `scroll-back` and `scroll-forw` actions should use as a default. The default value is 1. (Available as of Release 4.) (See "Actions.")

`signalInhibit` (class `SignalInhibit`)
> Specifies whether or not the entries in the Main Options menu for sending signals to *xterm* should be disallowed. The default is `False`.

`tekGeometry` (class `Geometry`)
> Specifies the preferred size and position of the Tektronix window.

`tekInhibit` (class `TekInhibit`)
> Specifies whether or not Tektronix mode should be disallowed. The default is `False`.

`tekSmall` (class `TekSmall`)
> Specifies whether or not the Tektronix mode window should start in its smallest size if no explicit geometry is given. This is useful when running *xterm* on displays with small screens. The default is `False`. (Available as of Release 4.)

`tekStartup` (class `TekStartup`)
> Specifies whether or not *xterm* should start up in Tektronix mode. The default is `False`.

`titeInhibit` (class `TiteInhibit`)
> Specifies whether or not *xterm* should remove `ti` or `te` termcap entries (used to switch between alternate screens on startup of many screen-oriented programs) from the TERMCAP string.

`translations` (class `Translations`)
> Specifies the key and button bindings for menus, selections, "programmed strings," etc. See "Actions" below.

`visualBell` (class `VisualBell`)
> Specifies whether or not a visible bell (i.e., flashing) should be used instead of an audible bell when Control-G is received. The default is `False`.

`waitForMap` (class `WaitForMap`)
> Specifies whether or not *xterm* should wait for the initial window map before starting the subprocess. The default is `False`. (Available as of Release 4.)

The following resources are specified as part of the `tek4014` widget (class `Tek4014`):

`width` (class `Width`)
> Specifies the width of the Tektronix window in pixels.

`height` (class `Height`)
> Specifies the height of the Tektronix window in pixels.

Reference Pages

fontLarge (class Font)
> Specifies the large font to use in the Tektronix window. (Available as of Release 4.) This font is toggled using the Large Characters item on the Tek Options menu.

font2 (class Font)
> Specifies font number 2 to use in the Tektronix window. (Available as of Release 4.) This font is toggled using the #2 Size Characters item on the Tek Options menu.

font3 (class Font)
> Specifies font number 3 to use in the Tektronix window. (Available as of Release 4.) This font is toggled using the #3 Size Characters item on the Tek Options menu.

fontSmall (class Font)
> Specifies the small font to use in the Tektronix window. (Available as of Release 4.) This font is toggled using the Small Characters item on the Tek Options menu.

As of Release 4, the resources that can be specified for the various menus are described in the documentation for the Athena SimpleMenu widget. The name and classes of the entries in each of the menus are listed below.

The mainMenu (title Main Options) has the following entries:

securekbd (class SmeBSB)
> Invokes the secure() action.

allowsends (class SmeBSB)
> Invokes the allow-send-events(toggle) action.

logging (class SmeBSB)
> Invokes the set-logging(toggle) action.

redraw (class SmeBSB)
> Invokes the redraw() action.

line1 (class SmeLine)
> A separator.

suspend (class SmeBSB)
> Invokes the send-signal(suspend) action on systems that support job control.

continue (class SmeBSB)
> Invokes the send-signal(cont) action on systems that support job control.

interrupt (class SmeBSB)
> Invokes the send-signal(int) action.

hangup (class SmeBSB)
> Invokes the send-signal(hup) action.

terminate (class SmeBSB)
> Invokes the send-signal(term) action.

kill (class SmeBSB)
> Invokes the send-signal(kill) action.

line2 (class SmeLine)
>A separator.

quit (class SmeBSB)
>Invokes the quit() action.

The vtMenu (title VT Options) has the following entries:

scrollbar (class SmeBSB)
>Invokes the set-scrollbar(toggle) action.

jumpscroll (class SmeBSB)
>Invokes the set-jumpscroll(toggle) action.

reversevideo (class SmeBSB)
>Invokes the set-reverse-video(toggle) action.

autowrap (class SmeBSB)
>Invokes the set-autowrap(toggle) action.

reversewrap (class SmeBSB)
>Invokes the set-reversewrap(toggle) action.

autolinefeed (class SmeBSB)
>Invokes the set-autolinefeed(toggle) action.

appcursor (class SmeBSB)
>Invokes the set-appcursor(toggle) action.

appkeypad (class SmeBSB)
>Invokes the set-appkeypad(toggle) action.

scrollkey (class SmeBSB)
>Invokes the set-scroll-on-key(toggle) action.

scrollttyoutput (class SmeBSB)
>Invokes the set-scroll-on-tty-output(toggle) action.

allow132 (class SmeBSB)
>Invokes the set-allow132(toggle) action.

cursesemul (class SmeBSB)
>Invokes the set-cursesemul(toggle) action.

visualbell (class SmeBSB)
>Invokes the set-visualbell(toggle) action.

marginbell (class SmeBSB)
>Invokes the set-marginbell(toggle) action.

altscreen (class SmeBSB)
>This entry is currently disabled.

line1 (class SmeLine)
>A separator.

Reference Pages

softreset (class SmeBSB)
    Invokes the soft-reset() action.

hardreset (class SmeBSB)
    Invokes the hard-reset() action.

line2 (class SmeLine)
    A separator.

tekshow (class SmeBSB)
    Invokes the set-visibility(tek,toggle) action.

tekmode (class SmeBSB)
    Invokes the set-terminal-type(tek) action.

vthide (class SmeBSB)
    Invokes the set-visibility(vt,off) action.

The tekMenu (title Tek Options) has the following entries:

tektextlarge (class SmeBSB)
    Invokes the set-tek-text(l) action.

tektext2 (class SmeBSB)
    Invokes the set-tek-text(2) action.

tektext3 (class SmeBSB)
    Invokes the set-tek-text(3) action.

tektextsmall (class SmeBSB)
    Invokes the set-tek-text(s) action.

line1 (class SmeLine)
    A separator.

tekpage (class SmeBSB)
    Invokes the tek-page() action.

tekreset (class SmeBSB)
    Invokes the tek-reset() action.

tekcopy (class SmeBSB)
    Invokes the tek-copy() action.

line2 (class SmeLine)
    A separator.

vtshow (class SmeBSB)
    Invokes the set-visibility(vt,toggle) action.

vtmode (class SmeBSB)
    Invokes the set-terminal-type(vt) action.

tekhide (class SmeBSB)
    Invokes the set-visibility(tek,toggle) action.

The `fontMenu` (title VT Fonts) has the following entries:

`fontdefault` (class `SmeBSB`)
>   Invokes the `set-vt-font(d)` action.

`font1` (class `SmeBSB`)
>   Invokes the `set-vt-font(1)` action.

`font2` (class `SmeBSB`)
>   Invokes the `set-vt-font(2)` action.

`font3` (class `SmeBSB`)
>   Invokes the `set-vt-font(3)` action.

`font4` (class `SmeBSB`)
>   Invokes the `set-vt-font(4)` action.

`fontescape` (class `SmeBSB`)
>   Invokes the `set-vt-font(e)` action.

`fontsel` (class `SmeBSB`)
>   Invokes the `set-vt-font(s)` action.

The following resources are useful when specified for the Athena Scrollbar widget (`scroll-Bar`, class `ScrollBar`):

`thickness` (class `Thickness`)
>   Specifies the width in pixels of the scrollbar.

`background` (class `Background`)
>   Specifies the color to use for the background of the scrollbar.

`foreground` (class `Foreground`)
>   Specifies the color to use for the foreground of the scrollbar. The ''thumb'' of the scrollbar is a simple checkerboard pattern alternating pixels for foreground and background color.

Emulations

The VT102 emulation is fairly complete, but does not support the blinking character attribute nor the double-wide and double-size character sets. *termcap* entries that work with *xterm* include ''xterm,'' ''vt102,'' ''vt100,'' and ''ansi.'' *xterm* automatically searches the *termcap* file in this order for these entries and then sets the TERM and the TERMCAP environment variables. Note that the ''xterm'' *termcap* entry distributed with X is not automatically installed. You must add it to */etc/termcap* yourself.

Many of the special *xterm* features (like logging) may be modified under program control through a set of escape sequences different from the standard VT102 escape sequences. (See Appendix E, *xterm Control Sequences*, in this guide.)

The Tektronix 4014 emulation is also fairly good. Four different font sizes and five different line types are supported. The Tektronix text and graphics commands are recorded internally by *xterm* and may be written to a file by sending the COPY escape sequence (or through the

Reference Pages

Tektronix menu; see below). The name of the file will be "COPY*yy-MM-dd.hh:mm:ss*", where *yy, MM, dd, hh, mm,* and *ss* are the year, month, day, hour, minute, and second when the COPY was performed (the file is created in the directory in which *xterm* is started, or the home directory for a login *xterm*).

Pointer Usage

Once the VT102 window is created, *xterm* allows you to select text and copy it within the same or other windows.

The selection functions are invoked when the pointer buttons are used with no modifiers, and when they are used with the Shift key. The assignment of the functions described below to keys and buttons may be changed through the resource database; see "Actions" below.

Pointer button 1 (usually the left) is used to save text into the cut buffer. Move the cursor to the beginning of the text, and then hold the button down while moving the cursor to the end of the region and release the button. The selected text is highlighted and is saved in the global cut buffer and made the PRIMARY selection when the button is released. Double-clicking selects by words. Triple-clicking selects by lines. Quadruple-clicking goes back to characters, etc. Multiple-click is determined by the time from button up to button down, so you can change the selection unit in the middle of a selection. If the key/button bindings specify that an X selection is to be made, *xterm* will leave the selected text highlighted for as long as it is the selection owner.

Pointer button 2 (usually the middle) "types" (pastes) the text from the PRIMARY selection, if any, otherwise from the cut buffer, inserting it as keyboard input.

Pointer button 3 (usually the right) extends the current selection. (You can swap "right" and "left" everywhere in the rest of this paragraph.) If pressed while closer to the right edge of the selection than the left, it extends/contracts the right edge of the selection. If you contract the selection past the left edge of the selection, *xterm* assumes you really meant the left edge, restores the original selection, then extends/contracts the left edge of the selection. Extension starts in the selection unit mode in which the last selection or extension was performed; you can multiple-click to cycle through them.

By cutting and pasting pieces of text without trailing new lines, you can take text from several places in different windows and form a command to the shell, for example, or take output from a program and insert it into your favorite editor. Since the cut buffer is globally shared among different applications, you should regard it as a "file" whose contents you know. The terminal emulator and other text programs should be treating it as if it were a text file, i.e., the text is delimited by newlines.

The scroll region displays the position and amount of text currently showing in the window (highlighted) relative to the amount of text actually saved. As more text is saved (up to the maximum), the size of the highlighted area decreases.

Clicking button 1 in the scroll region moves the adjacent line to the top of the display window.

Clicking button 3 moves the top line of the display window down to the pointer position.

Clicking button 2 moves the display to a position in the saved text that corresponds to the pointer's position in the scrollbar.

Unlike the VT102 window, the Tektronix window does not allow the copying of text. It does allow Tektronix GIN mode, and in this mode the cursor will change from an arrow to a cross. Pressing any key will send that key and the current coordinate of the cross cursor. Pressing button 1, 2, or 3 will return the letters "l," "m," and "r," respectively. If the Shift key is pressed when a pointer button is pressed, the corresponding uppercase letter is sent. To distinguish a pointer button from a key, the high bit of the character is set (but this bit is normally stripped unless the terminal mode is RAW; see *tty*(4) for details).

Menus

The Release 4 version of *xterm* has four different menus, titled Main Options, VT Options, Tek Options, and VT Fonts. The first three menus are available in Release 3 under the names xterm, Modes, and Tektronix. The VT Fonts menu is available as of Release 4.

Many of the menu items have also been renamed in Release 4; however, most items have not changed in functionality. The following sections describe the items available on the Release 3 and 4 menus. In the sections describing the various menu items, if an item has simply been renamed, the Release 3 name appears in parentheses after the Release 4 name.

Each menu pops up under the correct combination of key and button presses. Most menus are divided into two sections, separated by a horizontal line. The top portion contains various modes that can be specified. A check mark appears next to a mode that is currently active. Selecting one of these modes toggles its state. The bottom portion contains command entries; selecting one of these performs the indicated function. The menus are described in detail in the following sections.

Main Options Menu (Release 3: xterm Menu)

The Main Options menu (formerly xterm) is displayed when the Control key and pointer button 1 are simultaneously pressed in an *xterm* window. The modes section contains items that apply to both the VT102 and Tektronix windows. The modes can also be set by command line options when invoking *xterm*, or by entries in a resource startup file like *Xresources* (see Chapter 10, *Setting Resources*). The menu selections enable you to change your mind once *xterm* is running.

All of the commands on this menu (except for Redraw Window) send a signal that is intended to affect the *xterm* process (Send INT Signal, Send TERM Signal, etc.). Given that your operating system may recognize only certain signals, every menu item may not produce the intended function.

Four of these commands (Send HUP Signal, Send TERM Signal, Send KILL Signal, and Quit) send signals that are intended to terminate the *xterm* window. In most cases, you can probably end an *xterm* process simply by typing some sequence (such as Control-D or exit) in the window. Of course, the menu options may be helpful if the more conventional ways of killing the window fail.

Reference Pages

Main Options Menu Mode Toggles (On/Off)

Visual Bell
Causes your terminal window to flash whenever an event occurs that would ordinarily cause your terminal bell to ring. This item appears on the equivalent Release 3 menu (the xterm menu) only. In Release 4, it has been renamed Enable Visual Bell and moved to the VT Options menu.

Secure Keyboard
Ensures that all keyboard input is directed *only* to *xterm*. Used when typing in passwords or other sensitive data in an unsecure environment. (See "Security" later in this reference page.)

Allow SendEvents (Release 4 only)
Causes synthetic key and button events (generated using the X protocol `SendEvent` request) to be interpreted. Note that allowing such events creates a very large security hole.

Log to File (Release 3: Logging)
Logs *xterm* input/output into a file in your home directory called *XtermLog.xxxxx* where *xxxxx* represents the process ID number of the *xterm* process. Logging allows you to keep track of the sequence of data and, therefore, is particularly helpful while debugging code.

To display the data contained in the log file, at the *xterm* window prompt type:

```
more XtermLog.xxxxx
```

The output file is sent to your *xterm* window.

Be sure to turn Log to File off before displaying the log file in the *xterm* window. When Log to File is on, anything in the window is appended to the end of the log file. If you display the log file while logging is on, you will get into a continuous loop, much as if you typed `cat * > file`.

To find out the exact name of the log file, list the contents of your home directory, looking for a log file with an appropriate time and date. Note that if you turn logging on in multiple *xterm* windows, there will be multiple log files.

Main Options Menu Commands

Redraw Window (Release 3: Redraw)
Redraws the contents of the window. (If you are using the *uwm* window manager, you can also do this with the Redraw selection of the *uwm* WindowOps menu. Or you can refresh the entire screen with the *xrefresh* client or the Refresh Screen selection of the WindowOps menu. See Appendix B, *Using the uwm Window Manager*.)

Send STOP Signal (Release 3: Suspend program)
Suspends a process (sends the SIGTSTP signal to the process group of the process running under *xterm*, usually the shell). If your system

supports job control, you may also be able to suspend the process by typing Control-Z. If your system does not support job control, this menu item won't work either.

Send CONT Signal (Release 3: Continue program)
: Continues a process that has been suspended (technically speaking, this menu item sends the SIGCONT signal to the process group of the process running under *xterm*, usually the shell). The Send CONT Signals item is especially useful on systems with job control if you accidentally type Control-Z and suspend a process.

Send INT Signal (Release 3: Interrupt program)
: Interrupts a process (sends the SIGINT signal to the process group of the process running under *xterm*, usually the shell).

Send HUP Signal (Release 3: Hangup program)
: Hangs up the process (sends the SIGHUP signal to the process group of the process running under *xterm*, usually the shell). This usually ends up killing the *xterm* process, and the window disappears from the screen.

Send TERM Signal (Release 3: Terminate program)
: Terminates the process (sends the SIGTERM signal to the process group of the process running under *xterm*, usually the shell). This usually ends up killing the *xterm* process, and the window disappears from the screen.

Send KILL Signal (Release 3: Kill program)
: Kills the process (sends the SIGKILL signal to the process group of the process running under *xterm*, usually the shell). This ends up killing the *xterm* process, and the window disappears from the screen.

Quit
: Like Send HUP Signal, Quit sends the SIGHUP signal to the process group of the process running under *xterm*, usually the shell. This usually ends up killing the *xterm* process, and the window disappears from the screen.

Quit is separated from the earlier commands by a horizontal line, so it's easier to point at. Sending a SIGHUP signal with Quit is also slightly more gentle to the system than using Send KILL Signal.

See *signal*(3C) in the *UNIX Programmer's Manual* for more information on what each signal does.

VT Options Menu (Release 3: Modes Menu)

The VT Options menu (formerly Modes) menu sets various modes in the VT102 emulation and is displayed when the Control key and pointer button 2 are pressed in the VT102 window.

In the command section of this menu, the soft reset entry will reset scroll regions. This can be convenient when some program has left the scroll regions set incorrectly (often a problem when

Reference Pages

using VMS or TOPS-20). The full reset entry will clear the screen, reset tabs to every eight columns, and reset the terminal modes (such as wrap and smooth scroll) to their initial states just after *xterm* has finish processing the command line options.

VT Options Menu Mode Toggles (On/Off)

Most of these modes can also be set by command line options when invoking *xterm*, or by entries in a resource startup file like *Xresources* (see Chapter 10, *Setting Resources*). The menu selections enable you to change your mind once *xterm* is running.

Enable Scrollbar (Release 3: Scrollbar)

> Causes a scrollbar to appear on the left-hand side of the *xterm* window. Off by default.

Enable Jump Scroll (Release 3: Jump Scroll)

> Causes the window to move text several lines at a time rather than line by line. On by default.

Enable Reverse Video (Release 3: Reverse Video)

> Reverses the foreground and background colors. Off by default.

Enable Auto Wraparound (Release 3: Auto Wraparound)

> Wraps the text or data to the next line automatically when the cursor reaches the window border on input. On by default.

Enable Reverse Wraparound (Release 3: Reverse Wraparound)

> Allows the cursor to wrap around from the leftmost column to the rightmost column of the previous line. Allows you to backspace to the previous line and overstrike data or erase data with the space bar. Off by default.

Enable Auto Linefeed (Release 3: Auto Linefeed)

> Generates a linefeed automatically. This is useful if you are using a program that generates a carriage return without dropping down a line on your screen. Off by default. (This option is usually not needed on UNIX systems.)

Enable Application Cursor Keys (Release 3: Application Cursor Mode)

> Generates ANSI escape sequences rather than standard cursor movement when you use the arrow keys. This option may be useful when working with certain applications. Off by default.

The following table lists the ANSI characters generated by application cursors.

Cursor Key (Arrow)	Reset (Cursor)	Set (Application)
Up	ESC [A	ESC O A
Down	ESC [B	ESC O B
Right	ESC [C	ESC O C
Left	ESC [D	ESC O D

Enable Application Keypad (Release 3: Application Keypad Mode)

Generates a control function rather than a numeric character when you use the numeric keypad. Off by default.

Scroll to Bottom on Key Press

Indicates that pressing a key while using the scrollbar causes the cursor to be repositioned at the bottom of the scroll region. For example, if you have scrolled up the window to see past history, as soon as you begin typing your next command the cursor jumps to the bottom of the screen. Off by default.

Scroll to Bottom on Tty Output

Indicates that receiving output to the window (or pressing a key, if `stty echo` has been specified) while using the scrollbar causes the cursor to be repositioned at the bottom of the scroll region. In Release 4, on by default. (In Release 3, off by default; on automatically if the window has a scrollbar.) This mode can be toggled off, but is generally desirable to have.

Allow 80/132 Column Switching (Release 3: Allow 80/132 switching)

Allows *xterm* to recognize the DECCOLM escape sequence, which switches the terminal between 80- and 132-column mode. The DEC-COLM escape sequence can be included in a program (such as a spreadsheet) to allow the program to display in 132-column format. See Appendix E, *xterm Control Sequences*, for more information. Off by default.

Enable Curses Emulation (Release 3: Curses Emulation)

Enables the *curses* fix. Several programs that use the *curses* cursor motion package have some difficulties with VT102-compatible terminals. The bug occurs when you run the *more* program on a file containing a line that is exactly the width of the window and that is followed by a line beginning with a tab. The leading tabs may disappear. This mode causes the tabs to be displayed correctly. Off by default.

Enable Visual Bell   Causes your terminal window to flash whenever an event occurs that would ordinarily cause your terminal bell to ring. This item appears as

Reference Pages

Visual Bell on the Release 3 xterm menu. In Release 4, it has been renamed Enable Visual Bell and moved to the VT Options menu.

Enable Margin Bell (Release 3: Margin Bell)

Turns on the margin bell. Off by default.

Tek Window Showing   Shows the current contents of the Tektronix window; you cannot input to that window until you choose Switch to Tek Mode. Off by default. This item is a mode toggle on the equivalent Release 3 menu (Modes). In Release 4, it has been renamed and moved to the commands section, as described in "VT Options Menu Commands."

Show Alternate Screen (Release 3: Alternate Screen)

Informs you that you are looking at the alternate screen. You cannot select this mode from the menu. If a check mark appears beside this mode, you are viewing the alternate screen. Off by default.

VT Options Menu Commands

These commands can be invoked only from the menu; there are no alternative ways to perform the same functions.

Do Soft Reset (Release 3: Soft Reset)

Resets the terminal scroll region from partial scroll (a portion of the window) to full scroll (the entire window). Use this command when a program has left the scroll region set incorrectly.

Do Full Reset (Release 3: Full Reset)

Clears the window, resets tabs to every eight columns, and resets the terminal modes such as auto wraparound and jump scroll to their initial states.

Show Tek Window (Release 3: Tek Window Showing)

Shows the current contents of the Tektronix window; you cannot input to that window until you choose Switch to Tek Mode. Off by default. The Release 3 item appeared in the mode toggles section of the menu; the item has been renamed and moved to the commands section in Release 4.

Switch to Tek Mode (Release 3: Select Tek Mode)

Brings up a Tektronix window. You can input to this window.

Hide VT Window   Removes the VT window but does not destroy it. It can be brought back by choosing Select VT Mode from the Tek Options menu.

Tek Options Menu (Release 3: Tektronix Menu)

The Tek Options menu (formerly Tektronix) sets various modes in the Tektronix emulation, and is displayed when the Control key and pointer button 2 are pressed in the Tektronix window. The current font size is checked in the modes section of the menu. The PAGE entry in the command section clears the Tektronix window.

Tek Options Menu Mode Toggles (On/Off)

These modes can be set only from the Tek Options menu.

Large Characters #2 Size Characters #3 Size Characters Small Characters	Selecting one of these four options sets the point size of text displayed in the Tektronix window. The four options are mutually exclusive.
VT Window Showing	Shows the current contents of the VT102 window; you cannot input to that window until you choose Switch to VT Mode. This item is a mode toggle on the equivalent Release 3 menu (Tektronix). In Release 4, it has been renamed and moved to the commands section, as described below.

Tek Options Menu Commands

PAGE	Clears the Tektronix window.
RESET	Closes down the Tektronix window.
COPY	Writes a file of the Tektronix text and graphics commands.
Show VT Window (Release 3: VT Window Showing)	
	Shows the current contents of the VT102 window; you cannot input to that window until you choose Switch to VT Mode. The Release 3 item appeared in the mode toggles section of the menu; the item has been renamed and moved to the commands section in Release 4.
Switch to VT Mode (Release 3: Select VT Mode)	
	Makes the associated VT102 window active for input.
Hide Tek Window	Removes the Tektronix window but does not destroy it. It can be brought back by choosing Switch to Tek Mode from the VT Options menu.

VT Fonts Menu (Release 4)

Added in Release 4, the VT Fonts menu enables you to change the VT102 display font dynamically. The menu is displayed when the Control key and pointer button 3 are pressed in the VT102 window. All items on the menu toggle different display fonts. The items are mutually exclusive. A checkmark appears on the menu next to the current font.

Default Tiny Small Medium Large	Selecting one of these five options sets the point size of text displayed in the VT102 window. The Default font is the font specified when the *xterm* was run.
Escape Sequence	
	Allows you to select a font previously toggled using an escape sequence. See Chapter 6, *Font Specification*, for the escape sequence to use.

Reference Pages

Selection

Allows you to toggle a font whose name you've previously selected with the pointer or using the select button of the *xfontsel* client. See Chapter 6, *Font Specification*, for more information.

Security

X environments differ in their security consciousness. MIT servers, run under *xdm*, are capable of using a "magic cookie" authorization scheme that can provide a reasonable level of security for many people. If your server is using only a host-based mechanism to control access to the server (see *xhost*), then if you enable access for a host and other users are also permitted to run clients on that same host, there is every possibility that someone can run an application that will use the basic services of the X protocol to snoop on your activities, potentially capturing a transcript of everything you type at the keyboard. This is of particular concern when you want to type in a password or other sensitive data. The best solution to this problem is to use a better authorization mechanism than host-based control, but a simple mechanism exists for protecting keyboard input in *xterm*.

The Main Options menu (see "Menus" above) contains a Secure Keyboard entry which, when enabled, ensures that all keyboard input is directed *only* to *xterm* (using the `GrabKeyboard` protocol request). When an application prompts you for a password (or other sensitive data), you can enable Secure Keyboard using the menu, type in the data, and then disable Secure Keyboard using the menu again. Only one X client at a time can secure the keyboard, so when you attempt to enable Secure Keyboard it may fail. In this case, the bell will sound. If the Secure Keyboard succeeds, the foreground and background colors will be exchanged (as if you selected the Enable Reverse Video entry in the VT Options menu); they will be exchanged again when you exit secure mode. If the colors do *not* switch, then you should be *very* suspicious that you are being spoofed. If the application you are running displays a prompt before asking for the password, it is safest to enter secure mode *before* the prompt gets displayed, and to make sure that the prompt gets displayed correctly (in the new colors), to minimize the probability of spoofing. You can also bring up the menu again and make sure that a check mark appears next to the entry.

Secure Keyboard mode will be disabled automatically if your xterm window becomes iconified (or otherwise unmapped), or if you start up a reparenting window manager (that places a titlebar or other decoration around the window) while in Secure Keyboard mode. (This is a feature of the X protocol not easily overcome.) When this happens, the foreground and background colors will be switched back and the bell will sound in warning.

Character Classes

Clicking the middle mouse button twice in rapid succession will cause all characters of the same class (e.g., letters, white space, punctuation) to be selected. Since different people have different preferences for what should be selected (for example, should filenames be selected as a whole or only the separate subnames), the default mapping can be overridden through the use of the `charClass` (class `CharClass`) resource.

This resource is simply a list of *range*:*value* pairs, where the range is either a single number or *low-high* in the range of 0 to 127, corresponding to the ASCII code for the character or characters to be set. The *value* is arbitrary, although the default table uses the character number of the first character occurring in the set.

The default table is:

```
static int charClass[128] = {
/* NUL  SOH  STX  ETX  EOT  ENQ  ACK  BEL */
    32,  1,   1,   1,   1,   1,   1,   1,
/* BS   HT   NL   VT   NP   CR   SO   SI */
    1,   32,  1,   1,   1,   1,   1,   1,
/* DLE  DC1  DC2  DC3  DC4  NAK  SYN  ETB */
    1,   1,   1,   1,   1,   1,   1,   1,
/* CAN  EM   SUB  ESC  FS   GS   RS   US */
    1,   1,   1,   1,   1,   1,   1,   1,
/* SP   !    "    #    $    %    &    ' */
    32,  33,  34,  35,  36,  37,  38,  39,
/* (    )    *    +    ,    -    .    / */
    40,  41,  42,  43,  44,  45,  46,  47,
/* 0    1    2    3    4    5    6    7 */
    48,  48,  48,  48,  48,  48,  48,  48,
/* 8    9    :    ;    <    =    >    ? */
    48,  48,  58,  59,  60,  61,  62,  63,
/* @    A    B    C    D    E    F    G */
    64,  48,  48,  48,  48,  48,  48,  48,
/* H    I    J    K    L    M    N    O */
    48,  48,  48,  48,  48,  48,  48,  48,
/* P    Q    R    S    T    U    V    W */
    48,  48,  48,  48,  48,  48,  48,  48,
/* X    Y    Z    [    \    ]    ^    _ */
    48,  48,  48,  91,  92,  93,  94,  48,
/* `    a    b    c    d    e    f    g */
    96,  48,  48,  48,  48,  48,  48,  48,
/* h    i    j    k    l    m    n    o */
    48,  48,  48,  48,  48,  48,  48,  48,
/* p    q    r    s    t    u    v    w */
    48,  48,  48,  48,  48,  48,  48,  48,
/* x    y    z    {    |    }    ~    DEL */
    48,  48,  48, 123, 124, 125, 126,   1};
```

For example, the string "33:48,37:48,45-47:48,64:48" indicates that the exclamation mark, percent sign, dash, period, slash, and ampersand characters should be treated the same way as characters and numbers. This is very useful for cutting and pasting electronic mailing addresses and UNIX filenames.

Actions

It is possible to rebind keys (or sequences of keys) to arbitrary strings for input, by changing the translations for the `vt100` or `tek4014` widgets. Changing the translations for events other than key and button events is not expected, and will cause unpredictable behavior. The following actions are provided for use with the vt100 or tek4014 `translations` resource:

`bell([`*`percent`*`])`

Rings the keyboard bell at the specified percentage above or below the base volume.

`ignore()`

Ignores the event but checks for special pointer position escape sequences. This is useful for trapping events that might otherwise interfere with translations you might want to set.

`insert()`

A synonym for `insert-seven-bit()`.

`insert-seven-bit()`

Inserts the 7-bit USASCII character or string associated with the keysym that was pressed.

`insert-eight-bit()`

Inserts the 8-bit ISO Latin-1 character or string associated with the keysym that was pressed. The fallback translation associated with this action is `Meta<Keypress>`. That is, pressing Meta in conjunction with any key will get the 8-bit equivalent.

`insert-selection(`*`sourcename`*`[, ...])`

Inserts the string found in the selection or cut buffer indicated by *sourcename*. Sources are checked in the order given (case is significant) until one is found. Commonly-used selections include: PRIMARY, SECONDARY, and CLIPBOARD. Cut buffers are typically named CUT_BUFFER0 through CUT_BUFFER7.

`keymap(`*`name`*`)`

Dynamically defines a new translation table whose resource name is *name* with the suffix `Keymap` (case is significant). The keymap name `None` restores the original translation table. This is useful for loading translations that will be used with a particular application running in an *xterm* window. In the following example, `keymap` is used to define a set of special keys for entering commonly-typed words when running the *dbx* application:

```
*VT100.Translations: #override <Key>F13: keymap(dbx)
*VT100.dbxKeymap.translations: \
```

```
<Key>    F14:    keymap(None)\n\
<Key>    F17:    string("next") string(0x0d)\n\
<Key>    F18:    string("step") string(0x0d)\n\
<Key>    F19:    string("continue") string(0x0d)\n\
<Key>    F20:    string("print ") insert-selection(PRIMARY,CUT_BUFFER0)
```

When the user presses key F13, the *dbx* keymaps go into effect. Keys F15-F20 then print common *dbx* commands. F14 disables the translations on the "dbx" keys.

`popup-menu(`*menuname*`)`
> Displays the specified popup menu. Valid names (case is significant) include: `main-Menu`, `vtMenu`, `fontMenu`, and `tekMenu`.

`secure()`
> Toggles the secure keyboard mode described in the "Security" section, and is invoked from the Secure Keyboard entry in `mainMenu`.

`select-start()`
> Begins text selection at the current pointer location. See the section on "Pointer Usage" for information on making selections.

`select-extend()`
> Tracks the pointer and extends the selection. It should be bound only to motion events.

`select-end(`*destname* `[, ...])`
> Puts the currently selected text into all of the selections or cut buffers specified by *destname*.

`select-cursor-start()`
> Similar to `select-start`, except that it begins the selection at the current text cursor position.

`select-cursor-end(`*destname* `[, ...])`
> Similar to `select-end`, except that it should be used with `select-cursor-start`.

`set-vt-font(`d/1/2/3/4/e/s `[,`*normalfont* `[,` *boldfont*`]])`
> Sets the font or fonts currently being used in the VT102 window. The first argument is a single character that specifies the font to be used: `d` or `D` indicates the default font (the font initially used when *xterm* was started); 1 through 4 indicate the fonts specified by the `font1` through `font4` resources; `e` or `E` indicates the normal and bold fonts that may be set through escape codes (or specified as the second and third action arguments, respectively); and `i` or `I` indicates the font selection (as made by programs such as *xfontsel*) indicated by the second action argument.

`start-extend()`
> Similar to `select-start` except that the selection is extended to the current pointer location.

`start-cursor-extend()`
> Similar to `select-extend` except that the selection is extended to the current text cursor position.

`string(`*string*`)`
> Inserts the specified text string as if it had been typed. Quotation is necessary if the string contains whitespace or non-alphanumeric characters. If the string argument begins with the characters "0x", it is interpreted as a hex character constant.

Reference Pages

scroll-back(*count* [, *units*])
>   Scrolls the text window backward so that text that had previously scrolled off the top of the screen is now visible. The *count* argument indicates the number of *units* (which may be page, halfpage, pixel, or line) by which to scroll.

scroll-forw(*count* [, *units*])
>   Scrolls is similar to scroll-back except that it scrolls in the other direction.

allow-send-events(*on/off/toggle*)
>   Sets or toggles the allowSendEvents resource and is also invoked by the allowsends entry in mainMenu.

set-logging(*on/off/toggle*)
>   Toggles the logging resource and is also invoked by the logging entry in main-Menu.

redraw()
>   Redraws the window and is also invoked by the redraw entry in mainMenu.

send-signal(*signame*)
>   Sends the signal named by *signame* (which may also be a number) to the *xterm* subprocess (the shell or program specified with the −e command line option) and is also invoked by the suspend, continue, interrupt, hangup, terminate, and kill entries in mainMenu. Allowable signal names are (case is not significant): suspend, tstp (if supported by the operating system), cont (if supported by the operating system), int, hup, term, and kill.

quit()
>   Sends a SIGHUP to the subprogram and exits. It is also invoked by the quit entry in mainMenu.

set-scrollbar(*on/off/toggle*)
>   Toggles the scrollbar resource and is also invoked by the scrollbar entry in vtMenu.

set-jumpscroll(*on/off/toggle*)
>   Toggles the jumpscroll resource and is also invoked by the jumpscroll entry in vtMenu.

set-reverse-video(*on/off/toggle*)
>   Toggles the reverseVideo resource and is also invoked by the reversevideo entry in vtMenu.

set-autowrap(*on/off/toggle*)
>   Toggles automatic wrapping of long lines and is also invoked by the autowrap entry in vtMenu.

set-reversewrap(*on/off/toggle*)
>   Toggles the reverseWrap resource and is also invoked by the reversewrap entry in vtMenu.

`set-autolinefeed(`*on/off/toggle*`)`
> Toggles automatic insertion of linefeeds and is also invoked by the `autolinefeed` entry in `vtMenu`.

`set-appcursor(`*on/off/toggle*`)`
> Toggles the application cursor key mode and is also invoked by the `appcursor` entry in `vtMenu`.

`set-appkeypad(`*on/off/toggle*`)`
> Toggles the application keypad mode and is also invoked by the `appkeypad` entry in `vtMenu`.

`set-scroll-on-key(`*on/off/toggle*`)`
> Toggles the `scrollKey` resource and is also invoked from the `scrollkey` entry in `vtMenu`.

`set-scroll-on-tty-output(`*on/off/toggle*`)`
> Toggles the `scrollTtyOutput` resource and is also invoked from the `scrollttyoutput` entry in `vtMenu`.

`set-allow132(`*on/off/toggle*`)`
> Toggles the `c132` resource and is also invoked from the `allow132` entry in `vtMenu`.

`set-cursesemul(`*on/off/toggle*`)`
> Toggles the `curses` resource and is also invoked from the `cursesemul` entry in `vtMenu`.

`set-visual-bell(`*on/off/toggle*`)`
> Toggles the `visualBell` resource and is also invoked by the `visualbell` entry in `vtMenu`.

`set-marginbell(`*on/off/toggle*`)`
> Toggles the `marginBell` resource and is also invoked from the `marginbell` entry in `vtMenu`.

`set-altscreen(`*on/off/toggle*`)`
> Toggles between the alternative and current screens.

`soft-reset()`
> Resets the scrolling region and is also invoked from the `softreset` entry in `vtMenu`.

`hard-reset()`
> Resets the scrolling region, tabs, window size, and cursor keys and clears the screen. It is also invoked from the `hardreset` entry in `vtMenu`.

`set-terminal-type(`*type*`)`
> Directs output to either the `vt` or `tek` windows, according to the `type` string. It is also invoked by the `tekmode` entry in `vtMenu` and the `vtmode` entry in `tekMenu`.

`set-visibility(`*vt/tek, on/off/toggle*`)`
> Controls whether or not the `vt` or `tek` windows are visible. It is also invoked from

Reference Pages

the `tekshow` and `vthide` entries in `vtMenu` and the `vtshow` and `tekhide` entries in `tekMenu`.

`set-tek-text(`*large/2/3/small*`)`

Sets font used in the Tektronix window to the value of the resources `tektextlarge`, `tektext2`, `tektext3`, and `tektextsmall` according to the argument. It is also invoked by the entries of the same names as the resources in `tekMenu`.

`tek-page()`

Clears the Tektronix window and is also invoked by the `tekpage` entry in `tekMenu`.

`tek-reset()`

Resets the Tektronix window and is also invoked by the `tekreset` entry in `tek-Menu`.

`tek-copy()`

Copies the escape codes used to generate the current window contents to a file in the current directory beginning with the name COPY. It is also invoked from the `tekcopy` entry in `tekMenu`.

The Tektronix window also has the following action:

`gin-press(`l/L/m/M/r/R`)`

Sends the indicated graphics input code.

The default bindings in the VT102 window are:

```
Shift     <KeyPress>    Prior:          scroll-back(1,halfpage)\n\
Shift     <KeyPress>    Next:           scroll-forw(1,halfpage)\n\
Shift     <KeyPress>    Select:         select-cursor-start()\
                                        select-cursor-end(PRIMARY,CUT_BUFFER0)\n\
Shift     <KeyPress>    Insert:         insert-selection(PRIMARY,CUT_BUFFER0)\n\
          ~Meta         <KeyPress>:     insert-seven-bit()\n\
          Meta          <KeyPress>:     insert-eight-bit()\n\
Ctrl      ~Meta         <Btn1Down>:     popup-menu(mainMenu)\n\
          ~Meta         <Btn1Down>:     select-start()\n\
          ~Meta         <Btn1Motion>:   select-extend()\n\
Ctrl      ~Meta         <Btn2Down>:     popup-menu(vtMenu)\n\
~Ctrl     ~Meta         <Btn2Down>:     ignore()\n\
~Ctrl     ~Meta         <Btn2Up>:       insert-selection(PRIMARY,CUT_BUFFER0)\n\
Ctrl      ~Meta         <Btn3Down>:     popup-menu(fontMenu)\n\
~Ctrl     ~Meta         <Btn3Down>:     start-extend()\n\
          ~Meta         <Btn3Motion>:   select-extend()\n\
~Ctrl     ~Meta         <BtnUp>:        select-end(PRIMARY,CUT_BUFFER0)\n\
                        <BtnDown>:      bell(0)
```

The default bindings in the Tektronix window are:

```
          ~Meta    <KeyPress>:    insert-seven-bit()\n\
          Meta     <KeyPress>:    insert-eight-bit()\n\
Ctrl      ~Meta    <Btn1Down>:    popup-menu(mainMenu)\n\
Ctrl      ~Meta    <Btn2Down>:    popup-menu(tekMenu)\n\
```

```
Shift   ~Meta   <Btn1Down>:    gin-press(L)\n\
        ~Meta   <Btn1Down>:    gin-press(l)\n\
Shift   ~Meta   <Btn2Down>:    gin-press(M)\n\
        ~Meta   <Btn2Down>:    gin-press(m)\n\
Shift   ~Meta   <Btn3Down>:    gin-press(R)\n\
        ~Meta   <Btn3Down>:    gin-press(r)
```

An Obsolete Feature: Starting xterm from init

Warning: This feature is now obsolete. It is not supported in Release 4. If Release 3 is running at your site, this method may still be in use. However, sites using this method should switch to *xdm* instead.

On operating systems such as BSD 4.3 and Ultrix, the server and initial login window are normally started automatically by *init*(8).

By convention, the pseudo-terminal with the highest minor device number (e.g., *devttyqf* and *devptyqf*) is renamed for the lowest display number (e.g., *devttyv0* and *devptyv0*). Machines that have more than one display can repeat this process using *ttyqe* for *ttyv1*, and so on.

Once the pseudo-terminals are in place, a line similar to the following may be added to */etc/ttys* (replacing *Xqvss* with the appropriate server and putting it all on one line):

```
ttyv0 "/usr/bin/X11/xterm -L -geom 80x24+1+1 -display :0"
      xterm on secure window="/usr/bin/X11/Xqvss :0"
```

Sites that used to run X10 should note that the colon in the server display number is required.

Although the release will install both the X server and *xterm* in */usr/bin/X11* by default, many sites choose to make a copy of both of these programs on the root partition (usually in */etc*) so that they may still be used even if the partition containing */usr/bin/X11* isn't mounted.

Some versions of *init* have relatively small program name buffer sizes and treat all sharp signs as comment delimiters. Sites that wish to list large numbers of options on the *xterm* line will need to write a small shell script to execute the long *xterm* line. The best solution, of course, is to use *xdm*.

Other Features

xterm automatically highlights the window border and text cursor when the pointer enters the window (selected) and unhighlights them when the pointer leaves the window (unselected). If the window is the focus window, then the window is highlighted no matter where the pointer is.

In VT102 mode, there are escape sequences to activate and deactivate an alternate screen buffer, which is the same size as the display area of the window. When activated, the current screen is saved and replaced with the alternate screen. Saving of lines scrolled off the top of the window is disabled until the normal screen is restored. The *termcap* entry for *xterm* allows the visual editor *vi* to switch to the alternate screen for editing, and to restore the screen on exit.

In either VT102 or Tektronix mode, there are escape sequences to change the name of the windows and to specify a new log file name.

Reference Pages

Environment

xterm sets the environment variables TERM and TERMCAP properly for the size window you have created. It also uses and sets the environment variable DISPLAY to specify which bitmap display terminal to use. The environment variable WINDOWID is set to the X window ID number of the *xterm* window.

Bugs

The class name is XTerm instead of Xterm.

The −L option is no longer needed since the display manager, *xdm*, handles logging in much more cleanly. No more trying to match colors in */etc/ttys* or worrying about an unwanted login window. (The −L option has been removed in Release 4.)

xterm will hang forever if you try to paste too much text at one time. It is both producer and consumer for the *pty* and can deadlock.

Variable-width fonts are not handled reasonably.

This program still needs to be rewritten. It should be split into very modular sections, with the various emulators being completely separate widgets that don't know about each other. Ideally, you'd like to be able to pick and choose emulator widgets and stick them into a single control widget.

The focus is considered lost if some other client (e.g., the window manager) grabs the pointer; it is difficult to do better without an addition to the protocol.

There needs to be a dialog box to allow entry of the log file name and the COPY filename.

Many of the options are not resettable after *xterm* starts.

The Tek widget does not support key/button re-binding.

See Also

X, resize, pty(4), tty(4); Appendix E, *xterm Control Sequences*.

Authors

Far too many people, including:

Loretta Guarino Reid (DEC-UEG-WSL), Joel McCormack (DEC-UEG-WSL), Terry Weissman (DEC-UEG-WSL), Edward Moy (Berkeley), Ralph R. Swick (MIT-Athena), Mark Vandevoorde (MIT-Athena), Bob McNamara (DEC-MAD), Jim Gettys (MIT-Athena), Bob Scheifler (MIT X Consortium), Doug Mink (SAO), Steve Pitschke (Stellar), Ron Newman (MIT-Athena), Jim Fulton (MIT X Consortium), and Dave Serisky (HP).

Name

xwd – place window images in a dump file.

Syntax

xwd [*options*]

Description

xwd stores window images in a specially formatted window dump file. This file can then be read by various other X utilities for redisplay, printing, editing, formatting, archiving, image processing, etc. The target window is selected by clicking the mouse in the desired window. The keyboard bell is rung once at the beginning of the dump and twice when the dump is completed.

Options

xwd accepts the following options:

-help   Prints out the 'Usage:' command syntax summary.

-nobdrs

      Specifies that the window dump should not include the pixels that compose the X window border. This is useful when the window contents are included in a document as an illustration.

-out *file*

      Allows you to specify the output file on the command line. The default outputs to the standard output (*stdout*).

-xy   Applies to color displays only. The –xy option selects 'XY' pixmap format dumping instead of the default 'Z' pixmap format.

-root   Makes a dump of the entire root window.

-add *value*

      Specifies a signed value to be added to every pixel.

-frame

      Indicates that the window manager frame should be included when manually selecting a window. (Available as of Release 4.)

-display [*host*]:*server*[.*screen*]

      Allows you to specify the host, server, and screen to connect to. *host* is the machine, *server* is the server number, and *screen* is the screen number. For example,

          xwd -display *your_node*:**0.1 &**

      specifies screen 1 on server 0 on the machine *your_node*. If the host is omitted, the local machine is assumed. If the screen is omitted, the screen 0 is assumed; the server and colon (:) are necessary in all cases.

Files

XWDFile.h

X Window Dump File format definition file.

See Also

X, xdpr, xpr, xwud.

Author

Tony Della Fera, Digital Equipment Corp., MIT Project Athena;
William F. Wyatt, Smithsonian Astrophysical Observatory.

Name

xwininfo – window information utility for X.

Syntax

xwininfo [*options*]

Description

xwininfo is a utility for displaying information about windows. Depending on which options are choosen, various information is displayed. If no options are choosen, −stats is assumed.

The user has the option of selecting the target window with the mouse (by clicking any mouse button in the desired window) or by specifying its window id on the command line with the −id option. Or instead of specifying the window by its id number, the −name option may be used to specify the window by name. There is also a special −root option to quickly obtain information on the root window.

Options

xwininfo accepts the following options:

−help Prints out the 'Usage:' command syntax summary.

−id *id*

Allows the user to specify a target window *id* on the command line rather than using the mouse to select the target window. This is very useful in debugging X applications where the target window is not mapped to the screen or where the use of the mouse might be impossible or interfere with the application.

−name *name*

Allows the user to specify that the window named *name* is the target window on the command line rather than using the mouse to select the target window.

−root Specifies that the root window is the target window. This is useful in situations where the root window is completely obscured.

−frame

Causes window manager frames not to be ignored when manually selecting windows. (Available as of Release 4.)

−int Specifies that all X window ids should be displayed as integer values. The default is to display them as hexadecimal values.

−tree Causes the root, parent, and children windows' ids and names of the selected window to be displayed.

−stats

Causes various attributes of the selected window having to do with its location and appearence to be displayed. Information displayed includes the location of the window, its width, height, depth, border width, class, and map state, colormap ID (if any), backing store hint, and the location of its corners. If *xwininfo* is run with no options, −stats is assumed.

-bits Causes the display of various attributes pertaining to the selected window's raw bits and how the selected window is to be stored to be displayed. Information displayed includes the selected window's bit gravity, window gravity, backing store hint, backing planes value, backing pixel, and whether or not the window has save-under set.

-events
Causes the selected window's event masks to be displayed. Both the event mask of events wanted by some client and the event mask of events not to propagate are displayed.

-size Causes the selected window's sizing hints to be displayed. Information displayed includes: for both the normal size hints and the zoom size hints, the user supplied location, if any; the program supplied location, if any; the user supplied size, if any; the program supplied size, if any; the minimum size, if any; the maximum size, if any; the resize increments, if any; and the minimum and maximum aspect ratios, if any.

-wm Causes the selected window's window manager hints to be displayed. Information displayed may include whether or not the application accepts input, what the window's icon window # and name is, where the window's icon should go, and what the window's initial state should be.

-metric
Causes all individual height, width, and x and y positions to be displayed in millimeters, as well as number of pixels, based on what the server thinks the resolution is. Geometry specifications that are in $+x+y$ form are not changed.

-english
Causes all individual height, width, and x and y positions to be displayed in inches (and feet, yards, and miles if necessary), as well as number of pixels. -metric and -english may be used at the same time.

-all A quick way to ask for all information possible.

-display [*host*]:*server*[.*screen*]
Allows you to specify the host, server, and screen to connect to. *host* specifies the machine, *server* specifies the server number, and *screen* specifies the screen number. For example,

    xwinfo -display *your_node*:**0.1**

specifies screen 1 of server 0 on the machine *your_node*. If the host is omitted, the local machine is assumed. If the screen is omitted, screen 0 is assumed; the server and colon (:) are necessary in all cases.

Examples

The following is sample output taken with no options specified. (The Motif window manager was running on the display. See Chapter 8, *Other Clients*, for a discussion of how the *mwm* frame can affect *xwininfo*'s results.)

```
xwininfo ==> Please select the window about which you
         ==> would like information by clicking the
         ==> mouse in that window.

xwininfo ==> Window id: 0x40000e (xterm)

         ==> Absolute upper-left X:  12
         ==> Absolute upper-left Y:  29
         ==> Relative upper-left X:  0
         ==> Relative upper-left Y:  0
         ==> Width: 818
         ==> Height: 484
         ==> Depth: 8
         ==> Border width: 0
         ==> Window class: InputOutput
         ==> Colormap: 0x8006b (installed)
         ==> Window Bit Gravity State: NorthWestGravity
         ==> Window Window Gravity State: NorthWestGravity
         ==> Window Backing Store State: NotUseful
         ==> Window Save Under State: no
         ==> Window Map State: IsViewable
         ==> Window Override Redirect State: no
         ==> Corners:  +12+29  -322+29  -322-387  +12-387
```

Bugs

Using -stats and -bits together shows some redundant information.

See Also

X, xprop.

Author

Mark Lillibridge, MIT Project Athena.

Reference Pages

Name

xwud – X window image displayer.

Syntax

xwud [*options*]

Description

xwud is an X Window System window image undumping utility. *xwud* allows X users to display a window image saved in a specially formatted dump file, such as one produced by *xwd*.

As of Release 4, *xwud* allows you to specify the coordinates at which this image is displayed using the -geometry option. In prior releases, *xwud* displayed the window image at the coordinates of the original window from which the dump was taken.

Options

xwud accepts the following options:

-help   Prints out a short description of the allowable options.

-in *file*

    Allows the user to explicitly specify the input file on the command line. The default is to take input from standard input.

-new   Forces creation of a new colormap for displaying the image. If the image characteristics happen to match those of the display, this can get the image on the screen faster, but at the cost of using a new colormap (which on most displays will cause other windows to go technicolor). (Available as of Release 4.)

-noclick

    Clicking any button in the window will terminate the application, unless this option is specified. Termination can always be achieved by typing ’q’, ’Q’, or Control-c. (Available as of Release 4.)

-plane *number*

    Selects a single bit plane of the image to display. Planes are numbered with zero being the least significant bit. This option can be used to figure out which plane to pass to *xpr* for printing. (Available as of Release 4.)

-raw   Forces the image to be displayed with whatever color values happen to currently exist on the screen. This option is mostly useful when undumping an image back onto the same screen that the image originally came from, while the original windows are still on the screen, and results in getting the image on the screen faster. (Available as of Release 4.)

-std *map_type*

    Causes the image to be displayed using the specified standard colormap. The property name is obtained by converting the type to uppercase, prepending "RGB_", and appending "_MAP". Typical types are best, default, and grey. See *xstdcmap* for one way of creating standard colormaps. (Available as of Release 4.)

-vis *vis_type_or_ID*

Allows you to specify a particular visual or visual class. The default is to pick the "best" one. A particular class can be specified: StaticGray, GrayScale, StaticColor, PseudoColor, DirectColor, or TrueColor. Or Match can be specified, meaning use the same class as the source image. Alternatively, an exact visual ID (specific to the server) can be specified, either as a hexadecimal number (prefixed with "0x") or as a decimal number. Finally, default can be specified, meaning to use the same class as the colormap of the root window. Case is not significant in any of these strings. (Available as of Release 4.)

-display [*host*]:*server*[.*screen*]

Allows you to specify the host, server, and screen to connect to. *host* specifies the machine, *server* specifies the server number, and *screen* specifies the screen number. For example,

xwud -display *your_node*:**0.1**

specifies screen 1 on server 0 on the machine *your_node*. If the host is omitted, the local machine is assumed. If the screen is omitted, the screen 0 is assumed; the server and colon (:) are necessary in all cases.

-geometry *geometry*

The *xwud* window is created with the specified size and location determined by the supplied geometry specification. The -geometry option can be (and often is) abbreviated to -g, unless there is a conflicting option that begins with "g." The argument to the geometry option (*geometry*) is referred to as a "standard geometry string," and has the form *width*x*height*±*xoff*±*yoff*. (This option is available for use with *xwud* as of Release 4.)

Typically, you will want to specify only the position and let the size default to the actual size of the image.

-bg *color*

If a bitmap image (or a single plane of an image) is displayed, this option can be used to specify the color to display for the "0" bits in the image. (Available as of Release 4.)

-fg *color*

If a bitmap image (or a single plane of an image) is displayed, this option can be used to specify the color to display for the "1" bits in the image. (Available as of Release 4.)

-rv   If a bitmap image (or a single plane of an image) is displayed, this option forces the foreground and background colors to be swapped. This may be needed when displaying a bitmap image which has the color sense of pixel values "0" and "1" reversed from what they are on your display. (Available as of Release 4.)

Files

XWDFile.h

X Window Dump File format definition file.

See Also

X, xdpr, xpr, xstdcmap, xwd.

Author

Release 4 version by Bob Scheifler, MIT X Consortium;

Release 3 version by Tony Della Fera, Digital Equipment Corp. and MIT Project Athena, and William F. Wyatt, Smithsonian Astrophysical Observatory.

Part Four:

Appendices

This part of the book contains useful reference information.

System Management
Release 4 Standard Fonts
Standard Bitmaps
Standard Cursors
xterm Control Sequences
Translation Table Syntax
Athena Widget Resources
Glossary

Index

A

System Management

This appendix discusses various tasks involved in X Window System management, mostly from the UNIX point of view.

In This Appendix:

A
System Management

X exists in so many incarnations and runs on so many different versions of UNIX (not to mention other operating systems) that it is difficult to be definitive about system management. This appendix discusses several topics relevant to setting up the standard version of X (with UNIX) and keeping it running smoothly. The range of subjects discussed is somewhat broad. Here's an overview.

This appendix primarily focuses on ways in which you can set up X to run automatically:

* *xdm*, the display manager.

* *xinit*.

Prior to Release 4, X could also be started on BSD 4.3 systems by running *xterm* from */etc/ttys*. This method has been phased out in Release 4. System administrators should switch to *xinit* or *xdm*.

In addition to information relating to starting X, we've also included brief discussions of other topics relevant to X system management:

* Including X in your search path.

* Setting the terminal type for *xterm*.

* Managing fonts.

* Addressing security issues and access control.

* Redirecting console messages.

* Maintaining log files.

* Changing the color name database.

Given the various incarnations of X and UNIX, you should be sure to check your system's documentation for additional (or contrary) details.

Including X in Your Search Path

The various X clients are normally stored in the directory */usr/bin/X11*. In order to invoke them by name like any other UNIX program, you need to make this directory part of your search path.*

This is normally done from your *.cshrc* (C shell) or *.profile* (Bourne shell) file, using a command similar to this:

Bourne Shell:
```
PATH=/usr/ucb:/bin:/usr/bin:/usr/bin/X11:Other directories;
        export PATH
```

C Shell:
```
set path=( /usr/ucb /bin /usr/bin /usr/bin/X11 Other directories)
```

The exact list of directories will differ from system to system. Be aware that directories are searched sequentially from left to right, so a command with the same name in an earlier directory will be found and used before one in a later directory. Many users take advantage of this fact to run customized versions of programs by putting "." (the current directory) or a local tools directory first in their search path. This works fine but you should be aware that this provides a security loophole that can be taken advantage of by an experienced system cracker. It's much safer to put a period at the end of your path, or eliminate it entirely.

If you have already logged in before adding the above line to your *.profile* or *.cshrc* file, you should log out and log in again, or type in the path-setting command at your prompt, so that it takes effect for your current session.

Setting the Terminal Type

Several *termcap* entries work with *xterm*, including "xterm," "vt102," "vt100," and "ansi." The *xterm* program automatically searches the *termcap* file for these entries (in this order) and sets the TERM and TERMCAP environment variables according to the entry it finds.

We've found that the *termcap* entry called "xterm," which comes with the standard X distribution, provides very reliable operation. We suggest you copy this entry from the *xterm* source directory (the file is called *termcap*) and add it as the first entry in the */etc/termcap* file on your system. This will allow you to set your terminal type to xterm.

---

*This topic isn't really part of system management but since we assume most people know how to do it, we didn't want to clutter up Chapter 2, *Getting Started*, with unnecessary discussion. On the other hand, the information is critical for those who don't already know it, so we wanted to put it somewhere!

A Startup Shell Script

It's a basic principle of UNIX to let the computer do the work. Accordingly, you'd no doubt like to run various X clients automatically whenever you log in.

The best way to do this is to create a script that runs the clients you want. Depending on how X is set up on your system, you can execute this script in one of two ways:*

- If *xdm* is running X, name the script *.xsession* and put it in your home directory. When you log in, *xdm* will automatically execute your *.xsession* script.

- If you are starting X with *xinit*, name the script *.xinitrc* and put it in your home directory. Then put the command *xinit* at the end of your *.login* file. *xinit* normally starts the server and runs a single *xterm* as a client but if a file called *.xinitrc* exists in your home directory, *xinit* starts the server and executes *.xinitrc*.

Methods of starting X automatically with *xinit* or *xdm* are discussed later in this appendix.

What Should Go in the Script

With some variation depending on the specific environment, in most cases your startup script should:

- Set the DISPLAY environment variable.
- Load your resources file with *xrdb*.
- Start the window manager.
- Start other clients you want on your default display, such as *xterm*, *oclock*, *xload*, etc.
- Run a console *xterm* process in the foreground; terminating this process will terminate the login session.

The script can be either a C shell or Bourne shell script. We've included two versions of one sample script in Bourne shell syntax: one for a session run on a workstation; the other for an X terminal session. The scripts appear as Example A-1 and Example A-2.†

In writing a script, keep in mind this limitation: running *xterm* from inside a shell script only works if the script executes quickly—or does not terminate at all.

The problem involves the way that *xterm* sets up its controlling terminal (*/dev/tty*). If the *xterm*'s parent process has died by the time the *xterm* gets around to setting up its controlling terminal, then */dev/tty* is redefined properly. If the parent has not died, however, *xterm* uses the parent's controlling terminal as its own. If the parent dies at any time after that, */dev/tty* will become undefined for that *xterm* (and all processes spawned by it).

---

*If you are still starting the X server from the */etc/ttys* file, this will bring up an *xterm* window with a login prompt. In this case, you can run the script to start other clients from your *.login* file. Note, however, that this method of starting the X server is not supported in Release 4. Your system administrator should switch to *xinit* or *xdm*.

†Thanks to Dave Curry for his help in preparing these samples.

A C shell script that starts up a few *xterm*s and then exits will probably work because the *xterm*'s parent process (the script) has exited by the time the *xterm*s start defining their */dev/tty*. If, however, there is a *sleep* or another command that takes a long time in the script after the line invoking the *xterm*, the parent may still be around when the *xterm* defines */dev/tty*. Then, when the script finally exits, */dev/tty* becomes undefined for those *xterm*s.

If you want to use a C shell script, this problem can be avoided by enclosing commands in parentheses. This causes the shell to fork an extra time before executing the command, and thus disassociates the process from the controlling terminal before the process begins.

Whether you are using a C shell or Bourne shell script, you should make the last command in the script be one that opens a window, and run that command in the foreground. Then the script will not terminate until that final foreground command terminates—that is, when you kill the window. In this case, all the *xterm*s will have the script's controlling tty but since the script is guaranteed to hang around, this causes no problem.

If you want to run remote processes in your startup script, it's a good idea to set the DISPLAY variable inside the script. You can then run a client on a remote machine, but specify that the window be created on your local display by by using the DISPLAY variable as the argument to the -display option.

As explained in Chapter 3, *Working in the X Environment*, clients running on the local machine access the DISPLAY variable to determine on which physical display to create windows. Without explicit settings, both *xdm* and *xinit* will automatically set DISPLAY to unix:0.0 (or some variation thereof), which defaults to the local host.

If you only run processes on the local host, you don't have to deal with issues involving the DISPLAY setting. However, if you want to run a process on a remote machine and display the results locally, things become more complicated. A client running on a remote machine does not have access to the DISPLAY variable on the local machine. By default a client running on a remote machine checks the DISPLAY setting on *that* machine.

You can override the DISPLAY environment variable that a client accesses by using the -display option when you run the command. Think of -display as a pointer to the physical display on which you want the window to appear. In order to tell a client to connect to a display, you must identify it by its unique name on the network. (You cannot identify your display by the setting given to it by *xinit* or *xdm*—unix:0.0, :0.0, or some variation.)

We suggest you set the DISPLAY explicitly to the display's unique network name. For a workstation or other single-user system, you should determine the appropriate host name with the *hostname* command, as shown in the script below.

Note that the *hostname* command is a BSD command. For a System V equivalent, see your UNIX documentation. Note also that in this script, *sed* is used to strip domained-based hostnames such as *isla.ora.com* back to their initial term, the actual system name. If you are running in a standalone environment, this is not necessary.

Once DISPLAY is set, you can easily run a client on a remote machine and specify that the window be created on the local display, using a command line similar to:

```
% rsh oz xterm -display $DISPLAY
```

This command runs an *xterm* on the remote system oz, while the −display option directs that the window be opened on DISPLAY. Note that setting the DISPLAY variable using *hostname* (or another command) and then using the variable as an argument to −display makes the startup script portable.

Be aware that setting the DISPLAY variable in this way has some limitations, however. If you're using an X terminal, you cannot set DISPLAY using the *hostname* command. (This would set your DISPLAY variable to the display of the host to which your terminal is connected, rather than the terminal itself.) Instead you should explicitly set DISPLAY to the network name of your X terminal.* In Bourne shell syntax, you would set your DISPLAY variable to ncd5.camb.com:0.0 using the lines:

```
DISPLAY=ncd5.camb.com:0.0
export DISPLAY
```

You can then run a client on a remote machine using the −display option with an argument of DISPLAY, as described previously. However, since DISPLAY is set explicitly to a particular X terminal, a script using this sequence is not portable.

Example A-1 shows a startup Bourne shell script for a workstation, which would open windows on the display, as shown in Figure A-1. You can use this script even if you normally use the C shell for interactive use. Note that the comments should probably not be present in the working script. While they are ignored, they do slow down execution and on a loaded system can cause X to start up improperly.

Example A-1. Startup Bourne shell script for a workstation

```
#!/bin/sh

# Get hostname, strip the domain name if there is one

cpu=`hostname | sed -e 's/\..*//'`

# If no DISPLAY is set, set one.

if [ -z $DISPLAY ]
then
     DISPLAY=$cpu:0
fi

# Special-case the "bogus" non-network display names and
# make sure we can always execute remote clients

case $DISPLAY in
     unix:0.0|unix:0|:0.0|:0)DISPLAY="$cpu:0";;
esac
export DISPLAY

# Load resource definitions from .Xresources

xrdb -Dhostname=$cpu $HOME/.Xresources
```

---

*Some X terminals allow you to save the DISPLAY setting in ROM, which is accessed by *xdm* when you log in. If *xdm* is running X on your system and your X terminal stores its DISPLAY setting in this manner, it may not be necessary to set the DISPLAY variable in your startup script. Consult your system administrator and your X terminal documentation for details. In any case, though setting the DISPLAY variable in your startup script may be redundant, it cannot be harmful.

```
# Set keyclick off and invoke the screen saver after
# seven minutes of idleness
xset c off s 420
# Start the mwm window manager
mwm &
# Now start up some xterms
# Start an xterm in lower-left corner
xterm -geometry 80x22+0-0 &
# Place an xterm next to it
xterm -geometry 80x22+530-0 &
# remote xterm above (but below console xterm at top)
rsh ora xterm -geometry 80x28+0+135 -display $DISPLAY &
# Now start up other clients
# digital xclock in upper-right corner
xclock -digital -update 1 -geometry -0+0 &
# xcalc just below it;
xcalc -geometry -0+75 &
#xload at bottom of xcalc
xload -geometry -0+350 &

# Start a console xterm window.
# This is the only xterm that should be run in the foreground.
# Killing this window will shut down X.

# Use this line with xinit; comment out if you use xdm
exec xterm -C -geometry 80x5+0+0
# Uncomment this line if you use xdm
# exec xterm -C -ls -geometry 80x5+0+0
```

The script in Example A-2 starts the same session on the X terminal identified by the name ncd5.camb.com. Since this script runs the same clients as in the previous script, we've left out most of the comments. (Note that we're taking a slight liberty using the same geometry specifications for this X terminal session as for the previous workstation session; most X terminals have smaller dimensions.)

Example A-2. Startup Bourne shell script for an X terminal

```
#!/bin/sh
# Set the display
DISPLAY=ncd5.camb.com:0.0
export DISPLAY

# Load resource definitions from .Xresources

xrdb -load $HOME/.Xresources
```

```
xset c off s 420
mwm &
xterm -geometry 80x22+0-0 &
xterm -geometry 80x22+530-0 &
rsh ora xterm -geometry 80x28+0+135 -display $DISPLAY &
xclock -digital -update 1 -geometry -0+0 &
xcalc -geometry -0+75 &
xload -geometry -0+350 &

# Use this line with xinit; comment out if you use xdm

exec xterm -C -geometry 80x5+0+0

# Uncomment this line if you use xdm
# exec xterm -C -ls -geometry 80x5+0+0
```

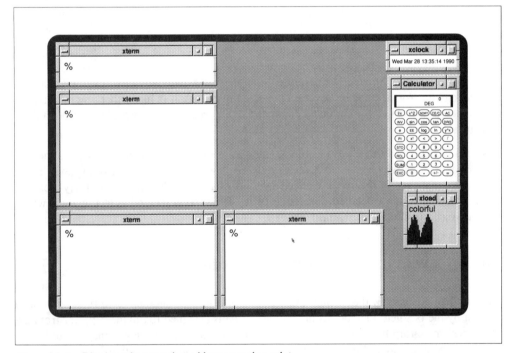

Figure A-1. Display after running either sample script

Note that all programs that create windows (and hence don't run quickly and then go away) are run in the background, with the exception of the final *xterm* window. This will cause the script to simulate the behavior of the console *xterm* normally started by *xinit* or *xdm*. The −C option specified with the console *xterm* window redirects messages sent to /dev/console to that *xterm* window. This option is only supported in some implementations of X; see your documentation. For additional information, see the section "Console Messages" later in this appendix.

System Management

You may want to start the console *xterm* window as an icon, using the `-iconic` option, so you're less likely to terminate the window inadvertently and end the session. In the example, though, we simply make the window only five lines high, so that we can still see console messages but won't be tempted to use it for most purposes.

Note that if you are using *xdm*, you want to run the final *xterm* with the `-ls` option, to make that window be your login shell. If you are using *xinit*, you should definitely *not* use this option! Since *xinit* is invoked from the end of the *.login* file (instead of directly by *xdm* before login), you will end up in an infinite loop.

Note that windows are actually arranged in a "tiled" fashion, with two large xterm windows side by side on the bottom of the screen, a smaller one (connected to a remote system) above, and the "desk accessories" lined up in the upper-left corner. This leaves some room free for new windows or for invoking the Root Menu menu on the root window. This is ideal for our purposes, which are mainly editing, formatting, and testing examples for books. Depending on what you do, another arrangement might be better.*

Starting X

In Chapter 2, *Getting Started*, we described how to start X manually. However, on a single-user workstation (or perhaps on several connected displays), it is likely that you might want X to come up automatically. In many commercial X ports, this may already have been done for you.

This section describes three ways to run X automatically. The first method involves the display manager, *xdm*, which can run X on a single display or several connected displays. Since the display manager is the recommended method of running X and is extremely flexible, we're including a fairly detailed discussion of it. The second method is to use *xinit*, which was introduced in Chapter 2, *Getting Started*.

Starting X with the Display Manager, xdm

Introduced in Release 3, the display manager, *xdm*, offers an alternative to running X with *xinit* (or by the obsolete method, from */etc/ttys*). *xdm* is designed to run the X server from the */etc/rc* system startup file. In its most basic implementation, the display manager emulates a *login* or *getty* on a standard terminal, keeping the server running, prompting for a user's name and password, and managing a standard login session.

---

*Note that this file was developed for and run on a Sun workstation. Differences in pixel sizes may make the coordinates and sizes of various windows come out differently on other hardware.

However, *xdm* has far more powerful and versatile capabilities. Users can design their own login sessions, using *.xsession* files. You can also customize special *xdm* files to manage several connected displays (both local and remote), and to set system-wide and user-specific X resources.

A not-so-obvious limitation of *xdm* is that it does not work well if you are using other window systems (in addition to X). If you want to use multiple window systems on the same hardware, you should continue to use *xinit* for the time being. Future releases of *xdm* should overcome these limitations.

The functionality of *xdm* has been expanded in Release 4, though many features have not changed since Release 3. The following sections describe the Release 4 version of *xdm*. Release 4 specific features are noted.

First, we'll give you the basics of using *xdm* to run X on a single display and then give you some tips on how to design your own user session and manage multiple displays.

Getting Started with xdm on a Single Display

To have *xdm* run X on a single display, the system administrator should perform three simple tasks:

1. Set up the *xdm* configuration file and other special files, as described in the next section.

2. Put the line */usr/bin/X11/xdm* at the end of */etc/rc* or other similar system startup file.

3. It's also a good idea to turn off the "console" in */etc/ttys* on a single-user workstation, although this is discretionary. (As we'll see, the display manager provides its own login window. Turning off the console prevents the standard UNIX prompt from being simultaneously displayed on the full screen when *xdm* is started. Keep in mind this will also prevent system messages from being sent to the console but they should still be saved in */usr/adm/messages*.) How you'd turn off the "console" depends on the version of UNIX you are running. The procedure and the system file you edit may differ from system to system. See the *getty*(8) and *init*(8) reference pages in your UNIX documentation for details.

Once you perform these steps, as long as UNIX is running, *xdm* should keep the X server running, allow users to log on and off, and manage a simple login session. The following sections describe the steps you need to get started with *xdm* in greater detail.

Setting Up the Configuration File and Other Special Files

In order to run X, *xdm* uses a configuration file and several special files that specify such things as the server, basic login session, and an error log file.

Be aware that *xdm should* be able to work in a very rudimentary fashion *without any* special files. However, a problem with Release 4 may require that at least two of the special files be present (namely, *xdm-config* and *Xservers*). These limitations should be removed by patches to the release. If this bug has been patched and *xdm* finds no special files, it will still start the server and a login *xterm* window. This default action can be very helpful, because it allows you to log in even if the special files have been inadvertently removed or corrupted.

Despite the potential to work in a rudimentary fashion without special files, *xdm* was not intended to be run in this way. For most purposes, system administrators will want to use and very likely customize the special files to have *xdm* run X in a manner more suitable for the particular system.

The configuration file and some prototypical special files can be found in the *config* directory under the *xdm* source directory. (Starting from the top of the X11 source tree, the directory is *mit/clients/xdm/config* .) Table A-1 lists some of the more commonly used special files for Release 4.

Table A-1. xdm Special Files

File	What it specifies
xdm-config	Configuration parameters.
Xservers	List of displays to manage.
xdm-errors	*xdm* error log file.
xdm-pid	Contains ID of the *xdm* parent process (Available as of Release 4).
Xresources	Resources to load (with xrdb).
Xsession	Default login session.
Xstartup	Startup procedure.
Xreset	Reset procedure.

As you can see, the file *xdm-pid* has been added in Release 4; it represents new functionality. The *Xstartup* and *Xreset* files can still be used to affect *xdm* in Release 4 but there are no default files. We'll discuss these and some of the other special files in greater detail later in this appendix.

Each of the special files can be specified by an *xdm* command line option. However, it's more efficient to specify the files—other than the single *xdm* configuration file—as resources and put those resources in the configuration file itself. The configuration file shipped with the standard version of X is called *xdm-config* and is shown in Figure A-2.

```
DisplayManager.servers:          /usr/lib/X11/xdm/Xservers
DisplayManager.errorLogFile:     /usr/lib/X11/xdm/xdm-errors
DisplayManager.pidFile:          /usr/lib/X11/xdm/xdm-pid
DisplayManager*resources:        /usr/lib/X11/xdm/Xresources
DisplayManager*session:          /usr/lib/X11/xdm/Xsession
DisplayManager._0.authorize:     true
DisplayManager*authorize:        false
```

Figure A-2. Default xdm-config file

These three *xdm-config* file entries have been added in Release 4:

```
DisplayManager.pidFile:        /usr/lib/X11/xdm/xdm-pid
DisplayManager._0.authorize:   true
DisplayManager*authorize:      false
```

These entries represent new *xdm* functionality, which will be discussed later in this appendix.

In effect, most of the entries in the default configuration file are just pointers to the other special files *xdm* uses. Notice also that, in most cases, the configuration file has the same syntax as any resource file. Release 4 introduces a variation from traditional resource syntax, which appears in this line:

```
DisplayManager._0.authorize:      true
```

The _0 represents the display name :0. Certain *xdm* resource variables can be display specific. When a display name is a component of an *xdm* resource specification, the parts of the display name should be connected by underscores, rather than by dots and colons (as is done when you specify a display name on the command line). This is because dots and colons have special meaning for the resource manager. (Dots separate resource variable components; a colon signals the end of the variable and the beginning of the value field. See Chapter 10, *Setting Resources*, for more information.) Underscores allow a display name to be treated as a single resource variable component. This syntax variance is applicable only to Release 4. The Release 3 version of *xdm* compensates for resource syntax anomalies—display name components are separated by dots.

In addition to the variables set in the default *xdm-config* file, you can specify several other display manager resources in the configuration file. See the *xdm* reference page in Part Three of this guide for a complete list of resource variables.

To get started using *xdm*, the system administrator should make a directory (*/usr/lib/X11/xdm* is suggested) and copy these default special files into it:

- *xdm-config*.

- *Xresources*.

- *Xsession*.

As we'll see later, each of the standard files can be customized but in many cases the defaults will be sufficient to run X on a single display.*

Next, the system administrator should create an *Xservers* file containing an entry for the local display. As we've said, if the Release 4 *xdm* has been updated with all relevant patches, the *Xservers* file is not necessary for *xdm* to run X on a single display. However, if you are running Release 4 without the relevant patches, *xdm* has a bug that requires you to set up an *Xservers* file before *xdm* can work properly. (The bug also requires an *xdm-config* file be

---

*For our purposes, we are talking about the default special files provided with the standard release of X. Keep in mind that you can rewrite the resource definitions in the *xdm-config* file to specify files of any name (in any directory) as the so-called special files. (The configuration file also can have any name you like and be stored in any directory). If you use a filename other than *xdm-config*, you need to specify that filename (and its explicit path) with the -config option after the *xdm* command. See the *xdm* reference page in Part Three of this guide for more information.)

present.) Since setting up an *Xservers* file is fairly simple to do and a good way to avoid potential problems, we recommend that you do so before placing the *xdm* command in one of the system startup files.

Most workstations can be run using an *Xservers* file made up of this line:

```
:0 local /usr/bin/X11/X
```

This *Xservers* file is probably adequate for most workstations. However, if X does not run properly on your single display, you should edit the *Xservers* file. See "The Xservers File" later in this appendix and the *xdm* reference page in Part Three of this guide for more information about file syntax.

The Standard Login Session

Once you copy the special files to */usr/lib/X11/xdm* and create a single-entry *Xservers* file, if you want *xdm* simply to run the X server on the local display, prompt for username and password, and run a simple login session, you should simply be able to add this line to the end of the */etc/rc* file:

```
/usr/bin/X11/xdm
```

(Depending on your version of UNIX, you may want to add this line to */etc/rc.local*, */etc/rc2* or some other file. Consult your operating system documentation. Regardless of the file to which it is added, the display manager should be the last process run.)

After this simple modification, when UNIX is put into multiuser mode, *xdm* automatically starts the X server and keeps it running.

xdm also takes over the login procedure for displays specified in the *Xservers* file, supplying username and password prompts normally provided by the *getty* and *login* programs. Without modification, *xdm* provides the login window pictured in Figure 2-1 of Chapter 2, *Getting Started*.

This login procedure is controlled by the authentication widget (part of the *xdm* program), which in effect "authenticates" the user and password. You can customize the login window by setting resources for the authentication widget in the *Xresources* file. (These resources must be set in the *Xresources* file in the directory */usr/lib/X11/xdm* to take effect. They cannot be set in a resources file in a user's home directory, since that file is not loaded into the resource manager until after the login procedure.) Among the customizable features are the login greeting (by default, *Welcome to the X Window System*), the size and position of the window, and colors and fonts of the text displayed or typed in the window. See the *xdm* reference page in Part Three of this guide for a complete list of resources.

Each time a user successfully logs on, *xdm* looks for a file called *.xsession* in the user's home directory. If that file exists and is an executable script, *xdm* runs it as the user's login session. The *.xsession* file should follow the general guidelines for startup scripts described earlier in this appendix.

If you've just set up *xdm*, users may not have written *.xsession* scripts. If *xdm* finds no *.xsession* file in a user's home directory, it provides a default session, consisting of these commands (excerpted from the standard *Xsession* file):

```
resources=$HOME/.Xresources
xrdb -load $resources

twm &

exec xterm -geometry 80x24+10+10 -ls
```

This default session has three elements. First, *xdm* checks the user's home directory for a file called *.Xresources*. If that file exists, it is loaded into the resource manager with *xrdb*. Second, the window manager, *twm*, is started. Third, the console *xterm* window is started with a login shell (-ls) in the foreground. In Motif environments, system administrators will want to edit the standard *Xsession* file so that the *mwm* window manager is automatically invoked.

After this basic session has been started, the screen looks something like Figure 2-3 and the user is ready to work.

Customizing xdm

The display manager can do far more than run the simple session described above. Any of the special files can be edited to customize the display manager for your site. For example, by editing the *Xservers* file, you can set up *xdm* to run multiple displays, such as X terminals.*

Remember that, if *xdm* has been modified with the proper Release 4 patches, *none* of the special files (not even the *xdm-config* file) is *absolutely necessary* to run X on a single display. In a worst-case scenario—if all the special files are removed or corrupted—*xdm* has reasonable defaults that will allow you to log in and work. Depending on your system configuration, you may elect not to use some of the special files. For example, the Release 4 *xdm* works well without *Xstartup* and *Xreset* files in many environments. As we've said, if no *Xsession* is specified, *xterm* is executed, etc. (If you decide not to use one of the special files listed in the default *xdm-config* file, remember to remove the pointer to it from the file!)

What the special files provide is the flexibility to configure *xdm* for your site, perhaps running X on several displays, each possibly with a different default session, different resources for the authentication widget, etc.

If you examine the default configuration file, you'll notice most of the resources are specified with loose bindings. This means that the specified resource (for example, *Xsession*) will apply to all displays being run by *xdm*. By using tight bindings in the configuration file, you

---

*Generally, this modification is *required* for *xdm* to run sessions on X terminals. However, as we'll see, an increasing number of X terminals do not require an *Xservers* file entry in order to be controlled by *xdm*. See "X Terminals and the XDM Control Protocol" later in this appendix.

can also specify resources that only take effect on a specific display. To specify a resource for a particular display, just insert the name of the display between `DisplayManager` and the final resource variable. For example, say *xdm* is running X on a workstation (named : 0) and a connected X terminal (`visual:0`). You could specify two different default sessions by using resource definitions (in the configuration file) similar to this:

```
DisplayManager._0.session:        /usr/lib/X11/xdm/Xsession.ws
DisplayManager.visual_0.session: /usr/lib/X11/xdm/Xsession.visual
```

Note that an *xdm* resource specification uses an underscore in place of the colon in a display name. (As discussed earlier, the use of underscores has been introduced in Release 4.) You should match the display name syntax for resources intended to be used on the same display. For example, you might have these `resources` variable settings to match the `session` resource specifications above:

```
DisplayManager._0.resources: /usr/lib/X11/xdm/Xresources.ws
DisplayManager.visual_0.resources: /usr/lib/X11/xdm/Xresources.visual
```

The following sections discuss some possible customizations of the default special files. With the vast number of possible system configurations and user preferences, you should consult the *xdm* reference page in Part Three of this guide for more information.

The Xservers File

As of Release 4, the *xdm* source directory contains two sample *Xservers* files, *Xservers.ws* and *Xservers.fs*, which illustrate file entries for workstations and file servers (such as X terminals), respectively. To run *xdm* on a single workstation, you should create an *Xservers* file using the *Xservers.ws* file as a guide. As we'll see later, in most circumstances, you must edit the *Xservers* file to specify additional displays for *xdm* to manage.

Each entry in the *Xservers* file usually has three or four elements: the display name, an optional display class, the display type, and the server program name (and its arguments, typically the display number). (Since an X terminal runs its own server, the final argument can be a comment, such as "Joe's X terminal.") Possible display types are described on the *xdm* reference page in Part Three of this guide.

Most workstations have a single display numbered 0 of the type *local*, as illustrated by the typical *Xservers* file entry for a workstation:

```
:0 local /usr/bin/X11/X
```

The display class part of the *Xservers* entry is new as of Release 4. The sample entry above does not contain a display class but it would normally be the second part, between the display name and type, as in:

```
:0 display_class local /usr/bin/X11/X
```

The display class is determined by the machine you are using and should be provided by the hardware vendor. The use of the display class is related to an underlying feature of the Release 4 *xdm*, the X Display Manager Control Protocol (XDMCP), which is described later in this appendix. For now suffice it to say that, in most circumstances, you do not have to supply a class name within an *Xservers* file entry.

For *xdm* to run sessions on most X terminals, you must add specifications for these displays to the *Xservers* file, using the sample file *Xservers.fs* from the *xdm* source directory as a template. For instance, say you have two X terminals hooked up to a workstation. (As of Release 4, most X terminals are of the display type *foreign*. In Release 3, most X terminals are of the display type *transient*.) Your *Xservers* file might look like this:

```
:0        local    /usr/bin/X11/X
visual:0  foreign  Lucy's Visual
ncd:0     foreign  Ricky's NCD16
```

Notice that the final element of each X terminal entry is a comment. Using this *Xservers* file, *xdm* provides login windows on the two X terminals, as well as the workstation, and runs a session for any user who logs on.

If you edit the *Xservers* file while the server is running, *xdm* will not be aware of the changes. You can make *xdm* reread the *Xservers* file (or another file specified by the resource `DisplayManager.servers`) by sending the *xdm* parent process a SIGHUP. Use the UNIX *kill* command with the `-HUP` option (for SIGHUP) and the process ID number of *xdm*.

It's likely there will be multiple *xdm* processes, since the program forks a child process for every display it's managing. As of Release 4, the ID of the parent process is stored in the file specified by the resource `DisplayManager.pidFile`—usually */usr/lib/X11/xdm/xdm-pid*.

```
% kill -HUP process-ID
```

If a new entry was added, the display manager starts a session on that display. If an entry has been removed, the display manager terminates any session on that display without notice and no new sessions will be started.

Once you edit the *Xservers* file to reflect the different displays you want to manage, you can enter other display-specific resources in the configuration file.

Be aware that communication problems can arise between the display manager and many autonomous displays (primarily X terminals). If the main display is powered off or reset, *xdm* may not detect that the server has been stopped and restarted, and thus may not send new login windows to connected displays. In the spring of 1989, the X Consortium proposed a standard protocol between displays and display managers that would avert these problems. The X Display Manager Control Protocol (XDMCP) was adopted and implemented by the Release 4 *xdm* but not all X terminals implement it yet. We'll discuss the goals of this protocol at greater length in "X Terminals and the XDM Control Protocol" later in this appendix. For now, be aware that the XDMCP will eventually eliminate the need for *Xservers* file entries for X terminals. Currently, however, chances are that your X terminal does not understand the XDMCP and requires an *Xservers* file entry.

The Xsession File and .xsession Scripts

Depending on the needs of your site, you can edit the *Xsession* file to make the default session anything you want. You can specify an alternative window manager, perhaps even use another program to load resources, and execute any combination of clients.

Another strength of *xdm* is that it provides for each user to design his or her own *.xsession* file. See "A Startup Shell Script" earlier in this appendix for more information on writing a *.xsession* file.

Be aware that if you're testing a *.xsession* script and it doesn't work, by default *xdm* will not let you log in (using the normal method) to fix it. However, *xdm* does provide an escape hatch for these situations, which is explained in the following section.

The Xresources File

The *Xresources* file is where you should specify resources for the authentication widget. See the *xdm* reference page in Part Three of this guide for a complete list of resource variables.

As of Release 4, the default *Xresources* file contains these event translations, which allow users to log in if a *.xsession* script doesn't work:

```
xlogin*login.translations: #override\
        <Key>F1: set-session-argument(failsafe) finish-field()\n\
        <Key>Return: set-session-argument() finish-field()
```

This translation table specifies that if you type the F1 key (rather than Return) after your password when logging in, a "failsafe" session, consisting of a simple login *xterm* window, will be executed. This will enable you to edit the non-functioning *.xsession* file. See the *xdm* reference page in Part Three of this guide for more information. (See Chapter 10, *Setting Resources*, and , for a discussion of event translations.)

The Error Log File

xdm errors are normally printed to the console. It's wise to redirect them to a file. The default configuration file sets the resource `DisplayManager.errorLogFile` to */usr/lib/X11/xdm/xdm-errors*. The *xdm-errors* file can be very helpful if you are testing various *xdm* configurations.

The xdm-pid File

Added to *xdm* as of Release 4, the *xdm-pid* file stores the ID number of the *xdm* parent process. If you edit the *Xservers* file while the server is running, *xdm* will not be aware of the changes. You can make *xdm* reread the *xdm-config* file and the *Xservers* file (or another file specified by the resource `DisplayManager.servers`) by sending the *xdm* parent process a SIGHUP.

To make *xdm* aware of changes to the *Xservers* file, use the UNIX *kill* command with the −HUP option (for SIGHUP) and the process ID number of *xdm* stored in the *xdm-pid* file. (See "The Xservers File" earlier in this appendix for an example.)

Xstartup and Xreset

As stated previously, the *Xstartup* and *Xreset* files mentioned in Table A-3 can still be used to affect *xdm* in Release 4 but there are no default files; thus, they are not specified in the default configuration file.

The *Xstartup* file is intended to be a script that is run as root before starting the user session. You might want to write a script containing commands to make fake entries in */etc/utmp*, mount users' home directories from file servers, display a message of the day, or abort the session if logins are not currently allowed.

The *Xreset* file is intended to be a script that is run as root after a user session has been ended. You might want to write a script to undo the effects of commands in *Xstartup*, perhaps removing fake entries from */etc/utmp*, or unmounting directories from file servers.

See the *xdm* reference page for more information about the *Xstartup* and *Xreset* files.

Security and the authorize Resource

In addition to pointers to several special files, the *xdm-config* file contains these resource specifications:

```
DisplayManager._0.authorize:    true
DisplayManager*authorize:    false
```

Available as of Release 4, the `authorize` resource represents a new method of security for X, which *xdm* can be set up to provide. The first resource specification above sets a user-based server access scheme to work on the local display. The second one turns the scheme off on all other displays. These defaults should be compatible with running X on the local display and most X terminals that might be connected to it. See "User-based Access: xdm and the .Xauthority File" later in this appendix and the *xdm* reference page in Part Three of this guide for more about authorization.

Stopping xdm and the Server

By default, *xdm* automatically restarts the server if the server is killed. If you don't want this boomerang effect, set this resource in the *xdm-config* file:

```
DisplayManager.DISPLAY.terminateServer: true
```

Then if you kill the server and all *xdm* processes, X will exit.

X Terminals and the XDM Control Protocol

The X Display Manager Control Protocol (XDMCP), introduced at Release 4, facilitates the connection of X terminals to remote hosts via *xdm*. From a user's standpoint, the main advantage of XDMCP is that it allows you to turn an X terminal off and on again, while maintaining the connection to the remote host. When you turn on an X terminal, *xdm* should automatically display a login window. The exchange of information between the X terminal and the remote host is invisible to the user. In fact, XDMCP and *xdm* are intended to make X terminals as easy to use as traditional character terminals. Under the X Display Manager Control Protocol, an X terminal basically requests a connection to a remote host, is recognized by the host, and is sent a login prompt by *xdm*.

Prior to the adoption of this protocol, *xdm* was not equipped to reconnect to X terminals that had been turned off and on again. In most cases, X terminals had to be left on at all times. If a terminal was turned off, it was often necessary to kill the associated *xdm* process; *xdm* would then restart itself and reestablish the connection, again displaying the login window.

XDMCP is intended to solve problems like this. Be aware, however, that the X terminals in question must be programmed to interpret XDMCP or modified to do so. At the time of Release 4, virtually no X terminals in the market supported XDMCP. Protocol-compatible X terminals should become available in increasing numbers by the fall of 1990. If you're using an older X terminal, chances are that the programs controlling it must be upgraded to communicate via XDMCP.

If you are using X terminals at your site, the way you set up *xdm* partially depends on whether the terminals can communicate via the XDMCP. If a terminal *can't* communicate in this way, the *Xservers* file must include an entry for it and the terminal must be left on at all times to maintain the connection to the host via *xdm*. If a terminal *can* communicate via the protocol, no *Xservers* file entry is necessary and the terminal can be turned on and off, while still maintaining the connection to the host. Refer your X terminal documentation to find out whether it's XDMCP compatible.

The XDMCP helps clarify the actual purpose of the *Xservers* file. The file is actually a list of displays to which *xdm* must perpetually maintain a connection. By contrast, the XDMCP is a dynamic mechanism whereby connections are made when requested by a display, such as a workstation or a newer X terminal, that can communicate via the protocol.

XDMCP also affects the *Xservers* file entry for the host. If you are running Release 4, it is recommended that the *Xservers* file entry for the host include a display class name, which should be provided by the hardware manufacturer. You can use this name in the *xdm-config* file to specify resources by display class, rather than by individual display.

Starting X with xinit

The *xinit* program is used to start the server and a first client program, by default an *xterm* window. Starting X manually with *xinit* is described in Chapter 2, *Getting Started*. You can also use *xinit* to start X automatically.

The easiest way to do this is to run *xinit* from your *.login* or *.profile* file. (If you are using System V, this may be the only reliable way to run *xinit*.)

xinit will look in your home directory for a file called *.xserverrc* to run as a shell script to start up the server. If there is no such script, *xinit* will start the server X on the display : 0.

xinit will also look in your home directory for a file called *.xinitrc* to run as a login script, such as the one described earlier in this appendix. If no such script is found, it will execute a login *xterm* window.

With System V only, you might try to run *xinit* from the */etc/inittab* terminal initialization file. This file is analogous to the BSD 4.3 */etc/ttys*. The */etc/inittab* file normally has an entry for each serial port on a system, plus several entries that are used during the boot process. Note that the concept of pseudo-terminals, or ptys (which X relies on) is foreign to System V. All System V servers will have had to do some system hacking to add support for ptys. How this is done will vary from system to system. As a result, we're going to beg off on describing *inittab* in detail, and refer you to your system documentation. Again, it is also possible that there will be problems with the controlling tty.

See the *xinit* reference page in Part Three of this guide for more information.

Server Access Control

X runs in a networked environment. Because of X's design, your workstation is no longer your private preserve but hypothetically can be accessed by any other host on the network. This is the true meaning of the server concept: your display can serve clients on any system, and clients on your system can display on any other screen.

The possibilities for abuse are considerable. However, there are two access control mechanisms, one host-based and one user-based. The host-based scheme involves a system file (*/etc/Xn.hosts*) and can be controlled using the *xhost* client. The user-based scheme involves authorization capabilities provided by the display manager, *xdm*, as of Release 4, and depends upon the newly introduced X Display Manager Control Protocol (XDMCP). As we'll see, since most X terminals cannot interpret the XDMCP at this time, the usefulness of this latter access control mechanism is currently somewhat limited.

These two access control methods are discussed briefly in the following sections. For more information, see the *Xserver*, *xhost*, *xdm*, and *xauth* reference pages in Part Three of this guide.

Host-based Access and the xhost Client

The */etc/Xn.hosts* file (where *n* is the number of the display) contains a list of systems that are allowed to access the server. By default, this file contains only the name of the local host. Edit this file so that it contains the list of systems you want to have access to your server on a regular basis.

The *xhost* client can be used to give (or deny) systems access to the server interactively, possibly overriding the contents of */etc/Xn.hosts*. (The *xhost* client can also be run from a startup script.) Note that this is really only sufficient for a single-user workstation environment, however.

Specifying a host name with an optional leading plus sign (+) allows the host to access the server, and specifying a host name with a leading minus sign (-) prevents a previously allowed host from accessing the server. Multiple hosts can be specified on the same line. Running *xhost* without any arguments prints the current hosts allowed to access your display.

For example, to add the hosts jupiter and saturn, and remove neptune:

```
% xhost +jupiter saturn -neptune
```

It is possible to remove the current host from the access list. Be warned that you can't undo this without logging out.

Note that when a remote system is denied access to your display, it means two things: that a person working on the remote system can't display on your screen, and that you can't use that remote system for running clients you want displayed on your screen.

User-based Access: xdm and the .Xauthority File

As of Release 4, the display manager and its control protocol (XDMCP) provide a user-based access control mechanism, which can be used to supplement or replace the host-based access mechanism discussed in the previous section. The Release 4 *xdm* can be set up to provide user authorization on a particular display (see "Security and the authorize Resource" earlier in this appendix). If authorization is enabled, when you log in, *xdm* places a machine-readable access code, known as a magic cookie, in a file called *.Xauthority* in your home directory. *xdm* also makes this magic cookie available to the server.

The *magic cookie* defined in a user's *.Xauthority* file is basically a secret code shared by the server and a particular user logged in on a particular display. When the user runs a client on the local display, the server checks to see whether the client program has access to the magic cookie. All processes started by the user in question have that access, and thus the server allows the client to be run on the display. Basically, under the magic cookie authorization scheme, a display becomes user-controlled. Once *xdm* creates an *.Xauthority* file for a user, each time the user logs on, *xdm* merges in authorization codes (magic cookies).

The access afforded by magic cookies is not as broad as that afforded by the host-based mechanism. When a system relies entirely on host-based access, any machine on the list of approved hosts can connect to the system. Thus, generally, any user logged on to an approved host can access any display connected to the system. This is somewhat feeble security. User-based access control is a little safer.

Be aware, however, that, currently, user-based access control cannot provide security for all X terminal users. This method of access control relies on the X Display Manager Control Protocol and few X terminals in the current market are programmed to understand the protocol. However, user-based access *can* be used effectively on workstations running Release 4 and on many of the newer X terminals.

The security mechanism provided by the magic cookie is evident in a situation in which another user tries to run a client on your machine. The server requires the client run by the other user to have access to the magic cookie shared exclusively between you and the server. The other user cannot provide the proper authorization code and thus cannot run a client on your host.

Of course, in many cases, users in a network will want to run clients on several machines (while displaying the client window on their local displays). This can be done if a user supplies authorization information associated with his local machine (or X terminal display) to the remote host. X developers have provided a new client, *xauth*, to allow users to transfer this information. Basically, *xauth* is a utility to manipulate *.Xauthority* files.

The most common use for *xauth* is to extract a user's authorization information for the current display, copy it to another machine, and merge it into the server's authorization records on the remote machine like this:

```
% xauth extract - $DISPLAY | rsh host2 xauth merge -
```

The dash (−) arguments indicate that extracted authorization records should be written to the standard output and that the *xauth* merge function should accept records from standard input. This command supplies the remote server with authorization information, allowing the user to run a remote shell on that host. See the *xauth* reference page in Part Three of this guide for more information.

If an installation is using remote file sharing, such as NFS, then sharing authorization records may not be an issue. If every user has a single home directory that is accessible to all machines, the machines have access to the necessary *.Xauthority* files at all times. In such an environment, users should be able to run programs on any of the networked machines without using *xauth*.

When user-based access control fails (for example, when a null or invalid magic cookie is offered to the server), host-based access takes over. To be more specific, say for example a user is logged on at an X terminal that is not XDMCP-compatible, and thus the user has no *.Xauthority* file (i.e., magic cookie). If that user tries to open a window on the remote console display, the client window cannot access a magic cookie. (The host interprets this as a null cookie.) Then host-based access control takes over. If the user in question is working on a system authorized in the */etc/Xn.hosts* file, he or she should be authorized to run a client on the console display.

Font Management

In Release 3, the X Consortium adopted the Bitmap Display Format (BDF) as the (non-exclusive) standard font format. (These files generally have a *.bdf* extension.) BDF font files are portable: they represent the characters of a font in ASCII.

In order to use BDF font files on a particular server, the files must be compiled to produce SNF (Server Natural Format) font files. (These files generally have a *.snf* extension.) Server Natural Format is particular to a given server. The server vendor must provide a program to convert BDF font files to SNF font files.

If you are using the standard version of X from MIT, the fonts shipped with X should be compiled when you build X. If you subsequently add BDF font files to the system, the files must be converted to SNF format. In the standard X environment, you convert BDF font files to SNF format using the program *bdftosnf*. The *showsnf* program displays the SNF font file so you can check that it compiled properly. See the *bdftosnf* and *showsnf* reference pages in Part Three of this guide for details.

Be aware that many vendors provide fonts designed for their own hardware in a format other than Bitmap Display Format. These files are not strictly portable. However, if you want to use vendor-supplied fonts with X, you may be able to convert them. The user-contributed part of the MIT X distribution includes tools to convert certain vendor supplied fonts to BDF. Then you can use *bdftosnf* to convert the BDF files to Server Natural Format.

Adding a Font to Your Server

In order to add one or more fonts to the standard server, you must:

- Convert the fonts from Bitmap Display Format to Server Natural Format.

- Add the fonts to the font database (*fonts.dir* file) used by the server.

- Make the server aware of the new fonts.

Converting Fonts and Updating fonts.dir

You perform the first two of these tasks using the *mkfontdir* command as follows:

1. Move the font files to the directory in which you want to store them (perhaps */usr/lib/X11/fonts/misc*). The files can be in Bitmap Display Format, Server Natural Format, or compressed in either form.

2. Run the *mkfontdir* command with the directory as an argument.

   ```
   % mkfontdir /usr/lib/X11/fonts/misc
   ```

   If necessary, *mkfontdir* uncompresses the new font file(s) and/or converts them to server natural format. (Thus, you don't have to run *bdftosnf* on BDF files first.)

   mkfontdir also adds an entry for each of the new fonts to the *fonts.dir* file. (You should edit the *fonts.alias* file if you want to add aliases for the new fonts.)

Making the Server Aware of Font Changes

Then, to complete the font installation process, the server must be made aware of the new fonts. The command:

```
% xset fp rehash
```

makes the server reread the font databases and alias files in the current font path. You should then be able to use any of the new fonts on the command line or in a resource file.

If you've added fonts to a directory not in the current font path, you must add that directory to the font path. You can inform the server of the new directory using *xset*. For example, say you add fonts to a directory called *newfonts*, a subdirectory of your home directory. The following command appends the directory ˜/*newfonts* to the server's font search path:

```
% xset fp+ ˜/newfonts
```

Then make the server reread the font databases and aliases file in the font path by issuing the command `xset fp rehash`.

In adding directories to the font path, the location of the plus sign is significant. The command:

```
% xset +fp ~/newfonts
```

adds *~/newfonts* to the beginning of the existing font search path.

You can remove a directory from the font path using either the `-fp` or `fp-` option. The location of the minus sign is not significant. To remove *~/newfonts* from the font path, enter:

```
% xset -fp ~/newfonts
```

or:

```
% xset fp- ~/newfonts
```

You can add or subtract multiple directories from the font path with a single invocation of *xset*. After the relevant `fp` option, the argument should be a comma-separated list of directories, as in the command:

```
% xset fp+ ~/newfonts,/usr/lib/X11/fonts/new
```

This command adds the directories *~/newfonts* and */usr/lib/X11/fonts/new* to the end of the current font path.

To set the font search path from scratch (rather than append to or subtract from the current path), enter:

```
% xset fp= fontdir1,fontdir2,fontdir3,...
```

To restore the default font path, enter:

```
% xset fp default
```

See the *xset* reference page in Part Three of this Guide for more information.

Console Messages

On a single-user workstation, it is likely that the screen used for running X is also used as the system console.

If X is started manually, the console will be the first window to appear on the screen. But if X is started from your *.login* file, console messages from the kernel may sometimes appear on the screen, overlaying the X windows. They make a nasty mess of the screen but the display can be refreshed and the console message erased by running the client *xrefresh* (described in Part Three of this guide).

Some implementations of X support a −C option to *xterm* that redirects messages sent to */dev/console* to that *xterm* window. If this option is supported, you should add the −C option to the console *xterm* in your startup file. After this window is mapped (displayed on the screen), all such messages are displayed there.

Log Files

The X server creates log files useful in fixing a problem that might occur. These files are located in */usr/adm*.

You should make provisions to trim these files periodically. As with all log files, you can do this automatically with an entry in the *crontab* file.

Changing the Color Name Database

The X Window System comes with a predefined set of colors, listed in the file */usr/lib/X11/rgb.txt*. You can use these color names to specify colors either on the command line or in a resources file. If you have the X sources, you can customize the color name database using this procedure.

1. Edit the *rgb.txt* source file, which is located in the *mit/rgb* directory, to change or add colors. The format of a line in the *rgb.txt* file is:

   ```
   red green blue color_name
   ```

   The red, green, and blue values are integers in the range 0 to 255; the color name is case-insensitive but must not include any special symbols. A typical entry in the *rgb.txt* file is:

   ```
   127 255 212              aquamarine
   ```

   See Chapter 9, *Command Line Options*, for more information about color specifications.

2. Run the *rgb* program using the makefile also located in the *mit/rgb* directory. This program converts the text file (*rgb.txt*) to a UNIX *dbm*(1) format file (*rgb.dir*), which is used as the color database. Just type:

   ```
   % make
   ```

3. Then install the new *rgb.dir* file in */usr/lib/X11* by typing:

   ```
   % make install
   ```

If the color name database gets corrupted in some way (e.g., written to accidentally), the server may not be able to find any colors with which to display. On a black and white workstation, you may get error messages similar to this:

```
X Toolkit Warning:  Cannot allocate colormap entry for White
X Toolkit Warning:  Cannot allocate colormap entry for Black
X Toolkit Warning:  Cannot allocate colormap entry for white
X Toolkit Warning:  Cannot allocate colormap entry for black
```

If you get errors of this sort, perform steps 2 and 3 in the procedure described above. This will overwrite the corrupted *rgb.dir* file.

B

Release 4 Standard Fonts

This appendix shows the standard display fonts available in Release 4 of the MIT X distribution. The images contained in this appendix are window dumps created with our own program, called xshowfonts, *the code for which is included.*

B
Release 4 Standard Fonts

This appendix includes pictures of some representative fonts from the standard X distribution in Release 4. Not every font may be supported by particular server vendors, and some vendors may supplement the set.

The standard fonts are stored in three directories:

Directory	Contents
/usr/lib/X11/fonts/misc	Six fixed-width fonts, the cursor font, other miscellaneous fonts.
/usr/lib/X11/fonts/75dpi	Fixed- and variable-width fonts, 75 dots per inch.
/usr/lib/X11/fonts/100dpi	Fixed- and variable-width fonts, 100 dpi.

Tables B-1 through B-3 list the fonts in each of the three Release 4 font directories. The first column lists the name of the file in which the font is stored (without the *.snf* extension); the second column lists the actual font name. See Chapter 6, *Font Specification*, for information about font naming conventions.

PICTURES of the different font families supplied in the MIT X11 distribution appear on subsequent pages. We show just the fonts in the *75dpi* directory. The *100dpi* directory contains the same fonts stored in the *75dpi* directory but for 100 dots per inch monitors. Keep in mind that all of the fonts in the *75dpi* and *100dpi* directories are available in 8-, 10-, 12-, 14-, 18-, and 24-point sizes. Each page shows fonts of various sizes, weights, and styles. We include the source for *xshowfonts.c*, the program we wrote to make these displays, at the end of the appendix.* We also show you, using *xfd*, one example of each of the unique character sets available.

All of the characters in each font are shown actual size, as they would appear on a 900 × 1180 pixel, 10" × 13.5" screen (Sun). On a screen with different pixel density, these fonts would appear in a different size.

Fonts that begin with many blank characters are shown with most leading blanks removed. Therefore, you can't always get the character number of each cell in the font by counting from the first cell we have shown. Use *xfd* to quickly determine the code for a particular cell.

---

*If you don't want to type this program in, you can obtain the source from uunet.uu.net via anonymous *ftp* or *uucp*. See the Preface for more information.

Table B-1. Fonts in the misc Directory

Filename	Font name
7x13B.snf	-misc-fixed-bold-r-normal- -13-120-75-75-c-70-iso8859-1
8x13B.snf	-misc-fixed-bold-r-normal- -13-120-75-75-c-80-iso8859-1
9x15B.snf	-misc-fixed-bold-r-normal- -15-140-75-75-c-90-iso8859-1
6x13B.snf	-misc-fixed-bold-r-semicondensed- -13-120-75-75-c-60-iso8859-1
6x10.snf	-misc-fixed-medium-r-normal- -10-100-75-75-c-60-iso8859-1
7x13.snf	-misc-fixed-medium-r-normal- -13-120-75-75-c-70-iso8859-1
8x13.snf	-misc-fixed-medium-r-normal- -13-120-75-75-c-80-iso8859-1
k14.snf	-misc-fixed-medium-r-normal- -14-130-75-75-c-140-jisx0208.1983-0
7x14.snf	-misc-fixed-medium-r-normal- -14-130-75-75-c-70-iso8859-1
7x14rk.snf	-misc-fixed-medium-r-normal- -14-130-75-75-c-70-jisx0201.1976-0
9x15.snf	-misc-fixed-medium-r-normal- -15-140-75-75-c-90-iso8859-1
10x20.snf	-misc-fixed-medium-r-normal- -20-200-75-75-c-100-iso8859-1
5x8.snf	-misc-fixed-medium-r-normal- -8-80-75-75-c-50-iso8859-1
6x9.snf	-misc-fixed-medium-r-normal- -9-90-75-75-c-60-iso8859-1
6x12.snf	-misc-fixed-medium-r-semicondensed- -12-110-75-75-c-60-iso8859-1
6x13.snf	-misc-fixed-medium-r-semicondensed- -13-120-75-75-c-60-iso8859-1
clB6x10.snf	-schumacher-clean-bold-r-normal- -10-100-75-75-c-60-iso8859-1
clB8x10.snf	-schumacher-clean-bold-r-normal- -10-100-75-75-c-80-iso8859-1
clB6x12.snf	-schumacher-clean-bold-r-normal- -12-120-75-75-c-60-iso8859-1
clB8x12.snf	-schumacher-clean-bold-r-normal- -12-120-75-75-c-80-iso8859-1
clB8x13.snf	-schumacher-clean-bold-r-normal- -13-130-75-75-c-80-iso8859-1
clB8x14.snf	-schumacher-clean-bold-r-normal- -14-140-75-75-c-80-iso8859-1
clB9x15.snf	-schumacher-clean-bold-r-normal- -15-150-75-75-c-90-iso8859-1
clB8x16.snf	-schumacher-clean-bold-r-normal- -16-160-75-75-c-80-iso8859-1
clB8x8.snf	-schumacher-clean-bold-r-normal- -8-80-75-75-c-80-iso8859-1
clI6x12.snf	-schumacher-clean-medium-i-normal- -12-120-75-75-c-60-iso8859-1
clI8x8.snf	-schumacher-clean-medium-i-normal- -8-80-75-75-c-80-iso8859-1
clR5x10.snf	-schumacher-clean-medium-r-normal- -10-100-75-75-c-50-iso8859-1
clR6x10.snf	-schumacher-clean-medium-r-normal- -10-100-75-75-c-60-iso8859-1
clR7x10.snf	-schumacher-clean-medium-r-normal- -10-100-75-75-c-70-iso8859-1
clR8x10.snf	-schumacher-clean-medium-r-normal- -10-100-75-75-c-80-iso8859-1
clR6x12.snf	-schumacher-clean-medium-r-normal- -12-120-75-75-c-60-iso8859-1
clR7x12.snf	-schumacher-clean-medium-r-normal- -12-120-75-75-c-70-iso8859-1
clR8x12.snf	-schumacher-clean-medium-r-normal- -12-120-75-75-c-80-iso8859-1
clR6x13.snf	-schumacher-clean-medium-r-normal- -13-130-75-75-c-60-iso8859-1
clR8x13.snf	-schumacher-clean-medium-r-normal- -13-130-75-75-c-80-iso8859-1
clR7x14.snf	-schumacher-clean-medium-r-normal- -14-140-75-75-c-70-iso8859-1
clR8x14.snf	-schumacher-clean-medium-r-normal- -14-140-75-75-c-80-iso8859-1
clR9x15.snf	-schumacher-clean-medium-r-normal- -15-150-75-75-c-90-iso8859-1
clR8x16.snf	-schumacher-clean-medium-r-normal- -16-160-75-75-c-80-iso8859-1
clR4x6.snf	-schumacher-clean-medium-r-normal- -6-60-75-75-c-40-iso8859-1
clR5x6.snf	-schumacher-clean-medium-r-normal- -6-60-75-75-c-50-iso8859-1
clR6x6.snf	-schumacher-clean-medium-r-normal- -6-60-75-75-c-60-iso8859-1
clR5x8.snf	-schumacher-clean-medium-r-normal- -8-80-75-75-c-50-iso8859-1

Table B-1. Fonts in the misc Directory (continued)

Filename	Font name
clR6x8.snf	-schumacher-clean-medium-r-normal- -8-80-75-75-c-60-iso8859-1
clR7x8.snf	-schumacher-clean-medium-r-normal- -8-80-75-75-c-70-iso8859-1
clR8x8.snf	-schumacher-clean-medium-r-normal- -8-80-75-75-c-80-iso8859-1
8x16.snf	-sony-fixed-medium-r-normal- -16-120-100-100-c-80-iso8859-1
8x16rk.snf	-sony-fixed-medium-r-normal- -16-120-100-100-c-80-jisx0201.1976-0
12x24.snf	-sony-fixed-medium-r-normal- -24-170-100-100-c-120-iso8859-1
12x24rk.snf	-sony-fixed-medium-r-normal- -24-170-100-100-c-120-jisx0201.1976-0
olcursor.snf	-sun-open look cursor-----12-120-75-75-p-160-sunolcursor-1
olgl10.snf	-sun-open look glyph-----10-100-75-75-p-101-sunolglyph-1
olgl12.snf	-sun-open look glyph-----12-120-75-75-p-113-sunolglyph-1
olgl14.snf	-sun-open look glyph-----14-140-75-75-p-128-sunolglyph-1
olgl19.snf	-sun-open look glyph-----19-190-75-75-p-154-sunolglyph-1
cursor.snf	cursor
deccurs.snf	decw$cursor
decsess.snf	decw$session
nil2.snf	nil2

Table B-2. Fonts in the 75dpi Directory

Filename	Font name
courBO10.snf	-adobe-courier-bold-o-normal--10-100-75-75-m-60-iso8859-1
courBO12.snf	-adobe-courier-bold-o-normal--12-120-75-75-m-70-iso8859-1
courBO14.snf	-adobe-courier-bold-o-normal--14-140-75-75-m-90-iso8859-1
courBO18.snf	-adobe-courier-bold-o-normal--18-180-75-75-m-110-iso8859-1
courBO24.snf	-adobe-courier-bold-o-normal--24-240-75-75-m-150-iso8859-1
courBOO8.snf	-adobe-courier-bold-o-normal--8-80-75-75-m-50-iso8859-1
courB10.snf	-adobe-courier-bold-r-normal--10-100-75-75-m-60-iso8859-1
courB12.snf	-adobe-courier-bold-r-normal--12-120-75-75-m-70-iso8859-1
courB14.snf	-adobe-courier-bold-r-normal--14-140-75-75-m-90-iso8859-1
courB18.snf	-adobe-courier-bold-r-normal--18-180-75-75-m-110-iso8859-1
courB24.snf	-adobe-courier-bold-r-normal--24-240-75-75-m-150-iso8859-1
courB08.snf	-adobe-courier-bold-r-normal--8-80-75-75-m-50-iso8859-1
courO10.snf	-adobe-courier-medium-o-normal--10-100-75-75-m-60-iso8859-1
courO12.snf	-adobe-courier-medium-o-normal--12-120-75-75-m-70-iso8859-1
courO14.snf	-adobe-courier-medium-o-normal--14-140-75-75-m-90-iso8859-1
courO18.snf	-adobe-courier-medium-o-normal--18-180-75-75-m-110-iso8859-1
courO24.snf	-adobe-courier-medium-o-normal--24-240-75-75-m-150-iso8859-1
courOO8.snf	-adobe-courier-medium-o-normal--8-80-75-75-m-50-iso8859-1
courR10.snf	-adobe-courier-medium-r-normal--10-100-75-75-m-60-iso8859-1
courR12.snf	-adobe-courier-medium-r-normal--12-120-75-75-m-70-iso8859-1
courR14.snf	-adobe-courier-medium-r-normal--14-140-75-75-m-90-iso8859-1

Table B-2. Fonts in the 75dpi Directory (continued)

Filename	Font name
courR18.snf	-adobe-courier-medium-r-normal--18-180-75-75-m-110-iso8859-1
courR24.snf	-adobe-courier-medium-r-normal--24-240-75-75-m-150-iso8859-1
courR08.snf	-adobe-courier-medium-r-normal--8-80-75-75-m-50-iso8859-1
helvBO10.snf	-adobe-helvetica-bold-o-normal--10-100-75-75-p-60-iso8859-1
helvBO12.snf	-adobe-helvetica-bold-o-normal--12-120-75-75-p-69-iso8859-1
helvBO14.snf	-adobe-helvetica-bold-o-normal--14-140-75-75-p-82-iso8859-1
helvBO18.snf	-adobe-helvetica-bold-o-normal--18-180-75-75-p-104-iso8859-1
helvBO24.snf	-adobe-helvetica-bold-o-normal--24-240-75-75-p-138-iso8859-1
helvBO08.snf	-adobe-helvetica-bold-o-normal--8-80-75-75-p-50-iso8859-1
helvB10.snf	-adobe-helvetica-bold-r-normal--10-100-75-75-p-60-iso8859-1
helvB12.snf	-adobe-helvetica-bold-r-normal--12-120-75-75-p-70-iso8859-1
helvB14.snf	-adobe-helvetica-bold-r-normal--14-140-75-75-p-82-iso8859-1
helvB18.snf	-adobe-helvetica-bold-r-normal--18-180-75-75-p-103-iso8859-1
helvB24.snf	-adobe-helvetica-bold-r-normal--24-240-75-75-p-138-iso8859-1
helvB08.snf	-adobe-helvetica-bold-r-normal--8-80-75-75-p-50-iso8859-1
helvO10.snf	-adobe-helvetica-medium-o-normal--10-100-75-75-p-57-iso8859-1
helvO12.snf	-adobe-helvetica-medium-o-normal--12-120-75-75-p-67-iso8859-1
helvO14.snf	-adobe-helvetica-medium-o-normal--14-140-75-75-p-78-iso8859-1
helvO18.snf	-adobe-helvetica-medium-o-normal--18-180-75-75-p-98-iso8859-1
helvO24.snf	-adobe-helvetica-medium-o-normal--24-240-75-75-p-130-iso8859-1
helvO08.snf	-adobe-helvetica-medium-o-normal--8-80-75-75-p-47-iso8859-1
helvR10.snf	-adobe-helvetica-medium-r-normal--10-100-75-75-p-56-iso8859-1
helvR12.snf	-adobe-helvetica-medium-r-normal--12-120-75-75-p-67-iso8859-1
helvR14.snf	-adobe-helvetica-medium-r-normal--14-140-75-75-p-77-iso8859-1
helvR18.snf	-adobe-helvetica-medium-r-normal--18-180-75-75-p-98-iso8859-1
helvR24.snf	-adobe-helvetica-medium-r-normal--24-240-75-75-p-130-iso8859-1
helvR08.snf	-adobe-helvetica-medium-r-normal--8-80-75-75-p-46-iso8859-1
ncenBI10.snf	-adobe-new century schoolbook-bold-i-normal--10-100-75-75-p-66-iso8859-1
ncenBI12.snf	-adobe-new century schoolbook-bold-i-normal--12-120-75-75-p-76-iso8859-1
ncenBI14.snf	-adobe-new century schoolbook-bold-i-normal--14-140-75-75-p-88-iso8859-1
ncenBI18.snf	-adobe-new century schoolbook-bold-i-normal--18-180-75-75-p-111-iso8859-1
ncenBI24.snf	-adobe-new century schoolbook-bold-i-normal--24-240-75-75-p-148-iso8859-1
ncenBI08.snf	-adobe-new century schoolbook-bold-i-normal--8-80-75-75-p-56-iso8859-1
ncenB10.snf	-adobe-new century schoolbook-bold-r-normal--10-100-75-75-p-66-iso8859-1
ncenB12.snf	-adobe-new century schoolbook-bold-r-normal--12-120-75-75-p-77-iso8859-1
ncenB14.snf	-adobe-new century schoolbook-bold-r-normal--14-140-75-75-p-87-iso8859-1
ncenB18.snf	-adobe-new century schoolbook-bold-r-normal--18-180-75-75-p-113-iso8859-1
ncenB24.snf	-adobe-new century schoolbook-bold-r-normal--24-240-75-75-p-149-iso8859-1
ncenB08.snf	-adobe-new century schoolbook-bold-r-normal--8-80-75-75-p-56-iso8859-1
ncenI10.snf	-adobe-new century schoolbook-medium-i-normal--10-100-75-75-p-60-iso8859-1
ncenI12.snf	-adobe-new century schoolbook-medium-i-normal--12-120-75-75-p-70-iso8859-1
ncenI14.snf	-adobe-new century schoolbook-medium-i-normal--14-140-75-75-p-81-iso8859-1
ncenI18.snf	-adobe-new century schoolbook-medium-i-normal--18-180-75-75-p-104-iso8859-1
ncenI24.snf	-adobe-new century schoolbook-medium-i-normal--24-240-75-75-p-136-iso8859-1

Filename	Font name
ncenI08.snf	-adobe-new century schoolbook-medium-i-normal--8-80-75-75-p-50-iso8859-1
ncenR10.snf	-adobe-new century schoolbook-medium-r-normal--10-100-75-75-p-60-iso8859-1
ncenR12.snf	-adobe-new century schoolbook-medium-r-normal--12-120-75-75-p-70-iso8859-1
ncenR14.snf	-adobe-new century schoolbook-medium-r-normal--14-140-75-75-p-82-iso8859-1
ncenR18.snf	-adobe-new century schoolbook-medium-r-normal--18-180-75-75-p-103-iso8859-1
ncenR24.snf	-adobe-new century schoolbook-medium-r-normal--24-240-75-75-p-137-iso8859-1
ncenR08.snf	-adobe-new century schoolbook-medium-r-normal--8-80-75-75-p-50-iso8859-1
symb10.snf	-adobe-symbol-medium-r-normal--10-100-75-75-p-61-adobe-fontspecific
symb12.snf	-adobe-symbol-medium-r-normal--12-120-75-75-p-74-adobe-fontspecific
symb14.snf	-adobe-symbol-medium-r-normal--14-140-75-75-p-85-adobe-fontspecific
symb18.snf	-adobe-symbol-medium-r-normal--18-180-75-75-p-107-adobe-fontspecific
symb24.snf	-adobe-symbol-medium-r-normal--24-240-75-75-p-142-adobe-fontspecific
symb08.snf	-adobe-symbol-medium-r-normal--8-80-75-75-p-51-adobe-fontspecific
timBI10.snf	-adobe-times-bold-i-normal--10-100-75-75-p-57-iso8859-1
timBI12.snf	-adobe-times-bold-i-normal--12-120-75-75-p-68-iso8859-1
timBI14.snf	-adobe-times-bold-i-normal--14-140-75-75-p-77-iso8859-1
timBI18.snf	-adobe-times-bold-i-normal--18-180-75-75-p-98-iso8859-1
timBI24.snf	-adobe-times-bold-i-normal--24-240-75-75-p-128-iso8859-1
timBI08.snf	-adobe-times-bold-i-normal--8-80-75-75-p-47-iso8859-1
timB10.snf	-adobe-times-bold-r-normal--10-100-75-75-p-57-iso8859-1
timB12.snf	-adobe-times-bold-r-normal--12-120-75-75-p-67-iso8859-1
timB14.snf	-adobe-times-bold-r-normal--14-140-75-75-p-77-iso8859-1
timB18.snf	-adobe-times-bold-r-normal--18-180-75-75-p-99-iso8859-1
timB24.snf	-adobe-times-bold-r-normal--24-240-75-75-p-132-iso8859-1
timB08.snf	-adobe-times-bold-r-normal--8-80-75-75-p-47-iso8859-1
timI10.snf	-adobe-times-medium-i-normal--10-100-75-75-p-52-iso8859-1
timI12.snf	-adobe-times-medium-i-normal--12-120-75-75-p-63-iso8859-1
timI14.snf	-adobe-times-medium-i-normal--14-140-75-75-p-73-iso8859-1
timI18.snf	-adobe-times-medium-i-normal--18-180-75-75-p-94-iso8859-1
timI24.snf	-adobe-times-medium-i-normal--24-240-75-75-p-125-iso8859-1
timI08.snf	-adobe-times-medium-i-normal--8-80-75-75-p-42-iso8859-1
timR10.snf	-adobe-times-medium-r-normal--10-100-75-75-p-54-iso8859-1
timR12.snf	-adobe-times-medium-r-normal--12-120-75-75-p-64-iso8859-1
timR14.snf	-adobe-times-medium-r-normal--14-140-75-75-p-74-iso8859-1
timR18.snf	-adobe-times-medium-r-normal--18-180-75-75-p-94-iso8859-1
timR24.snf	-adobe-times-medium-r-normal--24-240-75-75-p-124-iso8859-1
timR08.snf	-adobe-times-medium-r-normal--8-80-75-75-p-44-iso8859-1
luBIS10.snf	-b&h-lucida-bold-i-normal-sans-10-100-75-75-p-67-iso8859-1
luBIS12.snf	-b&h-lucida-bold-i-normal-sans-12-120-75-75-p-79-iso8859-1
luBIS14.snf	-b&h-lucida-bold-i-normal-sans-14-140-75-75-p-92-iso8859-1
luBIS18.snf	-b&h-lucida-bold-i-normal-sans-18-180-75-75-p-119-iso8859-1
luBIS19.snf	-b&h-lucida-bold-i-normal-sans-19-190-75-75-p-122-iso8859-1
luBIS24.snf	-b&h-lucida-bold-i-normal-sans-24-240-75-75-p-151-iso8859-1
luBIS08.snf	-b&h-lucida-bold-i-normal-sans-8-80-75-75-p-49-iso8859-1

Filename	Font name
luBS10.snf	-b&h-lucida-bold-r-normal-sans-10-100-75-75-p-66-iso8859-1
luBS12.snf	-b&h-lucida-bold-r-normal-sans-12-120-75-75-p-79-iso8859-1
luBS14.snf	-b&h-lucida-bold-r-normal-sans-14-140-75-75-p-92-iso8859-1
luBS18.snf	-b&h-lucida-bold-r-normal-sans-18-180-75-75-p-120-iso8859-1
luBS19.snf	-b&h-lucida-bold-r-normal-sans-19-190-75-75-p-122-iso8859-1
luBS24.snf	-b&h-lucida-bold-r-normal-sans-24-240-75-75-p-152-iso8859-1
luBS08.snf	-b&h-lucida-bold-r-normal-sans-8-80-75-75-p-50-iso8859-1
luIS10.snf	-b&h-lucida-medium-i-normal-sans-10-100-75-75-p-59-iso8859-1
luIS12.snf	-b&h-lucida-medium-i-normal-sans-12-120-75-75-p-71-iso8859-1
luIS14.snf	-b&h-lucida-medium-i-normal-sans-14-140-75-75-p-82-iso8859-1
luIS18.snf	-b&h-lucida-medium-i-normal-sans-18-180-75-75-p-105-iso8859-1
luIS19.snf	-b&h-lucida-medium-i-normal-sans-19-190-75-75-p-108-iso8859-1
luIS24.snf	-b&h-lucida-medium-i-normal-sans-24-240-75-75-p-136-iso8859-1
luIS08.snf	-b&h-lucida-medium-i-normal-sans-8-80-75-75-p-45-iso8859-1
luRS10.snf	-b&h-lucida-medium-r-normal-sans-10-100-75-75-p-58-iso8859-1
luRS12.snf	-b&h-lucida-medium-r-normal-sans-12-120-75-75-p-71-iso8859-1
luRS14.snf	-b&h-lucida-medium-r-normal-sans-14-140-75-75-p-81-iso8859-1
luRS18.snf	-b&h-lucida-medium-r-normal-sans-18-180-75-75-p-106-iso8859-1
luRS19.snf	-b&h-lucida-medium-r-normal-sans-19-190-75-75-p-108-iso8859-1
luRS24.snf	-b&h-lucida-medium-r-normal-sans-24-240-75-75-p-136-iso8859-1
luRS08.snf	-b&h-lucida-medium-r-normal-sans-8-80-75-75-p-45-iso8859-1
lubBI10.snf	-b&h-lucidabright-demibold-i-normal--10-100-75-75-p-59-iso8859-1
lubBI12.snf	-b&h-lucidabright-demibold-i-normal--12-120-75-75-p-72-iso8859-1
lubBI14.snf	-b&h-lucidabright-demibold-i-normal--14-140-75-75-p-84-iso8859-1
lubBI18.snf	-b&h-lucidabright-demibold-i-normal--18-180-75-75-p-107-iso8859-1
lubBI19.snf	-b&h-lucidabright-demibold-i-normal--19-190-75-75-p-114-iso8859-1
lubBI24.snf	-b&h-lucidabright-demibold-i-normal--24-240-75-75-p-143-iso8859-1
lubBI08.snf	-b&h-lucidabright-demibold-i-normal--8-80-75-75-p-48-iso8859-1
lubB10.snf	-b&h-lucidabright-demibold-r-normal--10-100-75-75-p-59-iso8859-1
lubB12.snf	-b&h-lucidabright-demibold-r-normal--12-120-75-75-p-71-iso8859-1
lubB14.snf	-b&h-lucidabright-demibold-r-normal--14-140-75-75-p-84-iso8859-1
lubB18.snf	-b&h-lucidabright-demibold-r-normal--18-180-75-75-p-107-iso8859-1
lubB19.snf	-b&h-lucidabright-demibold-r-normal--19-190-75-75-p-114-iso8859-1
lubB24.snf	-b&h-lucidabright-demibold-r-normal--24-240-75-75-p-143-iso8859-1
lubB08.snf	-b&h-lucidabright-demibold-r-normal--8-80-75-75-p-47-iso8859-1
lubI10.snf	-b&h-lucidabright-medium-i-normal--10-100-75-75-p-57-iso8859-1
lubI12.snf	-b&h-lucidabright-medium-i-normal--12-120-75-75-p-67-iso8859-1
lubI14.snf	-b&h-lucidabright-medium-i-normal--14-140-75-75-p-80-iso8859-1
lubI18.snf	-b&h-lucidabright-medium-i-normal--18-180-75-75-p-102-iso8859-1
lubI19.snf	-b&h-lucidabright-medium-i-normal--19-190-75-75-p-109-iso8859-1
lubI24.snf	-b&h-lucidabright-medium-i-normal--24-240-75-75-p-136-iso8859-1
lubI08.snf	-b&h-lucidabright-medium-i-normal--8-80-75-75-p-45-iso8859-1
lubR10.snf	-b&h-lucidabright-medium-r-normal--10-100-75-75-p-56-iso8859-1
lubR12.snf	-b&h-lucidabright-medium-r-normal--12-120-75-75-p-68-iso8859-1

Filename	Font name
lubR14.snf	-b&h-lucidabright-medium-r-normal--14-140-75-75-p-80-iso8859-1
lubR18.snf	-b&h-lucidabright-medium-r-normal--18-180-75-75-p-103-iso8859-1
lubR19.snf	-b&h-lucidabright-medium-r-normal--19-190-75-75-p-109-iso8859-1
lubR24.snf	-b&h-lucidabright-medium-r-normal--24-240-75-75-p-137-iso8859-1
lubR08.snf	-b&h-lucidabright-medium-r-normal--8-80-75-75-p-45-iso8859-1
lutBS10.snf	-b&h-lucidatypewriter-bold-r-normal-sans-10-100-75-75-m-60-iso8859-1
lutBS12.snf	-b&h-lucidatypewriter-bold-r-normal-sans-12-120-75-75-m-70-iso8859-1
lutBS14.snf	-b&h-lucidatypewriter-bold-r-normal-sans-14-140-75-75-m-90-iso8859-1
lutBS18.snf	-b&h-lucidatypewriter-bold-r-normal-sans-18-180-75-75-m-110-iso8859-1
lutBS19.snf	-b&h-lucidatypewriter-bold-r-normal-sans-19-190-75-75-m-110-iso8859-1
lutBS24.snf	-b&h-lucidatypewriter-bold-r-normal-sans-24-240-75-75-m-140-iso8859-1
lutBS08.snf	-b&h-lucidatypewriter-bold-r-normal-sans-8-80-75-75-m-50-iso8859-1
lutRS10.snf	-b&h-lucidatypewriter-medium-r-normal-sans-10-100-75-75-m-60-iso8859-1
lutRS12.snf	-b&h-lucidatypewriter-medium-r-normal-sans-12-120-75-75-m-70-iso8859-1
lutRS14.snf	-b&h-lucidatypewriter-medium-r-normal-sans-14-140-75-75-m-90-iso8859-1
lutRS18.snf	-b&h-lucidatypewriter-medium-r-normal-sans-18-180-75-75-m-110-iso8859-1
lutRS19.snf	-b&h-lucidatypewriter-medium-r-normal-sans-19-190-75-75-m-110-iso8859-1
lutRS24.snf	-b&h-lucidatypewriter-medium-r-normal-sans-24-240-75-75-m-140-iso8859-1
lutRS08.snf	-b&h-lucidatypewriter-medium-r-normal-sans-8-80-75-75-m-50-iso8859-1
charBI10.snf	-bitstream-charter-bold-i-normal--10-100-75-75-p-62-iso8859-1
charBI12.snf	-bitstream-charter-bold-i-normal--12-120-75-75-p-74-iso8859-1
charBI14.snf	-bitstream-charter-bold-i-normal--15-140-75-75-p-93-iso8859-1
charBI18.snf	-bitstream-charter-bold-i-normal--19-180-75-75-p-117-iso8859-1
charBI24.snf	-bitstream-charter-bold-i-normal--25-240-75-75-p-154-iso8859-1
charBI08.snf	-bitstream-charter-bold-i-normal--8-80-75-75-p-50-iso8859-1
charB10.snf	-bitstream-charter-bold-r-normal--10-100-75-75-p-63-iso8859-1
charB12.snf	-bitstream-charter-bold-r-normal--12-120-75-75-p-75-iso8859-1
charB14.snf	-bitstream-charter-bold-r-normal--15-140-75-75-p-94-iso8859-1
charB18.snf	-bitstream-charter-bold-r-normal--19-180-75-75-p-119-iso8859-1
charB24.snf	-bitstream-charter-bold-r-normal--25-240-75-75-p-157-iso8859-1
charB08.snf	-bitstream-charter-bold-r-normal--8-80-75-75-p-50-iso8859-1
charI10.snf	-bitstream-charter-medium-i-normal--10-100-75-75-p-55-iso8859-1
charI12.snf	-bitstream-charter-medium-i-normal--12-120-75-75-p-65-iso8859-1
charI14.snf	-bitstream-charter-medium-i-normal--15-140-75-75-p-82-iso8859-1
charI18.snf	-bitstream-charter-medium-i-normal--19-180-75-75-p-103-iso8859-1
charI24.snf	-bitstream-charter-medium-i-normal--25-240-75-75-p-136-iso8859-1
charI08.snf	-bitstream-charter-medium-i-normal--8-80-75-75-p-44-iso8859-1
charR10.snf	-bitstream-charter-medium-r-normal--10-100-75-75-p-56-iso8859-1
charR12.snf	-bitstream-charter-medium-r-normal--12-120-75-75-p-67-iso8859-1
charR14.snf	-bitstream-charter-medium-r-normal--15-140-75-75-p-84-iso8859-1
charR18.snf	-bitstream-charter-medium-r-normal--19-180-75-75-p-106-iso8859-1
charR24.snf	-bitstream-charter-medium-r-normal--25-240-75-75-p-139-iso8859-1
charR08.snf	-bitstream-charter-medium-r-normal--8-80-75-75-p-45-iso8859-1
techB14.snf	-dec-terminal-bold-r-normal--14-140-75-75-c-80-dec-dectech

Table B-2. Fonts in the 75dpi Directory (continued)

Filename	Font name
termB14.snf	-dec-terminal-bold-r-normal--14-140-75-75-c-80-iso8859-1
tech14.snf	-dec-terminal-medium-r-normal--14-140-75-75-c-80-dec-dectech
term14.snf	-dec-terminal-medium-r-normal--14-140-75-75-c-80-iso8859-1

Table B-3. Fonts in the 100dpi Directory

Filename	Font name
courBO08.snf	-adobe-courier-bold-o-normal--11-80-100-100-m-60-iso8859-1
courBO10.snf	-adobe-courier-bold-o-normal--14-100-100-100-m-90-iso8859-1
courBO12.snf	-adobe-courier-bold-o-normal--17-120-100-100-m-100-iso8859-1
courBO14.snf	-adobe-courier-bold-o-normal--20-140-100-100-m-110-iso8859-1
courBO18.snf	-adobe-courier-bold-o-normal--25-180-100-100-m-150-iso8859-1
courBO24.snf	-adobe-courier-bold-o-normal--34-240-100-100-m-200-iso8859-1
courB08.snf	-adobe-courier-bold-r-normal--11-80-100-100-m-60-iso8859-1
courB10.snf	-adobe-courier-bold-r-normal--14-100-100-100-m-90-iso8859-1
courB12.snf	-adobe-courier-bold-r-normal--17-120-100-100-m-100-iso8859-1
courB14.snf	-adobe-courier-bold-r-normal--20-140-100-100-m-110-iso8859-1
courB18.snf	-adobe-courier-bold-r-normal--25-180-100-100-m-150-iso8859-1
courB24.snf	-adobe-courier-bold-r-normal--34-240-100-100-m-200-iso8859-1
courO08.snf	-adobe-courier-medium-o-normal--11-80-100-100-m-60-iso8859-1
courO10.snf	-adobe-courier-medium-o-normal--14-100-100-100-m-90-iso8859-1
courO12.snf	-adobe-courier-medium-o-normal--17-120-100-100-m-100-iso8859-1
courO14.snf	-adobe-courier-medium-o-normal--20-140-100-100-m-110-iso8859-1
courO18.snf	-adobe-courier-medium-o-normal--25-180-100-100-m-150-iso8859-1
courO24.snf	-adobe-courier-medium-o-normal--34-240-100-100-m-200-iso8859-1
courR08.snf	-adobe-courier-medium-r-normal--11-80-100-100-m-60-iso8859-1
courR10.snf	-adobe-courier-medium-r-normal--14-100-100-100-m-90-iso8859-1
courR12.snf	-adobe-courier-medium-r-normal--17-120-100-100-m-100-iso8859-1
courR14.snf	-adobe-courier-medium-r-normal--20-140-100-100-m-110-iso8859-1
courR18.snf	-adobe-courier-medium-r-normal--25-180-100-100-m-150-iso8859-1
courR24.snf	-adobe-courier-medium-r-normal--34-240-100-100-m-200-iso8859-1
helvBO08.snf	-adobe-helvetica-bold-o-normal--11-80-100-100-p-60-iso8859-1
helvBO10.snf	-adobe-helvetica-bold-o-normal--14-100-100-100-p-82-iso8859-1
helvBO12.snf	-adobe-helvetica-bold-o-normal--17-120-100-100-p-92-iso8859-1
helvBO14.snf	-adobe-helvetica-bold-o-normal--20-140-100-100-p-103-iso8859-1
helvBO18.snf	-adobe-helvetica-bold-o-normal--25-180-100-100-p-138-iso8859-1
helvBO24.snf	-adobe-helvetica-bold-o-normal--34-240-100-100-p-182-iso8859-1
helvB08.snf	-adobe-helvetica-bold-r-normal--11-80-100-100-p-60-iso8859-1
helvB10.snf	-adobe-helvetica-bold-r-normal--14-100-100-100-p-82-iso8859-1
helvB12.snf	-adobe-helvetica-bold-r-normal--17-120-100-100-p-92-iso8859-1
helvB14.snf	-adobe-helvetica-bold-r-normal--20-140-100-100-p-105-iso8859-1

Filename	Font name
helvB18.snf	-adobe-helvetica-bold-r-normal--25-180-100-100-p-138-iso8859-1
helvB24.snf	-adobe-helvetica-bold-r-normal--34-240-100-100-p-182-iso8859-1
helvO08.snf	-adobe-helvetica-medium-o-normal--11-80-100-100-p-57-iso8859-1
helvO10.snf	-adobe-helvetica-medium-o-normal--14-100-100-100-p-78-iso8859-1
helvO12.snf	-adobe-helvetica-medium-o-normal--17-120-100-100-p-88-iso8859-1
helvO14.snf	-adobe-helvetica-medium-o-normal--20-140-100-100-p-98-iso8859-1
helvO18.snf	-adobe-helvetica-medium-o-normal--25-180-100-100-p-130-iso8859-1
helvO24.snf	-adobe-helvetica-medium-o-normal--34-240-100-100-p-176-iso8859-1
helvR08.snf	-adobe-helvetica-medium-r-normal--11-80-100-100-p-56-iso8859-1
helvR10.snf	-adobe-helvetica-medium-r-normal--14-100-100-100-p-76-iso8859-1
helvR12.snf	-adobe-helvetica-medium-r-normal--17-120-100-100-p-88-iso8859-1
helvR14.snf	-adobe-helvetica-medium-r-normal--20-140-100-100-p-100-iso8859-1
helvR18.snf	-adobe-helvetica-medium-r-normal--25-180-100-100-p-130-iso8859-1
helvR24.snf	-adobe-helvetica-medium-r-normal--34-240-100-100-p-176-iso8859-1
ncenBI08.snf	-adobe-new century schoolbook-bold-i-normal--11-80-100-100-p-66-iso8859-1
ncenBI10.snf	-adobe-new century schoolbook-bold-i-normal--14-100-100-100-p-88-iso8859-1
ncenBI12.snf	-adobe-new century schoolbook-bold-i-normal--17-120-100-100-p-99-iso8859-1
ncenBI14.snf	-adobe-new century schoolbook-bold-i-normal--20-140-100-100-p-111-iso8859-1
ncenBI18.snf	-adobe-new century schoolbook-bold-i-normal--25-180-100-100-p-148-iso8859-1
ncenBI24.snf	-adobe-new century schoolbook-bold-i-normal--34-240-100-100-p-193-iso8859-1
ncenB08.snf	-adobe-new century schoolbook-bold-r-normal--11-80-100-100-p-66-iso8859-1
ncenB10.snf	-adobe-new century schoolbook-bold-r-normal--14-100-100-100-p-87-iso8859-1
ncenB12.snf	-adobe-new century schoolbook-bold-r-normal--17-120-100-100-p-99-iso8859-1
ncenB14.snf	-adobe-new century schoolbook-bold-r-normal--20-140-100-100-p-113-iso8859-1
ncenB18.snf	-adobe-new century schoolbook-bold-r-normal--25-180-100-100-p-149-iso8859-1
ncenB24.snf	-adobe-new century schoolbook-bold-r-normal--34-240-100-100-p-193-iso8859-1
ncenI08.snf	-adobe-new century schoolbook-medium-i-normal--11-80-100-100-p-60-iso8859-1
ncenI10.snf	-adobe-new century schoolbook-medium-i-normal--14-100-100-100-p-81-iso8859-1
ncenI12.snf	-adobe-new century schoolbook-medium-i-normal--17-120-100-100-p-92-iso8859-1
ncenI14.snf	-adobe-new century schoolbook-medium-i-normal--20-140-100-100-p-104-iso8859-1
ncenI18.snf	-adobe-new century schoolbook-medium-i-normal--25-180-100-100-p-136-iso8859-1
ncenI24.snf	-adobe-new century schoolbook-medium-i-normal--34-240-100-100-p-182-iso8859-1
ncenR08.snf	-adobe-new century schoolbook-medium-r-normal--11-80-100-100-p-60-iso8859-1
ncenR10.snf	-adobe-new century schoolbook-medium-r-normal--14-100-100-100-p-82-iso8859-1
ncenR12.snf	-adobe-new century schoolbook-medium-r-normal--17-120-100-100-p-91-iso8859-1
ncenR14.snf	-adobe-new century schoolbook-medium-r-normal--20-140-100-100-p-103-iso8859-1
ncenR18.snf	-adobe-new century schoolbook-medium-r-normal--25-180-100-100-p-136-iso8859-1
ncenR24.snf	-adobe-new century schoolbook-medium-r-normal--34-240-100-100-p-181-iso8859-1
symb08.snf	-adobe-symbol-medium-r-normal--11-80-100-100-p-61-adobe-fontspecific
symb10.snf	-adobe-symbol-medium-r-normal--14-100-100-100-p-85-adobe-fontspecific
symb12.snf	-adobe-symbol-medium-r-normal--17-120-100-100-p-95-adobe-fontspecific
symb14.snf	-adobe-symbol-medium-r-normal--20-140-100-100-p-107-adobe-fontspecific
symb18.snf	-adobe-symbol-medium-r-normal--25-180-100-100-p-142-adobe-fontspecific
symb24.snf	-adobe-symbol-medium-r-normal--34-240-100-100-p-191-adobe-fontspecific

Release 4
Standard Fonts

Filename	Font name
timBI08.snf	-adobe-times-bold-i-normal--11-80-100-100-p-57-iso8859-1
timBI10.snf	-adobe-times-bold-i-normal--14-100-100-100-p-77-iso8859-1
timBI12.snf	-adobe-times-bold-i-normal--17-120-100-100-p-86-iso8859-1
timBI14.snf	-adobe-times-bold-i-normal--20-140-100-100-p-98-iso8859-1
timBI18.snf	-adobe-times-bold-i-normal--25-180-100-100-p-128-iso8859-1
timBI24.snf	-adobe-times-bold-i-normal--34-240-100-100-p-170-iso8859-1
timB08.snf	-adobe-times-bold-r-normal--11-80-100-100-p-57-iso8859-1
timB10.snf	-adobe-times-bold-r-normal--14-100-100-100-p-76-iso8859-1
timB12.snf	-adobe-times-bold-r-normal--17-120-100-100-p-88-iso8859-1
timB14.snf	-adobe-times-bold-r-normal--20-140-100-100-p-100-iso8859-1
timB18.snf	-adobe-times-bold-r-normal--25-180-100-100-p-132-iso8859-1
timB24.snf	-adobe-times-bold-r-normal--34-240-100-100-p-177-iso8859-1
timI08.snf	-adobe-times-medium-i-normal--11-80-100-100-p-52-iso8859-1
timI10.snf	-adobe-times-medium-i-normal--14-100-100-100-p-73-iso8859-1
timI12.snf	-adobe-times-medium-i-normal--17-120-100-100-p-84-iso8859-1
timI14.snf	-adobe-times-medium-i-normal--20-140-100-100-p-94-iso8859-1
timI18.snf	-adobe-times-medium-i-normal--25-180-100-100-p-125-iso8859-1
timI24.snf	-adobe-times-medium-i-normal--34-240-100-100-p-168-iso8859-1
timR08.snf	-adobe-times-medium-r-normal--11-80-100-100-p-54-iso8859-1
timR10.snf	-adobe-times-medium-r-normal--14-100-100-100-p-74-iso8859-1
timR12.snf	-adobe-times-medium-r-normal--17-120-100-100-p-84-iso8859-1
timR14.snf	-adobe-times-medium-r-normal--20-140-100-100-p-96-iso8859-1
timR18.snf	-adobe-times-medium-r-normal--25-180-100-100-p-125-iso8859-1
timR24.snf	-adobe-times-medium-r-normal--34-240-100-100-p-170-iso8859-1
luBIS08.snf	-b&h-lucida-bold-i-normal-sans-11-80-100-100-p-69-iso8859-1
luBIS10.snf	-b&h-lucida-bold-i-normal-sans-14-100-100-100-p-90-iso8859-1
luBIS12.snf	-b&h-lucida-bold-i-normal-sans-17-120-100-100-p-108-iso8859-1
luBIS14.snf	-b&h-lucida-bold-i-normal-sans-20-140-100-100-p-127-iso8859-1
luBIS18.snf	-b&h-lucida-bold-i-normal-sans-25-180-100-100-p-159-iso8859-1
luBIS19.snf	-b&h-lucida-bold-i-normal-sans-26-190-100-100-p-166-iso8859-1
luBIS24.snf	-b&h-lucida-bold-i-normal-sans-34-240-100-100-p-215-iso8859-1
luBS08.snf	-b&h-lucida-bold-r-normal-sans-11-80-100-100-p-70-iso8859-1
luBS10.snf	-b&h-lucida-bold-r-normal-sans-14-100-100-100-p-89-iso8859-1
luBS12.snf	-b&h-lucida-bold-r-normal-sans-17-120-100-100-p-108-iso8859-1
luBS14.snf	-b&h-lucida-bold-r-normal-sans-20-140-100-100-p-127-iso8859-1
luBS18.snf	-b&h-lucida-bold-r-normal-sans-25-180-100-100-p-158-iso8859-1
luBS19.snf	-b&h-lucida-bold-r-normal-sans-26-190-100-100-p-166-iso8859-1
luBS24.snf	-b&h-lucida-bold-r-normal-sans-34-240-100-100-p-216-iso8859-1
luIS08.snf	-b&h-lucida-medium-i-normal-sans-11-80-100-100-p-62-iso8859-1
luIS10.snf	-b&h-lucida-medium-i-normal-sans-14-100-100-100-p-80-iso8859-1
luIS12.snf	-b&h-lucida-medium-i-normal-sans-17-120-100-100-p-97-iso8859-1
luIS14.snf	-b&h-lucida-medium-i-normal-sans-20-140-100-100-p-114-iso8859-1
luIS18.snf	-b&h-lucida-medium-i-normal-sans-25-180-100-100-p-141-iso8859-1
luIS19.snf	-b&h-lucida-medium-i-normal-sans-26-190-100-100-p-147-iso8859-1

Filename	Font name
luIS24.snf	-b&h-lucida-medium-i-normal-sans-34-240-100-100-p-192-iso8859-1
luRS08.snf	-b&h-lucida-medium-r-normal-sans-11-80-100-100-p-63-iso8859-1
luRS10.snf	-b&h-lucida-medium-r-normal-sans-14-100-100-100-p-80-iso8859-1
luRS12.snf	-b&h-lucida-medium-r-normal-sans-17-120-100-100-p-96-iso8859-1
luRS14.snf	-b&h-lucida-medium-r-normal-sans-20-140-100-100-p-114-iso8859-1
luRS18.snf	-b&h-lucida-medium-r-normal-sans-25-180-100-100-p-142-iso8859-1
luRS19.snf	-b&h-lucida-medium-r-normal-sans-26-190-100-100-p-147-iso8859-1
luRS24.snf	-b&h-lucida-medium-r-normal-sans-34-240-100-100-p-191-iso8859-1
lubBI08.snf	-b&h-lucidabright-demibold-i-normal--11-80-100-100-p-66-iso8859-1
lubBI10.snf	-b&h-lucidabright-demibold-i-normal--14-100-100-100-p-84-iso8859-1
lubBI12.snf	-b&h-lucidabright-demibold-i-normal--17-120-100-100-p-101-iso8859-1
lubBI14.snf	-b&h-lucidabright-demibold-i-normal--20-140-100-100-p-119-iso8859-1
lubBI18.snf	-b&h-lucidabright-demibold-i-normal--25-180-100-100-p-149-iso8859-1
lubBI19.snf	-b&h-lucidabright-demibold-i-normal--26-190-100-100-p-156-iso8859-1
lubBI24.snf	-b&h-lucidabright-demibold-i-normal--34-240-100-100-p-203-iso8859-1
lubB08.snf	-b&h-lucidabright-demibold-r-normal--11-80-100-100-p-66-iso8859-1
lubB10.snf	-b&h-lucidabright-demibold-r-normal--14-100-100-100-p-84-iso8859-1
lubB12.snf	-b&h-lucidabright-demibold-r-normal--17-120-100-100-p-101-iso8859-1
lubB14.snf	-b&h-lucidabright-demibold-r-normal--20-140-100-100-p-118-iso8859-1
lubB18.snf	-b&h-lucidabright-demibold-r-normal--25-180-100-100-p-149-iso8859-1
lubB19.snf	-b&h-lucidabright-demibold-r-normal--26-190-100-100-p-155-iso8859-1
lubB24.snf	-b&h-lucidabright-demibold-r-normal--34-240-100-100-p-202-iso8859-1
lubI08.snf	-b&h-lucidabright-medium-i-normal--11-80-100-100-p-63-iso8859-1
lubI10.snf	-b&h-lucidabright-medium-i-normal--14-100-100-100-p-80-iso8859-1
lubI12.snf	-b&h-lucidabright-medium-i-normal--17-120-100-100-p-96-iso8859-1
lubI14.snf	-b&h-lucidabright-medium-i-normal--20-140-100-100-p-113-iso8859-1
lubI18.snf	-b&h-lucidabright-medium-i-normal--25-180-100-100-p-142-iso8859-1
lubI19.snf	-b&h-lucidabright-medium-i-normal--26-190-100-100-p-148-iso8859-1
lubI24.snf	-b&h-lucidabright-medium-i-normal--34-240-100-100-p-194-iso8859-1
lubR08.snf	-b&h-lucidabright-medium-r-normal--11-80-100-100-p-63-iso8859-1
lubR10.snf	-b&h-lucidabright-medium-r-normal--14-100-100-100-p-80-iso8859-1
lubR12.snf	-b&h-lucidabright-medium-r-normal--17-120-100-100-p-96-iso8859-1
lubR14.snf	-b&h-lucidabright-medium-r-normal--20-140-100-100-p-114-iso8859-1
lubR18.snf	-b&h-lucidabright-medium-r-normal--25-180-100-100-p-142-iso8859-1
lubR19.snf	-b&h-lucidabright-medium-r-normal--26-190-100-100-p-149-iso8859-1
lubR24.snf	-b&h-lucidabright-medium-r-normal--34-240-100-100-p-193-iso8859-1
lutBS08.snf	-b&h-lucidatypewriter-bold-r-normal-sans-11-80-100-100-m-70-iso8859-1
lutBS10.snf	-b&h-lucidatypewriter-bold-r-normal-sans-14-100-100-100-m-80-iso8859-1
lutBS12.snf	-b&h-lucidatypewriter-bold-r-normal-sans-17-120-100-100-m-100-iso8859-1
lutBS14.snf	-b&h-lucidatypewriter-bold-r-normal-sans-20-140-100-100-m-120-iso8859-1
lutBS18.snf	-b&h-lucidatypewriter-bold-r-normal-sans-25-180-100-100-m-150-iso8859-1
lutBS19.snf	-b&h-lucidatypewriter-bold-r-normal-sans-26-190-100-100-m-159-iso8859-1
lutBS24.snf	-b&h-lucidatypewriter-bold-r-normal-sans-34-240-100-100-m-200-iso8859-1
lutRS08.snf	-b&h-lucidatypewriter-medium-r-normal-sans-11-80-100-100-m-70-iso8859-1

Filename	Font name
lutRS10.snf	-b&h-lucidatypewriter-medium-r-normal-sans-14-100-100-100-m-80-iso8859-1
lutRS12.snf	-b&h-lucidatypewriter-medium-r-normal-sans-17-120-100-100-m-100-iso8859-1
lutRS14.snf	-b&h-lucidatypewriter-medium-r-normal-sans-20-140-100-100-m-120-iso8859-1
lutRS18.snf	-b&h-lucidatypewriter-medium-r-normal-sans-25-180-100-100-m-150-iso8859-1
lutRS19.snf	-b&h-lucidatypewriter-medium-r-normal-sans-26-190-100-100-m-159-iso8859-1
lutRS24.snf	-b&h-lucidatypewriter-medium-r-normal-sans-34-240-100-100-m-200-iso8859-1
charBI08.snf	-bitstream-charter-bold-i-normal--11-80-100-100-p-68-iso8859-1
charBI10.snf	-bitstream-charter-bold-i-normal--14-100-100-100-p-86-iso8859-1
charBI12.snf	-bitstream-charter-bold-i-normal--17-120-100-100-p-105-iso8859-1
charBI14.snf	-bitstream-charter-bold-i-normal--19-140-100-100-p-117-iso8859-1
charBI18.snf	-bitstream-charter-bold-i-normal--25-180-100-100-p-154-iso8859-1
charBI24.snf	-bitstream-charter-bold-i-normal--33-240-100-100-p-203-iso8859-1
charB08.snf	-bitstream-charter-bold-r-normal--11-80-100-100-p-69-iso8859-1
charB10.snf	-bitstream-charter-bold-r-normal--14-100-100-100-p-88-iso8859-1
charB12.snf	-bitstream-charter-bold-r-normal--17-120-100-100-p-107-iso8859-1
charB14.snf	-bitstream-charter-bold-r-normal--19-140-100-100-p-119-iso8859-1
charB18.snf	-bitstream-charter-bold-r-normal--25-180-100-100-p-157-iso8859-1
charB24.snf	-bitstream-charter-bold-r-normal--33-240-100-100-p-206-iso8859-1
charI08.snf	-bitstream-charter-medium-i-normal--11-80-100-100-p-60-iso8859-1
charI10.snf	-bitstream-charter-medium-i-normal--14-100-100-100-p-76-iso8859-1
charI12.snf	-bitstream-charter-medium-i-normal--17-120-100-100-p-92-iso8859-1
charI14.snf	-bitstream-charter-medium-i-normal--19-140-100-100-p-103-iso8859-1
charI18.snf	-bitstream-charter-medium-i-normal--25-180-100-100-p-136-iso8859-1
charI24.snf	-bitstream-charter-medium-i-normal--33-240-100-100-p-179-iso8859-1
charR08.snf	-bitstream-charter-medium-r-normal--11-80-100-100-p-61-iso8859-1
charR10.snf	-bitstream-charter-medium-r-normal--14-100-100-100-p-78-iso8859-1
charR12.snf	-bitstream-charter-medium-r-normal--17-120-100-100-p-95-iso8859-1
charR14.snf	-bitstream-charter-medium-r-normal--19-140-100-100-p-106-iso8859-1
charR18.snf	-bitstream-charter-medium-r-normal--25-180-100-100-p-139-iso8859-1
charR24.snf	-bitstream-charter-medium-r-normal--33-240-100-100-p-183-iso8859-1
techB14.snf	-bitstream-terminal-bold-r-normal--18-140-100-100-c-110-dec-dectech
termB14.snf	-bitstream-terminal-bold-r-normal--18-140-100-100-c-110-iso8859-1
tech14.snf	-bitstream-terminal-medium-r-normal--18-140-100-100-c-110-dec-dectech
term14.snf	-bitstream-terminal-medium-r-normal--18-140-100-100-c-110-iso8859-1

-adobe-courier-medium-o-normal--8-80-75-75-m-50-iso8859-1
-adobe-courier-medium-o-normal--10-100-75-75-m-60-iso8859-1
-adobe-courier-medium-o-normal--12-120-75-75-m-70-iso8859-1
-adobe-courier-medium-o-normal--14-140-75-75-m-90-iso8859-1
-adobe-courier-medium-o-normal--18-180-75-75-m-110-iso8859-1
-adobe-courier-medium-o-normal--24-240-75-75-m-

-adobe-courier-medium-r-normal--8-80-75-75-m-50-iso8859-1
-adobe-courier-medium-r-normal--10-100-75-75-m-60-iso8859-1
-adobe-courier-medium-r-normal--12-120-75-75-m-70-iso8859-1
-adobe-courier-medium-r-normal--14-140-75-75-m-90-iso8859-1
-adobe-courier-medium-r-normal--18-180-75-75-m-110-iso8859-1
-adobe-courier-medium-r-normal--24-240-75-75-m-

-adobe-courier-bold-o-normal--8-80-75-75-m-50-iso8859-1
-adobe-courier-bold-o-normal--10-100-75-75-m-60-iso8859-1
-adobe-courier-bold-o-normal--12-120-75-75-m-70-iso8859-1
-adobe-courier-bold-o-normal--14-140-75-75-m-90-iso8859-1
-adobe-courier-bold-o-normal--18-180-75-75-m-110-iso8859-1
-adobe-courier-bold-o-normal--24-240-75-75-m-1

-adobe-courier-bold-r-normal--8-80-75-75-m-50-iso8859-1
-adobe-courier-bold-r-normal--10-100-75-75-m-60-iso8859-1
-adobe-courier-bold-r-normal--12-120-75-75-m-70-iso8859-1
-adobe-courier-bold-r-normal--14-140-75-75-m-90-iso8859-1
-adobe-courier-bold-r-normal--18-180-75-75-m-110-iso8859-1
-adobe-courier-bold-r-normal--24-240-75-75-m-1

Foundry: adobe
Family: courier

-adobe-helvetica-medium-o-normal--8-80-75-75-p-47-iso8859-1
-adobe-helvetica-medium-o-normal--10-100-75-75-p-57-iso8859-1
-adobe-helvetica-medium-o-normal--12-120-75-75-p-67-iso8859-1
-adobe-helvetica-medium-o-normal--14-140-75-75-p-78-iso8859-1
-adobe-helvetica-medium-o-normal--18-180-75-75-p-98-iso8859-1
-adobe-helvetica-medium-o-normal--24-240-75-75-p-130-

-adobe-helvetica-medium-r-normal--8-80-75-75-p-46-iso8859-1
-adobe-helvetica-medium-r-normal--10-100-75-75-p-56-iso8859-1
-adobe-helvetica-medium-r-normal--12-120-75-75-p-67-iso8859-1
-adobe-helvetica-medium-r-normal--14-140-75-75-p-77-iso8859-1
-adobe-helvetica-medium-r-normal--18-180-75-75-p-98-iso8859-1
-adobe-helvetica-medium-r-normal--24-240-75-75-p-130-

-adobe-helvetica-bold-o-normal--8-80-75-75-p-50-iso8859-1
-adobe-helvetica-bold-o-normal--10-100-75-75-p-60-iso8859-1
-adobe-helvetica-bold-o-normal--12-120-75-75-p-69-iso8859-1
-adobe-helvetica-bold-o-normal--14-140-75-75-p-82-iso8859-1
-adobe-helvetica-bold-o-normal--18-180-75-75-p-104-iso8859-1
-adobe-helvetica-bold-o-normal--24-240-75-75-p-138-

-adobe-helvetica-bold-r-normal--8-80-75-75-p-50-iso8859-1
-adobe-helvetica-bold-r-normal--10-100-75-75-p-60-iso8859-1
-adobe-helvetica-bold-r-normal--12-120-75-75-p-70-iso8859-1
-adobe-helvetica-bold-r-normal--14-140-75-75-p-82-iso8859-1
-adobe-helvetica-bold-r-normal--18-180-75-75-p-103-iso8859-1
-adobe-helvetica-bold-r-normal--24-240-75-75-p-138-i

Foundry: adobe
Family: helvetica

-adobe-new century schoolbook-medium-i-normal--8-80-75-75-p-60-iso8859-1
-adobe-new century schoolbook-medium-i-normal--10-100-75-75-p-70-iso8859-1
-adobe-new century schoolbook-medium-i-normal--12-120-75-75-p-81-iso8859-1
-adobe-new century schoolbook-medium-i-normal--14-140-75-75-p-81-iso8859-1
-adobe-new century schoolbook-medium-i-normal--18-180-75-75-p-104-iso8859-1
-adobe-new century schoolbook-medium-i-normal--24-240-75-75-p-136-iso8859-1
-adobe-new century schoolbook-medium-r-normal--8-80-75-75-p-60-iso8859-1
-adobe-new century schoolbook-medium-r-normal--10-100-75-75-p-60-iso8859-1
-adobe-new century schoolbook-medium-r-normal--12-120-75-75-p-70-iso8859-1
-adobe-new century schoolbook-medium-r-normal--14-140-75-75-p-82-iso8859-1
-adobe-new century schoolbook-medium-r-normal--18-180-75-75-p-103-iso8859-1
-adobe-new century schoolbook-medium-r-normal--24-240-75-75-p-137-iso8859-1
-adobe-new century schoolbook-bold-i-normal--8-80-75-75-p-56-iso8859-1
-adobe-new century schoolbook-bold-i-normal--10-100-75-75-p-66-iso8859-1
-adobe-new century schoolbook-bold-i-normal--12-120-75-75-p-76-iso8859-1
-adobe-new century schoolbook-bold-i-normal--14-140-75-75-p-88-iso8859-1
-adobe-new century schoolbook-bold-i-normal--18-180-75-75-p-111-iso8859-1
-adobe-new century schoolbook-bold-i-normal--24-240-75-75-p-148-iso8859-1
-adobe-new century schoolbook-bold-r-normal--8-80-75-75-p-56-iso8859-1
-adobe-new century schoolbook-bold-r-normal--10-100-75-75-p-66-iso8859-1
-adobe-new century schoolbook-bold-r-normal--12-120-75-75-p-77-iso8859-1
-adobe-new century schoolbook-bold-r-normal--14-140-75-75-p-87-iso8859-1
-adobe-new century schoolbook-bold-r-normal--18-180-75-75-p-113-iso8859-1
-adobe-new century schoolbook-bold-r-normal--24-240-75-75-p-149-iso8859-1

Foundry: adobe
Family: new century schoolbook

b&h-lucida-medium-i-normal-sans-8-80-75-75-p-45-iso8859-1
-b&h-lucida-medium-i-normal-sans-10-100-75-75-p-59-iso8859-1
-b&h-lucida-medium-i-normal-sans-12-120-75-75-p-71-iso8859-1
-b&h-lucida-medium-i-normal-sans-14-140-75-75-p-82-iso8859-1
-b&h-lucida-medium-i-normal-sans-18-180-75-75-p-105-iso8859-1
-b&h-lucida-medium-i-normal-sans-19-190-75-75-p-108-iso8859-1
-b&h-lucida-medium-i-normal-sans-24-240-75-75-p-1

b&h-lucida-medium-r-normal-sans-8-80-75-75-p-45-iso8859-1
-b&h-lucida-medium-r-normal-sans-10-100-75-75-p-58-iso8859-1
-b&h-lucida-medium-r-normal-sans-12-120-75-75-p-71-iso8859-1
-b&h-lucida-medium-r-normal-sans-14-140-75-75-p-81-iso8859-1
-b&h-lucida-medium-r-normal-sans-18-180-75-75-p-106-iso8859-1
-b&h-lucida-medium-r-normal-sans-19-190-75-75-p-108-iso8859-1
-b&h-lucida-medium-r-normal-sans-24-240-75-75-p-1

b&h-lucida-bold-i-normal-sans-8-80-75-75-p-49-iso8859-1
-b&h-lucida-bold-i-normal-sans-10-100-75-75-p-67-iso8859-1
-b&h-lucida-bold-i-normal-sans-12-120-75-75-p-79-iso8859-1
-b&h-lucida-bold-i-normal-sans-14-140-75-75-p-92-iso8859-1
-b&h-lucida-bold-i-normal-sans-18-180-75-75-p-119-iso8859-1
-b&h-lucida-bold-i-normal-sans-19-190-75-75-p-122-iso8859
-b&h-lucida-bold-i-normal-sans-24-240-75-75-p-

b&h-lucida-bold-r-normal-sans-8-80-75-75-p-50-iso8859-1
-b&h-lucida-bold-r-normal-sans-10-100-75-75-p-66-iso8859-1
-b&h-lucida-bold-r-normal-sans-12-120-75-75-p-79-iso8859-1
-b&h-lucida-bold-r-normal-sans-14-140-75-75-p-92-iso8859-1
-b&h-lucida-bold-r-normal-sans-18-180-75-75-p-120-iso8859-1
-b&h-lucida-bold-r-normal-sans-19-190-75-75-p-122-iso8859
-b&h-lucida-bold-r-normal-sans-24-240-75-75-p-

Foundry: b&h
Family: lucida

-b&h-lucidabright-medium-i-normal--8-80-75-75-p-45-iso8859-1
-b&h-lucidabright-medium-i-normal--10-100-75-75-p-57-iso8859-1
-b&h-lucidabright-medium-i-normal--12-120-75-75-p-67-iso8859-1
-b&h-lucidabright-medium-i-normal--14-140-75-75-p-80-iso8859-1
-b&h-lucidabright-medium-i-normal--18-180-75-75-p-102-iso8859-1
-b&h-lucidabright-medium-i-normal--19-190-75-75-p-109-iso8859-1
-b&h-lucidabright-medium-i-normal--24-240-75-75-p-

-b&h-lucidabright-medium-r-normal--8-80-75-75-p-45-iso8859-1
-b&h-lucidabright-medium-r-normal--10-100-75-75-p-56-iso8859-1
-b&h-lucidabright-medium-r-normal--12-120-75-75-p-68-iso8859-1
-b&h-lucidabright-medium-r-normal--14-140-75-75-p-80-iso8859-1
-b&h-lucidabright-medium-r-normal--18-180-75-75-p-103-iso8859-1
-b&h-lucidabright-medium-r-normal--19-190-75-75-p-109-iso8859-1
-b&h-lucidabright-medium-r-normal--24-240-75-75-p-

-b&h-lucidabright-demibold-i-normal--8-80-75-75-p-46-iso8859-1
-b&h-lucidabright-demibold-i-normal--10-100-75-75-p-59-iso8859-1
-b&h-lucidabright-demibold-i-normal--12-120-75-75-p-72-iso8859-1
-b&h-lucidabright-demibold-i-normal--14-140-75-75-p-84-iso8859-1
-b&h-lucidabright-demibold-i-normal--18-180-75-75-p-107-iso8859-1
-b&h-lucidabright-demibold-i-normal--19-190-75-75-p-114-iso8859
-b&h-lucidabright-demibold-i-normal--24-240-75-75-

-b&h-lucidabright-demibold-r-normal--8-80-75-75-p-47-iso8859-1
-b&h-lucidabright-demibold-r-normal--10-100-75-75-p-59-iso8859-1
-b&h-lucidabright-demibold-r-normal--12-120-75-75-p-71-iso8859-1
-b&h-lucidabright-demibold-r-normal--14-140-75-75-p-84-iso8859-1
-b&h-lucidabright-demibold-r-normal--18-180-75-75-p-107-iso8859-1
-b&h-lucidabright-demibold-r-normal--19-190-75-75-p-114-iso885
-b&h-lucidabright-demibold-r-normal--24-240-75-75-

Foundry: b&h
Family: lucidabright

-adobe-times-medium-i-normal--8-80-75-75-p-42-iso8859-1
-adobe-times-medium-i-normal--10-100-75-75-p-52-iso8859-1
-adobe-times-medium-i-normal--12-120-75-75-p-63-iso8859-1
-adobe-times-medium-i-normal--14-140-75-75-p-73-iso8859-1
-adobe-times-medium-i-normal--18-180-75-75-p-94-iso8859-1
-adobe-times-medium-i-normal--24-240-75-75-p-125-iso8859

-adobe-times-medium-r-normal--8-80-75-75-p-44-iso8859-1
-adobe-times-medium-r-normal--10-100-75-75-p-54-iso8859-1
-adobe-times-medium-r-normal--12-120-75-75-p-64-iso8859-1
-adobe-times-medium-r-normal--14-140-75-75-p-74-iso8859-1
-adobe-times-medium-r-normal--18-180-75-75-p-94-iso8859-1
-adobe-times-medium-r-normal--24-240-75-75-p-124-iso8859

-adobe-times-bold-i-normal--8-80-75-75-p-47-iso8859-1
-adobe-times-bold-i-normal--10-100-75-75-p-57-iso8859-1
-adobe-times-bold-i-normal--12-120-75-75-p-68-iso8859-1
-adobe-times-bold-i-normal--14-140-75-75-p-77-iso8859-1
-adobe-times-bold-i-normal--18-180-75-75-p-98-iso8859-1
-adobe-times-bold-i-normal--24-240-75-75-p-128-iso8859-1

-adobe-times-bold-r-normal--8-80-75-75-p-47-iso8859-1
-adobe-times-bold-r-normal--10-100-75-75-p-57-iso8859-1
-adobe-times-bold-r-normal--12-120-75-75-p-67-iso8859-1
-adobe-times-bold-r-normal--14-140-75-75-p-77-iso8859-1
-adobe-times-bold-r-normal--18-180-75-75-p-99-iso8859-1
-adobe-times-bold-r-normal--24-240-75-75-p-132-iso8859-

Foundry: adobe
Family: times

-αδοβε-συμβολ-μεδιυμ-ρ-νορμαλ--8-80-75-75-π-51-αδοβε-φοντοπεχιφψχ
-αδοβε-συμβολ-μεδιυμ-ρ-νορμαλ--10-100-75-75-π-61-αδοβε-φοντοπεχιφψχ
-αδοβε-συμβολ-μεδιυμ-ρ-νορμαλ--12-120-75-75-π-74-αδοβε-φοντοπεχιφψχ
-αδοβε-συμβολ-μεδιυμ-ρ-νορμαλ--14-140-75-75-π-85-αδοβε-φοντοπεχιφψχ
-αδοβε-συμβολ-μεδιυμ-ρ-νορμαλ--18-180-75-75-π-107-αδοβε-φοντοπεχιφψχ
-αδοβε-συμβολ-μεδιυμ-ρ-νορμαλ--24-240-75-75-π-142-αδοβε

Foundry: adobe
Family: symbol

-b&h-lucidatypewriter-medium-r-normal-sans-8-80-75-75-m-50-iso8859-1
-b&h-lucidatypewriter-medium-r-normal-sans-10-100-75-75-m-60-iso8859-1
-b&h-lucidatypewriter-medium-r-normal-sans-12-120-75-75-m-70-iso8859-1
-b&h-lucidatypewriter-medium-r-normal-sans-14-140-75-75-m-90-iso8859-1
-b&h-lucidatypewriter-medium-r-normal-sans-18-180-75-75-m-110-is
-b&h-lucidatypewriter-medium-r-normal-sans-19-190-75-75-m-110-is
-b&h-lucidatypewriter-medium-r-normal-sans-24-240-

-b&h-lucidatypewriter-bold-r-normal-sans-8-80-75-75-m-50-iso8859-1
-b&h-lucidatypewriter-bold-r-normal-sans-10-100-75-75-m-60-iso8859-1
-b&h-lucidatypewriter-bold-r-normal-sans-12-120-75-75-m-70-iso8859-1
-b&h-lucidatypewriter-bold-r-normal-sans-14-140-75-75-m-90-iso8859-1
-b&h-lucidatypewriter-bold-r-normal-sans-18-180-75-75-m-110-iso8
-b&h-lucidatypewriter-bold-r-normal-sans-19-190-75-75-m-110-iso8
-b&h-lucidatypewriter-bold-r-normal-sans-24-240-75.

Foundry: b&h
Family: lucidatypewriter

-bitstream-charter-medium-i-normal--8-80-75-75-p-44-iso8859-1
-bitstream-charter-medium-i-normal--10-100-75-75-p-55-iso8859-1
-bitstream-charter-medium-i-normal--12-120-75-75-p-65-iso8859-1
-bitstream-charter-medium-i-normal--15-140-75-75-p-82-iso8859-1
-bitstream-charter-medium-i-normal--19-180-75-75-p-103-iso8859-1
-bitstream-charter-medium-i-normal--25-240-75-75-p-136-iso88

-bitstream-charter-medium-r-normal--8-80-75-75-p-45-iso8859-1
-bitstream-charter-medium-r-normal--10-100-75-75-p-56-iso8859-1
-bitstream-charter-medium-r-normal--12-120-75-75-p-67-iso8859-1
-bitstream-charter-medium-r-normal--15-140-75-75-p-84-iso8859-1
-bitstream-charter-medium-r-normal--19-180-75-75-p-106-iso8859-1
-bitstream-charter-medium-r-normal--25-240-75-75-p-139-iso88

-bitstream-charter-bold-i-normal--8-80-75-75-p-50-iso8859-1
-bitstream-charter-bold-i-normal--10-100-75-75-p-62-iso8859-1
-bitstream-charter-bold-i-normal--12-120-75-75-p-74-iso8859-1
-bitstream-charter-bold-i-normal--15-140-75-75-p-93-iso8859-1
-bitstream-charter-bold-i-normal--19-180-75-75-p-117-iso8859-1
-bitstream-charter-bold-i-normal--25-240-75-75-p-154-i

-bitstream-charter-bold-r-normal--8-80-75-75-p-50-iso8859-1
-bitstream-charter-bold-r-normal--10-100-75-75-p-63-iso8859-1
-bitstream-charter-bold-r-normal--12-120-75-75-p-75-iso8859-1
-bitstream-charter-bold-r-normal--15-140-75-75-p-94-iso8859-1
-bitstream-charter-bold-r-normal--19-180-75-75-p-119-iso8859-1
-bitstream-charter-bold-r-normal--25-240-75-75-p-157-

Foundry: bitstream
Family: charter

```
-bitstream-terminal-medium-r-normal--18-140-100-
-bitstream-terminal-bold-r-normal--18-140-100-1C
```

```
-dec-terminal-medium-r-normal--14-140-75-75-c-80-iso8859-1
-dec-terminal-bold-r-normal--14-140-75-75-c-80-iso8859-1
```

Foundry: bitstream
Family: terminal

Foundry: dec
Family: terminal

```
-misc-fixed-medium-r-normal--8-80-75-75-c-50-iso8859-1
-misc-fixed-medium-r-normal--9-90-75-75-c-60-iso8859-1
-misc-fixed-medium-r-normal--10-100-75-75-c-60-iso8859-1
-misc-fixed-medium-r-semicondensed--12-110-75-75-c-60-iso8859-1
-misc-fixed-medium-r-semicondensed--13-120-75-75-c-60-iso8859-1
-misc-fixed-medium-r-normal--13-120-75-75-c-70-iso8859-1
-misc-fixed-medium-r-normal--13-120-75-75-c-80-iso8859-1
-misc-fixed-medium-r-normal--14-130-75-75-c-70-iso8859-1
-misc-fixed-medium-r-normal--15-140-75-75-c-90-iso8859-1
-misc-fixed-medium-r-normal--20-200-75-75-c-100-iso8!
-misc-fixed-bold-r-semicondensed--13-120-75-75-c-60-iso8859-1
-misc-fixed-bold-r-normal--13-120-75-75-c-70-iso8859-1
-misc-fixed-bold-r-normal--13-120-75-75-c-80-iso8859-1
-misc-fixed-bold-r-normal--15-140-75-75-c-90-iso8859-1
```

Foundry: misc
Family: fixed

```
-schumacher-clean-medium-i-normal--8-80-75-75-c-80-iso8859-1
-schumacher-clean-medium-i-normal--12-120-75-75-c-60-iso8859-1
-schumacher-clean-medium-r-normal--6-60-75-75-c-40-iso8859-1
-schumacher-clean-medium-r-normal--6-60-75-75-c-50-iso8859-1
-schumacher-clean-medium-r-normal--8-80-75-75-c-50-iso8859-1
-schumacher-clean-medium-r-normal--8-80-75-75-c-60-iso8859-1
-schumacher-clean-medium-r-normal--8-80-75-75-c-70-iso8859-1
-schumacher-clean-medium-r-normal--8-80-75-75-c-80-iso8859-1
-schumacher-clean-medium-r-normal--10-100-75-75-c-70-iso8859-1
-schumacher-clean-medium-r-normal--10-100-75-75-c-80-iso8859-1
-schumacher-clean-medium-r-normal--10-100-75-75-c-50-iso8859-1
-schumacher-clean-medium-r-normal--10-100-75-75-c-60-iso8859-1
-schumacher-clean-medium-r-normal--12-120-75-75-c-60-iso8859-1
-schumacher-clean-medium-r-normal--12-120-75-75-c-70-iso8859-1
-schumacher-clean-medium-r-normal--12-120-75-75-c-80-iso8859-1
-schumacher-clean-medium-r-normal--13-130-75-75-c-80-iso8859-1
-schumacher-clean-medium-r-normal--13-130-75-75-c-60-iso8859-1
-schumacher-clean-medium-r-normal--14-140-75-75-c-80-iso8859-1
-schumacher-clean-medium-r-normal--14-140-75-75-c-70-iso8859-1
-schumacher-clean-medium-r-normal--15-150-75-75-c-90-iso88
-schumacher-clean-medium-r-normal--16-160-75-75-c-80-iso8859-1
-schumacher-clean-bold-r-normal--8-80-75-75-c-80-iso8859-1
-schumacher-clean-bold-r-normal--10-100-75-75-c-60-iso8859-1
-schumacher-clean-bold-r-normal--10-100-75-75-c-80-iso8859-1
-schumacher-clean-bold-r-normal--12-120-75-75-c-80-iso8859-1
-schumacher-clean-bold-r-normal--12-120-75-75-c-60-iso8859-1
-schumacher-clean-bold-r-normal--13-130-75-75-c-80-iso8859-1
-schumacher-clean-bold-r-normal--14-140-75-75-c-80-iso8859-1
-schumacher-clean-bold-r-normal--15-150-75-75-c-90-iso8859-1
-schumacher-clean-bold-r-normal--16-160-75-75-c-80-iso8859-1
```

Foundry: schumacher
Family: clean

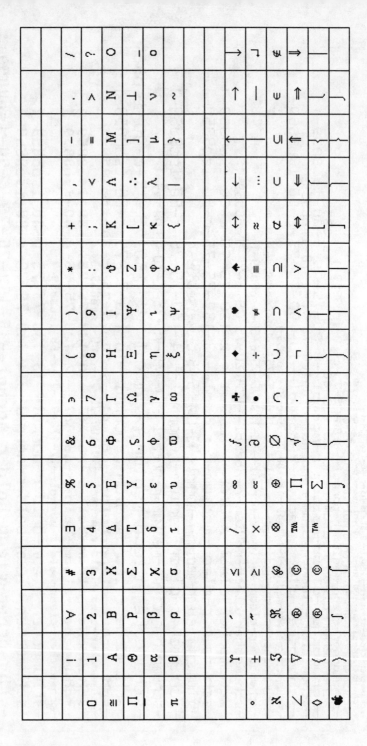

Encoding: adobe-fontspecific

X Window System User's Guide, Motif Edition

Encoding: dec-dectech

Encoding: iso8859

Encoding: jisx0201.1976

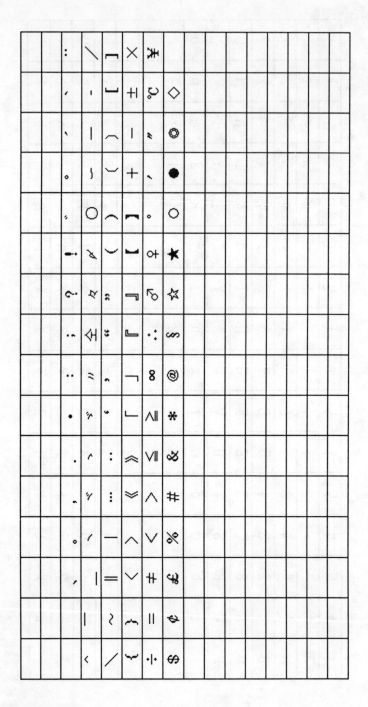

Encoding: jisx0208.1983

Encoding: jisx0201.1976

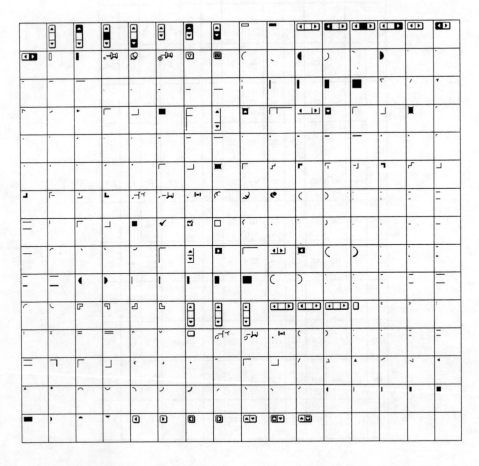

Encoding: sunolglyph

X Window System User's Guide, Motif Edition

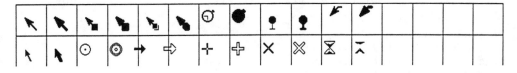

Encoding: SunOLcursor

Example B-1 is the source code for the *xshowfonts* program, which we used to create most of the illustrations in this appendix. If you don't want to type it in, you can find instructions for getting it online in the *Preface*.

Example B-1. xshowfont source listing

```
/* Dan Heller <argv@sun.com>, based on a design by Tim O'Reilly
 *
 * xshowfonts.c -
 *   Displays a set of fonts specified on the command line, from
 * a pipe, or typed into stdin.  Fonts can be specified as specific
 * or wildcard character strings.  A pixmap is created to
 * display all the fonts.  This is done by using the pixmap as the
 * pixmap image for a label widget.  Each font prints its own name
 * in its own font style -- the -phrase option prints the phrase
 * instead.
 *
 * All fonts are loaded first and scanned to determine the total
 * width and height of the pixmap first.  Then the fonts are
 * reopened again to actually render the fonts into the pixmap.
 * All this could be avoided by using XListFontsWithInfo()
 * rather than XListFonts() but since the list is potentially
 * very large, I didn't want to overload the server and client
 * with all those fonts + a very large pixmap.
 *
 * Usage: xshowfonts
 *    -s sorts the fonts in alphabetical order before displaying
 *       them.
 *    -v verbose mode for when input is redirected to stdin.
 *    -w width of viewport window
 *    -h height of viewport window
 *    -fg foreground_color
 *    -bg background_color
 *    -phrase "text string" (otherwise, name of font is used)
 *    -indicates to read from stdin.  Piping doesn't require
 *     the '-' argument.  With no arguments, xshowfonts reads
 *     from stdin anyway.
 *
 * Neat ways to use the program:
 *   xshowfonts -fg green -bg black "*adobe*"
 *   xshowfonts -sort "*"
 *   xshowfonts -phrase "The quick brown fox jumps over the lazy
 *              dog" "*times*"
 *   xlsfonts | xshowfonts -sort
 *   xshowfonts "*helvetica*"
 *
 * compile: (triple click and paste next line)
 *     cc -O -s xshowfonts.c -lXaw -lXt -lXmu -lX11 -o xshowfonts
 */

#include <stdio.h>
#include <X11/Intrinsic.h>
#include <X11/StringDefs.h>
#include <X11/Xaw/Label.h>
#include <X11/Xaw/Viewport.h>

struct _resrcs {
    int sort;
```

```
    int verbose;
    Pixel fg, bg;
    char *phrase;
    int view_width, view_height;
} Resrcs;

static XtResource resources[] = {
    { "sort", "Sort", XtRBoolean, sizeof (int),
     XtOffsetOf(struct _resrcs,sort), XtRImmediate,
        False },
    { "verbose", "Verbose", XtRBoolean, sizeof (int),
     XtOffsetOf(struct _resrcs,verbose), XtRImmediate,
        False },
    { "foreground", "Foreground", XtRPixel, sizeof (Pixel),
     XtOffsetOf(struct _resrcs,fg), XtRString,
        XtDefaultForeground },
    { "background", "Background", XtRPixel, sizeof (Pixel),
     XtOffsetOf(struct _resrcs,bg), XtRString,
        XtDefaultBackground },
    { "phrase", "Phrase", XtRString, sizeof (String),
     XtOffsetOf(struct _resrcs,phrase), XtRImmediate, NULL },
    { "view-width", "View-width", XtRInt, sizeof (int),
     XtOffsetOf(struct _resrcs,view_width), XtRImmediate,
        (char *)500 },
    { "view-height", "View-height", XtRInt, sizeof (int),
     XtOffsetOf(struct _resrcs,view_height), XtRImmediate,
        (char *)300 },
};

static XrmOptionDescRec options[] = {
    { "-sort", "sort", XrmoptionNoArg, "True" },
    { "-v", "verbose", XrmoptionNoArg, "True" },
    { "-fg", "foreground", XrmoptionSepArg, NULL },
    { "-bg", "background", XrmoptionSepArg, NULL },
    { "-phrase", "phrase", XrmoptionSepArg, NULL },
    { "-w", "view-width", XrmoptionSepArg, NULL },
    { "-h", "view-height", XrmoptionSepArg, NULL },
};

/* sort font according to these parameters.
 * font specs we're interested in:
 *    -fndry-fmly-wght-slant-*swdth-*adstyl-*pxlsz-ptsz- ....
 * foundry -- sort by foundry first; similar ones are always
 *            grouped together
 * weight -- medium, demi-bold, bold
 * slant -- roman, italic/oblique, reverse italic/oblique
 *          (i or o, r, ri, ro)
 * ptsize -- increase numerical order
 */
font_cmp(f1, f2)
char **f1, **f2;
{
    char fndry1[16], fmly1[64], wght1[32], slant1[3];
    char fndry2[16], fmly2[64], wght2[32], slant2[3];
    int n, m, ptsize1, ptsize2;
    char *font_fmt_str = "-%[^-]-%[^-]-%[^-]-%[^-]-%*[^0-9]%
        *d-%d-";
```

```
        n = sscanf(*f1, font_fmt_str, fndry1, fmly1, wght1, slant1,
                &ptsize1);
        m = sscanf(*f2, font_fmt_str, fndry2, fmly2, wght2, slant2,
                &ptsize2);
        if (m < 5 || n < 5)
        /* font not in correct format -- just return font names
         * in order */
        return strcmp(*f1, *f2);
        if (n = strcmp(fndry1, fndry2))
        return n; /* different foundries -- return alphabetical
                        * order */
        if (n = strcmp(fmly1, fmly2))
        return n; /* different families -- return alphabetical
                        * order */
        if (n = strcmp(wght1, wght2))
        return -n; /* weight happens to be correct in reverse
                           * alpha order */
        if (n = strcmp(slant1, slant2))
        return n; /* slants happen to be correct in alphabetical
                        * order */
        /* sort according to point size */
        return ptsize1 - ptsize2;
}

main(argc, argv)
int argc;
char *argv[];
{
    Widget topLevel, vp;
    char **list = (char **)NULL, **tmp;
    char buf[128];
    extern char **XListFonts();
    extern int strcmp();
    XFontStruct *font;
    Pixmap pixmap;
    GC gc;
    Display *dpy;
    int istty = isatty(0), redirect = !istty, i, j, total = 0;
    unsigned int w, width = 0, height = 0;

    topLevel = XtInitialize(argv[0], argv[0], options,
        XtNumber(options), &argc, argv);
    dpy = XtDisplay(topLevel);

    XtGetApplicationResources(topLevel, &Resrcs,
     resources, XtNumber(resources), NULL, 0);

    if (!argv[1] || !strcmp(argv[1], "-")) {
    printf("Loading fonts from input. ");
    if (istty) {
        puts("End with EOF or .");
        redirect++;
    } else
        puts("Use -v to view font names being loaded.");
    } else if (!istty && strcmp(argv[1], "-"))
    printf("%s: either use pipes or specify font names --
            not both.\n",
```

```
        argv[0]), exit(1);
   while (*++argv || redirect) {
    if (!redirect)
        if (!strcmp(*argv, "-"))
         redirect++;
        else
         strcpy(buf, *argv);
    if (redirect) {
        if (istty)
         printf("Fontname: "), fflush(stdout);
        if (!fgets(buf, sizeof buf, stdin) ||
               !strcmp(buf, ".\n"))
         break;
        buf[strlen(buf)-1] = 0;
    }
    if (!buf[0])
        continue;
    if (istty || Resrcs.verbose)
        printf("Loading
    tmp = XListFonts(dpy, buf, 32767, &i);
    if (i == 0) {
        printf("couldn't load font ");
        if (!istty && !Resrcs.verbose)
         printf("
        putchar('\n');
        continue;
    }
    if (istty || Resrcs.verbose)
        printf("%d font%s\n", i, i == 1? "" : "s");
    if (!list) {
        list = tmp;
        total = i;
    } else {
        i += total;
        if (!(list = (char **)XtRealloc(list, i *
                    sizeof (char *))))
        XtError("Not enough memory for font names");
        for (j = 0; total < i; j++, total++)
        list[total] = tmp[j];
    }
   }
   if (total == 0)
    puts("No fonts?!"), exit(1);
   printf("Total fonts loaded: %d\n", total);
   if (Resrcs.sort) {
    printf("Sorting fonts..."), fflush(stdout);
    qsort(list, total, sizeof (char *), font_cmp);
    putchar('\n');
   }
   /* calculate size for pixmap by getting the dimensions
    * of each font */
   puts("Calculating sizes for pixmap.");
   for (i = 0; i < total; i++) {
    if (!(font = XLoadQueryFont(dpy, list[i]))) {
        printf("Can't load font: %s\n", list[i]);
        continue;
```

```
    }
    if ((w = XTextWidth(font, list[i],
        strlen(list[i]))) > width)
        width = w;
    height += font->ascent + font->descent;
    XFreeFont(dpy, font);
    }
    width += 6;
    height += 6;
    /* Create pixmap + GC */
    printf("Creating pixmap of size %dx%d\n", width, height);
    if (!(pixmap = XCreatePixmap(dpy, DefaultRootWindow(dpy),
     width, height, DefaultDepth(dpy, DefaultScreen(dpy)))))
     XtError("Can't Create pixmap");
    if (!(gc = XCreateGC(dpy, pixmap, NULL, 0)))
     XtError("Can't create gc");
    XSetForeground(dpy, gc, Resrcs.bg);
    XFillRectangle(dpy, pixmap, gc, 0, 0, width, height);
    XSetForeground(dpy, gc, Resrcs.fg);
    XSetBackground(dpy, gc, Resrcs.bg);
    height = 0;
    for (i = 0; i < total; i++) {
     if (!(font = XLoadQueryFont(dpy, list[i])))
        continue; /* it's already been reported */
     XSetFont(dpy, gc, font->fid);
     height += font->ascent;
     if (Resrcs.phrase)
        XDrawString(dpy, pixmap, gc, 0, height,
         Resrcs.phrase, strlen(Resrcs.phrase));
     else
        XDrawString(dpy, pixmap, gc, 5, height, list[i],
                    strlen(list[i]));
     height += font->descent;
     XFreeFont(dpy, font);
    }
    vp = XtVaCreateManagedWidget("viewport", viewportWidgetClass,
        topLevel,
    XtNallowHoriz,      True,
    XtNallowVert, True,
    XtNwidth, Resrcs.view_width,
    XtNheight,     Resrcs.view_height,
    NULL);
    XtVaCreateManagedWidget("_foo", labelWidgetClass, vp,
    XtNbitmap,      pixmap,
    NULL);

    if (!redirect)
     XFreeFontNames(list);

    XtRealizeWidget(topLevel);
    XtMainLoop();
}
```

C

Standard Bitmaps

This appendix shows the bitmaps included with the standard distribution of the X Window System. These can be used for setting window background, cursor symbols, pixmaps, and possibly for application icon pixmaps.

C
Standard Bitmaps

A number of bitmaps are included with the standard distribution of the X Window System. These bitmaps can be used for setting window background pixmaps and possibly for application icon pixmaps.

The standard bitmaps are generally located in the directory */usr/include/X11/bitmaps*. Each bitmap is in standard X11 bitmap format in its own file. The *bitmap* application can be used to view these bitmaps in larger scale and to edit them (though their permissions normally do not allow overwriting).

You can use these bitmaps to set the background pattern of a window in any application that allows it. For example, if you wanted to change the root window background pixmap, you could do so using *xsetroot*:

```
xsetroot -bitmap /usr/include/X11/bitmaps/wide_weave
```

Note that the bitmaps that come in pairs, such as `cntr_ptr` and `cntr_ptrmsk`, are intended for creating pointer shapes. See Chapter 12, *Setup Clients*, for information on specifying a bitmap as the root window pointer.

The 63 bitmaps pictured on the following pages are included in the Release 4 standard distribution of X. Table C-1 lists those bitmaps that have been added to the standard distribution in Release 4.

Table C-1. Standard Bitmaps Available as of Release 4

calculator	dropbar7	dropbar8
escherknot	hlines2	hlines3
keyboard16	letters	mailempty
mailemptymsk	mailfull	mailfullmsk
menu10	menu12	menu16
menu8	noletters	plaid
terminal	vlines2	vlines3
xlogo11		

1x1	2x2	black	boxes	calculator
cntr_ptr	cntr_ptrmsk	cross_weave	dimple1	dimple3
dot	dropbar7	dropbar8	flagdown	flagup
flipped_gray	gray	gray1	gray3	hlines2
hlines3	icon	keyboard16	left_ptr	left_ptrmsk
letters	light_gray	mailempty	mailemptymsk	mailfull
mailfullmsk	menu10	menu12	menu16	menu8
noletters	opendot	opendotMask	plaid	right_ptr
right_ptrmsk	root_weave	scales	sipb	star
starMask	stipple	target	terminal	tie_fighter
vlines2	vlines3	weird_size	wide_weave	wingdogs
xfd_icon	xlogo11	xlogo16	xlogo32	xlogo64

Figure C-1. The Standard Bitmaps

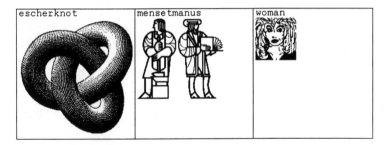

Figure C-1. The standard bitmaps (continued)

D

Standard Cursors

This appendix shows the standard cursor images that can be used by X programs.

D
Standard Cursors

Table D-1 lists the cursors available in the standard distribution of X from MIT; the cursor shapes themselves are pictured in Figure D-1.

To specify a cursor as an argument to a command line option, as the value of a resource variable, etc., strip the `XC_` prefix from the symbol name. For example, to specify the `XC_sailboat` cursor as the *xterm* pointer, you could enter the command:

```
% xterm -xrm 'xterm*pointerShape: sailboat'
```

Each cursor has an associated numeric value (to the right of the symbol name in the table). You may notice that the values skip the odd numbers. Each cursor is actually composed of two font characters: the character that defines the shape (pictured in Figure D-1), and a mask character (not shown) that sets the cursor shape off from the root (or other) window. (More precisely, the mask selects which pixels in the screen around the cursor are disturbed by the cursor.) The mask is generally the same shape as the character it underlies but is one pixel wider in all directions.

To get an idea of what masks look like, display the entire cursor font using the command:

```
% xfd -fn cursor
```

The *mwm* window manager uses several of the standard cursor symbols. In addition, *mwm* uses some Motif-specific cursors, which are illustrated in Figure 1-3 in Part One of this guide.

Table D-1. Standard Cursor Symbols

Symbol	Value	Symbol	Value
XC_X_cursor	0	XC_ll_angle	76
XC_arrow	2	XC_lr_angle	78
XC_based_arrow_down	4	XC_man	80
XC_based_arrow_up	6	XC_middlebutton	82
XC_boat	8	XC_mouse	84
XC_bogosity	10	XC_pencil	86
XC_bottom_left_corner	12	XC_pirate	88
XC_bottom_right_corner	14	XC_plus	90
XC_bottom_side	16	XC_question_arrow	92
XC_bottom_tee	18	XC_right_ptr	94
XC_box_spiral	20	XC_right_side	96
XC_center_ptr	22	XC_right_tee	98
XC_circle	24	XC_rightbutton	100
XC_clock	26	XC_rtl_logo	102
XC_coffee_mug	28	XC_sailboat	104
XC_cross	30	XC_sb_down_arrow	106
XC_cross_reverse	32	XC_sb_h_double_arrow	108
XC_crosshair	34	XC_sb_left_arrow	110
XC_diamond_cross	36	XC_sb_right_arrow	112
XC_dot	38	XC_sb_up_arrow	114
XC_dotbox	40	XC_sb_v_double_arrow	116
XC_double_arrow	42	XC_shuttle	118
XC_draft_large	44	XC_sizing	120
XC_draft_small	46	XC_spider	122
XC_draped_box	48	XC_spraycan	124
XC_exchange	50	XC_star	126
XC_fleur	52	XC_target	128
XC_gobbler	54	XC_tcross	130
XC_gumby	56	XC_top_left_arrow	132
XC_hand1	58	XC_top_left_corner	134
XC_hand2	60	XC_top_right_corner	136
XC_heart	62	XC_top_side	138
XC_icon	64	XC_top_tee	140
XC_iron_cross	66	XC_trek	142
XC_left_ptr	68	XC_ul_angle	144
XC_left_side	70	XC_umbrella	146
XC_left_tee	72	XC_ur_angle	148
XC_leftbutton	74	XC_watch	150
		XC_xterm	152

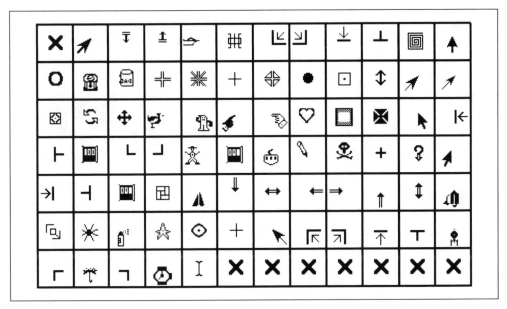

Figure D-1. The Standard Cursors

E

xterm Control Sequences

This appendix list the escape sequences that can be used to control features of an xterm *window or its terminal emulation.*

In This Appendix:

E
xterm Control Sequences

A standard terminal performs many operations in response to escape sequences sent out by a program. In emulating a terminal, *xterm* responds to those same terminal escape sequences. Under UNIX, programs use the *termcap* or *terminfo* database to determine which escape sequences to send out. For more information, see the standard UNIX man pages *termcap*(5) or *terminfo*(5), or the Nutshell Handbook *Termcap and Terminfo*, available from O'Reilly & Associates, Inc.

xterm Control Sequences

This appendix is based on two sources: the "Xterm Control Sequences" document, written by Edward Moy, University of California, Berkeley, for the X10 *xterm*; and X11 updates provided to the X Consortium by Skip Montanaro, GE Corporate Research & Development.

Definitions

C A single (required) character.

P_s A single (usually optional) numeric parameter, composed of one of more digits.

P_m A multiple numeric parameter composed of any number of single numeric parameters, separated by ⨪ character(s).

P_t A text parameter composed of printable characters.

VT102 Mode

Most of these control sequences are standard VT102 control sequences. There are, however, additional ones to provide control of *xterm*-dependent functions, like the scrollbar or window size.

`BEL`	Bell (Ctrl-G)
`BS`	Backspace (Ctrl-H)
`TAB`	Horizontal Tab (Ctrl-I)
`LF`	Line Feed or New Line (Ctrl-J)
`VT`	Vertical Tab (Ctrl-K)
`FF`	Form Feed or New Page (Ctrl-L)
`CR`	Carriage Return (Ctrl-M)
`SO`	Shift Out (Ctrl-N) → Switch to Alternate Character Set
`SI`	Shift In (Ctrl-O) → Switch to Standard Character Set
`ESC` `BEL`	Same as non-escaped BEL
`ESC` `BS`	Same as non-escaped BS
`ESC` `HT`	Same as non-escaped HT
`ESC` `NL`	Same as non-escaped NL
`ESC` `VT`	Same as non-escaped VT
`ESC` `NP`	Same as non-escaped NP
`ESC` `CR`	Same as non-escaped CR
`ESC` `SO`	Same as non-escaped SO
`ESC` `SI`	Same as non-escaped SI
`ESC` `#` `BEL`	Same as non-escaped BEL
`ESC` `#` `BS`	Same as non-escaped BS
`ESC` `#` `HT`	Same as non-escaped HT
`ESC` `#` `NL`	Same as non-escaped NL
`ESC` `#` `VT`	Same as non-escaped VT
`ESC` `#` `NP`	Same as non-escaped NP
`ESC` `#` `CR`	Same as non-escaped CR
`ESC` `#` `SO`	Same as non-escaped SO
`ESC` `#` `SI`	Same as non-escaped SI
`ESC` `#` `8`	DEC Screen Alignment Test (DECALN)
`ESC` `(` `BEL`	Same as non-escaped BEL
`ESC` `(` `BS`	Same as non-escaped BS
`ESC` `(` `HT`	Same as non-escaped HT
`ESC` `(` `NL`	Same as non-escaped NL
`ESC` `(` `VT`	Same as non-escaped VT
`ESC` `(` `NP`	Same as non-escaped NP
`ESC` `(` `CR`	Same as non-escaped CR
`ESC` `(` `SO`	Same as non-escaped SO

`ESC` `(` `SI`	Same as non-escaped SI
`ESC` `(` *C*	Select G0 Character Set (SCS)

$C = \boxed{0} \rightarrow$ Special Character and Line Drawing Set
$C = \boxed{1} \rightarrow$ Alternate Character ROM Standard Set
$C = \boxed{2} \rightarrow$ Alternate Character ROM Special Set
$C = \boxed{A} \rightarrow$ United Kingdom (UK)
$C = \boxed{B} \rightarrow$ United States (USASCII)

`ESC` `)` *C*	Select G1 Character Set (SCS)

$C = \boxed{0} \rightarrow$ Special Character and Line Drawing Set
$C = \boxed{1} \rightarrow$ Alternate Character ROM Standard Set
$C = \boxed{2} \rightarrow$ Alternate Character ROM Special Set
$C = \boxed{A} \rightarrow$ United Kingdom (UK)
$C = \boxed{B} \rightarrow$ United States (USASCII)

`ESC` `*` *C*	Select G2 Character Set (SCS)

$C = \boxed{0} \rightarrow$ Special Character and Line Drawing Set
$C = \boxed{1} \rightarrow$ Alternate Character ROM Standard Set
$C = \boxed{2} \rightarrow$ Alternate Character ROM Special Set
$C = \boxed{A} \rightarrow$ United Kingdom (UK)
$C = \boxed{B} \rightarrow$ United States (USASCII)

`ESC` `+` *C*	Select G3 Character Set (SCS)

$C = \boxed{0} \rightarrow$ Special Character and Line Drawing Set
$C = \boxed{1} \rightarrow$ Alternate Character ROM Standard Set
$C = \boxed{2} \rightarrow$ Alternate Character ROM Special Set
$C = \boxed{A} \rightarrow$ United Kingdom (UK)
$C = \boxed{B} \rightarrow$ United States (USASCII)

`ESC` `7`	Save Cursor (DECSC)
`ESC` `8`	Restore Cursor (DECRC)
`ESC` `=`	Application Keypad (DECPAM)
`ESC` `>`	Normal Keypad (DECPNM)
`ESC` `D`	Index (IND)
`ESC` `E`	Next Line (NEL)
`ESC` `H`	Tab Set (HTS)
`ESC` `M`	Reverse Index (RI)
`ESC` `N`	Single Shift Select of G2 Character Set (SS2)
`ESC` `O`	Single Shift Select of G3 Character Set (SS3)
`ESC`	Return Terminal ID (DECID)

xterm Control Sequences

`ESC` `[` `BEL`	Same as non-escaped BEL
`ESC` `[` `BS`	Same as non-escaped BS
`ESC` `[` `HT`	Same as non-escaped HT
`ESC` `[` `NL`	Same as non-escaped NL
`ESC` `[` `VT`	Same as non-escaped VT
`ESC` `[` `NP`	Same as non-escaped NP
`ESC` `[` `CR`	Same as non-escaped CR
`ESC` `[` `SO`	Same as non-escaped SO
`ESC` `[` `SI`	Same as non-escaped SI
`ESC` `[` `?` `BEL`	Same as non-escaped BEL
`ESC` `[` `?` `BS`	Same as non-escaped BS
`ESC` `[` `?` `HT`	Same as non-escaped HT
`ESC` `[` `?` `NL`	Same as non-escaped NL
`ESC` `[` `?` `VT`	Same as non-escaped VT
`ESC` `[` `?` `NP`	Same as non-escaped NP
`ESC` `[` `?` `CR`	Same as non-escaped CR
`ESC` `[` `?` `SO`	Same as non-escaped SO
`ESC` `[` `?` `SI`	Same as non-escaped SI
`ESC` `[` P_s `@`	Insert P_s (Blank) Character(s) (default = 1) (ICH)
`ESC` `[` P_s `A`	Cursor Up P_s Times (default = 1) (CUU)
`ESC` `[` P_s `B`	Cursor Down P_s Times (default = 1) (CUD)
`ESC` `[` P_s `C`	Cursor Forward P_s Times (default = 1) (CUF)
`ESC` `[` P_s `D`	Cursor Backward P_s Times (default = 1) (CUB)
`ESC` `[` P_s `;` P_s `H`	Cursor Position [row;column] (default = [1,1]) (CUP)
`ESC` `[` P_s `J`	Erase in Display (ED)

$P_s = \boxed{0} \rightarrow$ Clear Below (default)

$P_s = \boxed{1} \rightarrow$ Clear Above

$P_s = \boxed{2} \rightarrow$ Clear All

`ESC` `[` P_s `K`	Erase in Line (EL)

$P_s = \boxed{0} \rightarrow$ Clear to Right (default)

$P_s = \boxed{1} \rightarrow$ Clear to Left

$P_s = \boxed{2} \rightarrow$ Clear All

`ESC` `[` P_s `L`	Insert P_s Line(s) (default = 1) (IL)
`ESC` `[` P_s `M`	Delete P_s Line(s) (default = 1) (DL)
`ESC` `[` P_s `P`	Delete P_s Character(s) (default = 1) (DCH)
`ESC` `[` `T`	Track mouse

$\boxed{\text{ESC}}\boxed{[}\,P_s\,\boxed{\text{c}}$	Device Attributes (DA1)
$\boxed{\text{ESC}}\boxed{[}\,P_s\,\boxed{;}\,P_s\,\boxed{\text{f}}$	Cursor Position [row;column] (default = [1,1]) (HVP)
$\boxed{\text{ESC}}\boxed{[}\,P_s\,\boxed{\text{g}}$	Tab Clear

$P_s = \boxed{0} \rightarrow$ Clear Current Column (default)

$P_s = \boxed{3} \rightarrow$ Clear All

$\boxed{\text{ESC}}\boxed{[}\,P_s\,\boxed{\text{h}}$ Mode Set (SET)

$P_s = \boxed{4} \rightarrow$ Insert Mode (IRM)

$P_s = \boxed{2}\boxed{0} \rightarrow$ Automatic Linefeed (LNM)

$\boxed{\text{ESC}}\boxed{[}\,P_s\,\boxed{l}$ Mode Reset (RST)

$P_s = \boxed{4} \rightarrow$ Insert Mode (IRM)

$P_s = \boxed{2}\boxed{0} \rightarrow$ Automatic Linefeed (LNM)

$\boxed{\text{ESC}}\boxed{[}\,P_m\,\boxed{\text{m}}$ Character Attributes (SGR)

$P_m = \boxed{0} \rightarrow$ Normal (default)

$P_m = \boxed{1} \rightarrow$ Blink (appears as Bold)

$P_m = \boxed{4} \rightarrow$ Underscore

$P_m = \boxed{5} \rightarrow$ Bold

$P_m = \boxed{7} \rightarrow$ Inverse

$\boxed{\text{ESC}}\boxed{[}\,P_s\,\boxed{\text{n}}$ Device Status Report (DSR)

$P_s = 5 \rightarrow$ Status Report $\boxed{\text{ESC}}\boxed{[}\,\boxed{0}\,\boxed{\text{n}} \rightarrow$ OK

$P_s = 6 \rightarrow$ Report Cursor Position (CPR) [row;column] as
$\boxed{\text{ESC}}\boxed{[}\,r\,\boxed{;}\,c\,\boxed{\text{R}}$

$\boxed{\text{ESC}}\boxed{[}\,P_s\,\boxed{;}\,P_s\,\boxed{\text{r}}$ Set Scrolling Region [top;bottom] (default = full size of window) (DECSTBM)

$\boxed{\text{ESC}}\boxed{[}\,P_s\,\boxed{\text{x}}$ Request Terminal Parameters (DECREQTPARM)

$\boxed{\text{ESC}}\boxed{[}\,P_s\,$ *ND string NP*

OSC Mode

ND can be any non-digit Character (it's discarded)

NP can be any non-printing Character (it's discarded)

string can be any ASCII printable string (max 511 characters)

$P_s = \boxed{0} \rightarrow$ use string as a new icon name and title

$P_s = \boxed{1} \rightarrow$ use string as a new icon name only

$P_s = \boxed{2} \rightarrow$ use string as a new title only

$P_s = \boxed{4}\boxed{6} \rightarrow$ use string as a new log file name

$\boxed{\text{ESC}}\boxed{[}\,\boxed{?}\,P_s\,\boxed{\text{h}}$ DEC Private Mode Set (DECSET)

$P_s = \boxed{1} \rightarrow$ Application Cursor Keys (DECCKM)

$P_s = \boxed{2} \rightarrow$ Set VT52 Mode

xterm Control Sequences

$P_s = \boxed{3} \rightarrow$ 132 Column Mode (DECCOLM)

$P_s = \boxed{4} \rightarrow$ Smooth (Slow) Scroll (DECSCLM)

$P_s = \boxed{5} \rightarrow$ Reverse Video (DECSCNM)

$P_s = \boxed{6} \rightarrow$ Origin Mode (DECOM)

$P_s = \boxed{7} \rightarrow$ Wraparound Mode (DECAWM)

$P_s = \boxed{8} \rightarrow$ Auto-repeat Keys (DECARM)

$P_s = \boxed{9} \rightarrow$ Send MIT Mouse Row & Column on Button Press

$P_s = \boxed{3}\boxed{8} \rightarrow$ Enter TekTronix Mode (DECTEK)

$P_s = \boxed{4}\boxed{0} \rightarrow$ Allow 80 $\leftrightarrow$ 132 Mode

$P_s = \boxed{4}\boxed{1} \rightarrow$ *curses*(5) fix

$P_s = \boxed{4}\boxed{4} \rightarrow$ Turn On Margin Bell

$P_s = \boxed{4}\boxed{5} \rightarrow$ Reverse-wraparound Mode

$P_s = \boxed{4}\boxed{6} \rightarrow$ Start Logging

$P_s = \boxed{4}\boxed{7} \rightarrow$ Use Alternate Screen Buffer

$P_s = \boxed{1}\boxed{0}\boxed{0}\boxed{0} \rightarrow$ send VT200 Mouse Row & Column on Button Press

$P_s = \boxed{1}\boxed{0}\boxed{0}\boxed{3} \rightarrow$ send VT200 Hilite Mouse Row & Column on Button Press

$\boxed{\text{ESC}}\boxed{[}\boxed{?}P_s\boxed{l}$ DEC Private Mode Reset (DECRST)

$P_s = \boxed{1} \rightarrow$ Normal Cursor Keys (DECCKM)

$P_s = \boxed{3} \rightarrow$ 80 Column Mode (DECCOLM)

$P_s = \boxed{4} \rightarrow$ Jump (Fast) Scroll (DECSCLM)

$P_s = \boxed{5} \rightarrow$ Normal Video (DECSCNM)

$P_s = \boxed{6} \rightarrow$ Normal Cursor Mode (DECOM)

$P_s = \boxed{7} \rightarrow$ No Wraparound Mode (DECAWM)

$P_s = \boxed{8} \rightarrow$ No Auto-repeat Keys (DECARM)

$P_s = \boxed{9} \rightarrow$ Don't Send MIT Mouse Row & Column on Button Press

$P_s = \boxed{4}\boxed{0} \rightarrow$ Disallow 80 $\leftrightarrow$ 132 Mode

$P_s = \boxed{4}\boxed{1} \rightarrow$ No *curses*(5) fix

$P_s = \boxed{4}\boxed{4} \rightarrow$ Turn Off Margin Bell

$P_s = \boxed{4}\boxed{5} \rightarrow$ No Reverse-wraparound Mode

$P_s = \boxed{4}\boxed{6} \rightarrow$ Stop Logging

$P_s = \boxed{4}\boxed{7} \rightarrow$ Use Normal Screen Buffer

$P_s = \boxed{1}\boxed{0}\boxed{0}\boxed{0} \rightarrow$ Don't send Mouse Row & Column on Button Press

$P_s = \boxed{1}\boxed{0}\boxed{0}\boxed{3} \rightarrow$ Don't send Hilite Mouse Row & Column on Button Press

$\boxed{\text{ESC}}\boxed{[}\boxed{?}\, P_s\, \boxed{\text{r}}$ Restore DEC Private Mode

$P_s = \boxed{1} \rightarrow$ Normal/Application Cursor Keys (DECCKM)

$P_s = \boxed{3} \rightarrow$ 80/132 Column Mode (DECCOLM)

$P_s = \boxed{4} \rightarrow$ Jump (Fast)/Smooth (Slow) Scroll (DECSCLM)

$P_s = \boxed{5} \rightarrow$ Normal/Reverse Video (DECSCNM)

$P_s = \boxed{6} \rightarrow$ Normal/Origin Cursor Mode (DECOM)

$P_s = \boxed{7} \rightarrow$ No Wraparound/Wraparound Mode (DECAWM)

$P_s = \boxed{8} \rightarrow$ Auto-repeat/No Auto-repeat Keys (DECARM)

$P_s = \boxed{9} \rightarrow$ Don't Send/Send MIT Mouse Row & Column on Button
       Press

$P_s = \boxed{4}\boxed{0} \rightarrow$ Disallow/Allow 80 $\leftrightarrow$ 132 Mode

$P_s = \boxed{4}\boxed{1} \rightarrow$ Off/On *curses*(5) fix

$P_s = \boxed{4}\boxed{4} \rightarrow$ Turn Off/On Margin Bell

$P_s = \boxed{4}\boxed{5} \rightarrow$ No Reverse-wraparound/Reverse-wraparound Mode

$P_s = \boxed{4}\boxed{6} \rightarrow$ Stop/Start Logging

$P_s = \boxed{4}\boxed{7} \rightarrow$ Use Normal/Alternate Screen Buffer

$P_s = \boxed{1}\boxed{0}\boxed{0}\boxed{0} \rightarrow$ Don't send/send VT200 Mouse Row & Column on
       Button Press

$P_s = \boxed{1}\boxed{0}\boxed{0}\boxed{3} \rightarrow$ Don't send/send VT200 Hilite Mouse Row &
       Column on Button Press

$\boxed{\text{ESC}}\boxed{[}\boxed{?}\, P_s\, \boxed{\text{s}}$ Save DEC Private Mode

$P_s = \boxed{1} \rightarrow$ Normal/Application Cursor Keys (DECCKM)

$P_s = \boxed{3} \rightarrow$ 80/132 Column Mode (DECCOLM)

$P_s = \boxed{4} \rightarrow$ Jump (Fast)/Smooth (Slow) Scroll (DECSCLM)

$P_s = \boxed{5} \rightarrow$ Normal/Reverse Video (DECSCNM)

$P_s = \boxed{6} \rightarrow$ Normal/Origin Cursor Mode (DECOM)

$P_s = \boxed{7} \rightarrow$ No Wraparound/Wraparound Mode (DECAWM)

$P_s = \boxed{8} \rightarrow$ Auto-repeat/No Auto-repeat Keys (DECARM)

$P_s = \boxed{9} \rightarrow$ Don't Send/Send MIT Mouse Row & Column on Button
       Press

$P_s = \boxed{4}\boxed{0} \rightarrow$ Disallow/Allow 80 $\leftrightarrow$ 132 Mode

$P_s = \boxed{4}\boxed{1} \rightarrow$ Off/On *curses*(5) fix

$P_s = \boxed{4}\boxed{4} \rightarrow$ Turn Off/On Margin Bell

$P_s = \boxed{4}\boxed{5} \rightarrow$ No Reverse-wraparound/Reverse-wraparound Mode

$P_s = \boxed{4}\boxed{6} \rightarrow$ Stop/Start Logging

$P_s = \boxed{4}\boxed{7} \rightarrow$ Use Normal/Alternate Screen Buffer

$P_s = \boxed{1}\boxed{0}\boxed{0}\boxed{0} \rightarrow$ Don't send/send VT200 Mouse Row & Column on Button Press

$P_s = \boxed{1}\boxed{0}\boxed{0}\boxed{3} \rightarrow$ Don't send/send VT200 Hilite Mouse Row & Column on Button Press

$\boxed{\text{ESC}}\boxed{]}\,P_s\,\boxed{;}\,P_t\,\boxed{\text{BEL}}$	Set Text Parameters

$P_s = \boxed{0} \rightarrow$ Change Window Name and Title to P_t

$P_s = \boxed{1} \rightarrow$ Change Window Name to P_t

$P_s = \boxed{2} \rightarrow$ Change Window Title to P_t

$P_s = \boxed{4}\boxed{6} \rightarrow$ Change Log File to P_t

$P_s = \boxed{5}\boxed{0} \rightarrow$ Change Font to P_t

$\boxed{\text{ESC}}\boxed{\text{c}}$	Full Reset (RIS)
$\boxed{\text{ESC}}\boxed{\text{n}}$	Locking Shift Select of G2 Character Set (LS2)
$\boxed{\text{ESC}}$	Locking Shift Select of G3 Character Set (LS3)

Tektronix 4014 Mode

Most of these sequences are standard Tektronix 4014 control sequences. The major features missing are the alternate (APL) character set and the write-thru and defocused modes.

$\boxed{\text{BEL}}$	Bell (Ctrl-G)
$\boxed{\text{BS}}$	Backspace (Ctrl-H)
$\boxed{\text{TAB}}$	Horizontal Tab (Ctrl-I)
$\boxed{\text{LF}}$	Line Feed or New Line (Ctrl-J)
$\boxed{\text{VT}}$	Vertical Tab (Ctrl-K)
$\boxed{\text{FF}}$	Form Feed or New Page (Ctrl-L)
$\boxed{\text{CR}}$	Carriage Return (Ctrl-M)
$\boxed{\text{ESC}}\boxed{\text{ETX}}$	Switch to VT102 Mode
$\boxed{\text{ESC}}\boxed{\text{ENQ}}$	Return Terminal Status
$\boxed{\text{ESC}}\boxed{\text{LF}}$	PAGE (Clear Screen)
$\boxed{\text{ESC}}\boxed{\text{ETB}}$	COPY (Save Tektronix Codes to File)
$\boxed{\text{ESC}}\boxed{\text{CAN}}$	Bypass Condition
$\boxed{\text{ESC}}\boxed{\text{SUB}}$	GIN mode
$\boxed{\text{ESC}}\boxed{\text{FS}}$	Special Point Plot Mode
$\boxed{\text{ESC}}\boxed{\text{GS}}$	Graph Mode (same as $\boxed{\text{GS}}$)
$\boxed{\text{ESC}}\boxed{\text{RS}}$	Incremental Plot Mode (same as $\boxed{\text{RS}}$)
$\boxed{\text{ESC}}\boxed{\text{US}}$	Alpha Mode (same as $\boxed{\text{US}}$)
$\boxed{\text{ESC}}\boxed{8}$	Select Large Character Set

`ESC` `9`	Select #2 Character Set
`ESC` `:`	Select #3 Character Set
`ESC` `;`	Select Small Character Set
`ESC` `]` P_s `;` P_t `BEL`	Set Text Parameters

P_s = $\boxed{0}$ → Change Window Name and Title to P_t

P_s = $\boxed{1}$ → Change Icon Name to P_t

P_s = $\boxed{2}$ → Change Window Title to P_t

P_s = $\boxed{4}\boxed{6}$ → Change Log File to P_t

`ESC` `` ` ``	Normal Z Axis and Normal (solid) Vectors
`ESC` `a`	Normal Z Axis and Dotted Line Vectors
`ESC` `b`	Normal Z Axis and Dot-Dashed Vectors
`ESC` `c`	Normal Z Axis and Short-Dashed Vectors
`ESC` `d`	Normal Z Axis and Long-Dashed Vectors
`ESC` `h`	Defocused Z Axis and Normal (solid) Vectors
`ESC` `i`	Defocused Z Axis and Dotted Line Vectors
`ESC` `j`	Defocused Z Axis and Dot-Dashed Vectors
`ESC` `k`	Defocused Z Axis and Short-Dashed Vectors
`ESC` `l`	Defocused Z Axis and Long-Dashed Vectors
`ESC` `p`	Write-Thru Mode and Normal (solid) Vectors
`ESC` `q`	Write-Thru Mode and Dotted Line Vectors
`ESC` `r`	Write-Thru Mode and Dot-Dashed Vectors
`ESC` `s`	Write-Thru Mode and Short-Dashed Vectors
`ESC` `t`	Write-Thru Mode and Long-Dashed Vectors
`FS`	Point Plot Mode
`GS`	Graph Mode
`RS`	Incremental Plot Mode
`US`	Alpha Mode

xterm Control Sequences

F

Translation Table Syntax

This appendix describes the basic syntax of translation table resources, described in Chapter 10, Setting Resources.

In This Appendix:

F
Translation Table Syntax

This appendix explains some of the more complex aspects of translation table syntax. It probably gives more detail than the average user will need but we've included it to help clarify this rather complicated topic.

Event Types and Modifiers

The syntax of the translation table is sufficiently general to encompass a wide variety of events and circumstances. Event translations can be specified to handle characteristic user interface idioms like double clicking, dragging, or combining keyboard modifiers with pointer button input. To specify translations that use these features, it is necessary to learn more about the detailed syntax used to specify translations.

An activity susceptible to translation is a sequence of events and modifiers (that perform an action). Events are specified in angle brackets and modifiers precede the event they modify. The legal events that can be specified in a translation are as shown in Table F-1.

Table F-1. Event Types and Their Abbreviations

Event Name	Event Type	Abbreviations/Synonyms
`KeyPress`	Keyboard	`Key,KeyDown`
`KeyUp`	Keyboard	`KeyRelease`
`ButtonPress`	Mouse Button	`BtnDown`
`ButtonRelease`	Mouse Button	`BtnUp`
`Btn1Down`	Mouse Button Press	
.		
.		
`Btn5Down`		
`Btn1Up`	Mouse Button Release	
.		
.		
`Btn5Up`		

Event Name	Event Type	Abbreviations/Synonyms
`MotionNotify`	Mouse Motion	`Motion`, `MouseMoved`, `PtrMoved`
`ButtonMotion`	Motion w/any Button Down	`BtnMotion`
`Button1Motion`	Motion w/Button Down	`Btn1Motion`
.		.
.		.
`Button5Motion`		`Btn5Motion`
`EnterNotify`	Mouse in Window	`Enter`, `EnterWindow`
`LeaveNotify`		`LeaveWindow`, `Leave`
`FocusIn`	Keyboard Input Focus	
`FocusOut`		
`KeymapNotify`	Changed Key Map	`Keymap`
`ColormapNotify`	Changed Color Map	`Clrmap`
`Expose`	Related Exposure Events	
`GraphicsExpose`		`GrExp`
`NoExpose`		`NoExp`
`VisibilityNotify`		`Visible`
`CreateNotify`	Window Management	`Create`
`DestroyNotify`		`Destroy`
`UnmapNotify`		`Unmap`
`MapNotify`		`Map`
`MapRequest`		`MapReq`
`ReparentNotify`		`Reparent`
`ConfigureNotify`		`Configure`
`ConfigureRequest`		`ConfigureReq`
`GravityNotify`		`Grav`
`ResizeRequest`		`ResReq`
`CirculateNotify`		`Circ`
`CirculateRequest`		`CircReq`
`PropertyNotify`		`Prop`
`SelectionClear`	Intra-client Selection	`SelClr`
`SelectionRequest`		`SelReq`
`SelectionNotify`		`Select`

The possible modifiers of an event are listed in the table. The modifiers Mod1 through Mod5 are highly system-dependent, and may not be implemented by all servers.

Table F-2. Key Modifiers

Event Modifiers	Abbreviation
Ctrl	c
Meta	m
Shift	s
Lock	l
Any	
ANY	
None	
Mod1	1
.	.
.	.
Mod5	5

Detail Field

To provide finer control over the translation process, the event part of the translation can include an additional "detail." For example, if you want the event to require an additional keystroke, for instance, an A key, or a Control-T, then that keystroke can be specified as a translation detail. The default detail field is *ANY*.

The valid translation details are event-dependent. For example, to specify the above example for keypress events, you would use:

```
<Key>A
```

and:

```
Ctrl<Key>T
```

respectively.

Key fields can be specified by the keysym value, as well as by the keysym symbolic name. For example, the keysym value of the Delete key is 0xffff. Keysym values can be determined by examining the file *<X11/keysymdef.h>* or by using the *xmodmap* client. (See Chapter 12, *Setup Clients*, for information about *xmodmap*.) Unfortunately, with some translations the keysym value may actually be required, since not all keysym symbolic names may be properly interpreted.

Modifiers

Modifiers can be closely controlled to define exactly which events can be specified. For example, if you want the action to be performed by pointer button clicks but not by pointer button clicks with the Control or Shift key down, these limitations can be specified. Similarly, if you don't care if there are modifiers present, this can also be specified.

Table F-3 lists the available event modifiers.

Table F-3. Event Modifiers and their Meanings

Modifier	Meaning
None *<event>*	No modifiers allowed.
<event>	Doesn't care. Any modifiers okay.
Mod1 Mod	Mod1 and Mod2, plus any others (i.e., anything that includes m1 and m2).
!Mod1 Mod2*<event>*	Mod1 and Mod2 but nothing else.
Mod1 ~Mod2*<event>*	Mod1 and not Mod2.

Complex Translation Examples

The following translation specifies that function *f* is to be invoked when both the Shift key and the third pointer button are pressed.

```
Shift<Btn3Down>: f()
```

To specify that both the Control and Shift keys are to be pressed use:

```
Ctrl Shift<Btn3Down>: f()
```

To specify an optional repeat count for an activity, put a number in parentheses after the action. The number refers to the whole translation. To make the last example require a double-click, with both Control and Shift keys pressed, use:

```
Ctrl Shift<Btn3Down>(2): f()
```

The server distinguishes between single-clicks and double-clicks based on a pre-programmed timing interval. If a second click occurs before the interval expires, then the event is interpreted as a double-click; otherwise the event is interpreted as two single-clicks. The variable `clickTime` is maintained deep in the internals of X. Unfortunately, thus far there is no way to set this time interval to match user preference. Currently it is set to be 200 milliseconds.

A translation involving two or more clicks can be specified as (2+) in the previous example. In general, a plus sign following the number *n* would mean *n* or more occurrences of the event.

Multiple events can be specified by separating them with commas on the translation line. To indicate pressing button 1, pressing button 2, then releasing button 1, and finally releasing button 2, use:

```
<Btn1Down>,<Btn2Down>,<Btn1Up>,<Btn2Up>: f()
```

Another way to describe this action in English would be to say "while button 1 is down, click button 2." "Meaningless" pointer movement is generally ignored. In the previous case, for example, if pointer motion occurred while the buttons were down, it would not interfere with detection of the event. Thus, inadvertent pointer jiggling will not thwart even the most complex user-input sequences.

G

Athena Widget Resources

In This Appendix:

G
Athena Widget Resources

As suggested on the reference pages for various clients, you can set not only resources defined by the application itself, but also resources that apply to any of the widgets that make up the application. The reference page for the application sometimes lists the most important of these resources, but for fuller customization, you need to know more about each widget.

Unfortunately, the design of the X Toolkit is such that to really do the right thing, you probably need to know a bit more about Toolkit programming than the average user might like.

In this appendix, we provide both some introductory concepts about how widgets are used in X Toolkit programs, and reference information about each class of widgets. If you are a Toolkit programmer or other sophisticated user, feel free to skip right to the widget reference section later in this appendix.

The Widget Class Hierarchy

The first thing you need to know is how widgets are built.

Rather than starting each widget from scratch, the widget programmer starts with a copy of another, more basic widget, and modifies it. This process is called *subclassing* the widget, and the sequence of widgets leading up to the one you see is called its *class hierarchy*. Because of the way subclassing works, a widget *inherits* all of the characteristics of its superclasses, except those that are explicitly overridden or changed.

The class hierarchy starts with a class called Object, which defines some basic characteristics common to all widgets—namely the ability to understand resources, and to be linked to applications via a mechanism referred to as a callback. (When you click on a "quit" button, and the application quits, that is because the widget has communicated with the application via a callback.)

RectObj is a subclass of Object. RectObj adds various resources having to do with the fact that widgets are rectangular: width, height, borderWidth, and x, y positions. RectObj also adds resources for sensitivity—the fact that a widget can be temporarily "disabled" by a client (so for example, not allowing you to choose an option on a menu that would close a file if no file was open.)

Core is the first true widget in the class hierarchy. Object and RectObj don't have windows associated with them, and can never be "instantiated"— created and mapped to the screen. In fact, prior to Release 4, they were "invisible" even to Toolkit programmers, who simply assumed that Core was the root of the widget hierarchy.

The reason we now talk openly about Object and RectObj is that the R4 Toolkit supports a different class of object, known colloquially as a gadget, which is subclassed directly from RectObj, and does not have a window associated with it. It can be used only within a widget that understands how to manage gadgets, and allocates some of its own window space to display them. This is typically done when there are many identical widgets. (The only gadgets in the Athena widget set are the SmeBSB and SmeLine gadgets used to implement panes in a SimpleMenu widget. Motif offers its programmers both widget and gadget versions of many of its objects, including all kinds of command buttons.)

At any rate, for most purposes, you can still act as though Core is the root of the widget hierarchy, since all widgets are subclassed from it, and therefore share all of its resources. The phrase "Core resources" is a fluke of terminology that can be misleading to new users. Because it sounds meaningful just as a general term, it isn't clear that the Core resources are really the resources of a particular widget class (rather than something magically recognized as central or "core" by the X Toolkit.)

Let's take a brief look at the some of the Core resources, which appear in Table G-1. The list includes the resources inherited from Object and RectObj, plus those added by Core.

Table G-1. Core Resources

Name	Class	Default Value
background	Background	
borderColor	BorderColor	
borderWidth	BorderWidth	1
height	Height	0
width	Width	0
x	Position	0
y	Position	0

Some of these Core resources set obvious characteristics of a widget: background (color), borderColor, and borderWidth (in pixels). height and width specify the dimensions of the widget in pixels. x and y represent the x,y coordinates of the widget in relation to its parent.

Technically, foreground is *not* a Core resource. However, since foreground is defined by every widget class that does any drawing of lines or text, it can be assumed to be.

Note that Table G-1 isn't actually a complete list of all of the Core resources, but only of those that might be set by users. Some resources (such as callbacks) can only be set by programmers. The Toolkit doesn't even support a mechanism for understanding how to set them in a resource file. In addition, there are two resources that are so common that you might expect them to be Core resources, but which are not. They are defined individually by each of the widget classes that use them. This can be confusing, especially since they do correspond to standard X Toolkit options. But really, it is hair-splitting to worry about where they are defined—they are sufficiently standard to fall under the colloquial understanding of Core resources.

We'll say more about the subject of resource conversion later. First, though, let's finish describing the base classes provided by the X Toolkit, which are common to all Xt-based widget sets (including both Motif and the Athena widgets).

There is a special class of widgets whose job is to manage the size and/or position of other widgets. These are called Composite widgets, and all such geometry-managing widgets, are children of the Composite widget class. Composite inherits all of the characteristics of Core, and adds resources (settable only by the programmer) for identifying which widgets it should treat as its children.

Some simple geometry-managing widgets such as the Athena Box widget are direct subclasses of Core. However, there is another, more complex class of geometry-managing widget defined by the X Toolkit Intrinsics, called Constraint. A constraint widget defines special resources, called constraint resources, that apply to its children rather than to itself. They are actually resources of the constraint widget, but are specified as if they were resources of the child. The clearest example of constraint resources is provided by the Athena Form widget, which allows widgets to be positioned with respect to one another, so that they always keep the same arrangement, even when the Form is resized. For example, *xcalc* is implemented using a Form widget. Resources such as:

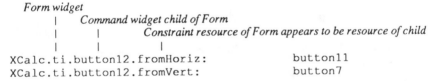

```
        Form widget
            |       Command widget child of Form
            |           |           Constraint resource of Form appears to be resource of child
            |           |           |
    XCalc.ti.button12.fromHoriz:            button11
    XCalc.ti.button12.fromVert:             button7
```

specify that button12 (label PI) should always be next to button11 (label x!), and over button7 (label 7). We'll return to this example later, when we talk about the instance hierarchy of widgets in an application.

At any rate, there is one other subclass of Composite that bears mention: the Shell widget class. Shell widgets are simple composite widgets; they manage only one child—the application's main window, and they make themselves exactly the same size, so that they are hidden behind it. Even though you never see them, though, Shell widgets are extremely important, since they are the widgets that know how to interact with the window manager. Shell introduces several resources of importance to the application programmer, but only one of importance to the user: geometry (class Geometry).

There are actually seven subclasses of Shell, three of which are for internal toolkit purposes and four of which are used by application programmers in different circumstances. For example, there is one kind of shell widget used for the main window of an application (class TopLevelShell) and another used as the parent of a popup widget like a dialog box (class OverrideShell) that should never be manipulated by the window manager. (Notice that *mwm* doesn't reparent dialogs—they don't get a titlebar of their own, and can't be moved independently—this is because they are children of an OverrideShell, which overrides window manager intervention.)

There is another class of shell widget, called a TransientShell, which is used for popups, but can be manipulated by the window manager. An application might use a TransientShell for a popup help window that would be allowed to remain on the screen, and could be moved or resized separately (but not iconified.) An ApplicationShell is used by an application that has more than one completely independent window, as the class for its secondary "top level" windows.

For all practical purposes, you don't need this much information about shell widgets. As we'll see shortly, the only reference to a shell widget in a resource specification is typically via the application name, which the shell widget takes as its own.

Returning to widgets that you actually do see and interact with, let's consider the class derivation of a widget like Command, which is used to implement buttons you can click on with the mouse to ask the application to do something.

The Athena Command widget is a subclass of the Label widget, which is a subclass of the Simple widget, which in turn is a subclass of Core. As a result, Command inherits all of the Core resources, plus the resources of the Athena Simple widget (for practical purposes, the cursor that is to be displayed when the pointer is in the window), plus the resources of the Label widget—such as the ability to display a label, in a particular font. Command adds the ability (defined by the programmer, not the user) to call a particular application function when the button is clicked on.

Figure G-1 shows the complete class hierarchy of the Athena widgets used in all of the standard MIT applications described in this book. The widgets shown in gray are defined by the X Toolkit intrinsics, and are common to all Xt-based widget sets, including Motif.

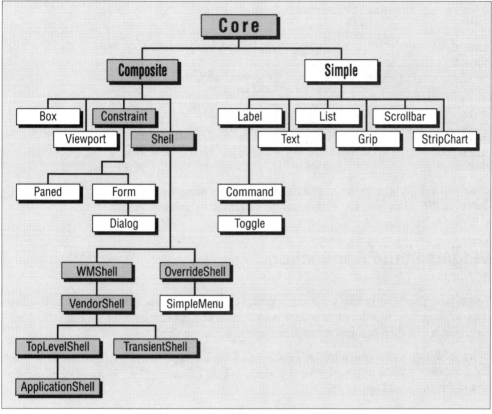

Figure G-1. Inheritance among the Athena widgets

The *listres* application, without any arguments, lists the inheritance hierarchy for each of the
Athena widgets. Given the name of any widget class, it lists all of the resources for that
widget, and which superclass they are inherited from. For example:

```
% listres label
WidgetClass          Instance   Class             Type
-----------          --------   -----             ----
label:   Core\Simple\Label
Core              accelerators   Accelerators      AcceleratorTable
Core          ancestorSensitive   Sensitive         Boolean
Core                background   Background        Pixel
Core          backgroundPixmap   Pixmap            Pixmap
Label                 bitmap   Pixmap            Bitmap
Core               borderColor   BorderColor       Pixel
Core              borderPixmap   Pixmap            Pixmap
Core               borderWidth   BorderWidth       Dimension
Core                 colormap   Colormap          Colormap
Simple                 cursor   Cursor            Cursor
Core                    depth   Depth             Int
Core           destroyCallback   Callback          Callback
```

Label	font	Font	FontStruct
Label	foreground	Foreground	Pixel
Core	height	Height	Dimension
Simple	insensitiveBorder	Insensitive	Pixmap
Label	internalHeight	Height	Dimension
Label	internalWidth	Width	Dimension
Label	justify	Justify	Justify
Label	label	Label	String
Core	mappedWhenManaged	MappedWhenManaged	Boolean
Label	resize	Resize	Boolean
Core	screen	Screen	Screen
Core	sensitive	Sensitive	Boolean
Core	translations	Translations	TranslationTable
Core	width	Width	Dimension
Core	x	Position	Position
Core	y	Position	Position

As we'll describe later in this appendix, not all of the resources listed by *listres* can be set in a resource file. However, this listing can provide a handy quick reference.

Widgets in the Application

Widget inheritance of resources from superclasses is an important part of the background to understanding how to affect the widget resources in the application, but it is not the whole story. Let's talk for a moment about how these widgets are used.

To make things more concrete, let's look at an actual application. *xclipboard* is a good choice. It uses several different widget classes, but isn't too complex. Figure G-2 illustrates the widgets that make up *xclipboard*.

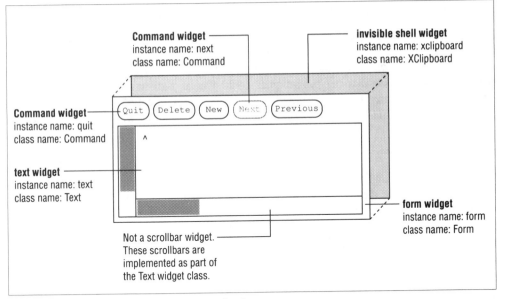

Command widget ──────
instance name: next
class name: Command

invisible shell widget
instance name: xclipboard
class name: XClipboard

Command widget ──────
instance name: quit
class name: Command

text widget ──────
instance name: text
class name: Text

Quit Delete New Next Previous

^

form widget
instance name: form
class name: Form

Not a scrollbar widget. ──────
These scrollbars are
implemented as part of
the Text widget class.

Figure G-2. Anatomy of an X Toolkit Application

Every Toolkit application begins with a call to a function called XtInitialize, which in looks something like this*:

```
top = XtInitialize( "xclipboard", "XClipboard", ... );
```

The first two arguments to this function give the instance name and class name of the application. This becomes the start of any resource specification for this application. And we know that if *xclipboard* has an app-defaults file, it will be called *XClipboard*, since that name is taken from the class name of the application. Notice that there's no magic here: this is under the explicit control of the application programmer. If he doesn't follow the conventions for the application's class and instance name, he'd better document what names he used here!

One of the things that XtInitialize does is create a TopLevelShell widget. The name before the equals sign, top, is the name that the programmer will use to refer to this widget whenever he needs to use it in the application. This is completely irrelevant to the name the widget publishes for itself as its instance name.

Next, the program begins to create the widgets in the application, using a function called XtCreateManagedWidget. The first widget to be created is the main application widget, which in this case is a Form widget.

```
parent = XtCreateManagedWidget("form", formWidgetClass, top, ... );
```

---

*Actually, modern Toolkit applications are supposed to use the more complex XtAppInitialize, but Xt-Initialize makes the concept clearer, and besides, it's what *xclipboard* actually uses.

The first argument to XtCreateManagedWidget is the instance name of the widget (form)—this is the name that will be used to refer to it in resource files. The second argument is a symbol identifying which widget class this widget should be.

Notice that the instance name is entirely arbitrary, and depends completely on the whim of the application programmer. Many applications that use only one instance of a widget class will give it an instance name that mirrors the class name, except in lower case, as was done here. But you can see that the programmer could just as well have given the widget the instance name "foo" or "main" or "grandma_moses." The implication is that unless the client's man page documents a widget instance name, you won't know what to use in a resource file.*

The class name, on the other hand, is a part of the definition of a widget's class. It is always the same.

The third argument is the widget's parent—the geometry-managing widget that this widget will be displayed inside, and which will control its size and position. Notice that the parent of the form is top—the shell widget created by XtInitialize. As noted earlier, Shell widgets take just one child, and resize themselves so they fit completely behind that child, and are invisible.

Remember, though, that the program's internal name for the shell widget is not important when it comes to resource specifications. The Shell widget takes its "resource name and class" from the XtInitialize call.

If you're following the flow of the argument, you can see that to refer to this widget in a resource file, you could use any of the following resource specifications:

xclipboard.form	*instance name for both the shell widget and form widget*
XClipboard.Form	*class name for both the shell widget and form widget*
XClipboard.form	*class name for the shell, and instance name for the form*
xclipboard.Form	*instance name for the shell, and class name for the form*

as well as any analogous loose bindings.

The form widget (named "parent" for internal reference within the application) is used in turn as the parent of the various command widgets and the text widget:

```
quit = XtCreateManagedWidget("quit", commandWidgetClass, parent, ... );
delete = XtCreateManagedWidget("delete", commandWidgetClass, parent, ... );
new = XtCreateManagedWidget("new", commandWidgetClass, parent, ... );
nextButton = XtCreateManagedWidget("next", commandWidgetClass, parent, ... );
prevButton = XtCreateManagedWidget("prev", commandWidgetClass, parent, ... );
text = XtCreateManagedWidget("text", textWidgetClass, parent, ... );
```

This "parent-child relationship" between composite widgets and their children is what is expressed in the instance hierarchy of the widget. So, for example, the Command widget instance named quit is a child of the Form widget instance named form, which in turn is a child of a Shell widget, which takes as its name the application name xclipboard.

---

*As of R4, all of the MIT client reference pages do list the instance names of all the widgets in the application.

What all this Means

The fully-specified instance name of any widget in an application is determined by the parent-child relationships of every widget in the application. First, there is always a shell widget, which takes as its name the application name. Then, there are one or more composite widgets, which contain other widgets. Finally, at the end of the chain, you have a simple widget, with the resources it defines, as well as the resources it inherits from its superclasses.

Don't confuse the class names of the widgets in the instance hierarchy with the class inheritance hierarchy of each widget. Figure G-3 tries to make the relationships clear.

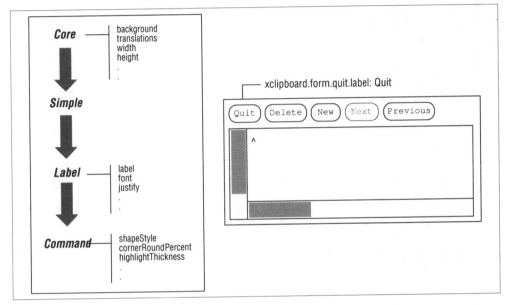

Figure G-3. Resource names and class inheritance

In Figure G-3, the `quit` widget gets its instance name from the relationship of widgets within the application. But it gets its resources from the class hierarchy of the widgets that the programmer used to develop the `Command` widget class.

Remember that the instance names of the widgets are completely arbitrary; even though it is not unusual to see a Form widget with the instance name `form`, there is nothing required about this. As a result, you need to look at the documentation for the application, not the widget, to find out the appropriate instance names.

The resources that a given widget class has are the result of its class inheritance hierarchy, which is defined by the widget programmer who originally designed the widget class. Thus, when you want to set resources for a widget like Command, you need to look not only in the section of this appendix that describes Command and its resources, but also the sections on each of its superclasses.

Complications

There are a number of provisos that modify this (hopefully by now clear and simple) picture:

- Even though a widget inherits a resource, it may not use it. For example, the Command widget class inherits the `borderWidth` resource from the Core widget class, but it does not actually use this information to redraw its border if you change the resource. A resource is just data you provide to the widget. Whether or not the widget does anything with that data is up to its designer. If you set a resource and nothing seems to happen, you might have done something wrong ... but you might also have set the resource correctly, and the widget simply chose to ignore it.

- Even when a widget does use a resource, you can't necessarily set it from a resource file. There are two reasons for this:

  — The programmer has the option to "hardcode" the value of a resource when creating a widget. If he does this, all resource specifications for that resource are ignored.

  — Some resources are designed only for programmer use. Some of these can't ever be specified in a resource file, since the data type of the resource isn't a text string, and the Toolkit doesn't provide any automatic conversion. (Things like colors or can be specified in resource files, even though a color name is not actually the color itself, because the X Toolkit automatically converts a color name to the appropriate internal format).

The following pages document only resources that are theoretically settable from resource files. (That is, if no converter exists, we've assumed that the resource is only for programmer use and have deleted it from the list.) However, there are many other resources listed that are most likely hardcoded by the programmer. Unfortunately, there is no way to tell in advance whether they will or will not be hardcoded in a particular application.

- The "default values" listed for each widget resource may or may not apply to an actual application. These are the default values for the widget. An application can override them, either in the program code, or in an application defaults file. But inasmuch as the defaults are reasonable, they will usually be unchanged.

With this background, you're now ready to navigate the widget reference information contained in this appendix. For each widget (or gadget) in the Athena widget set, we've given a brief description, a summary of its class hierarchy, a list of the new resources it defines, and its default translations and actions, if any.

Commercial Motif applications should document all of the appropriate resources for the Motif widgets they use.

Box

The Box widget provides geometry management of arbitrary widgets in a box of a specified dimension. Box moves but does not resize its children. The children are rearranged when the Box is resized, when its children are resized, or when children are managed or unmanaged. The Box widget always attempts to pack its children as closely as possible within the geometry allowed by its parent.

Box widgets are commonly used to manage a related set of Command widgets and are frequently called ButtonBox widgets, but the children are not limited to buttons.

The children are arranged on a background that has its own specified dimensions and color.

Resources

The following new resources are associated with the Box widget:

hSpace (class HSpace)
    Number of pixels to the left or to the right of each child. Default is 4.

orientation (class Orientation)
    Specifies whether the preferred shape of the box is tall and narrow (vertical, the default) or short and wide (horizontal).

vSpace (class VSpace)
    Number of pixels above or below each child. Default is 4.

Command

The Command widget is an area, often rectangular, that contains a text or pixmap label and calls an application function when "pressed" with a pointer button. This selectable area is sometimes referred to as a "button." When the pointer cursor is on the button, the button border is highlighted to indicate that the button is ready for selection. When a pointer button is pressed, the command widget indicates that it has been selected by reversing its foreground and background colors.

Resources

The following new resources are associated with the Command widget:

highlightThickness (class Thickness)
: The thickness of the line drawn by the highlight action.

shapeStyle (class ShapeStyle)
: Nonrectangular buttons may be created using this resource. Nonrectangular buttons are supported only on a server that supports the Shape Extension. If nonrectangular buttons are specified for a server lacking this extension, the shape is ignored and the widgets will be rectangular. The following shape names are currently supported: Rectangle, Oval, Ellipse, and roundedRectangle, in any case.

cornerRoundPercent (class CornerRoundPercent)
: When a ShapeStyle of roundedRectangle is used, this resource controls the radius of the rounded corner. The radius of the rounded corners is specified as a percentage of the length of the shortest side of the widget.

Translations and Actions

The following are the default translation bindings that are used by the Command widget:

```
<EnterWindow>:        highlight()
<LeaveWindow>:        reset()
<Btn1Down>:           set()
<Btn1Up>:             notify() unset()
```

With these bindings, the user can cancel the action before releasing the button by moving the pointer out of the Command widget.

The full list of actions supported by Command is as follows:

highlight()
: Displays the internal highlight border in the color (foreground or background) that contrasts with the interior color of the Command widget. This is normally bound to <EnterWindow> events, so the widget border is highlighted when the pointer enters the window.

unhighlight()
: Displays the internal highlight border in the color (foreground or background) that matches the interior color of the Command widget. This action is called internally by reset(), and does not need an explicit translation.

set()
: Enters the set state, in which notify is possible and displays the interior of the button, including the highlight border, in the foreground color. The label is displayed in the background color. This usually happens when a pointer button (button 1 by default) is pressed in the widget.

unset()
: Cancels the set state and displays the interior of the button, including the highlight border, in the background color. The label is displayed in

the foreground color. This action is called internally by reset(), and does not need an explicit translation.

reset()
    Cancels any set or highlight and displays the interior of the button in the background color, with the label displayed in the foreground color. This is normally bound to <Btu1Up> (along with notify()) to reset the button appearance to its normal state, once the button's callback function has been executed.

notify()
    Executes the callback list specified by callback, if executed in the set state. This is the action that actually calls the application function to be invoked.

Dialog

The Dialog widget prompts you for additional input. The typical Dialog widget contains three areas. The first line contains a description of the function of the Dialog widget, for example, the string *Filename:*. The second line contains an area into which you type input. The third line can contain buttons that let you confirm or cancel the Dialog input.

Dialog is not really a widget, but an interface to a widget. It might also be thought of as a compound widget. It includes a label widget, a command widget, and a text widget as components. These could theoretically appear as subwidgets in a resource specification.

Resources

The following new resources are associated with the Dialog widget:

icon (class Icon)
    The name of a pixmap to be displayed immediately to the left of the Dialog widget's label.

label (class Label)
    A string to be displayed at the top of the Dialog widget.

value (class Value)
    An initial value for the string field into which you will enter text. By default, no text entry field is available. Specifying an initial value for value activates the text entry field. If string input is desired but no initial value is to be specified, then set this resource to " " (empty string).

Form

The Form widget can contain an arbitrary number of children of any class. The Form provides geometry management for its children, including individual control of the position of each child. The initial positions of the children may be computed relative to the positions of other children. When the Form is resized, it computes new positions and sizes for its children.

Resources

The following new resource is associated with the Form widget:

defaultDistance
> Specifies the default value for `horizDistance` and `vertDistance`. This value is four pixels, by default. The default width of the Form is the minimum width needed to enclose the children after computing their initial layout, with a margin of `defaultDistance` at the right and bottom edges. If a width and height is assigned to the Form that is too small for the layout, the children will be clipped by the right and bottom edges of the Form.

Form is a subclass of Constraint, which means it has special kind of resources called constraint resources, which means that they apply to—and are specified as if they belong to—the child of the Form rather than to the Form itself. For example, *xcalc* uses a Form widget to organize its buttons. The resources below apply to the buttons, rather than to the Forms (e.g., xcalc.ti.button11.horizDistance : 4)

bottom (class Edge)

top (class Edge)

left (class Edge)

right (class Edge)
> Specify how to reposition the bottom, top, left, and right, respectively, of a child widget when the Form is resized. These resources can take one of five values. The values `ChainTop`, `ChainBottom`, `ChainLeft`, and `ChainRight` maintain a constant distance from an edge of the child to the top, bottom, left, and right edges, respectively, of the Form. The value `Rubber` (default) maintains a proportional distance from the edge of the child to the left or top edge of the Form. The proportion is determined from the initial position of the child and the initial size of the Form.

fromHoriz (class Widget)

horizDistance (class Thickness)
> Specify a child widget's horizontal position relative to another widget within the Form. `fromHoriz` is the name of the widget relative to which the child widget is placed, and `horizDistance` is the number of pixels separating the two widgets. For example, if `horizDistance` is 10, the child widget will be placed 10 pixels to the right of the widget defined in `fromHoriz`. If `fromHoriz` is not defined, then `horizDistance` is measured from the left edge of the Form.

fromVert (class `Widget`)

vertDistance (class `Thickness`)

> Similar to previous resources, except that `fromVert` and `vertDistance` position
> a child widget by a specified number of pixels *vertically* away from a specified widget.
> If no widget is specified for `fromVert`, then `vertDistance` is measured from the
> top of the Form.

resizable (class `Boolean`)

> TRUE if children are allowed to resize themselves. Default is FALSE.

Grip

The Grip widget provides a small region that allows button presses and button releases. The
Grip widget is typically used as an attachment point for visually repositioning an object (for
example, the pane border in a Paned widget).

Resources

The following Core resources may be useful with the Grip widget:

foreground, width, height, borderWidth.

Translations and Actions

The Grip widget does not declare any default event translation bindings, but it does declare a
single action routine named `GripAction` in its action table. The client specifies an arbitrary event translation table, giving parameters to the `GripAction` routine.

The following is an example of a `GripAction` translation table:

```
<Btn1Down>:      GripAction(press)
<Btn1Motion>:    GripAction(move)
<Btn1Up>:        GripAction(release)
```

Label

A Label is an non-editable text string or pixmap that is displayed within a window. The string may contain multiple lines of characters. It can be aligned to the left, right, or center of its window. A Label can be neither selected nor directly edited by the user.

Resources

The following resources are used by the Label widget:

bitmap (class Pixmap)
> Specifies a bitmap to display in place of the text label. In a resource file, the resource should be specified as the name of a file in the bitmap utility format that is to be loaded into a pixmap. The string can be an absolute or a relative filename. If a relative filename is used, the directory specified by the resource name bitmapFilePath or the resource class BitmapFilePath is added to the beginning of the specified filename. If the bitmapFilePath resource is not defined, the default directory on a POSIX-based system is */usr/include/X11/bitmaps*.

font (class font)
> The font of the label.

foreground (class Foreground)
> The color of the text string or pixmap.

internalHeight (class Height)
> Represents the distance in pixels between the top and bottom of the label text or bitmap and the horizontal edges of the Label widget. Default is 2 pixels.

internalWidth (class Width)
> Represents the distance in pixels between the ends of the label text or bitmap and the vertical edges of the Label widget. Default is 4 pixels.

justify (class Justify)
> Specifies left, center, or right alignment of the label string within the Label widget. One of the values left, center, or right can be specified.

label (class Label)
> Specifies the text string that is to be displayed in the button if no bitmap is specified. Note that the label may be hardcoded by the application.

resize (class Resize)
> A Boolean value that specifies whether the Label widget should attempt to resize to its preferred dimensions whenever XtSetValues is called for it. Default is True. Not usually set by users.

rowSpacing (class Spacing)
> Specify the amount of space in pixels between each of the rows in the list. The default is 6 pixels.

List

The List widget is a rectangle that contains a list of text strings formatted into rows and columns. When one of the strings is selected, it is highlighted, and an application callback routine is invoked. Only one string may be selected at a time. Note that most of the List resources are for application use.

Resources

The following resources are used by the List widget:

callback
> All functions on this list are called whenever the notify action is invoked. This resource cannot be set from within a resource file, but only within an application program.

columnSpacing (class Spacing)
> Specify the amount of space in pixels between each of the columns in the list. The default is 6 pixels.

Cursor (class Cursor)
> The cursor to be displaced when the pointer is in the List widget. Default is left-ptr.

defaultColumns (class Columns)
> Specifies the default number of columns, which is used when neither the width nor the height of the List widget is specified or when forceColumns is True. The default is 2.

forceColumns (class Columns)
> Specifies that the default number of columns is to be used no matter what the current size of the List widget is. The default is FALSE.

font (class Font)
> Specifies the font to be used to display the list.

foreground (class Foreground)
> Specifies the color to be used to paint the text of the list elements.

internalHeight (class Height)
> Represents a margin, in pixels, between the top and bottom of the list and the edges of the List widget. Default is 2 pixels.

internalWidth (class Width)
> Represents a margin, in pixels, between the left and right edges of the list and the edges of the List widget. Default is 4 pixels.

longest (class Longest)
> Specifies the length, in pixels, of the longest string in the current list. If the client knows the length, it should specify it; otherwise, the List widget computes a default length by searching through the list. This value is not typically set in resource files.

`numberStrings` (class `NumberStrings`)

Specifies the number of strings in the current list. If a value is not specified, the list must be `NULL`-terminated. This value is not typically set in resource files.

`pasteBuffer` (class `Boolean`)

If this is `True`, then the value of the string selected will be put into X cut buffer 0. The default is FALSE. (Normally, the selected item is simply passed to the application. For example, a filename might be passed to the application's "open" routine.)

`verticalList` (class `Boolean`)

If this is `True`, the elements in the list are arranged vertically; if `False`, the elements are arranged horizontally.

Translations and Actions

The List widget has three predefined actions: `Set`, `Unset`, and `Notify`. `Set` and `Unset` allow switching the foreground and background colors for the current list item. `Notify` allows processing application callbacks.

The following is the default translation table used by the List widget:

```
<Btn1Down>,<Btn1Up>:   Set() Notify()
```

These translations should not typically be modified by users, and may be hardcoded by the application.

MenuButton

The MenuButton widget is a subclass of the Command widget that is used to pop-up a menu. It is an area, often rectangular, that contains a text or pixmap label. This selectable area is referred to as a button. When the pointer cursor is on the button, the button border is highlighted to indicate that the button is ready for selection. When pointer button 1 is pressed, the MenuButton widget pops up the menu that has been named in the `menuName` resource.

Resources

MenuButton widgets have no new user-settable resources.

Translations and Actions

The following default translation bindings are used by the MenuButton widget:

```
<EnterWindow>:      highlight()
<LeaveWindow>:      reset()
<BtnDown>:      reset() PopupMenu()
```

With these bindings, the user can cancel the action before releasing the button by moving the pointer out of the MenuButton widget.

The actions supported by MenuButton are listed below:

`highlight(condition)`
Displays the internal highlight border in the color (`foreground` or `background`) that contrasts with the interior color of the Menu-Button widget. The conditions `WhenUnset` and `Always` are understood by this action procedure. If no argument is passed, `WhenUnset` is assumed.

`unhighlight()`
Displays the internal highlight border in the color (`foreground` or `background`) that matches the interior color of the MenuButton widget.

`set()`
Enters the set state, in which `notify` is possible, and displays the interior of the button, including the highlight border, in the foreground color. The label or pixmap is displayed in the background color.

`unset()`
Cancels the set state and displays the interior of the button, including the highlight border, in the background color. The label or pixmap is displayed in the foreground color.

`reset()`
Cancels any `set` or `highlight` action and displays the interior of the button in the background color, with the label or pixmap displayed in the foreground color.

`PopupMenu()`
Pops up the menu specified by the `menuName` resource.

Paned

The Paned widget manages children in a vertically or horizontally tiled fashion. You may resize these panes by using the *grips* that appear near the right or bottom edge of the border between two panes.

When you position the pointer on a grip, pressing the pointer button will display an arrow that indicates which pane is being resized. By keeping the pointer button down, you can move the pointer up and down (or left and right). This, in turn, changes the border between the panes, causing one pane to shrink and some other pane (or panes) to grow. The size of the Paned widget will not change.

The choice of alternate pane is a function of the `min`, `max`, and `skipAdjust` constraints on the other panes. With the default bindings, button 1 resizes the pane above or to the left of the selected grip, button 3 resizes the pane below or to the right of the selected grip, and button 2 repositions the border between two panes only.

Resources

The following new resources are associated with the Paned widget:

betweenCursor (class Cursor)
    Cursor for changing the boundary between two panes.

cursor (class Cursor)
    Pointer cursor image that displays, whenever the pointer is in this widget but not in any of its children (children may also inherit this cursor).

gripCursor (class Cursor)
    Cursor for grip when not active.

gripIndent (class GripIndent)
    Offset of grip from margin (in pixels). Default is 10.

gripTranslations (class Translations)
    Button bindings for grip.

horizontalBetweenCursor (class Cursor)
    Cursor to use for the grip when changing the boundary between two panes. Default is sb_up_arrow.

horizontalGripCursor (class Cursor)
    Cursor to use for the grips when they are not active. Default is sb_h_double_arrow.

internalBorderColor (class BorderColor)
    Internal border color of the widget's window. Default is XtDefaultForeground.

internalBorderWidth (class BorderWidth)
    Amount of space (in pixels) kept between panes. Default is 1.

leftCursor (class Cursor)
    Cursor used when resizing the pane to the left of the grip. Default is sb_left_arrow.

lowerCursor (class Cursor)
    Cursor used when resizing the pane below the grip. Default is sb_down_arrow.

orientation (class Orientation)
    Orientation to use in stacking the panes. This value can be either Vertical (the default) or Horizontal.

refigureMode (class Boolean)
    A Boolean that specifies whether the Paned widget should adjust its children. Default is TRUE.

X Window System User's Guide, Motif Edition

`rightCursor` (class `Cursor`)

> Cursor used when resizing the pane to the right of the grip. Default is `sb_right_arrow`.

`upperCursor` (class `Cursor`)

> Cursor used when resizing the pane above the grip. Default is `sb_up_arrow`.

`verticalBetweenCursor` (class `Cursor`)

> Cursor to use for the grip when changing the boundary between two panes. Default is `sb_left_arrow`.

`verticalGripCursor` (class `Cursor`)

> Cursor to use for the grips when they are not active. Default is `sb_v_double_arrow`.

Paned supports the following constraint resources. They can be specified to the Paned widget to indicate where a child widget should be positioned within the Paned widget.

`allowResize` (class `Boolean`)

> A Boolean that specifies whether to accept a child's request to resize. The default, `FALSE`, is to ignore such requests.

`max` (class `max`)

> Maximum height for pane. Default is to allow unlimited height.

`min` (class `min`)

> Minimum height for pane (in pixels). Default is 1.

`preferredPaneSize` (class `PreferredPaneSize`)

> Preferred size of pane. This default is dependent on the application.

`resizeToPreferred` (class `Boolean`)

> A Boolean that specifies whether to resize each pane to its preferred size when the Paned widget is resized. Default is `False`.

`showGrip` (class `ShowGrip`)

> A Boolean that specifies whether to show a grip for this pane. Default is `True`.

`skipAdjust` (class `Boolean`)

> By default, this resource is `FALSE`, meaning that the Paned widget will resize a pane automatically, whenever necessary. If this resource is `TRUE`, the Paned widget will skip the adjustment of the pane.

The Paned widget has no action routines of its own, as all actions are handled through the grips. The grips are each assigned a default Translation table.

```
<Btn1Down>:    GripAction(Start, UpLeftPane)
<Btn2Down>:    GripAction(Start, ThisBorderOnly)
<Btn3Down>:    GripAction(Start, LowRightPane)
<Btn1Motion>:  GripAction(Move, UpLeftPane)
<Btn2Motion>:  GripAction(Move, ThisBorderOnly)
<Btn3Motion>:  GripAction(Move, LowRightPane)
Any<BtnUp>:    GripAction(Commit)
```

The Paned widget interprets the GripAction as taking two arguments. The first argument may be any of the following:

Start   Sets up the Paned widget for resizing and changes the cursor of the grip. The second argument determines which pane will be resized, and can take on any of the three values shown above (UpLeftPane, ThisBorder-Only, LowRightPane).

Move   The internal borders are drawn over the current pane locations to animate where the borders would actually be placed if you were to move this border as shown. The second argument must match the second argument that was passed to the Start action that began this process. If these arguments are not passed, the behavior is undefined.

Commit   This argument causes the Paned widget to commit the changes selected by the previously started action. The cursor is changed back to the grip's inactive cursor. No second argument is needed in this case.

Scrollbar

The Scrollbar widget is a rectangular area that contains a slide region and a thumb (slide bar). A Scrollbar can be used alone (to provide a graduated scale) or within a composite widget (for example, a Viewport). A Scrollbar can be aligned either vertically or horizontally.

When a Scrollbar is created, it is drawn with the thumb in a contrasting color. The thumb is normally used to scroll client data and to give visual feedback on the percentage of the client data that is visible.

Resources

You can set the dimensions of the Scrollbar two ways:

- By using the width and height resources, as you can for all widgets.

- By using the Scrollbar resources length and thickness, which are independent of the vertical or horizontal orientation.

The following new resources are associated with the Scrollbar widget:

foreground (class Foreground)
> Thumb color.

length (class Length)
> Specifies the height for a vertical Scrollbar and the width for a horizontal Scrollbar. Default is 1 (pixel).

minimumThumb (class MinimumThumb)
> Smallest size, in pixels, to which the thumb can shrink. Default is 7.

orientation (class Orientation)

> Orientation of scrollbar. This value can be either XtOrientVertical (the default)
> or XtOrientHorizontal. Not usually set in resource files.

scrollDCursor (class Cursor)

> Cursor for scrolling down. Default is XC_sb_down_arrow.

scrollHCursor (class Cursor)

> Idle horizontal cursor. Default is XC_sb_h_double_arrow.

scrollLCursor (class Cursor)

> Cursor for scrolling left. Default is XC_sb_left_arrow.

scrollRCursor (class Cursor)

> Cursor for scrolling right. Default is XC_sb_right_arrow.

scrollUCursor (class Cursor)

> Cursor for scrolling up. Default is XC_sb_up_arrow.

scrollVCursor (class Cursor)

> Idle vertical cursor. Default is XC_sb_v_double_arrow.

shown (class Shown)

> Percentage the thumb covers. Default is 0.0.

thickness (class Thickness)

> Specifies the width for a vertical Scrollbar and the height for a horizontal Scrollbar.
> Default is 14 (pixels).

thumb (class Thumb)

> Thumb pixmap. Default is GrayPixmap.

topOfThumb (class TopOfThumb)

> Position on scroll bar. Default is 0.0.

Translations and Actions

The actions supported by the Scrollbar widget are:

StartScroll(*value*)

> The possible values are Forward, Backward, or Continuous.
> This must be the first action to begin a new movement.

NotifyScroll(*value*)

> The possible values are Proportional or FullLength. If the
> argument to StartScroll was Forward or Backward,
> NotifyScroll executes the XtNscrollProc callbacks and
> passes either the position of the pointer if its argument is Propor-
> tional or the full length of the scroll bar if its argument is Full-
> Length. If the argument to StartScroll was Continuous,
> NotifyScroll returns without executing any callbacks.

`EndScroll()`	This must be the last action after a movement is complete.
`MoveThumb()`	Repositions the scroll bar thumb to the current pointer location.
`NotifyThumb()`	Calls the `XtNjumpProc` callbacks and passes the relative position of the pointer as a percentage of the scroll bar length.

The default bindings for Scrollbar are:

```
<Btn1Down>:    StartScroll(Forward)
<Btn2Down>:    StartScroll(Continuous) MoveThumb() NotifyThumb()
<Btn3Down>:    StartScroll(Backward)
<Btn2Motion>: MoveThumb() NotifyThumb()
<BtnUp>:       NotifyScroll(Proportional) EndScroll()
```

Examples of additional bindings you might wish to specify in a resource file are:

```
*Scrollbar.Translations: \
 ~<KeyPress>f: StartScroll(Forward) NotifyScroll(FullLength) EndScroll()\n\
  <KeyPress>b: StartScroll(Backward) NotifyScroll(FullLength) EndScroll()\n\
```

Simple

The Simple widget defines characteristics that are inherited by non-composite widgets such as Labels, Lists, and Scrollbars. The Simple widget never appears in applications, but it does define resources that are inherited by its subclasses.

Resources

The following resources are associated with the Simple widget:

`cursor` (class `Cursor`)
    The cursor to use within the widget. Default is none.

`insensitiveBorder` (class `Insensitive`)
    The pixmap to use to indicate that the Simple widget cannot receive input. Default is `Gray`.

SimpleMenu

The SimpleMenu widget is a container for menu entries. It is a direct subclass of Shell. This is the only part of the menu that actually contains a window, since each menu pane is a gadget (a widget without a window). SimpleMenu "glues" the individual menu entries together into one menu.

Resources

The following new resources are used by the SimpleMenu widget:

backingStore (class BackingStore)
: Determines what type of backing store will be used for the menu. Legal values for this resource are NotUseful, WhenMapped, and Always. These values are the backing-store integers defined in <*X11/X.h*>. If default is specified (the default behavior) the server will use whatever it thinks is appropriate. This resource is typically set by the application.

bottomMargin, topMargin (class VerticalMargins)
: The amount of space between the top or bottom of the menu and the menu entry closest to that edge. Default is 0.

cursor (class Cursor)
: The shape of the mouse pointer whenever it is in this widget.

label (class Label)
: This label will be placed at the top of the SimpleMenu and cannot be highlighted. The name of the label object is menuLabel, and it is of the class specified by the LabelClass resource. Using this name, it is possible to modify the label's attributes through the resource database. When the label is created, the label is hard-coded to the value of label, and justify is hard-coded as XtJustifyCenter.

labelClass (class LabelClass)
: Specifies the type of Sme object created as the menu label. Possibilities are Sme, SmeBSB, or SmeLine.

menuOnScreen (class MenuonScreen)
: If the menu is automatically positioned under the cursor with the XawPosition-SimpleMenu action, and if this resource is True, then the menu is always fully visible on the screen. The default is True. This resource is usually set by the application.

overrideRedirect
: Determines the value of the override_redirect attribute of the SimpleMenu's window. The override_redirect attribute of a window determines whether a window manager may interpose itself between this window and the root window of the display. Usually set by the application program.

popupOnEntry (class PopupOnEntry)
: The XawPositionSimpleMenu action pops up the SimpleMenu with its label (or first entry) directly under the pointer, by default. To pop up the menu under another

entry, the application can set this resource to the menu entry that *should* be under the pointer when the menu is popped up. This allows the application to offer the user a default menu entry that can be selected without moving the pointer. Not usually settable by the user.

`rowHeight` (class `RowHeight`)

If this resource is 0 (the default), then each menu entry is given its desired height. If this resource has any other value, then all menu entries are forced to be `rowHeight` pixels high.

Translations and Actions

The following default translation bindings are used by the SimpleMenu widget:

```
<EnterWindow>:    highlight()
<LeaveWindow>:    unhighlight()
<BtnMotion>:  highlight()
<BtnUp>: MenuPopdown() notify() unhighlight()
```

With these bindings, the user can pop down the menu without activating any of the callback functions, by releasing the pointer button when no menu item is highlighted.

The actions supported by SimpleMenu are listed below:

`highlight()` — Highlights the menu entry that is currently under the pointer. Only an item that is highlighted is notified when the `notify` action is invoked. The look of a highlighted entry is determined by the menu entry.

`unhighlight()` — Unhighlights the currently highlighted menu item and returns it to its normal look.

`notify()` — Notifies the currently highlighted menu entry that it has been selected. It is the responsibility of the menu entry to take the appropriate action.

`MenuPopdown(menu)` — Built-in action to pop down a menu widget.

Sme

The Sme object is the base class for all menu entries that are children of SimpleMenu. While this object is intended mainly to be subclassed, it may be used in a menu to add blank space between menu entries.

Resources

The Sme object defines no new resources.

SmeBSB

The SmeBSB object is used to create a menu entry that contains a string, and optional bitmaps in its left and right margins. The parent is expected to be SimpleMenu. Since each menu entry is an independent object, the application is able to change the font, color, height, and other attributes of the menu entries, on an entry-by-entry basis.

Resources

The following resources are used by the SmeBSB object:

font (class Font)
: Specifies the font used by the menu entry.

foreground (class Foreground)
: Specifies the foreground color of the menu entry's window. This color is also used to render all 1's in leftBitmap and rightBitmap.

justify (class Justify)
: Specifies how the label is to be rendered between the left and right margins when the space is wider than the actual text. When specifying the justification from a resource file, the values left, center, or right may be used.

label (class Label)
: Specifies the string to be displayed in the menu entry. The exact location of this string within the bounds of the menu entry is controlled by the resources leftMargin, rightMargin, vertSpace, and justify.

leftBitmap (class LeftBitmap), rightBitmap (class RightBitmap)
: Specifies a name of a bitmap to display in the left or right margin of the menu entry. All 1's in the bitmap are rendered in the foreground color of the SimpleMenu widget, and all 0's will be drawn in the background color of the SimpleMenu widget. The programmer must ensure that the menu entry is tall enough and that the appropriate margin is wide enough to accept the bitmap. If care is not taken, the bitmap might extend into either another menu entry or this entry's label. This resource is typically set by the application.

leftMargin, rightMargin (class HorizontalMargins)
: Specifies the amount of space (in pixels) to leave between the edge of the menu entry and the label string.

vertSpace (class VertSpace)
: Specifies the amount of vertical padding to place around the label of a menu entry. The label and bitmaps are always centered vertically within the menu. Values for this

resource are expressed as a percentage of the font's height. The default value (25) increases the default height to 125% of the font's height.

SmeLine

The SmeLine object is used to add a horizontal line or menu separator to a SimpleMenu. Since each menu entry is an independent object, the application is able to change the color, height, and other attributes of the menu entries, on an entry-by-entry basis. This entry is not selectable, and does not highlight when the pointer cursor is over it.

Resources

The following resources are used by the SmeLine object:

foreground (class Foreground)
The foreground color of the menu entry's window.

lineWidth (class LineWidth)
The width of the horizontal line to be displayed.

stipple (class Stipple)
If a bitmap is specified for this resource, the line will be stippled through it. This allows the menu separator to be rendered as something more exciting than just a line. For instance, if the application defines a stipple that is a chain link, then menu separators will look like chains.

StripChart

The StripChart widget is used to provide a real-time graphic chart of a single value. This widget is used by *xload* to provide the load graph. It will read data from an application, and update the chart at the interval specified by update.

Resources

The following resources are used by the StripChart widget:

height (class Height)
The height of the stripchart. Default is 120 pixels.

highlight (class Foreground)
The color that will be used to draw the scale lines on the graph.

jumpScroll (class JumpScroll)
When the graph reaches the right edge of the window it must be scrolled to the left.

This resource specifies the number of pixels it will jump. Smooth scrolling can be achieved by setting this resource to 1.

minScale (class Scale)

> The minimum scale for the graph. The number of divisions on the graph will always be greater than or equal to this value. Default is 1.

update (class Interval)

> The number of seconds between graph updates. Each update is represented on the graph as a 1-pixel-wide line. Every update seconds, a new graph point will be added to the right end of the StripChart. Default is 10.

width (class Width)

> The width of the stripchart. Default is 120 pixels.

Text

A Text widget is a window that provides a way for an application to display one or more lines of text. The displayed text can reside in a file on disk or in a string in memory. An option also lets an application display a vertical Scrollbar in the Text window, letting the user scroll through the displayed text. Other options allow an application to let the user modify the text in the window or search for a specific string.

Three types of edit mode are available:

- Append-only
- Read-only
- Editable

Append-only mode lets the user enter text into the window, while read-only mode does not. Text may be entered only if the insertion point is after the last character in the window. Editable mode lets you place the cursor anywhere in the text and modify the text at that position. The text cursor position can be modified by using the keystrokes or pointer buttons defined by the event bindings. (See the section "Translations and Actions" below.)

Resources

The following resources are used by the Text widget:

autoFill (class AutoFill)

> A Boolean that specifies whether the Text widget will automatically break a line when the user attempts to type into the right margin Default is False.

bottomMargin (class Margin)

> Amount of space, in pixels, between the edge of the window and the edge of the text within the window. Default is 2.

dataCompression

> If True (the default), the AsciiSrc will compress its data to the minimum size

required. This will happen either every time the text string is saved or whenever the value of the string is queried.

displayCaret (class Output)
    A Boolean that specifies whether to display the text caret. Default is True.

displayPosition (class TextPosition)
    Character position of first line. Default is 0.

insertPosition (class TextPosition)
    Character position of caret. Default is 0.

leftMargin (class Margin)
    Left margin in pixels. Default is 2.

rightMargin (class Margin)
    Amount of space, in pixels, between the edge of the window and the corresponding edge of the text within the window. Default is 2.

scrollHorizontal

scrollVertical
    Control the placement of scrollbars on the left and bottom edge of the text widget. Possible values are XawtextScrollAlways, XawtextScrollWhenNeeded, and XawtextScrollNever (the default). Not settable from a resource file.

topMargin (class Margin)
    Amount of space, in pixels, between the edge of the window and the corresponding edge of the text within the window. Default is 2.

useStringInPlace
    If True, will disable the memory management provided by the Text widget, updating the string resource instead. Default is False.

Translations and Actions

Many standard keyboard editing facilities are supported by the event bindings. The following actions are supported:

Cursor Movement	Delete
Forward-character	Delete-next-character
Backward-character	Delete-previous-character
Forward-word	Delete-next-word
Backward-word	Delete-previous-word
Forward-paragraph	Delete-selection
Backward-paragraph	
Beginning-of-line	Selection
End-of-line	Insert-selection
Next-line	Select-word
Previous-line	Select-all
Next-page	Select-start

Cursor Movement	Delete
Previous-page	Select-adjust
Beginning-of-file	Select-end
End-of-file	Extend-start
Scroll-one-line-up	Extend-adjust
Scroll-one-line-down	Extend-end
New Line	Miscellaneous
Newline-and-indent	Redraw-display
Newline-and-backup	Insert-file
Newline	Insert-char
Kill	Display-caret
Kill-word	Focus-in
Backward-kill-word	Focus-out
Kill-selection	Search
Kill-to-end-of-line	Multiply
Kill-paragraph	Form-paragraph
Kill-to-end-of-paragraph	Transpose-characters
	No-op

- A page corresponds to the size of the Text window. For example, if the Text window is 50 lines in length, scrolling forward one page is the same as scrolling forward 50 lines.

- The delete action deletes a text item. The kill action deletes a text item and puts the item in the kill buffer (X cut buffer 1).

- The insert-selection action retrieves the value of a specified X selection or cut buffer, with fall-back to alternative selections or cut buffers.

Cursor Movement Actions

```
forward-character()
backward-character()
```
> These actions move the insert point forward or backward one character in the buffer. If the insert point is at the end (or beginning) of a line, this action moves the insert point to the next (or previous) line.

```
forward-word()
backward-word()
```
> These actions move the insert point to the next or previous word boundary. A word boundary is defined as a space, a tab, or a carriage return.

```
forward-paragraph()
backward-paragraph()
```
> These actions move the insert point to the next or previous paragraph boundary. A paragraph boundary is defined as two carriage returns in a row with only spaces or tabs between them.

```
beginning-of-line()
end-of-line()
```
These actions move to the beginning or end of the current line. If the insert point is already at the end or beginning of the line, no action is taken.

```
next-line()
previous-line()
```
These actions move the insert point up or down one line. If the insert point is currently *n* characters from the beginning of the line then it will be *n* characters from the beginning of the next or previous line. If *n* is past the end of the line, the insert point is placed at the end of the line.

```
next-page()
previous-page()
```
These actions move the insert point up or down one page in the file. One page is defined as the current height of the text widget. These actions always place the insert point at the first character of the top line.

```
beginning-of-file()
end-of-file()
```
These actions place the insert point at the beginning or end of the current text buffer. The text widget is then scrolled the minimum amount necessary to make the new insert point location visible.

```
scroll-one-line-up()
scroll-one-line-down()
```
These actions scroll the current text field up or down by one line. They do not move the insert point. Other than the scrollbars, this is the only way that the insert point may be moved off of the visible text area. The widget will be scrolled so that the insert point is back on the screen as soon as some other action is executed.

Delete Actions

```
delete-next-character()
delete-previous-character()
```
These actions remove the character immediately after or before the insert point. If a carriage return is removed, the next line is appended to the end of the current line.

```
delete-next-word()
delete-previous-word()
```
These actions remove all characters between the insert point location and the next word boundary. A word boundary is defined as a space, a tab or a carriage return.

```
delete-selection()
```
This action removes all characters in the current selection. The selection can be set with the selection actions.

Selection Actions

select-word()   This action selects the word in which the insert point is currently located. If the insert point is between words, it will select the previous word.

select-all()   This action selects the entire text buffer.

select-start() This action sets the insert point to the current pointer location, where a selection then begins. If many of these selection actions occur quickly in succession then the selection count mechanism will be invoked.

select-adjust()

This action allows a selection started with the select-start action to be modified, as described above.

select-end(name[,name, . . .])

This action ends a text selection that began with the select-start action, and asserts ownership of the selection or selections specified. A name can be a selection (e.g., PRIMARY) or a cut buffer (e.g., CUT_BUFFER0). Note that case is important. If no names are specified, PRIMARY is asserted.

extend-start() This action finds the nearest end of the current selection, and moves it to the current pointer location.

extend-adjust()

This action allows a selection started with an extend-start action to be modified.

extend-end(name[,name, . . .])

This action ends a text selection that began with the extend-start action, and asserts ownership of the selection or selections specified. A name can be a selection (e.g., PRIMARY) or a cut buffer (e.g., CUT_BUFFER0). Note that case is important. If no name is given, PRIMARY is asserted.

insert-selection(name[,name, . . .])

This action retrieves the value of the first (left-most) named selection that exists or the cut buffer that is not empty. This action then inserts it into the Text widget at the current insert point location. A name can be a selection (e.g., PRIMARY) or a cut buffer (e.g., CUT_BUFFER0). Note that case is important.

New Line Actions

`newline-and-indent()`
> This action inserts a newline into the text and adds spaces to that line to indent it to match the previous line. (Note: this action still has a few bugs.)

`newline-and-backup()`
> This action inserts a newline into the text *after* the insert point.

`newline()`
> This action inserts a newline into the text *before* the insert point.

Kill Actions

`kill-word()`
`backward-kill-word()`
> These actions act exactly like the `delete-next-word` and `delete-previous-word` actions, but they store the word that was killed into the kill buffer (CUT_BUFFER_1).

`kill-selection()`
> This action deletes the current selection and stores the deleted text into the kill buffer (CUT_BUFFER_1).

`kill-to-end-of-line()`
> This action deletes the entire line to the right of the insert point, and stores the deleted text into the kill buffer (CUT_BUFFER_1).

`kill-paragraph()`
> This action deletes the current paragraph. If the insert point is between paragraphs, it deletes the paragraph above the insert point, and stores the deleted text into the kill buffer (CUT_BUFFER_1).

`kill-to-end-of-paragraph()`
> This action deletes everything between the current insert point and the next paragraph boundary, and puts the deleted text into the kill buffer (CUT_BUFFER_1).

Miscellaneous Actions

`redraw-display()`
> This action recomputes the location of all the text lines on the display, scrolls the text to center vertically the line containing the insert point on the screen, clears the entire screen, and then redisplays it.

`insert-file([filename])`
> This action activates the insert file popup. The *filename* option specifies the default filename to put in the filename buffer of the popup. If no *filename* is specified the buffer is empty at startup.

insert-char()   This action may be attached only to a key event. It calls `XLookup-String` to translate the event into a (rebindable) Latin-1 character (sequence) and inserts that sequence into the text at the insert point position.

insert-string(*string*[,*string*, ...])
This action inserts each *string* into the text at the insert point location. Any *string* beginning with the characters "0x" and containing only valid hexadecimal digits in the remainder is interpreted as a hexadecimal constant and the corresponding single character is inserted instead.

display-caret(*state*,*when*)
This action allows the insert point to be turned on and off. The *state* argument specifies the desired state of the insert point. This value may be any of the string values accepted for Boolean resources (e.g., on, `True`, off, `False`, etc.). If no arguments are specified, the default value is `True`. The *when* argument specifies, for `EnterNotify` or `LeaveNotify` events, whether or not the focus field in the event is to be examined. If the second argument is not specified, or specified as something other than `always`, then if the action is bound to an `EnterNotify` or `LeaveNotify` event, the action will be taken only if the focus field is `True`. An augmented binding that might be useful is:

```
*Text.Translations: #override \
    <FocusIn>: display-caret(on) \n\
    <FocusOut>:display-caret(off)
```

focus-in()
focus-out()   These actions do not currently do anything.

search(*direction*,[*string*])
This action activates the search popup. The *direction* must be specified as either `forward` or `backward`. The string is optional and is used as an initial value for the "Search for:" string.

multiply(*value*) The multiply action allows the user to multiply the effects of many of the text actions. Thus the following action sequence:

```
multiply(10) delete-next-word()
```

will delete 10 words. It does not matter whether these actions take place in one event or many events. Using the default translations the key sequence Control-u, Control-d will delete 4 characters. Multiply actions can be chained; thus,

```
multiply(5) multiply(5)
```

is the same as:

```
multiply(25)
```

If the string `reset` is passed to the multiply action the effects of all previous multiplies are removed and a beep is sent to the display.

`form-paragraph()`

This action removes all the carriage returns from the current paragraph and reinserts them so that each line is as long as possible, while still fitting on the current screen. Lines are broken at word boundaries if at all possible. This action currently works only on Text widgets that use ASCII text.

`transpose-characters()`

This action will switch the positions of the character to the left of the insert point and the character to the right of the insert point. The insert point will then be advanced one character.

`no-op([`*action*`])` The no-op action makes no change to the text widget, and is used mainly to override translations. This action takes one optional argument. If this argument is `RingBell` then a beep is sent to the display.

Event Bindings

The default event bindings for the Text widget are:

```
char defaultTextTranslations[] = "\
      Ctrl<Key>F:          forward-character() \n\
      Ctrl<Key>B:          backward-character() \n\
      Ctrl<Key>D:          delete-next-character() \n\
      Ctrl<Key>A:          beginning-of-line() \n\
      Ctrl<Key>E:          end-of-line() \n\
      Ctrl<Key>H:          delete-previous-character() \n\
      Ctrl<Key>J:          newline-and-indent() \n\
      Ctrl<Key>K:          kill-to-end-of-line() \n\
      Ctrl<Key>L:          redraw-display() \n\
      Ctrl<Key>M:          newline() \n\
      Ctrl<Key>N:          next-line() \n\
      Ctrl<Key>O:          newline-and-backup() \n\
      Ctrl<Key>P:          previous-line() \n\
      Ctrl<Key>V:          next-page() \n\
      Ctrl<Key>W:          kill-selection() \n\
      Ctrl<Key>Y:          unkill() \n\
      Ctrl<Key>Z:          scroll-one-line-up() \n\
      Meta<Key>F:          forward-word() \n\
      Meta<Key>B:          backward-word() \n\
      Meta<Key>I:          insert-file() \n\
      Meta<Key>K:          kill-to-end-of-paragraph() \n\
      Meta<Key>V:          previous-page() \n\
      Meta<Key>Y:          stuff() \n\
      Meta<Key>Z:          scroll-one-line-down() \n\
      :Meta<Key>d:         delete-next-word() \n\
      :Meta<Key>D:         kill-word() \n\
      :Meta<Key>h:         delete-previous-word() \n\
      :Meta<Key>H:         backward-kill-word() \n\
      :Meta<Key>\<:        beginning-of-file() \n\
      :Meta<Key>\>:        end-of-file() \n\
      :Meta<Key>]:         forward-paragraph() \n\
```

```
            :Meta<Key>[:          backward-paragraph() \n\
            ~Shift Meta<Key>Delete:    delete-previous-word() \n\
             Shift Meta<Key>Delete:    backward-kill-word() \n\
            ~Shift Meta<Key>Backspace: delete-previous-word() \n\
             Shift Meta<Key>Backspace: backward-kill-word() \n\
            <Key>Right:           forward-character() \n\
            <Key>Left:            backward-character() \n\
            <Key>Down:            next-line() \n\
            <Key>Up:              previous-line() \n\
            <Key>Delete:          delete-previous-character() \n\
            <Key>BackSpace:       delete-previous-character() \n\
            <Key>Linefeed:        newline-and-indent() \n\
            <Key>Return:          newline() \n\
            <Key>:                insert-char() \n\
            <FocusIn>:            focus-in() \n\
            <FocusOut>:           focus-out() \n\
            <Btn1Down>:           select-start() \n\
            <Btn1Motion>:         extend-adjust() \n\
            <Btn1Up>:             extend-end(PRIMARY, CUT_BUFFER0) \n\
            <Btn2Down>:           insert-selection(PRIMARY, CUT_BUFFER0) \n\
            <Btn3Down>:           extend-start() \n\
            <Btn3Motion>:         extend-adjust() \n\
            <Btn3Up>:             extend-end(PRIMARY, CUT_BUFFER0)";
```

A user-supplied resource entry can use application-specific bindings, a subset of the supplied default bindings, or both. The following is an example of a user-supplied resource entry that uses a subset of the default bindings:

```
Xmh*Text.Translations: \
        <Key>Right:      forward-character() \n\
        <Key>Left:       backward-character() \n\
         Meta<Key>F:     forward-word() \n\
         Meta<Key>B:     backward-word() \n\
        :Meta<Key>]:     forward-paragraph() \n\
        :Meta<Key>[:     backward-paragraph() \n\
        <Key>:           insert-char()
```

An augmented binding that is useful with the *xclipboard* utility is:

```
*Text.Translations: #override \
    Button1 <Btn2Down>:   extend-end(CLIPBOARD)
```

The Text widget fully supports the X selection and cut buffer mechanisms. The following actions can be used to specify button bindings that will cause Text to assert ownership of one or more selections, to store the selected text into a cut buffer, and to retrieve the value of a selection or cut buffer and insert it into the text value.

`insert-selection(`*name*`[,`*name*`,...])`

> Retrieves the value of the first (left-most) named selection that exists or the cut buffer that is not empty and inserts it into the input stream. The specified name can be that of any selection (for example, PRIMARY or SECONDARY) or a cut buffer (i.e., CUT_BUFFER0 through CUT_BUF-FER7). Note that case matters.

`select-start()`   Unselects any previously selected text and begins selecting new text.

```
select-adjust()
```
`extend-adjust()` Continues selecting text from the previous start position.

`start-extend()` Begins extending the selection from the farthest (left or right) edge.

```
select-end(name[,name,...])
extend-end(name[,name,...])
```
        Ends the text selection, asserts ownership of the specified selection(s), and stores the text in the specified cut buffer(s). The specified name can be that of a selection (for example, PRIMARY or SECONDARY) or a cut buffer (i.e., CUT_BUFFER0 through CUT_BUFFER7). Note that case is significant. If CUT_BUFFER0 is listed, the cut buffers are rotated before storing into buffer 0.

Toggle

The Toggle widget is an area, often rectangular, containing a text or pixmap label. This widget maintains a Boolean state (e.g. True/False or On/Off) and changes state whenever it is selected. When the pointer is on the button, the button border is highlighted to indicate that the button is ready for selection. When pointer button 1 is pressed and released, the Toggle widget indicates that it has changed state by reversing its foreground and background colors, and its `notify` action is invoked. If the pointer is moved out of the widget before the button is released, the widget reverts to its normal foreground and background colors, and releasing the button has no effect. This behavior allows the user to cancel an action.

Toggle buttons may also be part of a radio group. A radio group is a list of Toggle buttons in which no more than one Toggle may be set at any time. A radio group is identified by the widget ID of any one of its members.

The difference between a Command widget and a Toggle widget is that a Command widget typically invokes an application function when it is invoked. A Toggle widget simply changes its state (and presumably the state of some application data.) Toggles are thus useful for mailing configuration settings, which can then be applied by an associated Command widget.

Resources

The following new resources are associated with the Toggle widget:

`radioGroup` (class `Widget`)
        Specifies another Toggle widget that is in the radio group to which this Toggle widget should be added. A radio group is a group of Toggle widgets, only one of which may be set at a time. If this value is NULL (the default), then the Toggle is not part of any radio group and can change state without affecting any other Toggle widgets. If the widget specified in this resource is not already in a radio group, then a new radio group is created containing these two Toggle widgets. No Toggle widget can be in multiple radio groups.

                                                        X Window System User's Guide, Motif Edition

`state` (class `State`)

    Specifies whether the Toggle widget is set (`True`) or unset (`False`). The default is `False`.

Translations and Actions

The following default translation bindings are used by the Toggle widget:

```
<EnterWindow>:        highlight(Always)
<LeaveWindow>:        unhighlight()
<Btn1Down>,<Btn1Up>:  toggle() notify()
```

The actions supported by Toggle are listed below:

`highlight(`*condition*`)`

    Displays the internal highlight border in the color (`foreground` or `background`) that contrasts with the interior color of the Toggle widget. The conditions `WhenUnset` and `Always` are understood by this action procedure. If no argument is passed, `WhenUnset` is assumed.

`unhighlight()`   Displays the internal highlight border in the color (`foreground` or `background`) that matches the interior color of the Toggle widget.

`set()`   Enters the set state, in which `notify` is possible, and displays the interior of the button in the foreground color. The label or pixmap is displayed in the background color.

`unset()`   Cancels the set state and displays the interior of the button, including the highlight border, in the background color. The label or pixmap is displayed in the foreground color.

`toggle()`   Changes the current state of the Toggle widget, setting the widget if it was previously unset, and unsetting it if it was previously set. If the widget is to be set and is in a radio group, then this action procedure may unset another Toggle widget, causing all routines on its callback list to be invoked. The callback routines for the Toggle to be unset are called before those for the Toggle to be set.

`reset()`   Cancels any `set` or `highlight` action and displays the interior of the button in the background color, with the label displayed in the foreground color.

Radio Groups

Two types of radio groups are typically desired by applications. In the first type, the default translations for the Toggle widget implement a "zero, or one of many" radio group. This means that no more than one button can be active, but no buttons need to be active.

The other type of radio group is "one of many" and has the more restricted policy that exactly one radio button will always be active. Toggle widgets can be used to provide this interface by modifying the translation table of each Toggle in the group:

```
<EnterWindow>:  highlight(Always)
<LeaveWindow>:  unhighlight()
<Btn1Down>,<Btn1Up>:   set() notify()
```

This translation table does not allow any Toggle to be unset unless another Toggle has been set.

Viewport

The Viewport widget consists of a frame window, one or two Scrollbars, and an inner window (usually containing a child widget). The size of the frame window is determined by the viewing size of the data that is to be displayed and the dimensions to which the Viewport is created. The inner window is the full size of the data that is to be displayed and is clipped by the frame window. The Viewport widget controls the scrolling of the data directly.

When the geometry of the frame window is equal in size to the inner window, or when the data does not require scrolling, the Viewport widget automatically removes any scroll bars. The `forceBars` resource causes the Viewport widget to display any scroll bar permanently.

Resources

The following new resources are associated with the Viewport widget:

allowHoriz (class Boolean)
> Flag to allow horizontal scroll bars. Default value is FALSE. Setting this resource to TRUE allows a Viewport child to increase in size horizontally.

allowVert (class Boolean)
> Flag to allow vertical scroll bars. Default value is FALSE. Setting this resource to TRUE allows a Viewport child to increase in size vertically.

forceBars (class Boolean)
> Flag to force display of scroll bars. Default value is FALSE. Normally, when the geometry of the frame window is equal in size to the inner window, or when the data does not require scrolling, Viewport automatically removes any scroll bars. Setting forceBars to TRUE causes the Viewport widget to display any scroll bar permanently.

useBottom (class Boolean)
> Flag to indicate bottom/top bars. Default is FALSE, meaning to put scrollbars on top.

useRight (class Boolean)
> Flag to indicate right/left bars. Default is FALSE, meaning to put scrollbars on the left.

Glossary

X uses many common terms in unique ways. A good example is "children." While most, if not all, of these terms are defined where they are first used in this manual, you will undoubtedly find it easier to refresh your memory by looking for them here.

Glossary

access control list   X maintains lists of hosts that are allowed access to each server controlling a display. By default, only the local host may use the display, plus any hosts specified in the *access control list* for that display. The list is found in */etc/Xn.hosts* where *n* is the number of the display. The access control list is also known as the host access list.

active window   The window where the input is directed. With a "pointer focus" window manager such as *twm*, you must put the pointer in a window to make it the active window. The *active window* is sometimes called the **focus window**.

ASCII   American Standard Code for Information Interchange. This standard for data transmission assigns individual 7-bit codes to represent each of a specific set of 128 numerals, letters, and control characters.

background   Windows may have a *background*, consisting of either a solid color or a tile pattern. If a window has a background, it will be repainted automatically by the server whenever there is an Expose event on the window. If a window does not have a background, it will be transparent. See also **foreground**.

background color   The color that determines the backdrop of a window, for example, on monochrome displays, the root window background color is gray.

background window   A shaded area (also called the **root window**) that covers the entire screen and upon which other windows are displayed.

binding   An association between a function and a key and/or pointer button. *twm* allows you to bind its functions to any key(s) on the keyboard, or to a combination of keys and pointer button (e.g., the Control key and the middle button on a 3-button pointer).

bitmap   A grid of pixels or picture elements, each of which is white, black, or, in the case of color displays, a color. The *bitmap* client allows you to edit bitmaps, which you can use as pointers, icons, and background window patterns.

border	A window can have a border that is zero or more pixels wide. If a window has a border, the border can have a solid color or a tile pattern, and it will be repainted automatically by the server whenever its color or pattern is changed or an `Expose` event occurs on the window.
client	An X application program. There are *client* programs to perform a variety of tasks, including terminal emulation and window management. Clients need not run on the same system as the display server program.
colorcell	An entry in a colormap is known as a *colorcell*. An entry contains three values specifying red, green, and blue intensities. These values are always 16-bit unsigned numbers, with zero being minimum intensity. The values are truncated or scaled by the server to match the display hardware. See also **colormap**.
colormap	A *colormap* consists of a set of colorcells. A pixel value indexes into the colormap to produce intensities of red, green, and blue to be displayed. Depending on hardware limitations, one or more colormaps may be installed at one time, such that windows associated with those maps display with true colors. Regardless of the number of installable colormaps, any number of virtual colormaps can be created. When needed, a virtual colormap can be installed and the existing installed colormap may have to be uninstalled. The colormap on most systems is a limited resource that should be conserved by allocating read-only colorcells whenever possible, and selecting RGB values from the predefined color database. Read-only cells may be shared between clients. See also **RGB**.
console xterm window	
	This *xterm* window is the first window to appear on your display. Exiting the console window kills the X server program and any associated applications. Also called the login *xterm* window.
default	A function-dependent value assigned when you do not specify a value. For example, specifying the −rv option with *xterm* reverses the foreground and background colors for the *xterm* window. If you do not specify this option, the default foreground and background colors are used.
depth	The *depth* of a window or pixmap is the number of bits per pixel.
device-dependent	Aspects of a system that vary depending on the hardware. For example, the number of colors available on the screen (or whether color is available at all) is a *device-dependent* feature of X.
display	A set of one or more screens driven by a single X server. The DISPLAY environment variable tells programs which servers to connect to, unless it is overridden by the −display command line option. The default is always screen 0 of (display) server 0 on the local node.

event	Something that must happen before an action can occur.

exposure Window *exposure* occurs when a window is first mapped, or when another window that obscures it is unmapped, resized, or moved. Servers do not guarantee to preserve the contents of windows when windows are obscured or reconfigured. Expose events are sent to clients to inform them when contents of regions of windows have been lost and need to be regenerated.

focus window The window to which keyboard input is directed. By default, the keyboard focus belongs to the root, which has the effect of sending input to whichever window has the pointer in it (if you are using a "pointer focus" window manager, such as *twm*). However, some clients may automatically take the focus, which means they may send input to a particular window regardless of the position of the pointer.

font A style of text characters. Fonts and X font naming conventions are described in Chapter 5, *Font Specification*. Samples of Release 4 screen fonts are pictured in Appendix E.

font directory By default, fonts are stored in three subdirectories of */usr/lib/X11/fonts*: called *misc*, *75dpi*, and *100dpi*. You can specify an alternative font search path for the server with the *xset* client.

foreground The pixel value that will actually be used for drawing pictures or text is referred to as the *foreground*.

foreground color The color in which the text in windows and menus, or graphics output are displayed.

geometry The specification for the size and placement of a window, which can be specified with the -geometry option. This option takes an argument of the form: `widthxheight±xoff±yoff`.

hexadecimal A base-16 arithmetic system, which uses the digits A through F to represent the base-10 numbers 10 through 15. *Hexadecimal* notation (called hex for short) is frequently used with computers because a single hex digit can represent four binary digits (bits). The table below shows the equivalence between hex digits and binary numbers.

Hex	Binary	Hex	Binary	Hex	Binary	Hex	Binary
0	0000	4	0100	8	1000	C	1100
1	0001	5	0101	9	1001	D	1101
2	0010	6	0110	A	1010	E	1110
3	0011	7	0111	B	1011	F	1111

X clients accept a special hexadecimal notation (prefixed by a # character) in all command line options relating to color. See Chapter 8, *Command Line Options*, for more information.

highlighter The horizontal band of color that moves with the pointer within a menu.

hot spot The reference point of a pointer that corresponds to its specified position on the display. In the case of an arrow, an appropriate *hot spot* is its tip. In the case of a cross, an appropriate hot spot might be its center.

icon A small symbol that represents a window but uses little space on the display. Converting windows to *icons* allows you to keep your display uncluttered.

input device Hardware device that allows you to input information to the system. For a window-based system, a keyboard and pointer are the most common input devices.

keyboard focus See **focus window**.

menu A list of commands or functions, listed in a small window, which can be selected with the pointer.

modifier keys Keys on the keyboard such as Control, Alt, and Shift. X programs recognize a set of "logical" *modifier key* functions that can be mapped to physical keys. The most frequently used of these logical keys is called the "meta" key.

mouse An input device that, when moved across a flat surface, moves the pointer symbol correspondingly across the display. The mouse usually has buttons that can be pressed to send signals that in turn accomplish certain functions. The mouse is one type of pointer device; the representation of the mouse on the screen is also called the **pointer**. (See **pointer**.)

occluding In a windowing system, windows may be stacked on top of each other much like a deck of cards. The window that overlays another window is said to *occlude* that window. A window need not completely conceal another window to be occluding it.

padding Space inserted to maintain alignment within the borders of windows and menus.

parameter A value required before a client can perform a function. Also called an argument.

pixel The smallest element of a display surface that can be addressed.

pointer A generic name for an input device that, when moved across a flat surface, moves the pointer symbol correspondingly across the display. A *pointer* usually has buttons that can be pressed to send signals that in turn accomplish certain functions. A mouse is one type of pointer device.

The pointer also refers to the symbol on your display that tracks pointer movement on your desk. Pointers allow you to make selections in menus, size and position windows and icons, and select the window where you want to focus input. A pointer can be represented by a variety of symbols. (See **text cursor**.) Some typical X pointer symbols are the I-beam and the skull and crossbones.

property	Windows have associated *properties*, each consisting of a name, a type, a data format, and some data. The X protocol places no interpretation on properties; they are intended as a general-purpose data storage and intercommunication mechanism for clients. There is, however, a list of predefined properties and property types so that clients can share information such as resize hints, program names, and icon formats with a window manager. In order to avoid passing arbitrary length property-name strings, each property name is associated with a corresponding integer value known as an atom.
reverse video	Reversing the default foreground and background colors.
RGB	An additive method for defining color in which tenths of percentages of the primaries red, green, and blue are combined to form other colors.
root window	A shaded area (also called the **background window**) that covers the entire screen and upon which other windows are displayed.
screen	A server may provide several independent *screens*, which may or may not have physically independent monitors. For instance, it is sometimes possible to treat a color monitor as if it were two screens, one color and one black and white.
scrollbar	A bar on the side of an *xterm* window that allows you to use the pointer to scroll up and down through the text saved in the window. The number of lines saved is usually greater than the number of lines displayed and can be controlled by the saveLines resource variable.
select	A process in which you move the pointer to the desired menu item or window and click or hold down a pointer button in order to perform some action.
selection	*Selections* are a means of communication between clients using properties and events. From the user's perspective, a selection is an item of data that can be highlighted in one instance of an application and pasted into another instance of the same or a different application. The client that highlights the data is the owner, and the client into which the data is pasted is the requestor. Properties are used to store the selection data and the type of the data, while events are

Glossary

used to synchronize the transaction and to allow the requestor to indicate the type of data it prefers and to allow the owner to convert the data to the indicated type if possible.

server   The combination of graphics display, hardware, and X server software that provides display services for clients. The *server* also handles keyboard and pointer input.

text cursor   The standard underscore or block cursor that appears on the command line or in a text editor running an *xterm* window. To make the distinction clearer, the cursor that tracks the movement of a mouse or other pointing device is referred to as the **pointer**. The pointer may be associated with any number of cursor shapes, and may change shape as it moves from window to window.

tile   A pattern that is replicated (as if laying a tile) to form the background of a window or other area. This term is also used to refer to a style of window manager or application that places windows side by side instead of allowing them to overlap.

window   A region on your display created by a client. For example, the *xterm* terminal emulator, the *xcalc* calculator, and the *bitmap* graphics editor all create windows. You can manipulate windows on your display using a window manager.

window manager   A client that allows you to move, resize, circulate, and iconify windows on your display.

Index

Index

C

C shell script, 558
calculator, 23
  (see also xcalc.)
calculator (xcalc), description, 175
  function of keys, 176
  terminating, 176
character set, 128
character-cell fonts, 122
class, definition, 236
  hierarchy (Athena) (see Athena class hierarchy)
  Object (Athena), 651-652
  RectObj (Athena), 651-652
  resource names, 236
click-to-type focus, (see explicit focus)
client, customizing, 24, 233
  definition, 21
  desk accessories, 172
  display manager, 23
  glossary definition, 694
  location of default values, 234
  removing, 191
  standalone, 23
  window manager, 22
clients, standard vs. Motif, 15-19
CLIPBOARD selection, 99
  (see also xclipboard.)
clock, 172
  (see also oclock, xclock.)
color, background (glossary definition), 693
  changing color name database, 578
  determining number available, 227
  displaying, 227
  for screen elements, 223
  foreground (glossary definition), 695
  hexadecimal specification, 226
  problems allocating, 578
  reverse video (glossary definition), 697
  RGB (glossary definition), 697
  RGB model, 226
  specifying root window (xsetroot), 289
color graphics, (see pixmap)
colorcell, definition, 227
  glossary definition, 694
  read-only, 229
  read/write, 229, 287
  shared, 228
colormap, 196, 287
  description, 227

glossary definition, 694
colors, previewing, 201, 225
command button, Maximize, 76
  Minimize, 76
command button widget (Athena), 18, 158
command buttons (bitmap), 151-157
command line options (client), 219-229, 233
  -background, 222
  -bd (border color), 222
  -bg (background), 222
  -border color, 222
  -borderwidth, 229
  -bw (border width), 229
  -fn (font), 222
  -foreground, 222
  -iconic, 221
  list of standard, 219
  -reverse, 222
  -title, 221
commands, bitmap editing, 150
  for terminating xterm window, 110
  Main Options menu, 108
  pointer, 151
  Tek Options menu, 115
  text editing widget, 188, 423
  VT Options menu, 112
Composite widget class (Athena), 653-654
console messages, 577
console xterm window, glossary definition, 694
Control key, 188, 423
conventions of book, xxvi
copying selections in xterm windows, 94
  and xcutsel, 99
Core widget class (Athena), resources, 652-653
cursor, cursor font, 625
customizing, clients, 24, 233
  mwm (icon box), 275
  mwm (.mwmrc file), 259
  mwm (system.mwmrc file), 260-267
  mwm (.xresources file), 259
  xdm, 567-571
cut buffer strings, 94
  vs. selections, 98

D

DEC VT102, 22
-def option (xsetroot), 288
default, glossary definition, 694
defaults, setting, 234

Index

G

generating display information, 200
  (see also xdpyinfo.)
geometry, glossary definition, 695
graphics, creating with bitmap, 147-157
  magnifying with xmag, 162
graphics utilities, 147-167
-gray option (xsetroot), 288
graymap, converting to another format, 165
  portable, 165
grayscale graphics, (see graymap)
grip, definition, 185
GUI (graphical user interface), xxi, 15

H

hexadecimal color specification, 226
  glossary definition, 695
highlighter, glossary definition, 696
hot spot, glossary definition, 696

I

icon, definition, 9
  glossary definition, 696
  starting window as, 221
-iconic option (X Toolkit), 221
icons, managing, 83-85
input device, glossary definition, 696
input focus, 34
instance, definition, 236
  resource names, 236
ISO Latin-1 character set, 128

K

keyboard, bell, 283
  preferences, 283
keyboard focus, 34
keyclick volume, 284
keys, Control, 188, 423
  Delete, 189, 424
  Meta, 72, 188, 423
  modifier, 72
keysym, values, 645
killing, client window, 191
  oclock, 193

server, 191
  xterm window, 110
killing a client, 174
killing windows, with Window Menu button, 80

L

led option (xset), 285
list fonts, 120
  (see also xlsfonts.)
list window tree, 196
  (see also xlswins.)
listres (list resources for widgets), reference
  page for, 345-346
listres (lists resources for widgets), 655-656
log files, 578
logging in, 23
logical, font convention, 120
  keyname, 72
loose bindings, 236

M

magnifying screen, 162
  (see also xmag.)
Main Options menu (xterm), 106
  commands, 110
  mode toggles, 108
managing icons, 83-85
  using Window Menu, 84
Maximize command button, 76
menus, glossary definition, 696
  mwm (window manager), 107
  Root Menu (mwm), 85-86
  Tek Options, 89, 114
  Tektronix (see Tek Options menu)
  VT Fonts, 113
  VT Options, 92, 111
  Window Menu (mwm), 80-85
  xterm (terminal emulator), 106
Meta key, 72, 188, 423
mkfontdir (create font databases), 576
  reference page for, 347
-mod option (xsetroot), 289
mode toggles, Main Options menu, 108
  Tek Options menu, 114
  VT Options menu, 112
Modes menu, (see VT Options menu)
modifier keys, 72

steps for, 33
System V, 572
with xinit, 33
xdm (display manager), 562-571
xinit (start X server), 572
startup scripts, 558, 570
system management, 555-578
system.mwmrc file, 260-267

T

Tek Options menu, commands, 115
description of items, 114
mode toggles, 114
Tek Options menu (xterm), 106
Tektronix 4014, 22
temporary xterm windows, running commands
in, 105
TERMCAP environment variable, 556
for xterm, 91
terminal emulator, 89
definition, 22
(see also xterm.)
terminal type, setting, 556
xterm, 90
terminating xterm window, 110, 221
text, copying and pasting, 94, 97, 99
switching buffer and selection (xcutsel), 99
text cursor, glossary definition, 698
text editing widget, 188, 423
Text widget (Athena), 183
tight bindings, 236
tile, 698
title area, description, 8
in xterm window, 30
-title option (X Toolkit), 221
titlebar, description, 8-9
Toolkit options, (see command line options)
toolkits, definition, 234
translation table, syntax, 643-647
twm (window manager), bringing up, 567

U

UNIX commands, running in temporary xterm,
105

V

vertical panes, 185
Viewport widget (Athena), 180
VPaned widget (Athena), 185
VT Fonts menu, description of items, 113
VT Fonts menu (xterm), 106
VT Options menu, Allow 80/132 Column
Switching, 112
description of items, 111
mode toggles, 112
VT Options menu (xterm), 106
VT102 (DEC), 22
Modes menu (see VT Options menu)
VT Options menu, 111

W

widget, attributes, 236
authentication, 566, 570
binding (loose vs. tight), 236
Box (Athena), 661
callback, 651
Command (Athena), 654, 661-663
command button (Athena), 18, 158
Command widget class (Athena), 659
Composite (Athena) (see Composite widget
class)
constraint (Athena) (see constraint widget
class)
Core (Athena) (see Core widget class)
defining conventions, 236
definition, 171
Dialog (Athena), 663
dialog box (Athena), 157
Form (Athena), 653, 664-665
Form widget class (Athena), 659
Grip (Athena), 665
hierarchy, 235
hierarchy (Athena) (see Athena class hierarchy)
inheriting resources, 659-660
instance names, 659
introduction, 651
Label (Athena), 654, 666
List (Athena), 667-668
MenuButton (Athena), 668-669
Paned (Athena), 669-672
push button (Motif), 18
quit (Athena), 659

Index

Index